ROUTLEDGE HANDBOOK OF ENVIRONMENTAL SECURITY

The *Routledge Handbook of Environmental Security* provides a comprehensive, accessible, and sophisticated overview of the field of environmental security.

The volume outlines the defining theories, major policy and programming interventions, and applied research surrounding the relationship between the natural environment and human and national security. Through the use of large-scale research and ground-level case analyses from across the globe, it details how environmental factors affect human security and contribute to the onset and continuation of violent conflict. It also examines the effects of violent conflict on the social and natural environment and the importance of environmental factors in conflict resolution and peacebuilding.

Organized around the conflict cycle, the handbook is split into four thematic sections:

* Section I: Environmental factors contributing to conflict;
* Section II: The environment during conflict;
* Section III: The role of the environment in post-conflict peacebuilding; and
* Section IV: Cross-cutting themes and critical perspectives.

This handbook will be essential reading for students of environmental studies, human security, global governance, development studies, and international relations in general.

Richard Matthew is Professor of Urban Planning, Public Policy, and Political Science and Associate Dean of Research and International Programs at the University of California, Irvine, USA.

Evgenia Nizkorodov is a research fellow at the University of California, Irvine Blum Center for Poverty Alleviation, USA.

Crystal Murphy is Associate Professor of Political Science and Director of the MA International Studies program at Chapman University, USA.

ROUTLEDGE HANDBOOK OF ENVIRONMENTAL SECURITY

Edited by Richard Matthew, Evgenia Nizkorodov, and Crystal Murphy with Kristen A. Goodrich, Ashley Hooper, Bemmy Maharramli, Maureen J. Purcell, and Paroma Wagle

LONDON AND NEW YORK

Cover credit: © Getty Images

First published 2022
by Routledge
2 Park Square, Milton Park, Abingdon, Oxon OX14 4RN

and by Routledge
605 Third Avenue, New York, NY 10158

Routledge is an imprint of the Taylor & Francis Group, an informa business

© 2022 selection and editorial matter, Richard Matthew, Evgenia Nizkorodov, and Crystal Murphy; individual chapters, the contributors

The right of Richard Matthew, Evgenia Nizkorodov, and Crystal Murphy to be identified as the authors of the editorial material, and of the authors for their individual chapters, has been asserted in accordance with sections 77 and 78 of the Copyright, Designs and Patents Act 1988.

All rights reserved. No part of this book may be reprinted or reproduced or utilised in any form or by any electronic, mechanical, or other means, now known or hereafter invented, including photocopying and recording, or in any information storage or retrieval system, without permission in writing from the publishers.

Trademark notice: Product or corporate names may be trademarks or registered trademarks, and are used only for identification and explanation without intent to infringe.

British Library Cataloguing-in-Publication Data
A catalogue record for this book is available from the British Library

Library of Congress Cataloging-in-Publication Data
A catalog record for this book has been requested

ISBN: 978-1-138-09229-7 (hbk)
ISBN: 978-1-032-14980-6 (pbk)
ISBN: 978-1-315-10759-2 (ebk)

DOI: 10.4324/9781315107592

Typeset in Bembo
by Apex CoVantage, LLC

CONTENTS

List of figures	*viii*
List of tables	*ix*
Contributing authors	*x*

1	Introduction	1
	Richard Matthew and Evgenia Nizkorodov	
2	Defining environmental peacebuilding	9
	Carl Bruch, David Jensen, and Monica Emma	

SECTION I
Environmental factors contributing to conflict   **27**

3	The geography(ies) of resource wars	29
	Michael T. Klare	
4	Extractives as a contributor to conflict	43
	Philippe Le Billon	
5	Land rights and land use as a contributor to conflict	55
	Jon D. Unruh	
6	Unpacking the complexity of water, war, and conflict	66
	Vandana Asthana	
7	Climate change as a contributor to conflict	82
	Alec Crawford and Clare V. Church	

SECTION II
The environment during conflict — 93

8 Environmental destruction during war — 95
Charles Closmann

9 The toxic legacy of war: landmines and explosive remnants of war — 107
Kenneth R. Rutherford and Paige Ober

10 The environmental spoils of war — 115
Päivi Lujala, Ashley Hooper and Maureen J. Purcell

11 Population displacement and the environment during war — 129
Evgenia Nizkorodov and Paroma Wagle

12 Natural disasters and armed conflict — 146
Colin Walch

13 Climate change, public health, and the conflict cycle — 155
James Orbinski, Richard Matthew, Evgenia Nizkorodov and Sifat Reazi

SECTION III
The role of the environment in post-conflict peacebuilding — 167

14 Natural resource governance reform and environmental
peacebuilding — 169
Michael D. Beevers

15 Urban dimensions of peacebuilding: green infrastructure
in Kigali, Rwanda, and Freetown, Sierra Leone, as a means
for more resilient peace — 179
Bemmy Maharramli

16 Peace parks in theory and practice: confronting the elephant
in the room — 189
Larry A. Swatuk

17 Integrating climate change adaptation into peacebuilding — 203
Richard Matthew

18 A paradigm for actionable and accessible local flood hazard information — 215
*Brett F. Sanders, Richard Matthew, Adam Luke, Kristen A. Goodrich,
Victoria Basolo, Ana Eguiarte, Danielle Boudreau and David L. Feldman*

Contents

SECTION IV
Cross-cutting themes and critical perspectives   **225**

19 Securitizing the environment   227
Rita Floyd

20 Environmental security discourse in the Anthropocene   240
Simon Dalby

21 The environment and human security: a water–food–energy
nexus approach   250
Florian Krampe, Anders Jägerskog and Ashok Swain

22 The environmental security debate in Nepal: a perspective
from the South   260
Bishnu Raj Upreti and Evgenia Nizkorodov

23 Environmental peacebuilding at the Tijuana–San Diego border   279
Kristen A. Goodrich and Kyle Haines

24 Gender and environmental security   290
Silja Halle

25 UN Environment's contribution to the emerging field of
environmental peacebuilding: key policy milestones
and lessons learned   303
David Jensen and Amanda Kron

26 Conclusion   326
Evgenia Nizkorodov and Richard Matthew

Index   *336*

FIGURES

2.1	Environmental opportunities and risks across the conflict life cycle	14
10.1	Kaplan–Meier survival estimates for conflict duration, 1946–2001	119
10.2	Smoothed hazard estimate for the event of peace	120
13.1	Factors contributing to public health	157
18.1	Newport Beach flood hazard viewer	219
18.2	Tijuana River Valley flood hazard viewer	219
18.3	Los Laureles Canyon flood hazard viewer	220
23.1	The canyon-estuary system: Los Laureles Canyon (MX) and the Tijuana River National Estuarine Research Reserve (US)	280
25.1	Environmental peacebuilding entry points in the SDGs	316

TABLES

4.1	Factors that influence the likelihood of conflict and potential degrees of resistance over mining projects	51
7.1	State fragility and climate vulnerability, 2020	83
10.1	Bivariate duration analysis of armed civil conflict, 1946–2001	121
10.2	Duration of armed civil conflict, 1946–2001	122
10.3	Onset of armed civil conflict, 1946–2003	124
11.1	Human and ecological impacts of settled and self-settled refugees in Lebanon	133
16.1	Transfrontier conservation areas in Southern Africa	196

CONTRIBUTING AUTHORS

Vandana Asthana, PhD, is a professor of international relations and environmental policy at Eastern Washington University, USA. Her regional area of expertise is South Asia. Her research includes publications on environment, water, climate, gender, and displacement challenges. She is the author of *Water Policy Processes in India: Discourses of Power and Resistance*, *Politics of the Environment*, and *Water Security in India and South Asia*.

Victoria Basolo, PhD, is a professor of urban planning and public policy at the University of California, Irvine, USA. Her research focuses on housing policy, environmental hazards, urban governance, and the consequences of urbanization. Her current work, initiated under the Fulbright Scholar Program, focuses on urbanization in Malta.

Michael D. Beevers, PhD, is an associate professor in the Department of Environmental Studies at Dickinson College, USA. His work has appeared in numerous journals and book chapters and his book, *Peacebuilding and Natural Resource Governance after Armed Conflict: Sierra Leone and Liberia*, was published by Palgrave Macmillan in 2019.

Danielle Boudreau is currently a National Reserve System Training Lead at the National Oceanic and Atmospheric Administration, where she leads a Coastal Training Program for the National Estuarine Research Reserve System, including 29 reserves located in 23 states and Puerto Rico. Previously, Ms. Boudreau served as a resilience initiative lead and a coastal management specialist at the Tijuana River National Estuarine Research Reserve in San Diego, California, USA.

Carl Bruch, JD, is the director of international programs at the Environmental Law Institute (ELI) and the founding president of the Environmental Peacebuilding Association (EnPAx) in Washington, DC, USA. He has edited more than ten books and authored more than 80 journal articles, book chapters, and reports.

Clare V. Church is a writer and researcher based in Aberystwyth, the United Kingdom. She is currently completing her doctoral studies. Her previous work with the International Institute

Contributing authors

for Sustainable Development focused on developing research and publications regarding the intersections among the environment, conflict, and peacebuilding.

Charles Closmann, PhD, is an associate professor of history at the University of North Florida, USA. Relevant publications include editing *War and the Environment* (2009) and "Feeling the Burn: Camp Blanding, Florida and the U.S. Military's Role in Forest Ecology, 1980s to 2010," in *FCH Annals*, 2021.

Alec Crawford is a senior policy advisor and lead, Environment, Conflict and Peacebuilding, at the International Institute for Sustainable Development (IISD). He works with both the Resilience and Economic Law and Policy programs. His publications include *Conservation and Peacebuilding in Sierra Leone* (2012), *Climate Change and Security in Africa* (2009), and *Conflict-Sensitive Conservation Practitioners' Manual* (2009).

Simon Dalby, PhD, is a professor of geography and environmental studies at Wilfrid Laurier University (Waterloo, Canada). His research focuses on climate change, environmental security, and geopolitics. He is the author of *Anthropocene Geopolitics: Globalization, Security, Sustainability* (University of Ottawa Press, 2020) and *Security and Environmental Change* (Polity, 2009) and co-editor of *Achieving the Sustainable Development Goals* (Routledge, 2019) and *Reframing Climate Change: Constructing Ecological Geopolitics* (Routledge, 2016).

Ana Eguiarte is the binational liaison at the Tijuana River National Estuarine Research Reserve on the US-Mexico border, where she has worked since 2008. Ms. Eguiarte has a rich history of working to establish and cultivate relationships with Mexican partners and maintain productive channels for formal and informal dialogue as well as partnerships for joint projects. She also coordinates the Mexican section of the Tijuana River Action Network, a cross-border collaborative addressing the conservation and restoration of the Tijuana River Valley watershed by engaging the public in stewardship and education activities. She also coordinates the temporary employment program for all residents of the Los Laureles Canyon, overseeing 430 employees. She received a bachelor of science degree in geography from the University of Guadalajara and a master's degree in environmental planning from El Colegio de la Frontera Norte.

Monica Emma is an international development and communications professional, working at the nexus of agriculture and food security and holding a bachelor's degree in international studies from American University. In her current position as a communications officer for Cultivating New Frontiers in Agriculture (CNFA), she specializes in employing digital and traditional communications tactics to elevate the voices of farmers and promote sustainable agricultural development.

David L. Feldman, PhD, is a professor of urban planning and public policy and political sciences and the director of Water UCI at the University of California, Irvine, USA. Dr. Feldman is the lead author for a US Climate Change Science Program report on climate and water. He is a member of the advisory board for two NSF research centers on water in the West and is also the co-principal investigator on an NSF-Partnership for International Research and Education project with Australian universities. Recent publications include *Water Politics – Governing Our Most Precious Resource* (2017) and *The Water Sustainable City: Science, Policy and Practice (2017).*

Contributing authors

Rita Floyd, PhD, is an associate professor in Conflict and Security at the University of Birmingham, UK. Her publications include *The Morality of Security: A Theory of Just Securitization* (CUP, 2019) and *Security and the Environment: Securitisation Theory and US Environmental Security Policy* (CUP, 2010).

Kristen A. Goodrich, PhD, is the Coastal Training Program Coordinator at the Tijuana River National Estuarine Research Reserve, USA, where she facilitates collaborative research and practice related to binational coastal resource management. She holds a PhD in social ecology from the University of California, Irvine.

Kyle Haines, PhD, graduated from the Department of Political Science at the University of California, San Diego (UCSD), and now serves as the field research lead at the UCSD Center on Global Justice, USA, where he coordinates field research with partner organizations and students on both sides of the border.

Silja Halle is the manager of the EU-UNEP Climate Change and Security Programme at the UN Environment Programme. She is co-author of *Gender, Climate and Security: Sustaining Inclusive Peace at the Frontlines of Climate Change* (2020) and Women and Natural Resources: Unlocking the Peacebuilding Potential (2013).

Ashley Hooper, PhD, earned her degree in urban and environmental planning and policy at the University of California, Irvine (UCI). She is currently a postdoctoral scholar with the Division of Teaching Excellence and Innovation at UCI. Her research interests include urban food systems and environmental justice.

Anders Jägerskog, PhD, is senior water resources management specialist at the Global Water Practice at the World Bank. He is the focal point at the World Bank for Transboundary Waters. He is also an associate professor (Docent) for Peace and Development Research, School of Global Studies, University of Gothenburg (Sweden). Some of his most recent publications include co-editing the *Routledge Handbook on Middle East Security* (2019 and *Water Politics in the Nile River Basin – Land Grabs, Energy Investments and Changing Hydropolitical Landscapes* (2016) and co-authoring *Emerging Security Threats in the Middle East: The Impact of Climate Change and Globalization* (2016).

David Jensen is the former head of the Environmental Peacebuilding Programme at UN Environment. He is a founding board member of the Environmental Peacebuilding Association and is also one of the core faculty members of the massive open online course on environmental security and sustaining peace. He is the coordinator or co-author of six flagship policy reports on risks and opportunities from natural resources across the conflict life cycle and is a is a co-editor of *Post-Conflict Peacebuilding and Natural Resource Management* (Routledge), a six-volume set of books on post-conflict peacebuilding and natural resource management.

Michael T. Klare, PhD, served as the Five College Professor of Peace and World Security Studies, a joint appointment at Amherst, Hampshire, Mount Holyoke, and Smith Colleges and the University of Massachusetts, Amherst, from 1985 to 2018. Since 2018, he has been a senior visiting fellow at the Arms Control Association, USA.

Florian Krampe, PhD, is the director of the Stochol International Peace Research Institute's (SIPRI) Climate Change and Risk Programme, specializing in peace and conflict research,

Contributing authors

environmental and climate security, and international security. Dr. Krampe is also a specially appointed professor at the Network for Education and Research on Peace and Sustainability at Hiroshima University, Japan. He has published in a variety of journals including *World Development*, *Sustainability Science*, and *Global Environmental Politics*.

Amanda Kron serves as an associate expert on climate change and environment at the Office of the UN High Commissioner for Human Rights (OHCHR). Prior to joining OHCHR, she worked as a legal advisor and project coordinator at the Crisis Management Branch of UN Environment Programme. She holds an LLM from Uppsala University, Sweden.

Philippe Le Billon, PhD, is a professor at the University of British Columbia with the Department of Geography and the Liu Institute for Global Issues. He works on linkages between environment, development, and security. He is the author of *Wars of Plunder: Conflicts, Profits and the Politics of Resources* (Oxford UP, 2013) and *Oil* (Polity Press, 2017 with Gavin Bridge), and editor of *Environmental Defenders: Deadly Struggles for Life and Territory* (Routledge, 2021 with Mary Menton).

Päivi Lujala, PhD, is a professor of geography and Academy of Finland Research Fellow at the Geography Research Unit, University of Oulu, Finland. Her publications include "Environmental and Land Defenders: Global Patterns and Determinants of Repression" (with Philippe Le Billon, Global Environmental Change, 2020).

Adam Luke, PhD, has a dual background in data science and hydrology. Dr. Luke completed his PhD in civil engineering at the University of California, Irvine (UCI). His research focused on (1) incorporating changing environmental conditions in flood risk assessment and coastal engineering design and (2) developing strategies for improving the visualization and communication of flood hazard data for non-expert end-users. He is currently working as a data scientist at Appriss, USA.

Bemmy Maharramli, PhD, is an associate director for strategic initiatives at the University of California, Los Angeles's (UCLA) Center for Community Engagement. She received her PhD in urban and environmental planning and policy from the University of California, Irvine (UCI). Her most recent publications include a book chapter on cities as a transformative nexus and journal manuscripts in press on civic ecology and community engagement.

Richard Matthew, PhD, is a professor of urban planning, public policy, and political science and an associate dean of research and international programs at the School of Social Ecology at the University of California, Irvine, USA. He is also the director of the UCI Blum Center for Poverty Alleviation. Dr. Matthew has done extensive field work in conflict zones in South Asia and East, Central, and West Africa. His research focuses on the environmental dimensions of conflict and peacebuilding; planetary health; and the co-production of flood risk models. He is the editor or co-editor of ten books including *Women's Perspectives on Human Security: Violence, Environment, and Sustainability* (2020), *The Social Ecology of the Anthropocene* (2015), and the four volume *Environmental Security* (2014).

Crystal Murphy, PhD, is an associate professor of political science and director of the MA International Studies program at Chapman University, USA. Dr. Murphy's research focuses on the political economy of conflict, humanitarianism, and development. She is author of *Microcredit Meltdown: The Rise and Fall of South Sudan's Post-Conflict Microcredit Sector*.

Contributing authors

Evgenia Nizkorodov, PhD, is a research fellow at the University of California, Irvine, Blum Center for Poverty Alleviation, USA. She examines collaborative solutions to the sustainable and resilient provision of critical resources and services, particularly fresh water. Notable publications include *The Social Ecology of the Anthropocene* (2015) and two journal publications on public-private partnerships.

Paige Ober is a project manager for New Columbia Solar in Washington, DC, USA. She holds master's degrees in international affairs (American University) and natural resources and sustainable development (University for Peace). She worked five years with the Center for International Stabilization and Recovery.

James Orbinski, MD, is a physician, author, and humanitarian. He is currently a professor at York University and the inaugural director of York's Dahdaleh Institute for Global Health Research in Toronto, Ontario, Canada. His current advocacy and research focus on climate change and planetary health. He has worked at providing medical humanitarian relief in situations of war, famine, epidemic disease, and genocide with Medicins Sans Frontieres/Doctors without Borders (MSF). As MSF's international president, he accepted the Nobel Peace Prize on its behalf in 1999. He is the author of *An Imperfect Offering: Humanitarian Action for the 21st Century*, which received the Canadian Governor General's Literary Award in nonfiction in 2008. He was the subject of the award-winning 2005 CBC documentary *Evil Revisited* and also of the film *Triage: Dr. James Orbinski's Humanitarian Dilemma*. Among his many awards, he became an Officer of the Order of Canada in 2009 "for his contributions as a physician who has worked to improve health care access and delivery in developing countries, and as an advocate for those who have been silenced by war, genocide and mass starvation".

Maureen J. Purcell is a PhD candidate in the social ecology core program at the University of California, Irvine, School of Social Ecology, USA. Her dissertation examines the potential of message framing to overcome affective snap judgments of climate change policy.

Sifat Reazi is a PhD candidate in the Department of Urban and Environmental Planning and Policy at the University of California, Irvine, USA. Her research interests center around the datafication of humanitarian work. Her doctoral dissertation looks particularly at app-based interventions for refugee camp management.

Kenneth R. Rutherford, PhD, is a professor of political science at James Madison University. He holds a PhD in government from Georgetown University and BA and MBA degrees from the University of Colorado, where he was inducted into its Hall for Distinguished Alumni. He co-founded the Landmine Survivors Network in 1995, became a leader in the International Campaign to Ban Landmines and wrote sections of the 1997 Mine Ban Treaty, and was a co-recipient of the Nobel Peace Prize in 1997. He has delivered presentations in nearly 40 countries and has published in numerous academic and policy journals, such as *World Politics*, and authored or co-edited five books, including *America's Buried History: Landmines in the Civil War* (2020) and *Landmines and Human Security: International Politics and War's Hidden Legacy* (2004).

Brett F. Sanders, PhD, is a professor of civil and environmental engineering, urban planning, and public policy at the University of California, Irvine, USA. Dr. Sanders is an expert in the development of flood hazard modeling systems and the use of flood simulation and visualization to support planning, preparedness, and emergency response needs. Recent publications include

"Collaborative Modeling with Fine-Resolution Data Enhances Flood Awareness, Minimizes Differences in Flood Perception, and Produces Actionable Flood Maps" in *Earth's Future* (2020) and "Going beyond the Flood Insurance Rate Map: Insights from Flood Hazard Map Co-production" in *Natural Hazards and Earth System Sciences* (2018).

Ashok Swain, PhD, is a professor and the head of the Department of Peace and Conflict Research and UNESCO chair of International Water Cooperation at Uppsala University, Sweden. His relevant publications include *Understanding Emerging Security Challenges: Threats and Opportunities* (2012), *Transboundary Water Management and the Climate Change Debate* (2015), and *Emerging Security Threats in the Middle East: The Impact of Climate Change and Globalization* (2016). He has also co-edited *Routledge Handbook on Environmental Conflict and Peacebuilding* (2018) and *Handbook of Security and the Environment* (2021).

Larry A. Swatuk, PhD, is a professor in the School of Environment, Enterprise and Development at the University of Waterloo, Canada, and Extraordinary Professor in the Institute for Water Studies at the University of the Western Cape, South Africa. He is author of *Water in Southern Africa* (UKZN Press).

Jon D. Unruh, PhD, is a professor in the Department of Geography at McGill University in Montreal, Canada. He has over 25 years of experience in developing and implementing research, policy, and practice on war-affected land and property rights in the Middle East, Latin America, Africa, and Asia.

Bishnu Raj Upreti, PhD, completed his degree in conflict management (2001) from Wageningen University and Research in the Netherlands. He is the executive chairperson of the Policy Research Institute (PRI), a government think tank in Nepal. His latest publications include "Nepal: Reflections on the Environmental and Human Security Debate" in the *Handbook of Security and the Environment* (2020) and "Nepal: The Role of the Military in Politics, 1990–2020" in the *Oxford Research Encyclopedia* (2021).

Paroma Wagle, PhD, received her PhD in urban and environmental planning and policy at the University of California, Irvine, USA. Dr. Wagle's research interests are in environmental policy, water policy, water conflicts, and access to basic urban services. She has worked predominantly in India, but also in Europe and the United States over her academic career.

Colin Walch, PhD, is a protection delegate at the International Committee of the Red Cross (ICRC) and a research affiliate at the Department of Peace and Conflict Research, Uppsala University. He previously was a post-doctoral researcher and lecturer at University of California, Berkeley.

1

INTRODUCTION

Richard Matthew and Evgenia Nizkorodov

The *Routledge Handbook of Environmental Security* is the first unified work to examine the linkage between environmental and human systems across all three stages of the conflict life cycle: pre-conflict, violent conflict, and post-conflict. The handbook brings together a diverse set of leading experts from academic and practitioner communities to provide a comprehensive overview of the risks posed by environmental shocks and stresses and the prospects for environmental peacebuilding. This book thus serves as a reference for both practitioners and scholars, presenting leading theories and causal mechanisms, policy recommendations, and critical avenues of further research.

Background

The end of the Cold War (1989–1992) and, in the assessments of many experts, the end of grand ideological rivalry, encouraged a broad rethinking of threat, vulnerability, and national security. At the same time, *Our Common Future* (WCED, 1987) and the 1992 Rio Earth Summit, undergirded by decades of interdisciplinary research worldwide, presented compelling scientific evidence of global environmental change so severe that it threatens the future of humankind (and many other species) and requires an extensive and urgent global response, captured in the concept of sustainable development. These two powerful discourses converged into an innovative and influential conversation among academics, activists, policymakers, and other interested stakeholders about the relationships between changes to the natural environment and human and national security imperatives. Complicated questions quickly emerged: How does and might environmental change affect the prospects for war and peace? Should the emphasis of security thinking and practice shift toward the human scale, or at least include it? Was the integrity of the living planet itself a security concern?

While thinkers from Plato and Thucydides to Thomas Malthus and Halford Mackinder have explored security from an environmental perspective, stressing both variables of geography and resource access, Homer-Dixon (1991, 1994, 1999) was among the first to examine the direct link between environment and violent conflict in the post–Cold War context of rethinking security (see also Dabelko & Matthew, 2000; Diamond, 1994; Deudney & Matthew, 1999; Matthew, Gaulin, & McDonald, 2003). While his arguments were influential in policy circles, especially in the United States during the Clinton-Gore era, and popularized by writers such

DOI: 10.4324/9781315107592-1

as Robert Kaplan (1994), they were downplayed or dismissed by many skeptics and critics (e.g., Lomborg, 2001). A decade later, however, the IPCC's Fourth Assessment Report (2007, also Cruz et al., 2007, arguments reinforced in IPCC, 2018) generated considerable interest in possible linkages between climate impacts and violent conflict, interest that often generated strong, but unevenly supported, predictions about where the world was headed (e.g., CNA, 2007; German Advisory Council, 2008; Gleick, 2012; McElroy & Baker, 2012; Sachs, 2005; Smith & Vivekananda, 2007; Stern, 2007; UNGA, 2009) Also, around this time, a second wave of more explicit evidence-based research began to take shape, modifying but also adding considerable weight to early conceptual claims (e.g., Floyd & Matthew, 2013; Kahl, 2006; Le Billon, 2015; Pearce, 2007; Welzer, 2012), although important and insightful critiques continued (e.g., Benjaminsen, Alinon, Buhaug, & Buseth, 2012; Slettebak, 2012).

Research interest also began to move in exciting new directions. For example, in response to the UNDP report (1994) focused on the concept of "human security," itself a controversial topic (e.g., Banuri, 1996; Paris, 2001; Suhrke, 1999; Tehranian, 1999), work began to emerge on how human security was being affected by environmental and climate change (e.g., Collier, 2007; Lonergan, 1999; Matthew, Barnett, McDonald, & O'Brien, 2009). This is an important area of inquiry and practice and a relationship that appears frequently in the following pages. Other research examined linkages between human migration, conflict, and conservation (e.g., Oglethorpe, Ericson, Bilsborrow, & Edmond, 2007).

Insofar as the conflict cycle is concerned, research on the environment during war and the environment post-war also expanded dramatically. Studying what happens to the natural environment during violent conflict is a challenging undertaking. Much has been learned from intrepid scholars venturing into high-risk geographies and also from the pioneering work of UNEP's Post-Conflict and Disaster Branch, which was established to evaluate the environmental impacts of conflict and which has produced numerous detailed assessment reports in over 20 countries. This field-based research demonstrates the high costs of some coping strategies during war, as people are forced to abandon farms and other livelihoods and turn to forest resources in order to survive while hiding. It also demonstrates that insofar as war slows economic activity, some forms of natural capital may actually benefit during periods of violent conflict. And it shows how natural resources have been used to fund war and how the state of war has facilitated the unregulated exploitation of natural resources for personal and corporate profit, creating incentives to continue the conflict. Analysis by Oli Brown (2013) concludes, for example, that 18 conflicts have been directly funded by natural resources since 1990.

Finally, and partly in response to the post–Cold War concept of "peacebuilding" introduced by the United Nations, considerable research has focused on the role of the environment and natural resources in peacebuilding processes (e.g., Conca & Dabelko, 2002; Matthew, Halle, & Switzer, 2002; UNEP, 2009.) The importance of environmental factors in conflict resolution and peacebuilding has led to a number of criticisms of peacebuilding programs and many recommendations for how these can be improved. Peacebuilding has been described by the United Nations as "a range of measures targeted to reduce the risk of lapsing or relapsing into conflict by strengthening national capacities at all levels for conflict management, and to lay the foundations for sustainable peace and development." These measures tend to fall into a handful of programming areas across the life cycle: basic services; restoring security; resettling people and facilitating a return to work; building governance capacity; and cooperation and confidence building such as creating opportunities for justice, truth, and reconciliation projects.

Unfortunately, since the end of the Cold War, peacebuilding activities have often resettled people, kick-started economies, and attracted investors in ways that are environmentally unsustainable. A decade after the initial investments, people in countries such as Rwanda and

Introduction

Sierra Leone have found the gains they experienced through the peacebuilding process partially offset because they have become more vulnerable to flooding (because they have been settled in floodplains), or soil erosion (because they are working steep hillsides), or respiratory ailments (because mining concessions have been granted quickly and without adequate assessments of their social and environmental impacts), and so on. Integrating environmental issues into peacebuilding and investing in climate resilience have, in the past decade, become widely accepted as essential.

Indeed, since about 2007, UNEP has led, with some success, an effort to address this deficiency in peacebuilding. Typically, its recommendations focus around building the capacity in a post-conflict country to assess environmental conditions and trajectories; manage natural resources sustainably; settle returnees and internally displaced persons (IDPs) with a better understanding of the potential ecological impacts of different decisions; handle land disputes that are often complicated by disagreements about the actual situation before the war, about the character and legitimacy of changes in ownership negotiated during the conflict, and low levels of trust in adjudicating systems; identify sustainable investment opportunities; and develop and implement a plan for adapting to climate change and building resilience to climate impacts.

Of course, there can be no final word when it comes to a complex evolving issue like the conflict cycle. Many factors can contribute to war and peace, and in a world characterized by multiple forms of inequality, widespread poverty, inflammatory social media, technologies that can confer tremendous destructive capacity into the hands of very small groups, frequent economic crises, and mounting pressure on some communities to move, it is impossible to predict the constellations of variables that will prove most volatile. Nonetheless, we believe a strong case can be made that the significance of the environment in violent conflict, human security, and peacebuilding will likely increase in the future. Research on planetary boundaries and tipping points suggests that humans have irreversibly altered fundamental ecosystem functions and biogeochemical cycles at an unprecedented rate and scale (Hoffmann, Irl, & Beierkuhnlein, 2019; Steffen et al., 2015; UNEP, 2019). Human-induced warming has reached a global average of 1°C above pre-industrial levels (IPCC, 2018) and is likely to reach 1.5°C of global warming by 2030. The IPCC warns that exceeding 1.5°C may result in detrimental and irreversible changes to ecological and human systems such as shifts in disease vectors, increased frequency and magnitude of natural disasters, decreased water supply and quality, sea level rise, and a drastic loss of biodiversity. These ecological impacts, coupled with a growing population, will ultimately increase competition for resources, displace millions of people from their home countries, and increase the likelihood of violent conflict (Black et al., 2011; Dalby, 2020; Duffy, 2016; Ionesco, Mokhnacheva, & Gemenne, 2017; Institute for Economics & Peace, 2020; Rigaud et al., 2018; Spijkers et al., 2019; Yilmaz, Zogib, Urivelarrea, & Demirbaş, 2019). Without robust mitigation and adaptation, low-income regions already have been and will continue to be disproportionately affected by these adverse impacts (IPCC, 2018, 2019; Goodrich & Nizkorodov, 2017).

Today, a third wave of research is unfolding, focused on investigating local cases, integrating gender, considering the impacts of powerful information technologies, investigating population displacement, and many other issues. The impacts of COVID-19, which include amplifying the vulnerability of many disadvantaged and marginalized communities to environmental and climate stresses and shocks, are briefly integrated into this volume and will certainly stimulate considerable research going forward (Dorussen, 2020; United Nations, 2020). In short, we are at a perfect moment for integrating and summarizing the findings of the past 30 years and for looking forward to where the field of environmental security is heading.

Road map of the book

The book begins with an overview of environmental peacebuilding. Bruch, Jensen, and Emma (Chapter 2) discuss three broad research themes within the field: 1) how resources (water, land, extractives) can directly or indirectly lead to or prolong conflict, 2) how the environment is degraded during conflict, and 3) the role of environmental management in post-conflict peacebuilding. The book structure mirrors these three themes. Each section examines the linkages and feedback between the environment and conflict before conflict, during conflict, and after conflict.

Section 1 provides a careful analysis of the complex linkages between resources and conflict. Klare (Chapter 3) argues that geography – and the uneven distribution of vital and valuable resources – plays a pivotal role in conflict. He illustrates how the distribution and consumption of oil has shaped international relations, conflict patterns, and world trade throughout the 20th century and reflects on how the development of multiple types of renewable and nonrenewable fuel will shape future resource wars and conflict in the 21st century. Le Billon (Chapter 4), on the other hand, argues that conflict is a complex social process that goes beyond geographic distribution of resources. Through a political ecology framework, Le Billon demonstrates how extractives and extractivism can reproduce and amplify conflict through interwoven socio-economic, historical, and political factors. This interplay between governance structures, resources, and anthropogenic change is highly prevalent in the remaining chapters of the section. In Chapter 5, Unruh utilizes five case studies to demonstrate how ineffective governance structures, unequal distributions of power, and tenuous land rights can stoke confrontation or conflict between actors. Meanwhile, Asthana (Chapter 6) reviews the hydrological and social elements of water scarcity – climate conditions, growing water demand, and resource management – as drivers of transboundary tensions and subnational conflicts.

A key consideration in mitigating the link between resource constraints and conflict is the role of climate change. Crawford and Church (Chapter 7) outline future climate change trends and impacts in fragile states and identify the links between climate change, governance, and conflict. The authors argue that while climate change will not directly result in violence, it will destabilize socio-economic livelihoods by stressing already overburdened institutions and governance mechanisms, increasing competition for natural resources, and displacing large numbers of people.

Section 2 focuses on the feedback between environmental and human systems during conflict. The section begins with an exploration of how direct and indirect environmental degradation can be used as a form of warfare. Drawing on military history, environmental history, and ecology, Closmann (Chapter 8) provides a global historical account of warfare that begins with the ancient world and ends in the modern era. Closmann argues that compared to prior conflicts, modern warfare causes more damage to natural resources and the environment and leads to long-term institutional changes that can have profound impacts on the future of the environment. Similarly, Rutherford and Ober (Chapter 9) highlight the toxic legacy of war by examining the environmental impact of landmines and explosive remnants of war (ERW). The process of removing and destroying weapons, as well as the soil contamination from the disposal and abandonment of weapon stockpiles, serves as an additional form of environmental degradation. The environment can also prolong the duration of conflict or lead to rising tensions within conflict-affected communities. In Chapter 10, Lujala, Hooper, and Purcell utilize a series of logistic and Weibull regression models to demonstrate that the presence of resources within a conflict zone will double the duration of conflict.

Introduction

Environmental factors such as displacement-induced environmental degradation, natural disasters, and climate change can also amplify conflict or increase human and ecological system vulnerabilities during wartime. In Chapter 11, Nizkorodov and Wagle illustrate the short- and long-term challenges of mitigating environmental impacts of population displacement through an analysis of Tanzania and the Syrian refugee crisis in Lebanon. Meanwhile, through a review of the literature from the 1990s to the present day, Walch (Chapter 12) presents three competing theories regarding the link between the environment, natural disasters, and conflict, urging scholars to pay additional attention to countries already affected by armed violence. Finally, Orbinski and colleagues (Chapter 13) draw on extensive field and research experience to explore the intersections between conflict, climate change, and public health; the authors also evaluate various governance and technical solutions that mitigate the adverse impacts of climate change on public health across the conflict cycle.

Section 3 examines the role of the environment in post-conflict peacebuilding, paying special attention to governance reform, sustainable development, and co-management of resources. Beevers (Chapter 14) provides a critical perspective on natural resource reform, arguing that long-term peace requires transforming pre-conflict power structures and systems of exploitation and corruption into a holistic approach to environmental protection and human well-being.

A key theme in Section 3, thus, is the importance of developing bottom-up – rather than top-down solutions – that protect the livelihoods of communities while promoting cooperation and peacebuilding. For example, Maharramli (Chapter 15) evaluates the opportunities and impacts of including green infrastructure in post-conflict peacebuilding; her analysis reveals that top-down approaches to post-conflict reconstruction and planning can increase the vulnerability of low-income populations. Meanwhile, Swatuk (Chapter 16) argues that the development of transboundary conservation areas and peace parks fails to account for the interests of those that inhabit the spaces where the parks will be established.

The section also examines the role of technology in aiding peacebuilding efforts. Matthew (Chapter 17) discusses the importance of integrating climate change resilience into peacebuilding and explores how recent advances in information and modeling technologies can facilitate this process. Sanders et al. (Chapter 18) provide an example of how community-engaged research can co-produce actionable science to reduce flood risk. This chapter demonstrates how very sophisticated information technologies can be used in low-resource high-vulnerability settings in a manner that enables the integration of local knowledge with other data streams in order to produce trusted decision support tools.

Finally, **Section 4** examines interdisciplinary themes that cut across the stages of the conflict life cycles, focusing heavily on the interdependencies and feedback between environmental and human systems. The section begins by tracing the evolving dialogue surrounding national security. Floyd (Chapter 19) argues that securitization theory enables us to understand how security discourse narratives are shaped, under what conditions they are accepted, and who the beneficiaries of the subsequent policies are. To illustrate how environmental issues are securitized, she traces the role of climate change and the environment in the broader securitization narratives of the United States, the EU, and other parts of the world. Dalby (Chapter 20), on the other hand, utilizes a historical lens to examine environmental security within the context of the Anthropocene: as we have entered a new geological epoch, environmental security thinking and sustainable development must evolve to match the rate of scale of planetary change.

Section 4 also identifies the specific linkages between the environment and traditional security considerations. For example, Krampe, Jägerskog, and Swain (Chapter 21) approach human and environmental security through a food-water-energy-nexus lens. Upreti and Nizkorodov (Chapter 22) build on the work of Dalby and Krampe *et al.* by highlighting broader human and environmental challenges in Nepal and the Global South. The four case studies in the chapter demonstrate that climate change institutional capacity, demographic pressure, and rising inequality play critical roles in shaping security, particularly in nation-states still recovering from conflict.

The section wraps up with critical perspectives from practitioners. Goodrich and Haines (Chapter 23) argue that conceptions of security at border regions must also address both social and ecological challenges; the authors draw on a decade of fieldwork at the Tijuana-San Diego border to identify a bottom-up adaptive governance approach that bolsters local capacity and enables transboundary cooperation. Halle (Chapter 24) explores a topic that is still underdeveloped in peacebuilding programming: the role of gender in natural resource management, environmental security, and post-conflict recovery. Her analysis of peacebuilding programming in Sudan and Colombia demonstrates how awareness of shifting gender dynamics during warfare, the inclusion of women in peace talks, and the direct involvement of women in implementation of peace agreements can lead to more equitable and effective solutions in the long term. Jensen and Kron (Chapter 25) present policy milestones in environmental peacebuilding and reflect on the lessons learned by the UN Environment Program and its partners from 20 years of fieldwork in conflict-affected countries.

Works cited

Banuri, T. (1996). Human security. In N. Naqvi (Ed.), *Rethinking security, rethinking development* (pp. 163–164). Islamabad: Sustainable Development Policy Institute.

Benjaminsen, T. A., Alinon, K., Buhaug, H., & Buseth, J. T. (2012). Does climate change drive land-use conflicts in the Sahel? *Journal of Peace Research, 49,* 97–111. https://doi.org/10.1177/0022343311427343

Black, R., Adger, W. N., Arnell, N. W., Dercon, S., Geddes, A., & Thomas, D. (2011). The effect of environmental change on human migration. *Global Environmental Change, 21,* S3–S11.

Brown, O. (2013). Encouraging peace-building through better environmental and natural resource management. *Energy, Environment, and Resources Briefing Paper #4.* Chatham House.

CNA (Center for Naval Analyses). (2007). *National Security and the Threat of Climate Change.* Retrieved from www.npr.org/documents/2007/apr/security_climate.pdf

Collier, P. (2007). *The bottom billion.* Oxford, UK: Oxford University Press.

Conca, K., & Dabelko, G. D. (Eds.). (2002). *Environmental peacemaking.* Washington, DC: Woodrow Wilson Center Press.

Cruz, R. V., Harasawa, H., Lal, M., et al. 2007. Asia. In M. L. Parry, et al. (Eds.), *Climate change 2007: Impacts, adaptation and vulnerability. Contribution of working group II to the fourth assessment report of the intergovernmental panel on climate change.* Cambridge, UK, and New York: Cambridge University Press. Retrieved March 15, 2012, from www.ipcc.ch/publications_and_data/ar4/wg2/en/ch10.html.

Dabelko, G., & Matthew, R. A. (2000). Environment, population, and conflict: Suggesting a few steps forward. *Environmental Change and Security Project Report, 6,* 99–103.

Dalby, S. (2020). Resilient earth: Gaia, geopolitics and the Anthropocene. In D. Chandler, K. Grove, & S. Wakefield (Eds.), *Resilience in the Anthropocene* (pp. 22–36). London, UK and New York, NY: Routledge.

Deudney, D., & Matthew, R. A. (Eds.). (1999). *Contested grounds: Security and conflict in the new environmental politics.* Albany, NY: SUNY Press.

Diamond, J. (1994). Ecological collapse of past civilizations. *Proceedings of the American Philosophical Society, 138,* 363–370.

Dorussen, H. (2020). Peacekeeping after Covid-19. *Peace Economics, Peace Science and Public Policy, 26*(3). https://doi.org/10.1515/peps-2020-0022

Duffy, R. (2016). War, by conservation. *Geoforum, 69,* 238–248.

Floyd, R., & Matthew, R. (Eds.). (2013). *Environmental security: Approaches and issues.* Oxford: Routledge.

German Advisory Council on Global Change. (2008). *World in transition: Climate change as a security risk.* London: Earthscan.

Gleick, P. H. (2012). Climate change, exponential curves, water resources, and unprecedented threats to humanity. *Climatic Change, 100*, 125–129.

Goodrich, K., & Nizkorodov, E. (2017). The science of the Anthropocene. In R. Matthew, K. Goodrich, K. Harron, B. Maharramli, & E. Nizkorodov (Eds.), *Continuity and Change in Global Environmental Politics: The Social Ecology of the Anthropocene* (pp. 3–32). The WSPC Reference Set on Natural Resources and Environmental Policy in the Era of Global Change.

Hoffmann, S., Irl, S. D., & Beierkuhnlein, C. (2019). Predicted climate shifts within terrestrial protected areas worldwide. *Nature Communications, 10*(1), 1–10.

Homer-Dixon, T. F. (1991). On the threshold: Environmental changes as causes of acute conflict. *International Security, 16*(2), 76–116.

Homer-Dixon, T. F. (1994). Environmental scarcities and violent conflict: Evidence from cases. *International Security, 19*(1), 5–40.

Homer-Dixon, T. F. (1999). *Environment, scarcity and violence*. Princeton, NJ: Princeton University Press.

Institute for Economics & Peace. (2020). *Ecological threat register 2020: Understanding ecological threats, resilience and peace*. Retrieved December 31, 2020, from http://visionofhumanity.org/reports.

Intergovernmental Panel on Climate Change (IPCC). (2007). *Climate change 2007: The physical science basis. Contribution of Working Group I to the fourth assessment report of the Intergovernmental Panel on Climate Change* [Solomon, S., D. Qin, M. Manning, Z. Chen, M. Marquis, K. B. Averyt, M. Tignor and H. L. Miller (Eds.)]. Cambridge and New York, NY: Cambridge University Press.

Intergovernmental Panel on Climate Change (IPCC). (2018). *Global warming of 1.5°C. An IPCC special report on the impacts of global warming of 1.5°C above pre-industrial levels and related global greenhouse gas emission pathways, in the context of strengthening the global response to the threat of climate change, sustainable development, and efforts to eradicate poverty* [Masson-Delmotte, V., P. Zhai, H.-O. Pörtner, D. Roberts, J. Skea, P. R. Shukla, A. Pirani, W. Moufouma-Okia, C. Péan, R. Pidcock, S. Connors, J. B. R. Matthews, Y. Chen, X. Zhou, M. I. Gomis, E. Lonnoy, T. Maycock, M. Tignor, and T. Waterfield (Eds.)]. Geneva, Switzerland: IPCC. Retrieved from https://www.ipcc.ch/sr15/

Intergovernmental Panel on Climate Change (IPCC). (2019). *Climate change and land: An IPCC special report on climate change, desertification, land degradation, sustainable land management, food security, and greenhouse gas fluxes in terrestrial ecosystems* [P. R. Shukla, J. Skea, E. Calvo Buendia, V. Masson-Delmotte, H.-O. Pörtner, D. C. Roberts, P. Zhai, R. Slade, S. Connors, R. van Diemen, M. Ferrat, E. Haughey, S. Luz, S. Neogi, M. Pathak, J. Petzold, J. Portugal Pereira, P. Vyas, E. Huntley, K. Kissick, M. Belkacemi, J. Malley, (Eds.)]. Geneva, Switzerland: IPCC.

Ionesco, D., Mokhnacheva, D., & Gemenne, F. (2017). *The atlas of environmental migration*. Geneva, Switzerland: International Organization for Migration.

Kahl, C. (2006). *States, scarcity, and civil strife in the developing world*. Princeton, NJ: Princeton University Press.

Kaplan, R. (1994). The coming Anarchy: How scarcity, crime, overpopulation, tribalism, and disease are rapidly destroying the social fabric of our planet. *The Atlantic Monthly*. Retrieved from http://theatlantic.com/politics/foreign/anarchy.htm

Leal Filho, W., Azul, A. M., Wall, T., Vasconcelos, C. R., Salvia, A. L., do Paço, A., . . . Mac-Lean, C. (2020). COVID-19: The impact of a global crisis on sustainable development research. *Sustainability Science*, 1–15.

Le Billon, P. (2015). Environmental conflict. In T. Perreault, G. Bridge, & J. McCarthy (Eds.), *The Routledge handbook of political ecology* (pp. 598–608). London, UK and New York, NY: Routledge.

Lomborg, B. (2001). *The skeptical environmentalist: Measuring the real state of the world*. Cambridge, UK: Cambridge University Press.

Lonergan, S. (1999). *Global environmental change and human security science plan, IHDP Report 11*. Bonn: IHDP.

Matthew, R. A., Barnett, J., McDonald, B., & O'Brien, K. L. (2009). *Global environmental change and human security*. Cambridge, MA: MIT Press.

Matthew, R. A., Gaulin, T., & McDonald, B. (2003). Elusive quest: Linking environmental change and conflict. *Canadian Journal of Political Science*, 857–878.

Matthew, R. A., Halle, M., & Switzer, J. (Eds.). (2002). *Conserving the peace: Resources, livelihoods, and security*. Geneva and Winnipeg: IISD Press.

McElroy, M., & Baker, D. J. (2012). *Climate extremes: Recent trends with implications for national security*. http://environment.harvard.edu/sites/default/files/climate_extremes_report_2012-12-04.pdf

Oglethorpe, J., Ericson, J., Bilsborrow, R., & Edmond, J. (2007). *People on the move: Reducing the impact of human migration on biodiversity.* Washington, DC: WWF and Arlington: CI.

Paris, R. (2001). Human security: Paradigm shift or hot air? *International Security, 26*(Fall), 87–102.

Pearce, F. (2007). *With speed and violence: Why scientists fear tipping points in climate change.* Boston: Beacon Press.

Rigaud, K. K., de Sherbinin, A., Jones, B., Bergmann, J., Clement, V., Ober, K., . . . Midgley, A. (2018). *Groundswell: preparing for internal climate migration.* Washington, DC: The World Bank.

Sachs, J. (2005). *Climate change and war.* Retrieved from www.tompaine.com/print/climate_change_and_war.php

Slettebak, R. T. (2012). Don't blame the weather! Climate-related natural disasters and civil conflict. *Journal of Peace Research, 49,* 163–176.

Smith, D., & Vivekananda, J. (2007). *A climate of conflict: The links between climate change, peace and war.* London: International Alert. Retrieved from www.international-alert.org/sites/default/files/publications/A_climate_of_conflict.pdf

Spijkers, J., Singh, G., Blasiak, R., Morrison, T. H., Le Billon, P., & Österblom, H. (2019). Global patterns of fisheries conflict: Forty years of data. *Global Environmental Change, 57.* https://doi.org/10.1016/j.gloenvcha.2019.05.005

Steffen, W., Richardson, K., Rockström, J., Cornell, S. E., Fetzer, I., Bennett, E. M., . . . Folke, C. (2015). Planetary boundaries: Guiding human development on a changing planet. *Science, 347*(6223), 1259855.

Stern, N. (2007). *The economics of climate change: The Stern review.* Cambridge, UK: Cambridge University Press.

Suhrke, A. (1999, September). Human security and the interests of states. *Security Dialogue, 30,* 265–276.

Tehranian, M. (Ed.). (1999). *Worlds apart: Human security and global governance.* London: I.B. Tauris.

United Nations. (2020). *COVID-10 in an urban world.* Retrieved from www.un.org/sites/un2.un.org/files/sg_policy_brief_covid_urban_world_july_2020.pdf

United Nations Development Programme (UNDP). (1994). *Human development report 1994.* Oxford: Oxford University Press.

United Nations Environment Programme (UNEP). (2009). *From conflict to peacebuilding: The role of natural resources and the environment.* Nairobi: UNEP.

United Nations Environment Programme (UNEP). (2019). *Global environmental outlook 6.* Retrieved from www.unep.org/resources/global-environment-outlook-6?_ga=2.227852510.2120879290.1614713659-1674902825.1613760489

United Nations General Assembly (UNGA). (2009, September11). *Climate change and its possible security implications: Report of the Secretary-General,* A/64/350.

Welch, C. (2017). Half of all species are on the move – and we're feeling it. *National Geographic,* online.www.nationalgeographic.com/news/2017/04/climate-change-species-migration-disease/#close

Welzer, H. (2012). *Climate wars: Why people will be killed in the 21st century.* Cambridge, UK: Polity Press.

World Commission on Environment and Development. (1987). *Our common future.* Oxford, UK: Oxford University Press.

Yilmaz, E., Zogib, L., Urivelarrea, P., & Demirbaş, S. (2019). Mobile pastoralism and protected areas: Conflict, collaboration and connectivity. *Parks, 25,* 6.

2
DEFINING ENVIRONMENTAL PEACEBUILDING

Carl Bruch, David Jensen, and Monica Emma

Over the past 50 years, there has been growing attention to the various linkages between armed conflict and the environment. This concern has evolved, largely in response to specific issues: targeting of the environment during the Viet Nam War and the 1990–1991 Gulf War; the proliferation of conflict diamonds, minerals, and other natural resources financing armed conflict in Liberia, the Democratic Republic of the Congo, Afghanistan, Colombia, and other countries; growing academic and military concern about the potential for scarcity of water, land, and other resources – as well as climate change – to cause conflict; evidence that competition for valuable resources drives conflict (the so-called resource curse); opportunities for confidence building and cooperation around natural resources and the environment; and efforts to manage natural resources and the environment after conflict to support post-conflict recovery (Matthew, 2015).

Even as the understanding of these linkages and operational experience has grown, it has generally been piecemeal and fragmented across the conflict life cycle. Typically, the roles that natural resources and the environment play in the conflict life cycle are divided into three main phases: before, during, and after conflict. Actors, mandates and objectives, and conceptual and operational frameworks will vary for each phase of the conflict life cycle. For example, before conflict, there is an emphasis on early warning and intervention to prevent escalation to violence. At this stage, development and environmental actors are important, and security and diplomatic actors often play important roles. During conflict, efforts seek to minimize the effects of conflict on the environment (including intentional effects, secondary effects, and the effects of survival strategies and the breakdown of governance) and to address the use of natural resources to finance armed conflict. In these efforts, security and humanitarian actors are most prominent; diplomatic actors are critical to peace mediation; and environmental NGOs, the government, and the private sector are also often important. After conflict, objectives shift to securing the peace, demobilizing and reintegrating ex-combatants, restoring livelihoods, rebuilding the economy, fostering inclusive governance, and supporting reconciliation and cooperation. Perhaps, the broadest array of actors are engaged in post-conflict recovery, including the security, humanitarian, development, environmental, and governance sectors at the local, national, and international levels.

Environmental peacebuilding integrates these diverse frameworks, objectives, and actors within an overarching framework that aims to maximize the positive peacebuilding potential of natural resources across the conflict life cycle while also mitigating potential risks.

Environmental peacebuilding is the process of governing and managing natural resources and the environment to support durable peace. It includes efforts to prevent, mitigate, resolve, and recover from violent conflict[1] and involves renewable natural resources (such as land, water, and fisheries), nonrenewable natural resources (such as minerals, oil, and gas), and ecosystems (including climate change and ecosystem services). It comprises and links diverse concepts and activities, such as governing natural resources and sharing benefits in a transparent manner to sustain peace and build confidence between stakeholders, preventing or reducing environmental threats to human health and livelihoods caused by violent conflict, using shared natural resources as an entry point for dialogue or as a basis for cooperation and trust building between divided groups, and developing natural resources in a conflict-sensitive manner. As such, environmental peacebuilding provides a framework for contextualizing and linking tools for managing environmental risks and opportunities across the conflict life cycle (see Figure 2.1).

This chapter defines and describes the emerging field of environmental peacebuilding. It starts with a brief overview of the academic and policy discourse on environment, conflict, and peace. This discourse has generated many of the threads that – when woven together – form the fabric of environmental peacebuilding. It then outlines the core dimensions and objectives of environmental peacebuilding, before providing an overview of the key dynamics and considerations across the conflict life cycle (before, during, and after conflict). The chapter concludes with consideration of the value of environmental peacebuilding as a framework linking and contextualizing related issues and thoughts on ways to build environmental peacebuilding looking forward.

Background: the need for a new approach

The concept of peacebuilding was first introduced by Johan Galtung (1967) as one of three approaches to peace, together with peacekeeping and peacemaking (Galtung, 1967). Galtung's definition of peacebuilding was notable for its focus on both positive and negative forms of peace. Positive peace goes beyond the absence of conflict (negative peace).[2] For Galtung, peacemaking generally focuses on de-escalating violence (negative peace), and peacebuilding aims to secure lasting peace that focuses more on positive peace. In 1992, the UN secretary-general published *An Agenda for Peace* (UN Secretary-General, 1992), which provided a much broader, more coherent, and more ambitious approach to peace that moved beyond peacekeeping to secure both positive and negative peace. In 2005, the UN Security Council created the UN Peacebuilding Commission to help member states build peace and learn from others' experiences (Lehtonen, 2016).

Even as peacebuilding was taking shape conceptually and operationally, there was growing political, popular, and academic attention to the linkages between the environment, conflict, and peace. This was not new. Concern for the environmental impacts of war goes back to the Old Testament, Babylonia, and Ancient Greece (Austin & Bruch, 2000; Gleick, 1993). In the modern era, the literature generally starts with the end of World War II, initially focusing on the scorched earth tactics of the Nazi army and the Cold War concerns about the implications of nuclear weapons (Conca & Dabelko, 2002; Deligiannis, 2012; Floyd, 2008).

International focus on environment and conflict began in many ways with the Viet Nam War and the strategic, widespread targeting of the environment (Westing & Pfeiffer, 1972; Zierler, 2011). The United States sprayed an estimated 19 million gallons of Agent Orange and other herbicides over 20,000 km^2 of forests and 2,000 km^2 of agricultural land in South Viet Nam, trying to remove cover for the Viet Cong (Operation Ranch Hand). It seeded clouds to slow the movement of Viet Cong troops and materiel (Operation Popeye), and it used massive

Defining environmental peacebuilding

bulldozers to scrape groundcover (Operation Rome Plow) (Certini, Scalenghe, & Woods, 2013; "Weather modification," 1974). Concern over the environmental damage of the Viet Nam War led to the negotiation and adoption of the 1976 Environmental Modification Convention and provisions in the two 1977 Protocols Additional to the Geneva Conventions (Bothe, 1991; Bouvier, 1991; Fleck & Bothe, 1999). Attention to the environmental consequences of armed conflict grew with the 1990–1991 Gulf War, calls for a Fifth Geneva Convention (to protect the environment), and work of the UN Compensation Commission (Austin & Bruch, 2000; Payne & Sand, 2011).

The end of the Cold War drove two new developments in the environment/conflict/peace nexus. The first was an interest in the environmental causes of conflict. Many argued that people and states would fight over scarce natural resources, such as land and water, and that these conflicts would be fueled by a changing climate (see Chapters 3–7; Homer-Dixon, 1994; Conca & Dabelko, 2002; Urdal, 2005; Deligiannis, 2012; Barnett & Morse, 2013; Dabelko & Dabelko, 1995). This generated talk of "water wars" and "climate wars" (Gleick, 1993; Westing, 1986; Elliott, 1991; Dolatyar & Gray, 1999; Yoffe, Wolf, & Giordano, 2003; Weinthal, Troell, & Nakayama, 2014). More recent analysis has nuanced these assertions, emphasizing the importance of government and societal institutions, and of leadership, in shaping whether a country navigates these stresses or descends into violence (Adger et al., 2014; Rüttinger, Smith, Stang, Tänzler, & Vivekananda, 2015). In this new conceptualization, climate change becomes a "threat multiplier" and a "conflict accelerant" (CNA, 2014; Nordås & Gleditsch, 2007; National Research Council, 2013; see also Crawford & Church, Chapter 7; Orbinski et al., Chapter 13).

The other prominent way that research suggests that the grievances related to the environment can drive conflict is through competition for valuable natural resources. The "resource curse" or the "paradox of plenty" seeks to explain the apparent negative correlation between natural resource wealth and reduced economic, political, and social performance (Auty, 1993; Karl, 1997; Collier & Venables, 2011; Ross, 2015). As with the discourse on conflict and resource scarcity, the literature on the resource curse has become more nuanced, as it has become apparent that natural resources are not inherently a curse, and the outcomes depend substantially on institutional capacity and political will (see Le Billon, Chapter 4).

The end of the Cold War also drove the proliferation of conflict resources – natural resources whose exploitation helps to finance armed conflict (Taylor & Davis, 2016; Le Billon, 2012). During the Cold War, the United States and the USSR often financed opposing sides in proxy wars. The end of the Cold War saw the funding for proxy wars dry up. While governments still had taxation and other traditional sources of financing, rebels had to find other sources of funding. This led to the rapid expansion in the use of conflict diamonds (in Angola, Liberia, Sierra Leone, and elsewhere), conflict timber (in Liberia, Cambodia, and elsewhere), conflict bananas (in Somalia), and conflict cacao (in Cote d'Ivoire) (UNEP, 2009). Between 1989 and 2017, more than 35 major armed conflicts were financed by revenues from diverse natural resources (Bruch, Jensen, Nakayama, & Unruh, in progress). In response, the UN Security Council adopted a series of resolutions banning trade in specific conflict resources from specific countries (Aldinger, Bruch, & Yazykova, 2018), and the international community established the Kimberley Process and domestic due diligence requirements (e.g., in the United States and the European Union) (Grant, 2012; Bone, 2012).

In response to the growing narrative about the potential environmental causes of conflict, researchers in the early 2000s started suggesting that shared interests in the environment could provide opportunities for cooperation, confidence building, and ultimately peacebuilding (Conca & Dabelko, 2002; Carius, 2006). This thinking coalesced into a distinct conceptual framework – with a growing body of experience – on environmental cooperation for peacebuilding. The most common natural resources around which people cooperated have been water, protected areas (so-called peace parks), and wildlife (Mehyar, Al Khateeb, Bromberg, & Koch-Ya'ari, 2014; Weinthal, 2016; Westrik, 2015; Walters, 2015).

The end of the Cold War also created an expanded space for UN activities in ending armed conflict, keeping the new peace, and recovering from armed conflict.

With the growing recognition of the role of natural resources in armed conflict, a growing number of peace agreements have addressed natural resources. Historically (from 1945 to 2015), only 15% of peace agreements addressed natural resources (Blundell & Harwell, 2016); from 1989 to 2004, this rose to 54% (Mason, Sguaitamatti, & Gröbli, 2016); and since 2005, every major peace agreement has included natural resource provisions (UN DPA & UNEP, 2015). The growth of environmental considerations in peace mediation reflects a substantial shift in how mediators and parties view the environment, and a growing body of literature considers when and how to address the environment in mediation processes (Dawes, 2016; UN DPA & UNEP, 2015).

Since the early 2000s, there has been a growing consideration of the relevance of natural resources to peacekeeping. From 1948, not a single peacekeeping mission for 55 years was mandated to address natural resource issues. With the end of the Cold War, UN peacekeeping missions became more multidimensional. Starting in 2003, with the mandate for the UN Mission in Liberia (UNMIL), the Security Council started giving explicit mandates to peacekeeping missions to address certain resources (often, conflict resources) to broadly help restore natural resource governance or to address the environmental impacts of peacekeeping operations (Ravier, Vialle, Doran, & Stokes, 2016). Additionally, the UN Department of Peacekeeping Operations and Department of Field Support adopted an Environmental Policy for UN Field Missions, and national militaries involved in peacekeeping missions also adopted environmental policies (Ravier et al., 2016; Waleij, Bosetti, Doran, & Liljedahl, 2016).

Theoretical and operational interest also grew in the role of the environment and natural resources after conflict. A series of 150 case studies examined experiences and lessons in managing natural resources in more than 70 conflict-affected countries.[3] These analyses showed that most stated objectives of post-conflict peacebuilding, including the security, political, economic, basic services, and social objectives, had environmental dimensions. Drawing on these analyses and others, the UN adopted systemwide guidelines on Natural Resource Management in Transition Settings (UNDG, 2013). Similarly, the African Development Bank developed a flagship report to inform environmental programming in conflict-affected settings (AfDB, 2014).

These different dimensions of the environment/conflict/peace nexus evolved largely independently. They were rarely connected directly with one another or across phases of the conflict life cycle. In some instances, theory preceded practice (e.g., with the resource curse, water wars, and environmental cooperation for peacebuilding), and in many instances, practice drove theoretical considerations (environmental consequences of war, conflict resources, peacekeeping, environmental considerations in peace mediation, and post-conflict natural resource management).

As thinking in these different areas grew – regarding environmental impacts, environmental causes, conflict resources, cooperative opportunities, and otherwise – scholars started seeing linkages among these areas. They coined a series of terms to describe the broader context, including "environmental security," "environmental peace," "environmental peacemaking," and "environmental peacebuilding" (Carius, 2006; Conca & Dabelko, 2002; Harari & Roseman, 2008). Recognizing that there has been some fluidity in the terms, this chapter adopts "environmental peacebuilding" to encompass the full range of environmentally related considerations across the conflict life cycle.[4]

Components and objectives of environmental peacebuilding

To the extent that environmental peacebuilding is understood as the environmental dimension of peacebuilding,[5] it follows the structure and objectives of peacebuilding – albeit using an environmental lens. While peacebuilding takes a different form in each context, it usually encompasses one or more of the following five dimensions:[6]

1   Security: Establishing safety and security, including through security sector reform and disarmament, demobilization, and reintegration of combatants;
2   Political: Redistributing power between groups and establishing a new social contract between the state and its citizens;
3   Economic: Generating economic growth, revenue, sustainable livelihoods, and employment;
4   Basic services: Delivering basic services such as waste management, water and sanitation, health care, and education; and
5   Social: Rebuilding relationships and trust between groups.

Environmental peacebuilding can make a critical contribution to each of the five dimensions of peacebuilding – for example, by securing resource-rich sites and restoring access (security); supporting the redistribution and sharing of benefits and revenue (political); enabling productive, sustainable, and rewarding livelihoods (economic); offering pathways for delivering access to basic services and food security (basic services); and providing platforms for dialogue and confidence building between stakeholders (social).

All these dimensions are supported by establishing and reforming institutions, laws, and practices as well as by restoring the rule of law and access to justice – in short, by improving governance. Governance is "the system of values, policies and institutions by which a society manages its economic, political and social affairs through interactions within and among the state, civil society and private sector" (UNDP, 2004, p. 1). Governance should be distinguished from management, which is the ensemble of day-to-day activities and technical decisions executing the decisions made through governance processes (Cook, 2014). Environmental peacebuilding relies on good resource governance and management at all levels, from local mechanisms to national laws to bilateral and multilateral agreements. It is particularly important to establish effective governance mechanisms and safeguards (1) at the national level for high-value resources that generate revenue and have the potential to trigger corruption and conflict as well as (2) at the local level for renewable resources that sustain livelihoods and ecosystem services. Local-level mechanisms are often based on a combination of statutory and customary frameworks, sometimes also integrating religious frameworks (Meinzen-Dick & Pradhan, 2016; Sait, 2013).

Phases of environmental peacebuilding

Recognizing that there are environmental dimensions of many conflict and peace dynamics, environmental peacebuilding can best be understood by reference to the conflict life cycle: environmental dimensions that can cause conflict or drive escalation to violence; the environment during armed conflict, both as a casualty and as a conflict driver; support to conflict resolution, peacemaking, and cooperation; and foster post-conflict recovery and reconciliation (see Figure 2.1). It is worth emphasizing that environmental peacebuilding includes both (1) discrete

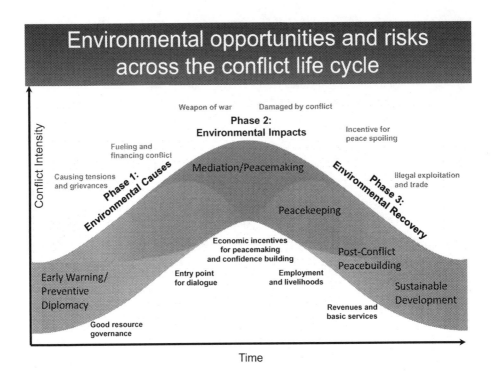

Figure 2.1 Environmental opportunities and risks across the conflict life cycle

consideration of specific dynamics and processes at specific points in the conflict life cycle and (2) cross-cutting consideration of how these dynamics and processes link across time. We will now consider the environmental dimensions of the four key phases of peacebuilding.

Onset and escalation of conflict

As noted earlier, environmental grievances can both generate latent or social conflict and can cause latent or social conflicts to escalate to violence. Common sources of grievances include scarce natural resources, competition over valuable natural resources (including inequitable benefit sharing) (see Klare, Chapter 3; Unruh, Chapter 5), and extreme pollution and environmental degradation. For example, in Bougainville, Papua New Guinea, the lack of benefit sharing and severe water pollution from the Panguna gold and copper mine drove a secessionist movement that escalated to civil war (Regan, 2017).

Recognizing that environmental grievances can be a contributing cause of conflict and can drive escalation to violence, conflict prevention increasingly considers environmental dimensions and interventions. Acknowledging that conflict dynamics are complex, the long-term factors that prevent social conflicts related to natural resources from escalating to violent conflicts are good governance and social resilience.[7] While there has been substantial debate over what constitutes "good" governance, analysis of diverse regional articulations highlights five key factors: rule of law, equity, participation and transparency, effectiveness, and accountability (Bruch, Muffett, & Nichols, 2016). Accordingly, efforts to prevent conflicts related to natural resources often emphasize transparency (e.g., the Extractive Industries Transparency Initiative), equity (e.g., in benefit sharing), and other good governance principles.

More recently, attention has emphasized resilience-based approaches to conflict prevention. In this framing, environmental governance, sustainable livelihoods, institutional capacity, and strong community relationships all contribute to social resilience, which can prevent conflict. The new scholarship argues that as institutions are further developed, social resilience will increase, and the capacity to prevent violent conflict will follow (UNEP, 2014; Rüttinger et al., 2015).

There are a growing number of efforts designed to address potential environmental causes of conflict or drivers that escalate conflict to violence. These include, for example, the Extractive Industries Transparency Initiative (EITI) (Epremian, Lujala, & Bruch, 2016; Sovacool, Walter, Van de Graaf, & Andrews, 2016), benefit-sharing funds (Binningsbø & Rustad, 2012), early warning systems (FEWS NET, n.d.), and early action funds and other interventions (Dumas, 2016). Experiences with these different approaches (and their respective theories of change) are providing a growing body of evidence. Just as research has led to more nuanced understandings of the dynamics related to the environmental causes of conflict, experience is leading to more nuanced understandings of the benefits and limitations of the proposed approaches to preventing escalation and supporting de-escalation of natural resource–related conflicts.

During armed conflict

Armed conflicts both affect the environment and are affected by the environment. As noted earlier, much of the academic and operational attention has focused on two issues: the deliberate targeting of the environment and conflict resources. It is important, though, to maintain a broader view of the relationship.

There are three main pathways by which armed conflict causes environmental damage and degradation: direct impacts, secondary impacts, and governance impacts. Direct impacts are caused by the intentional targeting or physical destruction of the environment from military operations. These include, for example, scorched earth tactics (including poisoning wells or leveling forests to remove cover); the use of particular weapons (including unexploded ordnance); the release of chemicals and waste from the bombing of industrial sites and infrastructure, creating environmental hotspots; and the environmental impacts of natural resource extraction by armed groups to finance conflict (Austin & Bruch, 2000; see also Closmann, Chapter 8). These direct impacts are often very visible and in the public eye.

Secondary impacts of armed conflict on the environment result from coping strategies to survive the socio-economic disruption and loss of basic services. Common examples of these impacts include liquidation of natural assets, displacement and temporary settlements, proliferation of informal economies (often as part of the broader conflict economy), and delivery of humanitarian and peacekeeping support (UNEP, 2009; see also Chapter 11). While being less in the public eye, secondary impacts are often more widespread and long-term than the direct impacts.

Governance impacts of armed conflict on the environment appear when conflicts disrupt state institutions, policy coordination, and social relationships between resource users (UNEP, 2009; Bruch et al., 2016). For example, armed conflict undermines environmental regulation, coordination, monitoring, and enforcement. Weakened governance, in turn, often supports a dramatic expansion of illegal and criminal exploitation of natural resources and the loss of land tenure security. Governance impacts, then, can be among the most severe and problematic.

Natural resources can also finance, drive, and otherwise affect armed conflict (see Lujala et al., Chapter 10). Once combatants start exploiting natural resources and their revenues to finance armed conflict, the natural resources can transform the conflict narrative. Once conflict resources take root in the conflict economy, it can be difficult to control, even after the conflict has ended. Rather than being a civilian object (protected by international law), conflict resources become a military objective that might be attacked, seized, or destroyed to deprive the other side from their benefits (Bannon & Collier, 2003; Le Billon, 2013; Ross, 2004).

Since the mid-1970s, there has been a steady development of international law seeking to prevent and punish wanton harm to the environment during armed conflict (Bothe, Bruch, Diamond, & Jensen, 2010; UNEP, 2009). While there has been an implementation and enforcement gap, this is starting to change. There are a growing number of national and international measures to operationalize international law, such as national legislation, military manuals, and dedicated environmental staff (Jacobsson, 2015; Austin & Bruch, 2000). Moreover, UN Security Council tools address conflict resources, including resolutions and presidential statements, peacekeeping mission mandates, sanctions, and panels of experts (Aldinger et al., 2018). There are also national tools to address conflict resources, including certification schemes, due diligence, consumer awareness campaigns, and prosecution (Bannon & Collier, 2003; Radics & Bruch, 2017).

Environmental peacemaking

Historically, there were four common reasons against including environmental provisions in peace agreements. There are many competing priorities during peace negotiations, and mediators and parties were concerned about overloading the negotiations. The vested interests of elites (often on the negotiating delegations) meant that they were not interested in addressing land, extractives, or other resources. There was also a perception that natural resources were economic issues that were not essential to resolving the conflict. Additionally, both negotiators and parties often lacked technical expertise and time to include robust provisions.

With the many resource-related conflicts of the 1990s, negotiators and parties started considering natural resources more frequently. Where resource provisions were not included – for example, in all but the final peace agreements for Sierra Leone – peace agreements often failed.

There are four key reasons that parties decided to include provisions related to natural resources and the environment in peace agreements: (1) grievances over natural resources were a contributing cause of conflict (as in Nepal, Sierra Leone, and Sudan); (2) natural resource revenues helped finance conflict (as in Angola, Cambodia, and Liberia); (3) natural resources were damaged by the conflict (as in Darfur and the DRC); and (4) the environment can be used collaboratively to build confidence and trust (Dawes, 2016; UN DPA & UNEP, 2015).

Of the many resources, land is the natural resource most commonly addressed in peace agreements, followed by extractive resources and water (UN DPA & UNEP, 2015). Provisions most often relate to resource access and ownership, allocation of the power to manage and develop natural resources, sharing of natural resource revenues and other benefits, and confidence-building measures.

There are some common strategies that inform how to address environmental considerations in peace negotiations (UN DPA & UNEP, 2015). First, natural resource–related issues should be addressed in a manner suited to their role in the conflict (cause, financing, casualty, etc.). The potential benefits from natural resources can provide an incentive to keep parties at the negotiating table. In many cases, a peace agreement does not provide a final solution to complex resource problems, but rather, establishes institutions and processes to address natural resource issues in the future (e.g., rather than setting forth the details of how to redistribute land, a peace agreement can create a process that will lead to land reform) (Unruh & Williams, 2013b). Due to the technical aspects of natural resource issues, it is often effective to establish a technical track on natural resources within the broader political negotiation. Moreover, technical support is often needed for one or more negotiating parties.

Post-conflict recovery

After armed conflict ends, there is a staggeringly broad effort to help countries recover. As mentioned earlier, post-conflict peacebuilding focuses on five core dimensions: security, political, economic, basic services, and social. Each of these has strong environmental components, and sound environmental management can improve post-conflict peacebuilding, while ignoring the environment can undermine peacebuilding efforts.

For example, the environment affects security efforts in many ways – and often in unexpected ways. Peacekeeping seeks both to physically dissuade violence (through a military presence) and to manage potential drivers of conflict. Six peacekeeping mandates have directly addressed natural resources, and 16 indirectly (UNEP, 2012). Peacekeeping operations can be more effective by working to restore the national and local governance of natural resources and by securing resource-rich sites that may finance conflict and otherwise serve as an incentive to spoil peacebuilding efforts (UNEP, 2012.). Typically, 50%–80% of ex-combatants seek to return to agriculture, so a high priority is on ensuring that they have the necessary land, water, inputs (seed, fertilizers, etc.), and capacity (UNEP & UNDP, 2013). Where the military and other security actors have been involved in the illicit extraction of and trade in natural resources, security sector reform needs to consider the environment. And efforts to remove landmines and unexploded ordnance need to ensure that there are governance systems in place to prevent land grabbing of the newly opened lands (Shimoyachi-Yuzawa, 2012).

After conflict, there are often political efforts to reform key natural resource sectors, including reviewing and maybe canceling resource concessions, securing resource rights, and changing how resources and their revenues are allocated and managed (Bruch et al., 2016). Tired from conflict, the government, private sector, and civil society are often willing to try approaches that had previously been rejected. There may be more transparency and participation, more community engagement, and more efforts to rebuild trust. Increasingly, countries and their international partners realize that governance and institutions are crucial in avoiding and managing conflict – and that neither resource abundance nor resource scarcity will inevitably lead to conflict.

The environment is a prominent feature in the economic dimensions of post-conflict peacebuilding. Natural resources such as land, timber, minerals, and oil and gas are often the primary assets readily available to governments to generate revenues, build infrastructure, enhance livelihoods, and ensure food security (Lujala & Rustad, 2012; Young & Goldman, 2015). Common strategies include the use of growth poles, resource corridors, value chains, and sustainable livelihood approaches (see Young & Goldman, 2015). In some instances, it is necessary to restore the productive capacity of natural resources (Jensen & Lonergan, 2012). The creation of resource-related jobs should take into account the specific (and sometimes differing) needs of men and women as well as key structural factors such as ownership of land.

The restoration and development of basic services can provide significant peace dividends by improving people's lives and showing the value of peace (and the cost of returning to conflict). The environment provides inputs and externalities to many basic services, including water, sanitation, waste management, and energy.

Common interests in natural resources – especially ones that cross boundaries – can be an entry point for social dialogue or as an initial platform for cooperation and trust building between divided groups (Karuru & Yeung, 2016; UNEP et al., 2013). If structured in a strategic manner, cooperation around shared environmental priorities can also extend into other areas of collaborative action. For example, regional economic integration in both Europe and Central America was characterized by post-conflict cooperation around natural resources that laid the ground for broader political cooperation (Bruch et al., 2012; King, Pastora, Salazar, & Rodriguez, 2016;). This is also the idea underpinning the concept of peace parks (Ali, 2007; Westrik, 2015; Walters, 2015; see also Swatuk, Chapter 16).

Conclusion and the way forward

One of the great challenges in conflict-affected settings is the combination of profound needs, high expectations, and hundreds of independent institutions,[8] each with their own mandates and resources. Environmental considerations cut across many of the peacebuilding objectives, and often, a single natural resource (e.g., minerals, land, or water) or environmental dynamic (e.g., climate change) can affect multiple peacebuilding objectives.

Environmental peacebuilding offers a broader perspective to better link and contextualize diverse peacebuilding activities across time, space, and objectives. Temporally, it helps to link the environmental causes of conflict and environmental impacts of conflict to consideration of those causes and impacts in the peace agreement and to recovery efforts after conflict. Spatially, environmental peacebuilding can help to see where different efforts are taking place to ensure that all groups are benefiting from peacebuilding, and not just those associated with the government (an important consideration in conflict-sensitive programming). Spatial considerations can also help to both predict conflicts and promote cooperation. And where a single resource is both limited and important for multiple objectives – for example, forests being important for government revenues, community livelihoods and food security, and conservation – coordination around that resource can help to ensure that activities pursuant to one objective do not undermine the ability to achieve other objectives (Altman, Nichols, & Woods, 2012).

Looking forward, there are three areas in environmental peacebuilding where researchers and practitioners will need to pay more attention.

First, different resources have different characteristics that affect their potential for conflict and peace (see Chapter 4). In many regards, certain resources tend to play similar roles and can be grouped together accordingly: extractive resources (minerals, oil, gas), land, water, and other renewable resources (including fisheries, forests, wildlife, agriculture, and livestock). Extractive resources, for example, are nonrenewable and tend to be high value, and as a result, are often a key driver of rent-seeking and inadequate benefit-sharing, and minerals, in particular, are often conflict resources. Oil, gas, and certain types of mining require substantial capital investment in infrastructure to extract and take years to bring online. Mismanagement of extractive resources has driven secessionist movements in Kurdistan (Iraq), Aceh (Indonesia), and Southern Sudan (now South Sudan), among other places (Collier & Hoeffler, 2012). Managed well, extractive industries can enable countries to recover and transition to a more sustainable economy by generating substantial revenues, reducing macroeconomic vulnerability (through diversification) and dependence on foreign economies, and creating infrastructure.

Unlike nonrenewable resources that often require large amounts of money, labor, and time to extract, renewable resources such as agriculture and fisheries are more readily exploited and can thus rapidly support livelihoods and food security. Land is not only an important economic asset and source of livelihood, but also closely linked to community identity, history, and culture

(Green, 2015). In Africa, land issues have played a substantial role in all but 3 of the more than 30 intrastate conflicts since 1990 (Unruh & Williams, 2013b). Due to their importance to livelihoods and local well-being, land and water have proven to be successful entry points for cooperation (Wolf, 2007).

Second, further attention needs to be paid to gender dimensions of environmental peacebuilding. It has become increasingly important to consider the relationship between gender, conflict, and natural resources beyond the traditional narrative of victimhood (Halle, Chapter 24). Rather than center on women as victims of violence when carrying out natural resource–related responsibilities, the focus has recently shifted to the role of natural resources in strengthening women's political and economic participation in conflict prevention and peacebuilding.

Women play a crucial role in natural resource management. They constitute approximately two-thirds of the livestock keepers and 30% of artisanal miners worldwide (UNEP et al., 2013). Furthermore, 43% of the agricultural labor force in developing countries is composed of women (Team & Doss, 2011). In conflict-affected settings, women serve as the primary managers of water and energy needs at both the household and community levels. Despite their potential to capitalize on the benefits of natural resources, women must overcome many obstacles relating to their own security, variation in the quality and availability of natural resources, and discriminatory laws and cultural practices. However, conflict poses a unique opportunity to surmount these challenges, as it is often followed by a shift in traditional roles and the division of labor (Team & Doss, 2011; UNEP et al., 2013).

Notwithstanding a growing body of literature on the topic and a growing understanding of the importance of gender-sensitive approaches (Dunn & Matthew, 2015; Karuru & Yeung, 2016; UNEP et al., 2013), experience in the field suggests both that there are a number of innovative and promising approaches, but that even so, the majority of approaches are often modest at best. This means that there is often a sense of what might work, but the evidence base is not as robust as it needs to be and political will is not as deep as it should be. Future peacebuilding efforts and research need to better integrate gender considerations from the start.

Third, there is a similar need to mainstream conflict-sensitive approaches to environmental and natural resource programming. Conflict sensitivity relies on the principles of "do no harm" and "do some good," in that the design of development interventions should either avoid raising the risk of violent conflict or lower the risk (Hammill, Crawford, & Craig, 2000). It is a widely accepted practice for interventions where baseline conflict risks are significant. There are usually five key steps in conflict-sensitive programming: (1) conducting a conflict assessment; (2) identifying the environment, resource, and climate linkages that could make conflict more likely; (3) mapping development plans against the identified environment-conflict risks; (4) modifying development plans to neutralize that risk; and (5) monitoring the risks and providing adequate warning. A growing number of institutions have adopted guidance, both generally and for the environment, conservation, and natural resources specifically (Ajroud et al., 2017; Hammill et al., 2000). In most cases, the approaches are based on experience and are considered good practice (or even best practice). However, the as yet modest body of experience means that these approaches are not necessarily based on a large-N evidence base.

In recent years, there has been a remarkable growth in environmental peacebuilding. Researchers are starting to collect and synthesize learning in the scholarship on diverse dimensions. Both quantitative and qualitative research are burgeoning, much of it transdisciplinary. People are increasingly exchanging approaches, experiences, and lessons. Learning to date is being translated into institutional policy and operational guidance. Universities and practitioners are offering courses on environmental peacebuilding and on related topics.[9] Furthermore, a new professional association is being created to provide an institutional architecture to support the ongoing development and maturation of the field.

There is still much to learn. Research has highlighted many risks and opportunities for governing the environment and natural resources to support a durable peace. Further work is needed on the vocabulary and the conceptual frameworks. Particular attention needs to be paid to what we know, what works, what does not, and why (Krampe, 2017). In many instances, though, the specific dynamics and reliable solutions are still in the process of being characterized and tested. Too few voices from conflict-affected countries are involved in the discourse, and many of the case studies are still unfolding, generating new learning. There is a companion need to determine how to measure and assess impact in environmental peacebuilding – which is essential if meaningful funding is to be committed. And there will be ongoing efforts to translate this growing understanding into practice through mandates, policy, guidance, hiring, and training.

There are numerous linkages between environment, conflict, and peace, and the evidence supporting the need for a theoretical and operational environmental peacebuilding framework to conflict is clearer than ever before. The linkages go both ways: conflict and peace are affected by the environment and, in turn, affect the environment. The diverse linkages are themselves linked temporally across the conflict life cycle, spatially across landscapes, and programmatically across peacebuilding objectives, and environmental peacebuilding provides an important framework for understanding and acting on these linkages.

Notes

1 While this chapter focuses on armed and violent conflict, the dynamics, approaches, and considerations apply to a large extent to latent and social conflict.
2 Efforts that support negative peace include, for example, early warning, negotiation of peace agreements, and peacekeeping. Efforts that support positive peace include regional political and economic integration and cooperation around shared water resources. For a more recent and detailed analysis on positive and negative peace, see Galtung and Fischer (2013).
3 See Lujala and Rustad (2012); Jensen and Lonergan (2012); Unruh and Williams (2013a); Weinthal, Troell, and Nakayama (2014); Young and Goldman (2015); and Bruch, Muffett, and Nichols (2016).
4 In contrast, "environmental security" is often framed either as addressing the environmental causes of conflict or as encompassing the environmental risks more broadly (but not necessarily addressing the positive opportunities presented by the environment) (Barnett, 2001; Dabelko & Dabelko, 1995). And "environmental peacemaking" often is understood to focus on the cooperative aspects of environmental peacebuilding in contrast to environmental security (e.g., Conca & Dabelko, 2002; Deligiannis, 2012).
5 As an alternative to framing environmental peacebuilding with reference to peacebuilding, others have framed environmental peacebuilding from other perspectives. For example, environmental peacebuilding may be grounded in sustainable development, as a rights-based approach, and from an ecocentric perspective (Conservation International, 2017; Brundtland, 1987).
6 These five categories are drawn from the UN General Assembly (2010).
7 For example, the risk of renewed conflict in countries with good governance drops rapidly after conflict, while countries characterized by poor governance are substantially more vulnerable to conflict relapse (Hegre & Nygård, 2015). And socially resilient communities are best prepared to employ the multilayered, multisector approaches needed to resolve disputes and prevent escalation to violence (Ganson & Wennmann, 2012).
8 For example, post-conflict Sierra Leone had more than 400 organizations working on its reconstruction, including 17 UN agencies, 95 international NGOs, and 200 local NGOs.
9 For instance, the United Nations Environment Program, the Environmental Law Institute, the University of California – Irvine, Duke University, and Columbia University partnered to develop a massive open online course (MOOC) on Environmental Security and Sustaining Peace (see www.epmooc.org/, 2019).

Works cited

Adger, W. N., Pulhin, J. M., Barnett, J., Dabelko, G. D., Hovelsrud, G. K., Levy, M., . . . Vogel, C. H. (2014). Human security. In *Climate change 2014: Impacts, adaptation, and vulnerability* (pp. 755–791). Fifth Assessment Report of the Intergovernmental Panel on Climate Change. Cambridge, UK: Cambridge University Press.

AfDB (African Development Bank). (2014). *From fragility to resilience: Managing natural resources in fragile states in Africa.* Tunis.

Ajroud, B., Al-Zyoud, N., Cardona, L., Edmond, J., Pavitt, D., & Woomer, A. (2017). *Environmental peacebuilding training manual.* Arlington, VA: Conservation International.

Aldinger, P., Bruch, C., & Yazykova, S. (2018). Revisiting securitization: An empirical analysis of environment and natural resource provisions in UN Security Council resolutions, 1946–2016. In A. Swain & J. Öjendal (Eds.), *Handbook of environmental conflict and peacebuilding.* London and New York: Routledge.

Ali, S. H. (Ed.). (2007). *Peace parks: Conservation and conflict resolution.* Cambridge, MA: MIT Press.

Altman, S. L., Nichols, S. S., & Woods, J. T. (2012). Leveraging high-value natural resources to restore the rule of law: The role of the Liberia Forest Initiative in Liberia's transition to stability. In P. Lujala & S. A. Rustad (Eds.), *High-value natural resources and post-conflict peacebuilding* (pp. 337–365). London: Routledge.

Austin, J. E., & Bruch, C. E. (Eds.). (2000). *The environmental consequences of war: Legal, economic, and scientific perspectives.* Cambridge, UK: Cambridge University Press.

Auty, R. M. (1993). *Sustaining development in mineral economies: The resource curse thesis.* London: Routledge.

Bannon, I., & Collier, P. (Eds.). (2003). *Natural resources and violent conflict: Options and actions.* Washington, DC: World Bank.

Barnett, J. (2001). *The meaning of environmental security: Ecological politics and policy in the new security era.* London: Zed Books.

Barnett, H. J., & Morse, C. (2013). *Scarcity and growth: The economics of natural resource availability* (Vol. 3). New York: Routledge.

Binningsbø, H. M., & Rustad, S. A. (2012). Sharing the wealth: A pathway to peace or a trail to nowhere? *Conflict Management and Peace Science, 29*(5), 547–566.

Blundell, A. G., & Harwell, E. E. (2016). *How do peace agreements treat natural resources?* Washington, DC: Forest Trends.

Bone, A. (2012). The Kimberley process certification scheme: The primary safeguard for the diamond industry. In P. Lujala & S. A. Rustad (Eds.), *High-value natural resources and post-conflict peacebuilding* (pp. 189–194). London: Routledge.

Bothe, M. (1991). The protection of the environment in times of armed conflict. *German Yearbook of International Law, 34,* 54.

Bothe, M., Bruch, C., Diamond, J., & Jensen, D. (2010). International law protecting the environment during armed conflict: Gaps and opportunities. *International Review of the Red Cross, 92*(879), 569–592.

Bouvier, A. (1991). Protection of the natural environment in time of armed conflict. *International Review of the Red Cross Archive, 31*(285), 567–578.

Bruch, C., Jensen, D., Nakayama, M., & Unruh, J. (In Progress). *Post-conflict peacebuilding and natural resources: The promise and the peril.* Washington, DC: Environmental Law Institute Press.

Bruch, C., Muffett, C., & Nichols, S. S. (Eds.). (2016). *Governance, natural resources and post-conflict peacebuilding.* London: Routledge.

Bruch, C., Wolfarth, R., & Michalcik, V. (2012). Natural resources, post-conflict reconstruction, and regional integration: Lessons from the Marshall Plan and other reconstruction efforts. In D. Jensen & S. Lonergan (Eds.), *Assessing and restoring natural resources in post-conflict peacebuilding* (pp. 343–362). London: Routledge.

Brundtland, G. H. (1987). *Our common future.* Report of the World Commission on environment and development. New York: United Nations.

Carius, A. (2006). Environmental peacebuilding: Conditions for success. *Environmental Change and Security Program Report, 12,* 59–75.

Certini, G., Scalenghe, R., & Woods, W. I. (2013). The impact of warfare on the soil environment. *Earth-Science Reviews, 127,* 1–15.

CNA. (2014). *National security and the accelerating risks of climate change.* Alexandria, VA.

Collier, P., & Hoeffler, A. (2012). High-value natural resources, development, and conflict: Channels of causation. In P. Lujala & S. A. Rustad (Eds.), *High-value natural resources and post-conflict peacebuilding* (pp. 297–312). London: Routledge.

Collier, P., & Venables, A. J. (Eds.). (2011). *Plundered nations? Successes and failures in natural resource extraction.* London: Palgrave Macmillan.

Conca, K., & Dabelko, G. D. (Eds.). (2002). *Environmental peacemaking.* Washington, DC: Woodrow Wilson Center Press.

Conservation International. (2017). *Policy center for environment and peace.* Retrieved from www.conservation. org/Projects/Pages/Policy-Center-for-Environment-and-Peace.aspx. Last visited: April 8, 2018.

Cook, C. (2014). Governing jurisdictional fragmentation: Tracing patterns of water governance in Ontario, Canada. *Geoforum, 56,* 192–200.

Dabelko, G. D., & Dabelko, D. D. (1995). Environmental security: Issues of conflict and redefinition. *Environmental Change and Security Project Report, 1*(1), 3–13.

Dawes, M. A. (2016). Considerations for determining when to include natural resources in peace agreements ending internal armed conflicts. In C. Bruch, C. Muffett, & S. S. Nichols (Eds.), *Governance, natural resources, and post-conflict peacebuilding* (pp. 121–146). London: Routledge.

Deligiannis, T. (2012). The evolution of environment–conflict research: Toward a livelihood framework. *Global Environmental Politics, 12*(1), 78–100.

Dolatyar, M., & Gray, T. (1999). *Water politics in the Middle East: A context for conflict or cooperation?* New York: Palgrave Macmillan.

Dumas, J. (2016). Preventing violence over natural resources: The Early Action Fund in South America. In C. Bruch, C. Muffett, & S. S. Nichols (Eds.), *Governance, natural resources, and post-conflict peacebuilding* (pp. 501–518). London: Routledge.

Dunn, H., & Matthew, R. (2015). Natural resources and gender in conflict settings. *Peace Review, 27*(2), 156–164.

Elliott, M. (1991). Water wars. *Geographical Magazine,* 28–30.

Epremian, L., Lujala, P., & Bruch, C. (2016). High-value natural resources revenues and transparency: Accounting for revenues and peace. In *Oxford research encyclopedia of politics.* Oxford, UK: Oxford University Press.

Famine Early Warning Systems Network (FEWS NET). (n.d.). *Home | Famine Early Warning Systems Network.* Retrieved from www.fews.net/.

Fleck, D., & Bothe, M. (Eds.). (1999). *The handbook of humanitarian law in armed conflicts.* Oxford, UK: Oxford University Press.

Floyd, R. (2008). The environmental security debate and its significance for climate change. *The International Spectator, 43*(3), 51–65.

Ganson, B., & Wennmann, A. (2012). *Confronting risk, mobilizing action: A framework for conflict prevention in the context of large-scale business investments.* Berlin: Friedrich Ebert Stiftung.

Galtung, J. (1967). *Theories of peace: A synthetic approach to peace thinking.* Oslo: International Peace Research Institute.

Galtung, J., & Fischer, D. (2013). Positive and negative peace. In *Johan Galtung: Pioneer of Peace Research* (pp. 173–178). Berlin: Springer.

Gleick, P. H. (1993). Water and conflict: Fresh water resources and international security. *International Security, 18*(1), 79–112.

Grant, J. A. (2012). The Kimberley Process at ten: Reflections on a decade of efforts to end the trade in conflict diamonds. In P. Lujala & S. A. Rustad (Eds.), *High-value natural resources and post-conflict peacebuilding* (pp. 159–179). London: Routledge.

Green, A. (2015). Social identity, natural resources, and peacebuilding. In H. Young & L. Goldman (Eds.), *Livelihoods, natural resources, and post-conflict peacebuilding* (pp. 19–40). London: Routledge.

Hammill, A., Crawford, A., & Craig, R. (2000). *Conflict-sensitive conservation: Practitioners' manual.* Winnipeg, Canada: International Institute for Sustainable Development.

Harari, N., & Roseman, J. (2008). *Environmental peacebuilding, theory and practice: A case study of the Good Water Neighbours project and in depth analysis of the Wadi Fukin/Tzur Hadassah communities.* Amman/Bethlehem/Tel Aviv: FoEME.

Hegre, H., & Nygård, H. M. (2015). Governance and conflict relapse. *Journal of Conflict Resolution, 59*(6), 984–1016.

Homer-Dixon, T. F. (1994). Environmental scarcities and violent conflict: Evidence from cases. *International Security, 19*(1), 5–40.

Jacobsson, M. (2015). *Second report on the protection of the environment in relation to armed conflicts.* New York: International Law Commission.

Jensen, D., & Lonergan, S. (Eds.). (2012). *Assessing and restoring natural resources in post-conflict peacebuilding.* London: Routledge.

Karl, T. L. (1997). *The paradox of plenty: Oil booms and petro-states.* Berkeley, CA: University of California Press.

Karuru, N., & Yeung, L. (2016). Integrating gender into post-conflict natural resource management. In C. Bruch, C. Muffett, & S. S. Nichols (Eds.), *Governance, natural resources, and post-conflict peacebuilding* (pp. 579–604). London: Routledge.

King, M. W., Pastora, M. G., Salazar, M. C., & Rodriguez, C. M. (2016). Environmental governance and peacebuilding in post-conflict Central America: Lessons from the Central American Commission for Environment and Development. In C. Bruch, C. Muffett, & S. S. Nichols (Eds.), *Governance, natural resources, and post-conflict peacebuilding* (pp. 777–802). London: Routledge.

Krampe, F. (2017). Toward sustainable peace: A new research agenda for post-conflict natural resource management. *Global Environmental Politics, 17*(4), 1–8.

Le Billon, P. (2012). Bankrupting peace spoilers: Can peacekeepers curtail belligerents' access to resource revenues. In P. Lujala & S. A. Rustad (Eds.), *High-value natural resources and post-conflict peacebuilding* (pp. 25–48). London: Routledge.

Le Billon, P. (2013). *Fuelling war: Natural resources and armed conflicts.* London: Routledge.

Lehtonen, M. (2016). Peacebuilding through natural resource management: The UN Peacebuilding Commission's first five years. In C. Bruch, C. Muffett, & S. S. Nichols (Eds.), *Governance, natural resources, and post-conflict peacebuilding* (pp. 147–164). London: Routledge.

Lujala, P., & Rustad, S. A. (Eds.). (2012). *High-value natural resources and post-conflict peacebuilding.* London: Routledge.

Mason, S. J., Sguaitamatti, D. A., & Gröbli, M. D. P. R. (2016). Stepping stones to peace? Natural resource provisions in peace agreements. In C. Bruch, C. Muffett, & S. S. Nichols (Eds.), *Governance, natural resources, and post-conflict peacebuilding* (pp. 71–120). London: Routledge.

Matthew, R. A. (Ed.). (2015). *Environmental security.* London: SAGE Publications.

Mehyar, M., Al Khateeb, N., Bromberg, G., & Koch-Ya'ari, E. (2014). Transboundary cooperation in the Lower Jordan River Basin. In E. Weinthal, J. J. Troell, & M. Nakayama (Eds.), *Water and post-conflict peacebuilding* (pp. 265–270). London: Routledge.

Meinzen-Dick, R., & Pradhan, R. (2016). Property rights and legal pluralism in post-conflict environments: Problem or opportunity for natural resource management? In C. Bruch, C. Muffett, & S. S. Nichols (Eds.), *Governance, natural resources, and post-conflict peacebuilding* (pp. 525–544). London: Routledge.

National Research Council. (2013). *Climate and social stress: Implications for security analysis.* Washington, DC: National Academies Press.

Nordås, R., & Gleditsch, N. P. (2007). Climate change and conflict. *Political Geography, 26*(6), 627–638.

Payne, C., & Sand, P. (Eds.). (2011). *Gulf War reparations and the UN Compensation Commission: Environmental liability.* New York: Oxford University Press.

Radics, O., & Bruch, C. (2017). The law of pillage, conflict resources, and jus post bellum. In C. Stahn, J. Iverson, & J. S. Easterday (Eds.), *Environmental protection and transitions from conflict to peace: Clarifying norms, principles, and practices.* Oxford, UK: Oxford University Press.

Ravier, S., Vialle, A. C., Doran, R., & Stokes, J. (2016). Environmental experiences and developments in United Nations peacekeeping operations. In C. Bruch, C. Muffett, & S. S. Nichols (Eds.), *Governance, natural resources, and post-conflict peacebuilding* (pp. 195–206). London: Routledge.

Regan, A. J. (2017). Bougainville: Origins of the conflict, and debating the future of large-scale mining. In C. Filer & P.-Y. Le Meur (Eds.), *Large-scale mines and local-level politics* (pp. 353–414). Canberra, Australia: ANU Press.

Ross, M. L. (2004). How do natural resources influence civil war? Evidence from thirteen cases. *International organization, 58*(1), 35–67.

Ross, M. L. (2015). What have we learned about the resource curse? *Annual Review of Political Science, 18,* 239–259.

Rüttinger, L., Smith, D., Stang, G., Tänzler, D., & Vivekananda, J. (2015). *A new climate for peace: Taking action on climate and fragility risks.* Berlin: Adelphi Research.

Sait, S. (2013). Unexplored dimensions: Islamic land systems in Afghanistan, Indonesia, Iraq, and Somalia. In J. Unruh & R. Williams (Eds.), *Land and post-conflict peacebuilding* (pp. 475–507). London: Routledge.

Shimoyachi-Yuzawa, N. (2012). Linking demining to post-conflict peacebuilding: A case study of Cambodia. In D. Jensen & S. Lonergan (Eds.), *Assessing and restoring natural resources in post-conflict peacebuilding* (pp. 181–197). London: Routledge.

Sovacool, B. K., Walter, G., Van de Graaf, T., & Andrews, N. (2016). Energy governance, transnational rules, and the resource curse: Exploring the effectiveness of the extractive industries transparency initiative (EITI). *World Development, 83*, 179–192.

Taylor, M. B., & Davis, M. (2016). Taking the gun out of extraction: UN responses to the role of natural resources in conflicts. In C. Bruch, C. Muffett, & S. S. Nichols (Eds.), *Governance, natural resources, and post-conflict peacebuilding* (pp. 249–276). London: Routledge.

Team, S. O. F. A., & Doss, C. (2011). The role of women in agriculture. *Economic Development Analysis Division (ESA) Working Paper No. 11.*

UNDG (United Nations Development Group). (2013). *Natural resource management in transition settings.* UNDG-ECHA Guidance Note. New York: United Nations.

UNDP (United Nations Development Programme). (2004). *Governance indicators: A users' guide.* Oslo.

UN DPA (United Nations Department of Political Affairs) & UNEP (United Nations Environment Programme). (2015). *Natural resources and conflict: A guide for mediation practitioners.* New York: United Nations.

UNEP (United Nations Environment Programme). (2009). *From conflict to peacebuilding: The role of natural resources and the environment.* Nairobi.

UNEP (United Nations Environment Programme). (2012). *Greening the blue helmets: Environment, natural resources, and UN peacekeeping operations.* Nairobi.

UNEP (United Nations Environment Programme). (2014). *Relationships and resources: Environmental governance for peacebuilding and resilient livelihoods in Sudan.* Nairobi.

UNEP (UN Environment Programme) & UNDP (UN Development Programme). (2013). *The role of natural resources in disarmament, demobilization and reintegration: Assessing risks and seizing opportunities.* Nairobi.

UNEP (UN Environment Programme), UN Entity for Gender Equality and the Empowerment of Women, UN Peacebuilding Support Office, and UN Development Programme. (2013). *Women and natural resources: Unlocking the peacebuilding potential.* New York.

United Nations Secretary-General. (1992, June 17). An agenda for peace. UN Doc. A/47/277.

UN General Assembly. (2010). *Report of the Secretary-General on peacebuilding in the immediate aftermath of conflict.* A/64/866 – S/2010/386. New York: United Nations.

Unruh, J., & Williams, R. (Eds.). (2013a). *Land and post-conflict peacebuilding.* London: Routledge.

Unruh, J., & Williams, R. C. (2013b). Lessons learned in land tenure and natural resource management in post-conflict societies. In J. Unruh & R. Williams (Eds.), *Land and post-conflict peacebuilding* (pp. 535–576). London: Routledge.

Urdal, H. (2005). People vs. Malthus: Population pressure, environmental degradation, and armed conflict revisited. *Journal of Peace Research, 42*(4), 417–434.

Waleij, A., Bosetti, T., Doran, R., & Liljedahl, B. (2016). Environmental stewardship in peace operations: The role of the military. In C. Bruch, C. Muffett, & S. S. Nichols (Eds.), *Governance, natural resources, and post-conflict peacebuilding* (pp. 223–247). London: Routledge.

Walters, J. T. (2015). A peace park in the Balkans: Cross-border cooperation and livelihood creation through coordinated environmental conservation. In H. Young & L. Goldman (Eds.), *Livelihoods, natural resources, and post-conflict peacebuilding* (pp. 155–166). London: Routledge.

Weather modification. (1974). *Hearings before the subcommittee on oceans and international environment of the Committee on Foreign Relations, United States Senate.* January 25 and March 20. Retrieved from www.scribd.com/document/332402260/top-secret-hearings-before-the-subcommittee-on-oceans-and-international-environment-january-25-and-march-20–1974

Weinthal, E. (2016). *State making and environmental cooperation: Linking domestic and international politics in Central Asia.* Cambridge, MA: MIT Press.

Weinthal, E., Troell, J. J., & Nakayama, M. (Eds.). (2014). *Water and post-conflict peacebuilding.* London: Routledge.

Westing, A. H. (Ed.). (1986). *Global resources and international conflict: Environmental factors in strategic policy and action.* New York: Oxford University Press.

Westing, A. H., & Pfeiffer, E. W. (1972). The cratering of Indochina. *Scientific American, 226*(5), 20–29.

Westrik, C. (2015). Transboundary protected areas: Opportunities and challenges. In H. Young & L. Goldman (Eds.), *Livelihoods, natural resources, and post-conflict peacebuilding* (pp. 145–153). London: Routledge.

Wolf, A. T. (2007). Shared waters: Conflict and cooperation. *Annual Review of Environment and Resources, 32*, 241–269.

Yoffe, S., Wolf, A. T., & Giordano, M. (2003). Conflict and cooperation over international freshwater resources: Indicators of basins at risk. *Journal of the American Water Resources Association, 39*(5), 1109–1126.

Young, H., & Goldman, L. (Eds.). (2015). *Livelihoods, natural resources, and post-conflict peacebuilding*. London: Routledge.

Zierler, D. (2011). *The invention of ecocide: Agent Orange, Vietnam, and the scientists who changed the way we think about the environment*. Athens, GA: University of Georgia Press.

SECTION I

Environmental factors contributing to conflict

3

THE GEOGRAPHY(IES) OF RESOURCE WARS

Michael T. Klare

Resource wars – violent conflicts in which the pursuit of natural resources constitutes a major impulse for battle – are almost always associated with some aspect of geography. This is so because vital and valuable resources – food and water, gold and diamonds, oil and iron ore – are unevenly distributed across the face of the planet, and so most human societies are regularly confronted with shortages of at least some of them; to overcome these deficiencies, a society can develop substitutes, trade what they have for what they lack, or employ military means to acquire the desired material, thereby igniting armed conflict. Most disputes over resources do not reach the point of violence, but when they do, they are usually intertwined with other factors, such as ethno-religious animosities, geopolitical rivalries, or corporate greed. Nevertheless, geography and resource predation have combined on many occasions to trigger conflict, often with far-ranging consequences.

Resource wars can take many forms but usually consist of attempts by one group (a tribe, nation, warlord, or empire) to gain control over or ensure access to a valuable resource deposit located on the territory of a different group. In the first category of resource wars are direct assaults by the forces of one tribe or nation on the lands of another for the purpose of plundering its resources, as in the European invasions of Africa and the Americas in the 15th through 19th centuries. Also included are wars intended to expand a nation's territory, as in the Czarist empire's drive to extend its rule in the Caucasus and Central Asia. In the second category are wars fought to overcome impediments to the flow of resources from foreign suppliers, as in anti-piracy operations in the Strait of Malacca, or to protect favored foreign suppliers against internal or external attack, as in US moves to defend Saudi Arabia following the Iraqi occupation of Kuwait. Resource wars can also erupt over the allocation of benefits from a shared resource supply, such as a major river system or an offshore resource reservoir. China and Vietnam, for example, have clashed over the rights to exploit undersea oil and gas reserves in their overlapping portions of the South China Sea (Klare, 2001).

As these examples suggest, geography usually plays a pivotal role in resource conflicts because of a dichotomy of some sort between the key actors involved and the location of the materials they covet. In the case of imperial plunder, the predatory party typically seeks to extract some desirable assets – they could be gold, silver, ivory, furs, spices, minerals, or human chattel – readily available in the target location but not at home. Alternatively, a tribe or nation may seek to expand its territory into that of other people so as to acquire more land for hunting,

29   DOI: 10.4324/9781315107592-4

logging, and farming – steps that could entail driving off the indigenous occupants of those spaces. Resource conflicts can also erupt over the location of boundaries and the ownership of contested border areas thought to be rich in resources of one sort or another, such as oil and natural gas reservoirs, or when an ethnic enclave incorporated into a multiethnic state seeks to break away and form its own nation, believing that rich resource deposits (typically of oil) found within its enclave will enable it to be self-financing (Le Billon, 2013).

"Vital" and "valuable" materials

Not all natural materials are prone to spark armed conflict over their control; what makes certain resources capable of inciting such violence is a perception that they possess certain distinctive characteristics that make them either *vital* or extremely *valuable*.

Vital resources are those that are considered essential for human survival, such as food and water, or for the effective functioning of modern industrial societies, such as oil and iron ore. What makes them distinctive, then, is what might be called their "essentiality." In contemporary terminology, such materials are said to be essential to "national security," and so, if necessary, it is considered legitimate to employ military force in securing adequate supplies of them. In modern times, oil has most often been invested with this unusual distinction, given its essential role in industry, transportation, and warfare. This was made explicit, for example, in the "Carter Doctrine" of January 1980, which affirmed the importance of Middle Eastern oil to the US economy and the need, therefore, to ensure the safety of its flow (Palmer, 1992, pp. 101–111). Any attempt by a hostile power to sever that flow, President Jimmy Carter told Congress, would be deemed "an assault on the *vital interests* of the United States of America" and so would be repelled "by any means necessary, including military force" (Carter, 1980; emphasis added). President George H.W. Bush also affirmed the "vital" nature of oil in August 1990 when announcing his decision to deploy US forces in Saudi Arabia to help defend that country against a possible attack from Iraq. Claiming that the United States "could face a major threat to its economic independence" if Saudi oil exports were blocked, he affirmed that "the sovereign independence of Saudi Arabia is of *vital interest* to the United States" (Bush, 1990; emphasis added). Because of this unique characteristic, oil has figured prominently in recent disputes over resources; however, it is conceivable that other natural materials will come to be viewed in this distinctive manner in the years ahead. Indeed, some analysts believe that water will come to be viewed through the same national security lens as is oil today when global warming has advanced and water supplies dwindle in many areas of the world (Chellaney, 2011; see also Asthana, Chapter 6).

Valuable resources, by contrast, lack the "essentiality" of vital resources but are coveted because of their rarity, attractiveness, or other unique properties. These include gold, silver, ivory, diamonds, animal pelts, exotic spices, stimulants, narcotics, and so forth. Throughout human history, avaricious leaders have been spurred by the allure of these materials to invade other lands and plunder their supplies of them. The Spanish conquest of South and Central America, for example, was largely propelled by the quest for gold and silver (Thomas, 2013). In more recent times, the procurement of such materials has not, for the most part, been deemed a matter of state policy and so has not triggered the use of force by established governments. However, assorted insurgent groups and warlord regimes have continued to employ armed violence in the extraction of especially valuable resources, whether to enrich their leaders or to finance their ongoing operations (Le Billon, 2013). For example, Jonas Savimbi, head of a rebel faction known as the National Union for the Total Independence of Angola (UNITA), until his death in 2002, was said by UN officials to have provided large sacks of diamonds – acquired through brutal tactics in Angola – to the rulers of neighboring states in exchange for their help in smuggling arms and ammunition to his beleaguered forces (UN, 2000).

The centrality of geography and geopolitics

Whatever the precise combination of factors in sparking resource conflicts, geography almost always plays a pivotal role. Geography enters this equation in several ways, beginning with the global *distribution* of major resource stocks and the political divisions or *boundaries* drawn across the earth by its human inhabitants.

The *distribution* of resources matters when supplies of a vital or valuable resource are highly concentrated in only a few locations, without corresponding to the areas of greatest need. Historically, human settlements have arisen where there is an abundance of vital materials, especially land and water; most societies, however, have always been in need of at least some materials only obtainable from a distant location. Under these circumstances, the area possessing a high concentration of the desired material will act as a powerful magnet for all those societies in lack thereof, leading them to cultivate trade ties and political alliances with those already in control of that place or to invade and occupy them. In the ancient Mediterranean world, swaths of arable land and deposits of valuable metals often acted in this fashion, attracting conquest and settlement by one aspiring power after the other (Starr, 1991, pp. 213–222, 313, 466–467). The Vikings, inhabitants of an especially resource-scarce region, were impelled to explore, invade, and settle other lands in search of farmland and other resources not easily accessible in ancient Scandinavia (Diamond, 2005, pp. 178–210). In modern times, oil has acted as a magnet in this manner, drawing the major industrial powers ever deeper into the political cauldron of the Middle East (Klare, 2005).

Boundaries matter in the resource/conflict equation for the obvious reason that they separate the territory of one polity from another and so determine who enjoys ownership over particular concentrations of vital and valuable resources and who does not. Throughout history, human societies have sought to increase the extent of territory (and thus their access to resources) by extending their boundaries as much as possible, whether through purchase or military means. The westward expansion of the United States, for example, was accompanied by constant battles over territorial claims between European settlers and Native populations, beginning with King Philip's War of 1675–1678 and ending with the Battle of Wounded Knee in 1890; along the way, the United States also fought a war with Mexico (1846–1848), resulting in a massive accretion of territory and resources (Greenberg, 2011). Since the establishment of the United Nations in 1945, the use of violence to expand a state's territory has become less frequent than in the past, but has not disappeared entirely: in 1980, Iraq invaded Iran with the apparent aim of annexing the oil-rich province of Khuzestan; in 1998–2000, Eritrea and Ethiopia fought over a disputed area in their joint border called Badme. But even as the frequency of disputes over *terrestrial* boundaries has diminished, fresh conflicts have arisen over contested *maritime* territories, especially when these areas are thought to house substantial reserves of oil and natural gas (Klare, 2013).

Geography also enters the equation in terms of differentiating between *supplying* states, *consuming* states, and *transit* states. *Supplying* states are those that possess more of certain resource than they consume domestically and so are in a position to export a portion of their supply to states that lack adequate domestic sources of that material. *Consuming* states, by contrast, are those that possess insufficient domestic stocks of a needed resource and so are dependent on imports to satisfy their requirements. Any given nation can, of course, be a supplier state with regard to one resource and a consumer state with respect to another. The Persian Gulf oil kingdoms, for example, are both suppliers of petroleum to consumers around the world and consumers of imported food and other vital materials. *Transit* states – an important but often overlooked actor in this equation – lie between those other two groups of states, housing the ports, canals, railroads, pipelines, and other infrastructure needed to transport resources from one to another. What occurs in these states can affect relations among supplier and consumers, especially if a disruption in deliveries from one to another causes disarray at the receiving end (Kalicki & Goldwyn, 2013). When Russia cut off natural gas supplies to Ukraine in 2006 and 2009 as punishment for that country's pro-Western orientation, countries further west in Europe also suffered, as they depended on the same pipelines used to deliver gas to Ukraine; in response, the European Union (EU) commenced a drive to reduce its reliance on Russian gas in the pursuit of "energy security" (Noël, 2013).

Finally, geography enters the equation in the form of *geopolitics*, or the competition among states for political and economic advantage beyond their borders. As argued by several influential analysts of world affairs, including Alfred Thayer Mahan (1840–1914), a former president of the US Naval War College; Halford Mackinder (1861–1947), a former director of the London School of Economics; Zbigniew Brzezinski (1928–2017), once the national security adviser to President Carter, nation-states are in perpetual competition with one another for access to and control over foreign markets, trade routes, key geographic features (such as strategically located ports and shipping lanes), and, of course, major resource deposits. The greater the degree of control a state exerts over all these assets, it is claimed, the stronger will be its economy and thus its ability to defend itself and defeat its rivals. States will, therefore, constantly seek advantage on this global chessboard; any miscalculation in this ongoing struggle could, in theory, portend painful and far-ranging consequences (Brzezinski, 2016; Crowl, 1986; Mackinder, 2004). A decision to go to war over access to vital resources, then, will usually be made in light of its effect on this larger competitive struggle, with each party involved attempting to calculate how its actions will affect the power balance among all other major actors. Conflict over resources is most likely to arise when geographical circumstances (discrepancies in the global distribution of vital or valuable materials) coincide with political factors (long-standing grievances, the ambitions of leaders, etc.) and a favorable geopolitical environment.

The inherited geographies of resource wars

It is hardly an exaggeration to say that the geography and political order of the contemporary world has largely been shaped by resources wars of the past, specifically the major European imperial powers' drive to conquer and exploit the resources of Asia, Africa, and the Americas, and by the resistance to invasion offered by the indigenous populations of those areas. As part of the colonial project, the imperial powers drew boundaries enclosing their appropriated territories, creating new divisions upon the land where none existed before and often separating ethnic kin from one another (Pakenham, 1992). In some cases, the colonial powers encouraged settlement in those new entities by members of their own population, who in time rebelled and established new nation-states; in others, they suborned members of the local population to serve as petty bureaucrats, some of whom later formed the nucleus of post-colonial regimes; in still others, leaders of the anti-colonial movements assumed this role. Whatever the trajectory of leadership formation, most post-colonial regimes have chosen to preserve the boundaries established by the imperial powers before them (Meredith, 2011).

With this in mind, the contemporary geographies of resource wars can best be grasped by locating the principal concentrations of vital resources upon this political matrix and then plotting the major flows of said materials from major suppliers to their principal consumers via key transit states. If we use the year 2000 as a benchmark, the vital resources we would be looking at are oil and natural gas, along with water, uranium, and certain specialty minerals, such as cobalt and platinum. With the exception of water (which is a vital necessity everywhere), most of the world's oil, gas, and industrial minerals were consumed by the older industrial powers, mostly members of the Organization for Economic Cooperation and Development (OECD); however, the production of these resources was largely concentrated in areas *outside* the OECD. For example, while the OECD accounted for an estimated 59% of all oil consumed worldwide in 2000, it produced only 29% of global oil output. A similar picture is seen in the case of natural gas and many other critical materials (IEA, 2017, pp. 644, 646). As a result of these discrepancies, there was a substantial flow of oil and gas from major non-OECD oil-producing countries, notably Russia and the Persian Gulf producers, to OECD countries. Accordingly, our global map of resource flows would show arrows leading from Africa, Latin America, and the Middle East to Europe, North America, and Japan, either traversing the major oceans or traveling by pipeline across connecting land areas.

This unique geography of resource distribution, consumption, and transportation played a commanding role in shaping world trade and international relations throughout most of the 20th century, with oil as a dominant feature. As petroleum became ever more vital to the functioning of modern industrial societies, the major oil-consuming nations became increasingly intent on ensuring access to their main sources of supply – leading, over time, to direct military and political involvement by the major consuming states in the affairs of their principal suppliers. This involvement was most highly concentrated in the Persian Gulf area, where a handful of countries – Iran, Iraq, Kuwait, Oman, Syria, and Saudi Arabia – were in possession of an estimated two-thirds of the world's proven oil reserves (Klare, 2001, pp. 27–80).

This saga of oil-related Western involvement in Gulf affairs began just before World War I, when the British Cabinet – prodded by First Lord of the Admiralty, Winston Churchill – nationalized the Anglo-Persian Oil Company (APOC, the forerunner to BP) in order to gain control over the APOC's concessions in southwestern Persia (now Iran). With war looming and the British converting their warships from coal to oil propulsion, Britain established a military protectorate over Persia and sent troops to the APOC concession area to ensure its safety (Yergin, 1991, pp. 134–149, 153–164). Believing that control over oil would be essential for success in all future wars, the British and French conducted secret diplomacy during World War I to divide up the territory of the crumbling Ottoman Empire, with each side seeking to gain control over promising oil reserves in the areas abutting Iran. Under the Sykes-Picot agreement of 1916, Britain was accorded most of what became Iraq, and France received Syria (Keay: 52–59). This arrangement – like so many in which the European powers established the boundaries of non-European spaces to facilitate the extraction of resources, while ignoring the wishes of their inhabitants – has remained a source of resentment and bloodshed from that moment on (Wright, 2016).

In the years following World War I, the major consuming powers sought to imitate Britain and France's behavior by seeking control over promising oil reserves of their own in the Middle East. The United States did not play a role in this scramble for foreign reserves until after World War II, as it was blessed with adequate domestic reserves of its own. During that war, however, President Franklin D. Roosevelt and his advisers concluded that US oil reserves were being depleted at a dangerous rate, and so this country would eventually become dependent on imports. To ensure that the United States would be assured of adequate oil supplies, Roosevelt tasked his staff with selecting a reliable overseas producer to supplement dwindling US reserves; this quest resulted in the selection of Saudi Arabia as America's chosen foreign supplier. To cement this relationship, Roosevelt met with King Abdul Aziz ibn Saud aboard the USS *Quincy* on February 14, 1945, and devised with him an arrangement by which the United States would protect the kingdom in return for assured access to Saudi oil (Stoff, 1980). In accordance with this arrangement, the United States established military bases in Saudi Arabia and undertook the task of arming and training the Saudi military (McNaugher, 1985).

At first, Washington hoped that Great Britain would continue to serve as regional gendarme in the Gulf area, thereby minimizing the need for an elaborate US military presence there. When Britain abandoned this role in 1971, Washington turned to its closest ally in the region, Shah Mohammed Reza Pahlavi of Iran, to serve in this capacity. With US support, the shah sought to transform Iran into a regional powerhouse, suppressing the Shiite clergy and all other voices of dissent in the process (Klare, 1984, pp. 108–126). When he was overthrown, in 1979, Washington was deprived of a key ally and also confronted with a largely hostile Iranian population, which resented US support for the overbearing shah. The result, after much deliberation and nail-biting in Washington, was the Carter Doctrine of January 1980, which assigned primary responsibility for protecting the flow of Persian Gulf oil to the United States.

As the United States did not at that time have any forces specifically earmarked for operations in the Gulf area, Carter created a new military organization, the Rapid Deployment Joint Task Force (RDJTF), to perform this mission. His successor, Ronald Reagan, elevated the RDJTF to a full-scale military command, the US Central Command (Centcom), with responsibility for all US designated deployment to the greater Gulf area. Reagan was also the first US president to implement the Carter Doctrine, ordering US naval forces to escort Kuwaiti oil tankers through the Gulf when they came under attack from Iranian gunboats during the Iran-Iraq War of 1980–1988 (Operation Earnest Will) (Palmer, 1992, pp. 112–149). As noted, this principle was again cited by President George W. Bush when ordering US forces to defend Saudi Arabia following the Iraqi invasion of Kuwait in August 1990 (Palmer, 1992, pp. 150–162). Centcom has taken on a wide variety of tasks in the years since its formation but retains its core function of ensuring the safety of the Persian Gulf oil flow.

While President George H.W. Bush's decision to expel Iraqi forces from Kuwait in 1991 was clearly in conformity with the Carter Doctrine and its pledge to ensure the free flow of Persian Gulf oil supplies, much debate has raged over the degree to which resource considerations figured in his son's decision to invade Iraq in 2003. Some analysts argue that a desire to gain control over Iraqi oil fields played a significant role in his decision; others say it played a minor role or none at all. Putting aside the issue of Iraqi oil, it certainly can be argued that the Iraqi regime was viewed in Washington as a threat to America's hegemonic presence in the Gulf and so was part of the larger geopolitical context in which oil was a critical factor (Cramer & Thrall, 2011). In any case, the US invasion altered the resource geography of the region, with Iraq now under the control of a Shiite-dominated regime with control over the nation's vast oil infrastructure (leaving the Sunnis feeling marginalized) and a Kurdish enclave in the northeast seeking to become independent (and finance itself with oil revenues).

The enunciation of the Carter Doctrine and the establishment of Centcom occurred at a time when the United States was experiencing declining oil production at home and becoming more dependent on supplies from abroad. By the second decade of the 21st century, however, the United States had become less reliant on imports as a result of its success in extracting oil from domestic shale formations. For some observers, this meant it was now possible to rescind the Carter Doctrine and reduce the US military presence in the Gulf. "If America can produce its own oil," *The Economist* opined in 2014, "[w]hy waste so much blood and treasure policing the Middle East?" (*The Economist*, 2014). Others, however, argued that the rest of the world continued to rely on oil from the Gulf, and so ensuring the safety of its flow remained a major US obligation. The uninterrupted flow of Persian Gulf oil is essential "to global economic stability," ExxonMobil chief executive officer Rex W. Tillerson asserted in 2012, before being chosen by Donald Trump to be secretary of state. Even if "we're no longer getting any oil from the Middle East," he continued, "a disruption of oil supplies from that region will have devastating impacts on global economies," making it a major US strategic concern (Tillerson, 2012). President Trump has not yet articulated a comprehensive strategic design for the greater Gulf region, but it is unlikely that he will diverge from the geopolitical logic articulated by Tillerson. It follows that Centcom will remain a major actor in the region and that protection of the oil flow will continue to be one of its ongoing responsibilities.

And so, at the time of this writing, the legacy of Western reliance on Persian Gulf oil supplies can still be detected in the politics and conflict dynamics of the greater Persian Gulf area. Even though the United States no longer relies on Middle Eastern oil for a significant share of its petroleum requirements, it remains fully embedded in the nexus of supply, demand, transportation systems, and military ties established in 1945, when President Roosevelt first determined that this country must possess secure access to Persian Gulf supplies.

Because of its colossal resource endowment, perennial instability, and vulnerability to outside pressures, the Persian Gulf has been the site of the greatest Western – and especially US – political and military involvement in foreign producing areas. But the imprint of such involvement can be seen in other areas of the world where a substantial resource endowment coincides with other factors. During the George H.W. Bush administration, for example, the United States made a concerted effort to increase its reliance on oil imports from Africa and the Caspian Sea area (thereby, lessening US dependence on the Gulf). As part of this drive, Bush stepped up US military aid to the governments of friendly oil-producing countries in these areas (Klare, 2008, pp. 123–128, 157–164, 211–219).

The future geographies of resource wars

As is evident from the above, the political and military dynamics that evolved over time in the Persian Gulf area arose from distinctive geographies of resource demand, distribution, and consumption. This was a very powerful nexus of factors, and it persisted for nearly a century. As we move deeper into the 21st century, however, it is likely that this nexus will begin to unravel as other fuels come to assume oil's prominent role and as existing systems of resource distribution, consumption, and transportation shift. Some of these shifts can be discerned now, and others will become increasingly evident with time; whether any of these will result in a complex nexus like that found in the Persian Gulf, with all its political and military dimensions, remains to be seen.

Of the shifts in resource valuation, distribution, and consumption now under way, none, perhaps, is as significant as those occurring in the realm of energy. To begin with, oil's dominant role in the global fuel mix is being challenged as natural gas becomes more popular as an energy source and concern over climate change leads to a greater emphasis on renewable sources of energy. The decline of oil as a major source of energy can be traced in the statistics and projections provided by the International Energy Agency (IEA) based in Paris. According to the 2017 edition of its *World Energy Outlook*, oil's share of world energy consumption dropped from approximately 37% in 2000 to 32% in 2015 and, under its "New Policies Scenario" (which assumes some but not drastic efforts to curb carbon emissions), is projected to decline even further to 27% of world consumption in 2040. At the same time, natural gas – the least carbon emitting of the fossil fuels – is expected to enjoy an expansion of its share, from 21% in 2000 to 25% in 2040 (IEA, 2017, p. 648). These ratios could change even more, the IEA notes, if governments around the world decide to make a determined effort to limit the increase in global warming to 2°C above the pre-industrial level – the largest increase, most scientists agree, that the planet can absorb without undergoing catastrophic consequences, such as the melting of the Greenland and Antarctica icecaps, and a resulting mean sea level rise of a meter or more (IPCC, 2014a, 2019). Under one such scenario provided by the IEA, oil's share of world energy consumption drops to 23% in 2040 while gas becomes the most prominent of the fossil fuels, with a 25% share; even more significant, renewables become the dominant source of world energy in this scenario, with a 29% share (IEA, 2017, p. 649)

The 2017 edition of the *World Energy Outlook* also reveals significant shifts in the patterns of energy production and consumption. While Russia and the Middle East will continue to supply the bulk of internationally traded oil, other producers are likely to gain prominence in Africa and the Americas, especially as advanced technology allows for intensified drilling in dense rock formations (usually shale) and ever-deeper offshore waters. Brazil, for example, is expected to become a major producer as its "pre-salt" fields (i.e., located below a thick layer of salt) beneath the deep Atlantic come on line (IEA, 2017, pp. 184–186). A similar picture prevails with respect to natural gas: while traditional suppliers like Russia and Algeria will continue to enjoy a significant market share, some new producers are gaining prominence as gas becomes more desirable (IEA, 2017, p. 346). One such producer is Turkmenistan, thought to possess the world's fourth largest reserves of natural gas (after Iran, Russia, and Qatar). Once a part of the USSR and closed off from international commerce, Turkmenistan is now sending gas to China via a newly constructed pipeline across Central Asia and is in talks with the EU about building another pipeline under the Caspian Sea to Azerbaijan and Georgia for onward shipment to Europe (Lain, 2015).

Global consumption patterns are also changing. Whereas the OECD countries accounted for 53% of total world energy consumption in 2000, by 2015 its share had dropped to 38% and in 2040 is projected to fall to just 29%. Meanwhile, non-OECD Asia, including China and India, is witnessing an explosion in demand. According to the IEA (2017), non-OECD Asia's share of world consumption jumped from 25% in 2000 to 38% in 2015, equaling that of the OECD, and is expected to reach 44% by 2040. This shift from the older industrial powers of the West to the rising powers of Asia is also reflected in the consumption of individual fuels, with an ever-increasing share of global oil and gas consumption expected to occur in non-OECD Asia. One consequence of this shift is the growing prominence of liquefied natural gas (LNG) in international energy commerce: whereas Europe has long obtained much of its imported gas via pipelines from Russia, gas consumers in Asia now obtain most of their gas in the form of LNG carried by ship (IEA, 382–397, 648, 696, 708, 716).

As these shifts in fuel preference and consumption patterns occur, we can expect to see corresponding adjustments in the geography and geopolitics of global resource flows, with the dominant paradigm of the 20th century – oil shipments generally traveling westward from Russia and the Middle East to OECD countries – being replaced by a more complex grid, involving oil and natural gas shipments largely traveling eastward from Russia, Central Asia, Africa, and the Middle East to China, India, and other rising Asian powers.

Most notable of these developments, of course, is the emergence of China as a major consumer of imported resources. As its economy has grown, so has its need for basic commodities of all sorts, ranging from oil, coal, and natural gas to minerals of all sorts, timber, and food products. China can acquire some of these materials at home but has to turn to foreign suppliers for an ever-increasing share of many of them. Regarding oil, for example, China was self-sufficient until the 1990s, but as the number of automobiles on its roads has grown, it has become increasingly dependent on imports. In 2016, for example, China produced 4.0 million barrels of oil per day and consumed 11.5 million barrels, producing an import requirement of 7.5 million barrels; by 2040, according to the IEA (2017), its consumption will rise to 15.5 million barrels per day while production falls to 3.1 million barrels, generating an import requirement of 12.4 million barrels (pp. 163, 186). A similar pattern will prevail in the case of natural gas and other vital materials, producing dramatic shifts in the global flow of resources (Economy & Levi, 2014; Lee, 2012).

As was the case with previous resource flows of vital materials, these new patterns have heightened the geopolitical significance of key producing areas and transit routes. As China has come to rely more heavily on oil and gas imports from the Caspian states, for example, it has exerted an ever more conspicuous political and military role in Central Asia, often filtered through the Shanghai Cooperation Organization (SCO), a regional economic and security organization sponsored by Beijing (Klare, 2008, pp. 132–137). Under its proposed "One Belt One Road" initiative – a continent-spanning web of railroads, highways, pipelines, and transmission lines – China intends to play an even more significant role in the economic development of this region (Blanchard & Flint, 2017).

The growing flow of oil and natural gas (in the form of LNG) from the Middle East and Africa to South and East Asia had also lent increased strategic significance to the Indian Ocean, the South China Sea, and the Strait of Malacca (which connects those two bodies of water). For India, which – like China – is becoming increasingly dependent on imported oil, the safety of these sea routes has acquired particular importance. "India's economic resurgence is directly linked to her overseas trade and energy needs, most of which are transported by sea," a 2007 strategic blueprint released by the Indian Navy declared. Accordingly, the blueprint noted, "the primary task of the Indian Navy towards national security" is to ensure the safety of these maritime trade flows "so that the vital tasks of fostering economic growth . . . can take place in a secure environment" (India MoD, 2007, p. 10). Chinese naval officials have also spoken of their country's need to defend these vital sea routes. "With the expansion of the country's economic interests, the navy wants to better protect the country's transportation routes and the safety of our major sea lanes," said Rear Admiral Zhang Huachen in 2010. "In order to achieve this, the Chinese navy needs to develop along the lines of bigger vessels and with more comprehensive capabilities" (see Wong, 2010).

China's concern over the protection of vital sea lanes is especially evident in the South China Sea, through which most of its resource imports flow. In addition to constituting a major maritime conduit for the delivery of vital raw materials (and the export of finished products), the South China Sea is believed to house vast undersea reserves of oil and gas that China seeks to exploit. Beijing insists that most of the South China Sea falls within its national maritime territory and so is its alone to exploit, but this has been challenged by other littoral states, including Brunei, Malaysia, Vietnam, and the Philippines, all of which claim development rights to certain portions of the sea. This has led, on occasion, to clashes between naval and coast guard vessels belonging to China and these other countries (ICG, 2012). To further demonstrate its intent to control this area, China has dredged sand from the ocean floor around some low-lying atolls in order to convert them into islands capable of housing military facilities of varying sorts, including airstrips and missile batteries (AMTI, 2017). The United States, for its part, asserts that these are international waters and that all countries enjoy an unimpeded "freedom of navigation" through the area; to demonstrate its intent to defend that right, the Pentagon has dispatched missile-carrying destroyers on "freedom of navigation operations" through the South China Sea, deliberately steering them near the Chinese-fortified island (Freund, 2017).

Michael T. Klare

The outlook for conflict

All these developments are deeply embedded in the geopolitical dynamics of the current era. Just as the US drive to gain control over the energy flows of the Persian Gulf was initially seen as part of a larger power struggle with the Soviet Union, and then with Iran and Iraq, the current US quarrel with China over free passage through the South China Sea is part of the larger geopolitical contest between these two countries for global preeminence in the post–Cold War era (Allison, 2017). The same principle applies to other areas that are gaining in strategic importance as a result of shifts in energy production and consumption. This is evident, for example, in the Indian Ocean region, where growing resource commerce has been accompanied by increased geopolitical competition among India, China, and the United States. All three countries have increased their naval presence in the region and attempted to establish or bolster local alliances (Kaplan, 2010). President Obama sought greater cooperation with India as part of his "pivot" to Asia (Obama, 2011), while President Trump has pursued a similar approach, calling it his "Indo-Pacific" strategy (Trump, 2017).

The question remains, will these new trade and diplomatic arrangements lead to increased friction and conflict as was true of older such arrangements? At this point, it is too early to provide a conclusive answer to this question. From a positive perspective, many of the aspects of the old energy paradigm that contributed to a high risk of violence are not present in the emerging energy system. Whereas the old paradigm entailed heavy reliance on one type of fuel – oil – obtainable only in a few, often volatile, areas, the new one features reliance on a larger spectrum of fuels and a wider range of suppliers and supply channels. This, by its very nature, reduces the risk of conflict, as major consuming states are less dependent on just one or two providers to supply the majority of their energy and so need not feel compelled to go to war to protect an especially vital source. The increase in LNG export and import facilities should contribute to this outcome, as it will become increasingly possible for major gas-consuming states to obtain their supplies from a range of foreign providers rather than rely on piped imports from just one or two suppliers. The advent of renewables will accelerate this trend, as the more states rely on locally generated green energy, the less they will need to import fossil fuels from abroad (IEA, 2017, pp. 281–329).

Nevertheless, it is impossible to rule out the prospect of future wars driven in part by resource competition. This is so because while the global picture may seem more conducive to the nonviolent resolution of resource disputes, it could erupt in places where unanticipated resource scarcities converge with mounting geopolitical tensions. A future war between India and Pakistan, for example, could impede energy flows through the Indian Ocean to China and Japan, inducing one or another of these countries, along with the United States, to intercede in the conflict. One such scenario was envisioned by the National Intelligence Council (NIC), an arm of the Central Intelligence Agency, in 2008. As part of its *Global Trends 2025* report, the NIC described a hypothetical naval encounter in the Indian Ocean in 2021 between Indian and Chinese warships under just such circumstances, precipitating US military intervention. Although full-scale war was averted in the NIC scenario, the NIC asserts that the likelihood of such occurrences is destined to grow as a result of growing competition for vital resources (NIC, 2008, pp. 77–79).

Complicating the question about the future potential for resource wars is the changing identity of what is considered a "vital" resource, and so worthy of fighting over. In 2008, when the NIC published its scenario of a future Sino-Indian naval clash, oil was assumed to retain its pivotal importance well into the future, thereby incurring a continuing risk of friction and conflict. As renewable forms of energy become more widely dispersed, however, oil could lose its pivotal status, and so the risk of war will be diminished. But this raises another question: Will other materials come to acquire the pivotal status of oil and, with it, the potential for international competition and conflict?

At present, no resource stands out as possessing the combination of features that made oil so central to global conflict dynamics. Natural gas may come to replace oil as the world's leading source of energy, but gas reservoirs are rather widely dispersed, and gas's most avid consumer – the United States – is also its leading producer, so the likelihood of US intervention over foreign supplies is very low. There is, admittedly, a risk of armed conflict over the control of disputed offshore deposits of gas, notably in the East China Sea, the South China Sea, and the eastern Mediterranean Sea, but these are likely to remain localized affairs; if the United States or other outside powers do intervene, it will be for geopolitical reasons, not to secure access to resources. Uranium could also acquire pivotal status if nuclear energy becomes the dominant power source of the future, placing a geopolitical spotlight on those few countries possessing large supplies of it, but at present, there is no indication that this will come to pass. Some analysts have suggested that unevenly distributed materials required for renewable energy systems, such as the lithium used in electric car batteries and/or the rare earth elements employed in hybrid vehicle engines, will trigger the sort of geopolitical contestation long associated with petroleum, but again, there is no indication at this time to assume this will occur (Stegen, 2015).

The one resource that has analysts worried more than any other when peering into the future is water. This is so because water is essential to survival, possesses no substitutes, and is unevenly distributed across the face of the planet, with many areas of high population growth located in areas of perennial water scarcity. To make matters worse, climate change is expected to reduce water supplies in many areas of the world, and, in many cases, those are precisely the areas that are already suffering from elevated levels of water stress. Some countries, therefore, are likely to experience a sharp decline in water availability – a particularly severe threat to nations of the Global South that are highly dependent on agriculture for employment and income (IPCC, 2014b, 2018). One outcome of all this is likely to be large-scale migration from rural areas to the cities, which are already swelling in population, and, for those plucky (or desperate) enough to make the attempt, migration to richer countries of the global North, where they can expect a hostile reception (IPCC, 2014b: 766–771).

Geography enters this picture in another way: many societies rely on water obtained from rivers – the Nile, the Jordan, the Indus, the Mekong, the Tigris-Euphrates system, and so on – that are shared by two or more countries as they make their way from their place of origin to exit into the ocean or other outlet. Here again, the imposition of human-made borders on Mother Nature's pristine landscape is a significant problem, as these rivers become cut into segments, with each country claiming the right to develop its own segment irrespective of its neighbors' needs. This can lead to conflict if, say, an upstream state attempts to dam the river and use its waters for local irrigation works, thereby reducing the supply for downstream countries (see Crawford & Church, Chapter 7). If the upstream country is powerful enough, as is the case of Turkey with respect to the Tigris-Euphrates and China with respect to the Mekong, it can generally do what it wants; however, if the downstream countries are stronger, as is Israel with respect to the Jordan and Egypt with respect to the Nile, violence is possible (Chellaney, 2013). A particular danger arises with the Brahmaputra, a river that arises in China but passes through India and Bangladesh before emptying into the Bay of Bengal. China has expressed its intention to dam the upper Brahmaputra (known locally as the Tsangpo) and divert some of its waters to drought-stricken areas of northeastern China – a prospect that has generated alarm in India, and led some there to say it would constitute an act of war and so require a military response (Chellaney, 2011, pp. 141–197).

Conclusion

Resource wars generally erupt from the confluence of several factors, of which geography typically plays a leading role. Historically, violent conflict has most often erupted when the desire of one society to possess or gain access to the resources of another has coincided with historical grievances, ethno-religious differences, and a favorable geopolitical environment. This convergence was especially evident in the Persian Gulf region during the peak of Western reliance on Middle Eastern oil supplies, when the major Western powers – beginning with the British and French and then led by the United States – viewed protection of those supplies as a major security imperative involving, as needed, the use of military force.

As the primary direction of flow of Middle Eastern oil shifts, from West to East, and as other sources of energy gain prominence, new resource geographies are emerging across the face of the planet. Whether these will also generate new clusters of economic, political, and military factors akin to that which developed around Persian Gulf oil supplies cannot be foreseen, but the possibility remains. Climate change is bound to play a significant role in determining the outcome, as it will both create new resource scarcities, especially of water, and influence decisions on energy choices. Ultimately, the prospect for friction and conflict over natural resources will depend on humanity's success in deploying renewable sources of energy and in finding cooperative solutions to other resource-related dilemmas, such as transboundary river systems.

Works cited

Allison, G. (2017). *Destined for war: Can America and China escape Thucydides's trap?* New York and Boston: Houghton Mifflin Harcourt.

Asia Maritime Transparency Initiative (AMTI). (2017). *Updated: China's big three near completion.* Retrieved June 29, 2018, from https://amti.csis.org/chinas-big-three-near-completion/

Blanchard, J. F., & Flint, C. (2017). The Geopolitics of China's maritime silk road initiative. *Geopolitics*, *22*(2), 223–245. https://doi.org/10.1080/14650045.2017.1291503

Brzezinski, Z. (2016). *The grand chessboard: American primacy and its geostrategic imperatives* (2nd ed.). New York: Basic Books.

Bush, G. H. W. (1990). *Address to the nation announcing the deployment of United States armed forces to Saudi Arabia.* Retrieved August 8, 2018, from www.presidency.ucsb.edu/ws/index.php?pid=18750

Carter, J. (1980). *State of the Union Address.* January 23, at www.jimmycarterlibrary.org

Chellaney, B. (2011). *Water: Asia's new battleground.* Washington, DC: Georgetown University Press.

Chellaney, B. (2013). *Water, peace, and war: Confronting the global water crisis.* Lanham, MD: Rowman and Littlefield.

Cramer, J. K., & Thrall, A. T. (Eds.). (2011). *Why did the United States Invade Iraq?* London and New York: Routledge.

Crowl, P. A. (1986). Alfred Thayer Mahan: The Naval Historian. In P. Paret (Ed.), *Makers of Modern Strategy from Machiavelli to the Nuclear Age* (pp. 444–477). Princeton: Princeton University Press

Diamond, J. (2005). *Collapse: How Societies Choose to Fail or Succeed.* New York: Viking Penguin.

Economy, E. C., & Levi, M. (2014). *By all means necessary: How China's resource quest is changing the world.* Oxford and New York: Oxford University Press.

Freund, E. (2017). *Freedom of navigation in the South China Sea: A practical guide.* Belfer Center for Science and International Affairs, Harvard Kennedy School, June 2017, at www.belfercenter.org/publication/freedom-navigation-south-china-sea-practical-guide

Greenberg, A. A. (2011). *Manifest destiny and American territorial expansion: A brief history with documents.* New York: Bedford/St. Martin's.

India, Integrated Headquarters Ministry of Defence (MoD). (2007). *Freedom to use the seas: India's maritime military strategy.* New Delhi: MoD.

Intergovernmental Panel on Climate Change (IPCC). (2019). *Special report on the ocean and cryosphere in a changing climate* (H.-O. Pö;rtner, D. C. Roberts, V. Masson-Delmotte, P. Zhai, M. Tignor, E. Poloczanska, . . . N. M. Weyer, Eds.). Retrieved from www.ipcc.ch/srocc/

Intergovernmental Panel on Climate Change (IPCC). (2018). *Global warming of 1.5°C. An IPCC Special Report on the impacts of global warming of 1.5°C above pre-industrial levels and related global greenhouse gas emission pathways, in the context of strengthening the global response to the threat of climate change, sustainable development, and efforts to eradicate poverty* (V. Masson-Delmotte, P. Zhai, H.-O. Pörtner, D. Roberts, J. Skea, P. R. Shukla, . . . T. Waterfield, Eds.). Retrieved from www.ipcc.ch/sr15/

Intergovernmental Panel on Climate Change (IPCC). (2014a). *Climate change 2014: Synthesis report*, at http://ar5-syr.ipcc.ch/ipcc/ipcc/resources/pdf/IPCC_SynthesisReport.pdf

Intergovernmental Panel on Climate Change (IPCC). (2014b). *Climate change 2014: Impacts, adaptation, and vulnerability*, Report of Working Group II, Part A New York and Cambridge: Cambridge University Press.

International Crisis Group (ICG). (2012). *Stirring up the South China Sea (II): Regional responses*. Brussels: ICG.

International Energy Agency (IEA). (2017). *World energy outlook 2017*. Paris: IEA.

Kalicki, J. H., & Goldwyn, D. L. (Eds.). (2013). *Energy and security* (2nd ed.). Washington, DC: Woodrow Wilson Center Press.

Kaplan, R. D. (2010). *Monsoon: The Indian Ocean and the future of American power*. New York: Random House.

Keay, J. (2003). *Sowing the wind: The seeds of conflict in the Middle East*. New York: W.W. Norton.

Klare, M. T. (2013). The growing threat of maritime conflict. *Current History* (January), 26–32.

Klare, M. T. (2008). *Rising powers, shrinking planet*. New York: Metropolitan Books.

Klare, M. T. (2005). *Blood and oil*. New York: Metropolitan Books.

Klare, M. T. (2001). *Resource wars: The new landscape of global conflict*. New York: Metropolitan Books.

Klare, M. T. (1984). *American arms supermarket*. Austin: University of Texas Press.

Lain, S. (2015, January 13). European energy security and Turkmenistan. *The Diplomat*. Retrieved from https://thediplomat.com/2015/01/european-energy-security-and-turkmenistan/

Le Billon, P. (2013). *Wars of Plunder*. Oxford and New York: Oxford University Press.

Lee, B., Preston, F., Kooroshy, J., Bailey, R., & Lahn, G. (2012). *Resources futures* (Vol. 1). London: Chatham House.

LeVine, S. (2007). *The oil and the glory*. New York: Random House.

Mackinder, H. (2004). The geopolitical pivot of history. *Geographical Journal, 13*(4), 1904.

McNaugher, T. L. (1985). *Arms and oil: US military strategy in the Persian Gulf*. Washington, DC: Brookings Institution.

Meredith, M. (2011). *The Fate of Africa: A history of the continent since independence*. New York: Public Affairs.

NIC (National Intelligence Council). (2008). *Global trends 2025: A transformed world*. Retrieved from https://www.dni.gov/files/documents/Newsroom/Reports%20and%20Pubs/2025_Global_Trends_Final_Report.pdf

Noël, P. (2013). European gas supply security: Unfinished business. In J. H. Kalicki & D. L. Goldwyn (Eds.), *Energy and security* (2nd ed., pp. 169–186). Washington, DC: Woodrow Wilson Center Press.

Obama, B. (2011). *Remarks by President Obama to the Australian Parliament*. November 17, at https://obamawhitehouse.archives.gov/the-press-office/2011/11/17/remarks-president-obama-australian-parliament

Pakenham, T. (1992). *The scramble for Africa: White man's conquest of the dark continent from 1876 to 1912*. New York: Avon Books.

Palmer, M. A. (1992). *Guardians of the Gulf*. New York: Free Press.

Starr, C. G. (1991). *A history of the ancient world* (4th ed.). Oxford: Oxford University Press.

Stegen, K. S. (2015). The security risks and rewards of renewable energies: Implications for the United States. In J. Deni (Ed.), *New realities: Energy security in the 2010s and implications for the US Military*. Carlisle, PA: US Army War College Press.

Stoff, M. B. (1980). *Oil, war, and American security*. New Haven: Yale University Press.

The Economist (2014, February 15). The petrostate of America. Retrieved from www.economist.com/news/leaders/21596521-energy-boom-good-america-and-world-it-would-be-nice-if-barack-obama-helped

Tillerson, R. W. (2012, June 27). *The new North American energy paradigm*. Address at the Council of Foreign Relations. Retrieved from www.cfr.org/north-america/new-north-american-energy-paradigm-reshaping-future/p28630

Thomas, H. (2013). *Rivers of gold: The rise of the Spanish Empire, from Columbus to Magellan*. New York: Random House.

Trump, D. (2017). *Remarks by President Trump at APEC CEO summit, Da Nang, Vietnam*. November 10, at www.whitehouse.gov/the-press-office/2017/11/10/remarks-president-trump-apec-ceo-summit-da-nang-Vietnam

UN. (2000). *Report of the panel of experts on violations of security council sanctions against UNITA*, UN Security Council doc. S/2000//203, March 10.

Wong, E. (2010). Chinese military seeks to extend its naval power. *New York Times*, April 23.

Wright, R. (2016). How the curse of Sykes-Picot still haunts the Middle East. *New Yorker*, April 30, at www.newyorker.com/news/news-desk/how-the-curse-of-sykes-picot-still-haunts-the-middle-east

Yergin, D. (1991). *The prize: The epic quest for oil, money and power*. New York: Simon and Schuster.

4
EXTRACTIVES AS A CONTRIBUTOR TO CONFLICT

Philippe Le Billon

Conflicts related to extractive resources such as fossil fuels and minerals have a prominent place on the environmental security agenda. In their most direct and prominent form, conflicts involve armed groups fighting over "strategic" and valuable resources such as oil or gold. A less prominent, but much more frequent, form of conflict involves local communities and environmental groups opposing extractive projects. Extractive sectors can also contribute to conflicts indirectly through their impact on environmental change, most notably climate change, although these links remain debated. In all these cases, extractive resources need to be understood as both material, such as through the pollution they can cause, and social, through their transformation and uses. Conflicts rarely occur over the raw materiality of resources. Rather, conflicts result from the complex array of uneven power relations around a resource, from its ownership to the disposal of its byproducts.

This chapter uses a political ecology perspective to understand resource-related violence "as a site-specific phenomenon rooted in local histories and social relations yet connected to larger processes of material transformation and power relations" (Peluso & Watts, 2001, p. 5). From this perspective, understanding conflicts around resources is not only about understanding the impact of resources on conflicts but also about grasping how the "environment comes to embody . . . violence and to reproduce it in various forms" (Nevins, 2003, p. 677). Such a perspective contrasts with "classical" theoretical arguments on conflicts and resources, including Hobbesian arguments interpreting resource conflicts as rational individualism in the absence of authority; neo-Malthusian accounts seeing resource conflicts as resulting from resource scarcity, including as a result of human population growth; positivist arguments seeing in resources opportunities or feasibility factors motivating and enabling conflicts; and, to a lesser extent, Schmittian arguments about the reification of historically complex identities through resource conflicts (Korf, 2011). Traditional geopolitical perspectives of resource conflicts have mostly drawn on Hobbesian and neo-Malthusian perspectives, with "resource wars" being defined as armed conflicts revolving around the "pursuit or possession of critical materials" – in essence violent scrambles over scarce and valuable resources (Klare, 2001, p. 25; see also Klare, Chapter 3). To paraphrase the Prussian war thinker von Clausewitz (1940), resource wars would thus be the continuation of resource politics by military means. Mostly used in reference to interstate conflicts over the control and supply of "strategic resources," conventional formulations of the

DOI: 10.4324/9781315107592-5

concept of resource wars are often associated with a narrow and militaristic notion of "resource security," and in particular, "energy security."

In contrast, a political ecology perspective on conflicts engages with the multiple forms of violence associated with resource control, access, exploitation, transformation, consumption, and disposal. Through their focus on uneven power relations and the ecological dimensions of resource-based political economies, political ecologists have put an emphasis on the "many violent ecologies of global inequalities" (Robbins, 2004, p. 1) as well as developed a sensibility to physical, structural, and symbolic violence – to use the typology proposed by Galtung (1990). Accordingly, political ecologists have explored how conflicts may involve physical violence conducted by armed combatants (Le Billon, 2013), structural and symbolic forms of violence affecting communities affected by extractive projects (Nevins, 2003), as well as the "slow violence" of insidious cumulative pollution (Nixon, 2011), or the cosmological violence of refusals to accept different ontologies of "nature" such as indigenous beliefs and values (Escobar, 2006; Blaser, 2013). Furthermore, a political ecology perspective does understand conflicts not only as outcomes, but rather, as social processes with the potential to bring about more equitable forms of resource control and access, notably in the interest of historically marginalized and dispossessed local communities.

This chapter outlines some of the major relations between extractive sectors and environmental conflicts. The first section covers the meaning of "extractives" and provides an overview of the major types of associated conflicts. The second section provides a brief historical review of extractive sector–related armed conflicts and discusses key factors and outcomes. The third section engages with the main causes of socio-environmental conflicts over resource extraction activities, with a focus on the contestation of extractive projects and repressive responses by governments and corporations. The final section concludes with a brief presentation of policy implications and options for further research.

Extractive sectors and conflicts

"Extractives" is a term increasingly used to define natural resource sectors involving the extraction – rather than the production – of primary commodities. Narrow definitions of extractive resources only include fossils fuels, metals, and minerals, while broader ones also include old-growth timber and wild fisheries. Water can also be considered as being extracted, especially if taken from fossil aquifers, but the renewable character of most water sources mean that it is rarely considered among extractive sectors. Farmland is even more rarely included within extractive resources, although it can be "grabbed" from local communities (see Unruh, Chapter 5), degraded to the point of soil exhaustion through poor agricultural practices, or converted to other uses such as residential use.

Extractive sectors vary widely in their scale, mode of extraction, and socio-environmental impacts. Artisanal mining, such as non-mercury-based manual gold panning performed by small communities in remote areas can have minimal impacts on the environment. In contrast, scaled-up and poorly regulated mechanized operations using mercury, dredges, and high-pressure pumps along river banks can have dramatic consequences upon entire watersheds. Large-scale industrial operations, such as open-pit mining and mountaintop removal mining can literally obliterate entire landscapes. Overall, most extraction processes have significant negative socio-ecological impacts, including the pollution and degradation of ecosystem services and health problems and loss of traditional livelihoods for local communities as well as direct and indirect contributions to greenhouse gas (GHG) emissions. Unsurprisingly, then, extractives are considered as major contributors to environmental conflicts, with about 40% of the 2,200 major environmental conflicts identified in the world for the past three decades being directly related to fossil fuels and minerals industries (Temper, del Bene, & Martinez-Alier, 2015).

Based on the concept of extraction, the term "extractivist" describes political regimes and political economies relying on extractive sectors for development purposes, often through the export of increased amounts of raw materials, rather than increasing the capture of value along the commodity chain or diversifying the economy (Martinez-Alier & Walter, 2016). The concept of extractivism is thus mostly employed to describe policies and economic relations maintaining countries in a situation of dependence on raw material exports – a situation generally associated with a wide range of problems, including economic distortions such as currency overvaluation or "Dutch disease" and chronic shocks related to high commodity price volatility as well as institutional effects such as the bolstering of authoritarian rule (Ross, 2015). Whereas dependency theory attributes such ill-effects to (neo)colonial processes perpetuating uneven power relations within the global economy, the "resource curse" paradigm mostly points at systemic domestic governance challenges and failures associated with resource dependence itself (Di John, 2011).

Extractive industries have frequently rejected the term "extraction," arguing that resources are in fact produced through the labor of "exploration" – the often arduous process of finding a resource – and "production" processes including vast amounts of capital, technological, and work inputs. Seeking to counter the negative image of extraction, some industry proponents promote concepts such as "sustainable mining", as rents can be reinvested to further develop the sector or alternative revenues, and "renewability", as reserves can generally be "created" through further investment into exploration (Whitmore, 2006). Extractive sector representatives also frequently narrow the causes of conflicts to poor governance by host authorities and "eco-populist" movements misrepresenting their industry to antagonize local populations and the broader public.

Trends in extractive sectors

The reshaping of the global economy over the past three decades – first around a Western project of neoliberalization and then around the rise of mostly Asian economies – affected extractive sectors and led to major fluctuations in primary commodity prices. Declining terms of trade for most primary commodities, and most notably oil from the mid-1980s through the early 2000s, resulted in a widespread economic downturn among extractive sector–dependent countries. Not least among these were many low-income countries, but also the Soviet Union and Persian Gulf countries such as Iraq, Iran, and even Saudi Arabia. The oil-related growth collapse contributed (even if only modestly) to the fall of the Soviet Union by cutting into government revenue and foreign currency access (Strayer, 1998). Iraq's military invasion of Kuwait, growing dissent in the Middle East, Iran's nuclear program, concerns over both "peak oil," and climate change put extractive sectors squarely on the international security agenda. The anticipated tragic fallout of the US invasion of Iraq, the Arab Spring, and the rise and fall of ISIS sustained close attention to the oil sector within the post-9/11 "War on Terror."

Low commodity prices in the 1990s accelerated the liberalization of resource sectors, with negative tax implications for many producing countries when prices rebounded a decade later. In contrast, cheap resources during the 1990s facilitated the rapid growth of industrializing countries, including China. The broader context of high public debts, structural adjustments, and democratization challenging authoritarian regimes led some ruling elites to seek survival through a privatization and criminalization of state institutions, with such "shadow states" personalizing control over export-oriented resource sectors (Reno, 1999). Concerns were voiced for the stability of countries highly dependent on extractive sector exports, most notably oil exporters such as Saudi Arabia (Jaffe & Manning, 2000).

The first decade of the 21st century saw a massive rise in commodity prices, notably as a result of Asian growth, while resource production levels in some conflict-affected countries such as Angola and Sudan soared as a result of investment flows from the late 1990s onward (Le Billon & Cervantes, 2009). The result was massive tax revenue windfalls for those governments able to capture a large proportion of resource revenues, but massive frustrations for populations whose ruling elites did not capture resource rents or kept them for themselves. After the doldrums of the 1990s, the resource boom of the 2000s provided greater financial incentives for peace and an increased military capacity on the part of governments, which implied a greater ability to negotiate peace or win militarily. The commodity price hike was not all positive, however. Rising prices also meant growing tensions within and between importing countries, most worryingly in the food sector, which contributed to massive popular upheavals, including the Arab Spring (Sommerville, Essex, & Le Billon, 2014). The challenges also remained acute for those countries benefiting from both higher oil prices and a transition to peace, most tragically for South Sudanese populations whose ruling elites squandered a significant oil windfall and plunged their country back into civil war shortly after gaining independence (Le Billon & Savage, 2016). Reflecting the cyclical character of extractive sectors, a return to low prices for most minerals after 2011 and oil since 2014 have again put strains on the public finances of extractives exporters but did not deter Russia and Saudi Arabia from becoming militarily involved in Syria and Yemen (Le Billon & Good, 2016).

Conceptualizing extractive sector conflicts

Understandings of extractive sector conflicts should account for a wide range of causes and processes involved. Extractive conflicts are often simplistically conceptualized as a zero-sum game over raw materials, whereby the supposedly intrinsic characteristics of resources – such as material scarcity or monetary value – would drive confrontational relations. This reductionist frame is rarely productive in terms of conflict prevention or resolution and can actually exacerbate extractive conflicts by narrowing the range of policy options available to address them (Le Billon, 2013). Instead, extractive sector–related conflicts should be considered as complex politicization and ecologization processes, whereby extractives are purposely politicized or pre-existing conflicts are reframed and rekindled through the extractive sector.

As political ecologist Paul Robbins (2004) points out, a *"politicization"* of environmental problems often occurs when "local groups . . . secure control of collective resources at the expense of others by leveraging management interventions by development authorities, state agents, or private firms," while the *"ecologization"* of pre-existing conflicts can be the result of "changes in conservation or resource development policy" that are then integrated and reinterpreted as part of broader and at times non-resource-related conflicts (p. 173). Resistance to a mining project, for example, can be the result of a broader political agenda of indigenous political resurgence, with ecological arguments against a mine being mobilized for the purpose of bolstering the rationale of indigenous dissent and self-governance. This argumentation, according to Robbins (2004), is based on three contributions: from feminist theory, which points at the effect of labor and power divisions unevenly distributing "access and responsibility for natural goods"; from property research, which understands "property systems as complex bundles of rights that are politically partial and historically contingent"; and from critical development studies, which show that development activities are "rooted in specific assumptions about the class, race, and gender of participants in the development process, often resulting in poorly

Extractives as a contributor to conflict

formed policy and uneven results" (p. 200). In this respect, many political ecologists consider that changes in environmental governance and resource development "will not occur without considerable struggle since they necessitate the transformation of a series of highly unequal power relationships upon which the present system is based" (Bryant & Bailey, 1997, p. 3).

Such perspective suggests at least five departures from the common understanding of extractive conflicts. First, conflicts related to extractive activities are always about the resource being extracted. For example, armed conflicts can integrate extractive sectors for funding purposes, as in the case of "conflict resources" benefiting belligerents (see Lujala et al., Chapter 10). As seen in Angola or the Philippines, rebel groups and government forces will at times collaborate rather than fight for the sake of enabling mutually profitable resource exploitation. While rebel groups may denounce the presence of foreign extractive companies for ideological and propaganda purposes, they may nonetheless prefer to tax them than forcibly close their operations through direct attacks (Quimpo, 2014).

Second, the characteristics of a resource and its mode of extraction can influence the contribution of extractives to conflict. The financial integration of extractive resources into war economies can be closely associated with the characteristics of particular resources and notably with what is often referred to as their "lootability" – the ability for insurgents to derive revenues from extractive sectors. Diamonds, for example, are more accessible to insurgents if located in shallow deposits in remote regions than if located deep in an underground mine close to the capital city (Lujala, 2009).

Third, conflicts are rarely, if ever, solely about extractive resources themselves – which notably contrasts with neo-Malthusian arguments considering a supposedly absolute scarcity of resources as an inherent risk of conflict. Rather, extractive conflicts should be understood as part of broader historical processes involving causes, symptoms, and consequences that can sometimes be only loosely connected with resources. For example, a conflict between a local community and mining company over alleged river contamination from potential tailing dam leakages should not be simply treated as a conflict over a "technical" issue (e.g., whether or not the dam leaks), but rather, within the broad scope of "traditional" socio-cultural practices associated with the river and relations between communities, the government, and the corporation that led to the implementation of the project (Hilson, 2002).

Fourth, conflicts should not be considered as always negative and destructive. Rather, they can constitute emancipatory struggles challenging deep-seated environmental injustice (Arsel, Hogenboom, & Pellegrini, 2016). Extractive conflicts, in this perspective, can also be interpreted as a productive contestation of the unjust allocation of costs and benefits within an often very uneven playing field. Furthermore, extractive projects can provide a "fix" through which broader frustrations and antagonisms come to be expressed, thereby offering the chance for transformative outcomes beyond those related to the targeted extractive project. Some resource sectors and modes of exploitation are more prone to conflicts and various forms of violence than others, notably because of exploitative or degrading social relations associated with resource projects and with the value attributed to the resources themselves or to the affected areas. Such is the case, for example, with large-scale open-pit mining for metals, which tends to result in protests by local communities affected by relative poverty and whose rural livelihoods are at risk in a context with few alternative options (Haslam & Tanimoune, 2016). Addressing these two underlying causes requires consideration of both historical inequalities and material conditions, such as perceptions of pollution, changes in landscapes, and livelihood transformations linked to resource extraction, but also the socio-political and environmental contexts in which extractive activities are to take place. What is generally required is a "deep contextualization," which allows for more fine-grained understandings of the many facets and complex relationships at work within extractive conflicts, including between and within the three main categories of actors involved – communities, companies, and governments.

Finally, conflicts involve various forms of violence, with different levels of severity. A first form of violence is associated with the direct physical consequences of armed conflicts associated with extractive sectors, such as forced displacement and death resulting from "resource wars," conflict resources, or cycles of contestation and repression about extractive projects resulting in violent protests, police brutality, or the execution of community and environmental activists (Bond & Kirsch, 2015; Global Witness, 2014; Le Billon, 2013). A second form of violence includes insidious forms of repression such as judicialization, criminalization, defamation, and intimidation against opponents to extractive projects (Birss, 2017; Le Billon & Middeldorp, 2019), which can have profound effects on the lives of targeted activists and community members (Rasch, 2017). Finally, there is violence associated with unrealized potential. Extractive sectors can improve the lives of populations in producing countries, but they often do not – especially for local populations in project areas. Failing to harness this potential and "spread the wealth" curtails opportunities, fosters inequalities, and arouses frustrations. Mismanagement, corruption, profit maximization, racism, and ethnocentrism can all contribute to this type of violence. The fairness, competence, and robustness of governing institutions thus matter a great deal for resource sectors to deliver "broad" development and, in turn, reduce the likelihood of conflict. Care should be taken, however, not to present the governance of resource sectors as the single cause of developmental failure or as its sole remedy. Neither should development be seen as a panacea for conflict risk. Rather, the iterative process between resource extraction and social development informs conflict patterns.

Extractives and "resource wars"

The global trend in armed conflicts involving extractives is generally perceived to have increased over the past three decades (Le Billon, 2013). The end of the Cold War led to a relative decline in US and Russian military support for insurgent groups. This led to greater attention by scholars and policymakers to the alternative sources of finances for armed groups, and notably those associated with extractive sectors. Many of the remaining armed conflicts in the 1990s were indeed tied to extractive sectors, contrasting with a downward trend in the number of wars in general. While some belligerents clearly fought over resources, many also simply had to rely more heavily on extractive revenues for lack of Cold War sponsors. Such reliance on "militarized commerce," rather than ideological sponsorship, raised concerns that wars were being waged for financial reasons and "greed," rather than for political and "grievance" motives. A view emerged that violent scrambles for resources among local warlords, regional powers, and international actors were a major feature of contemporary conflicts, particularly given the "declining" role of ideology in regional or local conflicts (Klare, 2001; Reno, 1999). Resource wars narratives mostly interpreted conflicts in several African countries during the 1990s as "diamond wars," while by the early 2000s, other narratives became concerned about international tensions over key resources, with the US-led invasion of Iraq putting the concept of resource war at the forefront of global anti-war activism (see Le Billon, 2013).

As with the Cold War, the US-led "War on Terror" at times rearticulated security threats and military strategies with corporate interests, while it also conflated concepts of freedom and security. In this case, this rearticulating process was aimed at regimes opposing the United States that were also reluctant to open their resources to Western or at least US companies, most prominently Iraq. Debates on oil and US security shifted as a result of 9/11, with US critics arguing that the "war on terror" provided one more convenient cover for a renewed "imperialist oil grab" in the region and others linking oil and terrorism and pointing to problems of authoritarian (and warmongering) governance in several oil-producing countries (Le Billon, 2005). As the Bush administration reframed the War on Terror to unleash it onto Iraq, first as a "preemptive" war and then as a "war of liberation," the US administration portrayed its Middle East foreign policy as broadening from securing a free flow of oil out of the Persian Gulf to promoting democracy in the region (Le Billon & El Khatib, 2004) – a claim some Republicans later sought to boost (and legitimate) in the context of the "Arab Spring" (Nikpour, 2011).

Most accounts of future resource wars are associated with a combination of rapidly increasing demand for raw materials, growing resource shortages, and contested resource ownership (Klare, 2008; see also Klare, Chapter 3). From this perspective, increasing demand for raw materials is mostly associated with the rapid growth of emerging economies such as China and India since the late 1990s (Zweig & Jianhai, 2005). Yet if most narratives stress the rapid industrialization and rise of consumerism in China as driving demand, part of these resources are redirected to the rest of the world in the form of exported manufactured goods, thereby pointing at broader responsibilities for resource consumption. Among the narratives of competitive resource control and contested resource ownership, many pit China against the United States. Both countries, from such a perspective, are seen as deploying aggressive "resource diplomacy," supporting (or toppling) dictatorships, and bolstering their military capacities and international bases. Oil, again, took center stage with geopolitical accounts focusing on the Persian Gulf and Iraq's oil field dispute with Kuwait, and the subsequent military invasion and US-led intervention. Besides relations with the United States, the Chinese "global quest for energy" is portrayed as a source of tensions, especially in Asia (Lee, 2005). Narratives of "peak oil" and other peaking of extraction for other resources also took center stage (Heinberg, 2007), along with climate change and its "threat multiplier" effects through food insecurity, forced migration, and institutional breakdown (Dalby, 2009; Sommerville et al., 2014). Among "critical" resources, rare earth metals came to draw much attention due to the concentration of production in China and restrictions put on exports by Chinese authorities (Massari & Ruberti, 2013).

Conflicts over extractive projects

Conflict with communities over resource extraction is an important dimension of the political economy of mineral extraction (Franks et al., 2014; Gamu, Le Billon, & Spiegel, 2015), and one particularly relevant in the shaping of resource frontiers – areas of resource exploitation at, or beyond, the reach of state authority (Exner, Lauk, & Zittel, 2015; Le Billon & Sommerville, 2016; Peluso, 2018; Silva-Macher & Farrell, 2014). The past two decades also witnessed increased struggles for environmental justice and resistance against extractive activities within the broader context of rising popular challenges to established elites and intensifying extractive sector development. The liberalization of extractive sector laws and investment codes, financialization of many commodity markets, and historically low domestic interest rates (Bridge, 2004), coupled with a decade of high commodity prices, deregulation, and technological innovations have allowed companies to advance the commodity frontier (Watts, 2015), affecting communities and ecosystems. Communities, many of them indigenous, in turn suffer the burdens of displacement, pollution, loss of resource-dependent livelihoods, unequal power relations, and social inequalities (Martinez-Alier & Walter, 2016). The ensuing conflicts are encompassed by a communications revolution that is connecting and making more visible many of these fights (Condé, 2017).

Three categories of extractive conflicts can be identified among conflicts over extractive projects (Arellano-Yanguas, 2012). The first category – *resistance conflicts* – is associated with local community opposition to extractive projects. Such conflicts often take the form of protests and blockades, which are in turn often responded to through repression on the part of the government and corporations. These conflicts often result from diverging ontologies and valuations of land, livelihoods, and communities (Martinez-Alier, 2001). The second category – *opportunity conflicts* – involves tensions over access to project benefits. In such cases, conflicts reflect – and are often instrumented – for the purpose of generating and securing opportunities including monetary compensation, land reallocation, infrastructure provision, wage labor, and subcontracts from the extractive company. Conflicts take place not only between a company and a recipient community, but also within and between communities (Horowitz, 2002). Conflict escalation can represent a tactical move on the part of companies and communities, each thinking that their opponent may back down and settle for less. Companies may call upon the intervention of the state, or private "security" organizations, to tip the balance through coercive means. A third category – *distributional conflicts* – results from tensions over the distribution of benefits controlled by the state, rather than companies. In its most drastic form, such conflicts can take the shape of secessionist demands and associated insurgency, as seen in the case of oil in the Niger Delta (Obi, 2010; Watts, 2004).

Factors in mining conflicts

Among extractive sectors, mining is the most geographically widespread and the most prone to conflicts (Temper et al., 2015). Many factors influence the likelihood of conflicts over mining projects, with some hindering or exacerbating resistance by local communities and others having mixed effects depending on the specific context of the project and characteristics of the community (Condé & Le Billon, 2017, see Table 4.1). Dependency toward extractive companies and political marginalization tend to reduce resistance to mining projects, especially when workers and mining towns depend on the mining company to subsist. Economically marginalized communities may also seek economic sustenance from extractive projects, but they can move toward resistance if they lack alternatives to the livelihoods that could be threatened by the project. Political and social marginalization can reduce or exacerbate resistance to mining, depending on the ways project and community characteristics play out, such as the degree of historical political and social marginalization versus the degree of livelihood dependence and alternatives.

Environmentally, the characteristics of the deposits and the modes of extraction influence to a large extent the type and intensity of impacts on ecosystems and communities. The locational characteristics of deposits and communities can also bear upon conflict likelihood. Remote communities can act more independently from the state, choosing either to negotiate directly with the mining company to accrue some benefits at the local level or to reject a mining project due to a strong attachment to and dependence on land. Another major dimension of conflict processes rests with the alliances built around affected communities. These alliances, often involving a mix of national and international social movements, co-produce and share new knowledge, strategies, and narratives combining both local demands relating to affected communities with broader demands for indigenous, territorial, and environmental rights (Condé, 2017).

Extractive companies have often tried to prevent or de-escalate conflicts through corporate social responsibility (CSR) programs. But these programs can have ambiguous effects. If well managed with good communication channels and genuine engagement of the community, they can prevent resistance. However, poorly designed or implemented programs can cause resistance to emerge or increase at later stages of the project, especially when communities are

Extractives as a contributor to conflict

Table 4.1 Factors that influence the likelihood of conflict and potential degrees of resistance over mining projects

Factors			Resistance likelihood		
			Decrease	*Mixed*	*Increase*
Project	Geography	Remoteness		X	
	Ore quality	Low grade			X
	Socio- environmental impacts	Open pit			X
		Community displacement			X
		Air and water pollutants			X
	Participation	Project driven		X	
Community	Marginalization	Economic			X
		Social	X		
		Political	X		
	Dependency	ASM			X
		Project-related labor	X		
		CSR		X	
	Place and territory	Prior-mining activities	X		
		Anti-extractivism			X
	Organization	Self-organization		X	
		Extra-local alliances		X	
	Trust	Institutional trust	X		
		Relational trust			X
	Participation	Community driven			X
Company	Size and capacity of company	Large		X	
		Medium			X
		Small	X		
	CSR			X	
	Compensation and grievance mechanisms			X	
	Participation	Corporate driven		X	
State	Pro-industry policies				X
	Inadequate planning				X
	Corruption				X
	Repression and criminalization of protest				X
	Participation	State driven	X		

Source: Condé and Le Billon, 2017.

not obtaining what they thought they negotiated for (e.g., "education" rather than simply a school building without teacher) or the impacts of the project start to be felt or are greater than expected.

More generally, distrust between communities, companies, and authorities is a clear driver of resistance. There is frequent distrust not only in the companies' CSR programs, but also in the information provided by companies and authorities over the project as well as the willingness or ability of authorities to defend the interest of communities and the environment over those of companies. Lack of community participation over decision-making, patterns of corrupt and repressive behavior by the state, as well as the frequent criminalization of community resistance, all tend to build a strong distrust of the state by affected communities. These factors, in turn, can result in an escalation of conflicts over extractive projects into protests, judicialization, and physical contention including lethal repression of protesters and the assassination of leaders. Factors affecting the complexity of escalation patterns include the participation of multiple actors, the range of empowerment strategies and conflict resolution mechanisms available, and the underlying causes of conflict, including divergent values and beliefs between project proponents and local communities (Yasmi, Schanz, & Salim, 2006).

Conclusion

Extractive sectors can influence the likelihood and course of environmental conflicts, making some conflicts more likely, nasty, and lengthy and turning what should be assets into liabilities. Not all extractive sectors influence conflicts in the same way. Characteristics such as relative location, level of economic dependence, mode of production and transportation, industry structure, revenue accessibility, and socio-environmental impact matter a great deal. This is not to say that extractives *cause* conflicts. Geology and biogeography are not destiny. But framing and transforming the environment into resources imply that values and interests will be at play, with often sharp divergences. The hybrid "socio-environmental" character of resources – as products of joint social and natural processes – thus requires paying attention to the physical materiality and geography of resources as well as to their historical conditions of production and multiple connections with social realms ranging from local cultural beliefs to global market trends.

Works cited

Arellano-Yanguas, J. (2012). Mining and conflict in Peru: Sowing the minerals, reaping a hail of stones. *Social Conflict, Economic Development and the Extractive Industry: Evidence from South America*, 89–111.

Arsel, M., Hogenboom, B., & Pellegrini, L. (2016). The extractive imperative and the boom in environmental conflicts at the end of the progressive cycle in Latin America. *The Extractive Industries and Society*, 3(4), 877–879.

Birss, M. (2017). Criminalizing environmental activism. *NACLA Report on the Americas*, 49(3), 315–322.

Blaser, M. (2013). Ontology and indigeneity: On the political ontology of heterogeneous assemblages. *Cultural Geographies*, 21, 49–58.

Bond, C. J., & Kirsch, P. (2015). Vulnerable populations affected by mining: Predicting and preventing outbreaks of physical violence. *The Extractive Industries and Society*, 2(3), 552–561.

Bridge, G. (2004). Mapping the bonanza: Geographies of mining investment in an era of neoliberal reform. *The Professional Geographer*, 56, 406–421.

Bryant, R., & Bailey, S. (1997). *Third world political ecology*. London: Routledge.

Condé, M. (2017). Resistance to mining. A review. *Ecological Economics*, 132, 80–90.

Condé, M., & Le Billon, P. (2017). Why do some communities resist mining projects while others do not? *Extractive Industries and Society*, 4(3), 681–697.

Dalby, S. (2009). *Security and environmental change*. Cambridge: Polity.

Di John, J. (2011). Is there really a resource curse? A critical survey of theory and evidence. *Global Governance*, *17*(2), 167–184.

Escobar, A. (2006). Difference and conflict in the struggle over natural resources: A political ecology framework. *Development*, *49*, 6–13.

Exner, A., Lauk, C., & Zittel, W. (2015). Sold futures? The global availability of metals and economic growth at the peripheries: Distribution and regulation in a degrowth perspective. *Antipode*, *47*(2), 342–359.

Franks, D. M., Davis, R., Bebbington, A. J., Ali, S. H., Kemp, D., & Scurrah, M. (2014). Conflict translates environmental and social risk into business costs. *Proceedings of the National Academy of Sciences*, *111*(21), 7576–7581.

Galtung, J. (1990). Cultural violence. *Journal of Peace Research*, *27*, 291–305.

Gamu, J., Le Billon, P., & Spiegel, S. (2015). Extractive industries and poverty: A review of recent findings and linkage mechanisms. *The Extractive Industries and Society*, *2*(1), 162–176.

Global Witness. (2014). *Deadly environment: The dramatic rise in killings of environmental and land defenders*. London: Global Witness.

Haslam, P. A., & Tanimoune, N. A. (2016). The determinants of social conflict in the Latin American mining sector: New evidence with quantitative data. *World Development*, *78*, 401–419.

Horowitz, L. (2002). Daily, immediate conflicts: An analysis of villagers' arguments about a multinational nickel mining project in New Caledonia. *Oceania*, *73*(1), 35–55.

Jaffe, A. M., & Manning, R. A. (2000). The shocks of a world of cheap oil. *Foreign Affairs*, *79*(1), 16–29.

Heinberg, R. (2007). *Peak everything*. Gabriola Island, BC: New Society Publishers.

Hilson, G. (2002). An overview of land use conflicts in mining communities. *Land Use Policy*, *19*(1), 65–73.

Klare, M. (2001). *Resource wars*. New York: Metropolitan.

Klare, M. (2008). *Rising powers, shrinking planet*. New York: Metropolitan.

Kirsch, S. (2012). Afterword: Extractive conflicts compared. A. Bebbington (Ed.), *Social conflict, economic development and extractive industry. Evidence from South America* (pp. 201–213). London and New York: Routledge.

Korf, B. (2011). Resources, violence and the telluric geographies of small wars. *Progress in Human Geography*, *35*, 733–756.

Le Billon, P. (2005). Corruption, reconstruction and oil governance in Iraq. *Third World Quarterly*, *26*(4–5), 685–703.

Le Billon, P. (2013). *Wars of plunder: Conflicts, profits and the politics of resources*. New York: Oxford University Press.

Le Billon, P., & Cervantes, A. (2009). Oil prices, scarcity and geographies of war. *Annals of the Association of American Geographers*, *99*(5), 836–844.

Le Billon, P., & El Khatib, F. (2004). From free oil to 'freedom oil': Terrorism, war and US geopolitics in the Persian Gulf. *Geopolitics*, *9*(1), 109–137.

Le Billon, P., & Good, E. (2016). Responding to the commodity bust: Downturns, policies and poverty in extractive sector dependent countries. *Extractive Industries and Society*, *3*(1), 204–216.

Le Billon, P., & Savage, E. (2016). Binding pipelines? Oil, armed conflicts, and economic rationales for peace in the two Sudans. *African Geographical Review*, *35*(2), 134–150.

Le Billon, P., & Sommerville, M. (2016). Landing capital and assembling 'investable land' in the extractive and agricultural sectors. *Geoforum*, *82*, 212–224.

Le Billon, P., & Middeldorp, N. (2019). Deadly environmental governance: Authoritarianism, ecopopulism and the repression of socio-environmental conflicts. *Annals of the American Association of Geographers*, *109*(2), 1–14.

Lee, P. K. (2005). China's quest for oil security: Oil (wars) in the pipeline? *Pacific Review*, *18*, 265–301.

Lujala, P. (2009). Deadly combat over natural resources: Gems, petroleum, drugs, and the severity of armed civil conflict. *Journal of Conflict Resolution*, *53*(1), 50–71.

Martinez-Alier, J. (2001). Mining conflicts, environmental justice, and valuation. *Journal of Hazardous Materials*, *86*(1), 153–170.

Martinez-Alier, J., & Walter, M. (2016). Social metabolism and conflicts over extractivism. In F. De Castro, B. Hogenboom, & M. Baud (Eds.), *Environmental governance in Latin America* (pp. 58–85). London: Palgrave Macmillan.

Massari, S., & Ruberti, M. (2013). Rare earth elements as critical raw materials: Focus on international markets and future strategies. *Resources Policy*, *38*(1), 36–43.

Nevins, J. (2003). Restitution over coffee: Truth, reconciliation, and environmental violence in East Timor. *Political Geography, 22*, 677–701.

Nikpour, N. (2011). Give Bush credit for the Arab Spring. *Sun Sentinel.*

Nixon, R. (2011). *Slow violence.* Cambridge, MA: Harvard University Press.

Obi, C. I. (2010). Oil extraction, dispossession, resistance, and conflict in Nigeria's oil-rich Niger Delta. *Canadian Journal of Development Studies/Revue canadienne d'études du développement, 30*(1–2), 219–236.

Peluso, N. L., & Watts, M. (2001). *Violent environments.* Ithaca: Cornell.

Peluso, N. L. (2018). Entangled territories in small-scale gold mining frontiers: Labor practices, property, and secrets in Indonesian gold country. *World Development, 101*, 400–416.

Quimpo, N. G. (2014). Revolutionary taxation' and the logistical and strategic dilemmas of the Maoist Insurgency in the Philippines. *Journal of Asian Security and International Affairs, 1*(3), 263–287.

Rasch, E. D. (2017). Citizens, criminalization and violence in natural resource conflicts in Latin America. *European Review of Latin American and Caribbean Studies, 103*, 131–142.

Reno, W. (1999). *Warlord politics and African states.* Boulder, CO: Lynne Rienner Publishers, 1999.

Robbins, P. (2004). *Political ecology.* Chichester, UK: Wiley-Blackwell.

Ross, M. L. (2015). What have we learned about the resource curse? *Annual Review of Political Science, 18*, 239–259.

Silva-Macher, J. C., & Farrell, K. N. (2014). The flow/fund model of Conga: Exploring the anatomy of environmental conflicts at the Andes – Amazon commodity frontier. *Environment, Development and Sustainability, 16*(3), 747–768.

Sommerville, M., Essex, J., & Le Billon, P. (2014). The 'global food crisis' and the geopolitics of food security. *Geopolitics, 19*(2), 239–265.

Strayer, R. W. (1998). *Why did the Soviet Union collapse? Understanding historical change.* New York: M.E. Sharpe.

Temper, L., del Bene, D., & Martinez-Alier, J. (2015). Mapping the frontiers and front lines of global environmental justice: The EJAtlas. *Journal of Political Ecology, 22*, 255–278.

Von Clausewitz, C. (1940). *On war.* Loschberg: Jazzybee Verlag.

Watts, M. J. (2004). Antinomies of community: Some thoughts on geography, resources and empire. *Transactions of the Institute of British Geographers, 29*(2), 195–216.

Watts, M. J. (2015). Securing oil. Frontiers, risk, and spaces of accumulated insecurity. In H. Apppel, A. Mason, & M. Watts (Eds.), *Subterranean estates: Life worlds of oil and gas* (pp. 210–236). Ithaca: Cornell University Press.

Whitmore, A. (2006). The emperors new clothes: Sustainable mining? *Journal of Cleaner Production, 14*(3), 309–314.

Yasmi, Y., Schanz, H., & Salim, A. (2006). Manifestation of conflict escalation in natural resource management. *Environmental Science and Policy, 9*, 538–546.

Zweig, D., & Jianhai, B. (2005). China's global hunt for energy. *Foreign Affairs*, 25–38.

5

LAND RIGHTS AND LAND USE AS A CONTRIBUTOR TO CONFLICT[1]

Jon D. Unruh

The role of rights to and use of lands in armed conflict has been linked to a wide range of fundamental reasons for fighting. From indigenous, autochthonous, and ethno-nationalist claims to religious, security, scarcity, and livelihood assertions or (re)settlement, political, restitution, environmental change, and extremist interests, the broad spectrum of land rights in war-affected scenarios are a reflection of an array of volatile problems that become reasons for engaging in armed conflict (e.g., Sait & Lim, 2006; Toal & Dahlman, 2011; Unruh & Williams, 2013;). Jensen et al. (2013) found that out of over 30 wars occurring between 1990 and 2009, land issues played a major role in all but three. And Alden-Wily (2008) concludes that over two-thirds of ongoing armed conflicts globally are driven at least in part by contested rights to land. While there are certainly other dilemmas that play significant roles in the onset of armed conflicts, land rights and land use comprise a common dilemma and will be the lens used in this chapter.

Pre-conflict ideas of the "unjustness" in the way the state dealt with land rights and land management for portions of a population can constitute an important aggregate force in violent means to right perceived wrongs. The importance of land rights and management problems as a contributor to civil conflict is reflected in the significant role that agrarian reform has played in many insurgent and revolutionary agendas. In El Salvador, grievances toward the landed elite and the state were at the core of the country's problems since the colonial era and a primary cause of the conflict in the 1980s. This was also the case in Zimbabwe's liberation war due to land expropriations by the Rhodesian state and in Mozambique's RENAMO war and Ethiopia's Derg war as a result of government villagization programs. Variants of such conditions also prevail in southern Mexico and in the way the land issue has been handled over the course of the conflict between the Palestinians and the Israelis. In the latter example, land confiscation for Israeli settlement building and the resulting Palestinian grievances have been significant in the overall conflict.

Perceptions of injustice regarding land and property can become especially problematic if they merge with other issues not necessarily related to land, but which in aggregate serve to further decrease the state's influence. This is a fundamental part of the situation in Somalia, where disputes over access to grazing and water resources quickly merged with a history of perceived wrongs done to clans and subclans on issues not directly about land. Animosities tied to historical events also have played a fundamental role in perceptions about who has legitimate access to what lands and properties in the Balkans. The social fluidity of conflict then allows for the opportunity to act, with outcomes resulting in a very different land tenure situation than what existed prior to a conflict.

The acknowledgment of the link between land rights/use and armed conflict parallels a wider recognition that the character of future instability will often comprise low-intensity conflict, with their origins buried deep within aggravating problems of inequitable access to and control over resources (e.g., Crossette, 2002; van Creveld, 1991; Sahnoun, 1996; Crocker, 1995). This chapter examines some of the more prominent linkages between land rights/use and armed conflict. Subsequent to a description of some of the more important components of land rights/use that contribute to armed conflict scenarios, five country cases are delineated where land rights/use have played a prominent role in the development of armed conflict.

Primary components of land rights and use contributing to conflict

Insecure land rights and land use: poverty and evictions

An important component of the world's rural poor exist within a set of property relations so insecure that they reside outside of the economic, social, and political domain relevant to stable peaceful states (de Soto, 2000). For this population, security of simple occupation of lands is so precarious that it compromises basic economic activities. The inability to predict continued access to one's residence and lands, however meagre these may be, significantly disrupts income generating and livelihood maintenance activities such as an itinerant job, small-scale trading and marketing of produce, daily household economic errands, or small-scale entrepreneurial and investment efforts. When widespread, such acute tenure insecurity hinders adequate governance; undermines even near-term personal and community planning; greatly distorts prices of property; prevents investments in housing and land; and reinforces poverty, criminality, and social exclusion (UN-HABITAT, 2001).

Such extreme tenure insecurity meshes with personal, food, and livelihood insecurity to produce a great vulnerability to even small livelihood shocks. Such a combination results in an overall human insecurity where livelihood unpredictability, desperation, frequent violence, and powerlessness in the face of local political machinations preclude the relative stability needed for tenure security to contribute to peaceful interaction. Layered on top of this is the correlation between increasing desperation (via poverty and personal and livelihood insecurity) and an increased willingness to just "take" land rights, particularly if criminality and/or weapons are pervasive and enforcement is lacking. The resulting confrontation about what land rights are possessed, to what degree, by whom, and for how long then fuels broader and more severe conflict.

The issue of forced evictions is especially difficult. Some 14 million people in the developing world are threatened by forced evictions (UN-HABITAT, 2001), in addition to the millions who have already been forcibly removed from residences in recent years and are acutely tenure insecure as a result. Forced evictions usually take place en masse, on urban or urbanizing land for either broad political reasons, or because land comes to have a significant value for select private interests. Forced evictions result in the destruction of social and survival networks and the degradation or destruction of the physical and social assets and savings of those affected. Costs of living jump significantly as patterns of health, education, and recreation are also destroyed (UN-HABITAT, 2001). Thus, forced evictions actively degrade what little the poor do have and dramatically increase conditions of human insecurity.

Forced evictions share several features worldwide: 1) evictions are most common in countries and parts of cities where land and property rights and use conditions are already the worst; 2) it is the poorest which are most subject to evictions, particularly mass evictions; 3) evictions are frequently violent, and include human rights abuses; 4) evictions always greatly compound the problem of insecure tenure (UN-HABITAT, 2001); and 5) mass evictions and demolition of residences and small-scale agricultural infrastructure often are the result of a political decision made about whole areas, against which the possession of title to small properties is unlikely to offer much protection or be offered in the first place. Such features can have especially pronounced security repercussions when large populations are subject to eviction because those evicted often develop or deepen political awareness while dislocated from home areas. As a result, land access problems can easily be placed within the larger political landscape. Alexander (1992) examines how such political awareness and mobilization can challenge authority structures and sources of legitimacy – two fundamental aspects of the land and conflict nexus.

Finally, those who have been forcibly evicted or are threatened with evictions comprise a ready-made constituency for political and violence-based opportunism. Such opportunism can run the range from criminality to mafia operations, to insurgent and extremist movements, particularly if an existing insurgent movement or extremist group desires to grow its constituency, which they frequently do.

Land rights and land management institutions

Extremely poorly functioning land rights and land management institutions are a common characteristic of conflict-affected states. A primary feature of such countries prior to periods of armed conflict is the very high number of ongoing land disputes. This becomes important more broadly in a worsening and self-perpetuating way because most civil institutions cannot endure the stresses of large-scale unresolved land conflicts in society. Thus, the repercussions of poorly functioning land rights and land management institutions degrade other institutions in society – courts, police, and other civil service institutions along with political institutions. Countries affected by or threatened by such problems usually lack the political and institutional capacity to resolve such a magnitude of land rights problems. This is especially the case where certain land rights issues are a national fundamental unresolved problem in society. If not dealt with, such issues can lead to an accumulation of aggressively confrontational ways of dealing with land rights problems that emerge from an increasingly divided society. The result is a buildup of competition, inequity, confrontation, grievance, resentment, and animosity, with no legitimate, fair way to manage these through a country's legal system and poorly functioning institutions.

While there are a variety of factors that can be part of a land rights contribution to periods of crisis (such as resource scarcity, poor land access, governance and political problems, identity, geography, history, ethnicity, grievance, religion), many countries are able to establish and operate legitimate and fair institutions to manage these, while countries that are affected by very large numbers of unresolved land conflicts are not. For countries thus affected, the problem is more complicated and difficult because alternative informal institutions and approaches (such as warlord, ethnic, mafia, or extremist approaches to land rights) can emerge from the absence of effective legal institutions. ISIS, al-Shabab, and al-Qaeda all operated their own approaches to land and property rights. These alternatives are able to operate within the fluidity, confrontation, and grievances of land conflict–ridden societies. Such crisis-based alternative informal institutions, which often originate within specific segments of a population, usually do not function in a fair manner in the context of broader society.

In addition, the variety of functioning state land tenure and land management institutions and processes that themselves cause large numbers of land conflicts is significant. These range from institutionalized forms of eviction, discriminatory policies, land confiscations, land speculation, crowding, acute tenure insecurity, and corruption in court procedures and court access. Often, the accumulation of institutionally caused land-related grievances, the lack of legitimate and workable alternatives, and the presence of weapons combine to provide for violence as an alternative way to resolve land disputes. In such situations, land tenure becomes a contributor to armed conflict. Such was the case with the eventual emergence of Shari'a courts in Somalia and, arguably, the Taliban in Afghanistan. Both were able to field their own mechanisms of enforcement for a variety of institutions, including land rights and use (Unruh, 2002). At times, they can constitute, as in the Balkans, a formal policy support of ethnic cleansing of lands. And in countries with poorly working or dysfunctional land tenure institutions, conditions are such that the state will, in many cases, be weak and of questionable legitimacy in the eyes of many in civil society.

Especially difficult in institutionally fragile states are disputes over land between participants in different and, in many cases, opposed tenure systems. This occurs together with an inability of these systems to connect in terms of how land disputes are resolved in ways that are viewed as peaceful, secure, and legitimate – and, therefore, respected. Left unattended, the overall land rights/use arrangement becomes inherently unwieldy with wider repercussions on agricultural productivity, food security, and the political problems associated with ideas about "home area," ethnicity, and areas gained or lost by different groups over time.

Customary versus statutory tenure systems: legal pluralism, tension, confrontation

The pervasiveness of the ongoing incompatibility between informal customary land tenure and formal state property rights regimes in the developing world has major repercussions for conflict, resource degradation, and development (Bruce & Migot-Adholla, 1994). Customary land tenure and use (also known as traditional, indigenous, or tribal land tenure – although technically these are somewhat different) in many areas of the developing world frequently exist in a state of substantial tension because they often operate in conflict with other forms of tenure. Often, customary tenure can develop to resist, evade, or oppose other forms of tenure – statutory, religious, other forms of customary tenure (i.e., one tribe's system versus another). Divisive tenure relationships between customary and other tenure forms, when lacking ways to resolve land rights/use problems legitimately, can cause or contribute to conflicts because alternative informal ways of resolving land problems are then sought, including violent means, particularly in fragile states. An additional problem is when statutory and/or customary tenure itself degrades, collapses, or becomes abusive and there is a reaction to this by the wider customary population. This was a primary contributor to the wars in Sierra Leone and Liberia (Unruh, 2008, 2009).

The effect of a natural or socio-political crisis in fragile states can leave the statutory and customary tenure systems in severe disarray, with little ability to provide for the land administration needs of the population. As a result, during and after a crisis, a wide variety of alternative or hybrid approaches to claiming and securing lands emerge. These can often be less directly connected to statutory and customary tenure systems and instead more connected to the crisis-related experiences of squatters, refugees, IDPs, migrants, combatants, the impoverished, the evicted, the neglected, militias, insurgents, religious groups, and opportunists.

The result of these processes can be the development of "legal pluralism" for land tenure, which is quite common in fragile states. Forms of legal pluralism are developed *on the ground* and *as needed* by the population at large (often relatively quickly) and are connected to both specific experiences and group membership. In such a context, attempts to intervene by the state can result in land-based legal pluralities being brought together in competition and confrontation relatively quickly. Competing claims can result in people abandoning features of pre-existing tenure systems (laws, norms, dispute resolution institutions) because the very large number of disputes and the lack of legitimate mechanisms to resolve them have made such features unworkable, or they believe there is little point in following tenure rules that others are not following. One of the most acute examples of incompatible legal pluralism regarding land resides in the Middle East, where the Israeli-Palestinian lands issue has vexed attempts at peacemaking for some time.

Narratives of grievance involving land rights and land use

The accumulation of grievances in a population about the way the state deals with land rights can constitute an important force in the contribution to conflict scenarios. Such grievances can range from simple disappointment to distrust of the state and its ability, willingness, or bias in handling land issues to the perception of the state as the enemy. The latter can be especially powerful if an accumulation of land-related grievances exist against the state due to land alienation and discrimination, corruption, or state intervention in agricultural production, dislocating agricultural and/or population programs, and heavy-handed approaches to enforcement of state decisions about land issues. Such an accumulation can result in what Ranger (1985) calls a "historical consciousness of grievances" with regard to land rights issues, which can become especially acute if such grievances merge with other issues not necessarily related to land (p. 1). In such cases, pluralistic approaches to land rights that resist, evade, or confront the state, once developed, can persist with considerable tenacity by justifying themselves with appeals made to perceived historical wrongs done to certain groups (Merry, 1988).

Narrative development among grievance-based constituencies prior to armed conflict occurs as negative events and processes regarding certain volatile land rights and use issues come to be seen as being connected to a broader pattern and to specific groups perceived to be responsible. Such groups can be ethnic, religious, linguistic, political, aligned along production systems (e.g., pastoralist, agriculturalist), or a mix of these. These events and processes can include exclusion; discrimination; armed encounters; dislocation; secondary occupation of land; claiming of lands; destruction of property; and ethnic, religious, linguistic, or livelihood "cleansing" of lands in a variety of forms. Over time, these perspectives spread, find fertile ground among others who feel similarly aggrieved, and can become both more simplified and acute. In aggregate, they produce collective or shared narratives of injustice that then serve to rationalize certain violent responses (Malkki, 1995; Toal & Dahlman, 2011). Often, the complex problem of land rights can become a framework through which grievance-related history and contemporary events and processes are interpreted within the constituencies of what then become two sides of an armed conflict.

The aftermath of the Arab Spring uprisings are an example of the role of narratives of grievance related to land rights and use. Due to the long period in which some governments preceding the uprisings were in power, and the manner in which they governed, what accumulated was a significantly large set of perceived injustices over a variety of issues including land rights. The long history of opposition to certain governments in the Middle East reflects a process of land confiscations, reallocation, poor performance of the rule of law regarding land rights, and importantly, the large role that lands and properties played in the patronage systems of governance. In aggregate, such acute land rights problems "form a common narrative that promises now to reshape new constitutions, legislation, policy formulation, social mobilization and transitional-justice processes for years to come" (Schechla, 2012, p. 2).

Land rights and land use cases

The five cases presented here represent a variety of specific scenarios where land rights and land use contribute significantly to armed conflict. In these cases, a number of "primary factors" noted earlier are at play, often interacting in synergistic ways.

Darfur (2003–present)

Land rights are at the heart of the war in Darfur and, for the different groups involved in the conflict, are complex, confused, sensitive, and volatile (DDPD, 2011; Flint and De Waal, 2008; Suiliman, 2011). In one of the most acute manifestations of the land rights problem, certain Arab pastoralists were easily recruited into the Janjaweed for two primary reasons: land and money (Flint and De Waal, 2008). During the pre-colonial sultanate period, the sedentary agriculturalist tribes acquired for themselves – or were granted – a large territory of land that became their homeland (Dar). The land tenure system operating within the Dars functions off of a framework of sultanate-era land grants or "hakura." Thus, the hakura-tenure system based on sedentary agriculture became the prevailing customary system over most of contemporary Darfur (O'Fahey & Abu Salim, 2003).

While agriculturalists occupying most of central and southern Darfur have their own Dars, the Arab camel nomads of North and West Darfur do not. This is due to the fact that the granting of tribal Dars during the sultanate era favored larger tribes and because, in the past, permanent forms of land claim were not important for nomadic pastoralists, who depended instead on transient rights of access. Thus, the various tribes of Darfur can be classified into land-holding (hakura practicing) and non-land-holding groups, with the alignment of these groups in the war falling out along this distinction (Unruh & Abdul-Jalil, 2014). From their perspective, Arab pastoralists of northern Darfur saw an opportunity within the tension between agricultural tribes and the state to correct a long-standing injustice of landlessness caused by the sultanate, customary, colonial, and independence legal land regimes by pursuing their acutely felt need for land and greater political participation in Darfur. At the same time, sedentary agriculturalists were (and continue to be) threatened by the increasing numbers of pastoralists and other outsiders who are able to gain access to their lands via statutory and Islamic law and violence, in an increasingly aggressive and confrontational way (Unruh, 2012). This pattern of land relationship constitutes one of the fundamental ingredients of the current civil war – control over land and political participation (and, thus, power) are inseparable in Darfur. As a result, political participation is kept away from the growing communities of migrants, such as the Zaghawa and the Arab pastoralists.

With such exclusionary political participation for the non-natives in place over time, land tenure insecurity for migrants became a serious problem, with the result being that fears about losing land access then drove the search for alternatives to the hakura system – such as statutory law, Islamic law, forms of resistance, and importantly, armed confrontation. Widespread pursuit of these alternatives within hakura-administered areas then eventually degraded the hakura system itself so that it began to have trouble functioning in a cohesive manner. Not surprisingly, those native to the hakura system resisted this degradation, also in a confrontational way. In this regard, the original hakura-granting documents became a target for destruction by the Janjaweed, in an attempt to reduce the customary legal basis for hakura claims. These documents, once only of historical interest, "today they are weapons of war" (O'Fahey, 2008).

Colombia (1964–present)

Beginning in the mid-1960s, with the FARC insurgency seizing large landholdings and redistributing it to those who labored on it, the conflict in Colombia developed over the decades to include right-wing paramilitaries, narco-traffickers, the Colombian armed forces and peasant groups, and large-scale commercial interests in land and territorial control (GMH, 2010; Posada, 2009). At the onset of the conflict, grievances generated by the takeover of peasant lands by more powerful interests led to the insurgents kidnapping large farm owners, which led many of the latter to depart the area, selling their haciendas very cheaply to narco-traffickers and others who would then establish a paramilitary presence in the area. Once the area was secured, the land would be sold on at a much higher price. Thus, in Colombia, the escalation of the war and the rise of land speculation based on the war was a parallel process (Posada, 2009).

When peace talks began in 2012 between the FARC insurgency and the Colombian government in an attempt to resolve the nearly 50-year civil war, land rights and rural development was the first item on the agenda (Economist, 2012); with the larger agrarian problem being both a cause and consequence of the war (Sanchez, 2010).

Yemen civil war (2014–present)

Land-related conflicts, grievances, and confusion are a primary component of the current instability in Yemen and resonate strongly in the current Houthi conflict, the Southern secession conflict, and al-Qaeda activities (al-Fadhli, 2012). Subsequent to the unification of northern and southern Yemen in 1990, the 30-year regime of Ali Abdullah Saleh sought to control land resources in the south, and this became one of the primary reasons the country fell into civil war in 1994 (Day, 2012). Prior to Yemen's Arab Spring in 2011, the proportion of cases in the primary courts that were about land and associated water resources is estimated to have been between 50% and 80% of all cases (YAVA, 2010). Land played a primary role in the patronage system of the Saleh government prior to its demise in 2012. Land confiscations and reallocation in order to punish some groups and individuals and reward others were commonplace in the Saleh regime and were important in propping up the government for the three decades it was in power.

The 1994 civil war, which erupted due to discontent in the south over unequal relations with the north, and the north's victory in that war led to two scenarios that further aggrieved the southern population. These were the dismissal of southerners from the country's military and civil services and a two-decade surge of land expropriations in the south by northern political, economic, and military elites and their associates (Hill, Salisbury, Northedge, & Kinninmont, 2013). The ongoing land issues in the south are a primary cause of the current secessionist movement and an opportunity for the involvement of al-Qaeda in the southern governorates (van Veen, 2014). Land grabs, tribal connections with lands, multiple claims, corruption, confiscations, and the lack of rule of law have combined to make the land rights issue a central feature of the ongoing discontent and instability in the south (see Salisbury, 2013; Schechla, 2013; YAVA, 2010).

Jon D. Unruh

Liberia (1989–1998 and 1999–2003)

Former American slaves were settled on the Liberian coast beginning in the 19th century, and a statutory system of land tenure was established in areas under their control. The settler society was exclusive and resided within an array of indigenous African coastal communities. Settler acquisition of lands was supported by a variety of (largely received) laws, including an early constitution (Sawyer, 2005; Wily, 2007). The initial decades of the 20th century saw often brutal subjugation of parts of the countryside, with the resulting tensions between the settlers and indigenous inhabitants reflected in long-standing land issues.

It is widely acknowledged that land problems were a primary factor in the cause and maintenance of the wars in Liberia (1989–1997 and 1999–2003) and the ensuing crisis (see GRC, 2007; Richards, 2005; Sawyer, 2005). Indeed, Bruce (2007) notes that early battles over land erupted due to fundamental differences in conceptions of land ownership between the Americo-Liberian settlers and indigenous inhabitants as early as 1822, the year Liberia was founded. Riddell and Dickerman (1986), citing Liebnow, note that during the Doe regime (1980–1990) "[l]and tenure is at the heart of rural discontent" (p. 102) Subsequent to the war, the Liberian Governance Reform Commission concluded that access to land was a root cause of the armed conflict (GRC, 2007). This occurred through the interaction between a contradictory and confused set of formal land laws, strongly held customary concepts about land, discriminatory "state sponsored customary law," and numerous ad hoc land and property norms connected to instability. With no legitimate way to deactivate these tensions, they became pervasive and then explosive.

Rampant land appropriation and land speculation eventually evolved into sources of acute uncertainty, grievance, and conflict. By the outbreak of the civil war in 1989, the legal mechanisms for acquiring land deeds, especially in areas under forms of customary tenure, was a highly contentious and volatile issue (GRC, 2007; Unruh, 2009). This included mechanisms for acquiring rights to lands that contained valuable timber and alluvial diamond and gold deposits, which then fueled the conflict (UNEP, 2004).

Sierra Leone (1991–2002)

Land issues in Sierra Leone were a significant source of the overall conflict (Keen, 2003; Richards et al., 2004). Amnesty International (1992) noted that in some areas of the country, land problems were so acute that joining the rebels sometimes led to the opportunity to take lands by force. Hussein and Gnisci (2005) argue that tensions over land contributed to the eruption or exacerbation of armed conflicts in all the Mano River countries (Sierra Leone, Guinea, Liberia) as well as in Cote d'Ivoire. Land disputes in Sierra Leone (endemic in the south), along with land allocation and access decisions, were nominally dealt with by chiefs, who utilized arbitrary, corrupt, self-serving approaches to such decisions. Keen (2003) indicates that the chieftaincy system was one of the primary contributors to the war due to long-standing and common abuses, particularly regarding land issues. As a result, some of the worst violence was focused on certain leadership elements in the customary system, and many chiefs were targeted by the insurgents and fled for the safety of the capital or abroad.

Richards et al. (2004) and Hussein and Gnisci (2005) explicitly identify the debilitation of customary and formal land and property institutions as a major cause of rural marginalization, disenfranchisement, and poverty prior to the war in Sierra Leone, all of which led to pronounced discontent. Richards et al. (2004) note that a particular problem was the "poverty and instability of large numbers of the rural youth 'spun off' from village society because of control exercised by village elders over land and marriage" (p. i).

Prior to the war, a number of informal "micro rule of law" systems involving land tenure emerged in the country. Primary among these were disenfranchised youth, chiefs, strangers, lineage members, women's groups, internally displaced persons and refugees. Disputes involving access to land between some of these groups created significant animosity in some areas of the country. Even subsequent to the war, animosity over land continues to varying degrees between disenfranchised youth and the chieftaincy structure and between the lineage landholders and disenfranchised youth, strangers, women's groups, and displaced persons. Much of the problem regarding the landholding lineages stems from the way they manage land with regard to other groups, driven by their own tenure insecurity.

Conclusion

This chapter introduced the reader to the significant role of land rights and land use in the development of contemporary armed conflicts. This chapter revealed that prior to armed conflict, when land use rights operate in dysfunction, they can cause tensions, confrontations, and ultimately be fought over. Such rights and uses can also be difficult to manage after a war.

As the field of environmental security matures, greater understanding is needed regarding the set of factors that constitute primary contributions to the onset of armed conflict. National and international security policies, especially in the developed West, are evolving to encompass much more than what has traditionally existed within the security domain. What will prove to be increasingly important in this regard is how intertwined security policy and approaches to poverty and development become. In this context, discussions about the condition of human security in the global economy (Thomas & Wilken, 1999) and security sector reform in a development context (Smith, 2001) will prove particularly useful as they are thrust to the fore for both the security and development communities.

Note

1 Portions of this chapter have previously appeared in the author's publications.

Works cited

Alexander, J. (1992). Things fall apart, the center can hold: Processes of post-war political change in Zimbabwe's rural areas. In Terrance Ranger & N. Bhehe (Eds.), *Zimbabwe's liberation war*. London: James Currey.

Alden-Wily, L. (2008). *Commons and conflict states: Why the ownership of the commons matters in making and keeping peace*. Washington, DC: Rights and Resources Initiative.

Al-Fadhli, A. H. (2012). *How are tribes changing in south-western Yemen? Report provided to the Office of the Special Representative of the Secretary General of the UN to Yemen*. Sana'a: United Nations.

Amnesty International. (1992). *Sierra Leone: The extrajudicial execution of suspected Rebels and Collaborators*. Report April 29, London.

Bruce, J. W., & Might-Adholla, S. E. (1994). *Searching for land tenure security in Africa*. Dubuque, Iowa: The World Bank and Kendall/Hunt Publishing Co.

Bruce, J. W. (2007). *Insecurity of land tenure, land law and land registration in Liberia: A preliminary assessment*. Washington, DC: The World Bank.

Crocker, C. (1995). What kind of role in African conflict resolution? In D. Smock & C. Crocker (Eds.), *African conflict resolution: The US role in peacemaking*. Washington, DC: US Institute of Peace Press.

Crossette, B. (2002). Leaders envision broad new role for UN council: Peacekeeping at issue – top officials attending session discuss causes of conflict in poorest nations. *New York Times*, September 8.

Day, S. (2012). *Regionalism and rebellion in Yemen: A troubled nation.* New York: Cambridge University Press.

de Soto, H. (2000). *The Mystery of capital: Why capitalism triumphs in the west and fails everywhere else.* New York: Basic Books.

Draft Darfur Peace Document (DDPD). (2011). *Draft Darfur peace document.* Doha, Qatar.

The Economist (2012, November 24). Land reform in Colombia: Peace, land and bread. *The Economist.*

Flint, F., & De Waal, A. (2008). *Darfur: A new history of a long war.* London: Zed Books.

GRC (Governance Reform Commission). (2007). *The way forward: Land & property right issues in the republic of Liberia.* Governance Reform Commission, Monrovia: Government of Liberia.

Grupo de Memoria Historica (GMH). (2010). *La tierra en disputa.* Bogota, Taurus.

Hill, G., Salisbury, P., Northedge, L., & Kinninmont, J. (2013). Yemen: Corruption, capital flight and global drivers of conflict. *A Chatham House Report,* September.

Hussein, K., & Gnisci, D. (2005). *Land, agricultural change and conflict in West Africa: Regional issues from Sierra Leone, Liberia, and Cote d'Ivoire, Phase I: Historical overview.* Issy-Les-Moulineaux, France: Sahel and West Africa Club/OECD.

Jensen, D., Crawford, A., Whitten, P., Bruch, C., Harris, A., & Brown, G. (2013). *Policy brief: Land and post-conflict peacebuilding.* Washington, DC: Environmental Law Institute.

Keen, D. (2003). Greedy elites, dwindling resources, alienated youths: The anatomy of protracted violence in Sierra Leone. *Internationale Politik und Gesellschaft,* (3), 67–94).

Malkki, L. (1995). *Purity and exile: Violence, memory, and national cosmology among Hutu refugees in Tanzania.* Chicago: University of Chicago Press.

Merry, S. (1988). Legal pluralism. *Law and Society Review, 22*(5), 869–896.

O'Fahey, R., & Abu Salim, M. (2003). *Land in Dar Fur: Charters and related documents from the Dar Fur Sultanate.* Cambridge: Cambridge University Press.

O'Fahey, R. (2008). *The Darfur Sultanate: A history.* New York: Columbia University Press.

Posada, A. (2009). *Guerreros y campesinos: El despojo de la tierra en Colombia.* Bogota: Groupo Editorial Norma.

Ranger, T. (1985). *Peasant consciousness and guerrilla war in Zimbabwe.* London: James Currey.

Richards, P. (2005). To fight or to farm? Agrarian dimensions of the Mano River Conflicts Liberia and Sierra Leone. *African Affairs, 104,* 571–590.

Richards, P., Archibald, S., Bruce, B., Modad, W., Mulbah, E., Varpilah, T., & Vincent, J. (2004). *Community cohesion in Liberia: A post-conflict rapid social assessment.* Monrovia: African Knowledge Associates.

Richards, P., Archibald, S., Bruce, B., Modad, W., Mulbah, E., Varpilah, T., . . . Dickerman, C. (1986). Land tenure profile: Liberia. In J. Riddell & C. Dickerman (Eds.), *Country profiles of land tenure: Africa 1986.* Madison, WI: Land Tenure Center, University of Wisconsin, Madison.

Riddell, J., & Dickerman, C. (1986). Land tenure profile: Liberia. In J. Riddell & C. Dickerman (Eds.), *Country profiles of land tenure: Africa 1986.* Madison, WI: Land Tenure Center, University of Wisconsin, Madison.

Sahnoun, M. (1996). Managing conflict after the Cold War. *Horn of Africa Bulletin, 8,* 1–35.

Sait, S., & Lim, H. (2006). *Land, law, and Islam: Property and human rights in the Muslim world.* London: Zed Books.

Salisbury, P. (2013). *Yemen's southern intifada.* Retrieved October 28, 2014, from http://mideastafrica.foreignpolicy.com/posts/2013/03/13/yemen_s_southern_intifada

Sanchez, G. (2010). *La tierra en disputa: Memorias de despojo y resistencia campesina en la costa Caribe (1960–2010).* Bogota: Grupo de Memoria Historica.

Sawyer, A. (2005). *Beyond plunder: Toward democratic governance in Liberia.* London: Lynne Rienner Publishers.

Schechla, J. (2013). *Lands of the Arab spring.* Digital Development Debates, Issue 10. Retrieved November 9, 2014, from www.digital-development-debates.org/issue-10-hunger – for-resources – lands-of-the-arab-spring.html.

Schechla, J. (2012). *Land grabs and the Arab Spring: A chronicle of corruption as statecraft.* Nairobi: Habitat International Coalition's Housing and Land-Rights Network.

Smith, C. (2001). Security sector reform: Development breakthrough or institutional engineering? *Journal of Conflict, Security, and Development, 1,* 5–19.

Suiliman, O. (2011). *The Darfur conflict: Geography or institutions?* New York: Routledge Press.

Thomas, C., & Wilken, P. (Eds.). (1999). *Globalization, human security and the African Experience.* Boulder: Lynne Rienner.

Toal, G., & Dahlman, C. (2011). *Bosnia remade: Ethnic cleansing and its reversal.* Oxford, UK: Oxford University Press.

UNEP (United Nations Environment Programme). (2004). *Desk study on the environment in Liberia.* Nairobi: UN Environmental Programme.

UN-HABITAT. (2001). *The global campaign for secure tenure: Implementing the HABITAT agenda.* Nairobi: UN-HABITAT. Retrieved from www.unchs.org/tenure/tenure.htm

Unruh, J. D. (2012). Land and legality in the Darfur conflict. *African Security, 5,* 105–128.

Unruh, J. D., & Williams, R. (2013). *Land and post-conflict peacebuilding.* New York: Earthscan.

Unruh, J. D., & Abdul-Jalil, M. A. (2014). Constituencies of conflict and opportunity: Land rights, narratives and collective action in Darfur. *Political Geography, 42,* 104–115.

Unruh, J. D. (2009). Land rights in postwar Liberia: The volatile part of the peace process. *Land Use Policy, 26,* 425–433.

Unruh, J. D. (2008). Land policy reform, customary rule of law and the peace process in Sierra Leone. *African Journal of Legal Studies, 2,* 94–117.

Unruh, J. D. (2002). Local land tenure in the peace process. *Peace Review, 14*(September), 337–342.

van Creveld, M. (1991). *The transformation of war.* New York: The Free Press.

Van Veen, E. (2014). *From the struggle for citizenship to the fragmentation of justice: Yemen from 1990 to 2013.* Conflict Research Unit, the Netherlands: The Clingendael Institute.

Vincent, J. (2004). *Community cohesion in Liberia: A post-conflict rapid social assessment.* Monrovia: African Knowledge Associates.

Wily, L. (2007). *So who owns the forest: An investigation into forest ownership and customary land rights in Liberia.* Brussels: Sustainable Development Institute/FERN.

YAVA. (2010). *Yemen armed violence assessment issue brief,* October 2. Geneva: *Small Arms Survey.* Retrieved from www.yemenviolence.org

6

UNPACKING THE COMPLEXITY OF WATER, WAR, AND CONFLICT

Vandana Asthana

Water is essential for life and the health of ecosystems and is a basic requirement for economic development. Water serves multiple purposes on multiple scales throughout the world and strongly dictates how civilizations emerged and flourished based on its availability, accessibility, and transportation. As demand and competition over water increases, the needs of users are often difficult to reconcile. The risk and uncertainty of climate change, projected to affect the hydrological cycle on multiple levels, adds to the challenges of intensified global competition for water. The recent "water wars" narrative in public and media discourse is a worrying trend, as water is presented as a highly conflict-laden challenge. In a world where water insecurity and conflict have become the predominant challenges of the 21st century, the following questions must be urgently addressed: What are the actual risks of rising competition over water resources? Does a real threat of armed conflict and instability center around water resources in developing countries?

This chapter seeks to unpack the complex link between water scarcity and the growing risks of armed conflict. The argument is advanced in four sections. The first section reviews the literature on water-related conflict. The second section defines the key factors that are considered causative in water scarcity and conflict. After a "reality check" on scarcity, availability, and demand in the third section, the fourth section reviews the spatial scale of conflict at the international and subnational levels. The article concludes that international armed conflict over water is both rare and unlikely, as processes of cooperation run parallel to the disputes, but on a subnational level, water conflict is pervasive and likely to increase in the absence of significant efforts to promote good governance over shared water resources.

Linking water resources and conflict

Literature seeking to answer the critical question of whether environmental change contributes to armed conflict has three predominant foci: revealing causal links between environmental degradation and violent conflict, uncovering lessons learned from peaceful responses to

DOI: 10.4324/9781315107592-7

environmental change in lieu of conflict, or mediating scarcity and conflict through technology and trade in an interdependent world.

1) Literature in the environmental change and conflict approach assumes a causative relationship between water scarcity and armed conflict.

> The perfect storm of food, water and energy shortages – caused by a combination of population growth, triggering new rural and urban demands, and global climate change . . . threatens to decrease the net available supply in many areas of the globe.
>
> (Tarlock & Wouters, 2009, p. 53)

Depletion and degradation of a resource have the potential to create conflict among competing user groups. This depletion, scholars contend, could affect internal state stability, leading to the forced migrations of environmentally vulnerable populations, which could in turn lead to interstate conflicts (Homer-Dixon, 1991, 1994; Libiszewski, 1992; Samson & Charrier, 1997; Westing, 1986;). On a subnational level, resource scarcity contributes to a diffuse form of conflict based on ethnicity, class, religious structures, and regime legitimacy. In the case of water resources, this school believes that violence in water at the international and national scales is an outgrowth of water shortages. The strategic rivalry over water can be attributed to several factors: the degree of scarcity in a basin, the extent to which supply is shared by more than one region or state, the relative power of the basin states, and the ease of access to alternative freshwater sources (Gleick, 1994).

2) The other approach also examines environmental change but seeks to learn from peaceful responses to environmental change. Ohlsson (1991), Libiszewski (1995), and Wolf (1998) argue that the risk of common environmental harm outweighs the option of war over water; scarcity of a resource compels states and subnational users to negotiate water agreements that prove resilient even when relations are extremely hostile. Cooperation among states and groups results as an outcome of similar environmental problems. This approach emphasizes cooperation between states over shared water resources like rivers and seas (Conca & Dabelko, 2002).

3) The third approach highlights that in a highly interdependent world, technological innovation and an efficient trading system provide alternatives for resource scarcity and could thus mitigate some of the challenges of acute environmental conflict (Allan, 2000; Deudney, 1991).

These approaches underscore the way in which water resource scarcity can lead to armed violence, enable cooperative arrangements and compacts for mutual benefit, or be mitigated through technology or trade.

Factors influencing water conflict

Against this background, what does conflict mean in relation to water in the global context? There exists a consensus of exploitation of water resources in several regions of the world. Although fresh water resource withdrawals show tremendous variations among countries based on geographical location and level of development, there are three main causes of water scarcity working separately and in combination with each other.

1) Demand-induced scarcity: Demand-induced scarcity exists when the demand for a specific renewable resource like water cannot be met by existing supply. For example, population growth or increase in per capita consumption can reduce the per capita availability of the resource over time.
2) Supply-driven scarcity: Supply-driven scarcity arises when a resource is degraded or depleted due to pollution or breakdown in infrastructure, reducing the local availability and supply of water (water pollution, lowered water tables, etc.). In such a situation, options for pursuing livelihood strategies become limited, leading to competition over water.
3) Structural scarcity: Structural scarcity occurs when groups face unequal access to a resource due to inequalities of ownership rights or as a consequence of unequal power relations leading to marginalization of certain groups due to race, ethnicity, or religion. Socio-economic barriers, gender dynamics, and cultural factors also contribute to structural scarcity in water.

These different drivers of scarcity create conditions of water conflict in most developing societies, but scholars caution against attempting to associate conflict with just shared water resources, as water conflict is a more complex and multicausal phenomenon.

Most water conflicts can be attributed to a lack of water security in the developing world. Water security can be defined as a unifying element in supplying humanity with drinking water, hygiene and sanitation, food and fish, industrial resources, energy, transportation and natural amenities, all dependent upon maintaining ecosystem health and productivity (UNEP, 2002). The key components of water security entail availability, access, and quality.

Availability and access: Availability refers to the physical presence of adequate water supplies for human needs. Water availability is reduced when water is moved, impounded, or transported by humans. States try to manage water resources for food, energy, and survival, but this finite yet renewable resource faces an aberrant hydrological cycle. Natural and anthropogenic factors like changing climate patterns and rainfall affect water availability. Water availability, however, does not automatically constitute water security, as security requires consistent and reliable availability of water. The availability of water for use at the right place and time, in the right quantity and quality, and the ability of people within a country or region to receive or gain access to clean freshwater constitute some of the key variables that define water security (Regmi, 2007). Rainfall patterns and precipitation as well as water release from dams constitute important aspects of reliability. For example, the timing of water flow can become a contested issue, especially among upstream and downstream users in the operation of dams.

Access to water is about structural inequity and challenges. Access involves issues that range from fundamental individual rights to national sovereignty rights over water resources. It also includes issues of fairness and justice that involve equity and affordability (Asthana, 2014). For example, if a government prioritizes urban water use over agriculture and diverts water from agriculture to the city, it might set the stage for conflict among user groups competing for the same resource. Competing claims for a limited quantity of water is the most obvious reason for water-related conflict. The causal factor in access may not necessarily be water availability itself, but the perceived injustice in the allocation of the available resource that reduces access and marginalizes the livelihoods of affected farmers.

Quality: Water quality is important for the potable needs of society, the quality and quantity of crops, and human health. Water quality is measured by assessing the physicochemical and biological properties of water against a set of standards to determine whether the water is fit for consumption. Water quality is affected by both point and nonpoint sources of pollution. Some of these sources include discharge of industrial effluent and domestic sewage into water bodies and contamination through agricultural runoff. Urbanization and industrialization are likely to be the defining processes and characteristics of most developing countries in the 21st century. Industrial growth, a priority for developing states, requires more water for activities such as cooling, boiling, processing, and so on to transform raw materials into industrial products. Due to these resource-intensive processes, wastewater released into water bodies by industries is highly toxic and contains suspended solids (heavy metals like lead and mercury, phosphates, fluorides, etc.), reducing water availability and posing severe health challenges to the population. Domestic sewage and urban waste are the major sources of pollution in the cities of developing countries, making water unfit for drinking purposes and other uses. Lack of effective pollution control measures, inadequate sewage infrastructure, and poor on-site sanitation add to the gravity of the situation. The reduced water availability due to poor water quality becomes contentious between those who cause it and those who are affected by it. The quality of water resources, thus, affects both its availability and access.

Abundance: Floods are a constant recurrence in mostly every season and in several regions of the world, temporarily displacing large populations who survive in the unhealthiest environments and remain vulnerable to an array of water-related hazards. In several parts of the world, water arrives in overwhelming quantities, flowing beyond its normal confines, devastating huge areas of human habitation and causing forced migration. Displacement caused by natural disasters like floods and other weather-induced events results in mass population movement that puts pressure on the existing and available resources of the host population. Floods often destroy natural resources, and a sudden influx of a climate- or weather-induced migrant can increase the risk of civil conflict. Reuveny (2007) cites three reasons why migration increases the probability of conflict: 1) economic and resource bases of the receiving areas is under pressure, promoting native-migrant contest; 2) environmental scarcity creates distrust between the area where migration originates and the host area; and 3) tensions increase if the host population and migrant population belong to different ethnic groups (see also Nizkorodov & Wagle, Chapter 11).

In addition to the variables discussed earlier, climate change studies suggest that there will be a significant impact on fresh water resources, water quality, and the water cycle (IPCC, 2018). Changes in rainfall and in the intensity and frequency of storms will impact soil and water conditions, food security, and water demand. The impact of climate change will be more severely felt in the Southern/developing countries because of changes in water availability, food insecurity, livelihood losses, and migration that could spill over boundaries (Matthew, 2013). How political leadership and powerful elites deal with adaptation measures will determine the potential conflict scenario among user groups.

While there is growing evidence of extensive water-related violence (Conca, 2012, p. 40), water is rarely a major reason for nations to go to war. Yet, conflicts over shared water supplies can exacerbate existing political tensions between nations and users. This implies that apart from the finiteness of the physical resource and its socio-economic component, the danger also comes from complex issues like ineffective governance, bad management practices, and institutional failures in governing water wisely. Inefficiency of water distribution systems, leaking pipes, proximity of sewage and drinking water pipes, and water loss due to lack of maintenance in urban and irrigation management systems are some examples of inept water governance. A highly corrupt hydro-bureaucracy with rent-seeking officials also forces people to compete for available water sources. The political challenge lies in designing water policies that regulate water availability and access in a world where exhaustion of surface and ground water resources is becoming a lived reality and a major concern. The following section reviews the current water challenges in global water availability and demand.

Global water availability and demand

Water covers nearly 70% of the earth's surface, but freshwater resources are limited to just 3% of the resource. Most of it is trapped in glaciers and snow packs or deep underground aquifers. Only 0.3% is available for human consumption (Gleick, 1993, p3). Uses of water include human consumption, irrigation, industrial use, energy, and recreational purposes.

The global population is currently estimated at 7.7 billion people (USCB, 2020). Future estimates are that population will reach 9.7 million by 2050, and most of the growth will occur in Asia and Africa (UN Population Division, 2019). Four anthropogenic trends – demand for food, water, and energy as well as climate change – will shape most countries' economic and political conditions and international relations. Two-thirds of the world's population currently lives in areas that experience water scarcity for at least one month in a year (Mekonnen & Hoekstra, 2016). About 73% of the affected people live in Asia (Burek et al., 2016). By 2025, 1.8 billion people are expected to be living in countries or regions with absolute water scarcity; two-thirds of the world population could be under water stress (WHO, 2017). It is estimated that one-third of the world's population will live in river basins marked by significant water deficits within a few decades.

Nearly half of the world's population (3.5 billion) lives in cities (Feldman, 2017). Developing countries account for 93% of urbanization globally, 40% of which is expansion of slums (UN Habitat, 2010). Access to clean water and sanitation therefore dominates the policy concerns of urban areas (UN Habitat, 2011). Today, at least two billion people use a drinking water source contaminated with feces (WHO, 2017). The demand for water in megacities is enormous, and by 2030, rapidly growing cities will compete for freshwater availability, generating tensions for water rights and water quality. The agricultural sector is the largest user of water resources, accounting for roughly 70% of all freshwater withdrawals globally and over 90% in most of the world's least-developed countries (WWAP, 2014). Impounding surface water for irrigation needs and hydropower and ground water exploitation for rural and urban needs have put both systems under stress. The nature of scarcity is thus complex and has "linkages with ecological, socio-political, temporal and anthropogenic dimensions" (Mehta, 2003, p. 5066).

Water scarcity is both natural and socially constructed. Natural water scarcity is a result of natural processes like variability in rainfall, climate, increasing sea water intrusions on land, natural leeching from soil, and so on. The natural factors increase the pH and alkalinity of the water, which limits water availability. The solution lies in alternative sources and adaptation measures suited to the natural climate. Socially constructed scarcity arises from inefficient use, prohibitive pricing, and failed state policies and decisions. Such scarcity is also experienced as real and tangible. This scarcity can be managed with efficacious water resource management practices to avoid conflict.

Another aspect of scarcity is tied to "virtual water trade," which comes with its own set of complications. The term "virtual water" describes the water needed to produce a commodity and refers to the exchange between water-use products produced in one place and consumed in another. For example, the MENA countries[1] are water-scarce countries. Saudi Arabia has the third lowest precipitation in the world and suffers from water scarcity. To meet the population's needs, it imports foods and vegetable products or outsources production of food in other parts of the world. Most of Saudi Arabia's food comes from the United States, Australia, and the Russian federation. The virtual water imports in cattle and meat products come from Brazil. Thus,

Saudi Arabia becomes an importer of the water embedded in the traded commodities. Several examples exist in the region where water "embedded" in traded products like agricultural goods explains the absence of conflict over water in these countries, as they compensate the shortfalls in water supplies by importing or outsourcing commodities that consume large quantities of water (Allan, 2000). However, on the other side, the struggle to grab land to outsource production by these countries in Asia and Africa can lead to conflict, as land grabs lock up prime farmlands for remote consumers (Conca, 2012), marginalizing local livelihoods. Virtual water trade then increases the potential of conflict, as land becomes scarce for subsistence farmers and residents. As competition over water and human dependence over the resource increases, will reduced water availability act as a catalyst for conflict? The subsequent section examines the risks for real interstate armed conflict.

Spatial scale of water conflict dynamics

There is ample evidence suggesting that disputes over water use, storage, allocation, diversion, and pollution are found in virtually all parts of the world. They can be categorized as international and subnational; subnational conflicts can be further subdivided between intrastate and user group conflicts in the community. If water resources are depleted in a sovereign state due to domestic activities of another sovereign state, the lack of availability of water may set the stage for international conflict. Absence of bilateral or multilateral water-sharing agreements aggravates the situation, leading to political tensions as upstream riparian states reduce water flow to downstream areas through diversions and water infrastructure projects (Asthana & Shukla, 2014; Liebscher, 2004;). At the subnational level challenges of allocation, equitable distribution and water availability arise as sectoral competition over water increases and water quality decreases. On a local level, conflicts arise over taps that flow only a few hours a day. A review of some of the case studies discussed below will unpack the causal links between water, war, and conflict.

Transboundary water conflicts

Most of the challenges of providing water security center around developing and emerging economies and are emblematic of the global water challenges. These countries are unique in their own ways of contested histories of conflict, hydrogeological dynamics, a growing population, and rapid economic growth. Due to population growth and socio-economic demands, water-dependent sectors such as agriculture, industry, and urban cities are often growing at an unprecedented rate in these regions. In countries with existing historical conflict, water becomes even more contentious, as it plays an important role in the economic life of the country.

Many rivers are shared by one or more states. Plans for sharing water supplies in international river basins remain a contentious political and diplomatic challenge. In Asia and Africa, more than 80% of states depend on upstream countries for water resources. Some examples include Syria, Pakistan, Egypt, Kuwait, Uzbekistan, Turkmenistan (Ragab & Prudhomme, 2002). Integrated river basin management due to the institutional and political limitations of riparian states, their internal demands, and upstream and downstream relations becomes challenging and contentious.

> With 268 major river systems of the world being shared by two or more nations draining almost 50% of the world's land area and serving 40% of the world's population, the

potential for conflict over the use, access and allocation of water flowing in these rivers increases given that states are self-serving and rarely operate under the same set of laws.

(Phelps, 2007, p. 382)

While fresh water conflicts have numerous causes, most transboundary conflicts exist due to three major practices prevalent among states. These are water diversion projects (when states transfer water from one basin to another); water impounding projects (when states build dams upstream and control water flows downstream, thus creating distrust among the participating basin countries); and when states disagree over allocation rights by citing historical use versus equitable sharing rights. Due to these practices, several examples over water conflict are found in scholarly, political, and media discourse. But do nations really go to war over water? A closer examination of three sensitive case studies in Asia and Middle East/Africa might help dispel the myth in popular discourse about the notion of "water wars."

One of the most visible areas of regional conflict that is partially related to control over water resources lies in the Middle East. The path of the Jordan River highly complicates the relationship among the river basin states of Israel, Lebanon, Syria, Jordan, and Palestine. Many scholars predict that these states may go to war over water, while there are others who explore the opportunity for cooperation in the basin. Over the years, the river has been extensively developed with dams, diversions, and canals. Israel has diverted the river to the Sea of Galilee as well as drained more than 300 mm^3/yr by boreholes and ground water extraction from the aquifer (Ragab & Prudhomme, 2002). As a result, the river flow has reduced, salinity has increased, and water quality has sharply deteriorated (De Chatel, 2014). Israel and Syria draw more water upstream while Jordan and Palestine, as downstream states, do not have equitable access and fair share of the river's water resources.

In a region as sensitive as the arid Middle East, water has always been an underlying source of political stress and leads many to believe that it was the prime motivator for the subsequent military conflicts. Structural scarcity and resource capture by Israel is considered a major motivator for conflict between Israel and its neighbors over the Jordan River. But will there be a future war over water in the basin? Evidence, however, points to the contrary. Israel's strategic control over water resources by occupation of territories is not the main cause of political tension in the region. The diversion projects on the Jordan River cannot be divested from the history of intense hostility and overall political conflict between Israel and its Middle Eastern neighbors, as the two are closely intertwined.

The second case study discusses the conflict over the Nile River Basin. Many water researchers conclude that the river basin conflict has the potential to cause a water war (Clarke, 1991; Gleick, 1993; Swain, 1996). Despite the Nile Basin Initiative of 1999 to use the river resources sustainably and equitably to ensure peace and prosperity of the region, Egypt and Ethiopia continue to oppose each other for allocation and control over water resources of the river basin. Egypt cites "historical rights" to two-thirds of the river's water flow, while Ethiopia demands an "equitable distribution" of water resources to all basin countries. As Egypt's population growth, land reclamation projects, urbanization, and demand for more food security increases in the 21st century, the pressure on water resources also increases proportionately. Consequently, the Nile causes a lot of political tension and low-intensity conflict between three riparian states: Egypt, Ethiopia, and Sudan (Leinhard & Strzepek, 2015; Swain, 2011).

Many contend that this conflict for strategic control over the river has shaped military and political developments in the region (Mohammed, 1997, p. 148). Even though Egypt is a virtual water importer, the extreme reliance on the river and the fear that the river will no longer flow into Egypt after the construction of the Renaissance Dam in Ethiopia heightens concerns in Egypt. A sense of mistrust guides the key players' decisions over the dam's ultimate use. The Renaissance Dam remains a test of the countries' willingness to implement a water-sharing agreement after serious technical analysis of variability of annual rainfall or minimum flows is agreed upon. Despite efforts from the international community to support basin wide cooperative agreements, differences exist over what constitutes significant harm to the players' party to the agreement. Lack of consensus on project management has led to a collapse in negotiations.

While Egypt has historically threatened war with Ethiopia, will Egypt really go to war over waters of the Nile? The possibility seems remote. Given the history of transboundary waters and the challenges of cooperative water resource management, scholars conclude that international relations over freshwater resources are overwhelmingly cooperative and most of the "commonly cited indicators linking freshwater to conflict proved unsupported by data" (Wolf, Yoffe, & Giordano, 2003; Wolf, 1999). In fact, basin states have worked to prevent escalation than cause war. The countries of the Nile Basin states are exploring further options of sharing a river that touches the lives of millions of people and chart the way for a solution through innovative political engagement of member states. Celebrating the regional Nile Day on February 22, 2018, the Ethiopian minister for water resources who is also the chairman of the Nile Council of Ministers (NILE COM) remarked that all countries pledge to harness the potential of the river to promote cooperative and sustainable socio-economic development of their countries. They pledge to acknowledge and increase the awareness of the importance of basin wide cooperation for win-win benefits vis-à-vis the consequences of noncooperation (NBI, 2018). The threat of war or military conflict could constitute a part of the foreign policy bargaining behavior of Egypt, but the practice of actual war seems a far-fetched reality. The evidence suggested, however, does not mean that there is no cause for concern, given changing weather patterns and the reality of climate change.

The last case study is set in South Asia where India's relations with its neighbors over the Indus and the Ganga-Brahmaputra river basins have been increasingly contentious. The region hosts 25% of the world's population and half of the world's poor (Asthana & Shukla, 2014). The region has contested histories with boundaries mediated by colonial rationality. The partition of India led to the partition of the subcontinent's river systems. The Indus River is governed by the Indus Water Treaty of 1960. Of the six river systems that the treaty constitutes, India and Pakistan got exclusive rights to three rivers each. As the upper riparian, India has rights to use Pakistan's riverine systems in the upper reaches but under certain restrictions. This treaty worked well despite a very volatile and insecure relationship between India and Pakistan and three border wars from 1965 to 1988 (Asthana & Shukla, 2014, p 246). But with the course of time, India's population and socio-economic requirements upstream conflicted with similar needs of Pakistan downstream.

Since 2009, India's plan to construct the Kishanganga hydroelectric project (KHEP) on the waters of the Kishanganga/Neelam River – a tributary of the Jhelum River allotted to Pakistan became the center of conflict between the two states. Pakistan's fear entailed reduced water flows that would threaten downstream agriculture, the mainstay of Pakistan's economy. But despite a history of war with India, Pakistan filed a complaint with the International Court of Justice citing provisions of the treaty that protected the existing use of the river. The court ruled in favor of India deciding that the KHEP is a "run of the river project" permitted under the treaty, allowing India to divert water from the river for power production. The court also ordered India to respect the Indus Water Treaty Provisions on water storage behind impoundments and urged both nations to use the Indus Water Commission – the governing body of the cooperative agreement to revisit the case seven years after KHEP is completed. In this contentious case of water impoundment and allocation rights under the treaty, Pakistan favored arbitration against war.

Another example hailed as a landmark water-sharing agreement between India and Bangladesh is the Farakka Water Treaty signed in 1996. The treaty determines the water-sharing arrangement between the two countries on the Ganga River, but its ability to foster cooperation on riparian rights is fraught with difficulties. Both India and Bangladesh face tremendous pressures to meet rising water demand, and every dry season, tensions rise between the two countries with Bangladesh accusing India of not honoring the terms of the treaty leading to reduced downstream flow. With a total of 54 rivers flowing from India into Bangladesh there will be little incentive to sustain long-term bilateral cooperative relationships as internal demands over water increase in both states. While there is increased concern on the future and viability of the Farakka Treaty and other potential water-sharing agreements, the pressure to secure some form of food and water security in both countries might compel them to explore some forms of cooperation.

Past examinations of international hot spots reveal some interesting findings and themes surrounding transboundary cases:

1) Mostly, these conflicts emanate from the perceived inequality in allocation, diversion, and impoundment practices discussed. Economic development goals highly influence proposals to divert water as the case studies demonstrate. A sense of urgency over increasing demands propels these projects. These projects are generally undertaken without paying adequate attention to the needs and rights of their co-riparian. For example, Bangladesh's allegations on India demonstrate that impounding water upstream by India fails to capture the economic and environmental challenges for the country downstream.

2) These case studies illustrate that despite intense rivalry, there is no evidence of countries going to war over water. None of the basin states referenced have shown any inclination to go to war over water, not even at critical junctures in the case studies discussed. The countries adopt a belligerent rhetoric when discussing water supplies, but there is no significant historical record of states fighting over water. Even in regions of contentious water politics and competing territorial claims, states have fallen short of outright violence. For example, water had little to do with the Arab-Israeli wars of 1967, 1973, and 1982, although it remained an underlying source of political stress and one of the most difficult topics of negotiations. While not a cause of war, water allocation, use, and storage disagreements were an impediment to peace (Wolf, 2000).

3) The transboundary freshwater dispute database project (1999) compiled by the Oregon State University of every reported conflict or cooperation between two or more nations highlighted four key findings. First, despite the potential for water-related disputes, the incidence of conflict is overwhelmed by the rate of cooperation. The database identifies 507 conflict-related events versus 1,228 cooperative events including 157 treaties. The clear implication is that violence over water is neither strategically rational, hydrologically effective, nor economically viable (Wolf, 2004). Second, while political rhetoric might be aggressive and combative, the target audience is the state's own domestic constituencies and *not* the rival state. The report argues that most conflict-related events are verbal, and more than two-thirds do not even have official sanctions. Third, the distribution of cooperative events covers a broad spectrum from quantity, quality, hydropower, and joint management to economic development. Examples originate in the most sensitive river basins in Asia – the Israel-Jordan Peace Treaty of 1994 and "picnic talks" on the Jordan River, the Mekong Agreement of 1995, the Indus Water Commission that survived three wars between India

and Pakistan (Asthana & Shukla, 2014), and all ten Nile basin states that continue to negotiate under the Cooperative Framework Agreement of the Nile Basin Initiative (Milas, 2013). Finally, water can act as a unifier, but also as an irritant as volatile interstate relations prevent cooperation among riparian states.

4) In most cases, prospective violence is more likely to occur because of inadequate institutional arrangements governing availability and access to water resources. Scarcity alone does not determine the likelihood for violent conflicts. There exists accumulating evidence that states respond poorly to international challenges because their water-sharing arrangements are ineffective or unable to adapt to changing needs. Of the world's 268 transboundary water basins, 158 lack any type of cooperative management framework. Of the 105 water basins with water institutions. Approximately, two-thirds include three or more riparian states (adjacent to rivers and streams), yet less than 20% of the accompanying agreements are multilateral (UNEP, 2002). This indicates that states lack the mechanisms, political will, and resources to manage shared water resources bilaterally or multilaterally and share potential benefits equitably (WWDR, 2015).

5) The *Global Trends 2030* report by the National Intelligence Council (2012) claims that while historically, water tensions have led to more water-sharing agreements than violent conflict, the increasing number of risks could change this past pattern, causing intrastate disruptions and interstate conflicts. States are unwilling to adapt to changing needs, and archaic institutional arrangements lack a foundation in best practices for water management (Conca, 2012). Given the risks, "intrastate disruptions and conflicts probably are more likely to be the immediate result as pressures build within countries for relief and migration from impacted areas puts added strains on other areas" (NIC, 2012, p. 67). Thus, most of these conflicts escalate around subnational and local scales.

The literature and the case studies point to the conclusion that "water wars" seem unlikely even among states with extensive rivalries. Modern history is testimony to the fact that the "water wars" hypothesis is short of empirical evidence. The International Water Event Database, a database that documents over 6,400 historical water-related events from 1948 to 2008, has identified no cases of outright war and armed conflict and fewer than 30 cases involving interstate violence of any kind (De Stefano, Edwards, de Silva, & Wolf, 2010). Most assessments find a very weak link between threat to water resources and outright war or armed conflict. In fact, there are more possibilities of a pervasive increase in subnational conflicts.

Subnational conflicts

If interstate conflicts are rare and unlikely, why is it that intrastate conflicts are so widespread? Several documented studies exist on extensive water violence between provinces, social groups, subregions and communities at the subnational level in the world (Bernauer, Bohmelt, & Koubi, 2012). For example, in the Western United States, the Colorado River has been the site of a long-range interstate dispute among seven basin states that share its water. In India, Pakistan, Nigeria, and many other developing countries, intrastate conflicts are immense. These conflicts draw attention to the roles of multiple user groups and the competing values they attach to water use and management within a state. These conflicts can be classified under the following six categories: 1) allocation conflicts between upstream and downstream states/provinces despite cooperative institutional agreements; 2) water-related infrastructure conflicts due to the construction of dams, reservoirs, and canals; 3) conflicts arising over water rights and equity over allocation of water to different users in a given geographic area that pits rural against urban populations, head- against tail-end irrigation water users, or industrial versus agricultural users; 4) distributive conflicts when a local municipal water utility raises water prices or privatizes water outsourcing to a corporation and disadvantages certain groups against the privileged elites; 5) water pollution conflicts that generally occur between industrial users of water and communities affected by the degradation of that water; and 6) other conflicts caused by natural disasters or inefficient governance. Some of the facts about these categories of conflicts are discussed below:

1) The Cauvery River in India study exemplifies allocation conflict between two upstream and downstream neighbors, Karnataka and Tamil Nadu, despite an existing cooperative institutional arrangement. Tamil Nadu cites historical use of the resource for irrigation, while Karnataka, a late starter in irrigation, calls for equitable distribution of water to meet its upstream needs. This intrastate conflict has continued to see violence since 1995, and as each lean season approaches, water distribution and release by the upper riparian becomes contentious. Violence flared in September 2016, when

> forty luxury buses were burnt in one depot in Bengaluru, two people were killed in police firing and a young boy committed suicide by self-immolation in Tamil Nadu. The damage to property is (was) reportedly valued at 25,000 crores.[2]
> (Janakarajan, 2016, p. 10)

The politicization of this dispute has fostered cumulative bitterness, violent outbursts, and damage to public property between the population of both states, making this dispute intractable.

2) Another case of subnational conflict common in most developing economies is water-related infrastructural projects like dams, canals, and reservoirs. Conflict occurs when the benefits of these projects accrue to a small coalition of beneficiaries at the cost of the vulnerable and poor population, who are forced to migrate. Dams are symbols of political pride and economic development for developing countries. Large water resource development projects have generated worldwide protests, as emerging economies continue to build dams. Dam protests are peaking, as Latin America moves ahead in a new wave of dam building in Chile, Brazil, Peru, and Ecuador. Extensive protests in Brazil over the Bela Ponte dam and in Laos over the Xayaburi dam are a few examples where indigenous populations, subsistence fishermen, and residents lose their livelihood and are forced to migrate. Conflict occurs as native populations do not wish to accept migrants from another area. (Nizkorodov & Wagle, Chapter 11).

3) Water demand for urban cities at the expense of rural farmers and conflict between head- and tail-end users in canal irrigation in South Asia and parts of Africa demonstrate serious issues of water rights and inequity that lead to water conflict (Asthana & Shukla, 2014). Urban rural water access is becoming more and more contentious across the globe as people migrate to the cities. Tensions are flaring in the American West as rural and urban interests squabble over a resource diminished by drought and strained by a growing population (Wines, 2014); China, India, and many countries in Asia experience similar conflicts, as municipalities divert water from agricultural lands to cities. The cities of Karachi in Pakistan and Chennai in India; the province of Bali in Indonesia; and the states of Colorado, Arizona, and Texas in the United States are just a few examples. In Tanzania and Sudan, clashes between herders and farmers scrambling for irrigation water and pastures for feeding animals are another manifestation of a user group conflict.

Inequity considerations related to groundwater usage have led to tension over access and ownership rights among water users. Bulk water exports by multinational corporations (MNCs) due to indiscriminate pumping of groundwater in many developed and developing societies has caused huge resistance and protests. Passions run especially high when industries buy agricultural land and pump groundwater to meet business needs, pushing tribes and farmers out of livelihood. Water exploitation by Coca-Cola in the Plachimada district in Kerala, India, for instance, dried up many water bodies and lakes on which the tribal population depended for their livelihood (Asthana, 2010). A long-term conflict ensued with the company until a court order forced it to move away from the village. This inequity lies in the capital-intensive nature of modern tube wells and drilling technology, where the sufferers are vulnerable populations, indigenous groups, and poor farmers.

4) Distribution conflict also arises within cities where the rich and powerful get more water at the expense of the urban poor. The involvement of private sector in many countries of Asia and Latin America to fix inefficiencies in water supply has seen violent protests due to economic pricing decisions unfavorable to the poor. Protests in Cochabamba in Bolivia, the riots in India, Peru, Brazil, and Lagos against privatization of water are contested as being a violation of the human right to water (Asthana, 2009; Huancayo, 2006; Langman, 2002; Lobina, 2000). Other forms of localized conflict occur in cities where inefficiency and poor maintenance of water services cause people to stand in line for hours: tempers run high when people scramble for the service that is limited to a few hours a day or even a few days a week.

5) Loss of water-related livelihoods due to poor water quality via industrial pollution can also create politically destabilizing movements. Protesters took to the streets in Dhaka and more than 50 people were injured over the potential ecological impacts of a proposed coal plant on fisheries (Schneider, 2016).

6) Local disasters also have cross-border implications. Floods, for example, are common in Bangladesh, but environmental destruction in Bangladesh caused ethnic conflict in India (Swain, 1996) due to clashes between the host and migrant populations.

An analysis of the different categories of conflict illustrates that subnational conflicts are increasingly pervasive as the economic value of water ecosystem services becomes more pronounced in society. However, stress on water resources is compounded by institutional inefficiency and failure of governance. For example, sub-Saharan Africa is a region where the heterogeneous and unequal distribution of water has caused many conflicts. However, civil wars in parts of Africa are driven not just by scarcity of resources but also by failed political machinery and marginalization of certain sections of populations based on religion or ethnicity. The legacy of apartheid still dominates water rights and distribution of water resources in South Africa. Similarly, civil war in Syria has been linked to drought made worse by climate change, forced migration, and antecedent political and economic factors (Fountain, 2015; Gleick, 2014). The impacts of poorly designed water governance policies at the subnational or national level are locally felt, but rarely do these episodic conflicts conclude in large-scale violence at an international scale.

The way forward

The global community cautions that water scarcity might lead to national and international conflicts. The media discourse also publicizes the possibility of "Water Wars."[3] These forecasts are not new, but there is increasing visibility of the prediction of water wars in the voices of international organizations, political leaders, and journalists. The water war scenario assumes a statistical correlation between water and conflict and foresees serious water scarcities having increasing potential for war among countries of the world. However, the cooperation scenario

> while freely admitting the possibility of conflict, it denies its inevitability. . . . The cooperation scenario further points to the possibility of co-operative arrangements for sharing river resources between the upstream and downstream countries, including treaties and joint river administrations.
>
> (Toset, 2000, 971–976)

What is the way forward?

On an international scale, well-designed and adaptable institutions can go a long way toward equitable and peaceful river management. The key to managing water resources is cooperative management within a river basin approach, but nations often lack the political will to create mechanisms for integrated river management based on transparency and accountability. The ratification of the UN Watercourses Convention that establishes a framework for the management of international waterways should be the first step. In addition, water compacts created among nations need to be grounded in scientific knowledge regarding the spatial distribution, quality, and quantity of the resource and the variability of precipitation (Phelp, 2007, p. 383). Some of the necessary variables of a successful cooperative management approach should include data sharing, understanding allocation in a growing society, institutional capacity, adaptability, appropriate dispute resolution mechanisms, formal treaties, and a friendly host environment. Countries need to tap water's peacebuilding potential and understand the risk of common environmental and social harm.

It is on a subnational and local scale that violence occurs. Evidence points in the direction that resource scarcity alone does not constitute widespread conflict. In most events, the challenge is less about water availability than institutional weaknesses in water resource management. Resource stress acts as a threat multiplier in countries that lack stable political mechanisms, making them more disposed to civil strife. The current governance of water resources "demonstrates that piecemeal legislation has failed to account for interdependencies among agencies, jurisdictions, and sectors" (Asthana & Shukla, 2014, p192). Countries need stronger policies to regulate and manage water resources, but political will along with a comprehensive framework of strong regulatory structures, transparency, and participation of stakeholders will go a long way in establishing good governance in the water sector. Climate change should be factored in while negotiating agreements to avoid future conflicts.

The challenges are enormous – scarcity, poverty, degradation, inefficiency, and institutional and governance weaknesses. Until these hurdles are overcome, water will remain a threat multiplier, and the process of constructing a peaceful resource community will remain a mixture of conflict and cooperation. While states may not necessarily go to war over water, resource management practices that could improve cooperation require trade-offs that might often come at a high political cost. Thus, cooperative resource management faces several obstacles due to the critical importance of water for human survival. Untangling this complex web to govern water wisely is the only hope for a peaceful and stable future. While cooperation has historically dominated conflict in water-related matters, unprecedented competition for water supplies and uncertainty of climate change impacts have increased the risk of conflict; states may be tempted to engage in unilateral decisions, leading to contentious politics and coercive diplomacy in place of cooperation.

Notes

1 Middle East and North Africa (MENA) countries consist of Algeria, Bahrain, Egypt, Iran, Iraq, Israel, Jordan, Kuwait, Lebanon, Libya, Morocco, Oman, Qatar, Saudi Arabia, Syria, Tunisia, the United Arab Emirates, and Yemen.
2 US$ 3.97 billion approximately.
3 For example, the BBC News (2018) recently reported on the *brewing* "water war" between Egypt and Ethiopia over the new River Nile dam. The Asia Sentinel (2017) also recently reported a story about the threat of a water war between India and China over failing to share critical hydrological flow data during flood season.

Works cited

Allan, A. J. (2000). *The Middle East water question.* I. B. Tauris.Sharing the Nile; Water politics. (2016, January 16). *The Economist, 418*(8972), 49–50. Retrieved from https://ezproxy.library.ewu.edu/login?url=https://search-proquest-com.ezproxy.library.ewu.edu/docview/1757163012?accountid=7305

Asia Sentinel. (2017, August 31). *India and China in a water war.* Retrieved October 11, 2020, from www.asiasentinel.com/p/india-china-water-war

Asthana, V., & Shukla, A. C. (2014). *Water security in India: Hope and despair.* New York: Bloomsbury.

Asthana, V. (2010). The water privatization process: Global politics and ecological struggles in India. In R. Ganguly & S. K. Pramanick (Eds.), *Globalization in India: New frontiers and emerging challenges.* New Delhi. PHI Learning.

Asthana, V. (2009). *Water policy processes in India: Discourses of power and resistance.* New York: Routledge.

BBC News. (2018, February 24). The 'water war' brewing over the new River Nile dam. Retrieved October 11, 2020, from www.bbc.com/news/world-africa-43170408

Bernauer, T., Bohmelt, T., & Koubi, V. (2012). Environmental changes and violent conflict. *Environmental Research Letters, 7,* 1–8.

Bernauer, T., Bohmelt, T., Buhaug, H., Gleditsch, P., Tribaldos, T., Weibust, E., et al. (2012). Water-Related Intrastate Conflict and Cooperation (WARRIC): A new event dataset. *International Interactions: Empirical and Theoretical Research in International Relations, 38*(4), 529–545.

Burek, P., Satoj, Y., Fischer, G., Kahil, M. T., Scherzer, A., Tramberend, S., Nava, L. F., Wada, Y., et al. (2016). *Water Futures and Solution – Fast Track Initiative (Final Report).* IIASA Working Paper. IIASA, Laxenburg, Austria: WP-16–006

Clarke, R. (1991). *Water: The international crisis.* London: Earthscan.

Conca, K., & Dabelko, G. (2002). *Environmental peacemaking.* Baltimore, MD: Johns Hopkins University Press.

Conca, K. (2012). Water and Violent Conflict. *Issues in Science and Technology, 29*(Fall 1), 39–49.

De Chatel, F. (2014). Baptism in the Jordan river: Immersing in a contested transboundary watercourse. *Wiley Interdisciplinary Reviews; Water, 1*(2), 219–227. http://dx.doi.org.ezproxy.library.ewu.edu/10.1002/wat2.1013

De Stefano, L., Edwards, P., de Silva, L., & Wolf, A. (2010). Tracking cooperation and conflict in international basins: Historic and recent trends. *Water Policy, 12,* 871–884.

Deudney, D. (1991). Environment and security: Muddled thinking. *Bulletin of Atomic Scientists, 47*(3), 23–28.

Feldman, D. L. 2017. *Water Politics – Governing our most precious resource.* UK: Polity Books.

Fountain, H. (2015, March 3). Researchers link Syrian conflict to a drought made worse by climate change. *The New York Times.* Retrieved from www.nytimes.com/2015/03/03/science/earth/study-links-syria-conflict-to-drought-caused-by-climate-change.html

Gleick, P. H. (1993). *Water in crisis: A guide to the world's fresh water resources.* Oxford: Oxford University Press.

Gleick. (1994). Water, war, and peace in the Middle East. *Environment, 36*(3), 6.

Gleick, P. (2014). Water, drought, climate change, and conflict in Syria. *Weather, Climate, and Society, 6*(3), 331–340. Retrieved from www.jstor.org/stable/24907379

Homer-Dixon, T. (1991). On the Threshold: Environmental changes as causes of acute conflict. *International Security, 16*(2), 76–116. https://doi.org/10.2307/2539061.

Homer-Dixon, T. (1994). Environmental scarcities and violent conflict: Evidence from cases. *International Security, 19*(1), 5–40. https://doi.org/10.2307/2539147.

Huancayo (2006). Peru's water industry, Quenching thirst. *The Economist*. Retrieved from www.economist.com/node/5526571

Intergovernmental Panel on Climate Change (IPCC). (2018). *Global Warming of 1.5°C. An IPCC Special Report on the impacts of global warming of 1.5°C above pre-industrial levels and related global greenhouse gas emission pathways, in the context of strengthening the global response to the threat of climate change, sustainable development, and efforts to eradicate poverty* (V. Masson-Delmotte, P. Zhai, H.-O. Pörtner, D. Roberts, J. Skea, P. R. Shukla, . . . T. Waterfield, Eds.). Retrieved from www.ipcc.ch/sr15/

Janakarajan, S. (2016, October 8). Need to rethink the Cauvery water dispute. *Economic and Political Weekly, L1*(41), 10–15.

Leinhard, J. H., & Strzepek, K. M. (2015, September 28). How to share water along the Nile. *The New York Times*. Retrieved from www.nytimes.com/2015/09/29/opinion/how-to-share-water-along-the-nile.html

Libiszewski, S. (1992). *What is an environmental conflict?* Occasional Paper No. 1. Environment and Conflicts Project. Bern and Zurich. Swiss Peace Foundation and Center for Security Studies and Conflict Research.

Libiszewski, S. (1995). *Water disputes in the Jordan basin region and their role in the resolution of the Arab-Israeli conflict Occasional Paper* (Vol. 13). Zurich: Center for Security Studies and Conflict Research.

Liebscher, H. (2004). Potential and acute water conflicts in transboundary river basins. *Hydrology and Water Resources Management-Germany, 48*(2), 71–79. Retrieved from https://ezproxy.library.ewu.edu/login?url=https://search-proquest-com.ezproxy.library.ewu.edu/docview/17724451?accountid=7305

Lobina, E. (2000). Cochabamba- Water War. *Focus* (PSI) Magazine, Public Services International, France, *7*(2).

Langmann, J. (2002). Betchel battles against Dirt Poor Bolivia. *San Francisco Chronicle*, February 2.

Matthew, R. A. (2013). Climate change and water security in the Himalayan Region. *Asia Policy, 16*. Retrieved from www.nbr.org/publications/element.aspx?id=671

Mehta, L. (2003, November 29). Contexts and constructions of water scarcity. *Economic and Political Weekly, 38*(48), 5066–5072. Retrieved from www.jstor.org/stable/4414344

Milas, S. (2013). *Sharing the Nile: Egypt, Ethiopia and the geo-politics of water*. London: Pluto Press. Retrieved from www.jstor.org/stable/j.ctt183p7hn

Mohammed, N. A. L. (1997). Environmental conflict in Africa. In N. P. Gleditsch (Ed.), *Conflict in the environment*. Netherlands: Kluwer Academic Publishers.

Mekonnen, M. M., & Hoekstra, A. Y. (2016). Four billion people facing severe water scarcity. *Science Advances February 12, 2016, 2*(2), e1500323. https://doi.org/10.1126/sciadv.1500323

Myers, N. (1987). *Not far afield: US interests and the global environment*. Washington, DC: World Resources Institute.

National Intelligence Council. (2012). *Global trends 2030 report: Alternative worlds*. Retrieved from www.dni.gov/files/documents/GlobalTrends_2030.pdf

Nexus Conference. (2012). *Messages from the Bonn 2011 Conference: The water, energy and food security Nexus – Solutions for a green economy*. Retrieved from www.water-energy-food.org/en/conference.html

NBI. (2018). Ethiopia's minister of water affairs addresses the press ahead of Regional Nile Day 2018. Retrieved from www.nilebasin.org/index.php/new-and-events/190-ethiopia-s-minister-of-water-affairs-addresses-the-press-ahead-of-regional-nile-day-2018

Ohlsson, L. (1991). Sustainable development of the greater Ganga: A case for regional cooperation. In L. Ohlsson (Ed.), *Regional conflict and conflict resolutions-case studies II Padrigue Papers* (Vol. 1, p. 43). Sweden: Gothenburg University.

Phelps, D. (2007). Water and conflict: Historical perspective. *Journal of Water Resources Planning and Management*. ASCE. September October, 382–395.

Population Division. (2019). *World population prospects 2019*. Population Division of the Department of Economic and Social Affairs of the United Nations Secretariat. https://population.un.org/wpp/

Ragab, R., & Prudhomme, C. (2002). Climate change and water resources management in arid and semi-arid regions: Prospective and challenges for the 21st century. *Biosystems Engineering, 81*(1), 3–34.

Regmi, A. R. (2007). *The role of group heterogeneity in collective action. A look at the intertie between irrigation and forests. Case studies from Chitwan, Nepal*. PhD Dissertation. Indiana University.

Reuveny, R. (2007). Climate change-induced migration and violent conflict. *Political Geography, 26*(6), 656–673.

Samson, P., & Charrier, B. (1997). *International freshwater conflict issues and prevention strategies*. Green Cross Draft Report.

Schneider, K. (2016, November 1). Protests over water safety, bank financing rock Bangladesh coal plants. *Circle of Blue Water News*. Retrieved from www.circleofblue.org/2016/world/protests-water-safety-bank-financing-rock-bangladesh-coal-plants/

Shukla, S. (2008, November 24). Rivers of conflict. *India Today*. Retrieved from https://ezproxy.library.ewu.edu/login?url=https://search-proquest-com.ezproxy.library.ewu.edu/docview/198739464?accountid=7305

Swain, A. (1996). Displacing the conflict: Environmental destruction in Bangladesh and ethnic conflict in India. *Journal of Peace Research, 33*(2), 189–204.

Swain, A. (2011). Challenges for water sharing in the Nile basin: Changing geo-politics and changing climate. *Hydrological Sciences Journal, 56*(4), 687–702. https://doi.org/10.1080/02626667.2011.577037

Tarlock, D., & Wouters, P. (2009). Reframing the water security dialogue. *Journal of Water Law, 20*(2–3), 53–60.

Toset, H., Gleditsch, N., & Hegre, H. (2000). Shared rivers and interstate conflict. *Political Geography, 19*(8), 971–996.

UN Habitat (United Nations Human Settlements Program). (2010). *State of the World's cities 2010/2011 report: Bridging the urban divide*. Nairobi: UN-Habitat.

UN Habitat. (2011). *World Water Day 2011: Water and urbanization. Water for Cities: Responding to the urban challenge. Final Report*. Nairobi: UN-Habitat.

UNEP (United Nations Environment Program). (2002). *The world's international freshwater agreements*. Nairobi: UNEP.

USCB (United States Census Bureau). (2020). US and world population clock. Retrieved from www.census.gov/popclock/

Westing, A. H. (Ed.). (1986). *Global resources and international conflict*. Oxford: Oxford University Press.

WHO. (2017). *Factsheet*. Retrieved from www.who.int/mediacentre/factsheets/fs391/en/

Wines. (2014, March 17). Drought and growth intensify conflict over water rights. *The New York Times*. Retrieved from www.nytimes.com/2014/03/17/us/wests-drought-and-growth-intensify-conflict-over-water-rights.html

Wolf, A. (1995). *Hydropolitics along the Jordan River: Scarce water and its impact on the Arab-Israeli conflict*. Tokyo: United Nations University Press.

Wolf, A. T. (1998). Conflict and cooperation along international waterways. *Water Policy, 1*(2), 251–265.

Wolf, A. T. (1999). The transboundary freshwater dispute database project. *Water International, 24*(2), 160–163.

Wolf, A. T. (2000). Hydro-strategic territory in the Jordan Basin: Water, War, and Arab- Israeli peace negotiations. In A. Hussein & A. Wolf (Eds.), *Water in the Middle East: A geography of peace*. Austin: University of Texas.

Wolf, A. T. (2004). *Regional water cooperation as confidence building: Water management as a strategy for peace*. Berlin: Adelphi Research.

Wolf, A. T., Yoffe, S. B., & Giordano, M. (2003). International waters: Identifying basins at risk. *Water Policy, (5)*, 29–60.

WWAP (United Nations World Water Assessment Program). (2014). *The United Nations World Water development report 2014: Water and energy* (pp. 22–26). Paris: UNESCO. http://unesdoc.unesco.org/images/0022/002257/225741E.pdf

WWDR The UN World Water Development Report. (2015). *Water for a sustainable world*. http://unesdoc.unesco.org/images/0023/002318/231823E.pdf

Yoffe, S., & Wolf, A. (1999). Water, conflict and cooperation: Geographical perspectives. *Cambridge Review of International Affairs, 12*(2), 197–213.

7

CLIMATE CHANGE AS A CONTRIBUTOR TO CONFLICT

Alec Crawford and Clare V. Church

The Central African Republic, Chad, South Sudan, Somalia, Yemen, the Democratic Republic of Congo: the 2016 Human Development Report by the United Nations Development Programme shows that the countries furthest from achieving the Sustainable Development Goals (SDGs) are also typically the countries most affected by instability, violence, and fragility. For these countries, a lack of peace and stability means that achieving lasting progress on health, education, equality, and other determinants of well-being will continue to be difficult, if not impossible.

The Sustainable Development Goals (SDGs) – the 17 commitments to sustainable development made by the international community in 2015, to be achieved by 2030 – are highly ambitious and very necessary. For those fragile states most in need of development progress, SDG 16, which involves the promotion of peaceful and inclusive societies for sustainable development, is most central to achieving well-being. Peace and stability are key foundational first steps for these countries as they work toward meeting their development goals.

Climate change will make the achievement of SDG 16 much more difficult for fragile states, as many are characterized by high levels of vulnerability and low adaptive capacities. In addition, many of these countries are also found in those regions where the worst climate impacts are anticipated, such as the Horn of Africa and the Sahel (see Table 7.1, noting that climate vulnerability data is not available for South Sudan). Fragile states are particularly vulnerable to the impacts of climate change for a number of reasons. Their institutions and governance processes and norms are weak. Their populations and economies continue to rely on climate-sensitive sectors like agriculture and pastoralism. They have complex histories of conflict and instability, which have hindered the growth of adaptive capacities. Poverty and inequality are often widespread. For many fragile states, the additional stress of climate change may overwhelm the capacity of households, communities, and governments to cope with and respond to climate change impacts.

Climate change is not expected to directly result in violence but is likely to contribute – at times subtly, at times significantly – to the causal network that generates conflict and threatens human security (Crawford, Dazé, Hammill, Parry, & Zamudio, 2015). It will, in the words of former UN secretary-general Ban Ki-moon, act as a "threat multiplier," exacerbating existing challenges and sources of tension such as weak governance, poverty, inequality, historical grievances, terrorism, and ethnic differences (UN General Assembly, 2009; see also Orbinski et al.,

DOI: 10.4324/9781315107592-8

Climate change

Table 7.1 State fragility and climate vulnerability, 2020

Top 12 most fragile states	Top 12 most climate-vulnerable states
1. Yemen	**1. Somalia**
2. Somalia	2. Niger
3. South Sudan	**3. Chad**
4. Syria	4. Guinea-Bissau
5. Democratic Republic of Congo.	5. Micronesia
6. Central African Republic	**6. Sudan**
7. Chad	7. Liberia
8. Sudan	8. Mali
9. Afghanistan	**9. Democratic Republic of Congo**
10. Zimbabwe	**10. Afghanistan**
11. Cameroon	11. Eritrea
12. Burundi	12. Uganda

States in bold are among the most fragile as well as the most climate vulnerable in the world.
Source: The Fund for Peace Fragile States Index 2020; Notre Dame Global Adaptation Index (ND-GAIN) 2020.

Chapter 13). By making many parts of the world hotter, drier, and less predictable, climate change could contribute to the root causes of conflict by overwhelming state institutions by placing additional stress on social, economic, and natural systems; undermining livelihoods and increasing competition for scarce natural resources; and displacing large numbers of people.

Climate change: trends, forecasts, and vulnerabilities

Some of the more severe predicted impacts of climate change are already being felt by communities across the globe. From a growing frequency in extreme weather events to global temperature increases to changes in precipitation rates to a rise in average sea level, climate change poses significant threats to human security worldwide, and to fragile states in particular.

Greenhouse gas emissions are at their highest levels in history, driving climate change and rising temperatures at an unprecedented rate (UN Sustainable Development, n.d.). From 1880–2012, land and ocean surface temperatures rose by 0.85°C, and the period from 1983 to 2012 was likely the warmest 30-year period of the last 1,400 years (IPCC, 2013). With current levels of atmospheric greenhouse gas and ongoing emissions trends, forecasts expect that global temperatures are more than likely to continue to increase by at least 2.0°C by the end of the century (IPCC, 2014, 2018). Failing to reduce GHG emissions 45% below 2010 levels by 2030 will result in a temperature increase of 3–4°C by 2100 (IPCC, 2018).

In addition, global mean sea level is predicted to rise by between 0.2 and 2.0 meters, and extreme weather events are expected to become more frequent and intense (NASA, 2016). Precipitation rates are also expected to change with the climate, though these changes will vary across regions: some will get drier, others wetter. Regardless, increased surface temperatures will speed up the rate at which this varying precipitation evaporates, further threatening vulnerable ecosystems. In dry, subtropical regions, for example, an increase in surface temperatures will contribute to a decrease in renewable surface water and the speed with which aquifers recharge. In other regions, particularly those that rely on meltwater and glacial rivers, changing precipitation rates and melting snow and ice will alter hydrological systems, affecting the quantity and quality of water resources (IPCC, 2014).

While these changes are global, their severity will vary by region, state, community, and household. Areas like the Sahel region of Africa, the Horn of Africa, North Africa and the Middle East, South Asia, and small island developing states (SIDS) are of particular concern, due to their histories of weak or fragile governance, reliance on natural resources, and geographic vulnerability to climate-related risks.

In the Sahel, temperatures have increased by nearly 1.0°C since 1970, a rate nearly twice the global average (Niang et al., 2014). In the past few decades, and especially in recent years, droughts have been severe and recurrent, and floods have occurred more frequently and with greater intensity. These fluctuations have contributed to an observed decrease in soil moisture and tree density as well as a decline in fruit-bearing trees (IPCC, 2014). These changes may be exacerbated further as temperatures continue to rise. According to the Intergovernmental Panel on Climate Change, the Sahel is a hotspot for climate change, and temperatures are expected to climb by between 3°C and 6°C over the 20th-century baseline (Collins et al., 2013). Coupled with rapid population growth, widespread poverty, and an economic reliance on farming and pastoralism, climate change has the potential to further destabilize regional governments' capacities to manage critical natural resources, mediate and resolve resource conflicts, and deliver basic services to their populations.

Similarly, the Horn of Africa is expected to be especially vulnerable to increases in temperature and the frequency of extreme weather events. Kenya, for example, experienced a temperature increase of 1.0°C from 1960 to 2006, and Ethiopia an increase of 1.3°C (Oxfam, 2011). While the region has experienced droughts and drought-related shocks in the past, they previously occurred every ten years or so, but now occur every five years or less (Oxfam, 2011). The region's short rainfall season of 2016, for instance, marked the third consecutive year of drought for the Horn of Africa, contributing to a rise in food insecurity and malnutrition (ROSEA, 2017a). Oxfam predicts that shifts in regional temperatures and precipitation rates in the region will cause a decline in the crop-growing period by up to 20% by 2090 and corresponding declines in maize and bean yields of 20% and 50%, respectively (Oxfam, 2011). For a region that already has 27 million people categorized as "severely food insecure," this decline in crop yields poses a significant threat to food security, economic livelihoods, and stability in the region (ROSEA, 2017b).

Fragile states in North Africa and the Middle East are expected to face myriad challenges related to extreme heat and reduced water availability and crop yields. From 1961 to 1990, temperatures in the region increased by about 0.2°C per decade, and this rate has since accelerated (World Bank, 2014). The World Bank (2014) further predicts that if temperatures increase by 2.0°C globally, regions in North Africa and the Middle East will warm by 3.0°C and experience unusually high extremes in temperatures throughout 30% of the summer seasons. With a global increase of 2.0°C, Tunisia's growing season could be shortened by two weeks, and crop yields in the entire region could decrease by up to 30% (Al Harazi, 2014). This could further jeopardize fragility in the region, which currently hosts 7 million refugees, 14 million internally displaced people, and 47 million people in need (ROMENA, 2017).

South Asia and SIDS are particularly susceptible to extreme weather events, sea level rise, coastal erosion, and the consequent loss of arable land. In South Asia, flooding threatens to inundate coastal communities in states like Bangladesh, while extreme heat and drought in India and Pakistan are expected to make densely populated agricultural areas nearly unlivable in the coming decades (Im, Pal, & Eltahir, 2017). Flooding and decreases in flows of glacier-fed rivers, like the Indus in Pakistan and India, may put a further strain on the surrounding communities' source of livelihoods and food security, as sources of freshwater become sparse and unreliable.

For small island states, the threat is existential: flooding damage and rising sea levels can cause the loss of livelihoods, settlements, economic stability, and the state's territorial integrity. In Kiribati, a country made up of 33 low-lying atolls and reef islands with a population of just over 114,000, sea levels averaged a rise of 3.7 millimeters a year since 1992 (Kiribati, n.d.). In recent years, the small island state observed heightened and more frequent storm surges that not only placed pressure on shorelines, but also destroyed settlements occupied since the early 1900s (Kiribati, n.d.). As sea levels continue to rise, Kiribati and other low-lying SIDS face the loss of settlements and the subsequent displacement of their populations to neighboring states.

The aforementioned regional hotspots, as demonstrated, already face a host of challenges related to their geographic vulnerability. Should climate change continue unabated, these regions and others are predicted to be met by a range of unprecedented climate-related shocks that threaten livelihoods, governance, and peacebuilding.

Climate change and conflict

The links between climate change and conflict have been the subject of significant research and discussion over the past decade: among governments, policymakers, academics, NGOs, and international organizations. The UN Security Council has held multiple debates on the subject, and the IPCC has been awarded the Nobel Peace Prize. The relationship is complex, and no one theory adequately captures if or how climate change might lead to increased tensions, instability, or conflict within and between states. What has emerged from the debate is a consensus that climate change can act as a contributing factor in the emergence of conflict – a "threat multiplier," as previously discussed. Drawing from the research, what follows is an examination of some of the ways in which climate change could contribute to conflict.[1]

Overwhelming state capacities and institutions

Weak governance is a key variable in determining whether climate change impacts contribute to the emergence or exacerbation of conflict. With stretched budgets and weak institutions, many fragile state governments already struggle to provide basic services to their populations and address their citizens' grievances relating to a host of development challenges: unemployment; protection from violence; corruption; income and gender inequality; and livelihood, food, and land tenure insecurity (Crawford, 2015a). The impacts of climate change, and the associated costs of addressing them, could overwhelm fragile state governments and further impede their already limited capacities to perform their basic functions.

The estimated costs of adaptation in the near term are substantial. Globally, UN Environment recently put the costs of adaptation at between $280 billion and $500 billion per year by 2050 (UNEP, 2016). This is the amount of money needed to reduce climate vulnerability to an acceptable level, and while the figure is global, it does give an indication of the scale of resources required to address climate change impacts. Fragile state governments will not be able to fund these activities from their own budgets; attempting to do so would only divert funding away from already limited spending on key public services like health, education, and infrastructure. A significant amount of the funding will have to come from the international community, but to date, the funding pledged for adaptation does not meet the demand. In a world of increasingly frequent droughts, floods, and storms and a scramble by many fragile state governments to respond to them, climate change could result in a further breakdown in the provision of public services. If they cannot respond to their constituents' needs due to climate change – in part because they do not have the resources or capacities to do so – fragile state governments could see of a weakening of the social contract they have with citizens and a challenge to the government's legitimacy. This governance vacuum could easily be exploited by terrorist groups and organized crime and could lead to the emergence of political instability, unrest, or conflict (see Barnett & Adger, 2007; Crawford et al., 2015; Matthew & Hammill, 2012; USAID, 2009; UNGA, 2009). Negative feedback loops could also emerge, where existing conflicts in fragile states restrict the capacity of communities or governments to effectively respond to climate change, in turn amplifying the impacts of a changing climate and potentially exacerbating the conflict itself, further reducing the ability of communities and states to adapt (USAID, 2009; Yande & Bronkhorst, 2011).

Undermining livelihoods and increasing natural resource competition

Livelihoods in fragile states are typically centered around natural resources: farming, herding, fishing, mining, logging, and so on. Climate change, by influencing precipitation patterns, the frequency of storms, sea level rise and temperature rates, will challenge most of these livelihood options, perhaps none more so than agriculture and pastoralism.

In a future that is hotter and where rainfall is more variable, farmers and herders will increasingly compete for land and water to maintain their livelihoods. However, arable land for farming and pasture is not increasing at the same rate as populations in many fragile states, and productivity gains are typically unable to make up the difference in many of these countries (Crawford, 2015a). By affecting where, when, and how much rain falls, and where food and fodder can be grown, climate change will likely accelerate competition for natural resources.

These dynamics are already playing out in many parts of the world. In the Sahel, northern pastoralists are extending further southward into zones traditionally dominated by crop agriculture, while farmers are expanding their crop production into the migratory corridors traditionally used by herders due to failed rains and population pressures (Crawford, 2015a). With fragmented migratory corridors and encroached-upon farming plots, both groups are struggling to maintain their incomes and are adapting by turning to each other's livelihoods to make ends meet (i.e., herders are supplementing their incomes with farming and vice versa). This results in the groups increasingly competing for the same dwindling resource base (Crawford, 2015a).

Complicating these dynamics, both in the Sahel and in others areas rife with state fragility, are the demographic and economic realities on the ground. In many fragile states, the population is young, growing, and rural: in South Sudan, for example, the median age is 18.6, the population is growing at 4.1% per year, and 81% of the population is rural, while for Somalia, the same figures are 16.5 years, 2.4% growth, and 60% rural (UNDP, 2016). Traditionally, many young people within these societies have followed their parents into farming and herding. However, the long-term viability of these livelihoods will increasingly be in question as temperatures increase and rainfall patterns change. Faced with a future in which pursuing traditional local livelihoods has been made increasingly difficult, and in which the government cannot offer viable alternatives for employment and income, an increasing number of youths will feel disempowered and adrift. For some, their hopelessness could in turn be exploited by armed groups, terrorist organizations, or criminal networks, which could offer the lure of income or purpose to those struggling to find both (Crawford, 2015a). Groups like the Islamic State in West Africa (formerly, Boko Haram) and Al-Qaeda in the Islamic Maghreb could try to recruit youths marginalized in the face of climate change, blaming that marginalization on both the fragile governments unable to address its impacts and the Western countries largely responsible for the problem (Crawford, 2015a).

Increased competition for dwindling natural resources will likely extend beyond village and farm borders to national borders. For many fragile states, particularly those situated in hot and, at times, dry areas like the Horn of Africa and the Sahel, surface and groundwater resources can be transboundary. As temperature and evapotranspiration rates increase, glacial runoff declines, and rainfall patterns become more variable and uncertain (IPCC, 2018), water interdependence between countries could trigger tensions, particularly as neighboring countries also face growing populations, increased demands for food production, and development progress (Crawford, 2015a). Water could be hoarded or diverted by upstream countries or withdrawn from aquifers at accelerating rates. Thankfully, there are mechanisms in place to manage cooperation around many transboundary waterways, including the Indus Waters Treaty between India and Pakistan and the Nile Basin Initiative, and cooperation rather than conflict has traditionally been the norm (see Asthana, Chapter 6). But it remains to be seen whether these governance mechanisms can withstand the pressures imposed by climate change and increased water demand.

Displacing large numbers of people

Migrants may make the decision to leave their homes for a number of reasons, many of which are indirectly or directly linked to the effects of climate change, including drought, flooding, undermined livelihoods, and coastal inundations. In the first three weeks of 2017, for example, 33,000 people were displaced due to drought in central and southern Somalia (ROSEA, 2017a). In efforts to escape failing crops and livestock, extreme heat, and competition over the little remaining resources, individuals choose to cross regional and international borders to evade poverty and search for better lives for their families.

This kind of climate-induced migration will bring migrants into contact and competition for resources (land, water) with host communities. In the Horn of Africa, drought-induced migration led herders to move into established farming areas and protected conservation zones, raising tensions on a local level (ROSEA, 2017a). In Kenya, Somalia, and Uganda, intercommunal conflict intensified and was exacerbated when significant populations fled from neighboring states, placing a significant strain on the already limited water and food resources (ROSEA, 2017a). Conflicts in the Sahel have displaced 4.9 million people, internally and across borders (OCHA, 2016). Thirty million people in the region already face food insecurity, and 4.7 million children under five are acutely malnourished. Host countries and communities are already struggling to meet the humanitarian needs of these populations: Chad, for example, is currently hosting nearly 400,000 refugees from the Central African Republic (CAR), Nigeria, and Sudan, while 4.3 million of its own citizens – one-third of the country's population – are categorized as food insecure (OCHA, 2016). This places significant additional pressure on the country's already scarce resources. A drought or flood could easily deepen the humanitarian crisis and exacerbate cross-border tensions.

The displacement of a large number of people can be both a precursor and result of conflict. The Syrian refugee crisis, for example, driven primarily by the country's ongoing civil war, has been exacerbated by changes in the local climate. Prior to the outbreak of the war, Syria suffered an extreme drought from 2006 to 2011, a drought that was, in part, attributed to climate change. This extreme weather event displaced more than two million people throughout the country, most of whom moved from rural areas into the country's cities (Baker, 2015). The Syrian government, already strained to provide the basic services required in these cities, was largely unable to adequately help those internally displaced, contributing to social unrest (Crawford, 2015c).

Climate-related conflict outbreaks can lead to the mass movement of people, toward the promise of peace in neighboring regions and countries. For those countries with already fractionalized societies, be it due to ethnicity, class, or otherwise, climate-related disasters may disrupt peacebuilding and drive communities into direct conflict over the remaining resources, infrastructure, and land. Schleussner, Donges, Donner, and Schellnhuber (2016), for example, found that 23% of conflict outbreaks in ethnically divided countries coincided with extreme climate-related events.

For small island developing states like Kiribati or Tuvalu, or low-lying coastal cities, populations face permanent displacement due to climate change. Scientists predict that sea level rise, coastal flooding, and an increased frequency of extreme weather events could lead to the land of more than 152 million people being completely submerged by 2100 (Kopp et. al., 2017). For governments seeking to adapt to this growing threat, climate change will require the relocation of entire populations to higher ground or foreign territories (UNHCR, 2017). This may place strains on host communities and countries, which will be particularly concerning for those host areas with existing weak governance, scarce resources, or limited options for livelihoods.

Recommendations

Climate change is expected to play a contributing role in many conflicts in the future, exacerbating existing challenges and tensions in those states already beset by weak governance, inequality, poverty, resource dependence, and historical grievances. This will, of course, not always be the case; despite their high levels of vulnerability to climate change, it would be wrong to assume that individuals and communities based in fragile states will automatically resort to violence when confronted with climate stress. Many such populations have, in fact, proven resilient to droughts, floods, and extreme heat in the past and have honed their adaptive capacities and coping mechanisms over decades of living in severe climates.

That said, it would be unwise to assume that the scale of climate-related change expected to occur in these regions has a precedent: the changes that are coming will be dramatic and far-reaching. There is a pressing need for action. Concerted international action on greenhouse gas mitigation is an obvious need. GHG inventories cannot continue to increase at current rates. But just as important, significant efforts will be also needed to strengthen the adaptive capacity and resilience of fragile states and their populations to respond to the impacts of climate change. Achieving SDG 16 will require action on SDG 13: Taking urgent action to combat climate change and its impacts. For fragile states, the two are mutually reinforcing.

Thankfully, sustainable development, international stability, adaptive capacity, and climate resilience are all achieved through similar investments – investments that will require the support of national governments and the international community. Statutory and customary governance and national institutions must be made stronger, and resource rights, particularly around water and land, must be made clear and inviolable. Investments in strengthening climate science must be made, to allow for the integration of well-understood climate risks and forecasts into key sectoral policies including water, health, agriculture, infrastructure, and disaster management. Support for research into new seed varieties, crop types, livestock breeds, and growing techniques is desperately needed as well as access to these innovations for those living in fragile states. Water management should be improved to reduce waste and inefficiency, thereby reducing the strain of increased demand and a variable supply. Early warning systems should be developed that ensure support arrives when and where it is needed, and mechanisms for regional cooperation around transboundary resources should be supported and enhanced (Crawford, 2015b).

Government policies aiming to strengthen adaptive capacity and respond to climate change impacts must be based on sound data and information (Mason, Kruczkiewicz, Ceccato, & Crawford, 2015). For fragile states, this is often very difficult, if not impossible: Haiti (population: 11 million), for example, has less than half the functioning weather stations (4) of the small Canadian province of Prince Edward Island (nine stations, population: 150,000) (NCAR, 2017). Data generation is crucial, but so is its interpretation and use: capacities must be strengthened among government staff and peacebuilding practitioners to ensure they have the skills and knowledge required to translate it into appropriate responses.

It is also important that, when operating in fragile states, peacebuilding and humanitarian organizations design programs that are climate resilient, taking into account the implications of near- and long-term climate risks and the role these risks can play as a contributing factor to driving future conflict. This could mean, for example, integrating drought and flood risks into decisions on where to establish refugee camps (see Nizkorodov & Wagle, Chapter 11) or thinking through how climate risks could influence the design and implementation of reintegration programs for ex-combatants. And while peacebuilding interventions should be climate resilient, climate change programming in fragile states should be conflict sensitive: designed and implemented to ensure that, at a minimum, the interventions do not increase the risk of conflict and that they instead enhance peacebuilding opportunities (Crawford et al., 2015). This would include, for example, ensuring that the benefits of adaptation programs are equitably distributed to all the relevant stakeholders.

Conclusions

Climate change and conflict are not inextricably linked. While changing temperatures, coastlines, and rainfall patterns will inevitably strain the resilience and adaptive capacities of many communities – particularly those in fragile states with weak governance – conflict and violence are not predetermined responses to a changing climate; many individuals and communities will continue to cope, albeit under increasingly difficult conditions. This should not, however, invite complacency, either from governments themselves or from the international community; climate change's role as a threat multiplier means that the risks are present, and a lack of action to address them could lead to significant human suffering. Meaningful international progress on mitigating climate change, coupled with full support for adaptation, will help to ensure that climate change impacts can be addressed peacefully, cooperatively, and in a way that strengthens fragile states. The achievement of the SDGs depends on it.

Note

1 For further reading on the subject, see, for example, Brown and Crawford (2009); Crawford et al. (2015); Smith and Vivekananda (2007); Tänzler, Maas, and Carius (2010); UN General Assembly (2009); United States Agency for International Development [USAID] (2009); Yande and Bronkhorst (2011).

Works cited

Al Harazi, F. (2014, November 24). Future impact of climate change visible now in Yemen. *The World Bank.* Retrieved December 19, 2017, from http://www.worldbank.org/en/news/feature/2014/11/24/future-impact-of-climate-change-visible-now-in-yemen

Africa Growth Initiative. (2017). *Foresight Africa: Top priorities for the continent in 2017.* Africa Growth Initiative at the Brookings Institution. Retrieved from www.brookings.edu/wp-content/uploads/2017/01/global_20170109_foresight_africa.pdf

Baker, A. (2015, September 7). How climate change is behind the surge of migrants to Europe. *Time*. Retrieved December 21, 2017, from http://time.com/4024210/climate-change-migrants/

Barnett, J., & Adger, W. (2007). Climate change, human security and violent conflict. *Political Geography, 26*, 639–655. Retrieved December 21, 2017, from http://citeseerx.ist.psu.edu/viewdoc/download?doi=10.1.1.322.3751&rep=rep1&type=pdf

Brown, O., & Crawford, A. (2009). *Climate change and security in Africa: A study for the Nordic-African Foreign Ministers Meeting*. Winnipeg: IISD. Retrieved December 21, 2017, from www.iisd.org/pdf/2009/climate_change_security_africa.pdf

Collins, M., Knutti, R., Arblaster, J., Dufresne, J.-L., Fichefet, T., Friedlingstein, P., . . . Wehner, M. (2013). Long-term climate change: Projections, commitments and irreversibility. In T. F. Stocker, D. Qin, G.-K. Plattner, M. Tignor, S. K. Allen, J. Boschung, . . . P. M. Midgley (Eds.), *Climate change 2013: The physical science basis. Contribution of working group I to the fifth assessment report of the intergovernmental panel on climate change*. Cambridge, UK and New York: Cambridge University Press.

Crawford, A. (2015a). Climate change and state fragility in the Sahel. *FRIDE*. Retrieved from www.iisd.org/sites/default/files/publications/climate-change-and-state-fragility-in-the-Sahel-fride.pdf

Crawford, A. (2015b). *Climate change, conflict and the sustainable development goals*. Winnipeg: International Institute for Sustainable Development.

Crawford, A. (2015c). Climate change intensifies the refugee crisis [Web blog post]. *International Institute for Sustainable Development*. Retrieved December 20, 2017, from www.iisd.org/blog/climate-change-intensifies-refugee-crisis

Crawford, A., Dazé, A., Hammill, A., Parry, J.-E., & Zamudio, A. N. (2015). *Promoting climate-resilient peacebuilding in Fragile States*. Winnipeg: International Institute for Sustainable Development.

Fund for Peace. (2020). *Fragile states index*. Retrieved March 20, 2021, from https://fragilestatesindex.org/data/

Im, E., Pal, J. S., & Eltahir, E. A. (2017). Deadly heat waves projected in the densely populated agricultural regions of South Asia. *Science Advances, 3*(8). https://doi.org/10.1126/sciadv.1603322

Intergovernmental Panel on Climate Change (IPCC). (2018). *Global warming of 1.5°C. An IPCC Special Report on the impacts of global warming of 1.5°C above pre-industrial levels and related global greenhouse gas emission pathways, in the context of strengthening the global response to the threat of climate change, sustainable development, and efforts to eradicate poverty* (V. Masson-Delmotte, P. Zhai, H. O. Pörtner, D. Roberts, J. Skea, P. R. Shukla, . . . T. Waterfield, Eds.). Retrieved from www.ipcc.ch/sr15/

Intergovernmental Panel on Climate Change (IPCC). (2014). *Climate change 2014: Impacts, adaptation, and vulnerability. Part A: Global and sectoral aspects. Contribution of working group II to the fifth assessment report of the intergovernmental panel on climate change*. Cambridge, UK and New York: Cambridge University Press. Retrieved from www.ipcc.ch/pdf/assessment-report/ar5/wg2/ar5_wgII_spm_en.pdf

Intergovernmental Panel on Climate Change (IPCC). (2013). Retrieved from https://www.ipcc.ch/site/assets/uploads/2018/03/WG1AR5_SummaryVolume_FINAL.pdf

Kopp, R. E., Deconto, R. M., Bader, D. A., Hay, C. C., Horton, R. M., Kulp, S., Strauss, B. H. (2017). Evolving understanding of Antarctic ice-sheet physics and ambiguity in probabilistic sea-level projections. *Earth's Future*. https://doi.org/10.1002/2017EF000663. Retrieved from http://onlinelibrary.wiley.com/doi/10.1002/2017EF000663/abstract;jsessionid=E2ACD77A62F72F28D42B1BCAA3D9F3AF.f02t01

Mason, S., Kruczkiewicz, A., Ceccato, P., & Crawford, A. (2015). *Accessing and using climate data and information in fragile, data-poor states*. Winnipeg: International Institute for Sustainable Development.

Matthew, R., & Hammill, A. (2012). Peacebuilding and adaptation to climate change. In D. Jensen & S. Lonergan (Eds.), *Assessing and restoring natural resources in postconflict peacebuilding*. London: Earthscan.

National Aeronautics and Space Administration (NASA). (2016, August 4). *Understanding sea level: Projections*. Retrieved December 18, 2017, from https://sealevel.nasa.gov/understanding-sea-level/projections/empirical-projections

National Center for Atmospheric Research (NCAR). (2017). *International weather stations data*. Retrieved from http://weather.rap.ucar.edu/surface/stations.txt

Niang, I., Ruppel, O. C., Abdrabo, M. A., Essel, A., Lennard, C., Padgham, J., & Urquhart, P. (2014). Africa. In V. R. Barros, C. B. Field, D. J. Dokken, M. D. Mastrandrea, K. J. Mach, T. E. Bilir, M. Chatterjee, . . . L. L. White (Eds.), *Climate change 2014: Impacts, adaptation, and vulnerability. Part B: Regional aspects. Contribution of working group II to the fifth assessment report of the intergovernmental panel on climate change* (pp. 1199–1265). Cambridge, UK and New York: Cambridge University Press.

Notre Dame. (2020). Notre Dame global adaptation initiative. *Country Rankings*. Retrieved March 21, 2021, from https://gain.nd.edu/our-work/country-index/rankings/

Office of the President Republic of Kiribati (Kiribati). (n.d.). *Coastal erosion*. Retrieved December 19, 2017, from www.climate.gov.ki/category/effects/coastal-erosion/

Oxfam. (2011). *Briefing on the Horn of Africa Drought: Climate change and future impacts on food security*. Retrieved from www.oxfam.org/sites/www.oxfam.org/files/briefing-hornofafrica-drought-climat-echange-foodsecurity-020811.pdf

OCHA. (2016). *Sahel 2017: Overview of humanitarian needs and requirements*. New York: UN Office of the Coordination of Humanitarian Affairs.

Schleussner, C.-F., Donges, J. F., Donner, R. V., & Schellnhuber, H. J. (2016, May 20). Armed-conflict risks enhanced by climate-related disasters in ethnically fractionalized countries. *Proceedings of the National Academy of Sciences of the United States of America, 113*(33). https://doi.org/10.1073/pnas.1601611113.

Smith, D., & Vivekananda, J. (2007). *A climate of conflict: The links between climate change, peace and war*. London: International Alert.

Tänzler, D., Maas, A., & Carius, A. (2010). Climate change adaptation and peace. *Wiley Interdisciplinary Reviews: Climate Change* 1(5), 741–750.

United Nations Development Programme. (2016). *Human development report 2016: Human development for everyone*. New York: UNDP.

United Nations Environment Program. (2016). *UNEP report: Cost of adapting to climate change could hit $500B per year by 2050*. Retrieved from www.un.org/sustainabledevelopment/blog/2016/05/unep-report-cost-of-adapting-to-climate-change-could-hit-500b-per-year-by-2050/

UNFCCC. (1992). *United Nations Framework Convention on Climate Change*. New York: United Nations, General Assembly. Retrieved from https://unfccc.int/resource/docs/convkp/conveng.pdf

United Nations General Assembly. (2009). *Climate change and its possible security implications*, A/64/350.

United Nations High Commissioner for Refugees. (UNHCR). (2017). *Climate change and disasters*. Retrieved December 21, 2017, from www.unhcr.org/climate-change-and-disasters.html

UNOCHA Regional Office for Asia and the Pacific (ROAP). (2016). *This is ROAP*. United Nations Office for the Coordination of Humanitarian Affairs. Retrieved from www.unocha.org/sites/dms/ROAP/Mainpage/This_Is_ROAP_Email.pdf

UNOCHA Regional Office for Middle East and North Africa (ROMENA). (2017). *Middle East and North Africa*. United Nations Office for the Coordination of Humanitarian Affairs. Retrieved December 19, 2017, from www.unocha.org/romena.

UNOCHA Regional Office for Southern and Eastern Africa (ROSEA). (2017a). *Horn of Africa: A Call for Action, February 2017*. United Nations Office for the Coordination of Humanitarian Affairs. Retrieved from https://reliefweb.int/sites/reliefweb.int/files/resources/HOA_CALL_FOR_ACTION_Leaf-let_Feb2017_1.pdf

UNOCHA Regional Office for Southern and Eastern Africa (ROSEA). (2017b). *Regional outlook for the Horn of Africa*. United Nations Office for the Coordination of Humanitarian Affairs. Retrieved December 19, 2017, from http://hornofafrica.unocha.org.

UN Sustainable Development. (n.d.). *Climate change – United Nations sustainable development*. Retrieved December 19, 2017, from www.un.org/sustainabledevelopment/

United States Agency for International Development (USAID). (2009). *Climate change, adaptation and conflict: A preliminary review of the issues* (CMM Discussion Paper No.1). Retrieved December 21, 2017, from http://pdf.usaid.gov/pdf_docs/Pnadr530.pdf

The World Bank. (2014). *Turn down the heat: Confronting the new climate normal*. International Bank for Reconstruction and Development/The World Bank.

Yande, P., & Bronkhorst, S. (2011). *Climate change and conflict: Conflict-sensitive climate change adaptation in Africa* (Policy & Practice Brief 14). ACCORD. Retrieved December 21, 2017, from www.files.ethz.ch/isn/137666/policy_practice14.pdf

SECTION II

The environment during conflict

8

ENVIRONMENTAL DESTRUCTION DURING WAR

Charles Closmann

For millennia, humans have altered their physical surroundings. Over 10,000 years ago, agricultural groups cleared vegetation for settlements and burned forests to create suitable lands for hunting or growing their crops. Several thousand years later, urbanization spread through Mesopotamia, the Indus Valley, and other parts of the world – a process that demanded massive amounts of mud, stone, wood, and other natural resources for construction. Such activities depleted forests and eroded soils while causing other environmental side effects. Since then, human societies have continued to modify the environment through farming, the growth of cities, and industrialization, among other actions (Penna, 2010, pp. 57–83, 108–141).

War has also transformed the environment for thousands of years, sometimes in profound and enduring ways. Like farming, the burning of forests, or the channelization of rivers, war has also caused erosion, species loss, and a fundamental alteration of ecosystems. Indeed, warring societies have often intentionally targeted many of the resources that have allowed human societies to flourish: In 705 BCE, for instance, the Assyrian Army demolished the Haldian waterworks, an example of intentional environmental warfare in the ancient Near East (Tucker, 2004a). Warring nations have continued to use such tactics since then, sometimes on landscapes heavily modified by human activities. In 1864, the Union Army of General William Tecumseh Sherman intentionally ravaged the Georgia countryside, sweeping up corn, grain, cattle, and other provisions while destroying what could not be carried off. While the long-term environmental consequences proved relatively short lived – Sherman did not salt the earth or intentionally pollute streams – the march through Georgia ripped asunder the vital ecological relationships between agriculture, people, and the Confederate Army (Brady, 2009). More recently, during the 1960s, the US Air Force intentionally sprayed over seven million acres of South Vietnam's forests with the defoliant Agent Orange in an effort to deny cover to Viet Cong and North Vietnamese troops. The immediate efforts for agriculture and ecosystems were devastating, while the long-term environmental consequences include the erosion of ecosystems suitable for the region's unique fauna (Westing, 1971; see also Hupy, 2008; Lanier-Graham, 1993, pp. 30–38; Westing, 1983).

Many other examples of wartime destruction of the environment have occurred, especially during the last 150 years. In some cases, the effects have been dramatic and long lasting, as in the example of the battlefield sites from World War I, where warring armies left thousands of craters and shattered forests and where soil and woodland ecosystems had not recovered after decades

(Hupy, 2008). In other cases, the effects are less dramatic, but more insidious: the toxic wastes leaking from abandoned World War II military sites in the South Pacific are a good example. The indirect effects of war in terms of marshaling resources for combat can also have long-lasting repercussions, while in other cases, warfare accelerates processes already underway during times of peace. As these examples show, wars have impacted environments in a variety of ways. Equally important, war has been a fundamental and radically transformative human activity, often inseparable from other human actions like the expansion of agriculture, the exploitation of natural resources, or the development of new technologies. For these reasons, the destruction inflicted upon the environment during war demands further study (Tucker, 2004a, 2011).

Yet while historians have studied the spectacle of war for centuries, the effect of war on the environment has only recently become a topic of their interest. Focusing on the dramatic ebb and flow of war, military historians have chronicled the decisions of great generals, the role of combat tactics, and the influence of new weaponry, among other things. Yet they have rarely made the environment (or nature) a focus of their study. Instead, as Richard Tucker and Edmund Russell (2004) point out, "Although military historians have long portrayed nature as a set of strategic obstacles – especially in the form of terrain and weather – they have rarely discussed the impact of warfare on the same terrain" (p. 1). A survey of articles in the *Journal of Military History* reveals that this remains mostly true. In fact, since 2011, about 8 of 29 articles deal with the environment in one way or another, most often in terms of how weather conditions shaped tactics.[1]

Scholars in the field of environmental history have also neglected the relationship between war and the environment. Defined as the study of the historical relationship between human societies and their physical surroundings, environmental history emerged "from the activist climate of the 1960s and 1970s," in the words of the present author, and focused mostly on the perceived "ecological crises" resulting from population growth, capitalist agriculture, and the disappearance of natural resources.[2] Perhaps because the consequences of routine human activities could have such important ecological consequences, these first-generation environmental historians were not drawn to the study of war.[3]

Yet even while historians were devoting little attention to this topic, scholars in other fields were exploring the effects of war on the environment as early as the 1970s. Most notably, ecologist Arthur Westing (1971, 1972) researched the effects of the US military's campaign of defoliation and crop destruction in South Vietnam. Westing followed up this work with several articles and books, including *Warfare in a Fragile World: Military Impact on the Human Environment* (1980) and an edited collection titled *Environmental Warfare: A Technical, Legal and Policy Appraisal* (1984). Like others writing at the height of the environmental movement, Westing (1971, 1980, 1984) was alarmed by the effects of modern warfare on the globe's diminishing natural resources. His pioneering work also contributed to major policy initiatives and protocols intended to limit the use of weapons targeted toward the destruction of the environment (Brauch, 2017). Other scholars working in this field since the 1970s have included biologists, anthropologists, political scientists, economists, lawyers, and military officers, among others. Conclusions from this work include, among other things: 1) that the international community must be aware of the ecological consequences of past wars in order to avoid future conflicts and 2) that the destruction of natural resources during war may lead to even more environmental and social instability during subsequent times of peace.[4]

Interest by historians in this topic increased in the 1990s and early 2000s. Some highly publicized episodes, such as the Iraqi Army's intentional destruction of oil fields during the first Gulf War and NATO's use of depleted uranium during the Kosovo conflict undoubtedly encouraged this interest.[5] Books that exemplified this new emphasis included Edmund Russell's *War and*

Nature: Fighting Humans and Insects with Chemicals from World War I to Silent Spring (2001) and Richard Tucker and Edmund Russell's edited collection, *Natural Enemy, Natural Ally: Toward an Environmental History of War* (2004). The present author's edited collection, *War and the Environment: Military Destruction in the Modern Age* (2009), also reflected this trend. By 2017, a growing number of environmental historians had added their voices, with publications on the environmental consequences of the Civil War, World War II, and a host of other topics (see Drake, 2015; Laakkonen, Tucker, & Vuorisalo, 2017).[6]

While much of this recent work remains a patchwork of scholarship – after all, there are an unlimited number of military conflicts to study – several themes have emerged in recent years. First, scholars have concluded that modern wars have inflicted far more damage on nature and natural resources than previous conflicts. Given the immense destructive capacity of modern weapons and the vast resources of modern states, this is hardly surprising. Second, the indirect effects of war on the environment, such as the expansion of oil production or the exploitation of tropical forests for lumber, have often been more enduring than the dramatic effects of artillery shelling, the bombing of cities, or the digging of trenches. Finally, the evolution or creation of state institutions (such as the US Chemical Warfare Service in 1917) during war can also have consequences that reverberate for decades, long after treaties of peace have been signed.[7]

This chapter turns now to a few examples to highlight these major themes.

War's effect on the environment: before the modern era

Even agricultural societies thousands of years ago engaged in total war against their enemies. In fact, early farming communities often waged devastating wars against one another, killing off combatants and civilians while also destroying food supplies, crops, and fields. In some cases, however, warfare actually increased biodiversity, especially in the uninhabited buffer zones where game animals were allowed to flourish. Such early warfare had few long-run environmental effects, mostly because early agricultural societies lacked the destructive capacity to inflict severe, widespread harm on the landscape or on natural resources. As Richard Tucker (2004a) notes, the exception to this general rule was when combatants used fire, especially when it was used in arid or semiarid regions, like Australia.

Warring armies in the ancient world also engaged in direct and deliberate environmental warfare. As stated earlier, marauding forces in the Fertile Crescent during the sixth and seventh centuries BCE attacked each other's irrigation systems, a tactic that could devastate a society reliant upon careful control of water in an arid region. Forests and crops also became a target of ancient armies. Like armies of the 20th century, the Assyrians burned the woodlands of their opponents in the Near East, a policy adopted by the Romans against the barbarian tribes of Germany and France centuries later (Hupy, 2008; Tucker, 2004a). Warring armies also assaulted the links between humans and the natural environment, salting fields to prevent crops from growing (the most notorious case being the Romans' salting of Carthage). Such tactics could result in widespread, devastating harm to the environment, especially in the Mediterranean with its hot, dry summers and short, cool winters. In Southern Italy, for example, years of pillaging between the Carthaginians and Romans from 219–201 BCE left denuded hills, erosion along rivers and streams, and malarial conditions along the devastated coast. Some effects – such as malaria – continued to plague Italy well into the 20th century (McNeill, 2004; Tucker, 2011).

Armies in the ancient world also needed vast quantities of resources to fight their wars. The Greeks and Romans desperately required lumber for the construction of warships, a requirement that could normally be fulfilled from the forests of Lebanon, Cyprus, Thrace, and Macedonia. The Romans' need for lumber (for the construction of ships and forts, the smelting of metals, and other purposes) likely resulted in deforestation and erosion in Italy and other parts of the Mediterranean (McNeill, 2004; Tucker, 2011).

War also plagued the globe during the period from 600 CE to 1500 CE. In medieval Europe, weaponry was no more powerful than in ancient times, and no major nation-states existed, so the environmental consequences of warfare tended to be local. Led by wealthy lords, warring armies continued to pillage the landscape, denuding forests and crops while also robbing from local peasants, many of whom absconded to other regions. A paradox of this era was that warfare and the spread of disease would have depopulated the landscape, allowing fields and woodlands to recover some of the vegetation and biodiversity lost as a result of war. In any event, while the immediate consequences of war during this era would have been obvious, the long-term consequences are difficult to assess. Much would have depended upon patterns of farming and recovery during subsequent times of peace (Tucker, 2004a).

Similar warfare probably afflicted China and India. In East Asia, marauding armies repeatedly targeted irrigation systems of the Yangtze and Yellow Rivers, vast infrastructures that supported the region's population with food and water. In India from the tenth century CE, imperial armies of the Delhi Sultanate and the Mughals launched massive campaigns of destruction, devouring the land as they marched across the central Indian plateau and other regions. As Stewart Gordon (2004) notes, "A Mughal army (and its opponents) generally wreaked environmental havoc wherever it went," as foraging troops stripped the countryside of fodder for horses and food for troops, sending local peasants fleeing with their possessions (p. 48). As in Europe, the short-term consequences for the environment were likely severe but localized, while the long-term effects demand more study (Gordon, 2004; Tucker, 2004a).

War's effect on the environment: the modern era

Warfare since the mid-1800s has been far more destructive of the environment than in previous time periods. Several factors explain why this is true. First, armies and navies became far more sophisticated, in part a result of the military revolution (1450 to about 1700), which consisted of the elaboration of large state bureaucracies, the construction of heavier forts, and the development of powerful weaponry. All such factors have enabled armies to inflict massive environmental destruction in times of war, while also exploiting natural resources on a global scale. Subsequent developments in the 19th and 20th centuries have also contributed to the destructive capacity of warfare. These include new steam-powered transportation systems, smokeless gunpowder, powerful new weapons, and the introduction of aircrafts, steel ships, and other technologies. The discovery of new chemicals has also contributed to destruction on an unprecedented scale (Hupy, 2008; Laakkonen et al., 2017, pp. 3–14; Lanier-Graham, 1993; McNeill, 2004; Westing, 1980, pp. 1–43).

One can also draw additional conclusions about warfare in the modern era. First, it is clear that combatant nations (or empires) continued to inflict direct harm on the environment, just as they had in the past. Also, warring armies sometimes intentionally targeted their enemy's natural resources, or the crops, pastures, and infrastructure that linked people to nature. Moreover, modern nation-states had a far greater capacity to modify landscapes, ecosystems, and natural resources "behind the lines" in the name of war than in earlier periods, with enduring long-term consequences. In addition, the development, deployment, and disposal of new chemicals during times of war have unleashed into the environment compounds that are unlikely to biodegrade quickly, surely a new feature of modern war. Finally, the transformation of state (or international) institutions as a result of war can have profound consequences for the conservation of natural resources, ecosystems, and human-modified environments. The following examples illustrate these points.

The American Civil War (1861–1865) represents a notable example of the power that one modern state had to wage war on the environment. A full year before General William Tecumseh Sherman's march through Georgia, Union troops under General Ulysses S. Grant foraged widely through the broken countryside of Mississippi in their campaign to capture the Confederate fort at Vicksburg. Grant ordered his cavalry to confiscate all corn, wheat, hogs, cattle, and farm implements that could in any way support the Union Army; everything else with a military purpose he ordered destroyed. In the words of historian Lisa Brady (2012), "Crippling the rebellion required destroying the means by which southerners, Confederate or not, managed and improved their environment" (p. 56). Grant's march through Mississippi was merely a prelude to the more notorious *chevauchée* raids by General Philip H. Sheridan in the Shenandoah Valley and Sherman in Georgia. These raids sundered the relationships between Southerners, the land, and the Confederate Army, fatally weakening the Southern cause (Brady, 2012, pp. 24–48, 49–59, 93–126). The North's access to superior weaponry, transportation systems, and other resources made these campaigns possible. In addition, the Industrial Revolution meant that larger armies could be provisioned, that artillery had much greater range, and that each soldier could carry hundreds of bullets. Battles now lasted longer than in the past, with much greater earthworks and destruction of trees and landscapes on a wider geographic scale (Hupy, 2008).

Other wars fought in the late 19th and early 20th centuries witnessed the deployment of industrial-era weapons and the intentional destruction of enemy environments. In the Boer War (1900–1902), the British used modern, breech-loading rifles against an enemy that also had access to modern weapons. As in the Civil War, battles lasted longer, with greater savagery than in the past. Attempting to break Boer resistance, the British intentionally demolished Boer farms and herded Boer families into concentration camps (Tucker, 2004a). The Dutch deployed similar tactics in West Borneo from 1868 to 1917. To bring the Iban people under their colonial rule, they conducted several punitive raids into the forest, destroying Iban longhouses, uprooting rice crops, and cutting down fruit trees. In the near term, such tactics forced the Iban to seek refuge in old-growth forests where they continued to practice swidden agriculture, while in the long term, the Ibans' farming practices probably resulted in the spread of secondary forest, *Imperata* grass, and poor soils (Wadley, 2007).

While conflicts of the late 19th and early 20th centuries certainly devastated fields, farms, and forests, nothing could compare to the environmental destruction of World War I. More powerful artillery created much of the devastation. Instead of cannons that fired a few hundred yards, World War I–era howitzers could fire high explosive shells at targets miles in the distance, gouging huge craters in the ground and ripping apart people, animals, soil, trees, farms, and drainage systems, among other things. By some estimates, the war decimated some 2.5 billion board feet[8] of French timber (although some of this estimate includes the effects of harvesting during the war). Modern artillery units could also fire many more rounds than in the past, sometimes hundreds of shells per hour. Meanwhile, soldiers on both sides built extensive trench systems to escape enemy artillery and the danger of snipers and machine-gun fire, defensive lines that stretched from the North Sea coast to the border with Switzerland. The environmental conditions in the trenches were horrifying: soldiers endured the stench of death, cold weather, and the terrifying noise of enemy fire (Brantz, 2009). Even years after the war ended, signs of such deadly battlefields remained. According to Joseph Hupy (2008),

> Today, over ninety years after the fighting has ended, the landscape has been drastically altered in areas where stalemate conditions prevailed along the western front. Once

> diverse forest communities contain near monoculture plantings and, in some areas, the landscape is so cratered that only stunted trees grow upon the hummocks dividing water filled craters.
>
> (p. 413)

Fighting in other theaters also inflicted damage on the environment. In the Alps, Austrian, German, and Italian soldiers used all the tools of modern society to create defensive positions, digging barracks into the rock, setting up electrical generators, and laying miles of barbed wire in the snow. Deforestation also led to inevitable soil erosion, avalanches, and the near extinction of some species of plants. Yet the visible destruction of the Alps was nowhere near as severe as that of the western front; in fact, many soldiers found the alpine battlefields to be both terrifying and stirring in their stark, cold beauty (Keller, 2009).

As in other modern wars, the more profound effects on the environment resulted from indirect actions taken to support the war. In order to construct trenches and barracks, British authorities cut some 50% of all suitable forests in Great Britain during a four-year period of war. Because of the German submarine blockade, the British also had to supply a major portion of the pit timber needed for coal mines from France (already being exploited) and from Scandinavia. After the war, such dire conditions encouraged the British Parliament to pass a Forestry Act of 1919, legislation that coincided with the establishment of a UK Forestry Commission and a major program of afforestation in the postwar years. British forest policy now shifted to the goal of supplying vital timber needs and away from the aesthetic preservation of woodlands. Wartime shortages of wood also influenced the American Expeditionary Force. Concerned about the dearth of suitable lumber in France, the United States sent forestry experts to France with a mandate to obtain all the lumber needed to supply American troops along the front. Working through the Twentieth Engineering Corps, American forestry troops harvested millions of board feet from French forests. The experience of harvesting French timber and working with skilled French experts also encouraged US experts to lobby for practices that encouraged the long-term economic use of American forests, and not the "wanton" exploitation that characterized timber harvesting before the war (West, 2003).

Other institutions and policies also emerged during the war with major long-term consequences. As Edmund Russell (2004) has demonstrated, Germany's deployment of poisonous gas in 1915 encouraged the major combatants to experiment with and develop their own chemical weapons. Great Britain, for instance, established laboratories to test thousands of compounds for use in war, while the United States transformed the civilian National Research Council into the Chemical Warfare Service (CWS), under the aegis of the US Army. In the United States, the CWS experimented with insecticides like arsenic in hopes of finding the perfect gas to penetrate enemy gas masks and kill enemy soldiers. After the war, research on insecticides and poisonous gases evolved in tandem; the US Bureau of Entomology even argued that the end of the war set the stage for a new war, on insects. The long-term consequences were profound, as the CWS and other government agencies now began to encourage the use of chemical agents on insect populations, sometimes with little regard for the valuable role that insects play in ecosystems (Russell, 2004). By 1942, the renamed Bureau of Entomology and Plant Quarantine eventually supported the development of Dichlorodiphenyltrichloroethane (DDT) as a powerful insecticide. In the Pacific theater of World War II, DDT would be used by US forces to kill the mosquitoes that carried malaria, a campaign that enjoyed remarkable success. Of course, the long-term consequences of the development of DDT after 1945 are also well known (Russell, 2004). Despite impressive work to date, there is still much to be learned about the topic of war and the environment during World War I.

Environmental destruction during war

We know somewhat more about World War II, another modern conflict of global proportions. Focusing on the measurable consequences of warfare, several important scholars in this field have agreed that World War II was the most environmentally destructive conflict of all times. Arthur Westing (1980, 1990) noted, for instance, that modern technology allowed warring powers to deliver massive sums of high explosives and other munitions, some 15 million kilograms daily (see also McNeill & Painter, 2009, p. 21). Comparing damage in World Wars I and II, Richard Tucker (2004b) observes that World War II "produced far greater damage to forests," . . . "this time on a global scale," than World War I (p. 121).

At the same time, however, some basic themes remain the same in comparing the two world wars. In both cases, the likely direct environmental effects of combat were probably less enduring than the indirect effects of marshaling resources for war. Likewise, both wars transformed some state and international institutions, although the transformations emerging from World War II have been more profound and consequential. Some things are different, however. The careless deployment (or unintentional loss) of toxic chemicals can have a potentially great effect on ecosystems and is one that demands further study by scholars from all fields (Tucker, 2004b; Westing, 1980, pp. 144–182). Likewise, we are still faced with the reality that several major nations possess nuclear weapons, a consequence of the deployment of atomic bombs during World War II.

Germany's invasion of the Soviet Union in 1941 illustrates the vast potential of modern armies to destroy the environment. The gigantic size of the armies deployed – millions of troops on both sides – and the ideological nature of the war almost guaranteed such destruction. Quickly outrunning their logistical support, the German Army scoured the land for food and supplies, stripping farms and fields, just as previous armies had done for thousands of years. The German attack also devastated pine and spruce forests in the Baltic States, while also laying waste to Soviet paper mills in this northern region. Attempting to deny their enemy any resources, the retreating Soviets engaged in a "scorched earth" policy, burning crops and carting off all food, fuel, and other valuable assets. The Soviets also relocated thousands of factories and countless animals, stores of grain, and other materials to locations east of the Urals.[9] As a result, the production of crops collapsed under German occupation, as did that of steel, cement, and other materials (Josephson et al., 2013, pp. 112–131).

Surprisingly, however, the landscape recovered after the war. Within a few years, Soviet citizens rebuilt farms and factories, while natural processes covered over the devastated landscape with greenery (McNeill, 2000, pp. 344–345). Some forests also recovered after the war, in part because Finland transferred vast forested tracks to the Soviet Union when the war ended, regions that today represent something of a "green belt" along the border between Russia and Finland (Rodgers, 1955; see also Laakkonen, 2004). Such contradictions complicate much of this history. While landscapes in the former Soviet Union have recovered, it is likely that wartime environmental damage to other theaters of World War II, with more fragile ecosystems, will be more enduring. In the South Pacific islands, for instance, the US military blasted channels through coral reefs for the movement of landing craft, while bulldozers scraped away fragile soils for the construction of runways (Lanier-Graham, 1993, pp. 26–27).

The Allies also inflicted massive damage on the built environment. Beginning in 1942, British and American bombers dropped about two million tons of bombs on the cities of Germany and Italy, with devastating consequences. Such raids killed up to 600,000 civilians while also destroying about 50% of all built areas in cities of more than 100,000 citizens. In some cities, of course, the damage was far worse: In Hamburg, Wuppertal, Remscheid, and Bochum, the figure exceeded 70%. Across Germany, about 45% of all housing stock had been destroyed during the war, while cities like Hamburg, Berlin, and Dresden were also covered in millions of cubic meters of rubble (Diefendorf, 2009). The raids also devastated the basic infrastructure that supplied water and sewer services to the general public. In Hamburg and Frankfurt, the raids destroyed several thousand miles of water and sewer lines, along with supporting lift stations, generators, and other infrastructure.[10] The effects on Japanese cities were equally horrifying. During the war, the United States conducted over 60 raids on the cities of that country, including a particularly devastating attack on Tokyo that killed about 79,000 people and left 1,000,000 people homeless (Russell, 2004).

Despite the obvious social and environmental destruction, most German and Japanese cities were able to rebuild quickly, although the built environment would never look the same. In some cases, modernist planning schemes influenced urban design, while in others, the demands of local property owners overrode any plans by progressive urban planners to create model cities. Instead, cities rebuilt in the aftermath of war often reflected a hodgepodge of modernist planning styles, drab cement construction, and historically accurate reconstructions of individual structures (Diefendorf, 2009).

Yet while easily visible environmental devastation could be repaired in short order, the indirect environmental consequences of World War II proved to be more enduring. After overrunning Southeast Asia, for instance, the Japanese quickly launched a major logging campaign in Burma, the Philippines, and Java in order to supply its army with lumber. The Japanese indiscriminately felled trees in national parks, forest preserves, and other fragile landscapes – a destructive campaign that encouraged local farmers to practice swidden agriculture in once forested areas and further degrade the environment. While forests remain to this date, the result since then (in conjunction with centuries of overlogging) has been "genetic erosion" and the loss of biodiversity in fragile ecosystems (Bankoff, 2010, p. 43). In the United States, the Forestry Service urged the exploitation and management of forests in the Pacific Northwest – a policy that expanded private timber harvesting in this region and the introduction of monoculture forestry with the goal of efficient production. A similar expansion of logging occurred in tropical Latin America. With respect to Costa Rica, Richard Tucker (2004b) notes, "There, as elsewhere in the tropical world, the war greatly accelerated the infrastructure for later exploitation" (p. 132). Numerous other examples exist of how things done "in the name of war" have done more to transform the environment than combat itself (McNeill, 2000, p. 344).

The careless handling and disposal of oil and toxic chemical substances was another distinctive feature of World War II, and one with potentially serious environmental consequences. As Arthur Westing has observed, hundreds of sunken merchant vessels and warships now litter the ocean floor, leaking millions of cubic meters of fuel oil. The warring nations – and especially the Soviet Union – also carelessly disposed of thousands of pounds of gas and chemical munitions, some of which is unlikely to degrade for many years. Such practices and the profligate waste of resources continued well into the Cold War, an unfortunate environmental legacy of the 20th century (Lanier-Graham, 1993, pp. 28–29; Westing, 1980, pp. 144–182).

Of course, the use of atomic weapons also distinguishes World War II. Not only did the dropping of two atomic bombs instantly kill thousands of people, but the deployment of these weapons also left the soil and water of Hiroshima and Nagasaki irradiated for long periods of time. As soon as the war ended, the United States expanded its nuclear arsenal and embarked upon a massive campaign of nuclear testing, one that did not end until a moratorium in 1993. Such tests in the Nevada desert and the South Pacific left virtually every part of the globe contaminated with some level of radiation while also destroying small islands and likely killing several thousand people with radiation. The United States has also left millions of pounds of radioactive nuclear waste scattered at sites around the country – an environmental problem that will take many years and billions of dollars to clean up (McNeill & Painter, 2009).

During the Cold War, some major powers continued to inflict massive damage on the environment. Most famously, the US Air Force intentionally dropped over 100 million pounds of the defoliants Agent Orange, Blue, and White on seven million acres of the jungles and mangrove swamps of South Vietnam. Intended to deny cover to the North Vietnamese and Viet Cong during the Vietnam War, these tactics resulted in the total or partial destruction of over 50% of the area sprayed in this act of environmental warfare. The result over the long run has been the replacement of upland forest with grasses, bamboo, and crops, and the creation of ecosystems that no longer support the distinctive and varied fauna that once thrived in these regions. The United States also intentionally devastated Vietnamese mangrove swamps with defoliants and deployed giant 20-ton rome plows to clear the landscape of potential cover for the enemy. In addition, the US Air Force dropped millions of bombs on North and South Vietnam, not only killing thousands of people, but devastating soils and forest ecosystems, many of which have not recovered (Bankoff, 2010). Although the United States' intentional attacks on the landscapes and resources of Vietnam during the 1960s are the most notorious and devastating example of such warfare during the Cold War, they are by no means the only ones to occur.

Conclusion

These examples highlight important lessons about the potential for warfare to transform environments. First, it is clear that modern armies have been able to inflict much greater harm on the environment than armies of the ancient or early-modern world. The enormous destructive potential of industrial-age weapons has made that possible. Yet even though 20th-century combat inflicted massive damage to landscapes, resources, and the human-created environment, the long-term effects could vary widely from location to location. It is likely that factors such as climate, soil, and topography have played a role in the ability of war-torn environments to recover over time, just as it is likely that subsequent human activities have also played a role in this process. In addition, the indirect effects of providing support for modern armies have probably had more significant long-term environmental consequences for forests, oceans, farms, and fields than the direct effects of combat. Finally, the institutional transformations that occur during war can also have profound consequences for the environment, long after a war has ended. With respect to the wars of the last century, one can draw hope from the fact that international agencies like the United Nations Environment Programme (UNEP) have begun to study the effects of war on the environment and are determined to put this issue on the agenda in the future.

Notes

1 See the tables of contents for *Journal of Military History*, accessed January 28, 2018, www.smh-hq.org/jmh.html.
2 I have derived my definition of environmental history from Merchant (2007, p. xv–xxii). Regarding comments about the roots of environmental history as a discipline, see Closmann (2009, p. 1–14); Oosthoek (1999); and Tucker and Russell (2004b). The phrase "ecological crisis" comes from historian Lynn White Jr. (1967).
3 The scope of research in environmental history is vast, so only a few pioneering studies are mentioned here. They include Nash's (1967) *Wilderness and the American*; Worster's (1979) *Dust Bowl: The Southern Plains in the 1930s*; Cronon's *Changes in the Land: Indians, Colonists, and the Ecology of New England* (2003) and *Nature's Metropolis: Chicago and the Great West* (1991); Tarr's (1996) *The Search for the Ultimate Sink: Urban Pollution in Historical Perspective*; and Merchant's (1989) *The Death of Nature: Women, Ecology and the Scientific Revolution*.

4 The extent of this work cannot be captured in a footnote, but a few examples include Austin and Bruch (2000), Peterson (1983), and Vayda (1976). For evidence of major themes, see UNE (2009, p. 1–44) and Westing (1991; 2017, p. 16)
5 Quite a few books address the renewed interest in the topic of war and the environment. For overviews, see Closmann (2009, p. 1–14) and Tucker and Russell (2004b). For two individual works, see Brown (1991) and Inati (2003).
6 See also various topics in the journal *Environmental History*.
7 For important work that emphasizes these themes, see Tucker and Russell (2004a); Closmann (2009); Kohlman (2015); and Laakkonen, Tucker, and Vuorisalo (2017).
8 A board foot is the unit of measurement for hardwood lumber. One board foot is one square foot of lumber that is one inch thick (or 144 cubic inches).
9 See Josephson et al. (2013, p. 112–131). Regarding the loss of forested land, see Rodgers (1955). Regarding the Soviets' relocation of industry and other resources, see Lieberman (1983).
10 Regarding Hamburg, see Meng (1993) and Drobek, (1950). Regarding Frankfurt, see Watson (1946).

Works cited

Austin, J. E., & Bruch, C. E. (Eds.). (2000). *The environmental consequences of war: Legal, economic, and scientific perspectives*. Cambridge, UK: Cambridge University Press.

Bankoff, G. (2009). Wood for war: The legacy of human conflict on the forests of the Philippines, 1565–1946. In C. E. Closmann (Ed.), *War and the environment: Military destruction in the modern age* (pp. 32–48). College Station, TX: Texas A&M University Press.

Bankoff, G. (2010). A curtain of silence: Asia's Fauna in the Cold War. In J. R. McNeill & C. R. Unger (Eds.), *Environmental histories of the Cold War* (pp. 32–48). Cambridge, UK: Cambridge University Press.

Brady, L. M. (2012). *War upon the land: Military strategy and the transformation of Southern landscapes during the American Civil War*. Athens and London: The University of Georgia Press.

Brady, L. M. (2009). Devouring the land: Sherman's 1864–1865 campaigns. In C. E. Closmann (Ed.), *War and the environment: Military destruction in the modern age* (pp. 49–67). College Station, TX: Texas A&M University Press.

Brantz, D. (2009). Environments of death: Trench warfare on the Western front, 1914–1918. In C. E. Closmann (Ed.), *War and the environment: Military destruction in the modern age* (pp. 68–91). College Station, TX: Texas A&M University Press.

Brauch, H. G. (2017). Preface. In A. H. Westing (Ed.), *Arthur H. Westing: Pioneer on the environmental impact of war* (pp. vii–x). Berlin: Springer.

Brown, L. R. (Ed.). (1991). *State of the world, 1991: A Worldwatch Institute report on progress toward a sustainable society*. New York: W.W. Norton.

Closmann, C. E. (Ed.). (2009). *War and the environment: Military destruction in the modern age*. College Station, TX: Texas A&M University Press.

Closmann, C. E. (Ed.). (2009). Introduction. In C. E. Closmann (Ed.), *War and the environment: Military destruction in the modern age* (pp. 1–9). College Station, TX: Texas A&M University Press.

Cronon, W. (2003). *Changes in the land: Indians, colonists, and the ecology of New England*. New York: Hill and Wang.

Cronon, W. (1991). *Nature's metropolis: Chicago and the great West*. New York: W.W. Norton, 1991.

Diefendorf, J. M. (2009). Wartime destruction and the postwar cityscape. In C. E. Closmann (Ed.), *War and the environment: Military destruction in the modern age* (pp. 171–192). College Station, TX: Texas A&M University Press.

Drake, B. A. (Ed.). (2015). *The blue, the gray, and the green: Toward and environmental history of the civil war*. Athens, GA: The University of Georgia Press.

Drobek, W. (1950). Das Wasser einer Millionenstadt. *Hamburger Echo*, Dezember 9, 1950.

Gordon, S. (2004). War, the military, and the environment: Central India, 1560–1820. In R. P. Tucker & E. Russell (Eds.), *Natural enemy, natural ally: Toward an environmental history of war* (pp. 42–64). Corvallis, OR: Oregon State University Press.

Hupy, J. P. (2008). The environmental footprint of war. *Environment and History, 14*(3), 405–421.

Inati, C. S. (2003). *Iraq: Its history, people, and politics*. Amherst: Humanity Books.

Josephson, P., Dronin, N., Mnatsakanian, R., Cherp, A., Efremenko, D., & Larin, V. (Eds.). (2013). *An environmental history of Russia*. Cambridge, UK: Cambridge University Press.

Keller, T. (2009). The mountains roar: The alps during the great war. *Environmental History, 14*(2), 253–274.

Kohlman, M. (2015). The American chemical warfare service in World War I and its aftermath: Brewing an end to war and ensuring a prosperous peace for science and industry. *Alberta Science Education Journal, 44*(1).

Laakkonen, S. (2004). War – An ecological alternative to peace? Indirect impacts of World War II on the Finnish environment. In R. P. Tucker & E. Russell (Eds.), *Natural enemy, natural ally: Toward an environmental history of war* (pp. 175–194). Corvallis, OR: Oregon State University Press.

Laakkonen, S., Tucker, R. P., & Vuorisalo, T. (Eds.). (2017). *The long shadows: A global environmental history of the Second World War.* Corvallis, OR: Oregon State University Press.

Lanier-Graham, S. D. (1993). *The ecology of war: Environmental impacts of Weaponry and Warfare.* New York: Walker and Company.

Lieberman, S. R. (1983). The evacuation of industry in the Soviet Union during World War II. *Soviet Studies, XXXV*(1), 90–102.

Meng, A. (1993). *Geschichte der Hamburger Wasserversorgung* (pp. 291–313). Hamburg: Medien-Verlag Schubert.

Merchant, C. (2007). *American environmental history: An introduction.* New York: Columbia University Press.

Merchant, C. (1999). *The death of nature: Women, ecology and the scientific revolution.* New York: Harper & Row.

Merchant, C. (1989). *The death of nature: Women, ecology and the scientific revolution.* New York: Harper & Row.

McNeill, J. R. (2004). Woods and warfare in World History. *Environmental History, 9*, 388–410.

McNeill, J. R. (2000). *Something new under the sun: An environmental history of the twentieth-century world.* New York: W.W. Norton & Company, Inc.

McNeill, J. R., & Painter, D. S. (2009). The global environmental footprint of the US Military. In C. E. Closmann (Ed.), *War and the environment: Military destruction in the modern age* (pp. 10–31). College Station, TX: Texas A&M University Press.

McNeill, J. R., & Unger, C. R. (Eds.). (2010). *Environmental histories of the Cold War.* Cambridge, UK: Cambridge University Press.

Nash, R. (1967). *Wilderness and the American mind.* New Haven, CT: Yale University Press, 1967.

Oosthoek, K. J. (1999). Environmental history: Between science and philosophy. *Environmental History Resources.* Retrieved April 29, 2018, from www.eh-resources.org/environmental-history-between-science-and-philosophy/

Penna, A. N. (2010). *The human footprint: A global environmental history.* West Sussex, UK: Wiley-Blackwell. p

Peterson, J. (Ed.). (1983). *The aftermath: The human and ecological consequences of nuclear war.* New York: Pantheon.

Rodgers, A. (1955). Changing locational patterns in the Soviet pulp and paper industry. *Annals of the Association of American Geographers, 45*(1), 85–104.

Russell, E. (2004). "Speaking of Annihilation": Mobilizing for war against human and insect enemies. In R. P. Tucker & E. Russell (Eds.), *Natural enemy, natural ally: Toward an environmental history of war* (pp. 142–175). Corvallis, OR: Oregon State University Press.

Russell, E. (2001). *War and nature: Fighting humans and insects with chemicals from World War I to Silent Spring.* Cambridge: Cambridge University Press.

Laakkonen, S. (2004). War – An ecological alternative to peace? Indirect impacts of World War II on the Finnish environment. In R. P. Tucker & E. Russell (Eds.), *Natural enemy, Natural ally: Toward an environmental history of war* (pp. 175–194). Corvallis, OR: Oregon State University Press.

Tarr, J. A. (1996). *The search for the Ultimate Sink: Urban pollution in historical perspective.* Akron, OH: University of Akron Press.

Tucker, R. P. (2011). War and the environment. *World History Connected, 8*(2), 1–5. Retrieved January 28, 2018, from http://worldhistoryconnected.press.illinois.edu/8.2/forum_tucker.html

Tucker, R. P. (2004a). The impact of warfare on the natural world: A historical survey. In R. P. Tucker & E. Russell (Eds.), *Natural enemy, natural ally: Toward an environmental history of war* (pp. 15–41). Corvallis, OR: Oregon State University Press.

Tucker, R. P. (2004b). The world wars and the globalization of timber cutting. In R. P. Tucker & E. Russell (Eds.), *Natural enemy, natural ally: Toward an environmental history of war* (pp. 110–141). Corvallis, OR: Oregon State University Press.

Tucker, R. P., & Russell, E. (Eds.). (2004a). *Natural enemy, natural ally: Toward an environmental history of war.* Corvallis, OR: Oregon State University Press.

Tucker, R. P., & Russell, E. (2004b). Introduction. In R. P. Tucker & E. Russell (Eds.), *Natural enemy, natural ally: Toward an environmental history of war* (pp. 1–14). Corvallis, OR: Oregon State University Press.

United Nations Environmental Programme. (2009). *From conflict to peacebuilding: The role of natural resources and the environment* (pp. 1–44). Nairobi, Kenya: United Nations Environmental Programme.

Vayda, A. P. (1976). *War in ecological perspective.* New York and London: Plenum Press.

Wadley, R. L. (2007). Slashed and burned: War, environment and resource insecurity in West Borneo during the late nineteenth and early twentieth centuries. *Journal of the Royal Anthropological Institute, 13,* 109–128.

Watson, K. S. (1946). The water supply in Frankfurt. *Water & Sewage Works, 93,* 261–266.

West, J. A. (2003). Forests and national security: British and American forestry policy in the wake of World War I. *Environmental History, 8*(2), 270–293.

Westing, A. H. (2017). *Arthur H. Westing: Pioneer on the environmental impact of war.* Berlin: Springer.

Westing, A. H. (1991). Environment and security: The case of Africa. *Ambio: Journal of the Human Environment, 20*(5), 167.

Westing, A. H. (1990). *Environmental hazards of war: Releasing dangerous forces in an industrialized world* (pp. 1–9). London: Sage Publishers.

Westing, A. H. (1984). *Environmental warfare: A technical, legal, and policy appraisal.* London and Philadelphia: Taylor & Francis.

Westing, A. H. (1983). The environmental aftermath of warfare in Viet Nam. *Natural Resources Journal, 23*(2), 365–389.

Westing, A. H. (1980). *Warfare in a fragile world: Military impact on the human environment.* London and Philadelphia: Taylor & Francis.

Westing, A. H. (1972). Herbicides in war: Current status and future doubt. *Biological Conservation, 4*(5), 322–327.

Westing, A. H. (1971). Ecological effects of military defoliation on the forests of South Vietnam. *BioScience, 21*(17), 893–898.

White Jr., L. (1967). Historical roots of our ecological crisis. *Science, 155,* 203–1207.

Worster, D. (1979). *Dust bowl: The Southern plains in the 1930s.* Oxford, UK: Oxford University Press.

9

THE TOXIC LEGACY OF WAR

Landmines and explosive remnants of war

Kenneth R. Rutherford and Paige Ober

Long life weapons – a toxic (and deadly) legacy

Tens of millions of explosive remnants of war (ERW), including 80 million landmines, are buried in over 80 countries worldwide. Thousands of men, women, and children live with the daily threat of ERW and landmines, including artisanal and improvised weaponry also known as improvised explosive devices (IEDs). These weapons kill thousands of people, most of whom are civilians, including many children and women, and will continue to do so long after the conflicts end.[1]

Landmines and ERW are examples of the toxic legacy of war. Armed conflict has left remnants of itself littered across countries that live long after it is over, enduring even after peace treaties are signed and soldiers return to their homes. Due to the evolving nature of war has meant that IEDs are quickly replacing landmines as strategic weapons used by nonstate actors and armed groups, including the so-called Islamic State and other terrorist organizations. IEDs and landmines pose an increasingly problematic international security risk due to their nature: they are extremely lethal, can be built using a number of accessible materials, and are relatively easy to construct at an industrial manufacturing level. Recent and current internal wars, such as those in Afghanistan, Bosnia and Herzegovina, Iraq, and Syria, are examples that landmines and IEDs are not being used as strategic tools against an opposing force, but rather to pursue a goal of economic and social destabilization, prevention of the return of refugees, and permanent denial of land. These particular toxic legacies of war affect all aspects of society: human health, economic development, and the surrounding environment in which a society exists.

ERW, landmines, and IEDs pollute the land, making it useless for production and unsafe for humans to walk for fear of losing limbs or life. Without nearby help, the unfortunate victim, which can include livestock and wildlife, usually dies alone. According to the International Committee for the Red Cross (1999), landmines killed or injured more than 24,000 people every year in the 1990s with a significant number of the victims being civilians. In that same decade, the US Government highlighted the global antipersonnel landmine crisis when the State Department estimated that between 59 million and 69 million antipersonnel landmines were deployed worldwide thereby making them "one of the most toxic and widespread pollution[s] facing mankind" (U.S. Department of State, 1993, p. 2).

107 DOI: 10.4324/9781315107592-11

More recent figures demonstrate the continued toxic legacy of war two decades later as it relates ERW and landmines. As of 2017, ERW in the form of cluster munitions contaminated 27 countries (Mine Action Review, 2017a). The European Union (2018) estimates Laos to be polluted with two million tons of munitions, of which 270 million are submunitions from cluster bombs. In comparison, global landmine infestation is even more widespread than cluster munitions. In 2017, 59 countries and three other areas (Kosovo, Nagorno-Karabakh, and Western Sahara) are estimated to be mined and continue to be a threat to civilians despite international efforts to ban their use and remove or render safe contaminating weapons (Mine Action Review, 2017b).

Landmines, ERW, and IEDs cause and create lasting harm across a wide swath of human society. In the early 1990s, the US State Department (1993) found that landmines exacerbate regional conflicts, hinder post-conflict reconstruction, seriously undermine infrastructure, and deny land to civilian use, thereby leading to overuse of existing land. Additionally, those people not killed by their encounter with these weapons are negatively impacted by their lasting and life-altering injuries (Rutherford, 2011). This includes lack of access to medical care as well as jobs and livelihoods that can accommodate their landmine-acquired disability, thereby removing these individuals from economic participation. Less well understood is the comprehensive environmental impact each conflict creates.

Within the past two decades, the global community has come together to alleviate the negative humanitarian effects of landmine use vis-a-vis international conventions on the prohibition of the use of landmines as well as post-conflict efforts to clear landmines from the landscape. When the Anti-Personnel Landmine Ban Treaty, also more commonly known as the Mine Ban Treaty (MBT), was signed in December 1997, it included a clause requiring the clearance of landmines, thus becoming one of the first weapons treaty in the world's history to have such a cleanup clause. The MBT was an unprecedented achievement that came about through the efforts of many people, including those who wanted to protect the environment and rehabilitate the land from the negative effects of war. The treaty formalized the humanitarian work known as "mine action," which seeks to remove landmines, ERW, and other explosive contaminants from the soil; propagate knowledge related to landmine safety (a task known as mine risk education); and support victims of landmines and other explosives. It is within the humanitarian framework of mine action that we will address the effects of landmines on the environment.

A history of mine action

Landmines were traditionally used by state military forces for defensive purposes, primarily to protect strategic locations or channel enemy forces into specific fire zone areas. Restricted to these particular military uses, landmine casualties were broadly confined to military personnel during combat engagement or related operations. Beginning with the Vietnam War, however, landmines became more widely used as an offensive tactic and by poorly trained military forces. Since many wars are now

> long-running, internal, and low intensity, [they] often involve[e] cash starved militaries for whom low-technology, low-cost landmines are a weapon of choice . . . [c]consequently, in wars today, mines are frequently placed in areas of high civilian concentration rather than being confined to discrete battlefields of limited size.
> (Human Rights Watch & Physicians for
> Human Rights, 1993, p. 9)

The result has been an increasing level of destructiveness to civilian communities. For example, the top three states hosting landmine-disabled populations are recently emerging from decades of internal conflict that entailed the use of mines by all parties.[2] According to the Landmine and Cluster Munition Monitor (2017), landmine and ERW casualties from 1999–2016 total 112,646. Landmine casualties, specifically, occurred in 30 countries during this time period.

After conflict, nongovernmental and governmental organizations often work together to address the task of humanitarian mine action (HMA). HMA is so named to separate it from military actions that are a part of warfare strategy. HMA has the sole purpose of removing threats from *human* populations, and priorities and goals for HMA are developed around the needs of human health and society. Of note is that protection of the environment within mine action activities is, indirectly, a protection of the environment since the health of human populations cannot be measured outside of the health of their surrounding environment. Methods for demining (removing landmines and ERW from the land) vary by type of mine being removed, the type of soil in which it is embedded, the surrounding vegetation, general topography and climate, among other factors. The common denominator here is, however, that the landmine or ERW must be either removed or made so that it is no longer a threat.

During the past few years, the Center for International Stabilization and Recovery (CISR) at James Madison University (JMU) partnered with a British EOD consultancy company, C King Associates Ltd., to conduct a preliminary study into the effects of aging on landmines. This project entailed examination and disassembly of several types of antipersonnel mines in an effort to investigate the characteristics of mines and how they change significantly as they grow older.[3] It is important to understand the aging process of landmines in the soil, as this information could potentially indicate the level of threat associated with legacy contamination. The literary review found little evidence of any systematic attempt to document the effects of aging, let alone to analyze their implications for mine action. The traditional assumption is that aging ammunition tends to become "unpredictable," which is often interpreted as "unstable." It is unclear to what extent, if any, rotted and rusted mines bleed chemical contamination into the soil, a potential source of pollution.

To date, there has been minimal detailed analysis of the deadly environmental impacts of Landmines, IEDs, and ERW in the soil.[4] The International Campaign to Ban Landmines, in May 1999, created an ad hoc working group, known as the "Ethics and Justice Working Group" (EJWG), who, in turn, created the Sub-Committee on Environmental Aspects that focused on Article 7 of the MBT, which stated that states are obligated to destroy stockpiled and planted landmines, and that, in either process, environmental standards may or may not be observed (Landmine and Cluster Munition Monitor, 2000). The EJWC never gained much traction and the topic remained largely unaddressed for over a decade and provides fertile ground for future research.

One potential reason for the research gap is that these weapons have been used so widely, especially during current wars, that the global community has had little time to study their environmental toxic legacy. Another reason could be that some of the locations, such as Afghanistan, Colombia, and Iraq which host the greatest amount of these weapons, have been experiencing conflict for the last few decades, providing little respite to learn about ongoing legacy effects beyond immediate physical damage to human bodies and social adaptations to their presence. At best, the community has been able to create guidelines for best practices to protect the environment during demining operations. These guidelines, known as the International Mine Action Standards (IMAS),[5] obligate national mine action authorities, UN agencies, and NGOs to comply with all standards necessary for mine action activities. In 2005, IMAS 10.70 "Safety and Occupational Health; Protection of the Environment" was first introduced and underwent its last revision in 2013. In February 2018, the IMAS Review Board, the body responsible for the management and upkeep of the international standards, voted to remove IMAS 10.70 and create a new standard, IMAS 07.13 "Environmental Management in Mine Action." The change between the two standards revolves primarily around the nature of IMAS 07.13, which, as its title indicates, focuses much more heavily on the management and monitoring of environmental protections throughout all stages of activities, from planning through implementation. The previous standard focused more closely on the implementation stage of mine action. Legally, all signatories to the MBT are obligated to follow IMAS standards.

The environmental impact of landmines and ERW

Despite the dearth of data relating to the direct environmental impact of landmines, there is more information related to the secondary or indirect effect of landmines and ERW, often as a corollary to the effect of these weapons on human populations; as human societies are a part of the ecological world, so the effects of war must be assessed as they relate to entire ecosystems, including the human element of those ecosystems.

We will examine the impact of landmines and ERW on the environment through three lenses and discuss generally what the impact of cleaning up explosive debris is on the environment. We will first review the relationship of landmines and ERW on population movement and then discuss how biodiversity is then affected by this. We will then look at the catch-22 of how the humanitarian action of cleaning up landmines, ERW, and IEDs can further impact ecological systems already damaged by war. Finally, we will discuss how the explosive chemicals in landmines and ERW can enter into the environment through various means.

Landmines create pressure on ecological systems

Groups of people driven from their homes by conflict often settle in refugee camps, and fear returning to their homes due to the presence of landmines. Prolonged stays in these camps can create stress on the surrounding area as large, densely packed human populations seek to use the dwindling resources around them – for example using trees and forests for firewood but, over time, needing to move further and further afield to find additional firewood, until areas of 2,200 hectares are denuded (UNEP, 2007). Alternatively, fear of conflict can prevent refugees from straying far beyond the camp, causing more damage in the immediate surrounding area. For more information regarding the specific environmental stresses caused by population displacement, please see Chapter 11 of this book.

However, it must be noted that in some cases, the abandonment of a locale previously inhabited by people can actually benefit the environment in terms of biodiversity and restoration of overworked systems by relieving the pressure of human populations and their behaviors on the local ecological system.

Landmines – a boon to biodiversity?

In some cases, landmines and ERW create a refuge effect, a safe zone, for certain parts of the ecological system. In these areas, where humans fear to go, the ecological system is free to grow and behave without the limiting influence of human harvesting of resources or hunting of wildlife. For example, the heavily mined DMZ area between North and South Korea is known for its thriving species of animals and birds not found in any other surrounding area (Gaynor et al., 2016).

The full effect of war and legacy war items on biodiversity relies on factors such as the sensitivity of the ecosystem, the nature of the warfare, and the timescale of the impact (Lawrence, Stenberger, Zolderdo, Struthers, & Cooke, 2015). Additionally, the impact on biodiversity is unevenly distributed across taxa. Mammals are more likely to be affected by war and the movement of people, which, combined with the presence of the charismatic mega fauna within this taxa, make mammals the most well-known nonhuman victims of war and legacy warfare objects. Think, for example, of the elephant populations in Southeast Asia, especially along the Thai–Myanmar border area where the massive creatures frequently set off antipersonnel landmines. Birds, fish, reptiles, and invertebrate are likely to experience the effects of landmines and warfare only indirectly since due to their weight they are unlikely to set off an explosive triggered to detonate under the weight of an average human. The effect of landmines on these populations can be either negative or positive, depending on the degree to which the supporting ecosystem was affected or protected (refuge effect) (Gaynor et al., 2016).

The ability of various species to survive in an area also depends on the degree to which the biome remains hospitable to their particular needs. Although landmines may not affect birds, fish, reptiles, and invertebrates through physical detonation as they do many mammals, particularly larger mammals, the act of removing landmines from the soil can have overarching effects on an entire ecosystem, as will be discussed in the following sections.

Landmines and mine action – a toxic connection

Part of the humanitarian demining process includes removing vegetation that presents an obstacle to detection and removal of mines and ERW. This can mean that entire groves of trees and brush are removed, or grass clipped short. When a mine is detected, it is dug up (to be disarmed or destroyed via controlled detonation at a later time) or exploded *in situ*. The depth to which a deminer must dig into the soil to ensure that there are no remaining threats after a hazard has been detected varies by each country's national standards and laws, but a common depth is 30 cm. The means by which mines are detected and removed also vary and can be, for our purposes, broadly divided into mechanical and nonmechanical means. Nonmechanical demining can include manual detection via a metal detector as well as detection through trained canines. Mechanical demining involves the use of large machine tillers or rakes to disturb explosives into detonation. An unfortunate side effect of demining is environmental disturbance and damage, in an area that likely already suffered disturbance due to conflict.

The choice of demining methodology is contingent on each situation, but all leave an impact. Potential effects include the removal of fertile topsoil, disturbed root and soil systems, and deforestation. All of these effects can lead to erosion. While manual-demining practices can lead to any of these effects, it is mechanical demining that has the greatest impact (Hoffman & Rapillard, 2015). Exploding munitions *in situ* can also damage topsoil and create means for erosion. The delicate topsoil erodes quickly, which can impact moisture availability, soil structure, and vulnerability to water flows. These changes in soil health negatively impact the productivity of the soil, which causes problems for future agricultural activity in the area or for the recovery of the ecosystem.

Beyond the act of demining, there is the consideration of how weapons are disposed. The most cost-efficient method is to burn the materials and propellants in a controlled detonation, a technique referred to as open burn/open detonation (GICHD, 2015, pp. 152–159). This technique is used globally to destroy munitions through HMA, as well as by militaries, such as the U.S. Armed Forces. In Radford, Virginia, at the Radford Army Ammunition Plant, cleanup of explosives left over from manufacturing or testing is disposed of through open burn

(Lustgarten, 2017). When ammunition is burned, the resulting chemical reaction produces gas and ash (Hoffman & Rapillard, 2015). Chemicals present in these gases can include "lead, mercury, chromium, and compounds like nitroglycerin and percholate" (Lustgarten, 2017, para. 2). These are all known health hazards, and indeed, the community surrounding the Radford Army Ammunition Plant has seen an increase in the rate of thyroid disease that is the highest in the state. Despite the US Congress banning American industries from using open burn as a method of disposing of waste due to concerns that the process would result in health and environmental hazards, the US military has used time granted for the transition to other methods to continue open burns.

Toxic chemicals

There are various means through which military products can contaminate the environment beyond the use and abandonment of landmines. We will review a few of the ways conflict remnants continue to impact after the cessation of war and then look at how landmines and ERW specifically cause chemical contamination.

Demolition and training sites, dumping of unused chemicals, as well as stockpiles of weapons (large accumulated stock of explosive ordnance – landmines, rockets, cluster munitions, grenades, etc.) – are all sources of military pollution. After World War II (WWII), chemical warfare agents like mustard gases and arsenic poisons were packaged in barrels and dumped directly into the ocean. Buried munitions and containers on the seafloor could introduce high levels of chemicals into surrounding area as the containers that hold them degrade and corrode. Similarly, ship wreckage poses some risk for marine environments, including oil leakage. Oil contamination in the Atlantic Ocean from WWII-era shipwrecks is estimated at 15 million tons. Additionally, the targeting of civilian infrastructure during war can lead to legacy contamination. During the Yugoslav Wars, the shelling of civilian infrastructure (manufacturing plants) in Kosovo resulted in emission of industrial chemicals into the environment (Lawrence et al., 2015).

During and after conflict, stockpiles of weapons can be abandoned or left to disintegrate where they lie, often exposed to the elements or in poorly constructed infrastructure. These unsafe storage practices lead to unplanned explosions, which not only pose a direct physical threat to human populations and surrounding living creatures but also create environmental hazards via prolonged burning of explosive fuel and other stored chemicals.

Even well-maintained stockpiles of weapons that are properly stored can contribute to environmental contamination. Governments across the globe destroy outdated stockpiles of weapons before they become too unstable to use or as a means through which to keep munitions out of the hands of non-state actors or terrorists (GICHD, 2015). This responsible action, however, is often completed through controlled open burn and detonation of these weapons to protect people and structures from the force of explosive impact; people are not protected from the toxic gases of the burning ammunition.

Mitigating the impact and toxic legacy of war on the environment

The MBT, and the treaties that followed it controlling the use of other conventional weapons, ensures the illegality of using landmines in the future. Although this is by no means a guarantee that new landmine contamination may not be laid into our soils and our environment, it does contribute to lessening the impact of this aspect of human warfare on our planet. The challenge remains in addressing the legacy contamination from past conflicts.

The toxic legacy of war

There is precedent for HMA work that is less intensive on the environment. Cultural heritage sites, being of great value and importance to societies, are demined when necessary with great care and sensitivity to preserve the integrity of the structure and the surrounding environs. Adjustments are made to the usual practice of demining while maintaining the appropriate standards that keep people safe. For example, the depth to which clearance is conducted is adjusted according to archaeological requirements; mines and ERW are not destroyed *in situ* but are disarmed and removed for destruction elsewhere. In a case where the cultural heritage site was also an environmental protection zone, deminers did not cut down vegetation during their search for hazards (Aldrich, Fiederlein, & Rosati, 2015). While these extra precautions can contribute to more environmentally sensitive demining operations, they also greatly decrease the pace of demining activities, which, in turn, translates into additional money spent. For a field that is already suffering from decreased donor funding, the expense of extra precautions for the environment may be too costly.

While open burn/open demolition is the most widely used and common method for destruction of explosives hazards in mine action, there are various other methods that better capture toxic gases. However, these methods are more expensive and require greater logistical sophistication to practically use. The addition of funding and technical support from donors and national governments could lead to increased use of these safer methods of disposal. Further research could be done on low-cost, easily transportable filters able to capture toxic gases during demolition.

Finally, integrated strategic planning between land-use priorities and demining methods could inform the way in which demining is done to prepare soil for agricultural or infrastructure development. This could be critical for preserving topsoil integrity between the time demining is completed and when development is ready to occur.

Any legally sanctioned demining operation within a country that is a signatory to the MBT is obligated under the newly adopted IMAS 07.13[6] to have an environmental policy and to understand the environmental context in which demining will occur before it occurs. They are required to identify and assess the environmental impact of all mine action activities and to determine strategies for environmental protection and mitigation of damages. Environmental Impact Assessments and monitoring mechanisms that inform reviews of procedures to improve methodology are also stipulated within IMAS 07.13. It is now up to the national mine action authorities, and other pertinent actors, to determine how they will comply with these guidelines and how strict to make the standards for demining in their own countries.

There is potential for the HMA field, 20 years into its existence and reaching greater levels of sophistication, to better address the environmental aspect of the field and to conduct further research. As the nature of warfare evolves, so will the field, and so must our response to and consideration of the impacts legacy contamination has on the human and ecological systems.

Notes

1 International states and other pertinent actors are currently in discussion to define the limit to which humanitarian organizations can address IED contamination in the course of post-conflict recovery actions. Therefore, for our purposes, we will be primarily addressing the effect of landmines and ERW on human and animal populations. This is for two reasons; 1) IEDs as a weapon have only in the past few years made increasing impact on human and animal populations and have, therefore, not been as studied for their environmental impact as conventional weapons and 2) the political sensitivities that surround the use of IEDs prevent proper calculation and dissemination of data around their use.

2 The ICRC estimates that Afghanistan, Angola, and Cambodia host the largest numbers of those disabled by landmines.

3 While this process is constantly observed in the field through the recovery of rotted, rusted, and damaged mines, it has never been adequately investigated.
4 See Meerschman et al. (2011) for studies related to heavy metal contamination related to unexploded ordnance and landmines in Ypres, France, from WW1.
5 See IMAS (n.d.) for the full overview of International Mine Action Standards.
6 IMAS 07.13 was approved by the IMAS Review Board in February 2018.

Works cited

Aldrich, L., Fiederlein, S., & Rosati, J. (2015). Clearance at cultural heritage sites. *The Journal of ERW and Mine Action, 19*(1), 30–36. http://commons.lib.jmu.edu/cisr-journal/vol19/iss1/10

European Union. (2018). *The European Union's support for mine action across the world. Joint staff working document*. Luxembourg: European Union.

Gaynor, K., Fiorella, K., Gregory, G., Kurz, D., Seto, K., Withey, L., & Brashares, J. (2016). War and wildlife: Linking armed conflict to conservation. *Frontiers in Ecology and the Environment, 14*(10), 533–542. https://doi.org/10.1002/fee.1433

Geneva International Centre for Humanitarian Demining (GICHD). (2015). *A guide to mine action* (5th ed.). Geneva: GICHD.

Hoffman, U., & Rapillard, P. (2015). Do no harm in mine action: Why the environment matters. *The Journal of ERW and Mine Action, 19*(1), 4–8. http://commons.lib.jmu.edu/cisr-journal/vol19/iss1/13

Human Rights Watch & Physicians for Human Rights. (1993). *Landmines: A deadly legacy*. New York: Human Rights Watch.

International Committee for the Red Cross (ICRC). (1999). *Landmines must be stopped*. Geneva: ICRC.

International Mine Action Standards (IMAS). (n.d.). *Standards and technical documents*. Retrieved March 21, 2021, from www.mineactionstandards.org/en/standards/

Landmine and Cluster Munition Monitor. (2000). Ethics and justice working group report. Retrieved December 6, 2017, from http://archives.the-monitor.org/index.php/publications/display?url=lm/2000/icbl/ethics.html

Landmine and Cluster Munition Monitor. (2017). *Cluster munition monitor 2017*. Retrieved March 21, 2021, from www.the-monitor.org/media/2582190/Cluster-Munition-Monitor-2017_web4.pdf

Lawrence, M., Stenberger, H., Zolderdo, A., Struthers, D., & Cooke, S. (2015). The effects of modern war and military activities on biodiversity and the environment. *Environmental Reviews, 23*(4), 443–460. https://doi.org/10.1139/er-2015-0039

Lustgarten, A. (2017, July 20). Open burns, Ill Winds. *ProPublica*. Retrieved March 21, 2021, from www. propublica.org/article/military-pollution-open-burns-radford-virginia

Meerschman, E., Cockx, L., Islam, M. M., Meeuws, F., & Van Meirvenne, M. (2011). Geostatistical assessment of the impact of World War I on the spatial occurrence of soil heavy metals. *Ambio, 40*(4), 417–424. http://doi.org/10.1007/s13280-010-0104-6

Mine Action Review. (2017a). *Clearing cluster munition remnants 2017: A report by mine action review for the 7th meeting of states parties to the convention on cluster munitions*. Geneva: Mines Advisory Group, Norwegian People's Aid, and The Halo Trust.

Mine Action Review. (2017b). *Clearing the mines 2017: A report by mine action review for the 16th meeting of states parties to the anti-personnel mine ban convention*. Geneva: Mines Advisory Group, Norwegian People's Aid, and The Halo Trust.

Rutherford, K. R. (2011). *Disarming states: The International Movement to Ban Landmines*. Santa Barbara, Denver and Oxford: Praeger Security International.

United Nations Environment Programme. (2007). *Population displacement and the environment: Sudan post-conflict environmental analysis*. https://postconflict.unep.ch/publications/sudan/05_displacement.pdf

US Department of State. (1993). *Hidden killers 1993: The global problem with uncleared landmines*. Washington, DC: US Department of State.

10

THE ENVIRONMENTAL SPOILS OF WAR

Päivi Lujala, Ashley Hooper and Maureen J. Purcell

Although there is evidence that countries rich in natural resources appear to be engaged in armed civil conflict more often than resource-poor countries, there is less agreement on why these resource-rich countries descend into civil strife. Two primary explanations have emerged: first, natural resources (especially those that are easily exploited) provide motivation and means for rebel uprisings; second, the abundance of natural resources leads to poor policy decisions, weakens state-capacity, and ultimately, invites conflict. These competing theoretical explanations have driven the majority of scholarship on the topic of civil unrest, accounting for direct mechanisms of conflict (i.e., greedy and aggrieved rebels) and indirect mechanisms (i.e., economic and political contributions to a weak state). Unfortunately, only a few measures are available to estimate rebel access to resources or resource revenues accruing to the state. As a result, proponents of both of these theoretical arguments tend to use similar measures in their analyses[1]; this is a major weakness, as the same variables are used in support of competing explanations.

As will be discussed, this chapter contributes to this theoretical debate by providing evidence that natural resources affect rebel movements *directly*. Using new data on localities of hydrocarbon (crude oil and natural gas) fields throughout the world and locations of gemstone resources, this chapter examines whether (1) valuable natural resources directly affect armed civil conflict and (2) the location of those resources (i.e., within or outside of conflict zones) influences the length of conflict duration.

Direct and indirect mechanisms of rebel conflict

Valuable natural resources can affect conflict directly by providing the rebels, or the rebel group leaders a source for personal enrichment or by financing rebellion efforts. Further, grievances resulting from unequal distribution of natural resource rents may create conditions for rebel conflicts, especially if a region with abundant natural resources is deprived of revenue flows but must bear extraction costs (e.g., pollution and degradation of land). For example, the Bougainvilleans' secessionist civil conflict in Papua New Guinea began with an attack on the local gold and copper mine in 1989 after the authorities and company refused to compensate for the pollution on the island (Le Billon, 2003).

While most rebel groups claim to fight for "noble" causes (e.g., human and political rights), some of them may hold more dubious goals: they seek to accumulate private wealth under the guise of more acceptable objectives. Ascribing to this explanation, rebel movements can be seen as any other economic entity; people fight when it pays better than their alternative sources of income (Collier & Hoeffler, 1998; 2004). Payoff from resources may be contingent on successful rebellion (e.g., in the form of achieving greater autonomy as in the case of Southern Sudan). Alternatively, the conflict itself, especially those with low intensity, may be beneficial to those rebels able to exploit resources during the conflict. For example, in Sierra Leone, rebels were able to spend longer periods concentrating on diamond mining and terrorizing civilians than on fighting the army.

Collier and Hoeffler (2005) consider the funding of rebel movements as the most likely explanation for the perceived link between primary commodity exports and conflict than greed. Unless rebel leaders are able to raise sufficient funds to feed, clothe, and arm group members, a conflict is unlikely to start no matter how severe their grievances. Furthermore, continuous financing is likely crucial to the survival of a rebel movement for an extended period. In many prolonged conflicts, rebels have had access to easily extractable natural resources (Fearon, 2004) (e.g., access to opium cultivation and gemstone mines supported rebel conflicts for decades in the Kachin and Shan States of Myanmar).

The indirect mechanisms from valuable natural resources to conflict focus on the state: dependence on natural resource extraction and exportation may have adverse effects on the economy, political institutions, and state, leading to poor policy choices and exposing the society to violent conflict (Fearon & Laitin, 2003). Since the early 1960s, most resource-rich countries have underperformed compared with resource-deficient countries. Abundant resources provide easily accruable rents that can sustain detrimental political structures, such as corruption and nepotism, which would not persist without those resources (Auty, 1998; Auty & Gelb, 2001). Furthermore, per capita incomes have grown two to three times faster in resource-poor countries (Auty, 1998; Sachs & Warner, 1995, 2001). Low-income levels, in turn, have been shown to increase the likelihood of conflict (Brunnschweiler & Lujala, 2017a, 2017b; Collier & Hoeffler, 2004; Miguel, Satyanath, & Sergenti, 2004). Political and economic inequality are likely sources of grievance, and low-income levels may lower the opportunity cost of joining a rebellion; these are both factors that may contribute to the outbreak of armed conflict. State capacity (especially its military power to defend itself) influences the odds of rebel successes and, in turn, may be affected by the country's natural resource base.

Several channels, both indirect and direct, may work simultaneously. It is relatively widely accepted that dependence on resource production and exportation is related to the conflict onset and that the indirect route is valid (see, e.g., Fearon & Laitin, 2003; Humphreys, 2005; de Soysa & Neumayer, 2007). Controversy still exists about resources' effect on the rebel movement itself because few empirical studies can convincingly show any link – or, indeed, the absence of such a link. For example, Collier and Hoeffler (2006) argue that oil exports relate to secessionist conflict; however, they are unable to control for whether or not oil production is actually located in the seceding region and, thusly, are unable to clarify whether major oil-exporting countries in general are more likely to experience a conflict over territory or whether it is the location of oil in the seceding region that is directly related to the conflict.

Where natural resources are located should not matter if the indirect channel is the only explanation for the perceived detrimental effect of resources on peace, as revenue flows from different sources and regions should have the same effect on the state. There is no reason to expect that, for example, revenues from offshore oil in Nigeria should have a different effect on state institutions than revenues from onshore production. By contrast, to have a direct effect on rebel movements, natural resources must, in most cases, be located near the (potential) rebel groups. Rebels that rely on looting resources to accumulate private wealth or to finance warfare need to have access to those resources; therefore, the fighting is likely to center near valuable and easily extractable resources.

Measuring natural resource base in empirical studies

Distinguishing among the different mechanisms linking resource abundance to armed conflict presents challenges, as there are relatively few ways to measure the resource base. Commonly, the export value of natural resources or specific resource type is normalized with respect to the size of the economy or total exports (Ross, 2004a); alternatively, rent estimates are used instead of export value (de Soysa & Neumayer, 2007). Despite showing that natural resources are likely to have a detrimental effect on peace, these measures have weaknesses (Ross, 2006) and findings are not always robust (Sambanis, 2004; Hegre & Sambanis, 2006). Importantly, they do not control for whether rebels had access to these resources.

To address this, Fearon (2004) coded conflicts in which rebels are known to have exploited lootable resources (e.g., gemstones and drugs). Despite finding that these conflicts tend to last substantially longer, this approach fails to account for cases where lootable resources were available in the conflict region, but where rebels were not known to exploit them or where conflict ended before the rebels could or needed to utilize them. Therefore, it is possible that use of natural resources may be merely an indication of prolonged conflict but not the cause, as rebels are forced to exploit natural resources to sustain long durations of fighting.

Resource data

In general, we would expect that, if natural resources have an effect on a rebel group, resources that are located in a conflict zone should have an effect on conflict. By contrast, resources located outside the conflict zone should have a different or no effect on conflict. To evaluate how the location of natural resources affects conflict, the analysis in this chapter uses datasets of hydrocarbon reserves and diamond occurrences throughout the world.

PETRODATA[2] assigns geographic coordinates for each region with hydrocarbon reserves and production; identifies whether oil, gas, or both are present; and includes temporal information on when hydrocarbons were first discovered and produced in each region (Lujala, Rød, & Thieme, 2007). PETRODATA covers the period 1946–2003 and includes 885 onshore regions and 379 offshore areas. In total, there are confirmed hydrocarbon fields in 111 countries, 98 of which had produced gas, oil, or both by 2003. For the duration analysis, six conflict-specific dummies are coded from PETRODATA. Both the conflict zones and the resource regions can be viewed in ArcGIS software, which ensures the spatial and temporal overlap of conflict zones and resource localities. For the onset analysis, the hydrocarbon dummies are coded at the country level.

To test the effect of a more lootable natural resource, a dummy variable for secondary diamond production is coded at both the conflict and the country level. Diamond data come from the DIADATA dataset, which provides coordinates for more than 1,000 diamond deposits throughout the world (Gilmore, Gleditsch, Lujala, & Rød, 2005). Dummies for primary diamond production, which requires considerable investment in technology, are also constructed from DIADATA. Other gemstones, such as rubies, sapphires, and opals, are relatively easily extractable, and thus, a similar dummy for gemstone production was created using GEMDATA (Flöter, Lujala, & Rød, 2007).

Dependent variable 1: duration of armed civil conflict

The empirical analysis uses conflict data for the period 1946–2003 from the annually updated UCDP/PRIO Armed Conflict Dataset (Gleditsch, Wallensteen, Eriksson, Sollenberg, & Strand, 2002; Harbom & Wallensteen, 2007). The dataset includes conflicts with a minimum of 25-battle-related deaths in a one-year period, capturing the low-intensity conflicts in the analysis. Internal and internationalized internal conflicts are included and merged together. An extension to the UCDP/PRIO dataset assigns exact start and end dates for conflicts in the dataset (Gates & Strand, 2004). The duration is measured in days although the year is kept as the observation unit because no other variable is measured for a shorter period. A reactivation of a conflict that has been inactive for more than two calendar years is treated as a new conflict. A new conflict is also coded if there has been a total change in the opposite side. Conflicts that were active in 2001 are censored as are conflicts that ended in 2001 but revived during the following 24 months. In total, dates are available for 252 distinct conflicts for the period 1946–2001. In duration analysis, it is desirable to control for the location of conflict, which is available from the same dataset.

Dependent variable 2: onset of armed civil conflict

Onset is also coded from the UCDP/PRIO Armed Conflict Dataset and covers the period 1946–2003. The dataset includes several countries with simultaneous civil conflicts. For example, Myanmar had several ongoing conflicts in the 1990s with six conflict onsets in total. As a country with an ongoing conflict may experience an outbreak of another civil conflict, it would be incorrect to censor the following conflict years. In total, the dataset includes 7,176 country years although many are lost during analysis because of missing control variables. Conflict onset is a relatively rare event (238 onsets), and consequently, onset is coded for only 3.3% of the country years.

Control variables

Included in the models are the following control variables: income level, as per capita income (Fearon & Laitin, 2003); a dummy for continent (Fearon & Laitin, 2003); a dummy for former colony (Fearon & Laitin, 2003); incompatibility, coded as territorial (1) or governmental (0) conflict type from the UCDP/PRIO Armed Conflict Dataset; social fractionalization, which uses linguistic heterogeneity (1 on a scale of 0–1) as a proxy (Alesina, Devleeschauwer, Easterly, Kurlat, & Wacziarg, 2003); level of democratization, using a continuum of autocratic (−10) to democratic (10) (Marshall & Jaggers, 2002); rough terrain, as a logged percentage of country than conflict area covered by mountainous terrain (Fearon & Laitin, 2003; UNEP, 2002); forest cover, as a percentage of conflict area covered by forest (FAO, 1999)[3]; and a dummy for rainy season, assigned for the region once 8mm of rainfall days in a month is recorded (GPCP, 2002).

The income variable is both lagged one year and logged. The original (Fearon & Laitin, 2003) variable is updated using the Penn World Tables 6.0 (Heston, Summers, & Aten, 2002) and World Bank Development Indicators (World Bank, 2002). The logged population data come from Fearon & Laitin and are updated from World Bank Development Indicators. A Polity IV variable (Marshall & Jaggers, 2002) was used to measure the level of democratization.

To include all conflict onsets, the conflict years following the onset are not deleted. To control for the possibility that a country with ongoing conflict is inherently more likely to experience an onset than a country without ongoing conflict, a dummy for ongoing conflict is included. Variables that count the years since the last outbreak of conflict, as suggested by Beck, Katz, and Tucker (1998), control for time dependence and correct for bias in standard errors. All analyses are clustered on country to calculate robust White Standard errors.

Duration analysis

In the UCDP/PRIO Armed Conflict Dataset, the mean conflict duration is 6.9 years. Incompatibility has a clear effect on the mean duration; conflicts over government last on average five years, but secessionist conflicts last for more than nine years. The distribution of duration is skewed; the median survival time is two years, and 75% of all conflicts end in eight years. Conflicts over territory, conflicts in regions with the presence of gemstones and hydrocarbons, and conflicts in regions with oil production last longer than their counterparts; the latter weakly so. Figure 10.1 shows the Kaplan–Meier estimates for conflict duration for selected variables and confirms territorial conflicts are longer.[4]

Figure 10.2 shows the smoothed estimate for the hazard of peace. Immediately after a conflict starts, the probability of peace increases for the first two years, decreasing over time. There is an increase in hazard rate for the longest conflicts but, as very few conflicts last longer than 35 years, the confidence intervals for the right-hand tail are large. The figure suggests that the correct survival model could have a lognormal or log-logistic form. A Weibull model is also possible although it imposes a monotonically decreasing hazard function on the conflict data. All the models presented here have been analyzed by using the three different distributions. The Weibull is preferred to the Cox model because it performs better.[5]

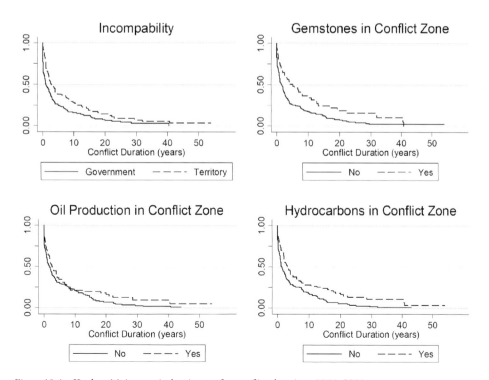

Figure 10.1 Kaplan–Meier survival estimates for conflict duration, 1946–2001.

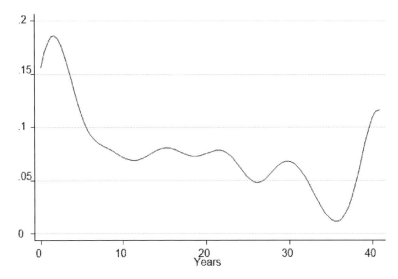

Figure 10.2 Smoothed hazard estimate for the event of peace.

Table 10.1 shows the results for the bivariate Weibull survival analyses. The coefficients are reported in time ratios, showing the multiplicative change in duration for one unit change in the independent variable. For example, if oil reserves are located in the conflict area, the conflict is predicted to last 2.2 times longer than a conflict without oil reserves inside the conflict zone. Resources located inside the conflict zone seem to prolong civil conflict. Oil and gas reserves both increase the duration as do secondary diamonds and gemstones, whose effects are similar enough to be aggregated to a single variable (all gemstones). Gas production does not seem related to the conflict length,[6] and primary diamonds are only weakly related to conflict. In the subsequent multivariate analysis, their effect is always insignificant, and the variable is dropped from the analysis.

Table 10.2 shows the main results for the duration analysis. Model 1 includes the dummies for the presence of hydrocarbon reserves and all gemstones, including secondary diamonds, in the conflict zone. As in the bivariate analysis, gemstones and hydrocarbons in the conflict zone more than double the conflict duration, and the effect is highly significant. Model 1 also includes various measures for rough terrain. Mountainous terrain and rainy season have the expected effect of seeming beneficial to rebels, but forest cover seems to decrease the length of conflict.

In Model 2, the dummy for incompatibility is added to the model; the effect is highly significant and, as predicted by the Kaplan–Meier estimate, conflicts over territory last three times longer than governmental conflicts. Model 2 also includes an intensity dummy for conflicts that had a relatively high casualty rate for at least one year.[7] Finally, in Model 3, the level of democracy is added to the analysis. The results show that democracies tend to fight longer wars.

In general, the inclusion of control variables weakens the effect of the hydrocarbon dummy but strengthens the effect of the gemstone variable.[8] Conflicts in which rebels have access to gems (including secondary diamonds) tend to last more than 2.5 times longer. These findings are in line with Fearon (2004), who finds the same positive effect for rebellions that profit from contraband production or trafficking. As secondary diamonds are frequently mentioned as a

The environmental spoils of war

Table 10.1 Bivariate duration analysis of armed civil conflict, 1946–2001.

Oil reserves,	2.171	Oil production,	1.79
Conflict zone	(2.60)	Conflict zone	(1.74)
	0.009		*0.082*
Gas reserves,	1.687	Gas production,	0.876
Conflict zone	(2.01)	Conflict zone	(0.40)
	0.044		*0.688*
Hydrocarbon reserves,	2.556	Hydrocarbon production,	1.752
Conflict zone	(3.34)	Conflict zone	(1.71)
	0.001		*0.088*
Secondary diamond prod.,	1.939	Gemstone production,	4.667
Conflict zone	(2.38)	Conflict zone	(4.96)
	0.017		*0.000*
Primary diamond production,	2.238	All gemstones,[a]	3.164
Conflict zone	(1.49)	Conflict zone	(4.37)
	0.137		*0.000*

Note: The table shows the time ratio form for bivariate Weibull survival analyses. For the description of the variables and the sources, see the text. Absolute robust z-values, adjusted over countries, in parentheses. $p < 0.1$ in italics.

a   The "All gemstones" variable does not include primary diamonds.

culprit for long conflicts, Model 4 tests the secondary diamond dummy alone. The results show that the dummy is highly significant, and the effect is similar to the dummy that includes other gemstones also.

The most interesting results concern the hydrocarbon dummy: the presence of hydrocarbons in the conflict area strongly increases the length of conflict, more than doubling the duration. Surprisingly, production is not necessary for this effect. Model 5 includes a hydrocarbon production dummy, which is not significant at the 0.1 level. Although the oil production dummy fares better (Model 7), the effect of production is weaker and less significant, as suggested by the Kaplan–Meier estimates and the bivariate analysis. The oil reserve dummy (Model 6) also performs weaker than the combined hydrocarbon measure. Running the model with a dummy that includes only the years between the discovery and the start of production shows a similar effect on the duration and is significant at the 0.02 level. This further illustrates that production is not necessary for the prolonging effect of hydrocarbons.

These results imply, first, that the presence of gas and oil lengthens the conflict, with the effect of oil seeming more salient. Second, production is not necessary for the adverse effect on duration; presence in the conflict region is sufficient. Therefore, it seems that the duration is lengthened not necessarily only by the financing available to rebels but also by the promise of future revenue flows originating from the region.

To determine if the analysis is picking up the effect of resource-rich countries generally having longer conflicts, Model 8 tests whether natural resources measured at the country level have the same effect on duration. The results show that these have no effect on conflict duration. Therefore, resources matter for conflict duration only when they are located inside the conflict area, implying that the prolonging effect of natural resources mainly works through their effect on rebel movements. If the impact of resource revenues on conflict operates only through their effect on government and other state institutions, we would have expected the country-level and conflict-level measures for resources to have a similar effect on conflict duration.

Päivi Lujala, Ashley Hooper and Maureen J. Purcell

Table 10.2 Duration of armed civil conflict, 1946–2001.

	1	2	3	4	5	6	7	8
ln Mountainous terrain,	1.124	1.104	1.092	1.099	1.096	1.092	1.094	1.120
conflict zone	(2.20)	(2.22)	(1.88)	(1.99)	(1.99)	(1.91)	(1.98)	(2.46)
	0.028	*0.027*	*0.060*	*0.046*	*0.046*	*0.056*	*0.048*	*0.014*
ln Forest cover,	0.928	0.899	0.889	0.898	0.887	0.885	0.885	0.892
conflict zone	(1.43)	(1.95)	(2.04)	(1.88)	(2.12)	(2.13)	(2.18)	(1.90)
	0.152	*0.051*	*0.041*	*0.060*	*0.034*	*0.033*	*0.029*	*0.057*
Rainy season,	1.915	1.806	1.548	1.897	1.697	1.615	1.703	1.883
conflict zone	(1.91)	(1.83)	(1.38)	(1.97)	(1.64)	(1.48)	(1.65)	(1.87)
	0.056	*0.067*	0.168	*0.049*	0.102	0.140	*0.100*	*0.061*
Incompatibility		3.356	3.135	2.901	3.333	3.270	3.338	2.557
		(4.58)	(4.47)	(4.15)	(4.64)	(4.56)	(4.66)	(3.63)
		0.000	*0.000*	*0.000*	*0.000*	*0.000*	*0.000*	*0.000*
Intensity		3.506	3.709	4.125	3.755	3.815	3.781	4.123
		(4.88)	(5.30)	(5.50)	(5.33)	(5.39)	(5.38)	(5.27)
		0.000	*0.000*	*0.000*	*0.000*	*0.000*	*0.000*	*0.000*
Democracy (lag)			1.050	1.052	1.049	1.051	1.050	1.050
			(1.99)	(2.06)	(1.97)	(2.02)	(2.02)	(2.13)
			0.047	*0.039*	*0.049*	*0.044*	*0.043*	*0.034*
All gemstones,[a]	2.632	3.149	2.938		2.937	2.884	2.934	
conflict zone	(3.65)	(4.49)	(4.34)		(4.21)	(4.22)	(4.24)	
	0.000	*0.000*	*0.000*		*0.000*	*0.000*	*0.000*	
Secondary diamonds,				2.400				
conflict zone				(3.21)				
				0.001				
Hydrocarbon reserves,	2.357	2.059	2.013	2.028				
conflict zone	(3.21)	(2.66)	(2.60)	(2.61)				
	0.001	*0.008*	*0.009*	*0.009*				
Hydrocarbon production,					1.595			
conflict zone					(1.50)			
					0.135			
Oil reserves,						1.798		
conflict zone						(2.07)		
						0.038		
Oil production,							1.679	
conflict zone							(1.66)	
							0.096	
All gemstones,[a]								1.539
country level								(1.21)
								0.226
Hydrocarbon production,								1.272
country level								(0.76)
								0.445

	1	2	3	4	5	6	7	8
p	0.473	0.505	0.511	0.506	0.508	0.509	0.508	0.499
	(11.45)	(10.87)	(10.82)	(11.10)	(11.13)	(11.05)	(11.10)	(11.53)
	0.000	*0.000*	*0.000*	*0.000*	*0.000*	*0.000*	*0.000*	*0.000*
No. of conflicts	252	252	248	248	248	248	248	248
Log-likelihood	–564.30	–547.12	–531.33	–533.63	–533.32	–532.43	–533.06	–537.81
Akaike Information Criteria	1142.60	1112.20	1082.70	1087.30	1086.60	1084.90	1086.10	1095.60

Note: The table shows the time ratio form for Weibull duration analysis. Absolute robust z-values, adjusted over countries, in parentheses. p < 0.1 in italics.
a   The "All gemstones" variable does not include primary diamonds.

Onset analysis

The onset analysis uses the location data for onshore and offshore hydrocarbon fields to study whether field location contributes differentially to the risk of conflict onset. Table 10.3 presents the results in odds ratios for logistic regressions.[9] Resource endowment may adversely affect regime type, its stability, and income level. To avoid the possibility that the resource dummies are merely picking up these indirect effects on peace, they are included in the analysis. In addition, poor countries generally tend to fight more conflicts, which may be due to factors such as the low opportunity cost of joining a rebellion (Collier & Hoeffler, 2004) or to low state capacity (Fearon & Laitin, 2003). Level of democracy has been shown to be related to conflict onset in a parabolic way; the most autocratic and democratic states are less likely to experience a conflict onset while regime types that have characteristics of both types fare worse (Hegre, Ellingsen, Gates, & Gleditsch, 2001). Therefore, both the linear and the square terms for regime type are included in the analysis. Political instability[10] has also been linked to conflict (Sambanis, 2004). Population size, social fractionalization, amount of mountainous terrain, and ongoing conflict are also controlled for.

Model 9 includes the control variables that mostly perform in coherence with the results of earlier studies. Countries that are more populous tend to have more conflict onsets. Income level has the expected negative sign but fails to be significant in this model. Democracy variables have the expected curvilinear relationship to onset; the most democratic and autocratic countries are less likely to experience a conflict, and the two variables are jointly significant. Instability is not significantly related to conflict. Linguistic fractionalization significantly predicts the conflict onset and mountainous countries tend to face a higher risk of onset, while the dummy variable for ongoing conflict is not significant.

Model 9 also includes a dummy for countries that produce secondary diamonds, the effect of which is considerable and highly significant, making the risk of conflict onset almost 1.5 times higher than that of a country without such production. This result complements an earlier study by Lujala, Gleditsch, and Gilmore (2005), who find that secondary diamond production is related to conflict onset for the post-1985 period.

In Model 10, the oil production dummy has a substantial and significant effect; oil production increases the risk of onset by a factor of 1.5. This result is in line with earlier studies that

Päivi Lujala, Ashley Hooper and Maureen J. Purcell

Table 10.3 Onset of armed civil conflict, 1946–2003.

	9	10	11	12	13
ln Population size	1.223	1.149	1.148	1.162	1.160
	(3.92)	(2.29)	(2.38)	(2.45)	(2.53)
	0.000	*0.022*	*0.017*	*0.014*	*0.011*
ln GDP per capita (lag)	0.827	0.777	0.773	0.736	0.731
	(1.45)	(2.00)	(1.96)	(2.59)	(2.59)
	0.147	*0.046*	*0.051*	*0.010*	*0.010*
Democracy score (lag)	1.011	1.014	1.014	1.02	1.021
	(0.72)	(0.96)	(0.95)	(1.54)	(1.53)
	0.471	0.335	0.344	0.123	0.126
Democracy score squared (lag)	0.993	0.993	0.993	0.993	0.993
	(3.10)	(3.17)	(3.17)	(3.15)	(3.19)
	0.002	*0.002*	*0.002*	*0.002*	*0.001*
Instability (lag)	1.166	1.155	1.163	1.153	1.160
	(0.84)	(0.78)	(0.82)	(0.78)	(0.81)
	0.401	0.433	0.413	0.434	0.420
Linguistic fractionalization	2.806	3.106	3.067	3.283	3.256
	(3.23)	(3.77)	(3.72)	(4.03)	(3.99)
	0.001	*0.000*	*0.000*	*0.000*	*0.000*
ln Mountainous terrain	1.128	1.129	1.126	1.125	1.122
	(3.06)	(3.18)	(3.12)	(2.97)	(2.94)
	0.002	*0.001*	*0.002*	*0.003*	*0.003*
Secondary diamonds	1.473	1.443	1.452	1.555	1.565
	(1.94)	(1.96)	(1.96)	(2.27)	(2.26)
	0.053	*0.050*	*0.049*	*0.023*	*0.024*
Oil production		1.503		1.401	
		(2.20)		(1.73)	
		0.028		*0.083*	
Onshore oil production			1.488		1.404
			(1.93)		(1.64)
			0.053		0.101
Offshore oil production			1.06		1.046
			(0.25)		(0.20)
			0.803		0.845
Ongoing conflict	1.025	0.992	0.983	0.968	0.959
	(0.12)	(0.04)	(0.09)	(0.18)	(0.22)
	0.903	0.966	0.930	0.859	0.825
Constant	0.009	0.013	0.013	0.01	0.01
	(7.01)	(6.19)	(6.42)	(6.29)	(6.47)
	0.000	*0.000*	*0.000*	*0.000*	*0.000*
Dummy for North Africa and Middle East				*Yes*	*Yes*
No. of conflicts	204	204	204	204	204
No. of country years	6322	6322	6322	6322	6322
Log-likelihood	–825.02	–822.51	–822.38	–819.37	–819.19

NOTE: The table shows the odds ratios for logistic estimations. Coefficients for time since last onset and cubic splines are not shown. Absolute robust z-values, adjusted over countries, in parentheses. $p < 0.1$ in italics.

find that oil producers and exporters are more likely to experience conflict onset. This chapter, however, seeks to clarify whether production location has an effect on conflict. Therefore, Model 11 differentiates between onshore and offshore production. From the results, it is clear that onshore oil production has a similar effect on conflict onset as oil production in general while offshore production fails to have any effect. Inclusion of oil dummies renders the GDP per capita significant: countries with higher income levels have lower risk of conflict onset.

If it were true that the mechanism from oil production worked only indirectly, for example, through the weak-state hypothesis, as access to and revenue from offshore production rarely fall to rebels, we would expect offshore oil production to have a similar positive effect on conflict onset as onshore production. There is no reason to expect revenue flows from either offshore or onshore production to have different impacts on state capabilities. However, the analysis shows no evidence for an adverse effect of offshore production, which, in turn, implies that the effect of onshore production should also work through other mechanisms. Models 10 and 11 are also estimated using an oil reserve dummy instead of production. The effect is weaker and less significant, suggesting that production is more relevant for the onset than the mere existence of reserves.[11]

Offshore production has been substantial only during the past 20–30 years; therefore, the weak and insignificant effect may be because the analysis period is too long to capture the effect. However, an analysis that only includes the past 20 years (1984–2003) reveals qualitatively the same results as the analysis of the full period. In fact, the effect of onshore production actually increases in both magnitude and significance while that of offshore production stays insignificant.

Gas production has no effect on conflict onset. When the pure gas production is added to the oil dummy, all three dummies perform worse than the corresponding dummies for oil production. This implies that pure gas production does not increase the risk of conflict onset.[12] As the value of gas production has been limited until the past 10–20 years, the study period may be too long to capture the effect of gas. However, analysis restricted to the past 20 years does not show qualitatively different results.

Conclusions

This chapter assessed how the temporal and spatial locations of natural resources relative to conflict zones overlap and affect conflict duration, uncovering whether natural resources affect rebel movement. This approach rectifies prior uncertainties in the identification of mechanisms through which natural resources and conflict interact. Indeed, results indicate that rebel access to secondary diamonds, other gemstones, or hydrocarbons in the conflict zone more than doubles the conflict duration. Resources located outside the conflict region do not have a prolonging effect on the duration. Interestingly, the duration analysis shows that production is not necessary for prolonging the conflict; the mere presence of hydrocarbons inside the conflict zone lengthens the conflict. This is further evidence for the view that the presence of hydrocarbons affects the rebel group directly rather than through their effect on the economy, political institutions, and state capacity because the revenue flows that potentially could affect the state are not always present. Furthermore, this suggests that rebels are forward-looking and engage in conflicts with promise of future revenues.

Besides finding support for the rebel-financing argument, these analyses also shed new light on the question of how resources affect conflict. Based on qualitative and quantitative research conducted up to 2004, Ross (2004a) concludes that oil is salient for conflict onset but not for duration. Further, he argues that evidence suggests that lootable resources affect only duration but not the risk of conflict onset. In contrast to these arguments, we find that oil substantially prolongs conflict when located inside the conflict zone, and secondary diamond production increases the risk of conflict onset by more than 40%.

Analysis of conflict onset further suggests that the resource location is important; onshore oil production increases the risk of conflict onset by 50% while offshore production has no effect. As there is no reason to expect that revenues from onshore and offshore oil production should affect the state differently, this implies that onshore oil production is salient for conflict through its impact on rebel movements. Furthermore, this implies that resources significantly alter the opportunities and incentives available for rebel groups. If the detrimental effect of natural resources on peace worked only through the weak-state channel, the relative location of resources should not matter. Together, these results suggest that rebel access to resources crucially shapes armed civil conflict. By examining the locality of hydrocarbons, this chapter provides evidence that nonlootable resources may have a great impact on rebel groups and their viability. The analysis also finds that a country with secondary diamond production has a 40% higher risk of conflict onset: a result that has not been documented earlier.

The results of the analyses in this chapter speak not only to themes relating to the role of the environment during conflict but also to how natural resources contribute to preconflict tension and conflict duration. By offering a new understanding of how natural resources directly impact the rebel groups (as opposed to weakening the capacity of the state), this chapter provides implications for post- and preconflict management of these natural resources. For example, instead of directing resources to building state capacity, aggrieved and economically disadvantaged rebel groups might be targeted for policy interventions. Furthermore, the results described herein lay a foundation to build a greater understanding of how natural resource extraction, production, and protection drive rebellious contingencies and fractures between state and corporate representatives and local citizens. This chapter complements others in this volume that shed light on the potential challenges that peacebuilders will face in the future, given the projected number of economically disenfranchised and climate refugees (see Crawford & Church, Chapter 7), the continued demand for and scarcity of natural resources, and the context of locality and access to resources for states, corporations, and citizens.

Notes

1 Share of (specific) natural resource exports, rents, or production volume to total exports or size of economy is commonly used variables.
2 PETRODATA and DIADATA are available at www.prio.no/CSCW/Datasets/Geographical-and-Resource.
3 All area calculations are conducted in ArcGIS 8.0 from Environmental System Research Incorporated (ESRI) based in Redlands, California.
4 Kaplan–Meier is a nonparametric estimate for the probability of conflict continuing past a specific point in time.
5 Appendix 1, which is available at www.prio.no/jpr/datasets together with the replication data, shows the base model using the lognormal and log-logistic distributions and compares the Weibull coefficients to the Cox model. The appendix also includes other models discussed in this section but that are not included in Table II.
6 Reserve dummy codes all the years after discovery. Production dummy includes only the years after production started.
7 For the conflicts in the UCDP/PRIO Armed Conflict Dataset, 75% of the conflict-country-years have fewer than 1,600 battle-related deaths (Lacina & Gleditsch, 2005). This figure is used as a cutoff point and a dummy for conflicts that exceeded this threshold for at least one year is included in the analysis. The dummy is used because the model is likely to omit variables that explain high levels of casualties.

8　The results for the resource variables in Model 3 are very robust to the inclusion of various control variables such as per capita income level, population size, and linguistic fractionalization. These control variables themselves are not related to conflict duration.

9　The odds ratio shows how many times the risk of conflict increases for one unit of change in the independent variable.

10　Instability is a dummy variable that takes value 1 if the country has experienced >2 change in the Polity IV index over the previous three years.

11　For these and other results discussed in this section but that are not included in Table III, see Appendix 2 (available at www.prio.no/jpr/datasets).

12　The gas dummies were also included separately in the analysis but none were found to be significant.

Works cited

Alesina, A., Devleeschauwer, A., Easterly, W., Kurlat, S., & Wacziarg, R. (2003). Fractionalization. *Journal of Economic Growth, 8*(2), 155–194.

Auty, R. M. (1998). Resource abundance and economic development: Improving the performance of resource-rich countries. *Research for Action 44.* Helsinki: World Institute for Development Economics Research (UNU/WIDER).

Auty, R. M., & Gelb, A. H. (2001). Political economy of resource-abundant states. In R. M. Auty (Ed.), *Resource abundance and economic development* (pp. 126–144). Oxford: Oxford Press.

Beck, N., Katz, J. N., & Tucker, R. (1998). Taking time seriously: Time-series-cross-section analysis with a binary dependent variable. *American Journal of Political Science, 42*(4), 1260–1288.

Brunnschweiler, C., & Lujala, P. (2017a). Economic backwardness and social tension. *Scandinavian Journal of Economics.* In press. 10.1111/sjoe.12281

Brunnschweiler, C., & Lujala, P. (2017b). Income and armed civil conflict: An instrumental variables approach. *Peace Economics, Peace Science and Public Policy, 23*(4), 1–7.

Collier, P., & Hoeffler, A. (1998). On the economic causes of Civil War. *Oxford Economic Papers, 50*(4), 563–573.

Collier, P., & Hoeffler, A. (2004). Greed and grievance in Civil War. *Oxford Economic Papers, 56*(4), 563–596.

Collier, P., & Hoeffler, A. (2005). Resource rents, governance, and conflict. *Journal of Conflict Resolution, 49*(5), 625–633.

Collier, P., & Hoeffler, A. 2006. The political economy of secession. In H. Hannum & E. F. Babbitt (Eds.), *Negotiating Self-Determination* (pp. 37–59). Lanham, MD: Lexington Books.

de Soysa, I., & Neumayer, E. (2007). Resource wealth and the risk of civil war onset: Results from a new dataset on natural resource rents, 1970–1999. *Conflict Management and Peace Science, 24*(3), 201–218.

FAO. (1999). Global forest cover map. *FRA Working Paper 19.* Retrieved from www.fao.org/docrep/007/ae157e/AE157E00.htm

Fearon, J. (2004). Why do some civil wars last so much longer than others? *Journal of Peace Research, 41*(3), 275–301.

Fearon, J. (2005). Primary commodity exports and civil war. *Journal of Conflict Resolution, 49*(5), 483–507.

Fearon, J., & Laitin, D. (2003). Ethnicity, insurgency, and civil war. *American Political Science Review, 97*(1), 75–90.

Flöter, A., Lujala, P., & Rød, J. K. (2007). 'The gemstone dataset codebook', *Mimeo, department of geography.* Trondheim: Norwegian University of Science and Technology.

Gary, I., & Reisch, N. (2005). *Chad's Oil: Miracle or Mirage?* Catholic Relief Services and Bank Information Center. Retrieved from www.bicusa.org/en/Project.7.aspx

Gates, S., & Strand, H. (2004, September 9–11). *Modeling the duration of civil wars: Measurement and estimation issues.* Paper prepared for the 2004 Meeting of the Standing Group on International Relations, The Hague. Retrieved from www.prio.no/Research-and-Publications/Publication/?oid=57322

Gilmore, E., Gleditsch, N. P., Lujala, P., & Rød, J. K. (2005). Conflict diamonds: A new dataset. *Conflict Management and Peace Science, 22*(3), 257–272.

Gleditsch, N. P., Wallensteen, P., Eriksson, M., Sollenberg, M., & Strand, H. (2002). Armed conflict 1946–2001: A new dataset. *Journal of Peace Research, 39*(5), 615–637.

GPCP. (2002). *Precipitation Climatology Project 2002.* Map series: Average Daily Precipitation. http://cics.umd.edu/~yin/GPCP/main.html

Harbom, L., & Wallensteen, P. (2007). Armed conflict, 1989–2006. *Journal of Peace Research*, *44*(5), 623–634.

Hegre, H., & Sambanis, N. (2006). Sensitivity analysis of the empirical literature on civil war onset. *Journal of Conflict Resolution*, *50*(4), 508–535.

Hegre, H., Ellingsen, T., Gates, S., & Gleditsch, N. P. (2001). Towards a democratic civil peace? Democracy, political change, and civil war, 1816–1992. *American Political Science Review*, *95*(1), 17–33.

Heston, A., Summers, R., & Aten, B. (2002). *Penn world table version 6.1*. Center for International Comparisons at the University of Pennsylvania (CICUP), October 2002. http://pwt.econ.upenn.edu/

Human Rights Watch. (2003). The Warri crisis: Fueling violence. *HRW Report*, *15*(18). http://hrw.org/reports/2003/nigeria1103/

Humphreys, M. (2005). Natural resources, conflict, and conflict resolution: Uncovering the mechanisms. *Journal of Conflict Resolution*, *49*(4), 508–537.

Keller, P. C. (1990). *Gemstones and their origins*. New York: Van Nostrand Reinhold.

Lacina, B. (2005, September 8–10). *Rebels as lobbyists: A political theory of asymmetrical insurgency*. Paper presented at the 3rd Annual General Meeting of the European Political Science Association, Budapest. Retrieved from www.stanford.edu/~blacina/BethanyLacinaPublications.html

Lacina, B., & Gleditsch, N. P. (2005). Monitoring trends in global combat: A new dataset of battle deaths. *European Journal of Population*, *21*(2–3), 145–165.

Le Billon, P. (2003). Fuelling war: Natural resources and armed conflict. *Adelphi Paper*, 357. Retrieved from www.geog.ubc.ca/~lebillon/adelphi357.pdf

Lujala, P. (2003). *Coca Bush, opium poppy and cannabis cultivation*. Mimeo, Department of Economics, Norwegian University of Science and Technology.

Lujala, P. Rød, J. K., & Thieme, N. (2007). Fighting over oil: Introducing a new dataset. *Conflict Management and Peace Science*, *24*(3), 239–256.

Lujala, P., Gleditsch, N. P., & Gilmore, E. (2005). A diamond curse? Civil war and a lootable resource. *Journal of Conflict Resolution*, *49*(4), 583–562.

Marshall, M. G., & Jaggers, K. (2002). *Polity IV dataset*. College Park, MD: Center for International Development and Conflict Management, University of Maryland. Retrieved from www.systemicpeace.org/polity/polity4.htm

Miguel, E., Satyanath, S., & Sergenti, E. (2004). Economic shocks and civil conflict: An instrumental variables approach. *Journal of Political Economy*, *112*(4), 725–754.

Ross, M. (2004a). What do we know about natural resources and civil war? *Journal of Peace Research*, *41*(3), 337–356.

Ross, M. (2004b). How do natural resources influence civil war? Evidence from thirteen cases. *International Organization*, *58*(winter), 35–67.

Ross, M. (2005). *Booty futures*. Mimeo, University of California, Los Angeles. Retrieved from www.polisci.ucla.edu/faculty/ross/bootyfutures.pdf

Ross, M. (2006). A closer look at oil, diamonds, and civil war. *Annual Review of Political Science*, *9*, 265–300.

Sachs, J. D., & Warner, A. M. (1995). Natural resource abundance and economic growth. *NBER Working Paper* W5398. Cambridge, MA: National Bureau of Economic Research, December.

Sachs, J. D., & Warner, A. M. (2001). The curse of natural resources. *European Economic Review*, *45*(4–6), 827–838.

Sambanis, N. (2004). What is civil war? Conceptual and empirical complexities. *Journal of Conflict Resolution*, *48*(6), 814–858.

UNEP. (2002). *Mountain watch*. Cambridge: UNEP World Conservation Monitoring Centre.

World Bank. (2002). *'World Development Indicators', CD-ROM*. Washington, DC: World Bank.

11
POPULATION DISPLACEMENT AND THE ENVIRONMENT DURING WAR

Evgenia Nizkorodov and Paroma Wagle

Conflict, mass migration, and the environment

Every minute, roughly 20 people are forcibly displaced as a result of violent conflict (UNHCR, 2020b). The threat of violence and persecution during war forces individuals to flee to low-conflict regions in their home countries and across international borders (Linscher, 2009). Presently, the number of displaced persons around the world is at a record high (UNHCR, 2020a, 2020b). At the end of 2019, 79.5 million people, or roughly one percent of the world population, were classified by the United Nations Refugee Agency (UNHCR) as forcibly displaced. Of this population, 26 million people were classified as refugees[1] and 45.7 million people as internally displaced persons[2] (UNHCR, 2020a). An additional 4.2 million individuals were asylum seekers[3] (UNHCR, 2020a).

Violent conflict and the impacts of forced displacement pose a development challenge to both displaced populations and host communities (World Bank, 2017a). Eight out of ten of the world's poorest countries have experienced or are experiencing large-scale violent conflict, resulting in high economic, social, and environmental costs (Stewart, 2002). Many countries and regions often faced cycles of repeated violence, with 90% of civil wars erupting in countries that had already experienced civil wars in the past 30 years (World Bank, 2011). Low- and middle-income countries are also more likely to host refugees and displaced persons: in 2016, developing countries bordering conflict zones hosted 84% of refugees (14.5 million people), with low-income countries providing asylum to 28% of the refugee population (roughly 4.9 million individuals) (UNHCR, 2016). In 2020, 80% of displaced individuals were located in countries and territories affected by acute food insecurity and malnutrition (UNHCR, 2020a). As displacement is typically a long-term, or even a permanent process (Loescher, Milner, Newman, & Troeller, 2007), the sudden influx and protracted stay of displaced populations can strain the economic and environmental resources of a host community (World Bank, 2017a). As a result of the increased resource competition, forced displacement creates or exacerbates economic, sociocultural, political, health, and environmental challenges in host environments (UNHCR, n.d.; Gomez & Christensen, 2010).

There is a pressing need to develop and implement sustainable practices in addressing large-scale displacement. Climate change and population growth are expected to intensify the existing competition for resources: by 2030, the share of global poor living in fragile and

129   DOI: 10.4324/9781315107592-13

conflict-affected situations is projected to increase from 17% to 46% (World Bank, 2017b). In short, the displacement of millions of people as a result of natural disasters and violent conflict (UNEP, 2011) will intensify the already pressing refugee crisis.

This chapter examines the environmental impact of displacement on host environments. Studies indicate that the environmental impact of displaced populations is a key variable in determining refugee–host relations (Berry, 2008) and can be a potential source of conflict if not mitigated (Conca & Wallace, 2009; Martin, 2005). Additionally, the well-being of displaced populations is linked directly to local resource use and environmental quality (UNHCR, n.d.-a). For example, rapid soil erosion and degradation from unsustainable practices can reduce agricultural yields, increasing food scarcity in a host region. Thus, this chapter examines the link between displacement and the environment by (1) illustrating the impact of self-settled and settled displaced populations on human and ecological systems; (2) overviewing the challenges of addressing the short- and long-term environmental impacts of displaced populations; and (3) providing policy, technology, and infrastructure recommendations that promote the well-being of displaced individuals, host communities, and ecological systems.

The environmental impact of forced displacement – settled and self-settled communities

Forced displacement can adversely impact ecological systems and the supply and quality of natural resources through the sudden influx of population in a host area (Martin, 2005). Degradation is most acute when displaced individuals first arrive in a host environment (Jacobsen, 1997). As the population increases – sometimes almost overnight – the resources, infrastructure, and institutions provided by host communities and relief agencies, such as the UNHCR, are insufficient for addressing the immediate needs of displaced persons and host communities.[4] In such scarce conditions, refugee populations will be forced to extract local resources to fulfill basic survival needs of water, shelter, and food (Jacobsen, 1997), consequently stressing local ecological systems (Oucho, 2007; Tafere, 2018). Overall, the large influx of displaced individuals to a host region, coupled with unsustainable practices by refugee and host communities over a prolonged period of time, can result in biodiversity loss, overextraction of water resources, soil erosion, land degradation, contamination of soil and water sources, increased indoor and outdoor air pollution, desertification, and the depletion of forests (Bernard, Aron, Loy, Muhamud, & Benard, 2020; Biswas & Tortajada-Quiroz, 1996; Imtiaz, 2018; Jaafar, Ahmad, Holtmeier, & King-Okumu, 2020; Oucho, 2007; Tafere, 2018; UNDP & UNEP, 2015; UNHCR, n.d.-a).

Studies have shown that the degree of environmental impact to a host country depends on the length of time refugees are displaced to an area, the size of the displaced population, the ratio of displaced to local people, the relationship between displaced individuals and host communities, the technology available to provide energy and construction materials, the nature of the local climate, and finally, the degree of international assistance for displaced persons and host countries (Black, 1994; Jacobsen, 1997; Oucho, 2007; Tafere, 2018). Large displaced populations (especially those in which the ratio of displaced persons is significantly higher than the host population) or refugee populations residing in protracted situations[5] are more likely to strain natural resource extraction in a host environment (Black, 1994). Additionally, tension and conflict between displaced individuals and host communities can increase the perceived competition for resources, hastening illegal or unsustainable resource extraction by local individuals (Allan, 1987; Berry, 2008; Martin, 2005). The infrastructure and layout of a settlement can also impact the rate of degradation (Jacobsen, 1997; UNHCR, n.d.-a, 2005). Close proximity to protected or vulnerable ecosystems increases the risk of irreversible harm and resource over-extraction in a region. Additionally, poor planning of roadways, settlements, and water and sanitation systems can lead to increased soil erosion, water pollution, and increased vulnerability to natural disasters.

One of the most influential factors in determining the scale and type of environmental impact is how refugees settle in a host country (Jacobsen, 1997; Oucho, 2007). When arriving in a host environment, refugees can either self-settle or be settled into a refugee camp. Self-settling is a process in which displaced persons settle among local community or informally occupy spaces as unregistered residents; aid from the local government and community is not guaranteed. Settled refugees, on the other hand, are displaced persons that are registered by the UNHCR and receive financial and/or resource assistance from the international organization (Jacobsen, 1997). Ultimately, this difference in resource provision for settled and self-settled populations can determine a displaced population's level of dependence on the natural resources of a host environment (Black, 1994).

The remainder of this section uses two case studies to illustrate the direct and indirect environmental impacts of settled and self-settled populations in a host region.

The environmental impact of settled camps

More than 6.6 million refugees and those in refuge-like situation live in camps, with 4.6 million residing in settled camps while 2 million reside in self-settled ones (UNHCR, n.d.-b), the ecological footprint of these camps can be significant. Settled camps may have higher environmental "start-up" costs than self-settled ones, as they require the clearing of terrain and the establishment of supportive infrastructure (roads, wells, hospitals, schools) for displaced communities (Jacobsen, 1997). Moreover, the high density of the population within camps can result in rapid land degradation through land cultivation, high levels of waste, and high levels of insecticide and pesticide use (Bernard et al., 2020; Imtiaz, 2018; Jacobsen, 1997; Oucho, 2007). Environmental degradation can also take place in protected areas in the direct vicinity of the camps as displaced communities move outside of camp boundaries to collect firewood and water, hunt bushmeat, and cultivate crops (Berry, 2008; Harper, 2016; Tafere, 2018).

A striking example of land and resource degradation surrounding settled camps is the degradation of protected forests in Tanzania during the conflicts in the Great Lakes region of Central Africa. Ethnic tension between the Tutsi and the Hutu forced refugees to flee from both the Burundian Civil War (1993–2006) and the Rwandan Genocide (1994). In a two-year time period, roughly 600,000 Burundian refugees relocated to Tanzania (Berry, 2008). The sudden onset of the Rwandan civil war resulted in an additional influx of a quarter-million Rwandans in a 24-hour time period (UNHCR, 2000). By 1995, settled refugees accounted for roughly 35% of the population in Kibondo (Veney, 2007, cited in Berry, 2008) and 39% in Ngara district (UNICEF, 2000).

Poor placement of the refugee camps, limited resources, and inadequate enforcement of protected forest boundaries resulted in severe environmental degradation. Despite the UNHCR's (2005) environmental guidelines to avoid placing refugees camps near fragile or protected areas, three out of four camps in Kibondo District were located within 15 km of forest reserves, with two camps only 500 meters away from reserve boundaries (Berry, 2008). The only provisions for shelter were plastic sheeting (UNHCR, 1997; Crisp, 2000). Food and water rations were insufficient to sustain refugee communities (UNHCR, 1997; Berry, 2008). As a result, refugees moved into protected reserves to ensure the provision of their basic needs. Despite the institutionalization of sustainable practices in protected areas (UNHCR, n.d.-a), limited program funding and the threat of conflict with refugees minimized the effectiveness of patrols around protected forest boundaries (Berry, 2008).

Areas surrounding refugee camps experienced bushfires; overuse and increased pollution of water resources; soil erosion; illegal harvesting of trees and forest resources; increases in diseases such as measles, malaria, dysentery, scabies, worms, and HIV/AIDS (Berry, 2008); and a 30% reduction of wild animal populations (Whitaker, 1999). The most severe forms of degradation in the area were deforestation and poaching (UNHCR, n.d.-a). Following the influx of refugees, Tanzania's wildlife population plummeted, resulting in a $100,000 loss of revenue for the local and central government, and roughly ten times that value for the country's private tourism industry (UNHCR, n.d.-a). The cost of rehabilitating Tanzania's Game Reserve population was $2.65 million. While the decline in wildlife was the result of both refugee and local community actions (Whitaker, 1999; Berry, 2008), the environmental degradation could have been largely avoided by placing the camps further from protected areas (UNHCR, n.d.-a).

The impact of self-settled individuals on host environments

Self-settled camps in rural and forest environments can result in similar patterns of environmental degradation to refugee camps, but at a lower magnitude (Jacobsen, 1997). Remote sensing imagery shows that self-settled population displacement can lead to a reduction of forest cover (Gorsevski et al., 2012) and overall biodiversity loss (Oucho, 2007) as populations move deeper into interior forests to escape conflict (Gorsevski et al., 2012; Nackoney et al., 2014). When population density is low and contamination of water and soil sources is minimal, the adverse environmental effects of self-settled camps in protected spaces can be reversible. Gorsevski *et al.* (2012), for example, found that over a ten-year time span, forest cover in South Sudan was partially regained following the return of displaced persons to their place of origin.

Self-settling can pose a unique environmental and development challenge. While refugees have greater flexibility in selecting locations and adopting more sustainable practices (Zetter, 1995; UNHCR, 2014), self-settled urban populations will most likely occupy high-risk, undesirable areas (ravines, hillside slopes, polluted areas); low-income, informal areas (slums); or public spaces such as squares or parks (UNHCR, n.d.-b, 2015a). As these informal settlements are formed without the involvement of the UNHCR or the host government, settlement layout and available resources are often inadequate, resulting in high concentrations of pollution and local resource extraction.

The majority of self-settled individuals relocate to urban spaces due to increased access to public services, greater economic opportunities, and an increased likelihood of supportive social tie networks (Brookings Institute, 2013). In fact, over 60% of refugees and 80% of IDPs reside in urban environments (Park, 2016). In low- and middle-income countries, the sudden increase in urban population density can exacerbate resource availability and strain public resource provision systems. For example, in 2014, Lebanon hosted 1.4 million refugees (MOE, EU, & UNDP, 2014). The population of displaced persons equated to 30% of the country's population, resulting in the highest concentration per capita of refugees in the world (Schlein, 2016). Seventy percent of the refugees lived below the poverty line, primarily clustered in low-income urban spaces or high-risk informal settlements at the outskirts of cities (MOE et al., 2014; Schlein, 2016). Following the refugee influx, urban population density in Lebanon increased 27%, resulting in stressed solid waste management systems and increased groundwater and land pollution, water stress, and air pollution (Jaafar et al., 2020; MOE et al., 2014). The estimated capital cost of addressing these environmental impacts is $3.43 billion (see Table 11.1).

Population displacement and the environment

Table 11.1 Human and ecological impacts of settled and self-settled refugees in Lebanon

	Human/Ecological System Impact	Abatement Strategy	Capital Cost (in Millions USD)	Operation & Management Costs
Solid waste management (SWM)	(1) Increased littering and contamination of land, soil, water, and groundwater by solid waste – 18% increase in infectious waste in environment – 52% increase in illegal dumping (2) Overstressing existing SWM systems – An additional 15.7% of solid waste generated by refugees	(1) Expansion of SWM infrastructure (2) Cleanup of land and water solid waste contamination	131.1	57.6
Water and Wastewater (WW) management	(1) Depletion of water resources – National water demand increased by 8%–12% (2) Deteriorating water quality – 63% of tested boreholes contaminated by fecal coliforms (3) Stressed WW management systems – WW generation increased 8%–14% – 40,000 tons of waste water pollution/year	(1) Expanding water infrastructure (storage, transmission, and distribution) systems (2) Improving water quality (3) Expansion of WW collection and treatment	1,287.3	Unknown
Air Quality	(1) Worsening air quality from increased transportation (2) Increased energy demand and strain on national electricity production (3) Increased pollution from residential heating Combined effect: 20% increase in emission of air pollutants	(1) Expansion of public transportation and mass transport systems (2) Meeting energy demands – changing fuel types, rehabilitating power plants, strengthening electrical network	1,986.8	139.0

(Continued)

Table 11.1 (Continued)

	Human/Ecological System Impact	Abatement Strategy	Capital Cost (in Millions USD)	Operation & Management Costs
		(3) Switching to bioenergy for residential heating		
Land Use and Ecosystems Health	(1) Informal settlement in high-risk areas (2) Deforestation and depletion of forest resources	(1) Managing informal settlement encroachment on agricultural and flood prone areas (2) Providing alternative fuel sources before winter	16.0	78.5
Total Cost			**3,421.2**	**275.1**

Table 11.1 shows the impact of refugees on human and ecological systems in Lebanon, the abatement strategies proposed by the Lebanese government to address these impacts, and the capital and operation & management costs (in millions of dollars) of abatement (adapted from (MOE et al., 2014).

A key concern of the Lebanese government and relief agencies has been managing the cost of increased public service and resource demands in a country where 40% of citizens face abject poverty (Schlein, 2016). The strain on resources and infrastructure systems has created tensions between local host communities and the displaced population. Moreover, the refugee crisis in Lebanon highlights the need for greater intervention in the design and placement of self-settled communities (UNHCR, 2014). In 2014, the government of Lebanon identified 45 vulnerable informal settlements (occupying 8.6% of the national territory). Located in flood plains and near agricultural plots, these settlements endangered both local and refugee well-being through increased vulnerability to natural hazards and the potential contamination of food and water resources (MOE et al., 2014).

As seen in Tanzania and Lebanon, self-settled and settled displaced populations can – directly or indirectly – lead to a number of adverse environmental consequences, including reduction of forest cover; biodiversity loss; pollution of air, land, and water resources; and increased health hazards. This degradation not only impacts the socioeconomic welfare of host communities but also worsens the livelihood of the refugees themselves (UNHCR, n.d.-a): decreased water quality will increase the risk of diseases in formal and informal settlements; deforestation rates can threaten the safety of women and children, who must walk further distances to acquire firewood (Shepherd, 1995); and decreased environmental quality of a region can incite conflict between refugees and host communities, spurring an additional wave of displacement (Martin, 2005). While some environmental harm is reversible (see Gorsevski et al., 2012), for low-income host communities with immediate needs and limited resources, abatement is costly. Preventing and minimizing these impacts will require an understanding of the trade-offs faced by displaced populations, host governments, and relief agencies during times of conflict and displacement.

The next section, therefore, examines the key economic, institutional, and social challenges of mitigating and abating the environmental impacts of forced displacement.

Challenges of addressing environmental impacts of displaced populations

A thorough literature review revealed three interrelated challenges of mitigating environmental effects of displacements: temporal constraints, funding limitations, and the complexity of coordinating multiple local and regional actors. Each challenge is described briefly below.

Short- and long-term temporal constraints

Two temporal constraints play a critical role in the ability of host governments to mitigate displacement-driven environmental degradation. The first is the need to provide relief and resources to large populations in a short period of time. During a sudden influx of mass migration, facilities and camps are set up quickly in emergency conditions, limiting opportunities for proper planning or environmental impact assessment (EIA) (Jacobsen, 1997; Kakonge, 2000). Location of campsites is based on security of political considerations (access to resources, ease of delivery, and minimization of conflict with host governments and communities), rather than environmental ones (Kakonge, 2000; Martin et al., 2017). For instance, Martin *et al.* (2017) argue that for political reasons, Aysaita camp in Ethiopia and Ali Addeh camp in Djibouti were placed in "environmentally-hostile, arid locations with minimal vegetation and variable access to sufficient water, particularly for livestock and growing vegetables" (p. 1). The insufficient assessment and knowledge of the environment in camp design can strain long-term resource availability and quality. Failure to consider groundwater replenishment when boring wells can drain aquifers and the failure to establish proper waste disposal practices can rapidly contaminate and deplete existing water sources (Hoerz, 1995, cited in Jacobsen, 1997).

The second facet is the long-term nature of displacement. Typically, displaced populations will only return to their home countries when the original cause of displacement is removed and economic opportunities and prospects of livelihood (provision of amenities such as water, medical aid, education, food, shelter) are better than or equal to the host location (UNEP, 2007). Moreover, displaced populations can only return when there is an opportunity for safe and affordable passage to their location of origin. Meeting these conditions requires a significant investment of resources, time, and coordination in the peacebuilding process. As a result, at the end of 2019, nearly 16 million people (roughly 78% of all refugees) under UNHCR's mandate were in a protracted situation (UNHCR, 2020c), with each situation lasting on average 26 years (UNHCR, 2015b). The majority of these 32 situations are found in the world's poorest and most conflict-ridden regions (Loescher et al., 2007).

Ultimately, these short- and long-term facets of displacement in fragile regions can strain international and host country funding, increase the likelihood of inefficiency, and lead to national- or local-level conflict.

Funding limitations

A key limitation in managing environmental impacts is funding mechanisms. For national non-government organizations and international relief agencies, funding – often collected in real time – is borrowed with the intent of repayment via fundraising campaigns. The current costs to meet refugee needs, however, still exceed available resources. Since 1994, the average annual per-capita cost for refugee support is approximately $220 to $270, a cost that barely covers basic needs for shelter, food, and fuel (UNHCR, n.d.-a).

In 2020–2021, the UNHCR required $8.633 billion to meet the needs of all displaced populations (UNHCR, 2020d). The income of the international agency was $4.283 billion, leaving a $4.353 billion (or 50.4%) funding gap. The international organization is entirely dependent on voluntary contributions (UNHCR, 2017b), with 89% of the financing coming from governments and the European Union and 8% from private donors (UNHCR, 2020d). While donor contributions have doubled since 2009, the donations have been insufficient for closing the funding gap (UNHCR, 2016).

The available funding is prioritized for fulfilling the basic needs of refugees, empowering communities of displaced persons, and promoting economic self-reliance (UNHCR, 2017b); as a result, financial constraints prevent the full realization of environmental management projects (Berry, 2008) and the implementation of sustainable management practices. Thus, while the UNHCR (n.d.-a, 2015a, 2016) has acknowledged the direct connection between sustainable environmental practices and the well-being of displaced populations, economic limitations and weak institutional enforcement of host communities[6] ultimately force humanitarian agencies to pursue a reactive – rather than a preemptive – environmental management approach (Berry, 2008; Harper, 2016; Jacobsen, 1997; Price, 2017; Tafere, 2018).

Coordination of multiple actors: inefficiency and the risk of additional conflict

The high number of actors involved – refugees, refugee origin states, relief agencies such as the UNHCR, the host state (Bariagaber, 1999), local actors (Crisp, 2000; Martin, 2005), and local and international nongovernmental organizations (UNHCR, 2005) – can not only lead to a more complex decision-making process but also spark or renew conflicts. The presence of multiple actors scrambling to meet the needs of vulnerable populations in emergency conditions can result in the duplication of mitigation strategies by multiple local groups (UNEP & UNHCR, 2000). As resources and expertise are siloed, this duplication results in strategies that are less effective in addressing the resource needs of displaced populations and in the enforcement of environmental guidelines.

The resource needs of displaced populations over a prolonged period of time can increase tension between host governments, refugees, and relief agencies. Host countries have the dual challenge of planning and providing for their own citizens and the long-term settlement (formal or informal) of a displaced population. Host countries, especially those with limited resources, feel obligated to provide for their own citizens. A sense of self-preservation, therefore, may lead a host country to either deny entry to thousands of refugees or view the actions of humanitarian agencies like the UNHCR as a threat to their economic and political security interests (Bariabager, 1999; Kirui & Mwaruvie, 2012). Such tensions may reduce overall cooperation between host governments and relief agencies, resulting in poor implementation and enforcement of environmental regulations and guidelines.

Resource needs can also increase tensions between local and host communities, especially when local communities believe that relief agencies prioritize the well-being of refugees over the local population. These perceived inequalities in resource access, combined with ethnic differences between displaced populations and local communities, can yield "unproductive conflict" or conflict that leads to noncooperative outcomes (Martin, 2005). In Kenya's Dadaab refugee camps, the provision of food, social services, and medical attention to refugees – resources that the local population could not afford – led to the resentment of the refugees despite both the host and refugee population being of Somali origin (Kirui & Mwaruvie, 2012). Similar conflicts have been documented globally for high-poverty regions that are in close proximity to refugee camps. This tension can ultimately result in the degradation of the local environment (Tafere, 2018). The presence of the refugees can produce a tragedy of the commons situation (Martin, 2005) in which local communities extract resources at an unsustainable rate to compensate for the "milk and honey" (i.e., the relief aid) received by refugees (Kirui & Mwaruvie, 2012, p. 164).

Policy, technology, and infrastructure recommendations

Mitigating the adverse environmental effects of degradation will require addressing feedbacks between environmental and human systems. This approach requires a long-term systems perspective in displacement policy and settlement design. In other words, international and national decisions must weigh the immediate benefits to refugees relative to long-term social, environmental, and political impacts. This section provides policy, technology, infrastructure, and system management strategy recommendations that address the challenges of mitigating the direct and indirect environmental impacts of population displacement.

Institutionalizing sustainable behaviors and practices

Effective management of resources and human well-being requires the institutionalization of environmental protection (Martin et al., 2017; UNHCR, 2014). Thus, national and local host governments must adopt regulatory measures that promote monitoring and enforcement of protected areas (Gorsevski et al., 2012), devalue protected bushmeat in local markets, (de Morode et al., 2007), provide sufficient water and sanitation resources (UNEP & UNHCR, 2000), and establish quantifiable environmental quality standards (rates of deforestation, levels of pollutants in soil and water levels, etc.). Additionally, international and national policies and conventions must be updated to include remedial and mitigation measures for environmental factors (UNEP & UNHCR, 2000).

Host governments and international agencies will also have to work directly with affected populations to ensure provision of resources and needs while minimizing long-term impact to the environment. To minimize the peak activities of environmental degradation, displaced populations must be provided with environmental guidelines and training on sustainable practices at the point of arrival into host communities (UNEP & UNHCR, 2000). Nongovernment organizations, relief agencies, and host governments can work with displaced populations to establish ecologically appropriate water management and agricultural practices[7] – can ensure the sustainable provision of resources (Hoerz, 1995, cited in Jacobsen, 1997; UNEP & UNHCR, 2000). Implementing these practices will require strengthening the coordination links between international agencies, NGO organizations, and local governments; active collaboration between the various actors can ultimately minimize duplication of relief and environmental management programs (UNEP & UNHCR, 2000; Oucho, 2007).

Tailored solutions – Environmental Impact Assessment (EIA), local knowledge, and technical approaches

With mass displacement happening in almost all regions of the world, and the inherent complexity of the refugee crises, a one-size-fits-all solution would not prove viable. Strategies for mitigating adverse environmental impacts of both large-scale migration and the protracted stay of refugees must be tailored to the local economic, political, and environmental context (Kibreab, 1997; Martin et al., 2017). The placement of settled camps and the types of intervention in informal settlements should be determined by not only the availability and quality of environmental resources but also the potential local and systemwide feedbacks between ecological and human health. Thus, there is a need for not only an EIA (Kakonge, 2000; Martin et al., 2017; Oucho, 2007; Price, 2017) but also incorporating local knowledge and expertise when selecting locations for refugee camps (UNEP & UNHCR, 2000). Collection of baseline data and follow-up assessment of environmental quality in settled and self-settled regions can allow for rapid responses to localized environmental degradation. Local knowledge can assist relief agencies in understanding the needs of and potential opportunities for refugees (Jacobsen & Fratzke, 2016); moreover, knowledge of topography and seasonal climate variations can decrease the ecological and human risks that emerge from poor site placement or camp design.

Technology can also assist in providing tailored solutions to environmental and human concerns in camps and self-settled populations. For instance, drone mapping, remote sensing, and three-dimensional modeling software allow planners to anticipate where water would collect in settlement sites (Luege, 2016) or can assist organizations in identifying sources of water supply, such as ground hole bore sites (Wendt et al., 2015); understanding the flow of water during natural disasters and high rain weather will minimize the contamination of water systems from overflowing latrines or other solid waste pollutants (Luege, 2016). Geospatial statistical analysis can also be used to uncover security and environmental concerns within refugee camps (Pierson, 2013). This mixed method approach would allow aid workers to flag rapidly expanding or high-density population clusters within camps and to monitor changes in environmental conditions in response to these population spikes. These geospatial methods can ultimately allow for effective resource allocation and rapid intervention strategies that are specific to each settlement community (Martin et al., 2017).

Increasing self-sufficiency and promoting a sense of community

Reducing ecological impacts of refugee displacement requires identifying effective and sustainable alternatives to settled camps for refugees (Martin et al., 2017). Camps are an "essential part of UNHCR's operational response" and facilitate the rapid provision of protection and supplies to displaced populations (UNHCR, 2014, p. 4). However, there is growing recognition that within refugee camps, displaced persons have limited economic and social opportunities – displaced populations receive limited protection by host governments, have limited freedom of movement in host countries, and lack employment and property rights (Kibreab, 1997; UNHCR, 2014). These restrictions force displaced populations to rely heavily on relief aid, placing a significant strain on national and international funding mechanisms. Increasing self-sufficiency of displaced populations can reduce the funding pressure on host governments and relief agencies. Self-sufficiency and coordinated efforts that build a sense of community can also reduce conflict between displaced populations and host communities. The dependence on international aid can heighten tensions between refugees and host populations (Martin, 2005); additionally, an inadequate provision of relief resources will force displaced populations to pursue environmentally degrading informal economic activities such as poaching (Berry, 2008), further inciting the risk of conflict between refugee and host communities.

Camp design of settled and self-settled spaces is a critical component of achieving self-sufficiency (UNEP & UNHCR, 2000). As the issue of displacement is a long-term one, settlement design must move away from the haphazard structures of temporary relief settlements. Instead, settlements must be envisioned as close-knit residential communities that can support large, self-sufficient populations for prolonged periods of time (Chamma & Arroyo, 2016; UNHCR, 2017a). To reduce dependence on food aid, refugees within camp settlements and self-settled spaces must be allocated agricultural plots and trained in subsistence farming agricultural practices (UNEP & UNHCR, 2000).

Additionally, to empower communities, displaced populations must be able to provide input or directly change day-to-day camp operations. A recent example of this phenomenon is Jordan's Zaatari camp. The camp was initially established in 2012 as a spontaneous emergency camp for Syrian refugees and rapidly expanded to host 80,000 displaced individuals by 2013 (Chamma & Arroyo, 2016). Given the rapid rate of expansion, the camp structure evolved more organically, with refugees setting up tents, shelters, and activities in areas that suited their own needs. While the informal expansion of the camp increased tension and conflict within camp boundaries,[8] the process also led to the formation of a market of roughly 3,000 refugee-operated shops and businesses in the camp center (Refugee International, 2016). The market allows for the provision of resources and sources of income (thus reducing reliance on international funding and the local environment) and serves as a source of "dignity, ownership, and pride" (Refugee International, 2016). The UNHCR has already begun formally experimenting with this new approach to settled refugee spaces: in Ethiopia, a pilot project in the rapidly expanding Dollo Ado refugee camp integrated a street grid format which included schools, water distribution points, markets, and health posts. In designing the new layout, the UNHCR staff coordinated directly with refugees to identify their pressing needs and "housing solutions that would be better suited to their lifestyles" (UNHCR, 2017a).

Another key element of increasing self-sufficiency is increasing the opportunities for cooperation and mediation between displaced populations and local communities (Martin et al., 2017; Smith et al., 2019). This collaboration requires improving channels of communication between funders, stakeholders, refugees, and local community members (Smith et al., 2019) to develop a shared interest and a shared identity between refugees and host communities (Conca & Wallace, 2009). Relief agencies and local governments should strive to develop joint development programs that seek to provide resources that benefit both local communities and refugee populations (Walton, 2012). Additionally, the establishment of joint environmental programs can promote cooperation and encourage accountability in resource management. For example, following rising tensions between host communities and settled refugees in Tanzania, village and refugee leaders, UNHCR staff, camp officials, and Ministry of Home affairs staff attended "good neighbor meetings" to develop mutually agreed upon guidelines for sharing and sustainably using local resources (Berry, 2008). To promote long-term cooperation, these programs should promote a flexible, "inclusive, and open process" (Martin, 2005, p. 341) of mediation that can capture the changing needs of both refugee and host populations.

Conclusion

This chapter examined the link between conflict-driven displacement and the environment; the large influx of populations for prolonged periods of time can – directly or indirectly – result in a number of adverse environmental effects, including deforestation, desertification, contamination of soil and water resources, the shifting of disease vectors, the depletion of aquifers, and increased air pollution. Funding limitations and the tensions between affected actors (relief agencies, the host government, nongovernment organizations) ultimately result in a reactive, rather than a preemptive, management approach to this degradation. Institutionalizing sustainable practices within settled and self-settled settings, contextualizing relief aid approaches to environmental conditions, and increasing self-sufficiency of displaced populations can address the challenges of mitigating displacement-driven environmental degradation.

Given the growing precarious situation of refugees and host countries, the importance of addressing environmental degradation and implementing sustainable practices is higher than ever. The global population crisis is at an all-time high. Vulnerable countries continue to have population influx from neighboring regions facing wars, ethnic conflict, or natural disasters. For instance, as we enter the tenth year of the Syrian refugee crises – the largest population displacement crises of our time with more than 5.6 million refugees and 6.1 million internally displaced people (Siegfreid, 2020) – the social, economic, and ecological impacts of this upheaval are still unknown.

It is important to note that the economic, social, political, and environmental pressure of displacement on host governments is only expected to increase in the future due to climate change effects and population growth. Climate change is expected to not only increase the frequency and magnitude of natural disasters but also intensify food and water scarcity (IPCC, 2014, 2018). The ability to adapt to these effects is unequal; low- and middle-income countries, particularly those already experiencing conflict or at risk of entering into conflict, are the most vulnerable to natural disaster events (iDMC, 2016). Coupled with the increased competition for resources as a result of population growth, climate change is expected to displace millions individuals. In fact, climate-driven displacement is already underway. Since 2008, an average of 26.4 million people have been displaced by natural disasters; this is equivalent to roughly one person being displaced every second (Yonetani, 2015). The World Bank estimates that, by 2050, Latin America, sub-Saharan Africa, and Southeast Asia will generate 143 million climate migrants (Rigaud et al., 2018).

Climate change and population growth will also create additional challenges in ensuring the well-being of displaced populations. For instance, since 2017, Bangladesh has faced a massive socioeconomic challenge of providing for the influx of more than 740,000 Rohingya people from neighboring Myanmar (Chan, Chiu, & Chan, 2018; UNHCR, 2020e). The government is struggling to provide for the rapidly growing number of refugees while refugees and host populations are struggling to overcome the wide cultural gap between the two communities (Sáez, 2018). The well-being and security of refugees are additionally threatened by flooding from monsoons and water-borne illnesses (CARE, 2018). Between May and July 2020, windstorms, heavy rains, landslide and soil erosion, and flooding have impacted more than 20,000 households in the camps (Relief Web, 2020). Reducing the risk of conflict and secondary conflict-driven displacement, thus, requires increasing the resilience of vulnerable communities to the effects of climate change and to the socioeconomic costs of hosting displaced individuals. Moreover, the increasing frequency of disaster-driven displacement requires the reconsideration of the rights and relief provided to refugees under the 1951 Convention (UNHCR, 2017c). Future research and international efforts should strive to determine the role of national and international relief in the protection of environmental refugees and IDPs.

Ultimately, it is imperative to establish sustainable practices for settled and self-settled displaced populations. Failure to address the challenge of mitigating the effects of disaster- and conflict-driven displacement can have irreversible effects on human and ecological systems.

Notes

1 The United Nations 1951 Convention Relating to the Status of Refugees and its 1967 Protocol defines a refugee as "someone who is unable or unwilling to return to their country of origin owing to a well-founded fear of being persecuted for reasons of race, religion, nationality, membership of a particular

social group, or political opinion" (p. 3). At the end of 2019, 20.4 million people were legally protected as refugees under UNHCR mandate. An additional 5.6 million Palestinian refugees received assistance and protection from the United National Relief and Work Agency (UNRWA) (UNHCR, 2020a).

2 Internally displaced persons (IDPs) are displaced individuals who are forced to flee their homes but do not cross international borders.

3 An individual seeking asylum is one who is applying for "the right to be recognized as a refugee and to receive legal protection and material assistance" (UNHCR 2020a) from relief agencies. The asylum seekers must demonstrate that he or she has fled violent conflict and persecution in his or her home country.

4 The UNHCR has set quantifiable goals for food, water, sanitation, and fuel provision in refugee camps. However, funding and infrastructure limitations prevent the relief agency from meeting these targets (Bruijn 2009). For example, the UNHCR standard for per capita daily food provision is 2,000 kilocalories. Yet, shortages of food in camps, particularly those in Sub-Saharan Africa, have resulted in camp malnutrition rates of 15% or more. For water and sanitation, the UNHCR requires a daily per capita of safe drinking water of at least 20 liters that water sources should be located a maximum of 200 meters from refugee camps and that there should be 20 or fewer people for each latrine. However, studies have shown that 40% of camps failed to provide an adequate water supply (Cronin *et al.* 2008), and 14%–28% of camps were unable able to meet the mandated distance for water sources (Bruijn 2009). Similarly, three-quarters of the camps did not meet the latrine requirements, resulting in an increased risk of waste contamination in the camps (Cronin *et al.* 2008).

5 The UNHCR (2016) defines a protracted refugee situation as "one in which 25,000 or more refugees from the same nationality have been in exile for five consecutive years or more in an asylum country" (p. 22).

6 Tafere (2018), for example, examined the environmental strategies and policies of Ethiopia, Kenya, Rwanda, Sudan, and Uganda for hosting displaced populations. The five countries host a total of 6.98 million sheltered persons in more than 57 refugee and IDP camps. The study found that the countries lacked the proper monitoring and enforcement mechanisms to implement environmental policies.

7 For example, one strategy is to work with communities to identify locations that reduce the likelihood of soil erosion, runoff, and the exacerbation of vulnerable ecological areas. Similarly, implementing small-scale irrigation techniques for subsistence farming can increase agricultural productivity and increase climate resilience by reducing local dependence on rainfall (UNEP & UNHCR, 2000).

8 During the expansion of Zaatari, several neighborhoods came under the control of quasi-mafia groups, inciting violence within camp settings (Refugee International, 2016).

Works cited

Allan, N. J. R. (1987). Impact of Afghan Refugees on the vegetation resources of Pakistan's Hindukush-Himalaya. *Mountain Research and Development, 7*(3), 200–204.

Bariagaber, A. (1999). States, international organisations and the refugee: Reflections on the complexity of managing the refugee crisis in the Horn of Africa. *The Journal of Modern African Studies, 37*(4), 597–619.

Bernard, B., Aron, M., Loy, T., Muhamud, N. W., & Benard, S. (2020). The impact of refugee settlements on land use changes and vegetation degradation in West Nile Sub-region, Uganda. *Geocarto International,* 1–19.

Berry, L. (2008). The impact of environmental degradation on refugee-host relations: A case study from Tanzania. *Research Paper No. 151.* UN Refugee Agency UNHCR. Retrieved November 1, 2017, from www.unhcr.org/47a315c72.pdf

Biswas, A. K., & Tortajada-Quiroz, H. C. (1996). Environmental impacts of the Rwandan refugees on Zaire. *Ambio, 25*(6), 403–408.

Black, R. (1994). Forced migration and environmental change: The impact of refugees on host environments. *Journal of Environmental Management, 42,* 261–277.

Brookings Institute. (2013). *Under the Radar: Internally displaced persons in non-camp settings.* Retrieved from www.brookings.edu/wp-content/uploads/2016/06/Under-the-radarIDPs-outside-of-camps-Oct-2013.pdf

Bruijn, B. (2009). *The living conditions and well-being of refugees.* United Nations Development Programme. Human Development Research Paper 2009/25.

CARE. (2018, April 30). *100,000 refugees at risk of landslides and flood in Monsoon, warns CARE.* Retrieved May 14, 2018, from www.care-international.org/news/press-releases/100000-refugees-at-risk-of-landslides-and-flood-in-monsoon-warns-care

Chamma, N., & Arroyo, C. M. (2016). *Rethinking refugee camp design: From "temporary" camps to sustainable settlements.* Paper presented at the Architecture in Emergency: Re-thinking the Refugee Crisis, Istanbul, Turkey.

Chan, E. Y., Chiu, C. P., & Chan, G. K. (2018). Medical and health risks associated with communicable diseases of Rohingya refugees in Bangladesh 2017. *International Journal of Infectious Diseases, 68,* 39–43.

Cohen, R., & Deng, F. M. (2008). Mass displacement caused by conflicts and one-sided violence: National and international responses. *SIPRI Yearbook,* 15.

Conca, K., & Wallace, J. (2009). Environment and peacebuilding in war-torn societies: Lessons from the UN Environment Programme's experience with postconflict assessment. *Global Governance, 15*(4), 485–504.

Crisp, J. (2000). Africa's refugees: Patterns, problems, and policy challenges. *Journal of Contemporary African Studies, 18*(2), 157–178.

Cronin, A. A., Shrestha, D., Cornier, N., Abdalla, F., Ezard, N., & Aramburu, C. (2008). A review of water and sanitation provision in refugee camps in association with selected health and nutrition indicators – the need for integrated service provision. *Journal of Water and Health, 6*(1).

de Morode, E., Smith, K. H., Homewood, K., Pettifor, R., Rowcliffe,. M., & Cowlishaw, G. (2007). The impact of armed conflict on protected-area efficacy in Central Africa. *Biology Letters, 3*(3). https://doi.org/10.1098/rsbl.2007.0010

Gomez, M. P., & Christensen, A. (2010). *The impacts of refugees on neighboring countries: A development challenge.* World Development Report 2011 Background Note. Washington, DC: World Bank.

Gorsevski, V., Kasischke, E., Dempewolf, J., Loboda, T., & Grossmann, F. (2012). Analysis of the impacts of armed conflict on the Eastern Afromontane forest region on the South Sudan – Uganda border using multitemporal Landsat imagery. *Remote Sensing of Environment, 118,* 10–20.

Hagenlocher, M., Lang, S., & Tiede, D. (2012). Integrated assessment of the environmental impact of an IDP camp in Sudan based on very high resolution multi-temporal satellite imagery. *Remote Sensing of Environment, 126,* 27–38.

Harper, A. (2016, December 10). A critical time for refugees and their environment (again). *UNHCR Innovation.* Retrieved October 10, 2020, from www.unhcr.org/innovation/critical-time-refugees-environment/

Imtiaz, S. (2018). Ecological impact of Rohingya refugees on forest resources: Remote sensing analysis of vegetation cover change in Teknaf Peninsula in Bangladesh. *Ecocycles, 4*(1) https://doi.org/10.19040/ecocycles.v4i1.89

Intergovernmental Panel on Climate Change (IPCC). (2018). *Global warming of 1.5°C. An IPCC special report on the impacts of global warming of 1.5°C above pre-industrial levels and related global greenhouse gas emission pathways, in the context of strengthening the global response to the threat of climate change, sustainable development, and efforts to eradicate poverty* [Masson-Delmotte, V., P. Zhai, H.-O. Pörtner, D. Roberts, J. Skea, P. R. Shukla, A. Pirani, W. Moufouma-Okia, C. Péan, R. Pidcock, S. Connors, J. B. R. Matthews, Y. Chen, X. Zhou, M. I. Gomis, E. Lonnoy, T. Maycock, M. Tignor, and T. Waterfield (Eds.)]. Retrieved from https://www.ipcc.ch/sr15/

Intergovernmental Panel on Climate Change (IPCC). (2014). *Climate change 2014: Impacts, adaptation, and vulnerability. Part A: Global and sectoral aspects. Contribution of working group II to the fifth assessment report of the intergovernmental panel on climate change* [C. B. Field, V. R. Barros, D. J. Dokken, K. J. Mach, M. D. Mastrandrea, T. E. Bilir, M. Chatterjee, K. L. Ebi, Y. O. Estrada, R. C. Genova, B. Girma, E. S. Kissel, A. N. Levy, S. MacCracken, P. R. Mastrandrea, and L. L. White (Eds.)].Cambridge, UK and New York, NY, USA: Cambridge University Press.

Internal Displacement Monitoring Centre (iDMC). (2016). *Global report on internal displacement.* Geneva, Switzerland: Norwegian Refugee Council.

Jaafar, H., Ahmad, F., Holtmeier, L., & King-Okumu, C. (2020). Refugees, water balance, and water stress: Lessons learned from Lebanon. *Ambio, 49*(6), 1179–1193.

Jacobsen, K. (2001). The forgotten solution: Local integration for refugees in developing countries. Working paper No. 45. *New Issues in Refugee Research.* UNHCR. Retrieved November 7, 2017, from www.unhcr.org/3b7d24059.pdf

Jacobsen, K. (1997). Refugees' environmental impact: The effect of patterns of settlement. *Journal of Refugee Studies, 10*(1), 19–36.

Jacobsen, K., & Fratzke, S. (2016). *Building livelihood opportunities for refugee populations: Lessons from past practice.* Washington, DC: Migration Policy Institute.

Kakonge, J. O. (2000). A review of refugee environmental-oriented projects in Africa: A case for environmental impact assessment. *Impact Assessment and Project Appraisal, 18*(1), 23–32.

Kibreab, G. (1997). Environmental causes and impact of refugee movements: A critique of the current debate. *Disasters, 21*(1), 20–38.

Kirui, P., & Mwaruvie, J. (2012). The dilemma of hosting refugees: A focus on the insecurity in North-Eastern Kenya. *International Journal of Business and Social Science, 3*(8), 161–171.

Rigaud, K. K., de Sherbinin, A., Jones, B., Bergmann, J., Clement, V., Ober, K., . . . Midgley, A. (2018). *Groundswell: Preparing for internal climate migration.* Washington, DC: World Bank.

Linscher, S. K. (2009). Causes and consequences of conflict-induced displacement. *Civil Wars, 9*(2), 142–155.

Loescher, G., Milner, J., Newman, E., & Troeller, G. (2007). Protracted refugee situations and the regional dynamics of peacebuilding. *Conflict, Security & Development, 7*(3), 491–501.

Luege, T. (2016). How drones can help improve refugee camps. *CartoBlog.* Retrieved January 10, 2017, from http://blog.cartong.org/2016/11/16/how-drones-can-help-improve-refugee-camps/

Martin, A. (2005). Environmental conflict between refugee and host communities. *Journal of Peace Research, 42*(3), 329–346. Retrieved from www.jstor.org/stable/30042304

Martin, S. F., Howard, D. A., Smith, L., Yossinger, N. S., Kinne, S., & Giordano, M. (2017). *Environmental resource management in refugee camps and surrounding areas: Lessons learned and best practices.* Georgetown University Walsh.

Ministry of Environment (MOE), Republic of Lebanon | EU | UNDP. (2014). *Lebanon environmental impact assessment of the Syrian conflict & priority interventions.* Retrieved November 1, 2017, from www.undp.org/content/dam/lebanon/docs/Energy%20and%20Environment/Publications/EASC-WEB.pdf

Nackoney, J. Molinario, G., Potapov, P., Turubanova, S., Hansen, M. C., & Furuichi, T. (2014). Impacts of civil conflict on primary forest habitat in northern Democratic Republic of Congo, 1990–2010. *Biological Conservation, 170,* 321–328.

Oucho, J. O. (2007). *Environmental impact of refugees and internally displaced person in Sub-Saharan Africa.* Keynote Address to the African Migration Alliance Biennial Workshop on Climate Change, Environment and Migration, East London, South Africa, November 15–16, 2007.

Park, H. (2016, November 25). The power of cities. *UNHCR Innovation.* Retrieved October 10, 2020, from www.unhcr.org/innovation/the-power-of-cities/

Pierson, L. (2013). Environmental geospatial statistics of Zaatari refugee camp. *Statistics Views.* Retrieved January 10, 2017, from www.statisticsviews.com/details/feature/5322231/Environmental-Geospatial-Statistics-of-Zaatari-Refugee-Camp.html

Price, R. (2017). *Environmental impact assessments in refugee crises.* Brighton, UK: Institute of Development Studies.

Refugee International. (2016). The difference a market makes: The case of Syrian refugee camps in Jordan. *Refugees International.* Retrieved January 10, 2017, from www.refugeesinternational.org/blog/2016/03/16/market

Relief Web. (2020). *Impact of the monsoon & COVID-19 containment measures.* Shelter and infrastructure damage in the Rohingya refugee camps. Site management sector Cox's bazar, Shelter/NFI Sector, Analysis Hub. Retrieved October 11, 2020, from https://reliefweb.int/sites/reliefweb.int/files/resources/20200820_acaps_report_impact_of_the_monsoon_covid-19_containment_measures.pdf

Sáez, L. (2018). Bangladesh in 2017: Bloggers, floods, and refugees. *Asian Survey, 58*(1), 127–133.

Schlein, L. (2016). Large Syrian refugee population in Lebanon sparks social tensions. *Voanews.* Retrieved December 14, 2017, from www.voanews.com/a/lebanon-syrian-refugees/3625462.html

Shepherd, G. (1995). *The impact of refugees on the environment and appropriate responses.* ODI HPN. Retrieved November 1, 2017, from http://odihpn.org/magazine/the-impact-of-refugees-on-the-environment-and-appropriate-responses/

Siegfried, K. (2020, March 11). The refugee brief –March 11, 2020. *UNHCR Refugee Brief.* Retrieved October 10, 2020, from www.unhcr.org/refugeebrief/the-refugee-brief-11-march-2020/

Smith, L., Howard, D. A., Giordano, M., Yossinger, N. S., Kinne, L., & Martin, S. F. (2019). Local integration and shared resource management in protracted refugee camps: Findings from a study in the horn of Africa. *Journal of Refugee Studies.* https://doi.org/10.1093/jrs/fez010

Stewart, F. (2002). Root causes of violent conflict in developing countries. *BMJ, 324,* 342–345.

Tafere, M. (2018). Forced displacements and the environment: Its place in national and international climate agenda. *Journal of Environmental Management*, *224*, 191–201. https://doi.org/10.1016/j.jenvman.2018.07.063

UNDP & UNEP. (2015). *Rapid Assessment of the Impact of the Syrian Refugee Influx on the Environment in Jordan*. Nairobi, Kenya: United Nations Environment Programme.

UNEP (2007). *Sudan – Post-conflict environmental assessment*. Nairobi, Kenya: United Nations Environment Programme.

UNEP. (2011). *Livelihood security: Climate change, migration and conflict in the Sahel*. Nairobi, Kenya: United Nations Environment Programme.

UNEP & UNHCR. (2000). *Report of the brainstorming on environmental impact of refugee settlement and flows in Africa 14–15 September 2000*. UN Compound, Gigiri, Nairobi, Kenya. Retrieved November 7, 2017, from http://ec.europa.eu/echo/files/evaluation/watsan2005/annex_files/UNEP/UNEP1%20-%20Environmental%20impact%20of%20refugees%20settlement%20and%20flows.pdf

UNHCR. (2020a). *Figures at a Glance*. UNHCR: The UN Refugee Agency. Retrieved October 15, 2020, from www.unhcr.org/en-us/figures-at-a-glance.html

UNHCR. (2020b). *Refugee statistics*. UNHCR: The UN Refugee Agency. Retrieved October 15, 2020, from www.unrefugees.org/refugee-facts/statistics

UNHCR. (2020c). *Protracted refugee situations explained*. Retrieved October 10, 2020, from www.unrefugees.org/news/protracted-refugee-situations-explained/

UNHCR. (2020d). UNHCR's 2020–2021 Financial Requirements. *Overview*. Retrieved October 10, 2020, from https://reporting.unhcr.org/sites/default/files/ga2020/pdf/Chapter_Financial.pdf

UNHCR. (2020e). Rohingya refugee response – Bangladesh. *Factsheet – Projection*. Retrieved October 11, 2020, from https://reliefweb.int/sites/reliefweb.int/files/resources/78231.pdf

UNHCR. (2017a). *Camps*. UNHCR. Retrieved December 15, 2017, from www.unrefugees.org/refugee-facts/camps/

UNHCR. (2017b). *Global appeal: 2017 update. Precarious futures, shared responsibilities*. Geneva, Switzerland: UNHCR.

UNHCR. (2017c). *Climate change, disasters, and displacement*. Geneva, Switzerland: UNHCR.

UNHCR. (2016). *Global trends: Forced displacement in 2016*. Geneva, Switzerland: UNHCR. Retrieved November 10, 2017, from www.unhcr.org/5943e8a34.pdf

UNHCR. (2015a). Managing and Supporting Spontaneous Settlements. *UNHCR Handbook for Emergencies* (4th ed.). Retrieved December 14, 2017, from https://emergency.unhcr.org/entry/85767

UNHCR. (2015b). *Global trends: Forced displacement in 2015*. Geneva, Switzerland: UNHCR. Retrieved January 2, 2018, from www.unhcr.org/576408cd7.pdf

UNHCR. (2014). *Policy on alternatives to camps*. Geneva, Switzerland: UNHCR. Retrieved from www.unhcr.org/en-us/protection/statelessness/5422b8f09/unhcr-policy-alternatives-camps.html

UNHCR. (2005). *UNHCR environmental guidelines*. Geneva, Switzerland: UNHCR.

UNHCR. (2000). Ch. 10: The Rwandan Genocide and its aftermath. In *The state of the world's refugees 2000: Fifty years of humanitarian action*. Geneva, Switzerland: UNHCR.

UNHCR. (1997). *The state of the world's refugees: A humanitarian agenda*. Oxford, UK: Oxford University Press and UNHCR.

UNHCR. (n.d.-a) *Refugee operations and environmental management: Selected lessons learned*. Geneva, Switzerland: UNHCR, Engineering and Environmental Services Section.

UNHCR. (n.d.-b). *Shelter*. Retrieved October 10, 2020, from www.unhcr.org/en-us/shelter.html#:~:text=More%20than%206.6%20million%20refugees,including%20aid%20dependency%20and%20isolation

UNICEF. (2000, 13 October). *UNICEF humanitarian action: Tanzania donor report update*. Retrieved August 30, 2021, from https://reliefweb.int/report/united-republic-tanzania/unicef-humanitarian-action-tanzania-donor-update-13-oct-2000

Walton, O. (2012). *Preventing conflict between refugees and host communities*. Birmingham, UK: Governance and Social Development Resource Center, University of Birmingham.

Wendt, L., Robl, J., Hilberg, S., Braun, A., Rogenhofer, E., Dirnberger, D., . . . Lang, S. (2015). Assisting groundwater exploration for refugee/IDP camps by remote sensing and GIS. *EGUGA*, 2912.

Whitaker, B. E. (1999). *Changing opportunities: Refugees and host communities in western Tanzania* (Working Paper No. 11). Geneva, Switzerland: UN High Commissioner for Refugees (UNHCR).

World Bank. (2017a). *Forcibly displaced. Toward a development approach supporting refugees, the internally displaced, and their hosts*. Washington, DC: International Bank for Reconstruction and Development/The World Bank.

Population displacement and the environment

World Bank. (2017b). *Fragility, conflict, and violence.* Retrieved December 15, 2017, from www.worldbank. org/en/topic/fragilityconflictviolence/overview#1

World Bank. (2011). *Conflict, security, and development.* World Development Report. Retrieved from http://web.worldbank.org/WBSITE/EXTERNAL/EXTDEC/EXTRESEARCH/EXTWDRS/0,, contentMDK:23256432~pagePK:478093~piPK:477627~theSitePK:477624,00.html

Yonetani, M. et al. (2015). *Global estimates 2015: People displaced by disasters.* Internal Displacement Monitoring Centre (iDMC) | Norwegian Refugee Council (NRC).

Zetter, R. (1995). *Shelter provision and settlement policies for refugees: A state of the art review.* Studies on Emergencies and Disaster Relief No. 2. Sweden: Nordiska Afrikainstitutet.

12

NATURAL DISASTERS AND ARMED CONFLICT

Colin Walch

The aim of this chapter is to review and understand the state-of-the-art research related to natural disasters and armed conflict. The review is based on studies published from the late 1990s until today in the most prominent political science and cross-disciplinary journals. This review chapter mainly focuses on potential short-run effects of natural disasters on armed conflict. I, therefore, do not explore long-term natural disasters that will have important effects in the future, such as sea-level rise.

The type of armed conflict explored in this review is collective, has two parties, and the aim is political rather than criminal.[1] These include both internal (civil wars) and interstate conflict but exclude criminal violence, such as the situation in some regions of Mexico and Brazil. While not properly considered as an armed conflict, food riots are still examined in the review given their growing numbers and prominence in existing literature. Three types of dependent variables to operationalize increase of armed conflict are most commonly used in the literature: onset of armed conflict, intensity of armed conflict, and duration of armed conflict.

A natural disaster is defined as an event "involving a natural hazard (e.g., flood, cyclone, landslide, volcanic eruption, and earthquake) which has consequences in terms of damage, livelihoods/economic disruption, and/or casualties that are too great for the affected area and people to deal with properly on their own" (Wisner, Blaikie, Cannon, & Davis, 2012, p. 30). Yet, there is agreement among scientists that, in strict terms, there is no such thing as a "natural disaster" (see Wisner et al., 2004). Indeed, natural disasters mark the interface between an extreme physical phenomenon and a vulnerable human population (O'Keefe, Westgate, & Wisner, 1976). Therefore, it is the combination of a natural hazard and a vulnerable human society that will result in a "natural disaster." It is important to remember that "natural" disasters have an important human component and are, therefore, not purely exogenous shocks. Natural disasters are usually categorized according to their impact speed: "rapid onset" and "slow onset." Rapid onset disasters are events that occur suddenly, often with little warning, including floods, fires, earthquakes, storms, wet and dry mass movements, and volcanic eruptions. Slow onset includes droughts and bouts of extreme temperature. Most existing research has looked at the impact of rapid onset disasters.

There are three main tendencies in the existing research on natural disasters and armed conflict. The first one argues that disasters generate insecurity, frustration, scarcity of important resources, and weakened enforcement of law and order, which are frequently suggested

DOI: 10.4324/9781315107592-14

to increase the likelihood of outbreaks of armed violence (see Brancati, 2007; Burke, Miguel, Satyanath, Dykema, & Lobell, 2009; Drury & Olson, 1998; Homer-Dixon, 1999; Miguel, Satyanath, & Sergenti, 2004; Nel & Righarts, 2008). By contrast, the second tendency in the literature claims that the likelihood of armed conflict and antisocial behaviors tend to drop during and after disasters (see Fritz, 1996; Kelman, 2011; Kreutz, 2012). Finally, the last trend is somehow fitting between these two extremes arguing that natural disasters do not have much effect on conflict dynamics, as economic and political variables remain the most important predictors of armed conflict (see Buhaug, 2010; Slettebak, 2012; Theisen, Gleditsch, & Buhaug, 2013; O'Loughlin, Linke, & Witmer, 2014). This chapter reviews and outlines, in turn, these three main trends in the literature. It concludes by suggesting avenues for future research.

Natural disaster increases armed conflict

One of the first studies arguing that natural disasters may increase conflict was written by Homer-Dixon in 1994. He argues that natural disasters, among other phenomena such as land degradation and population increase, create the scarcity of resources that, in turn, will increase armed conflict or fuel existing ones. He also argues that increased scarcity could trigger large movements of population, which could provoke ethnic conflict as migrants clash with indigenous populations (see also Nizkorodov & Wagle, Chapter 11). Using a series of single case studies, he provides examples of civil conflict that were partially caused by scarcity of resources. While his work has been criticized for lacking robust methodology (see Gleditsch, 1998), it is an important starting point in the literature on natural disasters and conflict.

The first cross-national quantitative studies aimed at testing the relationship between natural disasters and armed conflict came a bit later in 1998 and were conducted by Drury and Olson. They find a positive relationship between disaster severity and the level of political unrest, using a sample of 12 countries that experienced one or more disasters that killed at least 1,500 persons between 1966 and 1980. The positive association between disaster severity and the risk of conflict is illustrated in their study by six cases where severe natural disasters have been followed by armed conflict. Although path-breaking at its time, the study suffers from a sample that is limited both in time and in the number of countries included (see Slettebak, 2012, for a discussion on the limitations). Looking at a particular natural disaster, Brancati (2007) finds that earthquakes are significantly related to an increased risk of violent conflict. Nel and Righarts (2008) provide the first extensive cross-national analysis focusing specifically on natural disasters. Using a sample of 183 political units covering the period 1950–2000, they find a positive relationship between natural disasters and the risk of armed conflict. They argue that disaster creates resource scarcities and disorganizes the government, making it more vulnerable to unrest, especially in a country with predisasters existing tensions.

While much has been written since the late 1990s, it is possible to distinguish from previous literature three approaches which differently explain the links between disasters and conflict.

The first approach argues that natural disasters, mainly drought, may escalate competition over dwindling livelihoods, such as water, pasture, and cropland (cf. Homer-Dixon, 1999; Kahl, 2006). This neo-Malthusian model of conflict claims that natural disasters, by reducing essential resources for livelihood such as food and water, lead to fighting over the remaining resources. These scarcities have been found to be particularly conducive to communal violence in societies with little coping capacity (Fjelde & von Uexkull, 2012). In a similar vein, disaster may also increase migration, which will, in turn, increase competition over already dwindling resources and fuel communal conflict between the host population and the newcomers (Reuveny, 2007). Yet, both Collier and Hoeffler (2002) and de Soysa (2002) have argued that violent conflict is also particularly likely if there is an abundance of natural resources.

A second approach argues that natural disasters, especially drought and heat waves, can make individuals more likely to exhibit violent behavior toward others (Hsiang, Burke, & Miguel, 2013). In Africa, Burke et al. (2009) foresaw 393,000 additional battle-related deaths in the period leading to 2030 if temperatures continued to rise and new conflicts were as deadly as those in the period between 1981 and 2002. An increase of heat could potentially fuel civil wars on a larger scale as a result of individual-level aggression during temperature increases (Hsiang et al., 2013). Hsiang et al. (2013) build on a long line of research that links hot temperatures to individual aggression, including violent crime and riots. For example, a number of psychological studies indicate that people are more violent when temperatures are high (cf. Anderson, Bushman, & Groom, 1997; Larrick, Timmerman, Carton, & Abrevaya, 2011). Hsiang et al. (2013) also show that many civilizations, such as the Maya, collapsed as a result of climate shock and natural disasters. This literature is mostly driven by behavioral and psychological studies, and it considers civil war as an aggregate outcome of individual behaviors where formal and informal institutions do not play an active role in curbing or fueling hostilities (Wischnath & Buhaug, 2014). Burke, Hsiang, and Miguel (2015) addressed this critique by considering many types of human conflict in their review, including both interpersonal conflict – such as domestic violence, road rage, assault, murder, and rape – and intergroup conflict – including riots, ethnic violence, land invasions, gang violence, civil war, and other forms of political instability, such as coups. In their meta-analysis of 55 studies, they reach the same conclusion: deviations from moderate temperatures and precipitation patterns systematically increase the risk of conflict, often substantially, with average effects that are highly statistically significant. While they do not empirically explore the pathways linking disaster to an increase of violence, they indicate that much research supports a psychological pathway between heat waves and violence.

The third and most researched approach describes how natural disasters affect state stability and armed conflict via their impact on macroeconomic performance, agricultural output, and livelihood security. The loss of income from the disaster may affect conflict dynamics through three complementary processes: lowered opportunity costs of rebelling, increased opportunities for recruitment, and heightened grievances (Wischnath & Buhaug, 2014). Assuming that participating in armed conflict is a risky alternative source of income (Grossman, 1991), it seems probable that individuals who experience an economic shock due to a disaster might be more willing to join a rebel group. Faced with few economic alternatives from agriculture, individuals are more likely to value the expected short-term benefits and pay-offs of joining a rebel group. They are, therefore, more easily recruited by rebel groups (Collier & Hoeffler, 2001; Eastin, 2016; Wischnath & Buhaug, 2014). The impact of the disaster on economic stability may affect the government's ability to deal with insurgent activities (Le Billon & Waizenegger, 2007; Nel & Righarts, 2008). This may incentivize terrorist action by reducing the costs associated with attacking specific targets (Berrebi & Ostwald, 2011). The economic impact of a natural disaster on people's livelihood may increase the grievances of the population. Grievances may be further increased by absent or unfair aid assistance by the state following disaster and motivate a larger pool of individuals to join and/or support an active rebel group to redress their grievances. It is argued that collective identities among marginalized groups facilitate a shared perception of injustice, a significant factor when mobilizing the population for rebellion (Gurr, 1970; Wischnath & Buhaug, 2014). This may strengthen insurgent groups by increasing their capacity to recruit among disaster-affected populations (Eastin, 2016; Wischnath & Buhaug, 2014). Increased recruitment and troop size will, in turn, increase armed conflict intensity

(Wischnath & Buhaug, 2014) and systematically prolong the duration of armed intrastate conflicts (Eastin, 2016).

Natural disaster decreases armed conflict

On the other side of the debate, there are equally some scholars that argue that natural disasters could create windows of opportunity for peace. Already ahead of his time, Durkheim found that great social disturbances and wars tend to increase social integration, thereby reducing the risk of antisocial behavior (cited in Slettebak, 2012). In the 1960s, Fritz argued that:

> Even under the worst disaster conditions, people maintain or quickly regain self-control and become concerned about the welfare of others . . . antisocial behavior, such as aggression towards others and scapegoating are rare or nonexistent. Instead, most disasters produce a great increase in social solidarity among the stricken populace, and this newly created solidarity tends to reduce the incidence of most forms of personal and social pathology.
>
> (cited in Slettebak, 2012, p. 165)

Building on these findings, Kelman (2011) coined the term "disaster diplomacy." The argument is that disasters contribute to increased societal cohesion, an increased sense of unity in the face of adversity, or simply a widespread interest in maintaining fragile stability. Thus, disasters should reduce the individual propensity to engage in rebellion (Gleditsch & Nordas, 2014). Kelman (2011) argues that disaster-related activities often influence peace processes in the short term – over weeks and months – provided that a non-disaster-related basis already existed for the reconciliation. That could be secret negotiations between the warring parties or strong trade or cultural links. Over the long term, disaster-related influences disappear, succumbing to factors such as a leadership change, the usual patterns of political enmity, or belief that a historical grievance should take precedence over disaster-related bonds. The "disaster diplomacy school" has used a wide variety of case studies to demonstrate that disaster relief could influence the peace process in the short term by increasing, for example, the onset of negotiation and informal talks between the warring parties. Akcinaroglu, DiCicco, and Radziszewski (2011) similarly conclude that earthquakes "can promote rapprochement, political steps toward warmer relations that makes it difficult for interstate rivalry to continue" (p. 270).

In negotiation theory, the shock from the disaster may jolt "the mind and stimulates rethinking," opening up new avenues for negotiation (Pruitt, 2005, p. 4). Kreutz (2012) tests this argument by conducting a statistical analysis of the impact of natural disasters on the occurrence of new negotiations, ceasefires, and peace agreements. He argues that disasters provide ripe moments for negotiation during the civil war and provides support to disaster diplomacy, as natural disasters increase the likelihood that parties will agree to ceasefires but have less effect on the onset of talks or the signing of a peace agreement.

Finally, some scholars also argue that natural disasters may have pacifying effects on the conflict because they impact the resources and tactical environment where the rebel group operates (Salehyan & Hendrix, 2014; Walch, 2018). For example, with regard to communal conflict, some studies show that wetter years, associated with more abundant vegetation in eastern Africa, are on average more violent than drier years (Meier, Bond, & Bond, 2007; Witsenburg & Roba, 2009; Theisen, 2012). Similarly, Salehyan and Hendrix (2014) argue that natural disasters can affect the tactical environment and reduce the resource base for mobilization of armed violence. Indeed, most individuals will be more concerned with basic survival than with joining a rebel group (Salehyan & Hendrix, 2014, p. 241). Walch (2018) found that in the case of the Philippines, the New's People Army was weakened by both typhoons Bopha and Haiyan.

Natural disasters have little effect on armed conflict

Finally, there are also a number of researchers who believe that natural disasters do not play an important role in armed conflict, even in the region that is often seen as the most likely to be affected by conflict due to disaster: Africa. Indeed, O'Loughlin et al. (2014), using a new disaggregated dataset of violence and climate anomalies (measured as temperature and precipitation variations from normal) for sub-Saharan Africa, found that the location and timing of violence are influenced less by climate anomalies than by key political, economic, and geographic factors. While there is no doubt that natural disasters increase human suffering, economic and political variables remain the most important predictors of conflict (Slettebak, 2012). Case studies and ethnographic work seems to support these findings. For example, Benjaminsen, Alinon, Buhaug, and Buseth (2012) state on the basis of the Mopti region of Mali, at the heart of the Sahel, that there is "little evidence supporting the notion that water scarcity and environmental change are important drivers of intercommunal conflicts" (p. 108). Similarly, Omelicheva (2011) finds that when state fragility is taken into account, the risk of state failure in the aftermath of a disaster is minimal or disappears. Besley and Persson (2011) find that climatic disasters do not affect growth, but increase the risk of civil war, though only in fragile states. Finally, Bergholt and Lujala (2012) find that natural disasters have a negative effect on economic growth but that this does not translate into an increased risk of conflict. The IPCC (2014) seems to follow a similar argument, concluding that "collectively the research does not conclude that there is a strong positive relationship between warming and armed conflict" (p. 756).

On the whole, this literature argues that natural disasters may affect conflict under some conditions but that, most of the time, other sociopolitical factors are more important in explaining violence. Researchers suggest more clearly exploring these conditions. Comparative case studies, indeed, show that a similar natural disaster may sometimes have very different effects on conflict dynamics. For example, Beardsley and McQuinn (2009) found that the 2004 Indian Ocean Tsunami had different effects on the conflicts in Sri Lanka and Indonesia. While the tsunami triggered a set of peace talks in Indonesia, the disaster did not lead to any peace process in Sri Lanka. They linked this different outcome to the different types of rebel groups in Sri Lanka and Indonesia. In a similar vein, Walch (2014) argues that rebel groups are more likely to collaborate and start peace negotiation during disasters if the rebel groups are more dependent on civilians' welfare.

The way forward

This academic conundrum is explained by different factors. First, there is a difference in the operationalization of the main variables by the researchers in the field. For example, while the terms "disaster" and "conflict" refer to general concepts, they must be carefully operationalized at particular geographic, temporal, and social scales (Salehyan, 2014:2). There is an important difference among natural disasters in their effects on population and violent behavior. Operationalization choices are not trivial, and they often exaggerate results and make comparisons across studies approximate. Indeed, communal violence or riots are not comparable with civil war violence that pits a state army against a rebel group. Most existing research mainly explores civil conflict due to data availability. However, the organization of a rebel movement requires planning, resources, know-how, and leadership to start a conflict against the state. This takes time and requires many factors in addition to the grievances created by the disaster. Disaster may, therefore, have more direct effect on riots and communal violence that do not need such a level of organization. For example, Wischnath and Buhaug (2014) find that harvest loss is robustly associated with increased numbers of riots and political violence. As a result, being clearer on the unit of analysis and operationalization of the variables may lead to more nuanced and circumscribed conclusions.

Second, there is a need to specify causal mechanisms and context. Very often, the causal mechanism explaining the correlation between disaster and conflict is not empirically explored. For example, Brancati (2007) argues that disasters give rise to orphans who are prime targets for rebel recruitment (p. 721), but she does not have any data on actual recruitment or on rebel groups behavior. Much of the causal mechanism is assumed but not explored. In addition, coping capacity and ability to adapt to natural disasters are not similar in every society and community. These differences, together with ethnicity and formal and informal institutions among others, shape the impact of natural disasters on communities and society, but they most often remain uncounted for in existing research. Looking at the Philippines, for example, certain communities are more resilient to disaster and conflict than others (Walch, 2014). Not specifying the context leads to inappropriate generalizations and often to reductionist and near-deterministic narratives (Buhaug, 2015).

Third, it is important to explore the role of human agency and the behavior of armed actors in situations of natural disasters and armed conflict. Rebel groups may behave differently following a disaster; they collaborate with humanitarian actors to buy hearts and minds or take the opportunity to attack a weakened state (see Walch, 2014; Eastin, 2016). A growing number of case studies have been useful in highlighting agency, but quantitative studies should disaggregate violent events and actors more systematically.

The good news is that some ongoing research is addressing these issues and has been more precise in paying attention to contextual variables that condition the relationship between climatic stress and collective violence (see Bernauer, Böhmelt, & Koubi, 2012; Buhaug, 2015). There is a growing awareness that governance, institutional structures, and individuals' social positions and identities will shape human agency and violence in the wake of disaster. For example, there is evidence that the adverse effects of disaster on armed conflict are particularly significant in weak states already affected by conflict, where groups are heavily dependent on agriculture and are politically excluded (von Uexkull, Croicu, Fjelde, & Buhaug, 2016).

The current focus on mediating variables such as institutions is much needed to better understand and specify causal mechanisms. Examining institutions is increasingly important as they form the main mechanism to address armed violence and to adapt to a changing climate (Burke et al., 2015). Ngaruiya and Scheffran (2016) and Linke et al. (2017) highlight the role of informal institutions and traditional conflict resolution mechanisms in mitigating the security risks posed by erratic climatic conditions. Analyzing drought exposure and attitudes toward political violence in rural Kenya, they find that the effect of drought on attitudinal support for violence is dampened in areas where different ethnic communities engage in frequent dialogue about resource use and conflict. Linke et al. (2017) conclude that while environmental change and shortages of rainfall represent a stress for many households' livelihoods, certain formal or informal regulations may ameliorate these difficulties (p. 30). Future research should further examine the effects of formal and informal institutions as they may reduce the impact of disaster on people's livelihood and provide channels for conflict resolutions.

In conclusion, existing research as a whole has not identified a consistent causal relationship between natural disasters and armed conflict. The link between disaster and conflict is the strongest when it comes to riots and communal violence, as these types of violence require little planning, resources, or leadership. Yet, it is not clear how riots or communal violence may be linked to the onset of armed conflict. Another strong link has been found in countries already affected by armed conflict and high levels of ethnic tensions. This is not surprising, however, given that conflict has long been described as development in reverse. Indeed, there is clear evidence that armed conflict increases the vulnerability of societies to natural disasters (Wisner et al., 2004). Conflict poses numerous risks to countries and regions that are already vulnerable to the effects of disasters, creating a compounding effect. Hence, addressing vulnerabilities in countries highly exposed to armed conflict might be the best way to make societies more resilient to the destabilizing effects of natural disasters. Indeed, the adverse impact of intense violence on environmental vulnerability is probably many times greater than the effect of environmental shock on conflict risk. Similarly, disaster risk reduction in conflict-affected countries could improve the management of natural disasters and, therefore, make the country more stable in times of turmoil. Disaster risk reduction may also strengthen state legitimacy, a well-needed endeavor in regions affected by armed conflict. In the end, a natural hazard becomes a disaster because the society is vulnerable and exposed. Countries and communities vulnerable to natural disasters are very often equally vulnerable to armed conflict. As a result, more effort should be spent on specifying the factors that increase people's resilience to conflict and disasters instead of constantly trying to draw correlation between disaster and conflict. Strengthening the glue that holds societies together and promoting "no-regret" policies is likely to be the most efficient and cost-effective way to adapt to a world increasingly affected by natural disasters and avoid violent conflict as a result. In sum, disaster and conflict are related in other, less controversial, and quite possibly much more important ways than those considered in previous research. Viewing the disaster–conflict issues through the lens of resilience may open additional avenues for future research.

Note

1 Criminal violence does not include a political goal, such as taking over a government or create an independent state.

Works cited

Anderson, C., Bushman, B., & Groom, R. (1997). Hot years and serious and deadly assault: Empirical tests of the heat hypothesis. *Journal Personality and Social Psychology*, *73*(6), 1213–1223.

Anderson, C. (2001). Heat and violence. *Current Directions in Psychological Science*, *10*(1), 33–38.

Akcinaroglu, S., DiCicco, J., & Radziszewski, E. (2011). Avalanches and Olive branches: A multimethod analysis of disasters and peacemaking in interstate rivalries. *Political Research Quarterly*, *64*(2), 260–275.

Beardsley, K., & McQuinn, B. (2009). Rebel groups as predatory organizations: The political effects of the 2004 tsunami in Indonesia and Sri Lanka. *Journal of Conflict Resolution*, *53*(04), 624–645.

Benjaminsen, T. Alinon, K., Buhaug, H. & Buseth, J. T. (2012). Does climate change drive land-use conflicts in the Sahel? *Journal of Peace Research*, *49*(1), 97–111.

Bergholt, D., & Lujala, P. (2012). Climate-related natural disasters, economic growth, and armed civil conflict. *Journal of Peace Research*, *49*(1), 147–162.

Bernauer, T., Böhmelt, T., & Koubi, V. (2012). Environmental changes and violent conflict. *Environmental Research Letters, 7(1): 1–8.*

Berrebi, C., & Ostwald, J. (2011). Earthquakes, hurricanes, and terrorism: Do natural disasters incite terror? *Public Choice*, *149*(3/4), 383–403.

Besley, T., & Persson, T. (2011). The logic of political violence. *Quarterly Journal of Economics*, *126*(3), 1411–1445.

Brancati, D. (2007). Political aftershocks: The impact of earthquakes on intrastate conflict. *Journal of Conflict Resolution*, *51*(5), 715–743.

Buhaug, H. (2010). Climate not to blame for African civil wars. *Proceedings of the National Academy of Sciences, 107*(38), 16477–16482.

Buhaug, H. (2015). Climate–conflict research: Some reflections on the way forward. *WIREs Climate Change, 6*(3), 269–275.

Burke, M., Hsiang, S., & Miguel, E. (2015). Climate and conflict. *Annual Review of Economics, 7*, 577–617.

Burke, M. B., Miguel, E., Satyanath, S., Dykema, J. A., & Lobell, D. B. (2009). Warming increases the risk of civil war in Africa. *Proceedings of the National Academy of Sciences, 106*(49), 20670–20674.

Collier, P., & Hoeffler, A. (2002). On the incidence of civil war in Africa. *Journal of Conflict Resolution, 46*(1), 13–28.

Collier, P., & Hoeffler, A. (2001). *Greed and grievance in civil war*. Washington, DC: World Bank Press.

Drury, C., & Olson, S. (1998). Disasters and political unrest: An empirical investigation. *Journal of Contingencies and Crisis Management, 6*(3), 153–161.

de Soysa, I. (2002). Ecoviolence: Shrinking pie, or honey pot? *Global Environmental Politics, 2*(4), 1–34.

Eastin, J. (2016). Fuel to the fire: Natural disasters and the duration of civil conflict. *International Interactions, 42*(2), 322–349.

Fjelde, H., & von Uexkull, N. (2012). Climate triggers: Rainfall anomalies, vulnerability and communal conflict in sub-Saharan Africa. *Political Geography, 31*(7), 444–453.

Fritz, C. (1996). Disasters and mental health: Therapeutic principles drawn from disaster studies. In *Historical and comparative disaster series* 10. University of Delaware Disaster Research Center. Retrieved May 24, 2010, from http://dspace.udel.edu:8080/ dspace/handle/19716/1325.

Gleditsch, N. P. (1998). Armed conflict and the environment: A critique of the literature. *Journal of Peace Research, 35*(3), 381–400.

Gleditsch, N. P., & Nordas, R. (2014). Conflicting messages? The IPCC on conflict and human security. *Political Geography, 43*(1), 82–90.

Grossman, H. I. (1991). A general equilibrium model of insurrections. *The American Economic Review, 81*(4), 912–921.

Gurr, T. R. (1970). *Why men rebel*. Princeton, NJ: Princeton University Press.

Homer-Dixon, T. (1999). *Environment, scarcity, and violence*. Princeton, NJ: Princeton University Press.

Homer-Dixon, T. (1994). Environmental scarcities and violent conflict: Evidence from cases. *International Security, 19*(1), 5–40.

Hsiang, S. M., Burke, M., & Miguel, E. (2013). Quantifying the influence of climate on human conflict. *Science, 341*(6151), 1–14.

Intergovernmental Panel on Climate Change (IPCC). (2014). *Climate change 2014: Impacts, adaptation, and vulnerability. Part A: Global and sectoral aspects. Contribution of working group II to the fifth assessment report of the intergovernmental panel on climate change* (C. B. Field, V. R. Barros, D. J. Dokken, K. J. Mach, M. D. Mastrandrea, T. E. Bilir, . . L. L. White (Eds.). Cambridge, UK and New York: Cambridge University Press.

IPCC. (2007). *Impacts, adaptation and vulnerability. In fourth assessment report. Climate change 2007*. Geneva/ Cambridge, Switzerland: Intergovernmental Panel on Climate Change/Cambridge University Press. Retrieved from www.ipcc.ch

Kahl, C. (2006). *States, scarcity, and civil strife in the developing world*. Princeton, NJ: Princeton University Press.

Kelman, I. (2011). *Disaster diplomacy: How disasters affect peace and conflict*. London: Routledge.

Kreutz, J. (2012). From tremors to talks: Does natural disasters produce ripe moments for resolving separatist conflicts? *International Interactions, 38*(04), 482–502.

Larrick, R., Timmerman, T., Carton, A., & Abrevaya, J. (2011). Temper, temperature, and temptation: Heat-related retaliation in baseball. *Psychological Science, 22*(4), 423–428.

Le Billon, P., & Waizenegger, A. (2007). Peace in the wake of disaster? Secessionist conflicts and the 2004 Indian Ocean tsunami. *Transactions of the Institute of British Geographers, 32*(3), 411–427.

Linke, A., Frank, D. W., Witmer, F., Loughlin, J., McCabe, T., & Tir, J. (2017). Drought, local institutional contexts, and support for violence in Kenya. *Journal of Conflict Resolution, 62*(7), 1544–1578.

Meier, P., Bond, D., & Bond, J. (2007). Environmental influences on pastoral conflict in the horn of Africa, *Political Geography, 26*(6), 716–735.

Nel, P., & Righarts, M. (2008). Natural disasters and the risk of violent civil conflict. *International Studies Quarterly, 52*(1), 159–185.

Miguel, E., Satyanath, S., & Sergenti, E. (2004). Economic Shocks and Civil Conflict: An Instrumental Variables Approach. Journal of Political Economy, 112(4), 725–753.

Ngaruiya, G., & Scheffran, J. (2016). Actors and networks in resource conflict resolution under climate change in rural Kenya. *Earth System Dynamics Discussions*, 1–28.

O'Keefe, P., Westgate, K., & Wisner, B. (1976). Taking the naturalness out of natural disasters. *Nature*, *260*(5552), 566–567.

O'Loughlin, J., Linke, A., & Witmer, F. (2014). Effect of temperature and precipitation variability on the risk of violence in sub-Saharan Africa, 1980–2012. *Proceedings of the National Academy of Sciences*, *111*(47), 16712–19717.

Omelicheva, M. (2011). Natural disasters: Triggers of political instability? *International Interactions*, *37*(4), 441–465.

Pruitt, D. (2005). *Whither ripeness theory?* George Mason University, Working Paper No. 25.

Reuveny, R. (2007). Climate change-induced migration and violent conflict. *Political Geography*, *26*(6), 656–673.

Salehyan, I., & Hendrix, C. S. (2014). Climate shocks and political violence. *Global Environmental Change*, *28*, 239–250.

Slettebak, R. (2012). Don't blame the weather! Climate-related natural disasters and civil conflict. *Journal of Peace Research*, *49*(01), 163–176.

Theisen, O. M. (2012). Climate clashes? Weather variability, land pressure, and organized violence in Kenya, 1989–2004. *Journal of Peace Research*, *49*(01), 81–96.

Theisen, O. M., Gleditsch, N. P., & Buhaug, H. (2013). Is climate change a driver of armed conflict? *Climatic Change*, *117*(3), 613–625.

von Uexkull, N., Croicu, M., Fjelde, H., & Buhaug, H. (2016). Civil conflict sensitivity to growing-season drought. *Proceeding of the National Academy of Science*, *113*(44), 12391–12396.

Walch, C. (2018). Weakened by the storm: Rebel group recruitment in the wake of natural disasters in the Philippines. *Journal of Peace Research*, Forthcoming.

Walch, C. (2014). Collaboration or obstruction? Rebel group behavior during natural disaster relief in the Philip- pines. *Political Geography*, *43*, 40–50.

Wischnath, G., & Buhaug, H. (2014). Rice or riots: On food production and conflict severity across India. *Political Geography*, *43*, 6–15.

Wisner, B., Blaikie, P., Cannon, T., & Davis, I. (2004). *At risk, natural hazards, people's vulnerability and disasters* (2nd rev. ed.). London, USA: Routledge.

Wisner, B., Gaillard, J. C., & Kelman, I. (Eds.). (2012). *The Routledge handbook of hazards and disaster risk reduction*. London: Routledge.

Witsenburg, K., & Roba, A. (2009). Of rain and raids: Violent livestock raiding in Northern Kenya. *Civil Wars*, *11*, 514–538 (2009).

13

CLIMATE CHANGE, PUBLIC HEALTH, AND THE CONFLICT CYCLE

*James Orbinski, Richard Matthew, Evgenia Nizkorodov
and Sifat Reazi*

In the sixth *Global Environmental Outlook* report, UN Environment (2019) draws several conclusions about current and projected climate change impacts: "Climate change has become an independent driver of environmental change and poses a serious challenge to future economic development (well established) . . . . . Climate change poses risks to human societies through impacts on food, and water security (established but incomplete), and on human security, health, livelihoods and infrastructure. These risks are greatest for people dependent on natural resource sectors, such as coastal, agricultural, pastoral and forest communities; and those experiencing multiple forms of inequality, marginalization and poverty are most exposed to the impacts. . . . Climate change will amplify existing risks and create new risks for natural and human systems" (p. 27). The Sixth Assessmnt Report (AR6), which was just released by the Intergovernmental Panel on Climate Change (IPCC, 2021) underscores the growing gaps between climate change trends on the one hand, and mitigation and adaptation efforts on the other hand, and urges the world to take this issue more seriously to protect the health and welfare of the human species – and of many other species as well. Given the continuing growth in greenhouse gas emissions, it is not hard to imagine average global warming reaching 4–5 degrees Centigrade by 2100, placing humankind in a climate regime far beyond its evolutionary experience, a climate regime in which the homeostasis of critical human systems would experience radical stress.

Indeed, in "The 2020 report of The Lancet Countdown on Health and Climate Change," Watts et al. (2020) contend that

> A changing climate threatens to undermine the past 50 years of gains in public health, disrupting the wellbeing of communities and the foundations on which health systems are built. The effects of climate change are pervasive and impact the food, air, water, and shelter that society depend on, extending across every region of the world and every income group. These effects act to exacerbate existing inequities, with vulnerable populations within and between countries affected more frequently and with a more lasting impact (p. 134).

As global health comes under increasing threat due to the growing stresses and shocks of climate change, another significant driver of health outcomes, violent conflict, is also on the rise. According to Palik, Rustad, and Methi (2020), "In 2019, 54 state-based conflicts were recorded: two more than in 2018 and the same number as in 2016. This number is a record high since 1946. Thirty-five countries experienced civil conflicts and worldwide around 50,000 died in battle-related deaths" (p. 7). As the ICRC (2018) notes, not only is war on the rise, it is also in many ways different from the past, in ways that make it harder to manage and end. In particular, contemporary wars are protracted affairs, fought in dense urban settings by a wide array of armed combatants who are often embedded in larger transnational networks. They can be extremely hard to conclude, in part, because "they are often a tangled web of politically – motivated violence, terrorism and disproportionate reaction by states, inter-community and social violence, which often go hand-in-hand with economic crime" (para. 11).

Climate change and violent conflict are complex phenomena that interact in significant ways – climate change can amplify variables that are closely linked to the conflict cycle; the conflict cycle can increase vulnerability to climate change impacts. As UN Environment (2019) notes: "Wars and conflicts are major sources of pollution, especially air, water and soil pollution, waste, greenhouse gases and land degradation" (p. 10). And as many of the authors in this volume make clear, climate change can bolster the variables that make violent conflict more likely to occur and more difficult to end (see, e.g., Crawford & Church, Chapter 7). Taken together, these trends translate directly and indirectly into serious challenges for global health. Drawing on academic research and decades of field experience (Orbinski with MSF – Doctors without Borders in Somalia, Rwanda, and many other places; Matthew as a member of UN missions in Rwanda, the Democratic Republic of the Congo and Sierra Leone), this chapter examines interconnections and feedbacks among climate change, violent conflict, and public health.

Climate change, health, and the conflict cycle

Across a variety of metrics, public health has made significant gains in most of the world over the past century. For example, the Centers for Disease Control and Prevention (2011) notes that "during the previous century, great progress was made in raising life expectancy and reducing mortality among infants and young children through improvements in living conditions and activities to combat major infectious causes of death" (p. 817). And health experts Austin Frakt and Aaron Carroll (2019), in a review of some of these gains, identify: "major drops in the mortality of children under 5 (down more than 50 percent in the last three decades) . . . the halving of deaths of women at childbirth . . . significant decreases in death from malaria . . . a turnaround in the H.I.V. epidemic [and] . . . increased life expectancy in every country" (para. 8). But while the data are compelling that public health has made enormous progress in the span of a human lifetime, there are also growing concerns about the potential for significant public health setbacks in the span of another lifetime.

Much of this concern has been catalyzed by the science of climate change. Small increases in average temperature and relative humidity could make large areas between the tropics difficult if not impossible for human habitation (Xu, Kohler, Lenton, Svenning, and Scheffer, 2020). Salt-water intrusion into groundwater systems, resulting from both development and sea-level rise, is adding further pressure on public health in many densely populated, low-resource, and low-elevation coastal areas. Disease vectors are migrating, like most species on the planet, toward new and more congenial environments, often characterized by cooler temperatures, and more reliable water and food sources, exposing humans to new health risks. And the steady increase in severe weather events such as floods, heat waves, fires, and droughts all have large implications for human health.

So great are concerns about the health impacts of climate change, to both human and nonhuman species, that a new approach to research and policy has emerged in recent years captured in the concept of "planetary health." As Richard Horton explains in a 2016 *The Lancet* article:

> The definition is established – the health of human civilisations and the ecosystems on which they depend. But what does this mean? The core idea is the unity of the planet's natural and physical systems. And that the future health of our species demands a different level of investigation – not only of individuals and communities, but also of civilisations, the organisation and content of our cultures and societies. The predicaments our species faces are so severe that we must ask far-reaching questions about the capacity of our political, economic, and social institutions to adapt to and address those predicaments
>
> (p. 2462).

In the context of this chapter, it may be convenient to think of public health as the outcome of several clusters of variables:

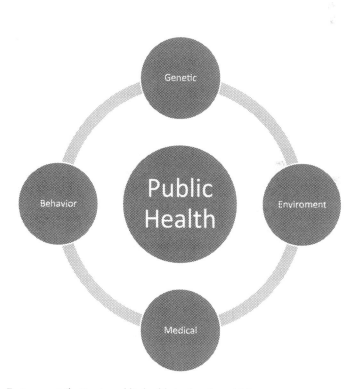

Figure 13.1 Factors contributing to public health (authors' graphic).

The relationship between human health and the environment is complex and exceptional, as the human body cannot survive absent regular environmental inputs (e.g., water and food), faces a broad array of environmental hazards (e.g., floods and heat waves), and also has to maintain a very precise body temperature in the context of ever-changing external conditions (e.g., ambient temperature and relative humidity). In the past century, significant gains to public health in most of the world were made in large measure due to improvements in environmental conditions related to large investments into water infrastructure, food production, sanitation, and waste management. Many other factors – including improved diets; public health systems; campaigns to reduce unhealthy habits such as smoking; and increase healthy habits such as meditation, sleep, and exercise; and improvements in medical treatments – buttressed these gains. Climate change is causing and likely to continue to cause reversals in the environmental cluster that will both undo past achievements and add new health-relevant stresses and shocks such as more frequent and intense heat waves.

Perhaps the best-known and most influential overview of the linkages between climate change and public health is *The Lancet Countdown*, an annual synthesis report that tracks 43 variables, a subset of which focus on direct health impacts:

- Health and heat including vulnerability to the extremes of heat, exposure of vulnerable populations to heat waves, heat-related mortality,; and change in labor capacity
- Health and extreme weather events including wildfires; flood and drought; lethality of extreme weather events
- Climate-sensitive infectious diseases including climate suitability for infectious disease transmission; and vulnerability to mosquito-borne diseases
- Food security and undernutrition including terrestrial food security and undernutrition, and marine food security and undernutrition
- Migration, displacement, and rising sea levels (adapted from Watts et al., 2020, p. 133)

The World Health Organization (WHO) also tracks linkages between climate change and global health, organizing evidence into three categories: direct impacts, indirect impacts, and social disruption. Much like *The Lancet Countdown*, the WHO explicitly focuses on health-relevant climate effects: higher temperatures; severe weather events; compromised drinking water supplies; poorer air quality; increasing vector-borne disease; and threats to food production, safety, and nutrition (WHO, 2003).

Insofar as the objectives of this chapter are concerned, it is important to note that climate change is also closely linked to violent conflict and the conflict cycle generally. Reports from the IPCC and the United Nations (UN) capture the findings of a large group of analysts who regard climate change as a "risk multiplier" (IPCC, 2014; Rüttinger, Smith, Stang, Tänzler, & Vivekananda, 2015; UN Security Council, 2011). Climate change is expected to escalate the intensity and magnitude of local resource competition, migration, extreme weather events, and disasters (Rüttinger et al., 2015), further increasing stress on already overburdened governance systems and institutions (Crawford & Church, Chapter 7). Regions with low resilience – that is, regions with low capacity to adapt to, recover from and flourish under conditions of ecological stress and change – are at higher risk of facing social unrest and division (Bowles, Butler, & Morisetti, 2015; CNA, 2007; Rüttinger et al., 2015). In fragile governmental systems, climate change can create a feedback loop whereby existing vulnerabilities worsen as scarce resources are shifted from resilience-building measures to emergency responses. This, in turn, can entrench societies further into conflict and unrest.

Climate change can also amplify the factors that lead to the forcible displacement of people. In 2019, UNHCR identified a record 79.5 million people as forcibly displaced; some through war, the majority due to environmental changes that dramatically – and often irreparably – disrupt traditional livelihoods and reduce livelihood options. A cascade of projections suggests this number is posed to increase steeply. For example, in its first *Groundswell Report*, The World Bank concluded that climate-induced internal migration could reach 143 million in Sub-Saharan Africa, Latin America, and South Asia (Rigaud et al., 2018); the Intergovernmental Science-Policy Platform on Biodiversity and Ecosystem Services (IPBES) projects that by 2050, 50–700 million people might be displaced by land degradation and climate change (IPBES, 2018); and the Secretariat of the United Nations Convention to Combat Desertification (UNCCD) has estimated that 135 million people could be displaced by drought by 2045 (UNCCD, 2019). The Institute for Economics & Peace (2020) has suggested that as many as 1.2 billion people might be highly vulnerable to climate change impacts – and thus highly vulnerable to forcible displacement.

While migration is a natural adaptive process used by both human and nonhuman species, and arguably the most persistent and reliable adaptive strategy in the history of humankind (Manning & Clayton, 2018), the numbers suggested earlier would be unprecedented. Where hundreds of millions of people might go to escape unbearably hot and humid conditions between the Tropics, contaminated groundwater along low-lying coastlines, small disappearing islands, or melting ice in the Arctic Circle is impossible to project. But building on current trends, one can imagine the continuing growth of peri-urban areas (Dutta et al., 2020; Matthew & McDonald, 2006). Marshall et al. (2009) explain that "'Peri-urban' . . . refers to the urban fringe and the geographic edge of cities as a place, it refers to the movement of goods and services between physical spaces and to the transition from rural to urban contexts as a process and finally, as a concept, it refers to an interface between rural and urban activities, institutions and perspectives" (p. 3). From a health perspective, this largely unregulated space that facilitates the comingling of domesticated and wild animals and birds, is often densely populated, lacks basic amenities, typically has multiple pathways into urban centers, and may also have an extensive interface with the broader world through rapid transportation systems, is fraught with risk. Indeed, a growing body of evidence has linked the emergence and spread of COVID-19 to both climate change and peri-urban space (Heyd, 2020; Horton & Horton, 2020; Yan Yam, 2020). It would scarcely be surprising to witness a migration of violent conflict into these areas as well.

As important as where people move to, is who is being compelled to move. Forced displacement often involves the migration of people who have very limited resources – little financial capital, possibly few marketable skills – which can create tension with other people along the journey and at whatever final destination they are ultimately able to settle in (see Nizkorodov & Wagle, Chapter 11). Arguments about the linkages between climate change and violent conflict tend to lean heavily on concerns about competition over scarce resources and migration. For example, Matthew, Brown, and Jensen (2009) argue that "attempts to control natural resources or grievances caused by inequitable wealth sharing or environmental degradation can contribute to the outbreak of violence. Countries that depend on the export of a narrow set of primary commodities may also be more vulnerable to conflict" (p. 8). Climate change has emerged as a primary driver of the types of environmental degradation that can be linked to displacement and conflict (Matthew, 2014, 2018).

In short, climate change and violent conflict are complex phenomena that interact in significant ways – climate change can amplify variables that are closely linked to the conflict cycle; the conflict cycle can increase vulnerability to climate change impacts. Moreover, when extreme weather and other climate events interact with conflict, there is a significant likelihood of generating "risk cascades" (Hammer et al., 2018). Risk cascades occur when several interrelated vulnerabilities trigger a series of public health risks. For example, as overcrowding by displaced populations interacts with poor hygiene and sanitation practices, the susceptibility to infectious disease and poor nutrition increases. Poor nutrition undermines the body's immunity and the ability it has to recover. As such, malnutrition is entangled with disease prevalence, recovery, and transmission.

Climate change can also have indirect effects on the health of displaced people. For example, severe weather events can damage formal and informal settlements, make aid and health resources difficult to access, and compromise water sources. Under such conditions, health risks follow vulnerable pathways – for example, a lack of shelter can expose displaced populations to meteorological and hydrological risks. These events can affect water quality and supply, increasing the likelihood of contracting communicable diseases. Respiratory illness and vector-borne disease pose serious threats to those living in substandard conditions (Hammer et al., 2018). While the direct effects of war are often discussed through the quantification of the wounded and killed, conflict also includes secondary and tertiary public health impacts that influence mortality and morbidity and can carry through long after a conflict has ended (Bowles, Butler, & Morisetti, 2015).

Alone or in tandem, climate change and violent conflict affect human health negatively.

Mitigating climate change impacts on health across the conflict cycle

Ideally, progress on mitigation and adaptation would increase quickly and dramatically, reducing the amplifying pressure of climate change impacts on both public health and the propensity for war. But 30 years after the first IPCC Assessment Report, there does not seem to be much basis for optimism. For example, in 2020, PBL, the Dutch equivalent of the US Environmental Protection Agency, which provides an annual estimate of all greenhouse gas emissions worldwide, reported that "global greenhouse gas (GHG) emissions have increased, on average, by 1.1% per year, from 2012 to 2019, which is a markedly lower growth rate than those seen in the first decade of this century (2.6%, on average) (para. 1)." The slope may be softening, but it is still climbing upward. And, this trend is poised to continue. At the Climate Ambition Summit held in December 2020, ten countries pledged to reach net zero emissions by 2050, bringing the total number of countries promising to reach this goal to 35 – or one-sixth of all countries. But, with the exception of China, which used the platform of this forum to announce a commitment to reduce its emissions to 65% of 2005 totals by 2030, these 35 countries and the rest of the world have basically no plans in place for the next decade, really no serious plans in place at all across any time frame. And of special concern, those countries that contribute large volumes of emissions – including Canada, India, and the United States – have not stepped forward with strong commitments.

The story is equally bleak on the adaptation front. In its 2019 report, *Adapt Now: A Global Call for Leadership on Climate Resilience*, the Global Commission on Adaptation noted that concrete examples of climate adaptation "are taking root and beginning to spread" worldwide, but acknowledged that "so far the response has been gravely insufficient" (p. 1). If considerably more effort is not made rapidly, then over the next three decades, we could witness 100 million people fall into extreme poverty, 500 million small farms decline or fail, and some five billion people living in conditions of water insecurity, a massive increase from the current 3.6 billion.

There is a very stark possibility that as climate change impacts worsen, global health will decline and violent conflict will increase in the twenty-first century. To avoid an overwhelming humanitarian crisis, world leaders will have to facilitate and support four types of initiative:

1   Under conditions of climate stress, millions of people – and many nonhuman species – may be forced to move. After World War II, the United States promoted three strategies designed to reduce the likelihood of a third world war: decolonization, democratization, and economic globalization. The reasoning was compelling – a world of territorially

defined, sovereign states, with trade-based economies and largely transparent political systems would have little incentive or opportunity to wage war. It has long been noted that this planetary restructuring generated rapid economic growth, not only producing an ample supply of goods and services to meet basic human needs (although distribution has been problematic) but also causing extensive environmental damage. The system also created massive legal – and often physical – barriers to human movement, barriers that are now becoming the faultlines of a new generation of conflict insofar as they confine people to areas – such as small island states, the hot and arid regions of sub-Saharan Africa, the water-stressed parts of South Asia, or the vulnerable countries in the Atlantic Hurricane Basin – that are becoming uninhabitable. There is a desperate need to rethink migration, protecting it as an adaptation strategy to the greatest extent possible.

2   Climate change and war will create enormous pressures on human health, and culturally and climatically sensitive grassroots public health systems will be critical for purposes of surveillance, education, and support.

3   Since 2016, under the auspices of the United Nations, a discussion has been haltingly unfolding around the need to improve coordination across humanitarian, peacebuilding, and development programs – the so-called humanitarian–development–peace nexus. While the obstacles to extensive coordination may prove insurmountable, some level of coordination seems desirable. For example, these activities overlap but are in large measure sequential; thus, digital platforms could be constructed allowing layers of information to aggregate from one phase to the next, creating opportunities to analyze transitions and identify best practices.

4   Finally, adaptive migration policies, grassroots public health systems, and the humanitarian–development–peace nexus all require resources. The fourth area of considerable importance is innovative financing, including crowdsourcing, private–public partnerships, environmental and social impact bonds, urban wealth assets, green investment portfolios, and microfinance institutions. All of these need to be energized, so the gap between needs and resources does not become a bridge too far.

The role of information technologies

Over the last several decades, the globe has undergone a digital revolution. The development of remote sensing technology and wireless communication has provided unprecedented opportunities to cost-effectively collect, store, aggregate, and process large sets of data (Susha et al., 2019). There is growing recognition that pooling data and analytical skills from diverse sources – citizens, public organizations, private companies, and NGOs – can lead to innovative solutions to pressing social challenges, enable effective decision-making policy-making, and improve the resilience of natural and human systems (Klievink et al., 2018; Susha et al., 2017; Robin et al., 2016). For instance, applying artificial intelligence (AI) and machine learning methods to large, nonlinear, or complex datasets can uncover relationships that were previously not detected through traditional statistical methods.

However, the supply and demand of data is often dispersed across geographies and sectors – conflicting legal jurisdictions, poor communications across sectors, the lack of a data-sharing culture, and the limited data science expertise of smaller nonprofit and civic organizations create data information gaps and delays in response time to crises (Verhulst, 2020). It is important to find ways to overcome these challenges so that information technologies – which have become universally accessible, highly portable, largely affordable, and easier to customize – can be deployed to assist in addressing the public health threats posed by climate change and violent conflict. Key areas of opportunity include:

- Developing early warning systems for conflict and disaster
- Developing surveillance systems for disease detection
- Developing predictive models that minimize uncertainty and can help in navigating conditions of extreme uncertainty
- Developed digital models for peacebuilding that can help communities shape and understand priorities, sequencing, and trade-offs
- Developing platforms for continuous stakeholder engagement, especially at the local level
- Developing AI solutions in critical areas such as WASH systems and food production

Finally, it is important to emphasize that powerful contemporary information technologies are intrusive and sensitive data can be used for a range of purposes, both positive and negative. While the digital revolution has rendered traditional notions of privacy obsolete (Enserink & Chin, 2015), sharing or analyzing sensitive data creates new ethical challenges (Susha et al., 2019). When datasets are shared, anonymization techniques may be absent (Raymond, 2016) or subjects can be reidentified through novel combinations or uses of datasets (Klein & Verhulst, 2017). Currently, there is no framework for data sharing or data use (Verhulst, 2020). Protocols need to be established to protect people and especially vulnerable and marginalized groups.

Another issue is the risk of misaligned policy responses. The outcomes of data science can appear to be very authoritative, even when uncertainty is very high. Imperfect inputs (datasets that are incorrectly aggregated, incomplete, or inaccurate), logics (assumptions underlying the model), or interpretations of data tools can introduce bias, reinforce historical discrimination, or result in negatively impactful policy decisions (Blumenstock, 2018; Janssen & Kuk, 2016; Klein & Verhulst, 2017). It is important not to create a false sense of confidence in outcomes. This risk can be mitigated by developing norms and procedures surrounding quality assurance checks of the data (Susha, Grönlund, & Van Tulder, 2019) and including third parties to verify the inputs and outputs of models (Mikhaylov et al., 2018; Patterson et al., 2019).

The COVID-19 effect

The coronavirus pandemic has had an enormous impact on public health. By the end of September 2021, Worldometer (2021) reported 234 million cases of COVID-19 worldwide and 4.79 million deaths. The pandemic also has had extensive indirect impacts as resources have been shifted to address immediate needs. For example, vaccination campaigns have been disrupted in 45 countries, putting more than 80 million children under the age of one at risk of vaccine-preventable diseases (UN Security Council, 2020). Looking ahead, the World Bank (2020) predicts that COVID-19 will increase income inequality, reduce social mobility (especially among vulnerable populations), increase food insecurity, and lower resilience to future shocks. Without intervention, COVID-19 will reduce inclusive growth (economic growth that is distributed fairly across society and creates opportunities for all) and will deepen inequality (World Bank, 2020, p. 22). In countries with weak health and governance structures, limited resources to combat the pandemic can exacerbate socioeconomic tensions, undermine local governance, and overall erode gains made to peace (UN Security Council, 2020) The United Nations Security Council (2020) argues that fragile and conflict-affected states will be the most affected by COVID-19 in the long term. Indeed, the pandemic has generated novel peacebuilding challenges and disrupted local peacebuilding efforts. Online peacebuilding platforms have emerged but require overcoming accessibility, trust, and capacity issues to succeed (Alberti & Clark, 2020; Eufemia et al., 2020).

One of the positive outcomes of the global pandemic has been further clarification around the ways in which big data can play an important role in disease management through developing early warning systems, contract tracing (through mobile data), screening, determining efficient allocation of resources, and forecasting the effects of an illness on a particular area or the whole population (Bachtiger, Peters, & Walsh, 2020; Chen et al., 2020; Wang et al., 2020). For example, data analysts in the United States combined Facebook's disease prevention maps (global maps with population density estimates) with Mapbox's global routing matrix engine to map the driving distance of each individual to a COVID-19 testing facility (Development Data Partnership, 2020). The visualization tool, which can be applied to any nation, can identify gaps in health care coverage and can enable more informed decision-making in expanding emergency health care services.

The pandemic may incentivize public and private agencies to consolidate public health and wastewater data to develop early warning systems for infectious diseases (Poch et al., 2020; see also Eggimann et al., 2017). Human biomarkers in wastewater can, at a neighborhood level, reveal rates of viral and bacterial infections, use of pharmaceuticals or personal care products, nutrition factors (e.g., obesity factors and sugar intake), and legal and illicit drug use (Eggimann et al., 2017; Garrido-Baserba et al., 2020; Moy de Vitry et al., 2019).

In short, COVID-19, which may have roots in climate change, has itself threatened public health in direct and indirect ways, underscored the special vulnerabilities of people living in conflict-affected regions, disrupted peacebuilding efforts, and almost certainly left a long-term impact of heightened vulnerability in many parts of the world. It has also helped us to understand the needs of people living in conditions of acute vulnerability and the ways in which information technologies might support efforts to manage risk. The lessons we learn from this turbulent year will surely be important ones, but their long-term value depends entirely on the willingness of people to heed those lessons.

Works cited

Alberti, C., & Clark, S. (2020). The challenge of peacebuilding during a pandemic. *LSE Covid 19 Blog*.

Bachtiger, P., Peters, N. S., & Walsh, S. L. (2020). Machine learning for COVID-19 – asking the right questions. *The Lancet Digital Health*, *2*(8), e391-e392.

Blumenstock, J. (2018). Don't forget people in the use of Big Data for development. *Nature*, *561*, 170–172. Retrieved from www.nature.com/articles/d41586-018-06215-5

Bowles, D. C., Butler, C. D., & Morisetti, N. (2015). Climate change, conflict and health. *Journal of the Royal Society of Medicine*, *108*(10), 390–395.

Centers for Disease Control and Prevention (CDC). (2011, June 24). Ten great public health achievements – worldwide, 2001–2010. MMWR Morb Mortal Wkly Rep., *60*(24), 814–818. PMID: 21697806.

Chen, C. M., Jyan, H. W., Chien, S. C., Jen, H. H., Hsu, C. Y., Lee, P. C., . . . Chan, C. C. (2020). Containing COVID-19 among 627,386 persons in contact with the Diamond Princess cruise ship passengers who disembarked in Taiwan: Big data analytics. *Journal of Medical Internet Research*, *22*(5), e19540.

CNA Corporation. (2007). *National security and threat of climate change*. Alexandria: The CNA Corporation.

Development Data Partnership. (2020, March 19). Addressing COVID-19 through Public-Private Data Partnerships – Where Do We Put New Testing Facilities? *Data Partnership*. Retrieved March 28, 2021, from https://datapartnership.org/updates/covid19-and-public-private-data-partnerships/

Dutta, D., Rahman, A., Paul, S. K. et al. (2020). Estimating urban growth in peri-urban areas and its interrelationships with built-up density using earth observation datasets. *Ann Reg Sci*, *65*, 67–82. https://doi.org/10.1007/s00168-020-00974-8

Eggimann, S., Mutzner, L., Wani, O., Schneider, M. Y., Spuhler, D., Moy de Vitry, M., . . . Maurer, M. (2017). The potential of knowing more: A review of data-driven urban water management. *Environmental Science & Technology, 51*(5), 2538–2553.

Enserink, M., & Chin, G. (2015). The end of privacy. *Science, 347*(6221), 490–491. https://doi.org/10.1126/science.347.6221.490

Eufemia, L., Lozano, C., Rodriguez, T., Del Rio, M., Morales-Muñoz, H., Bonatti, M., . . . Löhr, K. (2020). Peacebuilding in times of COVID-19: Risk-adapted strategies of cooperation and development projects. *Zeitschrift für Friedens-und Konfliktforschung,* 1–17.

Frakt, A., & Carroll, A. (2019, February 4). Giant strides in world health, but it could be so much better. *New York Times.* Retrieved from www.nytimes.com/2019/02/04/upshot/giant-strides-in-world-health-but-it-could-be-so-much-better.html

Garrido-Baserba, M., Corominas, L., Cortés, U., Rosso, D., & Poch, M. (2020). The fourth-revolution in the water sector encounters the digital revolution. *Environmental Science & Technology, 54*(8), 4698–4705.

Global Commission on Adaptation. (2019). Adapt now: A global call for leadership on climate resilience. https://files.wri.org/s3fs-public/uploads/GlobalCommission_Report_FINAL.pdf

Hammer, C. C., Brainard, J., & Hunter, P. R. (2018). Risk factors and risk factor cascades for communicable disease outbreaks in complex humanitarian emergencies: A qualitative systematic review. *BMJ Global Health, 3*(4), e000647.

Heyd, T. (2020). Covid-19 and climate change in the times of the Anthropocene. *The Anthropocene Review,* 205301962096179. https://doi.org/10.1177/2053019620961799

Horton, R. (2016). Offline: Planetary health – Gains and challenges. *The Lancet, 388*(10059), 2462. https://doi.org/10.1016/S0140-6736(16)32215-2

Horton, B., & Horton, P. (2020). COVID-19 and the climate emergency: Do common origins and solutions reside in the global agrifood system? *One Earth, 3*(1), 20–22. https://doi.org/10.1016/j.oneear.2020.06.006

ICRC. (2018). *Global trends of war and their humanitarian impacts.* Retrieved from www.icrc.org/en/document/global-trends-war-and-their-humanitarian-impacts-0

Institute for Economics & Peace (IEP). (2020). *Ecological threat register 2020: Understanding ecological threats, resilience and peace,* Sydney, September 2020. Retrieved December 31, 2020, from http://visionofhumanity.org/reports.

Intergovernmental Science-Policy Platform on Biodiversity and Ecosystem Services [IPBES]. (2018). *The assessment report on land degradation and restoration.* Bonn, Germany: Secretariat of the Intergovernmental Science-Policy Platform on Biodiversity and Ecosystem Services.

Intergovernmental Panel on Climate Change (IPCC). (2021). Climate Change 2021: The Physical Science Basis. Contribution of Working Group I to the Sixth Assessment Report of the Intergovernmental Panel on Climate Change. In Masson-Delmotte, V., P. Zhai, A. Pirani, S. L. Connors, C. Péan, S. Berger, N. Caud, Y. Chen, L. Goldfarb, M. I. Gomis, M. Huang, K. Leitzell, E. Lonnoy, J.B.R. Matthews, T. K. Maycock, T. Waterfield, O. Yelekçi, R. Yu and B. Zhou (Eds.). Camrbidge, UK: Cambridge University Press.

IPCC. (2014). *Climate change 2014: Impacts, adaptation, and vulnerability. Part A: Global and sectoral aspects. Contribution of working group ii to the fifth assessment report of the intergovernmental panel on climate change.* Cambridge: Cambridge University Press.

Janssen, M., & Kuk, G. (2016). Big and open linked data (BOLD) in research, policy, and practice. *Journal of Organizational Computing and Electronic Commerce, 26*(1–2), 3–13.

Klein, T., & Verhulst, S. (2017). Access to new data sources for statistics: Business models and incentives for the corporate sector. *PARIS21, Discussion Paper No. 10,*

Klievink, B., Van Der Voort, H., & Veeneman, W. (2018). Creating value through data collaboratives. *Information Polity, 23*(4), 379–397.

Manning, C., & Clayton, S. (2018). Threats to mental health and wellbeing associated with climate change. In S. Clayton, & C. Manning (Eds.), *Psychology and climate change* (pp. 217–244). Academic Press, 2018. https://doi.org/10.1016/B978-0-12-813130-5.00009-6

Marshall, F., Waldman, L., Macgregor, H., Mehta, L., & Randhawa, P. (2009). *On the edge of sustainability: Perspectives on peri-urban dynamics.* STEPS Working Paper 35, Brighton: STEPS Centre.

Matthew, R. (2018). Climate change adaptation and peacebuilding. In A. Swain (Ed.), *Routledge handbook of environmental conflict and peacebuilding* (pp. 108–120). London: Routledge Press.

Matthew, R. (2014). Integrating climate change into peacebuilding. *Climatic Change, 123,* 83–93. https://doi.org/10.1007/s10584-013-0894-1

Matthew, R., Brown, O., & Jensen, D. (2009). *From conflict to peacebuilding: The role of natural resources and the environment*. Geneva: UNEP.

Matthew, R. A., & McDonald, B. (2006). Cities under Siege: Urban planning and the threat of infectious disease. *Journal of the American Planning Association, 72*(1), 109–126.

Mikhaylov, S. J., Esteve, M., & Campion, A. (2018). Artificial intelligence for the public sector: Opportunities and challenges of cross-sector collaboration. *Philosophical Transactions of the Royal Society A: Mathematical, Physical and Engineering Sciences, 376*(2128), 20170357. Retrieved from www.ncbi.nlm.nih.gov/pmc/articles/PMC6107541/

Moy de Vitry, M., Schneider, M. Y., Wani, O. F., Manny, L., Leitão, J. P., & Eggimann, S. (2019). Smart urban water systems: What could possibly go wrong?. *Environment, al Research Letters, 14*(8), 081001.

Palik, J., Rustad, A., & Methi, F. (2020). *Conflict trends: A global overview, 2046–2019*. Oslo: PRIO Conflict Trends: A Global Overview, 1946–2019

Patterson, L., Doyle, M., & Gershuny, G. (2019). *Building an internet of water – A report from the 2017 to 2019 internet of water roundtables*. The Aspen Institute.

PBL. (2020). *Trends in global CO_2 and total greenhouse gas emissions; 2020 Report*. Retrieved from www.pbl.nl/en/publications/trends-in-global-co2-and-total-greenhouse-gas-emissions-2020-report

Poch, M., Garrido-Baserba, M., Corominas, L., Perelló-Moragues, A., Monclús, H., Cermerón-Romero, M., . . . Rosso, D. (2020). When the fourth water and digital revolution encountered COVID-19. *Science of the Total Environment, 744*, 140980.

Raymond, N. A. (2016). Beyond "do no harm" and individual consent: Reckoning with the emerging ethical challenges of civil society's use of data. In L. Taylor, L. Floridi, & B. van der Sloot (Eds.), *Group privacy* (pp. 67–82). Cham: Springer.

Rigaud, K. K., de Sherbinin, A., Jones, B., Bergmann, J., Clement, V., Ober, K., . . . Midgley, A. (2018). *Groundswell: Preparing for internal climate migration*. Washington, DC: The World Bank.

Robin, N., Klein, T., & Jütting, J. (2016). *Public-private partnerships for statistics: Lessons learned, future steps* (No. 8, p. 29). PARIS21 Discussion.

Rüttinger, L., Smith, D. F., Stang, G., Tänzler, D., & Vivekananda, J. (2015). *A new climate for peace: Taking action on climate and fragility risks*. An Independent Report Commissioned by the G7 Members.

Susha, I., Grönlund, Å., & Van Tulder, R. (2019). Data driven social partnerships: Exploring an emergent trend in search of research challenges and questions. *Government Information Quarterly, 36*(1), 112–128.

Susha, I., Janssen, M., & Verhulst, S. (2017). Data collaboratives as a new frontier of cross-sector partnerships in the age of open data: Taxonomy development. *Proceedings of the 50th Hawaii International Conference on System Sciences*, 2691–2700.

United Nations Convention to Combat Desertification [UNCCD]. (2019). *Land and human security*. Retrieved March 18, 2020, from www.unccd.int/issues/land-and-human-security

UN Environment. (2019). *Global environmental outlook 6*. Nairobi: UNEP. Retrieved from www.unep.org/resources/global-environment-outlook-6

UNHCR. (2020). *Figures at a glance*. Retrieved December 31, 2020, from www.unhcr.org/en-us/figures-at-a-glance.html

United Nations Security Council [UNSC]. (2011). *Statement by the President of the security council* (S/PRST/2011/15). Retrieved March 16, 2015, from www.securi- tycouncilreport.org/atf/cf/%7B65BFCF9B-6D27–4E9C-8CD3-CF6E4F- F96FF9%7D/CC%20SPRST%202011%205.pdf

UN Security Council. (2020, September 9). Weakest, Most Fragile States Will Be Those Worst Affected by COVID-19 in Medium, Long Term, Humanitarian Chief Tells Security Council. *United Nations*. Retrieved December 24, 2020, from www.un.org/press/en/2020/sc14296.doc.htm

Verhulst, S. G., & Young, A. (2019). The potential and practice of data collaboratives for migration. In *Guide to Mobile Data Analytics in Refugee Scenarios* (pp. 465–476). Cham: Springer.

Verhulst, S. G. (2020, April 2). The potential of Data Collaboratives for COVID19. *Medium*. Retrieved March 28, 2021, from https://medium.com/data-stewards-network/the-potential-of-data-collaboratives-for-covid19–682946da7bdc

Wang, C. J., Ng, C. Y., & Brook, R. H. (2020). Response to COVID-19 in Taiwan: Big data analytics, new technology, and proactive testing. *JAMA, 323*(14), 1341–1342.

Watts, N., Amann, M., Arnell, N., Ayeb-Karlsson, S., Beagley, J., Belesova, K., . . . Costello, A. (2020). The 2020 report of The Lancet Countdown on health and climate change: Responding to converging crises. *The Lancet, 397*(10269), 129–170. https://doi.org/10.1016/S0140-6736(20)32290-X

Worldometers. (2021, 30 March). *COVID-19 Coronavirus pandemic*. Retrieved March 30, 2021, from www.worldometers.info/coronavirus/

World Bank. (2020). *Poverty and shared prosperity 2020: Reversals of fortune.* Washington, DC: World Bank.

World Health Organization (WHO). (2003). *Climate change and human health: Risks and responses.* Geneva: World Health Organization.

Xu, C., Kohler, T. A., Lenton, T. M., Svenning, J. C., & Scheffer, M. (2020). Future of the human climate niche. *Proceedings of the National Academy of Sciences, 117*(21), 11350–11355. https://doi.org/10.1073/pnas.1910114117

Yan Yam, E. L. (2020). Climate change and the origin of SARS-CoV-2. *Journal of Travel Medicine.* https://doi.org/10.1093/jtm/taaa224

SECTION III

The role of the environment in post-conflict peacebuilding

14

NATURAL RESOURCE GOVERNANCE REFORM AND ENVIRONMENTAL PEACEBUILDING

Michael D. Beevers

In the 1990s, roughly 90% of all armed conflicts were internal and located in the developing world (Wallensteen & Sollenberg, 2001). Genocide, ethnic cleansing, child soldiers, hacking off limbs, executions, and other atrocities were commonplace, and a large majority of those killed were civilians (UNDP, 2002). Beyond the death and destruction, these conflicts were perceived as a threat to international security as problems like terrorism, organized crime, drug, weapons and human trafficking, disease, and refugees could spill over borders or "leap around the world" at a moment's notice (USAID, 2005, p. v). To assist and manage conflict-affected states, peacebuilding emerged as a novel form of international intervention. Ceasefires, peace agreements, peacekeepers, elections, and similar security measures were the priority of peacebuilding operations early on. High rates of conflict relapse, however, made it clear that peacebuilding efforts had to focus on not only ending conflict but also establishing the underlying conditions necessary to achieve long-term peace (Boutros-Ghali, 1992). Poverty and failed economic development were identified as key determinants of peacebuilding failure (Collier, Elliot, Hå, Reynal-Querol, & Sambanis, 2003). As such, the peacebuilding agenda increasingly stressed conventional development objectives of economic growth and poverty alleviation and emphasized that there can be "no development without security and no security without development" (Annan, 2005, p. 55; see also Paris, 2004). Peacebuilding efforts quickly expanded to include "sustainable development, the eradication of poverty and inequalities, transparent and accountable governance, the promotion of democracy, respect for human rights and the rule of law, and the promotion of a culture of peace and non-violence" (UNSC, 2001).

Natural resources became central to peacebuilding as evidence indicated that resources could trigger armed conflict and make peace difficult to sustain. Early scholarship argued that scarcities of renewable resources like land, water, and forests, worsened by environmental degradation, population growth, and inequitable distribution of land, could trigger violent conflict (Homer-Dixon, 1994). Other research contended just the opposite – that resource wealth increased the risk of conflict. Work by Collier and Hoeffler (1998) suggested that the presence of "lootable" natural resources provided insurgents with opportunities for self-enrichment and the revenues necessary for financing armed conflict (see also Lujala et al., Chapter 10). Rather than political or social grievances, they argued conflicts after the Cold War were mainly caused by a "selfish desire to loot the resources of others" (Collier & Hoeffler, 1999, p. 15). Related research found that states dependent on natural resource exports tend to be more corrupt, economically weak, impoverished, and authoritarian, all of which make armed conflict more likely (Ross, 2004; Collier, 2007). Indeed, between 1970 and 2008, between 29% and 56% of all armed conflicts involved natural resources (Rustad &Binningsbø, 2012).

In countries emerging from conflict, there is a governance vacuum. Peacebuilding affords a window of opportunity to reforms laws, policies, institutions, and practices, including how natural resources are governed. Over the last two decades, numerous governance reforms have been employed to end conflict and build peace. The governance reforms were principally designed by international actors to establish, perpetuate, or alter the "rules of the game" that dictate how society manages and values its natural resources.

I argue in this chapter that natural governance reforms to date have overwhelmingly focused on two fundamental and interrelated objectives that mirror the objectives of peacebuilding agenda more generally: *security* and *development*. Security and development reforms stress – on the one hand, extracting natural resources for economic growth, poverty alleviation and revenue generation, and on the other hand, instituting good governance provisions to ensure resources are not exploited, and resource revenues do not reignite conflict. These reforms deserve credit. In many places, the outright plunder of resources has ended, institutions are being rebuilt, laws are being implemented, and investments in extraction are showing promise (Bruch, Muffett, & Nichols, 2016). Yet, the reforms that focus on security and development objectives remain limited and contain "blind spots" that make peacebuilding more challenging. The reforms, for example, run the risk of recreating the very systems that historically led to exploitation, exclusion, and corruption and fail to adequately address elements related to the environment, livelihoods, and human rights that can reduce insecurities that people and communities, especially the most vulnerable and marginalized, often bear. More than that, security and development reforms tend toward competition and contention and reduce opportunities for cooperation and trust building so important to achieving a long-term peace.

This chapter proceeds as follows. It begins with an overview of efforts to improve natural resource governance to end armed conflict and build peace. The section highlights how the reforms primarily center on security and development objectives. It then goes on to discuss the limits and "blind spots" of natural resource governance reforms stressing why they pose a potential challenge to peacebuilding. The final section argues for a more holistic "environmental peacebuilding" agenda that infuses security and development reforms with measures pertaining to the environment, livelihoods, and human rights.

Governing natural resources for peace: a security and development agenda

In many post-conflict countries, natural resources were a key part of the economy, employment, and budgets before the wars (UNEP, 2009; Lujala & Rustad, 2012). Armed conflict destroys economies, intensifies poverty, leaves infrastructure in disrepair, and undermines the ability of governments to meet the basic needs of its citizens. High-value natural resources can help spur economic recovery, create jobs, alleviate poverty, and provide revenue for cash-strapped governments after conflicts end. Compared to other economic sectors (agriculture or manufactured goods, for example), resource extraction can ostensibly be carried out rapidly and often have robust revenue-generating potential, and if harnessed effectively can support reconstruction. Natural resources are also considered vital because entrenched poverty and weak economic growth – together with poor governance – produce a "conflict trap" (Collier, 2007). That is, continued conflict keeps people locked in cycles of poverty and underdevelopment, and poverty

Natural resource governance reform

and underdevelopment increase the risk of armed conflict. More than that, there is a presumption that that "development brings peace" (Bannon & Collier, 2003, p. 8). Put another way, rising incomes and more economic development can improve human well-being and make people less inclined to rebel.

It should not be surprising, then, that following armed conflict, international actors identify natural resources that can be extracted to support reconstruction and development efforts (Lujala, Rustad, & Kettenmann, 2016; World Bank, 2004). Attracting foreign direct investment in natural resource sectors and enacting "business friendly" governance reforms is generally a peacebuilding priority (Klein & Joras, 2016). The granting of contracts and concessions by governments for natural resource extraction regularly follow in the years after armed conflict (Rustad, Lujala, & Le Billon, 2012). In fact, there is substantial pressure on governments to liberalize their economies after conflicts end based on the underlying logic that pursuing free-market economic models will not only promote development but also reduce tensions and foster peace (Paris, 2004). The problem, of course, is that resource extraction in post-conflict countries is not straightforward. Enticing reputable companies can be difficult due to the business and investment risks involved. Political instability, poor infrastructure, and endemic corruption are often the norm in post-conflict countries, and legal and regulatory provisions dealing with taxes or property rights are uncertain or in flux. Moreover, if not governed properly, revenues from the exploitation of natural resources can reignite conflict. State institutions have little capacity and are not up to the task of governing resources effectively. This opens up opportunities for groups, be they former combatants or corrupt government leaders to compete for resource-rich areas or shape arrangements in their favor. As Le Billon (2012) argued, "Peace spoilers tend to hold on, or hang around, resource areas in hope of accessing funding for renewed hostilities" (p. 189).

Various interventions have been enacted to target the revenues from natural resources believed to have financed conflicts. The most publicized are UN sanctions that ban the import or export of so-called conflict resources to stop the flow of revenues to rebel groups or other combatants (Le Billon, 2003). Since 2003, the United Nation has imposed sanctions on at least eight countries (most frequently African countries) and predominantly targeted timber, oil, and diamonds. Another way to limit revenues was to directly control natural resources believed to have fueled conflict to keep belligerents (or potential belligerents) from exploiting the resources for nefarious purposes. Although reluctant to deploy UN peacekeepers directly to resource-rich areas, international actors have pressured governments to cancel or review resource contracts or concessions after conflicts end (Le Billon, 2012). By addressing resources contracts and opening them up to scrutiny, one can potentially sever the links between resources, revenues, and conflict. Another approach to secure natural resources and curtail the ability of rebels or potential rebels to exploit resource revenues are commodity-tracking schemes. These global governance schemes indirectly regulate natural resource extraction by tracking the illicit trade of otherwise legal commodities such as diamonds, minerals, and timber. The most advanced in this regard is the Kimberley Process Certification Scheme, which was created in 2000 (and came into full effect in 2003) to govern the global trade in rough diamonds, and the Forest Law Enforcement Governance and Trade initiative that encourages timber-producing countries to track timber and timber proceeds.

Paradoxically, the presence of natural resources can lead to economic and political dysfunction and ultimately a higher risk of renewed conflict. To ensure that resource extraction contributes to the development and the public interest, and at the same time does not jeopardize security, other governance reforms have been applied in countries emerging from armed conflict. These reforms reflect "good governance," which is a set of established principles about how governments should conduct themselves and manage resources and assets on behalf of its citizens (Lausche, 2011). Following international norms, natural resource governance reforms have tended to emphasize transparency, accountability, and public participation (Bruch et al., 2016). Transparency reduces the likelihood that revenues will be siphoned off by corrupt elites or societal groups in ways that undermine peace and development. Transparency also addresses the "resource curse" by exposing and rooting out corruption. More openness to information makes it possible for civil society groups and international actors to hold government officials and extractive companies accountable for revenue collected as well as important decisions and processes regarding extraction and the passing of laws and regulations (Le Billon, 2012). Transparency and accountability provisions certainly find their way into domestic laws and regulations regarding natural resources, but significant attention has been on international schemes to promote transparency and accountability. The Extractive Industries Transparency Initiative (EITI), for example, commits signatories to disclose payments from extractive industries (oil, gas, mining, timber). Under EITI, companies are required to disclose the payments they make to governments. By comparing payments received versus payments made, the objective is to address corruption and ensure that payments for resource extraction are funneled through official government channels. Public participation in resource-based decisions is important if extractive sectors are to become operational and have the support of local communities and the population at large. International peacebuilders emphasized the importance of consulting communities about resource extraction, especially given the lack of participation and inclusion in the past (Bruch et al., 2016). Public participation incorporates efforts to communicate with, and provide information to, local communities about environmental and social impacts, revenue sharing, and other community benefits as well as compensation for losses of land, jobs, livelihoods, or dwellings.

Although the earlier review is brief, I suggest that post-conflict natural governance reforms have focused on two fundamental and interrelated objectives: security and development. Development is concerned with efforts to harness the economic potential of natural resources to contribute to government, revenue, economic growth, and poverty alleviation. The argument is that if development proceeds apace, and incomes rise, security will be improved. Security denotes efforts to ensure that natural resource extraction goes forth in ways that will not foster renewed conflict. Illegal or unofficial extraction, or smuggling, could provide potential combatants or corrupt officials with the funds to reignite conflict or otherwise undermine development prospects. "Good governance," for its part, is the glue that binds security and development together through laws, regulations, institutions, policies, and practices that support among other things, accountability, transparency, and public participation. As Bannon and Collier (2003, 8) put it,

> building a more peaceful world is not just a matter of encouraging tolerance and consensus. It should involve a practical agenda for economic development and effective global governance of [natural resource] markets that have come to facilitate rebellion and corrupt governance.

(p. 8)

The limits and blind spots of the security and development agenda

Numerous factors determine whether a conflict will end or peace will be long lasting. No single factor causes conflict and a single factor will ensure peace. Natural resources, however, are correlated with conflict relapse. Rustad and Binningsbø (2012) found that the period of peace is 40% shorter when natural resources are involved. An influx of scholarly work has emerged to better understand the connection between natural resource governance and peacebuilding (see Bruch et al., 2016; Le Billon, 2012; Lujala & Rustad, 2012). We have a better idea about the range of governance strategies employed in the pursuit of peace and more clarity concerning how to design, implement, and assess natural resource governance initiatives. Nevertheless, attempts to govern natural resources after conflict have been characterized as a "limited success" (Rustad, Lujala, & Le Billon, 2012, p. 571). Natural resource governance has also had unintended consequences for peacebuilding (Rustad et al., 2012; Beevers, 2015). The reasons given range from ineffective government institutions, a lack of capacity, and corruption to a lack of commitment in terms of political will and financial resources. This is only part of the story, however. I argue later that the reforms that focus on security and development objectives are limited and contain "blind spots" that make peacebuilding more challenging.

Mirroring historical natural resource governance arrangements

Natural resource governance reforms that emphasize the dual objectives of security and development deserve praise. Efforts to address natural resource exploitation and manage resource revenues have generally helped to end the all-out plunder of natural resources (Lujala & Rustad, 2012). UN sanctions have arguably been effective at limiting access to resource revenues by rebel groups and other combatants (Le Billon & Nicholls, 2007). Commodity-tracking schemes like the Kimberley Process have helped formalize extraction in the resource trade and have curtailed illegal exploitation allowing more revenues to be collected by governments (Bone, 2012). State institutions have been strengthened, and new laws and regulations to manage the resource base, extraction processes, and related revenues and expenditures have improved. "Good governance" reforms have helped normalize transparency, improve accountability, and make public participation more widespread, thereby assisting the difficult task of managing resources for long-term development (Bruch et al., 2016). The reforms have been a tool for addressing corruption and mismanagement, and as resource extraction in post-conflict countries has increased, so too have official exports and government revenues. Yet, it is also clear that the governance reforms remain contentious and controversial because, I would argue, they mirror historical governing arrangements (Beevers, 2015).

First, the governance reforms of security and development accentuate the importance of state control over natural resources and extraction. This should not be surprising. The failure of states to govern resources has been linked to natural resource conflicts because either rebels are able to exploit natural resources or bad governance triggers the resource curse. States are also paradoxically deemed the most effective manager of natural resources due to their sovereign claim over territory and capacity to establish and enforce the "rules of the game" that govern society. States enforce property rights, and their agencies presumably have the knowledge and capacity to manage how land is used, resources are extracted, and the environment is protected. Local institutions, by contrast, are deemed incapable of governing resources sustainably or without conflict. What often goes unstated is that predatory state officials have long used their power to exploit natural resources, and control land for their own benefit, or the benefit of their patrons. Local communities are frequently denied access to, or use of, natural resources. Worse, their land and livelihoods are taken away and despoiled. In these instances, people do not receive a fair share of benefits and are excluded from decisions about how land and resources are distributed and used.

After conflict, simply reifying the state as the dominant authority in resource governance can recreate past disputes about land ownership and access to natural resources. In Liberia, for instance, efforts to restart the timber sector after the war went forward even though areas designated by the state for extraction had overlapping ownership arrangements. Long-standing disputes related to land became a point of serious contention (Beevers, 2016). The myopic focus on state-led extraction further delegitimizes other approaches to resource governance. Statutory legal frameworks created by states, for example, habitually dominate in a post-conflict setting although a variety of customary or ad hoc resource, land, and tenure arrangements exist (Unruh & Williams, 2013). This contributes to confusion about who owns the land and rekindles historical tensions and social conflicts around land and natural resources. Despite calls for more local or decentralized management structures and evidence that such structures provide higher livelihood and environmental benefits (Larson & Soto, 2008; Persha, Agrawal, & Chhatre, 2011), community-based management is scoffed at compared to centralized approaches.

Second, the idea that state-led resource extraction is a net positive for peace and development is being questioned. Well-governed natural resources are widely believed to have long-term positive effects if governed effectively (Collier & Venables, 2011). For this reason, restarting extractive industries is a peacebuilding priority, and governance reforms have focused on managing extraction and resource revenue in ways that enhance security and spur development. Still, in many post-conflict settings, challenges with resource extraction persist. In many places, anticipated revenue, employment, and community benefits of extraction have not materialized, and companies awarded concessions have violated the law (Beevers, 2015). Disagreements with communities continue to be ubiquitous, and issues related to land ownership, user rights, and public participation are a source of deep-seated tension and resentment (Beevers, 2016). Contracts between extractive companies and governments are repeatedly negotiated in secret and without stakeholder or community input. There is diminished faith that a system built on "patron-client" relations, and which treats people as passive objects of development can truly benefit local communities that were historically exploited and excluded from the benefits of resource extraction.

This is not to say that governance reforms are unimportant. It does raise questions as to whether the reforms go far enough to transform natural resource governance. The assumption is that the benefits of state-led resource extraction, coupled with "good governance," will "trickle down" to the people and generate positive outcomes for development and peace. Admittedly, reaping the rewards of current governance reforms will take many years. However, there is a risk of recreating the very systems of exploitation, exclusion, and corruption that have historically plagued so many post-conflict countries. In addition, the reforms that emphasize security and development need to be integrated with additional activities that focus on the environment, livelihoods, and human rights.

Blind spots: environment, livelihood, and human rights

Beyond the risk of recreating systems of exploitation, exclusion, and corruption, natural resource governance focused on security and development comes with significant "blind spots." Specifically, it focuses exclusively on "high-value" natural resources like timber, diamonds, and minerals and top-down "good governance" reforms. This is not unexpected given that armed conflicts are routinely blamed on these resources and formulas for addressing these issues focused on transparency, accountability, and the rule of law. This focus, while important, has rendered invisible elements related to the environment, livelihoods, and human rights that are both linked to natural resources and vital for peacebuilding success.

The environment and issues related to water, sanitation, shelter, food, and energy supplies have been largely overlooked during peacebuilding operations. Armed conflicts, directly and indirectly, damage environments and other natural assets that people rely on for their well-being. A failure to respond to environmental issues keeps people and communities vulnerable and insecure and locked into cycles of poverty and conflict that can be difficult to break. A lack of attention to the environment can also exacerbate tensions and make peacebuilding more challenging. As Conca and Wallace (2009) note, "at worst, tensions triggered by environmental problems or contested access to natural resources may lead to renewed conflict; more generally, a failure to meet basic environmental needs undercuts reconciliation, political institutionalization and economic reconstruction" (p. 486). Attention to the environment further helps bring dimensions of resource extraction (and development projects) and perverse land ownership arrangements that undercut livelihoods and create grievances to the forefront of conflict mitigation and peacebuilding.

Natural resource governance reforms tend to underemphasize livelihoods as well. Livelihoods, by definition, are the "capabilities, assets and activities required for a means of a living" (Scoones, 1998, p. 5). Livelihoods depend directly on the environment, natural resources, and land, and a failure to address people's livelihood needs certainly complicates peacebuilding (Young & Goldman, 2015). Without access to livelihoods, people and communities will remain marginalized and embedded in cycles of vulnerability and helplessness that can be difficult to escape. An inability to procure livelihoods can lead to conflict as strains linked to livelihoods increase. Thus, increased attention must be paid to factors that habitually impede the ability of people and communities to meet their livelihoods such as resource extraction, land ownership arrangements, and environmental degradation. Strengthening governance institutions and improving the provision of livelihoods can promote equitable access to natural resources and support local development and other economic opportunities. Livelihoods, by nature, are important to identity and, therefore, self-worth and dignity, which enhances livelihood opportunities for disempowered groups, including women.

Finally, the emphasis on security and development discounts rights-based approaches to natural resource governance. Rights-based approaches refer to norms that protect all people from human rights abuses and guarantees the right to life, personal and collective security, food, health, an adequate standard of living, the practice of culture, and freedom from discrimination. Human rights abuses are at times a root cause of armed conflict through "limited political participation, the quest for self-determination, limited access to resources, exploitation, forced acculturation, and discrimination" or the inability or unwillingness of the state to protect its citizens from social divisions or economic hardship (Parlevliet, 2002, p. 5). A reluctance to address abuses of human rights will make peacebuilding difficult (Parlevliet, 2017). Applied to natural resource governance, rights can help break cycles of vulnerability linked to the environment, livelihoods, and resource extraction. Local demands would more explicitly drive resource extraction and provide a powerful rationale for people and communities to be consulted to actively participate in decisions and have free, prior, and informed consent about actions that affect their land and resources. States, for their part, would be obligated to act as the responsible party that guarantees and safeguards these rights. Rights-based approaches provide a tool by which people and communities can press claims against predatory or corrupt states and support international and domestic reforms to enhance accountability, transparency, and the rule of law.

Opportunities for environmental peacebuilding

Security and development reforms stress, on the one hand, extracting natural resources for economic growth, poverty alleviation, and revenue generation, and on the other hand, emphasizing good governance to ensure resources were not exploited, and that the revenues did not reignite conflict. The reason for the focus on these reform elements is understandable. Armed conflicts have been linked to the revenues of natural resources, and extraction of these same resources is generally viewed as essential for peace and development. Efforts to address natural resources after conflicts have often helped end the worst of the resource plunder, and transparency and accountability have improved. However, I have argued in this chapter that the focus on security and development as the basis of natural resource governance reforms is ultimately insufficient for building robust and long-lasting peace. For one, contestation and controversy, and even violence, continue to plague post-conflict natural resource extraction. This is because the reforms mirror natural resource governance arrangements that have long produced antagonism and conflict. In fact, the reforms do not do enough to address the conditions that leave people and communities vulnerable, insecure and marginalized, and aggravate tensions by provoking competition and eroding trust. Prioritizing state-led resource extraction, for example, conflicts with community management of resources or legal pluralism and exacerbates grievances around land ownership, access to and benefits from extraction and livelihoods, which generally pits communities, extractive industries, and governments against each other. Second, the reforms ignore issues linked to the environment, livelihoods, and rights that are important to both governing natural resources and peacebuilding. Without adequate attention to the environment, livelihoods, and human rights, which are all deeply intertwined with natural resources, it will be difficult to fully address persistent human insecurities that are vital for achieving long-term peace.

The emphasis on security and development limits opportunities for environmental peacebuilding. Environmental peacebuilding, or environmental peacemaking, refers to the possibilities of using the environment and natural resources to foster cooperation and build trust in ways that not only consolidate peace but also transform societies (Conca & Dabelko, 2002; see also Bruch et al., Chapter 2). The environment and livelihoods are shared resources, the management of which can incite cooperation that over time builds trust and confidence among an array of actors. Dialogue and consultations open up pathways to resolve problems and devise solutions to issues related to water, land, food and agriculture, livelihoods and health while creating shared identities that can potentially overcome political and social barriers. Rights-based approaches similarly create opportunities for cooperation as societal groups become aware of their mutual rights to environmental sustainability, sustainable development, and livelihoods. Merging security and development approaches to natural resource governance with elements of environment, livelihoods, and rights has the potential to not only end conflicts but also open up new possibilities for peace.

Works cited

Annan, K. (2005). *In larger freedom: Towards development, security and human rights for all*. Report of the United Nations Secretary-General, A/59/2005. New York: United Nations.

Bannon, I., & Collier, P. (Eds.). (2003). *Natural resources and violent conflict*. Washington, DC: The World Bank.

Beevers, M. D. (2015). Governing natural resources for peace: Lessons from Liberia and Sierra Leone. *Global Governance, 21*(2), 227–246.

Beevers, M. D. 2016. Forest governance and post-conflict peace in Liberia: Emerging contestation and opportunities for change? *The Extractive Industries and Society, 3*(2), 320–328.

Bone, A. (2012). The Kimberley process certification scheme: The primary safeguard for the diamond industry. In P. Lujala & S. A. Rustad (Eds.), *High-Value Natural Resources and Post-Conflict Peacebuilding* (pp. 189–194). New York: Earthscan.

Boutros-Ghali, B. 1992. *An agenda for peace: Preventative diplomacy, peacemaking and peacekeeping*. New York: United Nations.

Natural resource governance reform

Bruch, C., Muffett, C., & Nichols, S. S. (Eds.). 2016. *Governance, natural resources, and post-conflict peacebuilding*. New York: Earthscan.

Conca, K., & Dabelko, G. D. (2002). *Environmental peacemaking*. Washington, DC: Woodrow Wilson Center.

Collier, P. (2007). *The bottom billion: Why the poorest countries are failing and what can be done about it*. Oxford: Oxford University Press.

Collier, P., & Hoeffler, A. (1998). On economic causes of civil war. *Oxford Economic Papers 50*. Oxford: Oxford University.

Collier, P., & Hoeffler, A. (1999). Justice-seeking and loot-seeking in civil war. *World Bank Paper*. Washington, DC: World Bank.

Collier, P., & Venables, A. (Eds.). (2011). *Plundered nations? Successes and failures in natural resource extraction*. Basingstoke: Palgrave-Macmillan Press.

Collier, P., Elliot, V. L., Hå, A. H., Reynal-Querol, M., & Sambanis, N. (2003). *Breaking the conflict trap: Civil war and development policy*. Washington, DC: World Bank.

Conca, K., & Wallace, J. (2009). Environment and peacebuilding in war-torn societies: Lessons from the UN environment programme's experience with postconflict assessment. *Global Governance*, *15*(4), 485–504.

Homer-Dixon, T. F. (1994). Environmental scarcities and violent conflict: Evidence from cases. *International Security*, *19*(1), 5–40.

Klein, D., & Joras, U. (2016). Natural resources and peacebuilding: The role of the private sector. In C. Bruch, C. Muffett, & S. S. Nichols (Eds.), *Governance, natural resources, and post-conflict peacebuilding* (pp. 931–949). New York: Earthscan.

Larson, A. M., & Soto, F. (2008). Decentralization of natural resource governance regimes. *Annual Review of Environment and Resources*, *33*, 213–239.

Lausche, B. (2011). *Guidelines for protected area legislation*. IUCN Environmental Policy and Law Paper 18. Gland, Switzerland: IUCN Environmental Law Center.

Le Billon, P. (2003). Getting it done: Instruments of enforcement. In I. Bannon & P. Collier (Eds.), *Natural resources and violent conflict* (pp. 215–286). Washington, DC: The World Bank.

Le Billon, P. (2012). *Wars of plunder: Conflicts, profits and the politics of resources*. New York: Columbia University Press.

Le Billon, P., & Nicholls, E. (2007). Ending resource wars: Revenue sharing, economic sanction or military intervention. *International Peacekeeping*, *14*(5), 613–632.

Lujala, P., & Rustad, S. A. (Eds.). (2012). *High-value natural resources and post-conflict peacebuilding*. New York: Earthscan.

Lujala, P., Rustad, S. A., & Kettenmann, S. (2016). Engines for peace? Extractive industries, host countries and the international community in post-conflict peacebuilding. *Natural Resources*, *7*(5), 239–250.

Paris, R. (2004). *At war's end: Building peace after civil conflict*. Cambridge: Cambridge University Press.

Parlevliet, M. (2002). Bridging the divide: Exploring the relationship between human rights and conflict management. *Track Two*, *11*(1), 8–43.

Parlevliet, M. (2017). Human rights and peacebuilding: Complementary and contradictory, complex and contingent. *Journal of Human Rights Practice*, *9*(3), 333–357.

Persha, L., Agrawal, A., & Chhatre, A. (2011). Social and ecological Synergy: Local rulemaking, forest livelihoods, and biodiversity conservation. *Science*, *331*(6024), 1606–1608.

Ross, M. L. (2004). How do natural resources influence civil war? Evidence from thirteen cases. *International Organization*, *58*(1), 35–67.

Rustad, S. A., & Binningsbø, H. M. (2012). A price worth fighting for? Natural resources and conflict recurrence. *Journal of Peace Research*, *49*(4), 531–546.

Rustad, S. A., Lujala, P., & Le Billon, P. (2012). Building or spoiling peace? Lessons from the management of high-value natural resources. In P. Lujala & S. A. Rustad (Eds.), *High-value natural resources and post-conflict peacebuilding* (pp. 571–621). New York: Earthscan.

Scoones, I. (1998). *Sustainable rural livelihoods: A framework for analysis. Institute of development studies working paper 72*. Brighton UK, University of Sussex: IDS.

Unruh, J., & Williams, R. C. (2013). *Land and post-conflict peacebuilding*. New York: Earthscan.

UNDP (United Nations Development Programme). (2002). *Human development report 2002: Deepening democracy in a fragmented world*. Oxford: Oxford University Press.

UNEP (United Nations Environment Programme). (2009). *From conflict to peacebuilding: The role of natural resources and the environment*. Geneva: UNEP.

UNSC (United Nations Security Council). (2001). *Statement by the President of the security council.* S/PRST/2001/5.

USAID (United States Agency for International Development). (2005). *Failed states strategy.* Washington, DC: USAID.

Wallensteen, P., & Sollenberg, M. (2001). Armed conflict, 1989–2000. *Journal of Peace Research, 38*(5), 629–644.

World Bank. (2004). *The role of the World Bank in conflict and development: An evolving agenda.* Washington, DC: World Bank.

Young, H., & Goldman, L. (Eds.). (2015). *Livelihoods, natural resources and post-conflict peacebuilding.* New York: Earthscan.

15

URBAN DIMENSIONS OF PEACEBUILDING

Green infrastructure in Kigali, Rwanda, and Freetown, Sierra Leone, as a means for more resilient peace

Bemmy Maharramli

The intersection between the environment and peacebuilding has often been imagined to be largely in remote forests and rural areas, where rich natural resources or alternatively the scarcity of natural resources can play a role in conflict. However, increasingly practitioners and scholars are recognizing the intersections, both direct and indirect, in the places that most people in the world live – cities. As discussed previously in the Handbook, environmental peacebuilding is defined as the integration of natural resource management across the conflict life cycle – from conflict prevention and mitigation to resolution and recovery – to build resilience in communities that have been affected by conflict (Environmental Peacebuilding Association, 2018; see also Bruch et al., Chapter 2). As Beevers (2015) notes, natural resources are central to driving or even financing conflict, and their governance can be central to peacebuilding and post-conflict recovery (see also Lujala et al., Chapter 10; Beevers, Chapter 14). As Floyd and Matthew (2013) demonstrate, the consideration of the environment in a large range of issues has propelled a rethinking of the links between human security and the environment, encompassing a diverse range of issues from conventional views of national security to poverty, public health, and natural disasters.

Green infrastructure is defined as a planned network of natural and/or seminatural areas that incorporate environmental features to strategically manage multiple ecosystem services, such as water filtration (e.g., wetlands), urban cooling, provisioning of community spaces, and more (Hansen & Pauleit, 2014; European Commission, 2013). Green infrastructure has been espoused as a way to ensure ecosystem service flow or operationalization of ecosystem service delivery to communities (Ahern, Cilliers, & Niemela, 2014). It has also been described as important to public health, with green infrastructure as a potential link between ecosystem services and ecosystem health (Stokols, Grzywacz, Mcmahan, & Phillips, 2003; Tzoulas et al., 2007). Cities are important places post-conflict as they are particularly vulnerable to violence (Goodfellow & Smith, 2013) and are subject to dramatic change (e.g., population changes). Therefore, this confluence of the vulnerability of cities post-conflict and green infrastructure is important to examine together. Green infrastructure can be seen as something that is both vulnerable during and after conflict as well as a tool to help strengthen the resilience of the city during recovery.

Urban Environmental Peacebuilding (UEPB) occurs in urban settings, as opposed to more rural settings, and brings with it its own set of circumstances, challenges, and opportunities. This chapter seeks to explore how urban green infrastructure is affected by conflict and evaluates its role in improving the resilience of post-conflict cities. To illustrate the opportunities and challenges of incorporating green infrastructure in post-conflict recovery and UEPB, the chapter examines two case studies – Kigali, Rwanda, and Freetown, Sierra Leone.

It is important to note that many ecosystems and watersheds are not restrained to municipal boundaries and are often more regional in scale. Therefore, while the chapter focuses on cities and the urban dimensions of natural resources, it acknowledges that the boundary between urban and rural areas is often blurry, with many connected and dynamic human and ecosystem service flows between the two and along with the urban–rural interface.

Major ways urban green infrastructure is impacted during conflict

There are urban dimensions and implications associated with conflict, with some links having been made between urbanization trends and conflict (Goodfellow & Smith, 2013). Generally speaking, green infrastructure can be impacted in a city in one or more of the following three ways: (1) direct conflict in a city; (2) displacement from a conflict in other areas to an urban area (e.g., the sanctuary city role); and/or (3) rebuilding, often hastily and unplanned, after conflict has affected a city in some way.

Critical infrastructure in a city can be strategic targets during conflict, or the urban area itself can be targeted as a prize to be captured (Goodfellow & Smith, 2013). If an urban area is situated as a direct part of the conflict, in addition to the great social and economic trauma that can be felt by a city's inhabitants, there can also be great damage to the green infrastructure the city relies upon, even without fully appreciating or realizing this reliance. For example, if a city is targeted or captured during a conflict, a host of environmental challenges can follow, such as reduced air quality, contamination of water resources and waste management systems, destruction of trees and safe parks or open spaces, and/or exposure (chronic or acute) to toxins. These can have disastrous consequences for public health.

During conflict, individuals may be displaced or will migrate away from conflict across international borders or to other parts of the same country. Generally, displaced individuals are now more likely to be found in urban areas than rural ones (Brookings Institute, 2013; Lynch, Maconachie, Binns, Tengbe, & Bangura, 2013). Sometimes, a city can be perceived as a more secure place related to other parts of the country or regions that are considered still too volatile (Goodfellow & Smith, 2013). These refugees or internally displaced individuals (IDPs) often face many new social, economic, and cultural challenges associated with starting over. In addition, displaced individuals coming into urban areas are often settled or self-settle into crowded, less desirable parts of the city where there is scant green space, higher levels of pollution and exposure to toxins, and poor waste management and water quality (see Nizkorodov & Wagle, Chapter 11). There is a lot of variation depending upon the context of the adopted country or city – with some refugees or IDPs beginning their new life in a sprawling urban slum and others crowded into a more established neighborhood, but with relative poverty compared to other parts of the city. The increase in urban density can create political backlash and tensions in a newly adopted city and country, such as xenophobia, racism, nationalism, etc. (see Nizkorodov & Wagle, Chapter 11), which has been evident by the recent upsurge in refugees from Syria to Europe and the rise of antiimmigrant, far-right political backlash that has come along with it.

And lastly, after a direct conflict or as a means to accommodate new migrants, cities will often rush to rebuild (whole cities or sections of a city) during or right after a conflict. Frequently, this building is unplanned and does not fully accommodate the needs of the residents. Understandably, after a conflict decision-makers and communities often want to quickly get the city up and running again to resume some sort of normalcy. However, this short-term rush to build can come at the cost of strategic planning and building a more livable city. It can be a missed opportunity to consider how the city – or a neighborhood within a city – might incorporate or leverage other elements, such as green infrastructure or urban natural capital to improve the environmental security, resilience, and quality of life for residents. Poorer neighborhoods within cities that are rebuilt rapidly are often vulnerable in both the short and long terms to floods, sea-level rise, landslides, urban heat island effects, and other natural disasters. The integration of green infrastructure across the built environment can help increase urban resilience, particularly for low-income communities.

In the following section, we provide a summary of the conflicts that took place in Rwanda and Sierra Leone, followed by an analysis of how this conflict both affected the green infrastructure and how green infrastructure can be a part of the solution in these two major cities in the aftermath of conflict.

Case studies: Kigali, Rwanda, and Freetown, Sierra Leone

These cities were selected because they were both devastated by civil war in the 1990s, and their capital cities were deeply affected during and after the conflict. Both countries have since focused on peacebuilding, rebuilding, and recovering post-conflict. In addition, in both cities, there have been potential missed opportunities to integrate green infrastructure as part of the peacebuilding efforts and overall strategic planning process. As will be shown, the lack of environmental consideration (e.g., green infrastructure) in these cities' approaches to UEPB has short- and long-term consequences that can make people vulnerable to human insecurity and human-induced environmental stressors.

Kigali, Rwanda

The Rwandan civil war was based upon long-standing colonial inflamed tensions between the Tutsi's and the Hutu's. War broke out in 1990 by the Rwandan Patriotic Front (RPF), which was based in neighboring Uganda (Wall, 2016). After three years of guerrilla warfare, a peace deal was brokered in 1993. However, after President Habyarimana's airplane was shot down and he was killed along with the President of Burundi, an extreme arm of the Hutu Power Movement initiated what has become known as the 1994 Rwandan Genocide – an onslaught of terror and murder targeting Tutsi's across the country. In less than one hundred days, 1–1.5 million Tutsi's and tens of thousands of Hutu's were killed. The conflict ended when RPF launched an offensive, led by Major General Paul Kagame, and won the war, taking over the city of Kigali. The war was followed by a four-year period focused on reflection and rebuilding of the government, initiating a period of abundance in substantial foreign expertise, assistance, and investment.

The end of the civil war and genocide left Kigali largely deserted and its infrastructure in tatters (Goodfellow & Smith, 2013). However, not long after, the city underwent a dramatic change in a short amount of time, in terms of both population and socioeconomic change. Many genocide survivors that arrived in the city came from other regions of the country. Kigali's population tripled between 1991 and 2001 (as cited in Goodfellow & Smith, 2013); the urban population growth rate increased dramatically to 18% in the five-year period after the genocide (1995–2000), with the city representing about 45% of the country's total population (UNEP, 2011). It has been noted that this growth rate was unlike anywhere else in the world.

However, Kigali has emerged as a unique city, or outlier, compared to other post-conflict cities. Despite all of the rapid changes and sensitive nature of the situation after the genocide, and against many predictions, the city has become one of the safest cities in the region (Goodfellow & Smith, 2013). In 2008, Kigali was awarded the UN-HABITAT Scroll of Honor Award for "many innovations in building a model, modern city"(UN-HABITAT, 2008, para 4). The reasons for this transformation are numerous and complex, but, in part, this unique trajectory has been because RPF was able to firmly consolidate its power in the city and throughout the country after the conflict.

The city's transformation was also driven by a large network of national and international actors and a high volume of international aid. Due to collective guilt developed countries felt for their failure to prevent or alleviate the genocide, there was a large outpouring of emergency aid to the individuals affected by warfare (e.g., refugees), and the RPF government, once it slowly began to gain legitimacy (Goodfellow & Smith, 2013). Between April and December 1994, roughly $1.4 billion in emergency assistance was given to Rwanda (RRN, 1996, cited in Goodfellow & Smith, 2013). In 2010, donor aid to Rwanda was close to $1 billion annually (MINECOFIN, 2010, cited in Goodfellow & Smith, 2013). This aid enabled the development of infrastructure within the city; as an example, in the 2000s, the World Bank funded $23.7 million local roads and drainage infrastructure projects in the low-income areas of the city (Goodfellow & Smith, 2013). The development community also provided assistance through broader budget support as well as increasing overall international legitimacy of the RPF government. Through international donor aid, Kigali was able to transform into a central node for international resource flows. The volume of aid has also resulted in a heavy presence of the international community (NGOs, aid workers, etc.) as well as a high number of elites and expatriates in the city, relative to other cities in the country. The city's governance is closely tied to the highest levels of the central state, demonstrating the strong links between the development elite and the central government.

In 2013, Rwanda unveiled its master plan for its capital city (see Government of Rwanda & Surbana, 2013) The government aimed to revitalize urban growth and to gain international credibility among development partners (e.g., World Bank, UNEP, and global financiers such as the Global Environmental Facility) by transforming the city space and pursuing low-carbon development (Government of Rwanda & Surbana, 2013; see also Hudani, 2020). The plan was developed by consultants from the United States and Singapore and identifies the following priority elements: social order, environmental conservation, and public order. A YouTube video describing the 2013 Master Plan conveys a model for how the city plans to be by 2040.[1] It also depicts the country's desire to be a "model city" and the region's leading hub for information and communication technologies, financial service, and logistics. The city is said to be very motivated to provide a "secure city" as a means of attracting investment and promoting sectors such as energy, finance, technology, and tourism. The environment and sustainability are firmly integrated in their vision, as illustrated by words and phrases such as, "sustainable infrastructure," "conserving nature," "sustainable communities with parks and public facilities nearby," "green transportation" (cycle lanes and pedestrian walkways), "affordable homes," "efficient resource management strategies," "green gateway," "wetlands and forests conserved for future generations," "wetland parks," and more. The video is very much a reflection of recent trends in urban planning.

Urban dimensions of peacebuilding

Another example of the country's priorities in terms of development is tourism – Rwanda has become world-renowned for its mountain gorilla tourism, with people often traveling through Kigali from all over the world to embark on this nature-based tourism. Observers note, however, that the international community should do a better job of making sure benefits are shared with the local communities (Maekawa, Lanjouw, Rutagarama, & Sharp, 2013).

While the environment has been identified as a priority in the city's Master Plan, the development and realization of green infrastructure as a means of improving the quality of life in the city lags behind. Much of the city's natural geography is characterized as a system of wetlands in the valley surrounded by steeper hills. With only 24% of the original wetland remaining, this ecosystem and its ecosystem services are threatened by unplanned development (UNEP, 2011). Residents cite access to safe and clean drinking water as a major concern and priority. In addition, poor waste management and sanitation (both urban sewage and drainage) remain a serious challenge, with many people relying upon pit latrines. Biological contamination of groundwater from pit latrines is a public health risk for people in the city. The construction of artificial/constructed wetlands, a form of green infrastructure, has been proposed as a solution.

As part of an effort to transform Kigali to a model city, there have been many wetland clearances for proposed business districts, which have displaced many people to outside of the city because of lack of formal housing, especially low-income housing, within the city. Kigali is also challenged by rapid demographic growth: the city is experiencing a growth rate of over 3%, and the rate of infrastructure and planned housing development has not kept pace with population growth (Baffoe, Ahmad, & Bhandari, 2020; UNEP, 2011). As a result, most of the country's housing demand is fulfilled through informal housing (UNEP, 2011). In 2011, 83% of the population resided in informal settlements and slums covering 62% of the city's land area (UNEP, 2011). In 2020, roughly every three in five people resided in informal settlements (Baffoe et al., 2020). These settlements consist largely of urban refugees, both from other regions in Rwanda in addition to refugees displaced from other conflicts in the region, such as the Democratic Republic of Congo (Hitayezu, Rajashekar, & Stoelinga, 2018; UNEP, 2011). These unplanned areas are especially prone to flooding and erosion, especially during the rainy season, which is further exasperated by the city's poorly constructed drainage infrastructure. As a result, the city has sunk, creating a host of challenges and disruptions for the residents, already living in below-par living conditions. For example, in May 2016, 49 people were killed because people built on the sides of hills that were prone to flooding after heavy rainfall (Davies, 2016). The flooding and associated landslides resulted in loss of homes, power, and destruction of roads. In addition, intensive land use around the city has affected water supply due to increased high sediment load in river water (UNEP, 2011).

Given the city's top-down approach and lack of inclusion of low-income and marginalized communities in the decision-making process (Baffoe et al., 2020; Goodfellow & Smith, 2013), many question the sustainability of the Kigali's path. Public debate in Kigali is very limited – there are strict constraints of public debate on ethnicity, grievances, etc., put in place by the central government that leave unresolved important conversations that the city and country should be having (Goodfellow & Smith, 2013). The lack of these thoughtful (and hard) conversations and reflections represents missed opportunities to propel collective healing and social development. The country is placing priority in working toward the UN Sustainable Development Goals, recently launching in 2017 a Sustainable Development Goal Center for Africa[2] located in Kigali. This center reiterates the city's closeness to the international development community, while also underlining the need for the city and country broadly to be more inclusive in its efforts toward meaningful progress.

Freetown, Sierra Leone

Civil war broke out in Sierra Leone in 1991. This conflict has been largely attributed to the lack of benefits sharing of the country's rich natural resources, specifically diamonds and minerals (UNEP, 2010). The leaders of a rebellion group, the Revolutionary United Front (RUF), claimed that the country's citizens were being excluded from the benefits of the diamonds and sufficient services by the government (Wall, 2016; Beevers, 2015). The RUF seized some of the diamond mines and financed their insurgency by smuggling the "blood diamonds" through neighboring Liberia, continuing the legacy of mismanagement of the country's natural resources. The civil war lasted about a decade (1991–2002), with about 50,000–70,000 people killed as a result of the conflict and an additional 2.6 million people were displaced (Kaldor & Vincent, 2006). Wall (2016) notes that many people sought protection from the United Nations (UN) in the capital of Freetown. After several failed peace attempts, the civil war finally ended in 2002 when a cease-fire was declared. However, the country's challenges in managing its natural resources post-conflict persist. Lynch et al. (2013) argue that even a decade after the war, Sierra Leone was "synonymous with poverty, poor governance, and 'blood diamonds'" (p. 33).

During the civil war, many rural regions survivors were traumatized and destabilized by the burning of villages and crops by rebel insurgents. As many as two million internally displaced person fled to Freetown (IDMC, 2004, cited in Lynch et al., 2013). Similar to Rwanda, Sierra Leone has faced sharp upward population growth and urbanization trends while also recovering from conflict and undergoing post-conflict processes. The civil war forced individuals to seek security in urban spaces, resulting in rapid urbanization. In 2010, 30%–40% of the country's population resided in urban areas, with roughly 1.5 million living in Freetown and the surrounding region (Lynch et al., 2013; UNEP, 2010). There are also major disparities between the rich and poor in Freetown, with visitors describing sprawling urban slums contrasting expansive mansions alongside the coast and hills.

The country has been identified as one of the most vulnerable to climate change, with high average rainfall and flooding that affects the country on a regular basis (UNDP, 2018b). Since the conflict, the government has recognized the importance of the environment and natural resources in peacebuilding and development, including highlighting the environment and natural resources in the country's, "Agenda for Change" (UNEP, 2010) and more recently with the UN Sustainable Development Goals. As a part of the UN Sustainable Development Goals, one of the focus areas of Sierra Leone is the environment and energy. In Freetown, this has included focusing on increasing capacity to disaster response, particularly from the risks of flooding (UNDP, 2018b).

However, with decision-makers eager to get the city up and running again, this has led to some hasty planning decisions or even a complete lack of planning, which have subsequently caused social and environmental problems. Geographically, Freetown is situated on one of the world's largest natural harbors and watersheds; the topography makes the city highly vulnerable to landslides and floods (World Bank, 2019). Approximately 38% of the development in Kigali between 1997 and 2015 has occurred in "medium- or high-risk areas" (World Bank, 2019, p. 29). Unplanned and urban growth has also resulted in the rapid deforestation of the hillsides surrounding the city, which increase the rate of stormwater run-off and intensifies the risk from floods and landslides (Korona, Rigon, Walker, & Sellu, 2018; UNEP, 2010, World Bank, 2019). The watershed is also treated by underdeveloped and unequally distributed water, sanitation, and hygiene (WASH) systems (UNEP, 2010). Damage to water and wastewater infrastructure during the war greatly increased the demand for the remaining water infrastructure. The city's elite developed an inefficient water diversion system, which further strains public resources

Urban dimensions of peacebuilding

(UNEP, 2010). Very poor solid and liquid waste management in Kigali – and all urban areas of the country – further contribute to water insecurity; for instance, most residents in Free-town's large informal settlements rely on pit latrines; the lack of WASH systems contaminating groundwater, and increasing the prevalence of water-related diseases such as cholera, typhoid, and malaria (Korona et al., 2018).

Another challenge that has been noted in Freetown has been food insecurity. The city was largely cut off from its rural hinterlands during the war and as such developed a tradition of urban and peri-urban (UPA) farming (Lynch et al., 2013). However, land tenure and access is often tenuous for those engaging in UPA, and cultivation often takes place on seasonally flooded wetlands (that tend to be state-owned). There is a lack of proper planning on where farming should and should not take place to ensure that this land use contributes to human security while also ensuring sustained ecosystem function and services from the larger watershed. UPA has continued since the war as a result of the net migration to Freetown, and efforts are being undertaken to address the issue of secure land use. One of the important benefits of UPA has been the development of community cultivation groups, which has contributed toward rebuild-ing civil society and engaging marginalized groups, like women and youth (Lynch et al. 2013).

Overall Freetown and Sierra Leone, in general, are suffering from poverty, poor governance, and overall lack of capacity to meet citizens' needs (Lynch et al., 2013; UNEP, 2010). This is evident in the country's very poor life expectancy, literacy rates, and overall human develop-ment. In 2018, the country was ranked 181st out of 189 countries in the Human Development Index (UNDP, 2018b). Given the pervasive inequality and development challenges that persist, the country remains volatile. This vulnerability is often expressed in Freetown with small-scale events of violence and insecurity, such as street gangs. This lack of skill and capacity is pervasive, particularly with uneducated and unskilled youth. In addition, there is a lack of participation and consultation in community decision-making, particularly concerning water, waste, and other environmental infrastructure that affects people's daily lives.

Comparing Kigali and Freetown

It is worth revisiting the three categories discussed earlier in the chapter, whereby cities can (1) play a role either directly in a conflict (e.g., captured or targeted); (2) serve as a hub where people are displaced during a conflict; and/or (3) serve as a concentrated rebuilding location post-conflict (at the expense of strategic planning, etc.). In the case of Kigali, the city was very much part of the direct conflict during the genocide and was left devastated and deserted after the conflict. In contrast, Freetown was viewed as a place of refuge: many people were displaced from other, more rural parts of the country that were more directly impacted by the conflict, such as the villages near mining areas that the rebellion group sought control over. In both cases, Kigali and Freetown have experienced a high influx of new migrants post-conflict. As their country's capitals, both cities have been a focal area for rebuilding after the conflict because of rapid population growth and urbanization in these cities and their strategic and symbolic importance.

While both Freetown and Kigali have experienced many similar environmental security challenges (poor water and waste management, destruction of wetlands, natural disasters, etc.), their contexts have been quite different. In Rwanda, given the intense donor support and desire of the country to improve its international reputation after the genocide, Kigali expe-rienced an enormous amount of financial and in-kind support domestically and internation-ally. Even though both countries have had explicit decentralization efforts (Wall, 2016), in Rwanda paradoxically this has actually served to cement the already consolidated power of the central government. Meanwhile, in Sierra Leone, low government capacity and extreme poverty remain serious challenges. Based on strong top-down support from the central government and international community and experts in Rwanda, the environment was identified as a strategic priority. In contrast, the reorganization of Freetown post-conflict has been more chaotic and piecemeal, and investments to improve the green infrastructure in the city for improved human security have been less supported. Socioeconomic progress was also undermined by an Ebola outbreak in 2014, which led to a contraction of mining activities throughout the country (USAID, 2016). However, there are some potential opportunities for more genuine bottom-up driven efforts for green infrastructure in Freetown that improves human security, such as the growth of a tradition of urban agriculture that has, in turn, fueled the development of community cultivation groups, which have provided multiple benefits for civil society and improved livelihoods. Overall because of the more intense focus and investment from the international donor community and one-sided consolidation of political power experienced in Kigali, the city has had a more unique and rapid development pathway toward being a "model African city." In contrast, Freetown has been on the more typical trajectory post-conflict – with more competing political interests that remain and challenges related to sporadic violence, widespread violence, pervasive poverty, and low capacity.

Both cities have faced very similar challenges in terms of intense population growth during their post-conflict period. As a result, there is rapid and unplanned development throughout the cities, expressing itself in poor urban infrastructure and deterioration of natural ecosystems/green infrastructure (e.g., watersheds and wetlands) that can provide important ecosystem services. Both cities also face similar challenges in terms of water security, waste management, destruction of green spaces (especially wetlands), and vulnerability to natural disasters.

Rwanda and Sierra Leone, similar to many developing countries, have had the international conservation community invest in and work in these countries. As mentioned, it seems that Rwanda has gotten more singular focus from the international conservation and development community, with Kigali benefiting as the hub of this resource flow (see Goodfellow & Smith, 2013). While in contrast, Sierra Leone has gotten attention from a more regional perspective, often lumped in with other countries either in the region or facing similar conflict or post-conflict situations. For example, the major international conservation nongovernmental organization, World Wildlife Fund (2018), has been involved in the mountain gorilla tourism in Rwanda, highlighting this and tour opportunities on their website. Another large international conservation organization, The Nature Conservancy (2009), discusses their efforts in both Sierra Leone and Sri Lanka that focus on peace through conservation.

Conclusion

As noted by Beevers (2015), peacebuilding brings the opportunity for new beginnings. And while expectations should be managed, with that comes the possibility of integrating green infrastructure in innovative ways not done previously or exceed what was before. In a relatively affordable way, the integration of green spaces and trees (e.g., urban canopy) in a city can represent a concrete, tangible way of progress that benefits people's human security through cleaner water; air; climate control; recreational, cultural, and spiritual spaces; and much more.

Cities are considered particularly vital places post-conflict, and if peacebuilding does not happen in a meaningful way, they can become sites of violence (Goodfellow & Smith, 2013). Whether it is from direct conflict, displacement, or rebuilding post-conflict in urban landscapes,

UEPB, together with other focal peacebuilding strategies (e.g., education, public health, economic development) to benefit and inclusively include people and communities that suffer from trauma or post-traumatic stress, has a role to play.

While this chapter focused on cities that recently suffered from devastating civil wars, like human-imposed conflict, natural disasters (also often driven in part by human actions) can wreak similar havoc on green infrastructure in cities. For example, a hurricane, as shown by the recent 2017 hurricane season, can wipe out islands and leave islands, such as Puerto Rico, with destroyed infrastructure, increased vulnerability to disease outbreaks, and overall erosion of resilience in all sectors (e.g., prolonged school closures).

In light of the many challenges the world is already seeing brought on from climate change (hurricanes, fires, drought, sea-level rise, and more), it is expected that the displacement of people to cities will only increase, increasing the potential for conflict and instability in urban setting. The process of strategically integrating urban green infrastructure into peacebuilding processes can facilitate more communication and cooperation among groups that typically do not work together or are recovering from conflict. Green infrastructure can be a strategy to improve the resilience of a city post-conflict, together with other sound social, environmental, and economic policies.

Notes

1 Kigali Master Plan YouTube Video: www.youtube.com/watch?v=8hG5avl-n6Y.
2 See http://sdgcafrica.org/tag/kigali/ for more information.

Works cited

Ahern, J., Cilliers, S., & Niemela, J. (2014). The concept of ecosystem services in adaptive urban planning and design: A framework for supporting innovation. *Landscape and Urban Planning, 125*, 254–259. https://doi.org/10.1016/j.landurbplan.2014.01.020.

Baffoe, G., Ahmad, S., & Bhandari, R. (2020). The road to sustainable Kigali: A contextualized analysis of the challenges. *Cities, 105*, 102838.

Beevers, M. (2015). Governing natural resources for peace: Lessons from Liberia and Sierra Leone. *Global Governance, 21*, 227–246.

Brookings Institute. (2013). *Under the Radar: Internally displaced persons in non-camp settings.* Retrieved from www.brookings.edu/wp-content/uploads/2016/06/Under-the-radarIDPs-outside-of-camps-Oct-2013.pdf

Environmental Peacebuilding Association. (2018). *About environmental peacebuilding.* Retrieved November 11, 2020, from www.environmentalpeacebuilding.org/about/

European Commission. (2013). *Green infrastructure: Enhancing Europe's natural capital.* SWD 155 final.

Davies, R. (2016, May 9). Rwanda – at least 49 killed in floods and landslides, 500 homes destroyed. *Floodlist.* Retrieved January 2018 from http://floodlist.com/africa/rwanda-floods-landslides-gakenke-muhanga

Floyd, R., & Matthew, R. (Ed.). (2013). *Environmental security: Approaches and issues.* London, Great Britain: Routledge.

Hansen, R., & Pauleit, S. (2014). From multifunctionality to multiple ecosystem services? A conceptual framework for multi functionality in green infrastructure planning for urban areas. *Ambio, 43*(4), 516–529. https://doi.org/10.1007/s13280-014-0510-2.

Hitayezu, P., Rajashekar, A., & Stoelinga, D. (2018). *The dynamics of unplanned settlements in the City of Kigali.* C-38312-RWA-1. Retrieved November 20, 2020, from www.theigc.org/wp-content/uploads/2019/02/Hitayezu-et-al-2018-final-report-v2.pdf

Goodfellow, T., & Smith, A. (2013). From urban catastrophe to 'Model' city? Politics, security and development in post-conflict Kigali. *Urban Studies, 50*(15), 3185–3202.

Government of Rwanda & Surbana. (2013). *City of Kigali mater plan 2013.* Retrieved November 20, 2020, from www.masterplan2013.kigalicity.gov.rw/Downloads/

Hudani, S. E. (2020). The green masterplan: Crisis, state transition and urban transformation in post-genocide Rwanda. *International Journal of Urban and Regional Research, 44*(4). https://doi.org/10.1111/1468-2427.12910

IDMC (Internal Displacement Monitoring Centre). (2004). *Sierra Leone executive summary*. Retrieved from http://www.internal-displacement.org/8025708F004CE90B/(httpCountrySummaries)/0372C6E093AFEFEB802570C00056B6D0%3fOpenDocument%26count%3d10000

Kaldor, M., & Vincent, J. (2006). Case study: Sierra Leone. *Evaluation of UNDP assistance to conflict-affected countries*. New York: United Nations Development Programme Evaluation Office. http://web.undp.org/evaluation/evaluations/documents/thematic/conflict/SierraLeone.pdf

Korona, B., Rigon, A., Walker, J., & Sellu, S. A. (2018). *Urban livelihoods in Freetown's informal settlements*. Freetown, Sierra Leone: Sierra Leone Urban Research Center (SLURC).

Lynch, K., Maconachie, R., Binns, T., Tengbe, P., & Bangura, K. (2013). Meeting the urban challenge? Urban agriculture and food security in post-conflict Freetown, Sierra Leone. *Applied Geography, 36*, 31–39.

Maekawa, M., Lanjouw, A., Rutagarama, E., & Sharp, D. (2013). Mountain gorilla tourism generating wealth and peace in post-conflict Rwanda. *Natural Resources Forum, 37*, 127–137.

MINECOFIN (Ministry of Finance and Economic Planning, Government of Rwanda). (2010). *Donor performance assessment framework (DPAF) FY 2009–2010*. Kigali: Ministry of Finance and Economic Planning, Government of Rwanda.

RRN (Relief and Rehabilitation Network). (1996). *The joint evaluation of emergency assistance to Rwanda: Study III principal findings and recommendations*. Network Paper No. 16, London: Overseas Development Institute.

Stokols, D., Grzywacz, J. G., Mcmahan, S., & Phillips, K. (2003). Increasing the health promotive capacity of human environments. *Human Environments*, 4–13.

Sustainable Development Goal Center For Africa. Retrieved from http://sdgcafrica.org/tag/kigali/.

The Nature Conservancy. (2009, June 8). *Peace through conservation: Liberia, Sierra Leone and Sri Lanka*. Retrieved January 2018 from https://blog.nature.org/conservancy/2009/06/08/peace-through-conservation-liberia-sierra-leone-and-sri-lanka/

Tzoulas, K., Korpela, K., Venn, S., Yli-Pelkonen, V., Kaźmierczak, A., Niemela, J., & James, P. (2007). Promoting ecosystem and human health in urban areas using Green Infrastructure: A literature review. *Landscape and Urban Planning, 81*(3), 167–178. https://doi.org/10.1016/j.landurbplan.2007.02.001.

United Nations Environment Programme. (2011). *Rwanda: From post-conflict to environmentally sustainable development*. Nairobi, Kenya: UNEP.

United Nations Environment Programme. (2010). *Sierra Leone environment, conflict and peacebuilding assessment*. Technical Report. Nairbob, Kenya: UNEP.

United Nations Development Programme. (2018a). *Solving Freetown's waste problem*. Retrieved from www.sl.undp.org/content/sierraleone/en/home/presscenter/articles/2018/solving-freetown-s-waste-problem-/

United Nations Development Programme. (2018b). *Energy and the environment*. Retrieved from www.sl.undp.org/content/sierraleone/en/home/ourwork/environmentandenergy/overview.html

United Nations-HABITAT. (2008). *The 2008 scroll of honour award winners*. Retrieved November 11, 2020, from https://mirror.unhabitat.org/content.asp?typeid=19&catid=827&cid=6586

USAID. Climate change risk profile. Sierra Leone. Fact sheet. Retrieved from www.climatelinks.org/sites/default/files/asset/document/2016%20CRM%20Fact%20Sheet%20-%20Sierra%20Leone.pdf

Wall, G. J. (2016). Decentralization as a post-conflict state-building strategy in Northern Ireland, Sri Lanka, Sierra Leone and Rwanda. *Third World Thematics, 1*(6), 898–920. doi.org/10.1080/23802014.2016.1369859.

World Bank. (2019). *Freetown: Options for Growth and Resilience*. World Bank Group. http://documents1.worldbank.org/curated/en/994221549486063300/pdf/127039-REVISED-PUBLIC2-14-19-Freetown-Report-Final-web2.pdf

World Wildlife Fund (WWF). (2018). *Rwanda & Uganda Gorilla Safaris*. Retrieved June 5, 2018, from www.worldwildlife.org/tours/rwanda-uganda-gorilla-safaris#

16

PEACE PARKS IN THEORY AND PRACTICE

Confronting the elephant in the room

Larry A. Swatuk

It has been many years since former South African President Nelson Mandela stated,

> I know of no political movement, no philosophy, no ideology, which does not agree with the peace parks concept as we see it going into fruition today. It is a concept that can be embraced by all. In a world beset by conflicts and division, peace is one of the cornerstones of the future. Peace parks are a building block in this process, not only in our region, but potentially the entire world.
>
> (PPF, n.d.)

This statement was part of Mr. Mandela's remarks made at the opening of the gate between the Kruger National Park in South Africa and the Limpopo National Park in Mozambique, thereby creating a transfrontier conservation area (TFCA) or "peace park" and symbolically marking a turn away from the violent history of the relations between these two countries. The ceremonial opening of the gate allowed seven elephants to pass from the South African side into Mozambique.

And so begins the problem with "peace," for peace park making – like peacemaking, in general – comes not only with benefits but also with a variety of costs: social, economic, ecological, political. In the intervening years, much has been written about peace parks and their potential. Yet, the empirical evidence shows very uneven outcomes, generally for very obvious reasons. In this chapter, I review the concept of the "peace park"; illustrate its extent across the world; profile some representative cases, with a focus on Southern Africa; and critically reflect on the past, present, and future of this phenomenon.

"Peace parks" defined

A "peace park," generally defined, is a comanaged area of land or sea that straddles the borders between two and more sovereign states. The primary aim of a "peace park" is the furtherance of peace and cooperation among neighboring states. It may or may not be a formally "protected area," defined by the International Union for Conservation of Nature (IUCN) as "a clearly defined geographical space, recognized, dedicated and managed, through legal or other effective means, to achieve the long-term conservation of nature with associated ecosystem services and

189　　DOI: 10.4324/9781315107592-19

cultural values" (Dudley, 2008, p. 8).[1] At the beginning of the twenty-first century, the IUCN promoted two definitions of transboundary conservation areas (Vasilijevic et al., 2015, p. 6):

- Transboundary Protected Area: "An area of land and/or sea that straddles one or more boundaries between states, sub-national units such as provinces or regions, autonomous areas and/or areas beyond the limits of national sovereignty or jurisdiction whose constituent parts are especially dedicated to the protection and maintenance of biological diversity, and of natural and associated cultural resources, and managed cooperatively through legal or other effective means."
- Parks for Peace: "Transboundary protected areas that are formally dedicated to the protection and maintenance of biological diversity, and of natural and associated cultural resources, and to the promotion of peace and cooperation."

Given that the IUCN (n.d.) is "a membership union composed of both government and civil society organizations" (para. 1), these definitions were widely accepted and formed the basis for conservation-focused planning, action, interpretation, and critical reflection. According to Vasilijevic et al. (2015, p. 6), by the early 2010s, it became clear that these definitions were deficient for at least four reasons: (i) the exclusive focus on protected areas was too narrow; (ii) the updated 2008 definition of "protected area" was poorly reflected in these definitions; (iii) the variety of models in existence goes beyond those suggested in the definition; and (iv) the inclusion of "subnational boundaries" added complexity and confusion to an already contested concept. In place of these two definitions, the IUCN has suggested four (in Vasilijevic et al., 2015):

- Transboundary Protected Area (TBPA): "A clearly defined geographical space that includes protected areas that are ecologically connected across one or more international boundaries and involves some form of cooperation."
- Transboundary Conservation Landscape and/or Seascape (TBCL/S): "An ecologically connected area that includes both protected areas and multiple resource use areas across one or more international boundaries and involves some form of cooperation."
- Transboundary Migration Conservation Area (TBMCA): "Wildlife habitats in two or more countries that are necessary to sustain populations of migratory species and involve some form of cooperation."
- Special Designation: A Park for Peace: "A Park for Peace is a special designation that may be applied to any of the three types of Transboundary Conservation Areas, and is dedicated to the promotion, celebration and/or commemoration of peace and cooperation."

The evolving definitions of transboundary conservation activities reflect the increasingly crowded landscape of initiatives related to interstate resource governance and management. Adding to the confusion are the numerous official designations attached to a wide variety of landscapes: biosphere reserves; Ramsar sites; World Heritage sites; and so on. The first "peace parks" are almost as old as the first national parks – Yellowstone National Park in the United States was established in 1872; Royal National Park in Australia was established seven years later. According to the Peace and Biodiversity Dialogue Initiative, "The first transboundary protected area was established by the Swedish and the Norwegian Peace Movements in 1914, to celebrate 100 years of peace between Sweden and Norway. In 1959 the area was named Morokulien" (Convention on Biological Diversity [CBD], n.d.). The most celebrated peace park is the Waterton-Glacier International Peace Park, established in 1932 "to commemorate the long history of peace and friendship between Canada and the United States and to emphasize both natural and cultural links" (Convention on Biological Diversity [CBD], n.d, para 2).[2] From these modest, but hopeful, beginnings, the number of TBCAs has grown dramatically, particularly since the late-1980s. Thorsell and Harrison (1990) reported an estimated 70 "border parks" involving 65 countries in Europe, North America, Asia, Africa, South and Central Americas. By 2007, the number of TBCAs had tripled to more than 227, comprising a total of 3,043 protected areas (Lysenko, Besancon, & Save, 2007) covering some 460 million hectares (Quinn, Broberg, and Freimund (2012).

What explains the present popularity in policy-making circles for peace park creation? The World Commission on Protected Areas (Sandwith, Shine, Hamilton, & Sheppard, 2001, p. 3) presents a long list of possible benefits:

- Promoting, celebrating, and/or commemorating peace and cooperation among people;
- Building trust, understanding, reconciliation, and cooperation between and among countries, communities, agencies, and stakeholders;
- Preventing and/or resolving tension across community or national boundaries, including over access to natural resources;
- Promoting the resolution of armed conflict and/or reconciliation following armed conflict;
- Supporting long-term cooperative conservation of biodiversity, ecosystem services, and natural and cultural values across boundaries;
- Promoting ecosystem management through integrated bioregional land-use planning and management;
- Sharing biodiversity and cultural resource management skills and experience, including cooperative research;
- Promoting more efficient and effective cooperative management programs;
- Promoting access to, and equitable and sustainable use of natural resources, consistent with national sovereignty; and
- Enhancing the benefits of conservation and promoting benefit-sharing across boundaries.

As suggested by this long list, "the orientation in conservation and development is always future positive" (Buscher, 2013, p. 107), revealing an almost unshakeable belief in the benefits to be had from peace park establishment irrespective of the complexity of the undertaking. Make no mistake, however, at the heart of the movement for TBCA establishment is conservation. For Ali (2010), "transboundary conservation is an essential part of meeting the goals of ecological regionalism. Since natural systems transcend political borders, management approaches must also aspire to transcend physical and cognitive barriers" (p. 25). Natural landscapes are overwhelmingly fragmented by human land-use decisions and practices. Thus, TBCAs are regarded as one means of recovering the natural rhythms of flora and fauna while reaping ancillary benefits such as trust-building and encouraging habits of cooperation among and between often antagonistic sovereign states (Conca & Dabelko, 2002). More than 15 years ago, Wolmer (2003) argued that TBCAs are "increasingly proposed as a means for the socio-economic upliftment and empowerment of previously marginalized communities who will be able to participate in, and derive benefits from the management and sustainable use of wild resources, principally via the economic incentives of hunting and ecotourism revenues" (p. 266). Such sentiments are echoed today, for example, in the newly developed MOOC (massive open online course) on Peace Parks Development and Management created by the UNDP, in partnership with the Secretariat of the Convention of Biological Diversity, its Peace and Biodiversity Dialogue Initiative (with financial support from the Ministry of Environment of the Republic of Korea), and

UNEP. The course is offered in five languages: English, French, Spanish, Russian, and Arabic. The first iteration of the course ran for three weeks during February 2019.

It is no accident that the number of peace-oriented TBCAs has tripled since 1990, for it is during this period that, among other things, (i) the Cold War ended; (ii) the Iron Curtain came down along with the Soviet Union; (iii) apartheid ended in South Africa; (iv) the first Earth Summit took place at Rio de Janeiro in 1992; (v) both environment and development were enfolded into "security" discourse; and (vi) global governance reached its zenith. This confluence of social forces created space for imagining collaborative governance for the achievement of global common goods (peace, biodiversity preservation), regional and national benefits (economic, social, and environmental), and possibly local economic and social development as well. It is this last "benefit" that has proved most elusive and problematic and to which I will return later.

Places, spaces, cases

Of the 227 established TBCAs identified by Lysenko et al. (2007), 22 are in North America, 24 are in South America, 46 are in Africa, 50 are in Asia, and 81 are in Europe. The character (size, shape, management and governance structures, primary goal) of the park/protected area varies dramatically across cases, typically reflecting factors such as its physical location and the drivers behind its establishment. I would argue that it is these factors – location and drivers behind establishment – that most closely determine the outcome of the TBCA's establishment relative to the goals stated at the outset of the initiative. In no particular order, the dominant drivers behind TBCAs seem to be:

- Biodiversity preservation – all conservation-oriented organizations from the local to the global
- A symbol of positive existing interstate relations – state actors such as Canada and the United States in relation to Waterton Glacier International Park
- A symbol of potentially positive future interstate relations – state actors such as the members of the Southern African Development Community (SADC) who share numerous borders and have endured numerous violent conflicts over time); but possibly also the two Koreas in relation to the Demilitarized Zone (DMZ) and India-Pakistan in relation to Kashmir and the Siachen Glacier
- Enhanced formal state(s) control of border regions – all state actors and many civil society and private sectors actors who stand to reap benefits from new initiatives such as ecotourism and infrastructure development
- Enhanced global governance of a "bioregion" – a primary goal of conservation organizations such as IUCN, WWF, donors such as GTZ and DfID, UN-affiliated organizations such as UNEP and the CBD
- Direct response to an ongoing conflict or security threat – peace-oriented civil society groups such as the Quakers who are involved in the Balkans Peace Park Project (B3P); state, NGOs, and IGOs who consider environmental cooperation as a possible soft entry point for peacemaking
- National economic wealth creation through tourism development – state and private sector actors in particular

What should be clear about this list is the near-total absence of the interests of those who inhabit the physical spaces where the park is intended to be established. Peace parks are, in the first instance, the result of deals made by powerful state and nonstate actors in the interest of ideologically driven concepts: conservationism; nationalism; developmentalism; regionalism. It is not that these ideals are inherently problematic; rather, their grand articulation – that is, global public goods; bioregional preservation; national economic development; regional integration – crowd out the needs and interests of those on the ground, at the place of the proposed intervention. In this way, peace parks mark a continuation of the struggle that conservationists have faced for decades: what to do about local people (see Adams and McShane, 1996)? As Duffy (2007), paraphrasing Neumann (1998), puts it: "[C]urrent demands from local communities for the power to control, use and access environmental resources are not the same as plans for local participation in externally driven conservation schemes and commitments to local benefit sharing" (p. 6).

While Katerere, Hill, and Moyo (2001) argue that all transboundary natural resource management initiatives must "ensure that communities and other stakeholders benefit from sustainable use of resources" (p. 9), others argue that private sector involvement in TFCA development is "turning conservation into a transnational business opportunity" (Chapin, 2004). For Milgroom and Spierenburg (2008), "the promotion of the Great Limpopo transfrontier conservation area was further enabled by neoliberal policy agendas adopted by southern Africa's governments" (p. 437). The consequences for local people have been problematic to say the least (Duffy, 2006).

Across much of the world, "national parks" were established at the frontier, or, in what critical geographers often call "borderlands" (Ramutsindela, 2017). Indeed, unlike the management-oriented literature that comes out of organizations such as the IUCN, critical geographers and political ecologists tend to use the term "transfrontier conservation areas" or TFCAs, for the term "frontier" helps denote the poor reach of the state into these spaces.[3] The frontier is a space occupied by groups who are not part of mainstream society, being generally located far from capital and primate cities.

However, the notion of "peace park" brings the margin to the center of politics. It relocates a remote landscape into the central imaginary of state-making (Duffy, 2001). Thus, having relegated indigenous and aboriginal people to these margins through the use of (initially colonial and/or imperial) force, the promulgation of parks and protected areas, both national and transnational, redefined "marginal lands" as centrally important to dominant cultures and often made first nations groups, aboriginal and indigenous peoples strangers in their own homes. Thus, peace parks reinvigorate the logic of "fortress conservation,"[4] the practice of which remakes subordinate social groups as problematic to the project of the preservation of "wild lands," "biological diversity," and so on (DeMotts, 2017). What we see, then, with the establishment of parks and protected areas at the frontier is ongoing contestations over the legitimate and authoritative use of physical space. Where indigenous populations are highly concentrated, the achievement of TBCA's stated goals has been limited, even highly contested (Buscher, 2013; DeMotts, 2017). This is particularly the case where land use rights have long been a source of social unrest, and the land allocated to the park is large and/or densely populated at the margins (King & Wilcox, 2008).

Where populations are small and the area remote, outcomes have been quite positive in relation to their stated intentions, for example, Waterton-Glacier International Park (457,614 ha) between Canada and the United States and the Transboundary Condor Peace Parks and Conservation Corridor in the remote mountains that act as a border between Ecuador and Peru. In each case, the local social costs of park establishment were minimal in comparison to the political capital generated by, in the Canada–US case, reaffirmation of peaceful relations and, in the Peru-Ecuador case, resolution of a long-simmering border dispute. Moreover, for state and international civil society actors, the limited local social costs are easily offset by the large ecological gains derived from biological diversity preservation, ecotourism, and opportunities for environmental education.

On the other hand, where populations are large and the area is central to the livelihoods of local communities, outcomes are mixed, at best. Two of the most well-known and well-cited cases of peace parks mismanagement involve South Africa: the Great Limpopo Transfrontier Park (GLTP) that includes Zimbabwe and Mozambique in addition to South Africa (DeMotts, 2017) and the Maloti-Drakensberg Transfrontier Park (MDTP) that involves Lesotho and South Africa (Buscher, 2013). As physical symbols of land alienation and exclusion, national parks have long been an object of derision by the majority of Africa's rural people (Grove, 1997; Koch, 1998). Linking existing parks together by obtaining more land is resulting in political difficulties; land claims lodged by South African communities forcibly removed from Kruger and Richtersveld National Parks (Fig, 1991; PLAAS, 2005; Swatuk, 2006; Wolmer, 2003) and the "induced volition" of some 7,000 people residing in the Limpopo National Park (Milgroom & Spierenburg, 2008) are well-known examples.[5]

The diversity of peace parks and TBCA initiatives means that there are many positive cases as well. These are highlighted in comprehensive collections such as Quinn, Broberg, and Freimund (2012), Ali (2007), and Vasilijevic et al. (2015). In line with the observations regarding size, location, and driving force, the most successful peace park efforts reflect particular geographic features such as mountains (e.g., Mont Blanc region involving France, Italy, and Switzerland), wetlands (e.g., Danube Delta between Ukraine and Romania), or even a combination of the two (e.g., Lake Titicaca between Bolivia and Peru). Other successful initiatives are those where joint management efforts yield environmental information useful to all states (e.g., the Barents Protected Area Network and the Kailash Sacred Landscape Conservation and Development Initiative) without challenging existing land use rights. Where an initiative carries symbolic importance, draws together people in activities that do not challenge existing land use rights, and results in obvious environmental gains, a transboundary conservation initiative is likely to succeed. A good example of this is the European Green Belt Initiative which comprises some 12,500 km of land, most of which formerly constituted the "Iron Curtain" dividing East from West.

Because of these particular successes, there are many attempts at mimicry. For example, the Greater Virunga Transboundary Collaboration between Rwanda, Uganda, and the Democratic Republic of Congo seems a perfect candidate for a peace park initiative. The area comprises numerous parks and protected areas in the mountainous border area between these three countries. The presence of charismatic mega fauna such as the mountain gorilla suggests to state policy-makers and international organizations that there is a huge potential for the expansion of tourism enterprise. The gorilla's presence on the IUCN Red List (Critically Endangered) draws a great deal of global attention to the initiative. Similar such initiatives are underway along the US–Mexico border and in the Cross River region of West Africa, involving Nigeria and Cameroon. The discovery of jaguar, long thought to be absent from the US–Mexico border region, has had a similar effect of drawing powerful conservation organizations to the region. Endangered species such as the Cross River gorillas or the tigers of the Sunderbans in South Asia and the borderlands between Indonesia and Bhutan draw similar sets of actors toward peace park establishment. Despite similarities of being locations far from the main centers of population, each of these cases presents particular difficulties to conservation initiatives of any sort. Duffy (2001) cautions those interested in developing peace parks against seeing TBCA as a radically new departure from existing processes, practices, and struggles over land use. While the use of environmental policy, processes, and practices in the interests of interstate and/or intercommunal peacemaking and peacebuilding still is relatively new in foreign policy circles, peace park establishment is nothing new to land-use planners of any kind (Duffy, 2006; King & Wilcox, 2008).

Focus on Southern Africa

All four of the IUCN delineated categories identified earlier – TBPA; TBCL; TBMCA; peace park – are present across the Southern African region, though the accepted nomenclature differs. Historically, the creation of parks and protected areas across the region is a consequence of colonial interests and interimperial rivalries. Parks established at the frontier – for example, between South Africa and Portuguese-controlled Mozambique – served several roles including acting as buffer zones between antagonistic states and peoples. Given the arbitrary delineation of state borders across the region, intact ecosystems were bifurcated as were families, communities, and other social forms such as Kingdoms and Chiefdoms. The leaders of the region's post-colonial states accepted the arguments regarding the ecological and economic values of protected areas, but these spaces continue to be contested by peoples living in and around parks. Over the course of the apartheid era, parks were important strategic sites for warring parties. Gorongosa in Mozambique and Kruger in South Africa housed the South African-supported rebel group, RENAMO, while Mavinga and Luengue-Luiana National Parks in the southeastern corner of Angola housed the South African-supported rebel group, UNITA. Many of these parks were heavily mined, and their rehabilitation since the end of the Cold War and apartheid has been slow to develop.

In the post-Cold War era, much was being made about the environment as a potential security risk (for an overview, see Swatuk, 2006). Across post-apartheid Southern Africa, a different narrative emerged, that is, the possibility of "nature to heal old wounds" (Koch, 1998). On February 1, 1997, after several years of experimentation with TFCA development along the South Africa–Mozambique border, the South African billionaire businessman turned philanthropist, Anton Rupert, established the Peace Parks Foundation (PPF).[6] The PPF is built around the sound idea that interstate action in support of biodiversity preservation through the interlinking of previously fragmented and contested parks and protected areas would facilitate peacebuilding in the region. Today, there are at least ten initiatives underway (see Table 16.1).

The logic of TFCAs from a conservationist standpoint is flawless. Increasing fragmentation of natural habitats due to the encroachment of human populations and resulting land-use change has put "nature under pressure" (Wegmann et al., 2014). The political expediency of colonial borders drawn along lines of latitude or longitude, across mountain tops and through the middle or along the shoreline of rivers and lakes, limited the movement of people and animals in a part of the world where survival – and the character of social formations – depended upon mobility: to follow the rains, to follow the animals. Connecting physical space through the removal of fences or the creation of corridors would enable the region's flora and fauna to recover some of its ancient rhythms and build collective resilience in a place where vulnerability had been long induced through fragmentation. As with natural systems, so with the region's states. The peace parks concept resonated loudly with southern Africa's leaders who were in the process of restructuring the Southern African Development Coordination Conference into the Southern African Development Community (SADC). The end of the Cold War facilitated this shift in perspective by quickly bringing to a close apartheid South Africa's practice of regional destabilization, the civil wars in Mozambique and Angola, South African dominance of Namibia, and apartheid rule in South Africa. As South Africa became a part of – not apart from – the region, so too did the opportunity

Larry A. Swatuk

Table 16.1 Transfrontier conservation areas in Southern Africa

Peace Park	Countries Involved	Size (in km²)	Remarks
Kavango-Zambezi (KAZA) TFCA	Angola, Botswana, Namibia, Zambia, Zimbabwe	520,000	Includes World Heritage sites (WHSs) and Ramsar site; joint management; five national integrated development plans (IDPs), one master IDP
Greater Limpopo TFCA (includes the Great Limpopo Transfrontier Park)	Mozambique, South Africa, Zimbabwe	GLTFCA: 100,000 GLTP: 35,000	GLTP includes three national parks and the Sengwe Corridor; a joint management board and several committees; in 2017, Greater Lebombos Conservancy became the first private landholding to join a TFCA
Lumbombo TFCA	Kingdom of eSwatini, Mozambique, South Africa	10,029	Includes five Ramsar sites; includes first marine TFCA
Malawi-Zambia TFCA	Malawi, Zambia	32,278	Includes two TFCAs: Nyika-North Luangwa and Kasungu-Lukusuzi; joint integrated management committee
/Ai/Ais-Richtersveld TFCA	Namibia, South Africa	5920	Joint management board; IDP; WHS; border post inside the TFCA
Kgalagadi TFCA	Botswana, South Africa	35,551	Joint management committee; IDP; WHS; true free movement of tourists within boundaries of TFCA
Greater Mapungubwe TFCA	Botswana, South Africa, Zimbabwe	5909	Bilateral technical committees; resource management committees; WHS
Maloti-Drakensberg Transfrontier Conservation and Development Area	Lesotho, South Africa	14,740	Two million people inside the TFCA; includes the Maloti-Drakensberg Park which is a transboundary WHS
Lower Zambezi-Mana Pools TFCA	Zambia, Zimbabwe	17,745	Currently in conceptual phase; WHS; Ramsar site
Liuwa Plains-Mussoma TFCA	Angola, Zambia	14,464	Currently in conceptual phase; IDP meeting 2013

arise to rethink the role of frontier parks, away from conflict toward cooperation (see Koch, 1998, for overview).

So, environmental and political goals of regional integration came together very nicely at a time when the world had embraced the concept of "environment and development" through the Rio process. Shortly following the collapse of the Berlin Wall and the fall of the Soviet Union, both environment and development became embedded within the discourse of security. As Duffield (2001) trenchantly observed, formerly excluded areas of the world became central to great power security as "the fear of underdevelopment" came to be regarded as "a source of conflict, criminalized activity and international instability" (p. 7). Border zones would have to be controlled. Peace parks offered a way for states to gain control of their own territories and reimagine "criminalized" spaces as "ecotourism destinations" with the help of international organizations such as the United Nation (through UNEP and financing instruments such as the UNDP GEF), international financial institutions such as the World Bank, donors of all types offering capital and expertise (from GIZ and USAID to WWF, Conservation International and the IUCN, just to name the most obvious and visible). Regional cooperation on protected areas development and management fits with SADC's broader initiative of regional integration for sustainable and equitable development (SADC, 2003), involving inter alia, numerous protocols such as the Protocol on the Development of Tourism in the Southern African Region wherein objective nine is "to aggressively promote the Region as a single but multifaceted tourism destination capitalizing on its common strengths and highlighting individual Member State's unique tourist attractions" (SADC, 1998, p. 5). At the 2018 INVESTOUR event held in Madrid, the World Tourism Organization pointed out that "international tourist arrivals in Africa grew by around 8% for the second consecutive year with 62 million arrivals registered for 2017." It was further noted that according to UNWTO research, "wildlife watching travel represents 80% of the total annual tourist arrivals to Africa" (State News Service, 2018).

The idea of an integrated system of protected areas fostering a more peaceful and prosperous region is part of a regional attempt to rebrand at least the southern part of the African continent (Buscher, 2013; Knott, Fyall, & Jones, 2015; Osei & Gbadamosi, 2011). Interest in rebranding – meaning, away from poverty, environmental degradation, and conflict toward prosperity, biodiverse resilience and cooperation – draws together local, national, regional, continental, and global state; NGOs; and private sector actors. Put simply, there is a great deal riding on the peace park concept. With the perceived benefits being so significant, critics of the initiative are being crowded out of the policy discourse by the sheer number and weight of influence of its supporters. As a result, there seem to be two camps talking past each other and working at cross purposes. Those who support TFCA development (states, conservation NGOs, IFIs) seem unwilling to countenance missteps and failures. Those who question the logic and methods of TFCA development (critical geographers, political ecologists, community-based organizations, activists) seem unwilling to see both the value in the concept and the advances made in many cases, not only in Southern Africa but also around the world.

As stated at the outset of this chapter, peace park numbers are growing, partly in response to the successes with their establishment across the SADC region. Granted, there are significant difficulties with the impact of land-use change on local communities. Vasilijevic et al. (2015) identify seven key activities to be undertaken en route to peace park establishment: (i) removal of international boundary fences; optimization of access points and transport routes to and within a TBCA; (iii) control of visitor movement and safety; (iv) involvement of local people; (v) harmonization of relevant laws and regulations; (vi) control of animal diseases and prevention of invasions of alien plants and animals; (vii) communications. These are practical activities that build trust and habits of cooperation. All of these actions have been undertaken in the eight promulgated TFCAs in SADC.

In addition, many of the SADC peace parks use global designations for subunits within the TFCA to generate stakeholder support for the broader project. As shown in Table 16.1, World Heritage Sites (WHS) and Ramsar Sites dot the TFCAs. Many of the WHS focus on cultural heritage, so there is an attempt to show meaningful respect for indigenous communities affected by the new land use designation. There are three important supports for peace park establishment that are present across SADC. One, the presence of a "champion" or "champions" to carry the idea forward, in this case, the PPF within the region but also IUCN and WWF internationally and SADC leaders regionally. Two, adequate finances, which are overwhelmingly generated internationally from bilateral (GIZ, SIDA, USAID) and multilateral (EU, World Bank) sources. And three, availability of technical expertise, which, in this case, comes from within the (especially South African) Parks Service and from external consultants (WWF, IUCN World Commission on Protected Areas). Because of this confluence of resources and supports, most of the TFCAs in the region have been able to construct Integrated Development Plans, create a variety of joint management committees, and technical committees (see Table 16.1).

One element that remains problematic is governance. In their important "best practice" guide to TBCA development and management, Vasilijevic et al. (2015, p. 45) distinguish between governance (which "is about process") and management (which "is about substance"), arguing that governance is about who sets the agenda; who brings together the appropriate people; how decisions are taken; who ensures that appropriate resources and conditions are available for effective implementation; who holds power, authority, and responsibility; and who is or should be held accountable. As stated earlier, peace park development is about land-use change. Across Southern Africa, parks are being established by influential actors convinced of their noble goals. As such, they are perhaps willfully blind to the socially contentious fact of extending a protected area around land that was taken from local people to establish the national park in the first place. While Vasilijevic et al. (2015, p. 47) are conscious of these facts, they argue that a way forward is collective or collaborative governance involving, among other things, local people's meaningful participation. Rare is the idea that the peace park should not be established. To fail to countenance this idea is to condemn the landscape to low-level forms of conflict and, to put it mildly, suboptimal outcomes. Where TFCAs and biodiversity corridors facilitate the movement of animals, they too often demand the removal of people indigenous to the area. The end result, as in the GLTFCA, is the continued militarization of conservation setting the state and "their animals" against the interests of citizens (DeMotts, 2017). Can TFCAs succeed where landscapes are replete with the unfinished business of demands for the return of "stolen lands"?

Conclusion

There are important lessons to be learned from Southern Africa for other regions and peace park initiatives. More than ten years ago, I wrote a short paper reflecting on the possibilities for multiple benefits (social, ecological, economic, political) to be derived from TFCA development in Southern Africa. Mounted by the Environmental Change and Security Program (ECSP) of the Woodrow Wilson Center for International Scholars, most of the papers delivered at this meeting ultimately made their way into Saleem Ali's edited collection on Peace Parks (Ali, 2007). In that collection, there are few dissenting voices, with perhaps only Rosaleen Duffy (2007) and Maano Ramutsindela (2007) falling into the category of the "unconvinced." As Ramutsindela (2007) put it: "It is important to understand that propositions for peace parks are grounded on assumptions about strategies for achieving piece. Currently the bioregionalism underpinning peace parks does not insulate the propositions for peace parks from socio-spatial processes affecting and regulating people's lives" (p. 80). Put simply, just because the park is in support of "peace," does not mean the process of its establishment will not be fraught with social conflict.

At the ECSP meeting, I flagged three issues to consider and made five recommendations. They are worth revisiting here. In terms of issues to consider:

- Peace parks must be set within local political ecology
- Peace parks cannot be considered separately from other conservation activities and their results
- Peace parks cannot be delinked from national/regional development strategies/priorities

As highlighted earlier, not only in the Southern African case but elsewhere in the world, it is very clear that history matters. Opportunities open themselves up at given historical moments and often close just as swiftly. The symbolism of those seven elephants crossing from South Africa into Mozambique holds several meanings: positive from conservationists' and national political leaders' points of view but quite negative from the view of people living in and around the GLTFCA. Privileging the mobility of animals over the livelihoods (and continuing immobilities) of local people simply reaffirms the chasm that exists between many governments and citizens across the Global South. "Consulting" these people during the establishment of the park development process will do little to right the wrongs of history.

The five recommendations I put forward in 2005 still remain relevant today:

(1) Accurately assess what has been achieved to date

An accurate assessment will only emerge where we dispense with naïve or arrogant approaches to conservation and biodiversity preservation. In 2004, Mac Chapin (2004) published a controversial article in WorldWatch where he accused the largest conservation organizations as lacking humility. I am not certain that it is a lack of humility; rather, it may be the overly technocratic and biocentric approach to conservation that continues to make it so difficult for these organizations to put people first.

(2) Put people first

Following the innovations made in regard to community-based natural resources management, the goals of transboundary natural resources management must be set and aligned with those of national parks, game reserves, and other forms of protected areas. This means putting people first and making social/economic benefits the primary motivating factor in TFCA processes, development, and establishment – and putting conservation at the service of the needs and interests of people living at the point of the intended intervention.

(3) Get local level buy-in

TBCA development privileges the central state and its machinery in the negotiation and management process. While it may be easier to deal with centralized agencies, supporters of peace parks must press for subsidiarity. Without local level buy-in, the initiative will fail.

(4) Monitor and benchmark

As highlighted by Sandwith et al. (2001), the potential benefits from parks are numerous and cut across economic, ecological, political, and sociocultural lines. But there has been little systematic information gathered on the performance of protected areas of all kinds. If stakeholders across the spectrum are expected to buy into peace parks, mechanisms must be developed for monitoring (e.g., biodiversity preservation, economic development, and gender empowerment) and benchmarking (e.g., job creation and forest regeneration) as well as the financial means to do so. A laundry list of potential benefits is not enough.

(5) Do not exaggerate achievements

Many claims regarding TFCA successes in Southern Africa are not true. States are very good at signing, and even ratifying into law, a wide variety of documents; implementation, however, is another matter altogether. The discrepancy between claims and outcomes is well documented by anthropologists, political economists, political ecologists, and others (see Andersson, de Garine-Wichatitsky, Cumming, Dzingirai, & Giller, 2013; Buscher, 2013; DeMotts, 2017). Perhaps there is space in the world of conservation policy making to invite in those most critical of TFCA initiatives and have an open conservation.

To this list, I would add a sixth:

(6) Do not be afraid to admit failure

In my reading of the literature, those most committed to peace park development are loathe to admit that there have been many mistakes. At the same time, and as stated earlier in this chapter, those most critical of peace park initiatives seem unable to acknowledge that there are not only successes – as shown earlier – but also significant possibilities. Is there a way to move toward each other? To find a "happy medium" where failure is but the necessary first step toward better practice? This, to me, is the "elephant in the room" that requires frank and open discussion. Perhaps the Wilson Center would like to host another conference?

Notes

1 The definition may be expanded to include six management categories: (Ia) strict nature reserve; (Ib) wilderness area; (II) national park; (III) natural monument or feature; (IV) habitat/species management area; (V) protected landscape or seascape; and (VI) protected area with sustainable use of natural resources. In relation to "who holds authority and responsibility for the protected area," the "IUCN defines four governance types": Type A: governance by government; Type B: shared governance (i.e., transboundary; collaborative; or joint); Type C: private governance; and Type D: governance by indigenous peoples and local communities. For more information, see the IUCN WPCA *Best Practice Guidelines for Protected Area Managers* series, available at www.iucn.org/pa_guidelines.

2 As described by Quinn (2012), prominent individuals were at the forefront of establishing the national parks in each of the United States and Canada that ultimately came to form Waterton-Glacier International Peace Park. The Peace Park itself resulted from sustained lobbying by civil society groups.

3 It should also be noted that "transfrontier" is the preferred nomenclature of the Peace Parks Foundation (see later).

4 Andersson et al. (2013), note that "people in Southern Africa have lived for a long time with wildlife and, for more than a century, within protected areas in which wildlife and other natural resources are preserved. In general, those now finding themselves living on the fringe of protected areas were legally denied access to these lands and their resources – a situation known as 'fortress conservation" (p. 3).

5 Decision makers in Africa's post-colonial states accepted not only their inherited sovereign borders but also the fact of national parks. Death (2016) provides a nuanced examination of the complex terrain of land use decision making across post-colonial Africa, highlighting the many ways in which different groups of people within and among states struggle to benefit from the fact of parks and protected areas. Often times, land claims are not confined to courts of law. Schroeder (in Broch-Due & Schroeder, 2000) illustrates how "In the mid-1970s, Maasai residents of southern Kenya were abruptly relocated from land that was subsequently enclosed within Amboseli National Park. . . . In response, the displaced groups began a systematic effort to kill many of Amboseli's most prized tourist attractions . . . not for sport or profit but as part of a desperate protest campaign designed to counter the growing threat tour operators posed to Maasai land rights" (p. 340).

6 See www.peaceparks.org.

Peace parks in theory and practice

Works cited

Adams, J. S., & McShane, T. O. (1996). The myth of Wild Africa: Conservation without illusion. Berkeley and Los Angeles, California: University of California Press.

Ali, A. (2002). A Siachen Peace Park: The solution to a half-century of international conflict? *Mountain Research and Development, 22*(4), 316–319.

Ali, S. (Ed.). (2007). *Peace parks, conservation and conflict resolution.* Cambridge, MA: MIT Press.

Ali, S. (2010). *Transboundary conservation and peace-building: Lessons from forest biodiversity conservation projects.* Yokohama: UNU-IAS Policy Report.

Andersson, J. A., de Garine-Wichatitsky, M., Cumming, D. H. M., Dzingirai, V., & Giller, K. E. (2013). People at wildlife frontiers in Southern Africa. In J. A. Andersson, M. de Garine-Wichatitsky, D. H. M. Cumming, V. Dzingirai, & K. E. Giller (Eds.), *Transfrontier conservation areas: People living on the edge* (pp. 1–11). London and New York: Routledge.

Broch-Due, V., & Schroeder, R. A. (Eds.). (2000). *Producing nature and poverty in Africa.* Uppsala: Nordiska Afrikainstitutet.

Brockington, D. (2002). *Fortress conservation: The preservation of the Mkomazi game reserve.* London: James Currey.

Buscher, B. (2013). *Transforming the frontier: Peace parks and the politics of neoliberal conservation in Southern Africa.* Durham, NC: Duke University Press.

Chapin, M. (2004, November). A challenge to conservationists. *WorldWatch,* 17–31.

Conca, K., & Dabelko, G. (2002). *Environmental peacemaking.* Baltimore and London: Johns Hopkins University Press; Washington, DC: Woodrow Wilson Center Press.

Convention on Biological Diversity. (n.d.). *Examples.* Retrieved November 9, 2020, from www.cbd.int/peace/about/peace-parks/examples/default.shtml

Death, C. (2016). *The green state in Africa.* New Haven and London: Yale University Press.

DeMotts, R. (2017). *The challenges of transfrontier conservation in Southern Africa.* London: Lexington Books.

Dudley, N. (Ed.). (2008). Guidelines for applying protected area management categories. *Best Practice Protected Area Guidelines Series, 21.* Gland, Switzerland: International Union for Conservation of Nature.

Duffield, M. (2001). *Global governance and the new wars: The merging of development and security.* London: Zed.

Duffy, R. (2007). Peace parks and global politics: The paradoxes and challenges of global governance. In S. H. Ali (Ed.), *Peace parks conservation and conflict resolution* (pp. 55–68). Cambridge, Mass: MIT Press.

Duffy, R. (2006). Global governance and environmental management: The politics of transfrontier conservation areas in Southern Africa. *Political Geography, 25,* 89–112.

Duffy, R. (2005). *Global politics and peace parks. Environmental change and security policy report 11* (pp. 67–69). Washington, DC: WWICS.

Duffy, R. (2000). *Killing for conservation: Wildlife policy in Zimbabwe.* Bloomington/Harare/Oxford: Weaver, James Currey and Indiana University Presses.

Duffy, R. (2001) Peace parks: The paradox of globalisation. Geopolitics, 6(2), 1–26.

Fig, D. (1991). Flowers in the desert: Community struggles in Namaqualand. In J. Cock & E. Koch (Eds.), *Going green: People, politics and the environment in Southern Africa* (pp. 112–128). Cape Town: Oxford University Press.

Gibson, C. C. (1999). *Politicians and poachers: The political economy of wildlife policy in Africa.* Cambridge: Cambridge University Press.

Grove, R. (1997). *Ecology, climate and empire: Colonialism and global environmental history 1400–1940.* Cambridge: White Horse.

International Union for Conservation of Nature (IUCN). (n.d.). *About.* Retrieved November 9, 2020, from www.iucn.org/about

Katerere, Y., Hill, R., & Moyo, S. (2001). *A critique of transboundary natural resource management in southern Africa.* Harare: IUCN ROSA.

King, B., & Wilcox, S. (2008). Peace Parks and jaguar trails: Transboundary conservation in a globalized world. *Geojournal, 71,* 221–231.

Knott, B., Fyall, A., & Jones, I. (2015). The nation branding opportunities provided by a sport mega-event: South Africa and the 2010 FIFA World Cup. *Journal of Destination Marketing and Management, 4*(1), 46–56.

Koch, E. (1998). Nature has the power to heal old wounds: War, peace and changing patterns of conservation in Southern Africa. In D. Simon (Ed.), *South Africa in Southern Africa: Reconfiguring the region* (pp. 54–72). London: James Currey.

Lysenko, I., Besancon, C., & Save, C. (2007). *2007 UNEP-WCMC Global List of Transboundary Protected Areas.*

Milgroom, J., & Spierenburg, M. (2008). Induced volition: Resettlement from the Limpopo National Park, Mozambique. *Journal of Contemporary African Studies, 26*(4), 435–448.

Neumann, R. P. (1998). *Imposing wilderness: Struggles over livelihood and nature preservation in Africa.* Berkeley: University of California Press.

Osei, C., & Gbadamosi, A. (2011). Re-branding Africa. *Marketing Intelligence and Planning, 29*(3), 284–304.

Peace Parks Foundation. (n.d.). *Our Journey.* Retrieved November 6, 2020, from www.peaceparks.org/about/our-journey/

Programme for Land and Agrarian Studies (PLAAS). (2005). *Umhlaba Wethu 3* (A quarterly bulletin tracking land reform in South Africa) (June). Retrieved December 1, 2018, from www.plaas.org.za/sites/default/files/publications-landpdf/Uw%2003.pdf.

Quinn, M. S., Broberg, L., & Freimund, W. (Eds.). (2012). *Parks, peace, and partnership: Global initiatives in transboundary conservation.* Calgary, AB: University of Calgary Press.

Ramutsindela, M. (2017). Greeing Africa's borderlands: The symbiotic politics of land and borders in peace parks. *Political Geography, 56,* 106–113.

Ramutsindela, M. (2007). Scaling peace and peacemakers in transboundary parks: Understanding glocalization. In S. H. Ali (Ed.), *Peace parks conservation and conflict resolution* (pp. 69–81). Cambridge, MA: MIT Press.

Southern African Development Community (SADC). (2003). *Regional indicative strategic development plan.* Gaborone: SADC.

SADC. (1998). *Protocol on the development of tourism in the SADC region.* Gaborone: SADC.

Sandwith, T., Shine, C., Hamilton, L., & Sheppard, D. (2001). Transboundary protected areas for peace and cooperation. *Best practice protected area guidelines series no. 7.* Gland, Switzerland: IUCN.

State News Service. (2018, January 18). *Brand Africa and Biodiversity Focus of the 9th Edition of INVESTOUR.* Press Release No.: 18006. Retrieved from https://www.unwto.org/global/press-release/2018-01-18/brand-africa-and-biodiversity-focus-9th-edition-investour

Swatuk, L. A. (2006). Environmental security. In M. M. Betsill, K. Hochstetler, & D. Stevis (Eds.), *International environmental politics* (pp. 203–236). Basingstoke: Palgrave Advances.

Swatuk, L. A. (2005). Peace parks in Southern Africa. *Environmental change and security policy report 11* (pp. 64–67). Washington, DC: WWICS.

Swatuk, L. A. (2002). Rio Minus Ten: The political economy of environmental degradation. *European Journal of Development Research, 14*(1), 264–275.

Thorsell, J., & Harrison, H. (1990). Parks that promote peace: A global inventory of transfrontier nature reserves. In J. Thorsell (Ed.), *Parks on the borderline: Experience in transfrontier conservation,* (pp. 4–21). Gland, Switzerland and Cambridge, UK: IUCN.

Van Amerom, M., & Buscher, B. (2005). Peace parks in Southern Africa: Brings of an African Renaissance? *Journal of Modern African Studies, 43*(2), 159–182.

Vasilijevic, M., Zunckel, K., McKinney, M., Erg, B., Schoon, M., Michel, T. R., & Groves, C. (2015). Transboundary conservation: A systematic and integrated approach. *Best practice protected areas guidelines series no. 23.* Gland, Switzerland: IUCN.

Walters, T. (2012). *Case study: The evolution of the Balkans Peace Park project.* Burlington, VT: Institute for Environmental Diplomacy and Security.

Wegmann, M., Santini, L., Leutner, B., Safi, K., Rocchini, D., Bevanda, M., . . . Rondinini, C. (2014). Role of African protected areas in maintaining connectivity for large mammals. *Philosophical Transactions of the Royal Society B, 369,* 1–8.

Wolmer, W. (2003). Transboundary conservation: The politics of ecological integrity in the Great Limpopo Transfrontier Park. *Journal of Southern African Studies, 29*(1), 261–278.

17

INTEGRATING CLIMATE CHANGE ADAPTATION INTO PEACEBUILDING[1]

Richard Matthew

Climate change impacts

Since the 1700s, human behavior has dramatically reduced natural carbon storage on the planet through agriculture, forestry, and urbanization and simultaneously increased greenhouse gas emissions through the extensive use of fossil fuels. As a result, the atmospheric concentration of carbon dioxide has jumped by 40% since the 1700s, from 280 parts per million (ppm) to 400 ppm in 2013 (IPCC, 2014a). This level of CO_2 is higher than it has been in the past three million years, and the average global temperature has increased as a result by approximately 0.8 degrees Celsius (IPCC, 2014a). In a business as usual scenario, carbon dioxide levels will exceed 450 ppm by 2040, and global warming will increase by 2.6–4.8 degrees Celsius by 2100 (IPCC, 2014a).

According to the IPCC's Fifth Assessment Report (2014a and b) because of climate change, humankind now faces a high risk of severe, long-term, and global impacts, including "substantial species extinction, global and regional food insecurity, consequential constraints on common human activities and limited potential for adaptation in some cases" (IPCC, 2014a, p. 19). Already 70% of the world's species are on the move, searching for more reliable access to water, food, and cooler temperatures (Welch, 2017; see also ICCA, 2020; Wordsell et al., 2020). These concerns are clearly reinforced by the conclusion of the 2019 Global Environmental Outlook report that we have reached or are closing in on irreversible levels of damage to each of the planet's principal socioecological systems: atmosphere, land, water, oceans, and biodiversity (UNEP, 2019). In a similar vein, according to the Ecological Threat Register, as many as 1.2 billion people are now highly vulnerable to and could be displaced by climate change impacts in the next few decades (IEP, 2020; see also Rigaud et al., 2018). This subset of humankind includes most of the world's indigenous peoples, traditional communities, and people living in extreme poverty in urban and peri-urban settings. These 1.2 billion people are most likely to be compelled to migrate due to the stresses and shocks of climate change, such as increases in food insecurity due to crop failure and declining nutritional values; water scarcity as the global hydrological system intensifies causing longer and more frequent droughts and as sea-level rise leads to saltwater contamination of groundwater reservoirs; changes in disease vectors, especially as tropical vectors, move north and south; increase in temperature and humidity that will make it difficult to maintain healthy metabolic function in some areas of the planet;

203   DOI: 10.4324/9781315107592-20

and more destructive extreme events such as floods, cyclones, heatwaves, droughts, and wildfires (Arora & Mishra, 2020; Heyd, 2020; Horton & Horton, 2020; IEP, 2020; IPCC, 2014a, 2014b; Rigaud et al., 2018; Thompson, 2020; UNHCR, 2020). People facing higher levels of exposure and sensitivity, and with fewer adaptive tools within reach due to high levels of poverty and marginalization, will likely experience significant health setbacks, lower economic productivity, the loss of traditional livelihoods, and growing pressure to move (Gemenne, 2011; Kabir et al., 2016; Rigaud et al., 2018).

Although linking complex processes such as population displacement to climate change is challenging, because, in this example, people move for many reasons, the concern expressed by the IPCC, World Bank, and others that hundreds of millions of people might be forced to evacuate coastal and arid areas for part of each year or permanently seems reasonable based on the evidence at hand (Gemenne, 2011; IPCC, 2014a, 2014b; Rigaud et al., 2018). Considerable research has demonstrated the enormous current and probable future impact of climate change on droughts and extreme weather events, and there is no obvious reason to assume people would not consequently be tilted into poverty, subject to health setbacks, and displaced in increasingly large numbers (Hallegatte, Green, Nicholls, & Corfee-Morlot, 2013; Hinkel et al., 2014; Hirabayashi, Kanae, Emori, Oki, & Kimoto, 2008; Hirabayashi et al., 2013; Lehner, Döll, Alcamo, Henrichs, & Kaspar, 2006; Mirza, 2003). Indeed, in recent years, tens of millions of people have been displaced by weather events, and especially by flooding.

Moreover, climate change will also lead to increases in less extreme weather events such as nuisance flooding, which can impose considerable costs on the health and welfare of a society. Moftakhari, AghaKouchak, Sanders, and Matthew (2017) have shown that in some cases, over time, the cumulative effect of nuisance flooding could equal or exceed that of extreme events. According to an estimate developed by Hallegatte et al. (2013), severe flooding alone could impose costs of $1 trillion US by mid-century – an enormous and unprecedented number that, in the wake of extremely destructive hurricanes Harvey, Maria, and Irma, in 2017, seems now quite plausible. Nuisance flooding would add substantially to that figure.

While considerable attention has focused on climate change amplifying extreme weather events, and flooding is emerging as the hazard with the greatest potential to cause widespread harm and displacement, climate change is having a variety of other impacts, and the trends for these are also alarming. Arid regions of the world are likely to experience increased water stress, heat waves, and extended droughts. In many projections, sub-Saharan Africa could experience steep declines in precipitation (IPCC, 2014a). Crop yields are also likely to decrease in parts of the world, which would expand food insecurity (IPCC, 2014a). Fish stocks, which are a primary source of protein for many countries, could decline dramatically under conditions of ocean warming and acidification.

There is another important aspect of climate change impacts that merits attention. As climate science improves, the sense of shared fate that perhaps helped unify global concern at the first Earth Summit and throughout the 1990s may be eroding, as it becomes clear that climate change could confer some benefits creating a twenty-first century divided between climate winners and climate losers. Russia, Scandinavia, Canada, and the United States, for example, all could gain arable land, longer growing seasons, better access to natural resources in the Arctic, and new trade routes. Ironically, primary beneficiaries tend to be already powerful countries, with well-developed economies – and high emission rates. This is in sharp contrast to the countries closer to the equator that are typically identified as in the front lines of negative climate change impacts, such as those in South Asia, the Middle East, and sub-Saharan Africa. Large sections of this region, still recovering from decades of colonial exploitation, have experienced long periods of instability and violence. This has led a number of analysts to explore the ways

Integrating climate change adaptation

in which climate change might affect regions where preexisting patterns of poverty, instability, and violent conflict could make adaptation very challenging. This is not to say that these regions lack understanding or ingenuity, but rather that their capacity to act might be stretched very thin by immediate social needs or being consumed by long-term violent conflict. The impacts of COVID-19 are still being assessed, but it is likely that the pandemic has diverted significant resources away from other pressing needs in many of these countries and pushed tens of millions of people into extreme poverty and insecurity (Barba, van Regenmortel, & Ehmke, 2020).

Climate change and the conflict cycle

As noted throughout this volume, there is a long history of linking environmental stress and competition over natural resources and land to violent conflict and other forms of insecurity. In antiquity, Thucydides (*The Peloponnesian War*) and Plato (*The Republic*) argued that states living within their ecological limits would be more stable and secure than those relying on imports. This line of thinking about ecological limits received a more explicit treatment in the work of economists such as David Ricardo and Thomas Malthus, who in 1798 argued that population growth would likely lead to resource scarcities that would, in turn, generate disaster and conflict. In the twentieth century, Fairfield Osborn drew on Malthus to explain World War II: "When will it be openly recognized that one of the principal causes of the aggressive attitudes of individual nations and of much of the present discord among groups of nations is traceable to diminishing productive lands and to increasing population pressures?" (Osborn, 1948, pp. 200–201).

Arguments linking resource scarcity to violent conflict picked up momentum as evidence of environmental stress improved in the 1970s and were popularized through works such as Garrett Hardin's (1968) article "The Tragedy of the Commons," Paul Ehrlich's (1968) *The Population Bomb*, and Donella Meadows, Meadows, Randers, and Behrens's (1972) *The Limits to Growth*. In 1977, Lester Brown argued that environmental issues were matters of national security; Richard Ullman (1983) contended that environmental stress should catalyze a rethinking of the concept of national security; and Norman Myers (1986) described environmental security as "ultimate security." Over the past 30 years, these seminal arguments have served as the platform for the field of environmental security, a protean concept that has supported a wide range of thinking, discussion, and policymaking.

A compelling conclusion of this volume is that environmental factors can be significant across the conflict cycle – for example, contributing to the outbreak of war (the desire by the Revolutionary United Front (RUF) to gain control of diamond fields in Sierra Leone); funding war (the imposition of levies on cacao in Cote d'Ivoire by both rebel and government forces to raise funds to purchase weapons and ammunition) (Lujala et al., Chapter 10); and as an element of peacebuilding in post-conflict countries (such as the reform of the diamond and forest sectors in the early days after the war in Liberia by President Ellen Johnson Sirleaf) (Jensen & Kron, Chapter 25).

Influential work on how environmental variables could contribute to the onset of violent conflict has been carried out by, among others, Homer-Dixon (1991, 1994, 1996, 1999) and Kahl (2006) focused on resource scarcity. At the same time, scholars such as de Soysa (2000), Klare (2001), Collier and Hoeffler (2002), and Collier (2008) argued that an abundance of high-value natural resources could also contribute to violent conflict. Early critiques of these largely conceptual arguments (e.g., Peluso & Watts, 2001; Korf, 2006) emphasized the complexity of war and dismissed this wave of scholarship as simplistic, an observation largely accommodated in more recent empirical research (see Floyd & Matthew, 2012).

In recent years, linkages have been tested using ethnographic methods, remote sensing, and large datasets. Hanson et al. (2009), for example, conclude that between 1950 and 2000, "118 of 146 conflicts (81%) took place wholly or partially within biodiversity hotspots. When we used the historical percentage of land covered by hotspots to generate an expected value, this proportion was highly significant (one-tailed; $\chi^2 = 456$, $p < 0.01$, df = 1)" (p. 580).

Once violent conflict erupts, natural resources can be used to finance war (or accumulated for personal gain), the environment may be targeted by combatants (such as the destruction of water systems by the RUF during the civil war in Sierra Leone) (Closmann, Chapter 8), environmental management may be disrupted (see Upreti & Nizkorodov, Chapter 22), and civilians fleeing the violence may place enormous pressure on the urban, protected or fragile environments to which they relocate (LeBillon, 2004, 2005, 2012; Brown, 2013). Finally, the role of the environment in the post-conflict period has also been examined through research identifying how environmental factors can be fruitfully integrated into conflict resolution and peacebuilding processes (Ali, 2007; Conca & Dabelko, 2002; Matthew, Hall, & Switzer, 2002; for an overview, see Ide et al., 2021).

This research has served as the platform for research on how climate change might affect the conflict cycle. Accelerated by the 2007 IPCC report, these arguments have tended to be quite speculative although they are beginning to be more data-driven. For example, Hsiang, Meng, and Cane (2011) has written that

> using data from 1950 to 2004, we show that the probability of new civil conflicts arising throughout the tropics doubles during El Niño years relative to La Niña years. This result, which indicates that ENSO may have had a role in 21% of all civil conflicts since 1950, is the first demonstration that the stability of modern societies relates strongly to the global climate.
>
> (p. 438)

Much of the work to date builds on projections and speculation in IPCC reports, where considerable attention is given to how climate stress could amplify problems in turbulent regions of South Asia and Africa (2007, 2014a, 2014b). The planet's mid-latitude countries have heightened exposure to many natural hazards, and they also often have greater sensitivity due to poverty and low governance capacity. They are, in a sense, the contemporary antithesis of sustainable development. This assessment lends itself, unfortunately, to the easy integration of negative impressions of these regions that are not scientifically informed, so one must be alert to the possibility that some reports unwittingly fuse climate science to popular Western impressions of Africa and South Asia and consequently exaggerate vulnerability and underestimate ingenuity and capacity.

With this caveat in mind, some of the most familiar and influential assertions include:

- "climate change acts as a threat multiplier for instability in some of the most volatile regions of the world" (CAN, 2007, pp. 6–7; see also Orbinski et al., Chapter 13).
- "Climate change will overstretch many societies' adaptive capacities within the coming decades" (German Advisory Council on Global Change, 2008, p. 1).
- There are "46 countries – home to 2.7 billion people – in which the effects of climate change interacting with economic, social and political problems will create a high risk of violent conflict" (Smith & Vivekananda, 2007, p. 3).
- "Over the next few years – driven by a combination of natural variability, a warmer climate from the effects of greenhouse gases, and a more vulnerable world in general – the

Integrating climate change adaptation

risk of major societal disruption from weather and climate-related extreme events can be expected to increase. These stresses will affect water and food availability, energy decisions, the design of critical infrastructure, use of the global commons such as the oceans and the Arctic region, and critical ecosystem resources." These stresses "will affect both poor and developed nations with large costs in terms of economic and human security" (McElroy & Baker, 2012, p. 4).

- "The impact of climate change will challenge and reduce the resilience of people and communities to varying degrees. . . . In some contexts, this can increase the risk of instability or violence. This is a particular problem in conflict-prone or conflict-affected contexts where governance structures and institutions are often weak, regardless of climate change" (Vivekananda, 2011, p. 8).

Opposing this speculation, Slettebak (2012), among others, writes

> Rather than over-emphasizing conflict as a result of climate change, I would recommend keeping the focus on societal development, including building resilience against adverse effects of climate change. While this promises the possibility of alleviating the danger of climate change, it can also lead to strengthened societies in the face of natural disaster and civil war.
>
> (p. 175)

Against this context, there are a handful of claims that have emerged that seem compelling and robust. First, in large measure, anthropogenic climate change amplifies phenomena such as floods, droughts, and heat waves that occur naturally. The impacts of such phenomena on human societies are partly determined by where people settle, the defense systems they build, and so on (Sanders et al., 2020). We have an increasingly crowded planet with a great deal of brittle infrastructure and urban and peri-urban space rapidly expanding on coastal and riverine flood plains as well as in arid regions (Marshall, Waldman, MacGregor, Mehta, & Randhawa, 2009; OECD/SWAC, 2020). As noted earlier, it is very difficult to distinguish between "natural" severe weather events and those "caused" by climate change. Together, this suggests that when exploring linkages to the conflict cycle, it would be more accurate to replace "climate change" with a more inclusive term such as "anthropogenic climate change and natural climate variability." Admittedly, this is a bit unwieldy.

Second, the vast literature on violent conflict makes it clear that simple causal models are very misleading. Violent conflict has links to deep structural issues such as colonization, poverty, inequality, regime type, and identity as well as to more immediate variables such as recession and corruption. Individuals and groups at different levels can also play critical roles, as can military plans and technological innovations. Human psychology may provide important insights into the propensity for group violence. When many variables shape outcomes, small changes in one might have an enormous impact (complexity science), but it may also be very hard to isolate the signal of any given variable. Even a very large effect could be hard to identify. So at this point, it is perhaps most accurate to suggest that links between anthropogenic climate change and natural climate variability, on the one hand, and the conflict cycle, on the other hand, may very well vary from case to case. And often, climate impacts will be indirect, amplifying variables related to war such as poverty and weak governance capacity (Crawford & Church, Chapter 7).

Third, and related to the earlier point, recent research is expanding the dependent variable to include a broader range of negative social outcomes. The idea is that climate change might contribute to many other forms of violence such as human insecurity, health setbacks, crime, murders, protests, riots, pandemics, and terrorism. Insofar as peacebuilding is concerned, the conflict cycle is a logical starting point, but we should be aware of other relationships to violence, and the types of adaptation and resilience responding to these might require and might be possible within the context of peacebuilding.

Fourth, climate change is a global phenomenon, which suggests that in some sense it is introducing turbulence at a planetary level. For example, if tens of millions of people are displaced by rising temperatures and humidity, drought, and flood in many parts of the planet, then this might influence how any one society responds to migratory pressure on its own borders – and this response might differ (e.g., it might be much more aggressive) from what it would have been if the broader pattern of displacement did not exist. A sort of general systemwide climate effect might lead to less generous particular responses.

Fifth, earlier I noted how some countries could benefit from climate change. One important example is the potential of Arctic nations to gain access to the vast mineral wealth that has for millennia been locked under an impenetrable sheet of ice. This suggests that climate change could be highly disruptive in other contexts as well, by changing the value of assets such as land and water. The implications for current power relationships are potentially enormous.

Sixth and finally, the concept of winners and losers has another variant. Some countries, and regions within countries, have more capacity to adapt than others. The state of California recently experienced a five-year drought (2012–2016). Many wealthy coastal communities had responded to an earlier drought in 2007–2009 by investing in water efficiency and were largely self-sufficient and unaffected by the more recent drought. Poor communities, on the other hand, had not adapted to the likelihood of more frequent drought events, and they experienced enormous hardship (Pincetl & Hogue, 2015). It is easy to imagine this scenario playing out globally, at which point the arguments of Harald Welzer (2012) – that where extreme poverty and climate hardship intersect, violence could erupt – seem very reasonable.

Peacebuilding

At the end of the Cold War, seeing new hope for international cooperation and alarmed by violent civil wars being fought in places like Angola, Rwanda, Sierra Leone, and Somalia, Boutros Boutros-Ghali introduced the concept of peacebuilding in *An Agenda for Peace* (1992). Since that time, the concept has evolved through deliberation and practice, especially inside the United Nations (United Nations, 2001; United Nations, 2006; UNDP, 1994; UNGA, 2009). While there is not a single definition used by everyone, the following statement captures current thinking quite well:

> Peacebuilding involves a range of measures targeted to reduce the risk of lapsing or relapsing into conflict by strengthening national capacities at all levels for conflict management, and to lay the foundations for sustainable peace and development. Peacebuilding strategies must be coherent and tailored to specific needs of the country concerned, based on national ownership, and should comprise a carefully prioritized, sequenced, and therefore relatively narrow set of activities aimed at achieving the above objectives.
>
> (United Nations, 2007)

A 2004 study carried out by the Peace Research Institute of Oslo identified four aspects of peacebuilding based on a review of 336 projects that were funded by Germany, the Netherlands,

Norway, and the United Kingdom (Smith, 2004). This framework for organizing peacebuilding into a set of core functions was adopted by the Organization for Economic Co-operation and Development (OECD) in 2008, and by a variety of UN agencies (e.g., UNEP, 2009). The framework organizes peacebuilding into four functional domains: (1) social, economic, and environmental; (2) governance and political; (3) security; and (4) truth and reconciliation. Other researchers have weighed in with slightly different frameworks. Barnett, Kim, O'Donnell, and Sitea (2007) focus on stability creation, restoration of state institutions, and socioeconomic recovery (p. 49). De Coning (2008) identifies security and rule of law, politics and governance, socioeconomic recovery, and human rights (p. 47).

These theorizations do capture the format of early peacebuilding initiatives and make clear that in the 1990s peacebuilding was largely about prompting post-conflict states toward something that resembled Sweden or Canada. But, the early track record was not especially successful. Following the first round of peacebuilding, so to speak, Hun Sen assumed full control over Cambodia; UN peacekeepers watched helplessly as an incredibly brutal genocide took place in Rwanda; and Charles Taylor played a key role in three wars after the UN mission left Liberia. The UN failed forward, and peacebuilding has improved over time. It shifted its focus to capacity building for both government and civil society. It sought to avoid areas in which other donors were active and focus on meeting needs where they were not. It made clear that post-conflict programs had to be largely designed and led by the people they would affect and that the character of peacebuilding would inevitably be highly contextual.

Has the evolution of peacebuilding been successful? Assessments vary (Berdal, 2009; Call & Cousens, 2008; Chetail, 2009; Doyle & Sambanis, 2006; Fortna, 2008; Howard, 2008; Tschirgi, 2004). Many argue that there is a huge gap between resources and needs (United Nations, 2013). Others contend that peacebuilding is shaped by Western agendas and ideology and needs to have more local input and content (Chandler, 1999; Chopra, 2000) For some, post-conflict societies are simply being recolonized with Western institutions and values (Bendaña, 2005; Pugh, 2008).

But two things are certain. First, almost no one else is rallying to help post-conflict states meet immediate needs and build capacity for sustainable development and climate resilience. So, the role of the United Nation remains critical. Second, although much has been written about the links between climate change and the conflict cycle, climate change adaptation has not been integrated into peacebuilding except in ad hoc and piecemeal ways.

Climate change adaptation and peacebuilding

Thus, there is an opportunity, especially through the United Nations, and a need, given the ways in which climate change has been linked to the conflict cycle, to focus on the prospects for integrating climate change adaptation into peacebuilding activities. In earlier work with Anne Hammill (Hammill & Matthew, 2010) and alone (Matthew, 2014), we identified two major obstacles to this integration. First, there is considerable tried and true programming, generally adaptable to local contexts, for many peacebuilding priorities – disarming, demobilizing, and reintegrating combatants; crafting conditions attractive to foreign investors; building capacity in core civil society and government areas; establishing reconciliation processes; and so on. There is considerably less proven content for climate change adaptation in post-conflict states. Consequently, peacebuilding lacks familiar climate programs that can be easily integrated into national reconstruction plans and funded.

Second, the time scales for conventional peacebuilding and climate change adaptation are not easy to align. Donors and societies emerging from war typically have immediate and pressing needs and are looking for fairly quick results, whereas climate change adaptation may impose costs early on, with the promise of benefits in the future.

To this, I would now add a third obstacle. In 2015, the Paris Agreement created a general framework for climate action designed to be globally inclusive, but this has not yet matured into clear policies, programs, and funding opportunities for post-conflict states. Under such conditions of uncertainty, climate change adaptation is easily delayed in peacebuilding operations.

Nonetheless, in earlier work, we developed an approach to thinking about how climate change adaptation could be integrated into conventional peacebuilding areas (see Matthew, 2014, p. 89). We further argued that principles for this integration ought to be established, perhaps modeled on the OECD's (2007) principles for effective engagement in fragile states, and an inventory of appropriate adaptation tools and best practices needs to be created. To this, I would add that climate change adaptation is not likely to succeed if it is not fully responsive to the needs, values, experiences, knowledge, and assets of the communities that will be affected by it. While a national climate action plan is essential, in the context of peacebuilding, trusted and inclusive community-based development of climate change adaptation projects and programs is critical.

The costs of not acting are becoming increasingly clear. In 2017, for example, mudslides in Freetown, the capital of Sierra Leone, destroyed homes and killed as many as a thousand people (Trenchard, 2018). The area received three times its normal rainfall in July 2017, creating a lot of mud in the hills. Unfortunately, during the post-conflict era, deforestation and unplanned and unregulated construction amplified vulnerability considerably, transforming a natural hazard into a flood and mudslide disaster. It is well-known, however, that mud and rain are a deadly combination in a hilly city where people build in areas of heightened vulnerability. Mud flows very quickly, and being at least twice the weight of water, it is extremely difficult to stop and can overwhelm neighborhoods, destroying houses and killing people, in a matter of minutes. If some attention had been given to climate resilience, then perhaps this tragedy would not have happened. This is a story playing in different parts of the planet, as war and disaster overlap.

Looking ahead, several things seem essential to this integration. First, as the case of Sierra Leone suggests, building community-level resilience, and harnessing the ingenuity and assets of a community to this effort, is essential. While supporting work being carried out at a community level can be expensive and challenging in peacebuilding situations, information technologies such as Zoom have made it much easier to maintain constant and sophisticated communication flows.

Second, this, in turn, requires improvements in the ability to quickly assess climate vulnerability, build adequate warning systems, and access funds to support climate action in post-conflict settings. Two recent developments are promising in this regard. On the one hand, earlier emphasis on hard infrastructure solutions is ceding to the realization that soft, often nature-based solutions are affordable, can use local materials, and can adapt as conditions require. For example, during the peacebuilding phase in Sierra Leone, beaches were mined for sand needed to rebuild Freetown. Beaches, however, are a natural defense against sea-level rise and ocean surges. Building to high tide marks, disrupting sediment flows, and mining beaches all increase vulnerability to climate change impacts – and, in the case of Sierra Leone, also reduce a natural asset that might attract tourism. Using alternative building materials and adopting beach nourishment practices would have protected and enhanced climate resilience. On the other hand, our ability to integrate multiple forms of big data, real-time observations, and local knowledge – whether these are available in structured or unstructured forms – to build models, run future scenarios, and assess trade-offs and costs of different interventions, has improved dramatically in a very short time. It is now relatively easy to train local stakeholders and codevelop

Integrating climate change adaptation

models of climate vulnerability in ways that lead to shared understanding and trust in science (Goodrich et al., 2020; Houston et al., 2017; Sanders et al., 2020).

Third, climate change affects variables associated with instability and conflict such as poverty, water access, and food security, and therefore, a particular focus on building climate-sensitive capacity in these areas, where immediate needs are being met, is especially important.

Fourth, during consultations around plans for post-conflict recovery, points of intersection need to be identified and trade-offs need to be openly discussed so that informed decisions can be made that are broadly understood.

Fifth, absent a more concrete framework for coordinating and funding global climate action, there is no easy reference point for this integration – it is held hostage by broader forces of inertia, which seems remarkably unfair given the heightened sensitivity to climate impacts in post-conflict states.

Note

1 This chapter is a substantially revised version of Matthew, R. (2018) Climate Change Adaptation and Peacebuilding in Swain A (ed) *Routledge Handbook of Environmental Conflict and Peacebuilding*. Routledge Press, 108–120. The research benefited from work carried out while preparing another edited volume and especially the chapter Goodrich K. and Nizkorodov E. (2016) "The Science of the Anthropocene" in Matthew R Harron C Goodrich K Maharramli B and Nizkorodov E *The Social Ecology of the Anthropocene* World Scientific/Imperial Press, London, 3–32; from previous work done on climate change and peacebuilding with Anne Hammill; and from informal conversations about what we know about the links between climate change and conflict with Marc Levy at Columbia University.

References

Ali, S. (2007). *Peace parks: Conservation and conflict resolution*. Cambridge, MA: MIT Press.

Arora, N. K., & Mishra, J. (2020). COVID-19 and importance of environmental sustainability. *Environmental Sustainability, 3*(2), 117–119. https://doi.org/10.1007/s42398-020-00107-z

Barba, L., van Regenmortel, H., & Ehmke, E. (2020). *Shelter from the Storm: The global need for universal protection in times of COVID-19*. Oxfam. Retrieved from www.oxfam.org/en/research/shelter-storm-global-need-universal-social-protection-times-covid-19

Barnett, M., Kim, H., O'Donnell, M., & Sitea, L. (2007). Peacebuilding: What is in a name? *Global Governance, 13*, 35–58.

Bendaña, A. (2005). From peacebuilding to statebuilding: One step forward and two steps back? *Development, 48*(3), 5–15.

Berdal, M. (2009). *Building peace after war*. London: International Institute for Strategic Studies.

Boutros-Ghali, B. (1992). *An agenda for peace: Preventive diplomacy, peacemaking and peacekeeping*. Retrieved September 1, 2017, from http://journals.sagepub.com/doi/abs/10.1177/004711789201100302

Brown, L. (1977). *Redefining national security*. Worldwatch Institute Paper 14. Washington, DC: Worldwatch Institute.

Brown, O. (2013). Encouraging peacebuilding through better environmental and natural resource management. *Chatham House Briefing Paper, 4, 1–8*.

Call, C., & Cousens, L. (2008). Ending wars and building peace: International responses to war-torn societies. *International Studies Perspectives, 9*, 1–21.

Chandler, D. (1999). *Bosnia: Faking democracy after Dayton*. London: Pluto.

Chetail, V. (Ed.). (2009). *Post-conflict peacebuilding: A lexicon*. Oxford: Oxford University.

Chopra, J. (2000). The UN's kingdom in East Timor. *Survival, 42*(3), 27–40.

CAN. (2007). *National security and the threat of climate change*. Retrieved September 1, 2017, from http://securityandclimate.cna.org/.

Collier, P. (2008). *The bottom billion: Why the poorest countries are failing and what can be done about it*. Oxford and New York: Oxford University Press.

Collier, P., & Hoeffler, A. (2002). *Greed and grievance in civil war*. Working Paper, Oxford: Centre for the Study of African Economies.

Conca, K., & Dabelko, G. (Eds.). (2002). *Environmental peacemaking*. Washington, DC: Woodrow Wilson Center.

De Coning, C. (2008). Understanding peacebuilding: Consolidating the peace process. *Conflict Trends, 4*, 45–51.

De Soysa, I. (2000). The resource curse: Are civil wars driven by rapacity or paucity?. In M. Berdal & D. Malone (Eds.), *Greed & grievance: Economic agendas in civil war* (pp. 113–135). Boulder: Lynne Rienner.

Doyle, M., & Sambanis, N. (2006). *Making war and building peace: United Nations peace operations*. Princeton, NJ: Princeton University Press.

Ehrlich, P. (1968). *The population bomb*. New York: Sierra Club/Ballantine Books.

Floyd, R., & Matthew, R. A. (Eds.). (2012). *Environmental security: Frameworks for analysis*. London: Routledge.

Fortna, V. (2008). *Does peacekeeping work? Shaping Belligerents' choices after civil war*. Princeton, NJ: Princeton University Press.

Gemenne, F. (2011). Why the numbers don't add up: A review of estimates and predictions of people displaced by environmental changes. *Global Environmental Change, 21*, S41–S49.

German Advisory Council on Global Change. (2008). *World in transition: Climate change as a security risk*. London: Earthscan.

Goodrich, K. A., Basolo, V., Feldman, D. L., Matthew, R. A., Schubert, J. E., Luke, A., . . . Sanders, B. F. (2020). Addressing pluvial flash flooding through community-based collaborative research in Tijuana, Mexico. *Water, 12*(5), 1257. https://doi.org/10.3390/w12051257

Hallegatte, S., Green, C., Nicholls, R. J., & Corfee-Morlot, J. (2013). Future flood losses in major coastal cities. *Nat. Clim. Change, 3*(9), 802–806.

Hammill, A., & Matthew, R. A. (2010). Peacebuilding and climate change adaptation. *St. Antony's International Review, 5*(2), 89–112

Houston, D., Cheung, W., Basolo, V., Feldman, D., Matthew, R., Sanders, B., . . . Luke, A. (2017). The influence of hazard maps and trust of flood controls on coastal flood spatial awareness and risk perception. *Environment and Behavior, 51*(4), 347–375.

Hanson, T., Brooks, T. M., Fonseca, G. A. B., Hoffmann, M., Lamoreux, J. F., Machlis, G., . . . Pilgrim, J. D. (2009). Warfare in biodiversity hotspots. *Conservation Biology, 23*, 578–587.

Hardin, G. (1968). The tragedy of the commons. *Science, 162*, 1243–1248.

Heyd, T. (2020). Covid-19 and climate change in the times of the Anthropocene. *The Anthropocene Review*, 205301962096179. https://doi.org/10.1177/2053019620961799

Hinkel, J., Lincke, D., Vafeidis, A. T., Perrette, M., Nicholls, R. J., Tol, R. S. J., . . Levermann, A. (2014). Coastal flood damage and adaptation costs under 21st century sea-level rise. *Proc. Natl. Acad. Sci., 111*(9), 3292–3297.

Hirabayashi, Y., Kanae, S., Emori, S., Oki, T., & Kimoto, M. (2008). Global projections of changing risks of floods and droughts in a changing climate. *Hydrological Sciences Journal, 53*(4), 754–772.

Hirabayashi, Y., Mahendran, R., Koirala, S., Konoshima, L., Yamazaki, D., Watanabe, S., . . . Kanae, S. (2013). Global flood risk under climate change. *Nationalism and Climate Change, 3*(9), 816–821.

Homer-Dixon, T. (1991). On the threshold: Environmental changes as causes of acute conflict. *International Security, 16*, 76–116.

Homer-Dixon, T. (1994). Environmental scarcities and violent conflict: Evidence from cases. *International Security, 19*, 5–40.

Homer-Dixon, T. (1996). Debate between Thomas Homer-Dixon and Marc A. Levy. *Environmental Change and Security Project Report*, 49–60.

Homer-Dixon, T. (1999). *Environment, scarcity, and violence*. Princeton, NJ: Princeton University Press.

Horton, B., & Horton, P. (2020). COVID-19 and the climate emergency: Do common origins and solutions reside in the global agrifood system? *One Earth, 3*(1), 20–22. https://doi.org/10.1016/j.oneear.2020.06.006

Howard, L. (2008). *UN peacekeeping in civil wars*. Cambridge, UK: Cambridge University Press.

Hsiang, S. M., Meng, K. C., & Cane, M. A. (2011). Civil conflicts associated with global climate change. *Nature, 476*, 438–441.

ICCA Consortium. (2020). *Defending territories of life and their defenders*. Retrieved December 31, 2020, from www.iccaconsortium.org/index.php/defending-territories-of-life/defending-territories-of-life-and-their-defenders-policy/

Ide, T., Bruch, C., Carius, A., Conca, K., Dabelko, G. D., Matthew, R., & Weinthal, E. (2021). The past and future (s) of environmental peacebuilding. *International Affairs, 97*(1), 1–16. https://doi.org/10.1093/ia/iiaa177

Institute for Economics & Peace (IEP). (2020). *Ecological threat register 2020: Understanding ecological threats, resilience and peace*. Retrieved on March 12, 2021, from http://visionofhumanity.org/reports

Intergovernmental Panel on Climate Change (IPCC). (2007). *Working group II report: Climate change impacts, adaptation, and vulnerability*. Retrieved September 1, 2017, from www.ipcc.ch/

Intergovernmental Panel on Climate Change (IPCC). (2014a). *Climate change 2014: Synthesis report. Contribution of working groups I, II and III to the fifth assessment report of the intergovernmental panel on climate change*. Geneva.

Intergovernmental Panel on Climate Change (IPCC). (2014b). *Climate change 2014: Impacts, adaptation, and vulnerability. Part A: Global and sectoral aspects. Contribution of working group II to the fifth assessment report of the intergovernmental panel on climate change*. Cambridge: Cambridge University Press.

Kabir, R., Khan, H., Ball, E., & Caldwell, K. (2016). Climate change impact: The experience of the coastal areas of Bangladesh affected by cyclones Sidr and Aila. *Journal of Environmental and Public Health*, 2016, 1–9.

Kahl, C. H. (2006). *States, scarcity, and civil strife in the developing world*. Princeton, NJ: Princeton University Press.

Klare, M. T. (2001). *Resource wars: The new landscape of global conflict*. New York: Henry Holt and Company.

Korf, B. (2006). Cargo cult science, armchair empiricism and the idea of violent conflict. *Third World Quarterly*, 27(3), 459–476.

LeBillon, P. (Ed.). (2004). *The geopolitics of resource wars: Resource dependence, governance and violence*. London: Frank Cass.

LeBillon, P. (2005). *Fueling war: Natural resources and armed conflict*. Adelphi paper no. 373. London: Routledge.

LeBillon, P. (2012). *Wars of plunder: Conflicts, profits and the politics of resources*. London: Hurst & Co Publishers Ltd.

Lehner, B., Döll, P., Alcamo, J., Henrichs, T., & Kaspar, F. (2006). Estimating the impact of global change on flood and drought risks in Europe: A continental, integrated analysis. *Clim. Change*, 75(3), 273–299.

Malthus, T. (1798). *An essay on the princple of population*. Retrieved September 10, 2017, from http://oll.libertyfund.org/titles/malthus-an-essay-on-the-principle-of-population-1798-1st-ed

Marshall, F., Waldman, L., MacGregor, H., Mehta, L., & Randhawa, P. (2009). On the Edge of Sustainability: Perspectives on Peri-urban Dynamics, *STEPS Working Paper 35*. STEPS Centre.

Matthew, R. A. (2014). Integrating climate change and peacebuilding. *Climatic Change*, 123, 83–93.

Matthew, R. A, Halle, M., & Switzer, J. (Eds.). (2002). *Conserving the peace: Resources, livelihoods and security*. Geneva: IUCN/IISD.

McElroy, M., & Baker, D. J. (2012). *Climate extremes: Recent trends with implications for national security*. Retrieved September 10, 2017, from http://environment.harvard.edu/sites/default/files/climate_extremes_report_2012-12-04.pdf

Meadows, D. H., Meadows, D. L., Randers, J., & Behrens III, W. W. (1972). *Limits to growth*. New York: New American Library.

Mirza, M. M. Q. (2003). Climate change and extreme weather events: Can developing countries adapt? *Climate Policy*, 3(3), 233–248.

Moftakhari, H. R., AghaKouchak, A., Sanders, B. F., & Matthew, R. A. (2017). Cumulative hazard: The case of nuisance flooding. *Earth's Future*, 5, 214–223.

Myers, N. (1986). The environmental dimension to security issues. *The Environmentalist*, 6, 251–257.

Organization for Economic Cooperation and Development (OECD). (2007). *Effective engagement in fragile states*. Retrieved September 15, 2017, from www.oecd.org/document/12/0,3746,en_2649_33693550_42113676_1_1_1,00.html

OECD/SWAC. (2020). *Africa's Urbanisation Dynamics 2020: Africapolis, Mapping a New Urban Geography*, West African Studies, OECD Publishing. https://doi.org/10.1787/b6bccb81-en

Osborn, F. (1948). *Our Plundered Planet*. New York: Grosset & Dunlap.

Peluso, N., & Watts, M. (Eds.). (2001). *Violent environments*. Ithaca: Cornell University Press.

Pincetl, S., & Hogue, T. S. (2015). California's new normal? Recurring drought: Addressing winners and losers. *Local Environment*, 20(7), 850–854.

Pugh, M. (2008). Corruption and the political economy of liberal peace. *International Studies Association annual convention paper*, San Francisco.

Rigaud, K. K., de Sherbinin, A., Jones, B., Bergmann, J., Clement, V., Ober, K., . . . Midgley, A. (2018). *Groundswell: preparing for internal climate migration*. Washington, DC: The World Bank.

Sanders, B. F., Schubert, J. E., Goodrich, K. A., Houston, D., Feldman, D. L., Basolo, V., et al. (2020). Collaborative modeling with fine-resolution data enhances flood awareness, minimizes differences in flood perception, and produces actionable flood maps. *Earth's Future*, 7, e2019EF001391. https://doi.org/10.1029/2019EF001391

Smith, D. (2004). *Towards a strategic framework for peacebuilding: Getting their act together: Overview report of the Joint Utstein Study of Peacebuilding*. Retrieved from www.prio.org/Publications/Publication/?x=153

Smith, D., & Vivekananda, J. (2007). *A climate of conflict: The links between climate change, peace and war*. London: International Alert. Retrieved from www.international-alert.org/pdf/A_Climate_Of_Conflict.pdf

Slettebak, R. T. (2012). Don't blame the weather! Climate-related natural disasters and civil conflict. *Journal of Peace Research*, *49*, 163–176.

Thompson, A. (2020). A running list of record-breaking natural disasters in 2020. *Scientific American*. Retrieved from www.scientificamerican.com/article/a-running-list-of-record-breaking-natural-disasters-in-2020/

Trenchard, T. (2018, April 8). Life doesn't go on after the mudslides in Sierra Leone. *NPR*. Retrieved March 22, 2021, from www.npr.org/sections/goatsandsoda/2018/04/08/599526907/life-doesnt-go-on-after-the-mudslides-in-sierra-leone

Tschirgi, N. (2004). *Post-conflict peacebuilding revisited: Achievements, limitations, challenges*. New York: International Peace Academy.

Ullman, R. (1983). Redefining security. *International Security*, *8*

United Nations. (2001). *No exit without strategy. Report of the Secretary-General* S/2001/394. New York: United Nations.

United Nations. (2006). *Note of guidance on integrated missions*. New York: United Nations.

United Nations. (2007). *Secretary general policy committee statement*. Reported on Peacebuilding Initiative website. Retrieved September 5, 2016, from www.peacebuildinginitiative.org/index.cfm?pageId=1764

United Nations. (2013). *Financing peacekeeping*. New York: United Nations. Retrieved September 15, 2017, from www.un.org/en/peacekeeping/operations/financing.shtml.

United Nations Development Programme (UNDP). (1994). *Human development report 1994*. Oxford: Oxford University Press.

United Nations Environment Programme (UNEP). (2019). *Global environmental outlook 6*. Retrieved from www.unep.org/resources/global-environment-outlook-6?_ga=2.227852510.2120879290.1614713659-1674902825.1613760489

United Nations Environment Programme (UNEP). (2009). *From conflict to peacebuilding: The role of natural resources and the environment*. UNEP.

UNGA. (2009). *Report of the secretary-general on peacebuilding in the immediate aftermath of conflict*, June 11, 2009 A/63/881-S/2009/304

UNHCR. (2020). *Figures at a Glance*. Retrieved December 31, 2020, from www.unhcr.org/en-us/figures-at-a-glance.html

Vivekananda, J. (2011). *Practice note: Conflict-sensitive responses to climate change in South Asia*. International Alert. Retrieved March 22, 2021, from www.international-alert.org/sites/default/files/IFP_ClimateChange_ConflictSensitiveResponsesAsia_EN_2011.pdf

Welch, C. (2017). Half of all species are on the move – and we're feeling it. *National Geographic*. Retrieved from online.www.nationalgeographic.com/news/2017/04/climate-change-species-migration-disease/#close

Welzer, H. (2012). *Climate wars: Why people will be killed in the 21st century*. Polity Press.

Wordsell, T., Kumar, K., Allan, J. R., Gibbon, G. E. M., White, A. M., Khare, A., & Frechette, A. (2020). Rights-based conservation: The path to preserving Earth's biological and cultural diversity? *Rights and Resources Initiative*, 1–43.

18

A PARADIGM FOR ACTIONABLE AND ACCESSIBLE LOCAL FLOOD HAZARD INFORMATION

Brett F. Sanders, Richard Matthew, Adam Luke, Kristen A. Goodrich, Victoria Basolo, Ana Eguiarte, Danielle Boudreau and David L. Feldman

In 1992, in the wake of the Cold War, the United Nations Secretary-General Boutros Boutros-Ghali identified peacebuilding as a global priority and offered a blueprint for action titled *An Agenda for Peace*. 1992 was also the year of the first Earth Summit, held in Rio, where considerable attention was given to climate change and biodiversity loss. It is not surprising that, since that time, one line of research and discussion has focused on the intersections among climate change, natural disasters, violent conflict, and peacebuilding (Conca & Dabelko, 2002; Matthew, Halle, & Switzer, 2002; Gleick, Iceland, & Trivedi, 2020).

Although research to date has been, in important ways, inconclusive and contested,[1] largely due to the complexity of contemporary war and the challenges of tracing and weighting environmental variables in this context, several evidence-based areas of concern have emerged (Ide et al., 2021; Null & Herzer-Risi, 2016). In the 2000s, partly in response to the Intergovernmental Panel on Climate Change's *Fourth Assessment Report*, research explored the possibility that natural disasters might contribute to the initiation or continuation of violent conflict (Harris, Keen, & Mitchell, 2013; Nelson, 2010), that conflict-affected countries might have a heightened vulnerability to disasters and vice versa (Smith & Vivekananda, 2007), and that violent conflict was more likely to occur in fragile environments (Hanson et al., 2009; Matthew, Jensen, & Brown, 2009). The concept of disaster diplomacy took shape in response to concerns about a significant intersection between disasters and violent conflicts (Streich & Mislan, 2014).

As this strand of research matured and the body of evidence expanded (Peters & Budimir, 2016), arguments in support of both conflict-sensitive approaches to climate change adaptation and integrating climate change resilience-building into peacebuilding activities gained traction (Matthew, 2014; Tanzler, Carius, & Maas, 2013). Recent work adds considerably to the claim that natural disasters can prolong conflict (Eastin, 2016), and conflict zones are emerging as an important arena for disaster risk reduction programming (Peters, 2017). Concerns about the intersections among climate change, natural disasters, violent conflict, and peacebuilding now inform international policy discussion at the highest levels (Peters, Mayhew, Slim, van Aalst, & Arrighi, 2019).

In this context, it is not surprising that evidence is also growing around the ways in which flooding, the most common and destructive natural disaster, might contribute to violent conflict, perhaps by prolonging its duration (Ghimire, Ferreira, & Dorfman, 2015). As noted in the *Ecological Threat Register*, in the past 30 years, 71% of natural disasters have been flood and storm events (Institute for Economics & Peace, 2020). There are many examples of devastating floods occurring in conflict-affected countries including Sudan (2007), Pakistan (2010, 2013, 2014, and 2019), Colombia (2010), Afghanistan (2013), Myanmar (2015), and Nepal (2020). It thus makes sense to consider how recent advances in environmental modeling, high-performance computing, and increasing capacity to collect fine-scale geospatial data at low cost make it possible to envision local level, fine-scale flood hazard models simulating flooding at spatial and temporal scales comparable to how people experience flooding. This technology presents new opportunities to improve the targeted communication of flood risks and accelerate a much-needed shift in adoption of vulnerability reduction measures.

Researchers have been focused for several decades on advancing numerical methods for solving the shallow-water equations to describe the movement of surface water over the land surface (Sanders, 2017). Predicting the dynamics of flooding has served as the primary motivation of these studies based on the potential to improve early warning systems, emergency preparedness and response efforts, and the delineation of flood plains for planning and insurance purposes. Recent research has focused on speeding up model execution through parallel computing (Brodtkorb, Sætra, & Altinakar, 2012; Castro, Ortega, de la Asunción, Mantas, & Gallardo, 2011; Sanders, Schubert, & Detwiler, 2010; Vacandio, Dal Palú, & Mignosa, 2014) and upscaling with subgrid models (also called porosity models) that account for the bulk effect of fine-scale features with relatively coarse computational cells (Casulli & Stelling, 2011; Guinot, Sanders, & Schubert, 2017; Özgen, Zhao, Liang, & Hinkelmann, 2016; Sanders & Schubert, 2019; Sanders, Schubert, & Gallegos, 2008; Soares-Frazão, Lhomme, Guinot, & Zech, 2008). Accuracy is also of paramount consideration when developing flood models and addressing sources of uncertainty (Bates, 2012; Dottori, Di Baldassarre, & Todini, 2013), and the numerous aspects of model development including the grid resolution and required data gathering will hinge on the types of outputs that are needed from the model and the decision points that will be informed. Collaborative flood modeling (CFM) has now emerged as a process by which the decision needs of model developers and the decision needs of community-level stakeholders are both met, and the process itself contributes to an atmosphere of greater cooperation with improved dialogue among stakeholders and higher levels of trust (Dawson et al. 2011; Evers et al. 2012; Goodrich et al., 2020; Hagemeier-Klose & Wagner, 2009; Lane et al., 2011; Maskrey, Mount, Thorne, & Dryden, 2016; Meyer et al. 2012; Luke et al., 2018; Pasche et al., 2009; Sanders et al., 2020; Steinfuhrer et al., 2009).

In the remainder of this chapter, we show a process by which modeling flood hazards can be undertaken collaboratively with end users of flood hazard information, resulting in hazard maps tailored to local decision-making needs and widely accessible through an online visualization system. We also show three applications of CFM at contrasting sites: an affluent urban site in southern California exposed to coastal flooding, a peri-urban site in southern California exposed to fluvial flooding, and an urban site in Tijuana, Mexico, exposed to pluvial flooding. We believe that the success of CFM at these three sites, and the coproduction of maps that inform a wide range of decision-making needs, demonstrates high potential to support community level stakeholders in conflict-affected countries (on coproduction, see Lemos et al., 2018). Results demonstrate potential for high-risk communities to begin building resilience throughout the peacebuilding process – not only for flood events but potentially for all natural hazards.

Materials and methods

CFM was applied at Newport Beach (NB) and Tijuana River Valley in Southern California, and in the Los Laureles Canyon (LLC) in Tijuana, Mexico. The NB site in Orange County, California, is characterized by an urbanized embayment where development on lowland topography is vulnerable to flooding from a combination of extreme high tides, waves, and rainfall. The TRV site in San Diego, California, consists of a mix of open spaces that offer riparian and estuarine wetland habitat and residential properties on large lots that often include equestrian amenities. The TRV is vulnerable to flooding from high flows down the Tijuana River, from lateral inflows draining from local catchments, and from extreme high tides and waves. The LLC site consists of steep topography that is densely developed. Upstream, development practices in highly erosive conditions leads to significant amounts of sediment conveyed by flood waters that result from intense rainfall, and the former (combined with solid waste) contributes to the latter through blockages of channels and culverts downstream.

The ParBreZo hydrodynamic model (Kim, Sanders, Famiglietti, & Guinot, 2015) was used for flood hazard modeling at all three sites. ParBreZo solves the two-dimensional shallow-water equations on an unstructured grid of triangular and/or quadrilateral cells using Godunov-type finite volume schemes capable of resolving subcritical, supercritical, and trans-critical flows with sharp fronts. This capability proved important based on the range of important flooding mechanisms across the three sites including overtopping of sea walls in NB, supercritical channel flows with hydraulic jumps in TRV and LLC, and the dynamic spreading of flood water over irregular topography at all three sites. Additional models and data were used to model the drivers of flooding including rainfall, runoff, extreme high tides, and waves. At all three sites, the ParBreZo model was configured with a model domain that encompassed areas vulnerable to flooding, and ParBreZo internal and external boundary conditions were specified using data or models of the flood drivers. Hence, flooding is simulated as a time-dependent and spatially distributed process to realistically capture how one would experience flooding during an extreme event.

Flooding can result from many different combinations of flood drivers, so there are countless ways in which flood model scenarios can be configured to inform and stimulate two-way dialogue about flooding. Two types of scenarios were utilized here: historical scenarios and probabilistic scenarios. To model historical scenarios, contemporaneous measurements of flood drivers were used as boundary conditions for the model including measurements from nearby tide gages, wave gages, stream gages, and rainfall gages. In some cases, additional modeling was required to transform measurements into useful boundary data. For example, wave transformation models and wave overtopping models were applied to compute an equivalent overtopping flow rate that accounts for waves at NB, as described by Gallien, Sanders, and Flick (2014). Probabilistic modeling scenarios, on the other hand, required boundary conditions representative of a specific return period (e.g., 20-year event). This is challenging in the coastal zone where flooding can occur as the result of combinations of multiple extreme and nonextreme flood drivers that may or may not be independent (Moftakhari, Salvadori, AghaKouchak, Sanders, & Matthew, 2017). Luke et al. (2018) describe the approach that was developed and used in the FloodRISE project, which assumes that an extreme event can occur when any one of the flood drivers occurs at an extreme level (based on univariate frequency analysis) accompanied by other drivers at expected (nonextreme) levels. Once simulations were completed for all important drivers, results were synthesized in a post-processing step to create a single flood hazard visualization representative of the chosen return level and to create a visualization of the annual probability of flooding of at least ankle depth water. All modeling scenarios were executed using a shared memory (OpenMP) version of ParBreZo on 16 cores of a 64 core high-performance computing node of the UC Irvine High-Performance Computing (HPC) system.

CFM was achieved through an iterative process involving four phases of stakeholder engagement (Goodrich et al., 2020):

1   Expert consultations – Resulting in Version 1 Flood Hazard Maps
2   Household surveys – Resulting in Version 2 Flood Hazard Maps
3   Focus group meetings – Resulting in Version 3 Flood Hazard Maps
4   Training sessions and outreach

The first phase of engagement focused on collecting system data (e.g., topography and flood defenses) and two-way communication between modelers and local authorities about flooding to establish a baseline flood hazard model that captured important flooding mechanisms and accounted for important flood drivers (e.g., rainfall, streamflow, and extreme high tides). The second phase of engagement focused on testing the interest in, and usability of, metric resolution flood hazard visualizations among the general public. This provided useful feedback on details such as color schemes and legends, and the limitations of digital communications among segments of the population (e.g., the elderly) who infrequently use computers (Feldman et al., 2016). The third phase of engagement targeted end users of flood hazard information including planners, public works officials, emergency response personnel, business owners, nongovernmental organizations, and residents and led to changes in proposed flood hazard maps (e.g., legends, descriptions, and flooding scenarios) as well as the creation of new flood hazard maps had not previously been conceived by the modeling team (Luke et al., 2018; Sanders et al., 2020).

To facilitate access and allow users to toggle between maps, pan, and zoom, an online flood hazard map viewer was prepared for each site using ArcGIS Online (ESRI, Redlands, California). In the fourth phase of engagement, training sessions were held at a computer laboratory where end users were guided through available information on the flood hazard viewer.

Results

FloodRISE flood hazard viewers display flood hazard maps for NB (bit.ly/floodrisenb), TRV (bit.ly/floodrise_TRV), and LLC (bit.ly/floodrisell). When the power of shallow-water models to predict depth and velocity at metric resolution is combined with the interests of end users for flood hazard information, the result is a wide variety of flood hazard maps including maps of flood depth, maps of the product of depth and velocity which serves as a proxy for flood force, maps of shear stress which bears on erosion potential, maps of flood duration, and maps of flood probability. The viewers for NB, TRV, and LLC hosted a total of 27, 14, and 14 flood hazard maps, respectively, and a few examples are shown here. First, Figure 18.1 shows the map of the Year 2035 flood depth corresponding to a 100-year return period. Note here the use of a body scale which was developed to communicate the flood hazard in an intuitive way as well as a quantitative scale. An outcome of the focus group meetings was the need for both qualitative and quantitative scales of flood hazard information. Note also that the predicted flood depth accounts for multiple flood drivers (extreme high tides, waves, and precipitation), but the complexity of methods required to account for multiple flood drivers need not complicate the presentation of the result.

Management of erosion and sediment is a major challenge in TRV, and this is reflected in the production of a flood hazard map depicting maximum shear stresses using both a quantitative scale and qualitative scale corresponding to the consequence of the shear. Figure 18.2 shows a

A paradigm –local flood hazard information

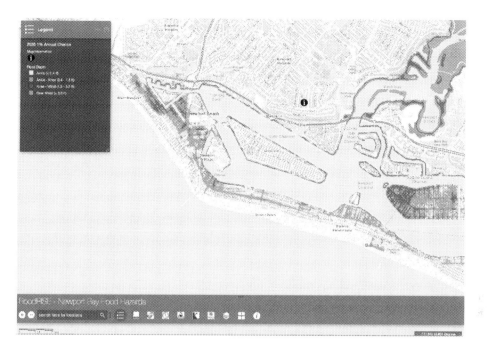

Figure 18.1 Newport Beach flood hazard viewer configured to show the 100-year return period flood depth with an intuitive body scale while accounting for multiple flood drivers.

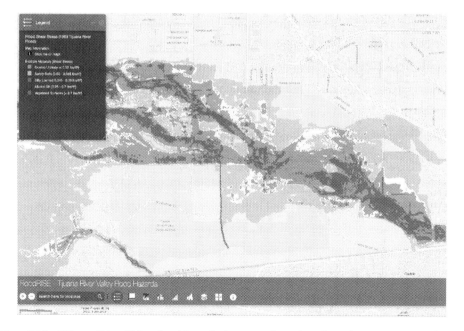

Figure 18.2 Tijuana River Valley flood hazard viewer configured to show shear stresses using both a quantitative scale and a qualitative scale that informs the susceptibility to erosion. The viewer displays both historical flood events and engineering design scenarios (e.g., 100-year return period) to make the information useful to multiple end users.

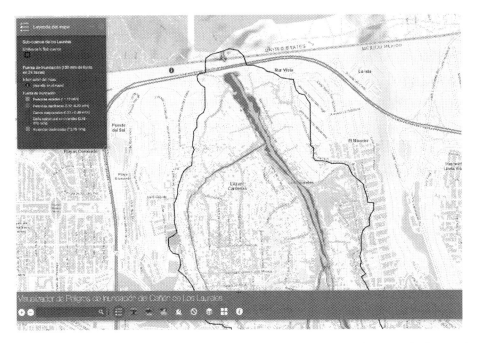

Figure 18.3 Los Laureles Canyon flood hazard viewer configured to show flood force using both a quantitative scale (product of depth and velocity) and a qualitative scale that indicates consequences.

map of shear stress corresponding to a historical flood event, one that occurred in 1983 amidst a strong El Nino. Use of a historical event to depict the hazard is one of several options provided by the viewer, in addition to two specific return periods (5- and 100-year events). Interaction with stakeholders reinforced the fact that communication of probabilities and return periods, while common among engineers, poses challenges that can be overcome by presenting historical events that are often more easily relatable among diverse end users of flood hazard information.

Human security is a major concern in LLC due to the potential for erosion and fast moving flood waters. Figure 18.3 shows a map of flood force with both a quantitative and qualitative scale corresponding to consequences. This is a good example of the power of fine scale shallow-water models to depict hazardous conditions that can develop along streets as a result of intense rainfall, here equal to a rainfall depth of 100 mm which corresponds to a 100-year return period event. End users stated a strong preference for naming these maps based on the amount of rainfall, and not the probability, because the former is much more easily understood during extreme events based on weather reports.

Implications for peacebuilding

The FloodRISE project achieved two-way communication about flooding between modeling experts and local stakeholders through the process of shallow-water modeling; this process has resulted in trusted flood hazard maps that meet end-user needs and preferences for information. Several examples of context-sensitive decision-support are shown herein, which validates the potential of the method to succeed under varied environmental and social conditions. These findings highlight the value of shallow-water models for at risk communities, consisting of stakeholders with varied educational backgrounds, interests, and worldviews, to orient themselves with respect to the best available science about flooding at the local scale. Moreover, this experience suggests that the implementation of much needed vulnerability reduction measures to reduce the consequences of flooding can be enhanced through a collaborative process of shallow-water modeling and visualization.

The opportunity to introduce a community-engaged process of codeveloping flood (and other hazard) risk maps into peacebuilding contexts has been enabled by (1) remarkable advances in environmental modeling, HPC, and increasing capacity to collect fine-scale geospatial data at low cost that together make it possible to envision local level, fine-scale hazard models simulating events at spatial and temporal scales comparable to how people experience them and (2) the increasing ubiquity of associated hardware and software, both of which can generally be introduced even into challenging conflict-affected areas as seen recently in peacebuilding countries such as Colombia (Defelipe, 2018). We believe, informed by both relevant literature and the direct peacebuilding experience of one of the authors (Matthew served on United Nations peacebuilding missions in Rwanda and Sierra Leone), that the implications for peacebuilding are exciting and compelling.

First, as noted throughout this volume, the broad trends in natural hazards, and especially in climate change-related impacts, suggest a future of more frequent, intense, and compounded events as populations continue to swell in vulnerable regions (such as coastal areas), infrastructure ages, forced displacements increase, the planet continues to warm, and the pace of adaptation and mitigation action remains relatively slow and uneven. The intersection between these trends and conflict-affected areas has been noted by many researchers and stressed in this chapter. In terms of the various aspects of peacebuilding – such as improving security, welfare, and representation (Schwarz, 2005) – the importance of characterizing hazard risk and building resilience at all levels of society seems broadly relevant and dangerous to delay.

Second, peacebuilding is often framed in terms of capacity building for both state and civil society (Leonardsson & Rudd, 2015). The approach outlined in this chapter may be effective on both fronts, generating trusted, actionable decision support tools that can be informed by shared scientific evidence, local knowledge, and the values and aspirations of both local and national entities.

Third, introducing state-of-the-art data collection methods and spatial analysis techniques into a conflict affected country in a manner that can be applied even in extremely remote contexts might mitigate against the historical tendency of such investments to deepen the digital divide, or rely on outsiders, both of which might reflect economic imperatives but might also track along other forms of social division (Webster et al., 2004; Ide et al., 2021). Our own research has capitalized on dramatic reductions in costs and the growing ability to create interfaces and trainings that make this type of information widely accessible and usable to a wide range of stakeholders.

Finally, a critical focus of peacebuilding is the extent and character of its empowerment functions – what local capacity is being activated, how are rural–urban and other divisions managed from this perspective, what is being crafted on prior power relationships, and so on (Gizelis, 2009; Maschietto, 2016). Our approach has the potential to be broadly inclusive and empowering, supporting coordination across stakeholders while also potentially improving bargaining position and increasing autonomy for local decision-makers.

Acknowledgments

This research was made possible by a grant from the National Science Foundation (Grant #DMS-1331611), who support is gratefully acknowledged. The research team is also indebted

Brett F. Sanders, et al.

to the communities who contributed time, knowledge, and energy to this project and numerous individuals who helped with the acquisition of critical data.

Note

1 Walch (Chapter 12), for instance, reviews three competing research narratives that link natural disasters and conflict.

References

Bates, P. D. (2012). Integrating remote sensing data with flood inundation models: How far have we got? *Hydrological Processes, 26*(16), 2515–2521.

Brodtkorb, A. R., Sætra, M. L., & Altinakar, M. (2012). Efficient shallow water simulations on GPUs: Implementation, visualization, verification and validation. *Computers & Fluids, 55*, 1–12.

Castro, M. J., Ortega, S., de la Asunción, M., Mantas, J. M., & Gallardo, J. M. (2011). GPU computing for shallow water flow simulation based on finite volume schemes. *Comptes Rendus Mécanique, 339*(2–3), 165–184.

Casulli, V., & Stelling, G. S. (2011). Semi-implicit subgrid modelling of three-dimensional free-surface flows. *International Journal for Numerical Methods in Fluids, 67*(4), 441–449.

Conca, K., & Dabelko, G. (Eds.). (2002). *Environmental Peacemaking*. Baltimore, MD: Johns Hopkins University Press.

Dawson, R. J., Ball, T., Werritty, J., Werritty, A., Hall, J. W., & Roche, N. (2011). Assessing the effectiveness of non-structural flood management measures in the Thames Estuary under conditions of socio-economic and environmental change. *Global Environmental Change, 21*(2), 628–646.

Defelipe, S. (2018). Connecting technology to peace: This is how we are going in Colombia. IMPACTOT(C. https://impactotic.co/en/technologies-for-peace-what-the-tic-ministry-leaves-to-the-new-government/

Dottori, F., Di Baldassarre, G., & Todini, E. (2013). Detailed data is welcome, but with a pinch of salt: Accuracy, precision, and uncertainty in flood inundation modeling. *Water Resources Research, 49*(9), 6079–6085.

Eastin, J. (2016). Fuel to the fire: Natural disasters and the duration of civil conflict. *International Interactions, 42*(2), 322–349. https://doi.org/10.1080/03050629.2016.1115402

Evers, M., Jonoski, A., Maksimovič, Č., Lange, L., Ochoa Rodriguez, S., Teklesadik, A., . . . Makropoulos, C. (2012). Collaborative modelling for active involvement of stakeholders in urban flood risk management. *Natural Hazards and Earth System Sciences, 12*(9), 2821–2842.

Feldman, D., Contreras, S., Karlin, B., Basolo, V., Matthew, R., Sanders, B., . . . Serrano, K. (2016). Communicating flood risk: Looking back and forward at traditional and social media outlets. *International Journal of Disaster Risk Reduction, 15*, 43–51.

Gallien, T. W., Sanders, B. F., & Flick, R. E. (2014). Urban coastal flood prediction: Integrating wave overtopping, flood defenses and drainage. *Coastal Engineering, 91*, 18–28.

Ghimire, R., Ferreira, S., & Dorfman, J. H. (2015). Flood-Induced Displacement and Civil Conflict. *World Development, 66*, 614–628. https://doi.org/10.1016/j.worlddev.2014.09.021

Gizelis, T.-I. (2009). Gender empowerment and United Nations peacebuilding. *Journal of Peace Research, 46*(4), 505–523. https://doi.org/10.1177/0022343309334576

Gleick, P., Iceland, C., & Trivedi, A. (2020). *Ending conflicts over water: Solutions to water and security challenges.* Washington, DC: World Resources Institute.

Goodrich, K. A., Basolo, V., Feldman, D. L., Matthew, R. A., Schubert, J. E., Luke, A., . . . Contreras, S. (2020). Addressing pluvial flash flooding through community-based collaborative research in Tijuana, Mexico. *Water, 12*(5), 1257.

Guinot, V., Sanders, B. F., & Schubert, J. E. (2017). Dual integral porosity shallow water model for urban flood modelling. *Advances in Water Resources, 103*, 6–31.

Hagemeier-Klose, M., & Wagner, K. (2009). Evaluation of flood hazard maps in print and web mapping services as information tools in flood risk communication. *Natural Hazards and Earth System Sciences, 9*(2), 563–574.

Hanson, T., Brooks, T. M., Da Fonseca, G. A. B., Hoffmann, M., Lamoreux, J. F., Machlis, G., . . . Pilgrim, J. D. (2009). Warfare in biodiversity hotspots. *Conservation Biology, 23*, 578–587. https://doi.org/10.1111/j.1523-1739.2009.01166.x

Harris, K., Keen, D., & Mitchell, T. (2013). *When disasters and conflicts collide: Improving links between disaster resilience and conflict*. Research Report. London: Overseas Development Institute.

Ide, T., Bruch, C., Carius, A., Conca, K., Dabelko, G., Matthew, R., & Weinthal, E. (2021, January). The past and future(s) of environmental peacebuilding, *International Affairs*, 97, 1–16. https://doi.org/10.1093/ia/iiaa177

Institute for Economics & Peace. (2020). *Ecological threat register 2020: Understanding ecological threats, resilience and peace*. Retrieved from http://visionofhumanity.org/reports

Kim, B., Sanders, B. F., Famiglietti, J. S., & Guinot, V. (2015). Urban flood modeling with porous shallow-water equations: A case study of model errors in the presence of anisotropic porosity. *Journal of Hydrology*, *523*, 680–692.

Lane, S. N., Odoni, N., Landström, C., Whatmore, S. J., Ward, N., & Bradley, S. (2011). Doing flood risk science differently: An experiment in radical scientific method. *Transactions of the Institute of British Geographers*, *36*(1), 15–36.

Lemos, M. C., Arnott, J. C., Ardoin, N. M. et al. (2018). To co-produce or not to co-produce. *Nat Sustain*, *1*, 722–724. https://doi.org/10.1038/s41893-018-0191-0

Leonardsson, H., & Rudd, G. (2015). The 'local turn' in peacebuilding: A literature review of effective and emancipatory local peacebuilding. *Third World Quarterly*, *36*(5), 825–839. https://doi.org/10.1080/01436597.2015.1029905

Luke, A., Sanders, B. F., Goodrich, K. A., Feldman, D. L., Boudreau, D., Eguiarte, A., . . . Matthew, R. A. (2018). Going beyond the flood insurance rate map: Insights from flood hazard map co-production. *Natural Hazards and Earth System Sciences*, *18*(4), 1097–1120.

Maschietto, R. (2016). *Beyond peacebuilding: The challenge of empowerment promotion in Mozambique*. New York: Springer.

Maskrey, S. A., Mount, N. J., Thorne, C. R., & Dryden, I. (2016). Participatory modelling for stakeholder involvement in the development of flood risk management intervention options. *Environmental Modelling & Software*, *82*, 275–294.

Matthew, R. A. (2014). Integrating climate change and peacebuilding. *Climatic Change*, *123*(1), 83–93.

Matthew, R., Halle, M., & Switzer, J. (2002). *Conserving the peace: Resources, livelihoods and security*. Geneva: International Institute for Sustainable Development.

Matthew, R. A., Jensen, D., & Brown, O. (2009). *From conflict to peacebuilding: The role of natural resources*. Nairobi: UNEP.

Meyer, V., Kuhlicke, C., Luther, J., Fuchs, S., Priest, S., Dorner, W., . . . Palka, G. (2012). Recommendations for the user-specific enhancement of flood maps. *Natural Hazards and Earth System Sciences*, *12*(5), 1701.

Moftakhari, H. R., Salvadori, G., AghaKouchak, A., Sanders, B. F., & Matthew, R. A. (2017). Compounding effects of sea level rise and fluvial flooding. *Proceedings of the National Academy of Sciences*, 201620325.

Nelson, T. (2010). When disaster strikes: On the relationship between natural disaster and interstate conflict. *Global Change, Peace & Security*, *22*(2), 155–174. https://doi.org/10.1080/14781151003770788

Null, S., & Herzer-Risi, L. (2016). *Navigating complexity: Climate, migration, and conflict in a changing world*. Discussion Paper. Office of Conflict Management and Migration. USAID. Retrieved from www.climatelinks.org/resources/navigating-complexity-climate-migration-and-conflict-changing-world

Özgen, I., Zhao, J., Liang, D., & Hinkelmann, R. (2016). Urban flood modeling using shallow water equations with depth-dependent anisotropic porosity. *Journal of Hydrology*, *541*, 1165–1184.

Pasche, E., Manojlovic, N., Schertzer, D., Deroubaix, J. F., Tchguirinskaia, I., El Tabach, E., . . . Garvin, S. (2009). The use of non structural measures for reducing the flood risk in small urban catchments. In P. Samuels, S. Huntington, W. Allsop, & J. Jarrop (Eds.), *Flood risk management: Research and practice* (pp. 132–133). Boca Raton, FL: CRC Press.

Peters, K. (2017). *The next frontier of disaster risk reduction: Tackling disasters in fragile and conflict affected contexts*. Research Report. London: Overseas Development Institute.

Peters, K., & Budimir, M. (2016). *When disasters and conflicts collide: Facts and figures*. Briefing Paper. London: Overseas Development Institute.

Peters, K., Mayhew, L., Slim, H., van Aalst, M., & Arrighi, J. (2019). *Double exposure: The humanitarian implications of intersecting climate and conflict risk*. ICRC – International Committee of the Red Cross, Working Paper 550.

Sanders, B. F. (2017). Hydrodynamic modeling of urban flood flows and disaster risk reduction. *Oxford Research Encyclopedia of Natural Hazard Science.* https://doi.org/10.1093/acrefore/9780199389407.013.127

Sanders, B. F., & Schubert, J. E. (2019). PRIMo: Parallel raster inundation model. *Advances in Water Resources, 126,* 79–95.

Sanders, B. F., Schubert, J. E., Goodrich, K. A., Houston, D., Feldman, D. L., Basolo, V., . . . Contreras, S. (2020). Collaborative modeling with fine-resolution data enhances flood awareness, minimizes differences in flood perception, and produces actionable flood maps. *Earth's Future, 8*(1), e2019EF001391.

Sanders, B. F., Schubert, J. E., & Detwiler, R. L. (2010). ParBreZo: A parallel, unstructured grid, Godunov-type, shallow-water code for high-resolution flood inundation modeling at the regional scale. *Advances in Water Resources, 33*(12), 1456–1467.

Sanders, B. F., Schubert, J. E., & Gallegos, H. A. (2008). Integral formulation of shallow-water equations with anisotropic porosity for urban flood modeling. *Journal of Hydrology, 362*(1), 19–38.

Schwarz, R. (2005). Post-conflict peacebuilding: The challenges of security, welfare and representation. *Security Dialogue, 36*(4), 429–446. https://doi.org/10.1177/0967010605060447

Smith, D., & Vivekananda, J. (2007). *A climate of conflict: The links between climate change, war and peace.* London: International Alert.

Soares-Frazão, S., Lhomme, J., Guinot, V., & Zech, Y. (2008). Two-dimensional shallow-water model with porosity for urban flood modelling. *Journal of Hydraulic Research, 46*(1), 45–64.

Steinführer, A., de Marchi, B., Kuhlicke, C., Scolobig, A., Tapsell, S., & Tunstall, S. (2009). Recommendations for flood risk management with communities at risk. *TU Delft Report T11–07–14.* Helmholz Unweltforschungszentrum (UFZ).

Streich, P. A., & Mislan, D. B. (2014). What follows the storm? Research on the effect of disasters on conflict and cooperation. *Global Change, Peace & Security, 26*(1), 55–70. https://doi.org/10.1080/147 81158.2013.837040

Tanzler, D., Carius, A., & Maas, A. (2013). The need for conflict sensitive adaptation to climate change. In G. Debalko, L. Herzer, S. Null, M. Parker, & R. Stickler (Eds.), *Backdraft: The conflict potential of climate change adaptation and mitigation.* Environmental Change and Security Program Report 14:2. Washington, DC: Woodrow Wilson International Centre for Scholars.

Vacandio, R., Dal Palú, A., & Mignosa, P. (2014). GPU-enhanced finite volume shallow water solver for fast flood simulations. *Environmental Modeling & Software, 57,* 60–75.

Webster, F., Blom, R., Karvonen, E., Melin, H., Nordenstreng, K., & Puoskari, E. (2004). *The information society reader.* London: Routledge.

SECTION IV

Cross-cutting themes and critical perspectives

19

SECURITIZING THE ENVIRONMENT

Rita Floyd

When it comes to the meaning of environmental and climate security, views differ widely, and sometimes even emotions run high.[1] The chapters comprising this volume show that different proponents (including practitioners and scholars) of environmental or climate security have distinct views on who or what is to be made secure. Some hold that it is states (e.g., because of the possibility of climate change causing or playing a casual role in violent conflict). Some – usually defense practitioners – wish to secure militaries' ability to train and fight, believing that both are compromised by, for example, environmental legislation to meet environmental targets as well as adverse weather conditions. Some wish to secure people from the myriad ill effects of climate change (including crop failure, loss of livelihoods, infectious disease, rising sea levels), while others hold that it is the biosphere itself that needs securing and that humans are only a small part of the larger whole that James Lovelock (2000) successfully referred to as Gaia. We can see that there is also disagreement on what referents[2] are to be secured from, specifically the actual physical effects of climate change or socioeconomic effects.

Proponents of the different views of who is threatened by climate change and who should be secured also disagree on who should or can most usefully provide security. Specifically, does the climate threat's transnational nature require a move away from national security toward some form of "world government"? These different accounts of environmental and climate security[3] are also informed by a different view of the meaning of security. Those scholars and practitioners interested in national security or the role of the military in the provision of climate security or even as a referent object (e.g., securing military bases from sea-level rise) are interested in environmental/climate security primarily to the extent to which it compromises national security, for example, because of the climate–conflict linkage.[4] This perspective is complicated by the notion that security threats are not intentionally caused by human beings, unlike terrorism. Climate change is not intended by one group and employed against another group; instead, climate change is a side effect of the burning of fossil fuels human beings need to fuel their economies and in their daily modern lives. While scholars interested in environmental security as human security or biosphere security (ecological security) tend to work with a much broader notion of security, true security is not only about more than freedom from threats but also about freedom from want. In other words, achieving true security requires emancipation away from state and militaristic notions of security (Booth, 2007; Dalby, 2009).

One of my two aims in this chapter is to demonstrate that for all its many flaws, the beauty about the logic of the Copenhagen School's securitization theory is that we can use this theory[5] to analyze the relationship between the natural environment and security. This analysis can occur without *inter alia* needing to make decisions on the moral or analytical primacy of the referent object, taking sides in the debate over the causality of the environment in conflict creation, or without deciding on the meaning of security. In other words, securitization theory allows us to study the linkage between the environment/climate and security while remaining neutral on any of these contentious issues. This analytical detachment is nowhere clearer than in the Copenhagen School's treatment of the subject. Compelled by empirical events they included an "environmental sector of security" into their now seminal study *Security: A new framework of analysis* (1998) in spite of the fact that – at the time – at least two of the school's three authors did not believe that intent-lacking threats have a rightful place in Security Studies (Floyd, 2010).

The use of securitization theory might then be a natural choice for anyone who does not have a stake (personal, institutional, or normative) in the "environmental/climate security debate" (Floyd, 2008) but who wishes to understand who securitizes, when, what issues, and with what outcome. However, securitization theory is not without its flaws. The original Copenhagen School theory associated with Ole Wæver, Barry Buzan, and Japp de Wilde contains a number of contested statements concerning the precise nature of the exception, the role of the audience, the nature of desecuritization, and much else. The theory also contains a number of contradictions regarding when securitization succeeds and how precisely it operates. This is important in the given context because the second aim in this chapter is to show that studies on the securitization of the environment/climate change have enabled analysts and practitioners to understand this relationship better and see the interests of various stakeholders more clearly. Empirical studies of the securitization of climate change/environmental security have also helped advance, refine, and redefine securitization theory in some of the key contested areas as well as to confirm revisions by other scholars. My claim is that environmental and climate security research has changed securitization theory for the better, while securitization theory has enabled a much better understanding of the practice of environmental and climate security.

The chapter is structured as follows: Section 1 provides a brief overview of the meaning of securitization theory; Section 2 examines key empirical studies in which authors have applied securitization theory; and Section 3 shows how empirical studies in this sector have challenged securitization theory.

What is securitization?

Securitization theory holds that in international relations an issue becomes a security threat not because it refers to something real (i.e., an objective threat) but because it has become constructed as such through a particular process called securitization. The securitization process involves a securitizing actor – this could be not only a state but also a regional organization, or even influential individual persons (i.e., persons with large amounts of social and political capital) – who declares a referent object (the thing threatened and in need of protection) existentially threatened unless something is done immediately (point of no return) to counter/defend against the threat. In very early versions of the theory (pre-1998), this speech act element took primacy of place, with Wæver (1995), the theory's originator, declaring that "with the help of language theory, we can regard 'security' as a speech act" (p. 55). The key point in this observation was that it enabled first Wæver and later the Copenhagen School to emphasize the social construction of security. The Copenhagen School sometimes refers to security as a

Securitizing the environment

self-referential practice (Buzan, Wæver, & de Wilde, 1998, p. 24), which captures the idea that no issue, or even threat, is a *security threat* unless it is constructed as such by powerful actors (Wæver, 2011).

In later writings, the goalposts concerning the precise social construction of security moved, but the overall idea of security's self-referential nature did not. Thus, by 1998, the speech act is directed at an audience that according to the Copenhagen School has to "accept" the speech act so that the use of extraordinary emergency measures becomes legitimate (Buzan et al., 1998, p. 25). Notably, however, for the Copenhagen School, to "accept" does not mean that the audience has to consent to either the threat narrative or the proposed security measures but only that securitizing actors have to argue their case. The latter has led to the criticism of a western liberal state-centric bias defined by democratic deliberation, while it has also been pointed out that if security depends on audience acceptance, security cannot also be tantamount to a performative illocutionary speech act in the way Wæver previously suggested (Balzacq, 2005). According to Balzacq (2011), we can retain both elements (speech act theory and intersubjectivity) only if we theorize audience acceptance as perlocution, that is, "the causal response to a linguistic act," a central element of speech act theory (p. 6). He argues: "[in] any intersubjective process such as securitization, the purpose is to prompt a significant response from the other (perlocutionary effect); unless this happens there is no securitization" (Balzacq, 2011, p. 6).

In the 1998 book, the performative power of speech is further weakened by the attention now focused on policy change following on from linguistic securitization. Thus, although the Copenhagen School holds that audience acceptance merely legitimizes the move away from ordinary politics by breaking established rules, they also hold that "[t]ypically, the agent will override such rules, because by depicting a threat the securitizing agent often says someone cannot be dealt with the normal way" (Buzan et al., 1998, p. 26). And more strongly still: "A successful securitization thus has three components (or steps): existential threats, emergency actions, and effects on interunit relations by breaking free of rules" (Buzan et al., 1998, p. 26; see also DeWilde, 2008, p. 597).

This is not the place to go into the countless debates over the meaning of securitization as they have evolved in Security Studies. What matters for our purposes here is that speech is an important aspect in the construction of security for securitization scholars whatever their notion of successful securitization. Thus, even those scholars who believe that securitization merely "exists" at the point of audience acceptance, but "succeeds" only once policy change has occurred, language and the securitizing move matter to be able to locate the onset of securitization (Floyd, 2016). The study of the effects of securitization (i.e., policy change), however, goes much beyond discourse analysis and often comprises interviews with key stakeholders, use of statistical data, and the qualitative study of documents that may not be publicly available (Karyotis, 2012).

Examples of studies of securitization of the environmental/climate change

Securitization theory has been applied to a number of different empirical cases; the majority[6] of these tend to be comparative in nature, looking at either securitization by the same or similar actors over two different periods or securitization by the same actor across time. Meanwhile, other studies compare the securitization of climate change in different countries or regions, sometimes spanning different levels of analysis. In this section, some of the most prominent cases are examined to demonstrate what precisely a securitization lens has added to our understanding of climate and environmental security.

In 2009, Nicole Detraz and Michelle Betsill analyzed the implications of the first United Nations Security Council (UNSC) debate on climate change. Theirs is a primary example of a comparative study of the securitization of climate change across time. That is, by establishing securitization, they are able to show a discursive shift. Thus, they show that although this debate marks a turning point in the linguistic securitization of climate change globally, much of it builds on a prior historical debate linking climate change and security found in global actors such as the UN Framework Convention on Climate Change and the Intergovernmental Panel on Climate Change. They argue that at the global level, both debates are dominated by the environmental security as human security discourse, whereby the focus is on the reduction of quality of life for human beings by climate change (see Dalby, Chapter 20; Upreti & Nizkorodov, Chapter 22). However, unlike in the historical debate, they find that there has been a shift in the discourse insofar as the 2007 debate increasingly features (about 20% of the debate) the climate–conflict narrative. The linkage of climate change to traditional hard security issues of "bombs and war" is pushed especially by members of the small Pacific island states whose very existence is in danger from climate-induced rising sea levels. Although the authors do not make this inference, it is likely that leaders of these states revert to traditional security narratives because they fear that the plight of individual human beings is still not considered on par with the threat of war. It is interesting that the majority of speakers also questioned the suitability of the UN Security Council to aid with the problem of climate change, in that way querying whether the issue should be securitized at this level or in this way. The bulk of resistance to this idea came from the developing world (with the exception of small island states), presumably because of greater confidence in the principle of sovereignty (versus humanitarian) intervention in these places (Buzan, 2004).

My own study on securitization of US environmental security policy during the Clinton and Bush administrations (Floyd, 2010) is an example of a comparative study between different administrations in the same country. Although climate change played a comparatively small role in the Clinton administration, climate change was repeatedly listed as one of the key drivers of environmental change. Provided we can accept that policy change is indicative of successful securitization and does not have to be exceptional in the Copenhagen School sense (Trombetta, 2011), the environment was successfully securitized by the Clinton administration. A key puzzle central to this study was: why did the Clinton administration not make use of extraordinary measures legitimized by securitization to the stated referent object of security – the American people? I argue that while the administration's narrative prioritized the American people, the myriad of actors within the national security establishment that become involved in the provision of environmental security did so because they all gained from securitization, usually by keeping or even expanding their mandate at a time when the national security apparatus was threatened with downsizing. In other words, securitization was agent-benefiting as opposed to referent-object benefiting, with the securitizing actor ultimately insincere in their promise to safeguard the American people from global environmental change.

My study also shows that while a skeptical and antigreen George W. Bush had no interest in the securitization of the environment, *desecuritization* (the unmaking of securitization) was enabled by the events of 9/11 and the onset of the war on terror, which gave a massive financial boost to the security and defense establishment, and thus eradicated the need for smaller nontraditional security discourses (Floyd, 2010).

Jarrod Hayes and Janelle Knox-Hayes' (2014) study of the securitization of climate change in the United States and the European Union is a typical example of a comparative study across different countries/regions. They found that discourses concerning climate change differ

Securitizing the environment

significantly in both regions, but that domestic factors and/or cultural attitudes influence both the tone and nature of the discourse significantly in both regions. They argue that in the United States, the issue was securitized under President Obama to overcome "public uncertainty and disengagement" encouraged by the Bush administration's desecuritization of environmental issues (Hayes & Knox-Hayes, 2014, p. 90). Specifically, Obama wanted the United States to join a global climate regime, believing that the security narrative would strike a chord with the American public. Much of this is corroborated by von Lucke, Wellmann, and Diez (2014), who argue that think tanks and research organizations funded by the military are particularly keen to make the link between climate change and overt violent conflict not only to improve US defense policy but also to convince new, conservative audiences that more progressive climate policies were needed. One might add that in the days of the war on terror, the military also made the link between global climatic change and terrorism, in part, I suspect, because, at that time, to be heard, all security narratives had to be linked up with this "macrosecuritization," the idea that global level security narratives can shape and influence lower level securitizations (Buzan & Wæver, 2009).

With regard to the European Union, Hayes and Knox-Hayes (2014) find no security narrative, but rather the European Union sees the problem of climate change as an opportunity to assume Global leadership. In my view, the latter is comparable to the European Commission's drive toward greater integration in the face of terrorism (Argomaniz, Bures, & Kaunert, 2015). Lacking often real foreign policy potential and arguably a democratic mandate, the commission has an incentive to cease on security problems, to foster greater integration, while this very process ensures self-securitization.[7]

Arguably, however, Hayes and Knox-Hayes (2014) analysis of the European Union ignores that the 2008 Solana report on *Climate Change and International Security* identifies conflict over resources, economic loss, loss of territory, and border disputes as threats driven by climate change, which are by and large traditional security concerns. It also ignores that a 2011 joint article by the European External Action Service which argued along similar lines. What is true, however, is that these key documents are essentially a departure from the European Union's global outlook which is much closer to the UN's human environmental/climate security narrative. I have suggested elsewhere that we can explain this discrepancy using a theoretical framework of ideational fragmentation, which is

> the phenomenon that diverse organisations/actors' choice of discourse on any given issue is influenced by who they are, specifically by their relative strengths (i.e. what they can (uniquely) offer and do about the issue) and their (perceived) weaknesses (i.e. how precisely the issue affects them, or even in what sense the issue renders them insecure)
>
> (Floyd, 2015, p. 137)

I have also suggested that "the main reason why the EU prioritizes the climate-conflict angle [is that] as an organization with no or limited military capabilities, it has repeatedly proved weak in situations of conflict in Europe and elsewhere" (Floyd, 2015, p. 137).

Perhaps, Hayes and Knox-Hayes (2014) ignore these factors because the solution sought by the European Union to climate change is a global environmental regime. Germany, as the leading power in Europe, might well play a key role in this. von Lucke et al. (2014) find that in Germany, the climate–conflict discourse plays almost no role. Indeed, a major difference they identify between Germany and the United States is that the former foresees no role for military strategies in the provision of climate security, and perhaps as a consequence, the German military's climate security discourse tends toward the environmental security as human security narrative (von Lucke et al., 2014, p. 871).

Research on the securitization of climate change is not restricted to countries of the Global North. As part of a book study, Diez, von Lucke, and Wellman (2016) examine the securitization of climate change in Mexico and Turkey in addition to Germany and the United States. In the case of Mexico, their analysis shows, among other things, how foreign actors (think tanks, NGOs) contributed to the securitization of climate change in Mexico by pushing particular threat narratives onto the domestic agenda. These narratives were picked up by the Mexican media or Mexican NGOs. They determine that in Mexico, the securitization was relatively successful when compared to Turkey as well as the parallel politicization of climate change. They found that environmentalist president Felipe Caldrón "did not exclusively rely on securitisation to advance his climate agenda . . . he also politicised the issue by portraying climate as an environmental issue . . . by discussing it as a question of sustainable development, moral responsibility, international justice and economic opportunity" (Diez et al., 2016, pp. 106–107). The parallel politicization of climate change had a limiting effect on the effect and consequences of securitization. In other words, the persuasiveness and motivational power of securitization was dampened by the fact that climate change was already an issue, albeit not a security one (see also von Lucke, 2016). In their study of Turkey, however, they show that a complete lack of politicization may mean that securitization does not succeed because, in such cases, conditions are not susceptible to the message of urgency and importance contained within securitization.

Delf Rothe's (2016) study *Securitizing Global Warming: A Climate of Complexity* is an example of a comparative securitization analysis not only across regions but also involving different levels of analysis featuring the United Nations at the international level, the European Union at the regional level, and the United Kingdom at the national level. His study shows that while many disparate and even conflicting discourses on the linkage between climate change and security exist, globally the securitization of climate change is informed/driven by a "discourse coalition around the notion of climate security" (Rothe, 2016). The latter features the following recurring elements (or in Rothe's terms "nodal points") that climate change is a threat multiplier and that climate-induced migration is inevitable; it relies on poignant examples (notably the fate of small island states), and it utilizes powerful images. While not all of these constitutive parts emerged at the level of the Union Nation (notably Rothe credits the threat multiplier logic to the Center for Navel Analysis report from 2007), Rothe finds that the climate security coalition is driven by the United Nation and he goes on to show how this narrative comes to influence climate security policies at the regional level (notably the European Union in their relations with their Mediterranean neighbors) and even nationally insofar as this same discourse comes to inform governmental ministries and organizations in the United Kingdom. As such, he concurs with Oels (2012) that we are witnessing the "Climatization of the security field [which] means that existing security practices are applied to the issue of climate change and that new practices from the field of climate policy are introduced into the security field" (p. 197).

The section of case studies advanced here shows that scholars utilizing a securitization lens do not *need* to engage into debates over which is the appropriate discourse. Instead, they have shown that the focus can be: What kind of actors securitize? How precisely do they do so? What do actors mean by climate security? Why do they revert to discourses of climate security? And under what circumstances are they likely to succeed? Such analysis is valuable because it takes a step back from the spirited debates over methods in environmental conflict research and from the normative focus on environmental and climate security more generally.

Environmental and climate security implications for securitization theory?

In recent years, securitization theory has proved so popular that it is no longer correct to speak of one theory of securitization; instead there are many disparate theories of securitization, (almost) all of which agree on a number of basic assumptions (Balzacq, Léonard, & Ruzicka, 2016). Securitization scholars have questioned and revised practically all aspects of the Copenhagen School's original securitization theory, including the nature of threats and referent objects, the role and nature of the audience, the nature of securitization, the meaning of desecuritization and its normative value, and much besides. In this section, I argue that research on the securitization of the environment and climate change has contributed important insights to this ongoing revision. We shall see that many studies in this empirical area have either led to the advancement of revisions of securitization theory or helped confirm revisions made by securitization scholars working in different fields. For ease of navigation, contributions can be divided into conceptual and supplementary components.

Conceptual contribution

In our time, it is commonplace to consider the environment or climate change as a security threat and the biosphere and individuals as possible referent objects of security. This was not always so, only a relatively short time ago, when the Copenhagen School first started to take shape. Wæver (1995) and Buzan (1997) both held that "intentions" structure the field of security studies (Floyd, 2010, p. 46), while Wæver wrote in 1995 that "the concept of security refers to the state" and that *"neither individual security nor international security exists"* (Wæver, 1995, p. 49). The Copenhagen School and their individual members do not hold this now, and I believe that research on the securitization of the environment, which has shown that a) in practice, intent-lacking threats are securitized and b) that securitization can take place beyond the state has played a part in this.

Research in this area has also contributed to a better understanding of the relevant audience in securitization. The nature and function of the audience is a prominent issue in Securitization Studies due to its relative under theorization in the Copenhagen Schools work (for some of the most significant revisions, see Balzacq, 2011; Salter, 2011, Léonard & Kaunert, 2011; Roe, 2008; Côté, 2016). Environmental security scholars have contributed to our understanding of the audience by suggesting that relevant audiences can encompass international actors, for example, the international community of states or a global public as well as the electorate within states (Floyd, 2010; Oels, 2012). In line with this, scholars have put forward interesting suggestions on how we can study audience acceptance, including, for example, studying international opinion polls on whether or not climate change is a serious threat might be helpful (Brauch, 2009). In the context of his analysis of the securitization of climate change, Rothe (2016), in turn, has suggested that the traditional sender–receiver logic of speaker and audience is misplaced and that securitization arises from reciprocal processes of communication – or discursive struggles – in which the common meaning of security (threats) is collectively established (Rothe, 2016). In this process, there are no passive audiences and active speakers – only communicative actors with different roles and subject positions.

Moreover, alongside scholars working on empirical cases other than the environment/climate change (Heck & Schlag, 2013), research in this area is challenging the idea that securitization occurs only through speech, with technologies, practices, and visual images (notably remote sensing) playing an important role (Rothe, 2017). Although "visual securitization" has not been theorized by the original members of the Copenhagen School, it is worthwhile noting that, in 2009, Wæver noted that the polar bear has become a symbol for climate change and that this symbol helps bring "home" the abstract and distant (in time, and for many in place) threat narrative of climate change (Wæver, 2009). That images can aid with securitization has also been a feature of Rothe's (2016) analysis discussed earlier.

Finally, research on the securitization of environmental/climate change has also served to redefine what counts as an instance of successful securitization. The Copenhagen School's notion of the same is tightly wedded to the idea that security − or rather, the policy change it leads to − is tantamount to the exception. The Copenhagen School's view of the exception is one of executive unilateralism propagated by Carl Schmitt (Williams, 2003; Neal, 2010). Executive unilateralism holds that the executive "has an inherent authority to decide both that there is an emergency and what measures are appropriate in responding to it" (Dyzenhaus, 2010, p. 45). The reality of the securitization of climate change is problematic for this logic because although the issue has been securitized in language, and policy change occurred, exceptional policy measures are usually not seriously part of an agenda.[8] Instead, most policy-makers, practitioners, and scholars advocate a new binding environmental regime. Instead of arguing that securitization of climate security has failed, however, the majority of securitization scholars (for exceptions, see, e.g., McDonald, 2012a) have taken this finding to question the logic of the exception informing the Copenhagen School's framework. Julia Trombetta (2011), for example, has argued that the fact that security in the environmental sector takes a different form to the logic of the exception prescribed by the Copenhagen School shows just how narrow and unreflective the School's notion of security is. If, so she argues, the practice of security is definitive of its meaning, then we ought to allow for other notions of security than those wedded to the exception. Similar arguments have been advanced in security studies previously (Huysmans, 1998; Bigo, 2002), simultaneously (Salter, 2011) and subsequently (Bourbeau, 2014; Floyd, 2016; von Lucke, Wellmann, & Diez, 2014; Rothe, 2016). By now, the "logic of the routine" alongside the "logic of exception" has become well established in securitization studies (Bourbeau, 2014).

Not everyone agrees, however. Olaf Corry (2012) argues that instead of securitization, climate change has undergone a process of riskification. His work is an important contribution on the difference between risks, "the *conditions of possibility for harm*", and threats '*direct causes of harm*" (Corry, 202, p. 12). He argues that "the *risk of terrorism* or even the *risk of nuclear war* relates to factors that make terrorism or nuclear war possible, that is, the vulnerability of societies with political tensions or the existence of nuclear weapons and weak international regimes. In contrast, the threat of terror is connected to "particular agents believed to exist and have malicious intent and capability to commit acts of terror" (Corry, 2012, p. 12). The key difference is that threats can be defended against, whereas risks can only be managed. As Corry (2012) explains, contrary to securitization which "involves a plan of action to defend a valued referent object against a threat" (p. 13), riskification implies a plan of action to govern the conditions of possibility for harm. The referent-object itself rather than an enemy becomes the primary target of risk programs − something to be changed and governed rather than something to be defended as such' (ibid. 13). While Methman and Rothe (2012), Rothe (2016), von Lucke et al. (2014), and von Lucke (2016) show that in the climate sector securitization and riskification can and often do coexist, just as they do in the war on terror, Corry's paper does much to flesh out and differentiate the logic of risk from the logic of security (see Aradau and van Munster, 2007).

Finally, greater conceptual clarity has been achieved not only regarding security and risk but also regarding desecuritization. My own study of the Bush administration's treatment of the environment has shown that the Copenhagen School's notion of desecuritization "as the process whereby issues are moved out of 'the threat-defense sequence and into the ordinary public sphere' where they can be dealt with in accordance with the rules of the (democratic) political system" is wanting (Floyd, 2010). Thus, in addition to such wide reading of politicization, it can also be defined narrowly as resting with political authority. For desecuritization, this means that it may result in politicization or depoliticization (Hansen, 2012). In the environmental sector of security, these findings have been substantiated by Sebastian Biba (2016) in his study on the spring 2010 Mekong crisis.

Supplementary contribution

As I have argued throughout this chapter, the Copenhagen School's securitization theory is an analytical framework. As such, it is not strictly necessary for securitization scholars to take a position on normative questions pertaining to who or what should be made secure, or even whether a particular securitization was justified (Taureck, 2006). In practice, however, and especially in the environmental and the societal sector of security, scholars find it difficult to remain silent on normative issues. There are a number of reasons for this, especially in the societal sector that is essentially concerned with the securitization of migration. Certainly, it is a normative dilemma of writing and speaking security, whereby the scholar risks (contributing to) securitization simply by writing/speaking about an issue in security language (Huysmans, 2002). In part as a response to this, the Copenhagen School is not completely silent on normative questions. Considering, however, that they do not believe real threats can be known, there is no reason for securitization to occur. Instead, because securitization necessarily involves depoliticization, de-democratization, and that security measures have negative effects on some actors, their overall preferred option and normative recommendation is desecuritization.

One look at Environmental Security Studies confirms that securitization (in discourse or policy change) can have negative consequences. Veterans of the environmental security as human security approach (notably Barnett, 2001; Dalby, 2002, 2009; see also Dalby, Chapter 20) have long pointed out that apocalyptical world visions such as that contained in Robert Kaplan's coming anarchy (1994) – whereby an ill-functioning environment in the Global South is the harbinger of death, destruction, conflict, and by means of unchecked environmental migration poses a security threat to the Global North – will achieve nothing but deepen existing chasms between the two worlds, without making anyone truly secure. These scholars have also warned against the militarization of the environment (Barnett, 2001; Deudney, 1991). In line with these important earlier works, Detraz and Betsill (2009) in their analysis of the UNSC's discussion on climate change warn of the inclusion of the environmental conflict discourse into these debates precisely because of the negative effects this is likely to have. von Lucke et al. (2014) corroborate these claims while also discussing the contextual argument that, in some instances, for example, in the United States – references to national security might be necessary to bridge political divides and kick start progressive climate action (see also Diez et al., 2016, pp. 149–152).

In spite of this, the majority of securitization scholars working on the securitization of the environment/climate change seem not to be happy with simply siding with desecuritization over securitization. In my view, there is a simple reason for this: most people believe climate change is a real and existential threat to a referent object they value and wish to see survive. Desecuritization as a normative strategy only works if and when real threats are ignored; because only in the absence of real threats, is it possible to argue that desecuritization is *ceteris paribus* better than securitization.

The possibility of just securitization seems further increased by the fact that securitization does not mean Schmittian exceptionalism. Yet this is not so, von Lucke et al. (2014) find evidence to suggest that "risk-based securitization" brings with its own negative consequences (notably "a less extreme but permanent and infinite state of emergency" and is unlikely to be better than a "security-based securitization") (p. 873). Nevertheless, the fact that securitization does not necessarily mean militarization or Copenhagen School-style exceptionalism all feed toward the idea of morally right, just, or positive securitization. Yet to argue, thus, is difficult from within the Copenhagen School that commences from an interest in the social construction of threats, not a concern with real threats to real people, and which is why some scholars (notably McDonald, 2012b) make the case for an emancipatory environmental security discourse, not with reference to the Copenhagen School, but inspired by the Critical Theory of the Aberystwyth School, whose explicit objective is the creation of a more inclusive and just world, free from oppression and harmful security practices (Booth, 2007).

My own research on just securitization, however, shows that normative theorizing and securitization theory can be combined (Floyd, 2019). Informed by the just war tradition that theories the morality of war, Just Securitization Theory consists of a number of universal moral principles that seek to capture: 1) the circumstances under which securitization is morally permissible; 2) the issues that have to be taken into consideration when securitizing; and 3) what desecuritizing actors are morally required to do to justly unmake securitization. Principles include just reason for securitization, just referent object, right intention, proportionality, and reasonable chance of success. While this theory is not restricted to the just securitization of climate change, the impetus for this theory comes from my previous work of environmental security (Floyd, 2010) that first considered – contrary to the Copenhagen School – the possibility of morally right securitization.

Conclusion

This chapter detailed the landscape of environmental/climate security and securitization theory. I have argued that securitization theory allows researchers to study climate/environmental security without being bogged down in methodological or normative controversies common to other approaches to environmental security. Securitization theory is essentially an analytical tool that enables researchers to study how issues, including climate change, become considered security threats, without assuming/theorizing that any one entity or thing is objectively threatened by global warming. The chapter showed the utility of securitization analysis by focusing on a number of prominent empirical studies analyzing the securitization of climate change in different states, regions, as well as at the global level (the United Nation). These studies deliver important insights on what climate security means and also on the effects of lifting climate change out of ordinary politics. Despite being able to offer these important insights, securitization theory is not without its flaws. Indeed, the growing subfield of Securitization Studies is concerned with revising and refining almost all aspects of the original Copenhagen School's framework. I have shown in this chapter that empirical studies in the field of environmental and climate security have enabled researchers to offer or confirm important revisions and improvements of securitization theory, concerning many contested issues, for example, on whether securitization is tied to the exception, the nature of the audience, the importance images in securitization, the definition of securitization vis-à-vis riskification, the meaning of desecuritization, as well as the possibility of thinking ethically about securitization. In sum, we can now say that environmental/climate security as a practice and securitization theory exist in fruitful symbiosis, as, indeed, do many other sectors of security and securitization.

Notes

1 As Sarah Saublet and Vincent Larvieière (2016) argue, in the "enviro-security" field emotions may run high not only because researchers care about the referent object but also because (especially in the environmental conflict literature) there is a fair amount of petty competition, backstabbing, and war occurring.
2 A referent object refers to something that is threatened and needs to be protected. A referent can be a person, social group, object, institution, ecosystem, or any other phenomenon that is the focus of security policy or discourse.
3 I purposefully say environmental and climate security because the climate security debate is in many ways a rehash of an earlier, less publicly prominent debate that concerned the linkage between environmental degradation and security (see Floyd, 2008).
4 Some recognize, however, that human insecurity can be a precursor to violent conflict (see, e.g., Barnett & Adger, 2007).
5 See Balzacq and Guzzini (2015) for a discussion of theory in securitization theory.
6 Hans Guenther Brauch (2009) provides a comprehensive overview of factors involved in the securitization of climate change up until 2009.
7 Jean-Claude Juncker's drive to building a Security Union and a Defense Union can be explained in this way. By being seen to provide security and defense in the face of the migrant crisis, terrorism, and other threats, the EU secures itself from fragmentation brought about by BREXIT, the rise of anti-EU parties across Europe, and the EURO-zone crisis. Thus, the suggested levels of security and defense cooperation require greater integration.
8 Oels (2012) points out that "It is only a few people, like former US Vice-President Al Gore, who actually call for the urgency and resolve that has previously been seen only when nations mobilized for war" (p. 191).

Works cited

Aradau, C., & Van Munster, R. (2007). Governing terrorism through risk: Taking precautions, (un) knowing the future. *European Journal of International Relations, 13*(1), 89–115.

Argomaniz, J., Bures, O., & Kaunert, C. (2015). A decade of EU counter-terrorism and intelligence: A critical assessment. *Intelligence and National Security, 30*(2–3), 191–206.

Balzacq, T. (2005). The three faces of securitization: Political agency, audience and context. *European Journal of International Relations, 11*(2), 171–201.

Balzacq, T. (2011). A theory of securitization: Origins, core assumptions, and variants. In T. Balzacq (Ed.), *Securitization theory: How security problems emerge and dissolve* (pp. 1–30). London: Routledge.

Balzacq, T., & Guzzini, S. (2015). Introduction: 'What kind of theory – if any – is securitization?'. *International Relations, 29*(1), 97–102.

Balzacq, T., Léonard, S., & Ruzicka, J. (2016). 'Securitization' revisited: Theory and cases. *International Relations, 30*(4), 494–531.

Barnett, J., & Adger, W. N. (2007). Climate change, human security and violent conflict. *Political Geography, 26*(6), 639–655.

Barnett, J. (2001). *The meaning of environmental security: Ecological politics and policy in the new security era.* London: Zed Books.

Biba, S. (2016). From securitization moves to positive outcomes: The case of the spring 2010 Mekong crisis. *Security Dialogue, 47*(5), 420–439.

Bigo, D. (2002). Security and immigration: Toward a critique of the governmentality of unease. *Alternatives, 27*(1_suppl), 63–92.

Booth, K. (2007). *Theory of world security* (Vol. 105). Cambridge, UK: Cambridge University Press.

Bourbeau, P. (2014). Moving forward together: Logics of the Securitisation Process. *Millennium, 43*(1), 187–206.

Brauch, H. G. (2009). Securitizing global environmental change. *Facing Global Environmental Change,* 65–102.

Buzan, B. (2004). *From international to world society?* Cambridge: Cambridge University Press.

Buzan, B., & Wæver, O. (2009). Macrosecuritisation and security constellations: Reconsidering scale in securitisation theory. *Review of International Studies, 35*(2), 253–276.

Buzan, B., Wæver, O., & de Wilde, J. (1998). *Security and new framework for analysis*. Boulder: Lynne Rienner.

Corry, O. (2012). Securitisation and 'riskification': Second-order security and the politics of climate change. *Millennium, 40*(2), 235–258.

Côté, A., 2016. Agents without agency: Assessing the role of the audience in securitization theory. *Security Dialogue, 47*(6), 541–558.

Dalby, S. (2002). *Environmental (In) Security*. John Wiley & Sons, Ltd.

Dalby, S. (2009). *Security and environmental change*. Polity.

Detraz, N., & Betsill, M. M. (2009). Climate change and environmental security: For whom the discourse shifts. *International Studies Perspectives, 10*(3), 303–320.

Deudney, Daniel. (1991). The case against linking environmental degradation and national security. *Millennium, 19*(3), 461–476.

Diez, T., von Lucke, F., & Wellmann, Z. (2016). *The Securitisation of Climate Change: Actors, Processes and Consequences*. Routledge.

Dyzenhaus, D. (2010). The "organic law" of ex parte Milligan. In Austin Sarat (Ed.), *Sovereignty, emergency, legality* (pp. 16–56). Cambridge: Cambridge University Press.

EU (2011). Council Conclusions on EU Climate Diplomacy, 3106th Foreign Affairs Council Meeting, Brussels, 18 July 2011. Joint Reflection Paper by the High Representative and the Commission 'Towards a renewed and strengthened European Union Climate Diplomacy', 9 July 2011

Floyd, R. (2019). *The morality of security: A theory of just securitization*. Cambridge: Cambridge University Press.

Floyd, R. (2016). Extraordinary or ordinary emergency measures: What, and who, defines the 'success' of securitization? *Cambridge Review of International Affairs, 29*(2), 677–694.

Floyd, R. (2015). Global climate security governance: A case of institutional and ideational fragmentation. *Conflict, Security & Development, 15*(2), 119–146.

Floyd, R. (2010). *Security and the environment*. Cambridge: Cambridge University Press.

Floyd, R. (2008). The environmental security debate and its significance for climate change. *The International Spectator, 43*(3), 51–65.

Hansen, L. (2012). Reconstructing desecuritisation: The normative-political in the Copenhagen School and directions for how to apply it. *Review of International Studies, 38*(3), 525–546.

Hansen, L. (2011). 'Theorizing the Image for Security Studies: Visual Securitization and the Muhammad Cartoon Crisis', *European Journal of International Relations, 17*(1), 51–74

Hayes, J., & Knox-Hayes, J. (2014). Security in climate change discourse: Analyzing the divergence between US and EU approaches to policy. *Global Environmental Politics, 14*(2), 82–101.

Heck, A., & Schlag, G. (2013). Securitizing images: The female body and the war in Afghanistan. *European Journal of International Relations, 19*(4), 891–913.

Huysmans, J. (2002). Defining social constructivism in security studies: The normative dilemma of writing security. *Alternatives, 27*(1_suppl), 41–62.

Huysmans, J. (1998). Desecuritization and the aesthetics of horror in political realism. *Millennium: Journal of International Studies, 27*(3), 569–589

Kaplan, R. D. (1994). The coming anarchy. The Atlantic *February, 273*, 44–76.

Karyotis, G. (2012). Securitization of migration in Greece: Process, motives, and implications. *International Political Sociology, 6*, 390–408

Léonard, S., & Kaunert, C. (2011). Reconceptualizing the audience in securitization theory. In T. Balzaq (Ed.), *Securitization theory: How security problems emerge and dissolve* (pp. 57–76). London: Routledge.

Lovelock, J., & Lovelock, J. E. (2000). *Gaia: A new look at life on earth*. Oxford Paperbacks.

McDonald, M. (2012a). The failed securitization of climate change in Australia. *Australian Journal of Political Science, 47*(4), 579–592.

McDonald, M. (2012b) *Security, the environment and emancipation: Contestation over environmental change*. Abingdon: Routledge.

Methman, C., & Rothe, D. (2012). Politics for the day after tomorrow: The logic of the apocalypse in global climate politics. *Security Dialogue, 43*(4), 323–344.

Neal, Andrew (2010). *Exceptionalism and the Politics of Counter-terrorism: Liberty, Security and the War on Terror*. Abingdon: Routledge.

Oels, A. (2012). From 'securitization' of climate change to 'climatization' of the security field: Comparing three theoretical perspectives. *Climate Change, Human Security and Violent Conflict*, 185–205.

Roe, P. (2008). 'Actor, audience (s) and emergency measures: Securitization and the UK's decision to invade Iraq'. *Security Dialogue*, *39*(6), 615–635.

Rothe, D. (2017). Seeing like a satellite: Remote sensing and the ontological politics of environmental security. *Security Dialogue*, *48*(4), 334–353

Rothe, D. (2016). *Securitizing global warming: A climate of complexity*. Abingdon: Routledge.

Salter, M. B. (2011). When securitization fails: The hard case of counter-terrorism programs. In T. Balzacq (Ed.), *Securitization theory: How security problems emerge and dissolve* (pp. 116–132). London: Routledge.

Saublet, S., & Larivière, V. (2016). Mapping the 'enviro-security' field: Rivalry and cooperation in the construction of knowledge. *European Political Science*.

Taureck, R. (2006). Securitization theory and securitization studies. *Journal of International Relations and Development*, *9*(1), 53–61.

Trombetta, Maria J (2011). Rethinking the securitization of the environment: Old beliefs, new insights. In T. Balzacq (Ed.), *Securitization theory: How security problems emerge and dissolve* (pp. 135–149). London: Routledge.

von Lucke, F. (2016). Linking climate change and security in Mexico: Explorations into an attempted securitisation in the Global South. *Journal of International Relations and Development*. Online First

von Lucke, F., Wellmann, Z., & Diez, T. (2014). What's at stake in securitising climate change? Towards a differentiated approach. *Geopolitics*, *19*(4), 857–884.

Wæver, O. (2011). Politics, security, theory. *Security Dialogue*, *42*(4–5), 465–480.

Wæver, O. (2009). Klimatruslen – en sikkerhedspolitisk analyse. *Tidsskriftet Politik*, *12*(1), 5–26

Wæver, O. (1995). *Securitization and desecuritization. On security* (Ronnie D. Lipschutz, Ed.) (pp. 46–87). Columbia University Press.

Wilde, J. H. (2008). Environmental security deconstructed. *Globalization and Environmental Challenges*, 595–602.

Williams, Michael C. (2003). Words, images, enemies: Securitization and international politics. *International Studies Quarterly, 47*(4), 511–531.

20

ENVIRONMENTAL SECURITY DISCOURSE IN THE ANTHROPOCENE

Simon Dalby

Anthropocene formulations

The Anthropocene is a relatively new term that encapsulates the implications of recent earth system science understandings of how life works as part of the complex processes that link the biosphere to other parts of our planet. It is a geological term, one that emphasizes the scale of the role humanity is now playing. It implies that earlier thinking about the environment, as the given context for humanity, does not adequately encompass the scale and speed of contemporary change; neither do scientific studies that focus on particular landscapes or ecosystems, rather than thinking about the earth as a single interconnected system that is being radically transformed by the actions of the rich and powerful parts of humanity (Hamilton, 2017). This change in perspective implies that the conceptual discussions of environmental security drawn from the 1980s debates about sustainable development need a substantial update. Getting the context right matters for both academic analysis and policy prescription.

The sheer scale of the transformation wrought by the fossil fuel-powered global economy became increasingly clear in the 1990-era scientific investigations of the planetary system. In addition to climate change, deforestation, the extension of artificial fertilizer production with large-scale nitrogen and phosphorus flows added into ecosystems, the ozone issue, loss of biodiversity, and large-scale destruction of ocean fish stocks were increasingly understood as factors in the transformation of the earth (see Goodrich & Nizkorodov, 2016). At an International Geosphere Biosphere Project meeting, Nobel Prize winning scientist Paul Crutzen became unhappy with participants using the conventional geological designation of the present as the Holocene and blurted out that we now live in the Anthropocene (Crutzen, 2002). His thinking was that recent changes were on such a scale that effectively humanity was living in a new geological period. This term gradually made its way into the scientific discussion and subsequently was on the front pages of both the *National Geographic Magazine* (Kolbert, 2011) and the *Economist* in the first half of 2011, then into much wider circulation.

The Anthropocene has become a term that summarizes the much larger shift in perspective that earth system science has brought about whereby the rich and powerful, fossil fuel burning part of humanity is understood as a geological scale forcing mechanism in the earth system (Bonneuil & Fressoz, 2016). No longer is the environment seen as a given context for the human drama, but now something that humanity is actively remaking and reorganizing so

DOI: 10.4324/9781315107592-24

that the context is now part of the human story, not a mere backdrop to the story of modernity and human progress (Hamilton, Bonneuil, & Gemenne, 2015). These changes have accelerated in the last three-quarters of a century through the period of the Cold War and its aftermath as fossil-fueled economic activity has dramatically expanded and its consequences have reached all parts of the earth system. Hence, the increasing use of the term "great acceleration" refers to the era since the end of the Second World War when the petroleum-fueled automobile mode of consumption economy spread rapidly (McNeill & Engelke, 2016).

Environmental security/sustainable development

While concerns about environmental damage and resource availability for human activities are not new, their crystallization into a cluster of issues under the rubric of environmental security came about in the latter years of the Cold War in the late 1980s. Issues of development, environment, and security intersected in a series of reports by various international commissions considering aspects of the human condition and the politics of survival in the face of nuclear war, economic difficulties, and environmental degradation. These policy issues coalesced in the discussions in the World Commission on Environment and Development (WCED). Its conclusions published in 1987 in *Our Common Future*, popularly known as the "Brundtland Report" after the Norwegian Chair of the Commission, synthesized many of the themes of the larger discussion.

Environmental disasters, notably the chemical leak in Bhopal, India, that killed hundreds of people in 1984 and the nuclear reactor meltdown at Chernobyl in the Soviet Union two years later, coupled with the discovery of a major depletion of the ozone layer over the Antarctic, heightened awareness of the unintended consequences of technological industrialization. Crucially, all these events emphasized the interconnectedness of humanity, the vulnerability of environmental systems, and the potential for technological innovation to lead to artificial disasters and unforeseen consequences. Studies of the likely impacts of nuclear war linked environmental matters directly to the dangers of the Cold War geopolitical confrontation and enhanced nascent understandings of the earth as an interconnected system increasingly influenced by human activities (Turco, Toon, Ackerman, Pollack, & Sagan, 1983).

These concerns built on earlier fears of pollution hazards in developed countries and worries about food shortages and famine plaguing poorer nations in Africa and Asia. Resource shortage worries from the 1970s, highlighted by the OPEC oil crisis in the mid-1970s, price rises in petroleum, and the disruptions to various development strategies that resulted, generated a sense of crisis that linked numerous human problems, even if the global economy continued to grow. The hugely popular report on the *Limits to Growth* in the early 1970s (Meadows, Meadows, Randers, & Behrens, 1972) suggested that there were biophysical limits to the expansion of the global economy and that resource shortages would inevitably lead to a collapse of the industrial economy if it continued to grow, regardless of these constraints.

Developing nations were especially concerned that developed states would use these environmental ideas in ways that would stymie their growth and in the process prevent the economic growth that was widely deemed necessary to alleviate poverty. Tackling all these issues together was a tall order, and the WCED addressed these by trying to combine concerns about the need for development with recognition that functional environmental conditions were a necessary prerequisite. Development would have to be environmentally sustainable if the long-term future for all of humanity was to be secured. Likewise, failure of development might, as *Our Common Future* warned, lead to conflict and environmental destruction. Nuclear warfare would also lead to environmental disaster and to the end of practical development efforts.

One of the factors that worried *Our Common Future's* authors, in particular, was climate change; although in the 1980s while alarm about nuclear winter did accelerate climate modeling efforts, they were not clear on the degree of sensitivity of the world's climate to increases in carbon dioxide in particular. Likewise, the losses to global biodiversity due to development and, in particular, deforestation involved in extending agricultural land were obviously a growing problem, too. The WCED's activities fed into the 1992 "Earth Summit" held in Rio de Janerio where both the Convention on Biodiversity and the Framework Convention on Climate Change (UNFCCC) were launched amid considerable fanfare. However, through the 1990s, progress on both these conventions was very slow despite such high-profile initial attempts to grapple with climate as the Kyoto Protocol to the UNFCCC.

Environmental security thus emerged as the necessary condition for sustainable development, and in an interesting linked formulation, sustainable development was understood as the policy framework that would deliver environmental security. The logic is neatly circular, but that did not lead to a clear comprehension of just how interconnected environmental matters were with habitat and climate change. The overarching formulation of the planet as one being remade by human activity had to wait until the new millennium when the earth system sciences insights have been crystallized around the idea of the Anthropocene, a new geological age shaped by the actions of the rich and powerful part of humanity (Davies, 2016).

Environmental security discourse

But for all the apparently sensible formulations in *Our Common Future*, there were numerous difficulties with both its diagnosis of the problems to which sustainable development was supposedly the answer and how new modes of development that did not perpetuate the exhaustion of resources and environmental change were to be formulated and implemented. Likewise, while the arguments that nuclear war would cause environmental damage, and by lofting huge quantities of smoke and debris into the atmosphere, at least temporarily cool the planet in a "nuclear winter" that would badly disrupt agriculture, were clear, it was far from clear what the relationships between resource scarcity and conflict were, especially in developing states. Still largely rural and agricultural, even if their urban populations were growing rapidly, it was not clear how these fragile economies might degenerate into conflict over resource scarcities. However, the assumption was widespread that they would.

Early attempts in the 1990s to provide clear understandings of these phenomena suggested that simple models of scarcity causing violence were not accurate, but the complexity of the linkages defied easy summation (Baechler, 1998; Homer-Dixon, 1999). Fears of such things as water wars turned out to be exaggerated; although difficulties across state boundaries are frequent, cooperation is far more likely given common interests in sensible management of shared resources (see Asthana, Chapter 6). Likewise, it is unlikely that states, in what is now known as the Global South, could use military means to deal with the inequities in the global economy or to rectify the damage caused by climate change, a matter where historically industrialized countries have caused the bulk of the greenhouse gas emissions that are the cause of the problem.

Indeed, the cause of much of the violence in the Global South after the Cold War seemed to have much more to do with struggles to control the revenue from resources being extracted there for export to global markets or fights by subsistence peoples and peasant farmers to hang onto their land or their forest homes in the face of rapid encroachment by commercial agriculture and resource companies (Peluso & Watts, 2001; see also Le Billon, Chapter 4). Critical scholars pointed to these factors as more important to understanding social change in the global south than more general fears of shortages and failures of development as the source of environmental insecurity (Suliman, 1999). Environmental matters clearly are important in rural societies dependent upon local resources for livelihoods. But assuming that indigenous sources of scarcity, for which development was supposedly the solution, was the cause of conflict, was to misread the politics and economic conditions that shaped rural discontent. How the environment was invoked in security discussions became a topic of serious scholarly discussion, which, in turn, has substantial policy implications in terms of how it is interpreted as either a cause of conflict or a matter of a backdrop that provides a context for them (Dalby, 2002).

This debate about environment and conflict became an important policy matter a couple of decades later when accelerating climate change coupled with American thinking on the war on terror lead to numerous analyses that linked environmental change to insurgencies and failed states, places apparently in need of military interventions to prevent terrorism spreading. In this version of the environmental security discourse, remote places in the Global South are seen as potentially threatening to the larger political system. Insecurity is about political instabilities and the potential of remote rural areas to breed terrorists and insurgencies. Now climate change, with the droughts, floods, and storms it brings, is understood as a threat multiplier or even a catalyst for conflict (CNA, 2014). These dangers require being taken seriously as they are a threat to American national security, in particular, in the context of the "war on terror," and subsequent military efforts in many places.

But while the 1990s discussion on environmental security as rural instability and violence has been appropriated and linked to climate security in American, and in some cases European, formulations of security (Hardt, 2018), simultaneous developments in earth system science, and political thinking from smaller southern states endangered by climate change have increasingly suggested a very different discourse on environmental security. This line of thinking suggests that the causes of insecurity come from the industrialized parts of the world, and the global economy, which is so dependent on the combustion of fossil fuels to literally keep everything moving. The increasingly disrupted environments of the Global South, where many of the victims of climate change-induced extreme weather events live, are not the cause of insecurity but bear the consequences of activities for which they bear little responsibility (Chaturvedi & Doyle, 2015). Which geopolitical assumptions structure policy matter greatly in terms of how environmental security plays out in the coming decades.

Anthropocene concepts: planetary boundaries and a safe operating space

While *Our Common Future* paid attention to the ozone depletion problem and highlighted the potential importance of climate change, back in the 1980s much less was known about how climate change might affect the earth. The nuclear winter discussion accelerated climate modeling and emphasized the key point highlighted by the ozone depletion problem that human actions were on a scale that could change the function of the system as a whole. Researchers began to actively try to link changes in one part of the system and understand the interconnections between the biosphere, lithosphere, atmosphere, hydrosphere, and what has recently increasingly been called the technosphere (Zalasiewicz, 2017).

Research under the auspices of the International Geosphere Biosphere Project and rapidly growing sophistication of global climate models gradually pieced the interconnections between earth system components together, suggesting that life itself is a crucial part of the system. James Lovelock (1979) had suggested much earlier that life itself was an important regulatory phenomenon in the operation of the earth system in his famous Gaia Hypothesis. While the mechanisms that made this regulation happen, wherein life tends to operate to maintain the overall planetary system in conditions that favor life, were not clear, and the geological record on these matters has not necessarily revealed all the causal connections in many of the major transitions, the importance of life in the system has come to be recognized.

The growing appreciation of our new context, captured in the increasingly wide use of the term Anthropocene, changes the discussion of environmental dimensions of security (Dalby, 2009). No longer can simple assumptions of resource scarcities be invoked as the cause of violence. The global context in which environments are enmeshed is now an increasingly artificial one. While climate change gets most of the attention, the larger discussion of the human dimensions of global change emphasizes the numerous ways ecological systems are being changed and the fact that many other species are being driven to extinction in the process as humanity expands its ecological niche to dominate most parts of the earth system. Vulnerabilities to environmental hazards are hence increasingly a matter of artificial factors, both directly in terms of how economic and infrastructures shape human living and fail at crucial moments and indirectly in that the artificial systems that make human life possible are being impacted by climate change and less predictable weather systems.

Earth system science has tried to encapsulate all this in a series of discussions of what is called the safe operating system for humanity and formulated a number of planetary boundaries within which it is argued, humanity can flourish (see Rockström et al., 2009; Steffen et al., 2018). The noteworthy point about the Holocene was that over the last 12 thousand years while the climate, in particular, has fluctuated, it has operated within a remarkably consistent range. Unlike the hundreds of thousands of years prior to the end of the last ice age, the Holocene was very stable, providing conditions within which humanity has flourished. This, the authors of the safe operating space idea argue, is the set of conditions within which we know human civilization can flourish. If fossil fuel consumption and the other economic activities of the present push the earth out of these stable conditions, it is not at all clear that civilization can continue to function (Steffen et al., 2015, 2018). Rapid fluctuations of climate would make agriculture to feed billions very difficult. Continued acidification of the ocean will further compromise fish stocks and threaten a major source of protein for humanity. The continued destruction of biodiversity might break crucial ecological linkages too. Overall, this still hangs the threat of major warfare if political elites choose to try to use violence to maintain some form of control over events in a rapidly changing world (Glikson, 2017).

Thus, the discussion of the Anthropocene requires a very different formulation of environmental security, one that focuses on global trends and the need to maintain the earth system within something approximating Holocene parameters (Steffen et al., 2015). This is not about rural populations becoming conflict-prone and posing problems to the existing geopolitical order. Instead, this discourse is about the consequences of that geopolitical order and how the search for security understood in terms of affluence produced by endless economic growth has changed the environmental context quite fundamentally. Security in these terms is about shaping the future configuration of the global biosphere and deciding on how much climate change will happen in the coming decades.

For small island nations and poor states with vulnerable coastlines, climate change and the consequent rise of sea levels is a threat to national survival. The actions of fossil fuel burning parts of humanity are rendering low-lying states increasingly insecure. They do not have military options to attempt to defend themselves. Likewise, many states with large agricultural economies are increasingly vulnerable to variable weather patterns, storms, and rainfall events. This is what environmental security means now as the full significance of the formulation of humanity as a geological scale actor becomes clear.

Good or bad Anthropocene?

Much of the Anthropocene discussion in popular discussions and social sciences has simply used the term to refer to the traditional pessimistic view of global environmental degradation and as a call to redouble efforts to protect nature from human depredations. This view of the Anthropocene is about the technologically induced disaster; the sediments left for the long-term geological future of the planet will record the extinction of numerous species and quite possibly radioactive trace elements left behind by the nuclear wars yet to be fought over shrinking resource bases (Glikson, 2017). Humanity is the instigator of the sixth planetary extinction event that may spiral into our own demise if we fail to change our course and recognize that we are part of a rapidly changing biosphere and need to live accordingly (Kolbert, 2014). Dystopian fictions are not new to modernity, but the sense of ecological disaster that this interpretation of the Anthropocene invokes has regenerated doom-laden scenarios of our future world. Some of the more pessimistic contemporary views simply argue that current human actions will render the world uninhabitable (Wallace-Wells, 2017).

Here the narratives of disaster follow some of the arguments made in the *Limits to Growth* discussion in the 1970s (Meadows et al., 1972), where resource depletion and environmental damage were bound to constrain human numbers, perhaps drastically so. The current trajectories in terms of planetary boundaries and the violations of the safe operating space formulation in the Anthropocene discussion certainly give great cause for alarm, the climate change, and biodiversity loss figures, which alone could be enough to change the earth system into a new mode of operation, are alarming. While it is difficult to keep many species alive when their habitats are removed, as is the case in deforestation, it will also be difficult to bring carbon dioxide levels down later this century assuming that humanity does finally build a civilization not dependent on combustion to make so many things work. But these are the kind of considerations that are essential to any serious discussion of environmental security that takes the Anthropocene formulation as the premise for analysis or policy prescription.

Although overdue, the Paris Climate Agreement of 2015 does suggest the beginning of a framework to deal with climate issues and to begin to reduce the emissions of greenhouse gases. The agreement commits all states to work toward this end, but leaves the methods whereby it will be achieved to states that can develop their own policies. Critics argue that efforts to date have been inadequate. The arguments about how to proceed at subsequent Conference of the Parties (COPs) suggest that progress will continue to be slow in the face of the need to act rapidly to turn energy systems around and build infrastructure that is much less dependent on carbon fuels. Failure to do so is likely to lead to a "bad" Anthropocene with dire dystopian futures ahead, futures that are grist to the mill of the current generation of science fiction writers exploring what an ecologically transformed world might look like (Bacigalupi, 2015).

Part of the uncertainties about the future lies in the speed with which technological and social innovation will play out, and about how hard governments will push new ways of making things so as to reduce the rate of climate change. These political decisions are key to whether the Anthropocene turns out to be "good" or "bad" for future generations (Dalby, 2016). More optimistic evaluations of the possibilities becoming available due to technological innovation suggest that while time is short, disaster can be averted if best practices and a clear recognition of the interconnectedness of ecology and economy are worked into practical arrangements (Rockström & Klum, 2015). Highly optimistic accounts of the future, and the possibilities of a "good" Anthropocene, are frequently premised on assumptions of what new technological devices will be capable of, and of new modes of growing food, and such things as farming the oceans in novel ways to provide for affluent future humanity (Ackerman, 2014).

However, notwithstanding the consensus among governments that climate changes need to be tackled, a view that has been institutionalized in the Paris Agreement (Falkner, 2016), the contemporary international political landscape is frequently occupied by nationalism and xenophobic rhetoric that insists on separations and sovereignty understood in terms of territory and fixed borders to enforce separations. Assumptions that separations are the key to security run in direct opposition to the ecological insights about an interconnected and rapidly changing world that are encapsulated in the idea of the Anthropocene (Dalby, 2018). In a view of the world that emphasizes these interconnections, security is about facilitating linkages and allowing migrations rather than building walls and assuming that threats in a rapidly changing world can be geographically constrained. While territorial administration remains the basis for much governance, as the Paris Agreement makes clear, now cooperation and common efforts are needed to deal with problems that imperil our common future.

Geopolitics or global security?

Sharply contrasting assumptions about the appropriate context for thinking about security thus structure notions of policy priorities. The political difficulties of thinking through how to cooperate are worsened by the rising inequities in the global economy and the resentment that runs through much populist discourse that invokes external threats to supposedly separate political communities. Where climate change might be understood to be a common threat to much of humanity, the counterarguments specify attempts to deal with climate as the problem because it challenges ways of life dependent on the profligate use of gasoline and other fossil fuels (Dalby, 2017). Thus, in these arguments, what needs to be secured is supplies of mainly fossil fuel energy so that the current consumption lifestyles of North Americans, in particular, can continue uninterrupted.

The contrasts here are stark. The earth system analyses make clear that greenhouse gas emissions have to be curtailed rapidly and pose consumption-based modes of life as the problem for future generations. As Bruno Latour's (2017) epigraph at the beginning of this chapter suggests the future is not practical if we are to have a future at all. In his terms, the "new climate regime" we are living within requires that we reconsider what the future we desire might look like. Clearly, continuing to try to burn our way to perpetual prosperity is impossible if there is any hope of maintaining the planet in conditions approximating the last dozen millennia. That insight has been very slow to penetrate into official discussions of climate policy or to galvanize publics to demand that dramatically different modes of the economy be constructed urgently. But that is what is needed if the next phase of the Anthropocene is to avoid destabilizing the climate system so much that feeding the many billions of humans now living, increasingly in urban systems, remains possible. If environmental security is a meaningful concept in present circumstances, then these are the political choices it has to address.

Much of the discussion of climate change so far has happened within a political understanding of the world in which it is assumed that environmental regulations, technical changes in the industry, and market mechanisms are the appropriate way to deal with the issue (Falkner, 2016). Protest groups, social movements, and numerous nongovernmental organizations whose members pay attention to the scientific discussion of climate change and Anthropocene themes repeatedly try to speed up the official state responses to climate dangers. But despite numerous efforts, change is still slow.

The rise of China as the world's factory in the last couple of decades raises the question of whether emissions should be counted in terms of the final use of the product rather than where the production of transportation emissions occurs on the way to the final user. Taking a holistic view, as the Anthropocene perspective requires, suggests that national statistics are frequently misleading. Moving pollution offshore may clean up environments in one place but does not solve the overall problem if it has merely been relocated (O'Lear, 2016), all of which suggests that the existing state structure with rival states as the key political activity is failing as a mode of governance that can provide security in meaningful ways to humanity in the long run (Harris, 2013). Who decides which mode of security will prevail is now a crucial part of the politics of the Anthropocene. How what needs to be secured is portrayed, and where the sources of danger are specified in these portrayals, is a key question for contemporary geopolitics.

Securing the global environment

The Anthropocene formulation, as a summation of the implications of the earth system science findings, suggests quite clearly that decisions made by governments and corporations in the coming years will profoundly affect the future trajectory of the climate system and determine which species survive to populate the earth in the future. This is no longer a matter of traditional environmental protection, of preventing the worst consequences of pollution, or providing refuges for wildlife and parks so humans can enjoy 'nature.' Focusing on the earth as a complex system in which human activities are now a major force requires some clear thinking about what it is that needs to be secured. Traditional models of national security derived from the Cold War period are completely inadequate; indeed, in many ways, they are the problem. We now face a much more dynamic world, one where security has to be rethought in terms of adapting to rapid change, and sometimes unpredictable events that require thinking in terms of transformations and enhanced forms of resilience (Kareiva & Fuller, 2016).

Thus, Anthropocene formulations of security require asking very different questions of state institutions and tackling sustainability at the largest of scales much more seriously than has so far been the case even in the promising aspirational statements in the 2015 Sustainable Development Goals (United Nations, 2015). What kind of environment are we collectively making? Is it one dominated by rapidly growing greenhouse gas concentrations or one that constrains fossil fuel use while expanding the use of alternative forms of energy use? Do we continue with existing forms of agriculture that extend even further the conversion of habitats into fields and appropriate remaining water supplies to irrigate monocultures? Or, do we think about modes of permaculture and innovative ways of making food that allow relatively undisturbed habitats so that the diversity of life on the planet can be maintained?

These choices will require much more than the kind of minor adjustments to market arrangements that efforts to constrain climate change have so far attempted (Angus, 2016). Security, in terms of the long-run viability of the biosphere rather than simply securing short-term access to fossil fuels and agricultural land, is a very different proposition than current versions of "national security" that still understand state rivalries in economic, and sometimes, in military terms to be most important. The old future of fossil-fueled technological expansion is not the route to any meaningful notion of environmental security in the next phase of the Anthropocene. The assumption that a world will continue to exist in a form that allows such priorities among political elites is no longer tenable if the insights drawn from discussions of the Anthropocene are incorporated into security thinking. "To put it baldly: in the face of what is to come, we cannot continue to believe in the old future if we want to have a future at all" (Latour, 2017, p. 245).

Which future policy-makers aim to secure matters greatly; if long-term survival is the key, then as Bruno Latour (2017) suggests, we need to think about futures very differently from those that were popular in the twentieth century. Nothing less is necessary if the next phase of the Anthropocene is going to be shaped by policies that aim to secure the ability to adapt and to

Simon Dalby

rapidly develop modes of the economy that can be sustained in the long run so as not to destroy the systems that make the biosphere conducive to human flourishing.

Works cited

Ackerman, D. (2014). *The Human Age: The World Shaped by Us*. Toronto: Harper Collins.

Angus, I. (2016). *Facing the Anthropocene: Fossil Capitalism and the Crisis of the Earth System*. New York: Monthly Review Press.

Bacigalupi, P. (2015). *The Water Knife*. New York: Knopf.

Baechler, G. (1998). Why Environmental Transformation Causes Violence: A Synthesis *Environmental Change and Security Project Report* 4, 24–44.

Bannon, I., & Collier, P. (Eds.). (2003). *Natural Resources and Violent Conflict: Options and Actions*. Washington, DC: World Bank.

Bonneuil, C., & Fressoz, J-B. (2016). *The Shock of the Anthropocene*. New York: Verso.

Chaturvedi, S.& Doyle, T. (2015). *Climate Terror: A Critical Geopolitics of Climate Change*. London: Palgrave Macmillan.

CNA Military Advisory Board (2014). *National Security and the Accelerating Risks of Climate Change*. Alexandria, VA: CNA Corporation.

Crutzen, P. J. (2002). Geology of Mankind – The Anthropocene *Nature* 415, 23.

Dalby, S. (2002). *Environmental Security*. Minneapolis: University of Minnesota Press.

Dalby, S. (2009). *Security and Environmental Change*. Cambridge: Polity.

Dalby, S. (2016). Framing the Anthropocene: The Good, the Bad, and the Ugly. *The Anthropocene Review* 3(1). 33–51.

Dalby, S. (2017). Firepower: Geopolitical Cultures in the Anthropocene *Geopolitics*. http://dx.doi.org/10.1080/14650045.2017.1344835

Dalby, S. (2018). Geopolitics in the Anthropocene. In Al Bergeson and Christian Suter (Eds.), *The return of geopolitics* (pp. 149–166). Zurich: Lit.

Dauvergne, P. (2016). *Environmentalism of the rich*. Cambridge, MA: MIT Press.

Davies, J. (2016). *The Birth of the Anthropocene*. Berkeley: University of California Press.

Edwards, P. N. (2010). *A vast machine: Computer models, climate data, and the politics of global warming*. Cambridge, MA: MIT Press.

Falkner, R. (2016). The Paris Agreement and the New Logic of International Climate Politics *International Affairs* 92(5), 1107–1125.

Glikson, A. (2017). *Plutocene: Blueprints for a Post-Anthropocene Greenhouse Earth*. Berlin: Springer.

Goodrich, K., & Nizkorodov, E. (2016). The Science of the Anthropocene. In R. Matthew, K. Goodrich, K. Harron., B. Maharramli, & E. Nizkorodov (Eds.), *Continuity and change in global environmental politics: The social ecology of the Anthropocene*. The WSPC Reference Set on Natural Resources and Environmental Policy in the Era of Global Change (pp. 3–32). Singapore: World Scientific Publishing Co.

Hamilton, C. (2017). *Defiant Earth: The Fate of Humans in the Anthropocene* Cambridge: Polity.

Hamilton, C., Bonneuil, C., & Gemenne, F. (Eds.). (2015). *The Anthropocene and global environmental crisis: Rethinking modernity in a new epoch*. Abingdon: Routledge.

Hardt, J. N. (2018). *Environmental Security in the Anthropocene*. London: Routledge.

Harris, P. G. (2013). *What's Wrong with Climate Politics and How to Fix It*. Cambridge: Polity.

Homer-Dixon, T. (1999). *Environment, Scarcity, and Violence*. Princeton: Princeton University Press.

Kareiva, P., & Fuller, E. (2016). Beyond Resilience: How to Better Prepare for the Profound Disruption of the Anthropocene *Global Policy* 7/S1, 107–118.

Kolbert, E. (2011). Enter the Anthropocene: The Age of Man *National Geographic* March. Cover Story.

Kolbert, E. (2014). *The Sixth Extinction: An Unnatural History*. New York: Henry Holt.

Latour, B. (2017). *Facing Gaia: Eight Lectures on the New Climatic Regime* Cambridge: Polity.

Lovelock, J. E. (1979). *Gaia A new look at life on Earth*. Oxford: Oxford University Press.

McNeill, J. R., & Engelke, P. (2016). *The Great Acceleration: An Environmental History of the Anthropocene since 1945* Cambridge, MA: Harvard University Press.

Meadows, D. H., Meadows, D. L., Randers, J., & Behrens, W. W. III. (1972). *The Limits to Growth*. New York: Universe Books.

O'Lear, S. (2016). Geopolitics and climate science: The case of the missing embodied carbon. In S. O'Lear & S. Dalby (Eds.), *Reframing climate change: constructing ecological geopolitics* (pp. 100–115). London: Routledge.

Peluso, N., & Watts, M. (Eds.). (2001). *Violent environments*. Ithaca, NY: Cornell University Press.

Rockström, J. et al. (2009). Planetary boundaries: Exploring the safe operating space for humanity. *Ecology and Society*, *14*(2), 32.

Rockström, J., & Klum, M. (2015). *Big world small planet: Abundance within Planetary Boundaries*. Stockholm: Max Strom.

Selby, J., & Hoffman, C. (Eds.). (2015). *Rethinking Climate Change, Conflict and Security* London: Routledge.

Steffen, W., Rockström, J., Richardson, K., Lenton, T. M., Folke, C., Liverman, D., . . . Donges, J. F. (2018). Trajectories of the Earth System in the Anthropocene. *Proceedings of the National Academy of Sciences*, *115*(33), 8252–8259.

Steffen, W., Richardson, K., Rockström, J., Cornell, S. E., Fetzer, I., Bennett, E. M., . . . Folke, C. (2015). Planetary boundaries: Guiding human development on a changing planet. *Science*, *347*(6223).

Suliman, M. (1999). *Ecology, Politics and Violent Conflict*. London: Zed.

Turco, R., Toon, O. B., Ackerman, T. P., Pollack, J. B., & Sagan, C. (1983). Nuclear Winter: Global consequences of multiple nuclear explosions. *Science*, *222*, 1283–1292.

United Nations (2015). *Transforming our world: The 2030 agenda for sustainable development*. Retrieved from https://sustainabledevelopment.un.org/post2015/transformingourworld/publication (A/RES/70/1)

Wallace-Wells, D. (2017). The Uninhabitable Earth *New York Magazine* 9 July.

World Commission on Environment and Development (1987). *Our Common Future*. Oxford: Oxford University Press.

Zalasiewicz, J., Williams, M., Waters, C. N., Barnosky, A. D., Palmesino, J., Rönnskog, A. S., . . . Wolfe, A. P. (2017). Scale and diversity of the physical technosphere: A geological perspective. *The Anthropocene Review*, *4*(1), 9–22.

21

THE ENVIRONMENT AND HUMAN SECURITY

A water–food–energy nexus approach

Florian Krampe, Anders Jägerskog and Ashok Swain

Human security, defined as the opportunity for all people "to meet their most essential needs and to earn their own living is closely linked to the environmental security debate" (UNDP, 1994, p. 24). In the original outline of the human security concept by UNDP in 1994, environmental security was one of the seven components of human security. Indeed, the connection between environmental and human security is one of the most crucial links that contribute to the fate of fragile and conflict-affected states. In these geographies, the link between environmental factors and human security is often more pronounced. In many regions, concern for human and soft security threats outweighs that of conventional, military security concerns (Krampe & Swain, 2016).

Conceptually, human security helps in shifting the referent object from the state to the individual. The international community prefers to use this concept while trying to influence development programs in fragile states. Among the two critical ingredients of what constitutes human security, the components of "freedom from fear" have been seen to be analytically more coherent than the components of "freedom from want"[1] in the context of peacebuilding and reconstruction in conflict-affected states. The advantage of the "freedom from fear" vision is that it is coherent and easier to act upon; thus, this idea has been supported and promoted by the international community more than the "freedom from want" conception of human security. However, there is no doubt that policies toward "freedom from want" are equally important for the long-term security and stability of fragile and conflict-affected countries (Swain, 2012).

In particular, the water–food–energy nexus is critical regarding the link between environment and human security as it fundamentally affects livelihoods. Indeed, a growing body of literature shows how environmental degradation and change fundamentally affect the livelihood of people around the world, especially through pathways related to water, food, and energy. In fragile and conflict-affected states, environmental change in particular exacerbates societal instability and is linked to sustained conflict (Swain & Jägerskog, 2016; Uexkull, Croicu, Fjelde, & Buhaug, 2016; van Baalen & Mobjörk, 2017).

The relationship between the environment and human security also offers opportunities (Krampe, 2017). Human security is not a defensive security concept, but rather a concept that "acknowledges the universalism of life claims" and is "embedded in a notion of solidarity among people" (UNDP, 1994, p. 24). As such, the relationship focuses on the rise of cooperative solutions in the face of environmental change (Krampe, 2017; Wallensteen & Swain,

DOI: 10.4324/9781315107592-25   250

1997, p. 702). Ken Conca (2001) was among the first to outline a theory, suggesting that "carefully designed initiatives for environmental cooperation" could facilitate peace (p. 227). Peace, in this case, meant "several dependent variables that might be affected by environmental cooperation," such as perceptions of other actors, actors' cost–benefit calculations, and broader societal changes (Conca, 2001, p. 227). Subsequent empirical assessments of this relationship focused on two mechanisms that could possibly affect these variables: "changing the strategic climate" – that is, influencing the cost–benefit calculations of states to make conflict less appealing – and "strengthening post-Westphalian governance" – that is, affecting society broadly by disseminating new transnational norms (Conca & Dabelko, 2002, p. 9). Like previous studies, the case studies suggested that environmental issues may provide an entry point for cooperation (Conca & Dabelko, 2002).

In this chapter, we provide a state-of-the-art overview of the interlinkages of the environment and human security by looking at both the risks and opportunities. We provide specific linkages to the key determinants of human security, namely food, water, and energy and illustrate the connection with case studies.

Water

Water is a key component of human security. Human security, as defined earlier, clearly encompasses the need for both access to water and adequate sanitation for humans. The vulnerabilities that are associated with a lack of water security are fundamental to address, from both a human and national security perspective. As outlined by Falkenmark (1986), water scarcity in the Middle East and North Africa (MENA) region as well as in other parts of the world was, indeed, an issue that a few decades back had received far too little attention. Unless it was addressed, it was argued by scholars that this would become a major issue going far beyond the environmental concerns that it had previously raised. Analyzing the lack of water for producing the required food in the region as populations were growing in the Middle East and North Africa led researchers to proclaim that we were about to see wars over water in the decades to come (Starr, 1991; Bullock & Darwish, 1993).

Adding fuel to the flames, much of the water in scarce regions as well as worldwide is shared by two or more nations. Around 276 river basins cross the political boundaries of two or more countries, and there exist over 300 shared groundwater aquifer systems (Transboundary Freshwater Dispute Database, n.d.). However, the outcome, in the MENA region as well as elsewhere, has been different than many predicted. Most countries that shared a river have engaged in primarily cooperative behavior (Jägerskog, Swain, & Öjendal, 2014). One key reason for this is related to the political economy and the import of "virtual water," that is, the embedded water that is in, for example, food. Looking at the trade patterns for the MENA region showed that since the 1970s and 1980s, countries have been compensating for their shortage of water with primarily imported virtual water in the form of food (Allan, 2001). This has challenged the predominant historical narrative in the region that stresses the importance of food self-sufficiency (i.e., that a country should be able to produce the food needed domestically from national resources). Nowadays, almost all countries in the MENA region rely on imported water (in its virtual form).

Furthermore, the functional cooperation that had, in some cases, been established over the common resources meant that there often was something of a water regime in place in which the exchange of views could take place. It was assumed, based on largely idealist/functionalist thinking, that this exchange could be used to further cooperation in other sectors. This, however, has not been clear in the MENA region where limited cooperation over water has not improved cooperation in other sectors (Jägerskog, 2009). While there is scarce evidence for wars over water, it is recognized that conflict and cooperation coexist, in the MENA region as well as in most places where countries share a river, lake, or groundwater resource (Zeitoun & Mirumachi, 2008; see also Asthana, Chapter 6). In addition, Zeitoun and Warner (2006) have noted that it is important to analyze the *quality* of the cooperation, highlighting that it is often the dominant party in a river basin that dominates the interaction. For effective cooperation to emerge, it is important to promote equitable approaches and water sharing.

While, in many cases, water security has not been a traditional security issue (Swain & Jägerskog, 2016), it has entered the security discussions through a human security perspective in which the global water and sanitation challenges have been highlighted. But in the last few years, the increasing focus on climate change has also resulted in a deepening of the discourse on water and security. It has been noted that many agreements on water are often volumetrically based, meaning that the water-sharing agreement is defined as country X receiving a predefined water allocation and country Y also receiving a predefined volume. However, as noted by Fishhendler (2004) and reemphasized by Falkenmark and Jägerskog (2010), this is becoming increasingly challenging as agreements focusing on volumetric allocations are defined by an average figure. When adjusting for climate change, the fluctuations are larger than previously noted and predefined allocations are not likely to be fulfilled. Thus, some agreements are likely to become obsolete, and in some cases, this could generate conflict by way of design. Water is increasingly becoming a weapon of war. Although this is not an entirely new phenomenon, it has been happening to a much larger extent than earlier considered in the Syria conflict, primarily by Daesh/ Isis and other actors. Here, water is being used as a tool in a war/conflict with the aim to achieve some other goals, for example, of geopolitical or strategic nature (Swain & Jägerskog, 2016).

Furthermore, the increased focus on water as a component of conflict and the need to secure water for the population in times of conflict are receiving increased attention. In fragile situations where conflict often has become protracted, the provision of water security for people is often very challenging because of weak institutional capacity, security concerns, and damaged infrastructure, which simultaneously undermines the social contract[2] in many of the affected countries (Sadoff, Borgomeo, & de Waal, 2017). Fragility and conflict are also a major driver for migration. In some instances, it has been claimed that water and climate change have been the main drivers of migration. However, while migration has been driven by decreased access to freshwater (e.g., in Syria prior to the civil war), a clear link among migration, drought, and conflict has yet to be established. For example, poor water governance in the case of Syria led to a situation of limited or no adaptive capacity when the drought in 2006–2008 was longer than normal, while in the neighboring Jordan and Israel, the consequences were very different despite a prolonged drought (Swain & Jägerskog, 2016).

In sum, water has been receiving increasing attention in the security debate, which, overall, is positive as it highlights the overall importance of water for human security. However, when presumed causal linkages and/or deterministic predictions are being made that ignore the politics and history of regions, conclusions are not likely to accurately reflect the full picture. Water needs to be situated in the bigger picture of political relations between states and while it can be used as weapon in war, it is not the reason for war (Jägerskog et al., 2014).

Food

Like water, food is linked to the basic sustenance of human life, making it critical for human security. Indeed, its link to freedom from want is strongly echoed in FAO's definition, which states that food security exists when "when all people, at all times, have physical, social and economic access to sufficient, safe and nutritious food that meets their dietary needs and food preferences for an active and healthy life" (FAO, IFAD, UNICEF, WFP, & WHO, 2017, p. 107). As such, an emphasis on food security is part of the UN's Human Development concept: Goal 2 "Zero Hunger" of the Sustainable Development Goals, a key global policy framework, aims to "End hunger, achieve food security and improved nutrition, and promote sustainable agriculture" (UN SDGs, 2015).

The risks of food security stem from multiple sources and are often very complex. Food security is closely linked not only to climate and environmental change, which increase the probability of droughts and uncertainties of precipitation, but also to mismanagement through various actors, as has been demonstrated in the recent food crises in 2008 and 2010 (De Châtel, 2014; Sternberg, n.d.; Wheeler & Braun, 2013). The effects of conflicts appear to be the biggest threat to food security, as a recent FAO report on the state of the world's food security stresses. The report puts the number of people affected by both hunger and conflict at 489 million, or roughly 60% of the 815 million people suffering worldwide from hunger and malnutrition (FAO et al., 2017). The report further details that the connection between conflict and hunger is especially notable "where the food security impacts of conflict were compounded by droughts or floods, linked in part to the El Niño phenomenon" (FAO et al., 2017, p. xi). The compounded interlinkages of climate change, environmental degradation, bad governance, social decay, and armed conflict strongly affect the food-security situation and continue to exaggerate the human costs of war long after active combat has ceased (Krampe, 2016). The Lake Chad Basin is one of the key examples of this dynamic.

Multiple stressors converge in the Lake Chad region, which lies at the southern end of the Sahara Desert. In the region around the lake, which borders Nigeria, Chad, Cameroon, and Niger, unemployment, depleted resources, poverty, and conflict interact with climate change. Prolonged severe droughts have contributed to a massive shrinking of Lake Chad, a main source of livelihood for millions of inhabitants (Gao, Bohn, Podest, McDonald, & Lettenmaier, 2011; Wirkus & Boege, 2006). The resulting livelihood insecurity and extreme poverty have exacerbated tensions between pastoralists, farmers, and fishers (Thébaud & Batterbury, 2001; UNSC, 2017). As insurgencies have increasingly spread from Nigeria across the region, the fragile security situation has intensified, causing increasing cross-border displacement of populations (UNSC, 2017). The ongoing insurgency in the region and the continued shrinking of Lake Chad are causing a massive humanitarian crisis, intensifying the fragile security situation, and increasing the cross-border displacement of populations. According to the Report of the Secretary-General, "some 10.7 million people across the Lake Chad Basin region currently need humanitarian assistance, including 8.5 million in Nigeria" (UNSC, 2017, p. 2). Roughly, 7.2 million people currently suffer severe food insecurity in the region, of which 4.7 million are located in the north-eastern Nigeria (UNSC, 2017).

The interconnectedness of food security, natural resources, peace, and conflict is not new to anyone familiar with fragile and conflict-affected states. In the outbreak of the Syrian Civil War in 2011, food insecurity was among the factors exacerbating human insecurity and grievances among the population. As Swain and Jägerskog (2016) remark:

> Recurring droughts, increased farming costs, and decades of neglect by the regimes made the situation further worse. However, the reasons for the uprisings were certainly not limited to the food prices and jobs. Not only was the region affected by growing poverty, inequality, and food insecurity, but also political oppression defined the relationship between rulers and the ruled.
>
> (p. 26)

Rising food prices and increasing food insecurity also played a role in the uprising in Egypt. Indeed, research suggests that the outbreak of violent protests in Egypt is linked both to global food price peaks and to drought in China's eastern wheat belt in the late 2010 and early 2011 (Lagi, Bertrand, & Bar-Yam, 2011; Sternberg, 2012). In addition, drought and wildfires in Russia and Ukraine in 2010, unusually cool wet weather in Canada and heavy rainstorms in Australia's wheat growing regions further affected global wheat prices (Femia & Werrell, 2013).

Overcoming the challenge of food security, environmental degradation, and ongoing conflict is difficult, as it is critical to guarantee human security in the endeavor. Building peace in post-conflict countries is rarely, if ever, straightforward. International actors often face insurmountable challenges when programming and implementing their projects. Yet, as has been pointed out, "food security faces natural and anthropogenic threats such as loss of productive land and water, climate change and declining crop productivity, . . . all of which are potentially amenable to solutions provided by science and technology" (Teng & Oliveros, 2015, p. 1). Yet, aside from science and technology, politics is crucial for the resolution and sustainable facilitation of peace. There is a tendency, especially among UN agencies – often due to their mandate – to treat issues such as food security and natural resources as technical issues in need of a technical solution (Aggestam, 2015; Krampe, 2016c). This approach is doomed to fail because, fundamentally, access to food, land, and other natural resources – like the conflicts themselves – are deeply political processes.

Research indicates two potential pathways to overcoming these challenges. First, it is essential to acknowledging the complex underlying dimensions of the problem (Stoett et al., 2016). In fact, the most detrimental effects of environmental change on human security stem from its role in the background to conflict. Actors' motivations as well as contextual factors "like dependence on agriculture for livelihoods, patterns of exclusionary ethnic rule, and low levels of economic development affect whether a given climate 'shock' results in violence" (Hendrix, 2017, p. 251). In fact, by stressing this complexity (and moving away from overly deterministic explanations), research on the links between climate change and conflict has made tremendous progress in recent years. Increasingly, a consensus has been established among researchers, policy actors, and practitioners that climate change and variability is, in fact, a security concern and often a threat multiplier, rather than a cause of conflict (Mobjörk et al., 2016; among others Swain, Swain, Themnér, & Krampe, 2011). New research findings highlight the pathways through which climate change does contribute to political violence (Hsiang, Burke, & Miguel, 2013; Mobjörk et al., 2016; van Baalen & Mobjörk, 2017) as well as to prolong and intensify already ongoing conflicts at the local or subnational level (Uexkull et al., 2016).

Second, both states and international state actors have to understand the state – society relationship – before, during, and after crisis. Supporting government efforts to focus on the state–society relationship is necessary because a state that focuses on the delivery of services to those it is supposed to serve is a state that cares about its inhabitants and provides human security (Brinkerhoff, Wetterberg, & Dunn, 2012; Krampe, 2016b; Migdal, 2001). Service delivery is fundamental in two ways: one, it reduces vulnerability and increases resilience and two, it reduces distrust toward the government. Without a certain level of trust between state and society, shocks cannot be adequately addressed.

Energy

Energy is closely linked to human well-being and progress across the world. Energy provision is a critical component of increased social and economic development (Toman & Jemelkova, 2003). Besides our regular dependence for domestic use, agriculture, manufacturing, transportation, construction, health, and social services also depend on the access to energy. The crucial role of energy in societal development was also highlighted in the Rio+20 conference (United Nations General Assembly, 2012) – access to sustainable modern energy services helps eradicate poverty, save lives, improve health, and supply basic human needs. There is a significant correlation between an inadequate supply of energy and economic underdevelopment.

While access to electricity has increased over the last decade,[3] more than 840 million people still live without access to electricity (WHO, 2019). The majority of these individuals are located in developing countries; in 2018, only 47% of individuals in Sub-Saharan Africa had access to electricity (IEA et al., 2020). If current actions to meet SDG 7 are not accelerated, it is estimated that roughly 650 million people will still be left without access to electricity in 2030 (WHO, 2019). Nine out of ten of these individuals will be living in sub-Saharan Africa. More than 2.6 billion people worldwide also do not have access to clean cooking facilities and rely on solid fuels such as wood, coal, and charcoal for subsistence (IEA, 2020). Therefore, it is important that the access to electricity must be environmental and socially sustainable (World Bank, 2013). Population growth, urbanization, and increasing demands for more food, goods, and services have put further challenges to energy supplies and energy structure, which is presently dominated by fossil fuels.

A new and powerful source of energy, oil, was discovered in 1859 in the United States. The exploitation of oil became a precondition for industrialization and economic development. It also brought a significant change to the way wars were being fought on the ground, in the air, and on and under the seas (see Klare, Chapter 3). Oil quickly transformed how nation states achieve their economic and military security (SIPRI, 1974). However, oil, like water, is unevenly distributed around the world, which gave oil producing nations a very significant strategic importance. The most plentiful oil reserves in the world are clustered in one part of the Middle East, primarily in the Arabian Gulf region. Due to technological development, it is now possible to access new reserves of natural gas, which were before inaccessible and financially impractical. Natural gas is replacing oil for electricity generation and some oil exporting countries have also started allocating gas for domestic energy supply. Moreover, gas also brings export revenues as good as oil, though the economically profitable gas export requires large and long-term infrastructure expenses.

The major oil-producing countries in the Middle East region are governed by nondemocratic political systems, weak or nonexistent political institutions, and regimes with very little political legitimacy (Swain & Jägerskog, 2016). It can be argued that oil and gas have helped empower nondemocratic authoritarian regimes in the region (Ross, 2001). Most of these regimes, through lavish spending and low taxes, have strategically used increased oil and gas revenue to nullify public opposition, buy loyalties at home, and cultivate friends and partners abroad (Youngs, 2008). Oil and gas revenue has changed the balance of power between state and society in most part of the region (Tetreault, 2008). It has brought a false sense of economic security in the policy-making of many countries. Regimes have used the oil and gas money to suppress civil society and prevent popular institutions from bringing checks on authority. However, the lack of basic democratic rights increases possibilities for violent revolutions in the region. While the regime and a few elites control the rich oil resource, the rapidly increasing population in the region suffers from poverty, unemployment, and worsening human development conditions. There is no doubt that the regimes in the region are highly unstable. The political instability raises question about the long-term oil production capacity of the region due to external sanctions, ethnic unrests, and changing investment environment.

In the face of global climate change, many hope to slow the pace of global warming by reducing the consumption of fossil fuels and increasingly shifting to renewable sources of energy

(Klare, 2015). The dominant use of oil and gas for electricity generation continues because these fuels are considered to be cheaper than available renewable energy technologies (Becker & Fischer, 2013). The coast advantages of nonrenewable fossil fuels over renewable resources for power generation wane in the long run as technology improves and oil and gas become more expensive. Adapting to renewable energy sources can become an instrument for improving energy security as well as an approach for mitigating greenhouse gas emissions. In the long term, renewable sources can improve reliability of electricity supplies while reducing energy costs. It is, therefore, not surprising that there has been increasing global interest in switching from traditional fossil fuel-based power generation to renewable energy sources.

For example, around the world and in the Middle East, solar has become the fastest growing method to produce energy. In the Middle East, environmental pollution and greenhouse gas emissions have been major challenge. The region is one of the highest per capita energy consumers in the world. Solar energy can enable actors to reduce fossil fuel dependence, has sufficient capacity to meet needs of users while minimizing environmental harms, and has low operating costs. Tax breaks for solar developers and subsidies for installing the technology further incentivize the adoption of solar energy. The Middle East provides an extremely suitable environment for the development of solar energy with its large open areas that receive sunlight. Strong political will backed by substantial investment in renewable energy sector can be the key in meeting the challenges of energy security of the Middle East region, in particular, and the world, in general.

Conclusion

This chapter examined the linkages between the environment and human security and outlined how the discourse on the topic has evolved over the last decades. While interlinkages between water, food, and energy were not traditionally considered security issues, they are increasingly evolving into intersecting security threats if not addressed in a coherent and effective manner (Swain & Jägerskog, 2016). Approaching this complex area through a water–energy–food nexus perspective is arguably an important way to overcome some of these challenges. A nexus approach identifies both trade-offs and opportunities for improving the water, food, and energy security in regions such as the Middle East, North Africa, and the Sahel region. To promote improved livelihood opportunities, there is a need for deeper analysis of these linkages that avoids oversimplification and is not overly deterministic. Likewise, improving livelihoods through a water–food–energy nexus must be an important goal for international and state actors. A long-term vision for increased human security and improved ecological outcomes is critical and must equally put people and their agency vis à vis the state and their environment at the center.

Notes

1 "Freedom from want" enlarges the boundary of the human security by including poverty, hunger, disease, natural disaster, and displacement. Meanwhile, "freedom from fear" includes threats directed at human safety and security, like armed conflict, terrorism, ethnic expulsion, illegal trade, and criminal violence. These forms of threats are visibly violent in nature and easy to identify and securitize (Swain, 2012).
2 The social contract refers, in principle, to the basic premises upon which a society is formed and upheld, including expectations what a government should provide in terms of basic services (e.g., water and sanitation).
3 In 2010, more than 1.3 billion people, or approximately one in five globally, lacked access to electricity (IEA, 2011).

Works cited

Aggestam, K. (2015). Desecuritisation of water and the technocratic turn in peacebuilding. *International Environmental Agreements: Politics, Law and Economics*, *15*(3), 327–340. http://doi.org/10.1007/s10784-015-9281-x

Allan, J. A. (2001). *The Middle East Water Question: Hydropolitics and the Global Economy*, London, I.B. Tauris.

Becker, B., & Fischer, D., 2013. Promoting renewable electricity generation in emerging economies. *Energy Policy*, Volume 56, pp. 446–455.

Bullock, J., & Darwish, A., 1993, *Water Wars: Coming Conflicts in the Middle East*. London: St Dedmundsbury Press.

Brinkerhoff, D. W., Wetterberg, A., & Dunn, S. (2012). Service Delivery and Legitimacy in Fragile and Conflict-Affected States. *Public Management Review*, *14*(2), 273–293. http://doi.org/10.1080/14719037.2012.657958

Conca, K. (2001). Environmental Cooperation and International Peace. In P. Diehl & N. P. Gleditsch (Eds.), *Environmental Conflict* (pp. 225–247). Boulder and Oxford: Westview Press.

Conca, K., & Dabelko, G. (Eds.). (2002). *Environmental peacemaking*. Washington, DC: Woodrow Wilson Centre Press and The Johns Hopkins University Press.

De Châtel, F. (2014). The Role of Drought and Climate Change in the Syrian Uprising: Untangling the Triggers of the Revolution. *Middle Eastern Studies*, *50*(4), 521–535. http://doi.org/10.1080/00263206.2013.850076

FAO, IFAD, UNICEF, WFP, & WHO. (2017). *The State of Food Security and Nutrition in the World. fao.org*. Rome.

Falkenmark, M., & Jägerskog, A. (2010, July). Sustainability of transnational water agreements in the face of socio-economic and environmental change. In A. Earle, A. Jägerskog, & Öjendal (Eds.), *Transboundary water management: Principles and practice*. London: Earthscan

Falkenmark, M. (1986). Freshwater: Time for a modified approach. *Ambio*, *15*(4), 192–200.

Femia, F., & Werrell, C. E. (2013). Climate Change Before and After the Arab Awakening: The Cases of Syria and Libya. In *The Arab Spring and Climate Change*. Washington, DC: climateandsecurity.files.wordpress.com.

Fishhendler, I. (2004). Legal and institutional adaptation to climate uncertainty: A study of international rivers. *Water Policy*, *6*(4), 281–302.

Gao, H., Bohn, T. J., Podest, E., McDonald, K. C., & Lettenmaier, D. P. (2011). On the causes of the shrinking of Lake Chad. *Environmental Research Letters*, *6*(3), 034021. http://doi.org/10.1088/1748-9326/6/3/034021

Hendrix, C. S. (2017). A comment on "climate change and the Syrian civil war revisited." *Political Geography*, *60*, 251–252. http://doi.org/10.1016/j.polgeo.2017.06.010

Hsiang, S. M., Burke, M., & Miguel, E. (2013). Quantifying the Influence of Climate on Human Conflict. *Science*, *341*(6151), 1235367–1235367. http://doi.org/10.1126/science.1235367

International Energy Agency. (2020). SDG7: Data and Projections. Retrieved November 13, 2020, from www.iea.org/reports/sdg7-data-and-projections/access-to-clean-cooking

International Energy Agency. (2011). *Energy for all, Financing access for the poor, special early excerpt of the World Energy Outlook 2011*. Paris: International Energy Agency.

International Energy Agency, International Renewable Energy Agency, United Nations Statistics Division, The World Bank, & The World Health Organization. (2020). Tracking SDG 7. The Energy Progress Report. Retrieved November 13, 2020, from https://trackingsdg7.esmap.org/

Jägerskog, A. (2009). Functional water co-operation in the Jordan River Basin: Spillover or spillback for political security. In H. G. Brauch, U. O. Spring, J. Grin, C. Mesjasz, P. Kameri-Mbote, C. Behera . . . H. Krummenacher (Eds.), *Facing global environmental change: Environmental, human, energy, food, health and water security concepts. hexagon series on human and environmental security and peace*, vol. 4. Berlin, Heidelberg, New York, Hong Kong, London, Milan, Paris, Tokyo: Springer-Verlag, 2008, i.p.

Jägerskog, A., Swain, A., & Öjendal, J. (Eds.). (2014, October). *Water security, a four volume set of SAGE major works*. London: SAGE Publications.

Klare, Michael T. (2015, Winter–Spring). "Climate change blowback: The threats to energy security. *SAIS Review of International Affairs*, *35*(1), 61–72.

Krampe, F. (2016a). *Building sustainable peace: Understanding the linkages between social, political, and ecological processes in post-war countries*. PhD thesis, Uppsala University.

Krampe, F. (2016b). Empowering peace: Service provision and state legitimacy in Nepal's peace-building process. *Conflict, Security & Development, 16*(1), 53–73. http://doi.org/10.1080/14678802.2016.1136 138

Krampe, F. (2016c). Water for peace? Post-conflict water resource management in Kosovo. *Cooperation and Conflict.* http://doi.org/10.1177/0010836716652428

Krampe, F. (2017). Toward Sustainable Peace: A New Research Agenda for Post-Conflict Natural Resource Management. *Global Environmental Politics, 17*(4), 1–8. http://doi.org/10.1162/GLEP_a_00431

Krampe, F., & Swain, A. (2016). Human Development and Minority Empowerment. In O. P. Richmond, S. Pogodda, & J. Ramovic (Eds.), *The Palgrave Handbook of Disciplinary and Regional Approaches to Peace.* Basingstoke.

Lagi, M., Bertrand, K. Z., & Bar-Yam, Y. (2011). The Food Crises and Political Instability in North Africa and the Middle East. *SSRN Electronic Journal.* http://doi.org/10.2139/ssrn.1910031

Migdal, J. S. (2001). State in Society. Cambridge: Cambridge University Press.

Mobjörk, M., Gustafsson, M.-T., Sonnsjö, H., van Baalen, S., Dellmuth, L. M., & Bremberg, N. (2016). *Climate-Related Security Risks.* Solna: Stockholm International Peace Research Institute.

Sadoff, C. W., Borgomeo, E., & de Waal, D. (2017). *Turbulent waters: Pursuing water security in fragile contexts.* World Bank, Washington, DC. © World Bank.

Ross, M L. (2001). Does Oil Hinder Democracy? *World Politics, 53,* 325–361.

Starr, J. R. (1991). Water Wars. *Foreign Policy, 82,* 17–36.

Sternberg, T. (2012). Chinese drought, bread and the Arab Spring. *Applied Geography, 34,* 519–524. http://doi.org/10.1016/j.apgeog.2012.02.004

Sternberg, T. (n.d.). Chinese Drought, Wheat, and the Egyptian Uprising: How a Localized Hazard Became Globalized. In *The Arab Spring and Climate Change.* climateandsecurity.files.wordpress.com.

Stockholm International Peace Research Institute (SIPRI). (1974). *Oil and security.* Stockholm: Almqvist & Wiksell.

Stoett, P., Daszak, P., Romanelli, C., Machalaba, C., Behringer, R., Chalk, F., et al. (2016). Avoiding catastrophes: Seeking synergies among the public health, environmental protection, and human security sectors. *The Lancet Global Health, 4*(10), e680 – e681. http://doi.org/10.1016/S2214-109X(16)30173-5

Swain, A., & Jägerskog, A. (2016). *Emerging security threats in the Middle East: The impact of climate change and globalization.* Lanham, MD: Rowman and Littlefield Publishers.

Swain, A. (2012). *Understanding emerging security challenges: Threats and opportunities,* London: Routledge.

Swain, A., Swain, R. B., Themnér, A., & Krampe, F. (2011). *Climate change and the risk of violent conflicts in Southern Africa.* Global Crisis Solutions.

Teng, P., & Oliveros, J. (2015). Challenges and Responses to Asian Food Security. *Cosmos, 11*(01), 3–20.

Tetreault, M. A. (2008). The political economy of middle Eastern oil. In J. Schwedler & D. J. Gerner (Eds.), *Understanding the contemporary middle East* (3rd ed., pp. 255–279). Boulder, CO: Lynne Rienner Publishers.

Thébaud, B., & Batterbury, S. (2001). Sahel pastoralists: Opportunism, struggle, conflict and negotiation. A case study from eastern Niger. *Global Environmental Change, 11*(1), 69–78. http://doi.org/10.1016/S0959-3780(00)00046-7

Toman, M., & Jemelkova, B. (2003). Energy and Economic Development: An assessment of the State of Knowledge. *The Energy Journal, 24*(4), 93–112.

Transboundary Freshwater Dispute Database (TFDD). (n.d.). Data and Datasets. Retrieved November 13, 2020, from https://transboundarywaters.science.oregonstate.edu/content/data-and-datasets

Uexkull, von, N., Croicu, M., Fjelde, H., & Buhaug, H. (2016). Civil conflict sensitivity to growing-season drought. *Proceedings of the National Academy of Sciences, 113*(44), 12391–12396. http://doi.org/10.1073/pnas.1607542113

United Nations Development Programme (UNDP). (1994). *Human development report 1994.* Oxford: Oxford University Press.

United Nations General Assembly. (2012). *The Future We Want,* Rio+20 United Nations Conference on Sustainable Development.

United Nations Security Council (UNSC). (2017). *Report of the Secretary-General on the situation in the Lake Chad Basin region*

United Nations Sustainable Development Goals. (2015). Goal 2: Zero Hunger. Retrieved November 13, 2020, from www.un.org/sustainabledevelopment/hunger/

van Baalen, S., & Mobjörk, M. (2017). Climate Change and Violent Conflict in East Africa: Integrating Qualitative and Quantitative Research to Probe the Mechanisms. *International Studies Review*. http://doi.org/10.1093/isr/vix043

Wallensteen, P., & Swain, A. (1997). Environment, Conflict and Cooperation. In D. Brune, D. Chapman, M. Gwynne, & J. Pacyna (Eds.), *The Global Environment. Science, Technology and Management* (Vol. 2, pp. 691–704). Weinheim: VCH Verlagsgemeinschaft mbH.

Wheeler, T., & Braun, von, J. (2013). Climate Change Impacts on Global Food Security. *Science, 341*(6145), 508–513. http://doi.org/10.1126/science.1239402

Wirkus, L., & Boege, V. (2006). Transboundary water management on Africa's international rivers and lakes: Current state and experiences. In *Transboundary Water Management in Africa*. ds80-237-152-15. dedicated.hosteurope.de.

World Bank. (2013). *Energy-the facts*. Washington, DC: World Bank.

World Health Organization. (2019, May 21). More people have access to electricity than ever before, but world is falling short of sustainable energy goals. Retrieved November 13, 2020, from www.who.int/news/item/21-05-2019-more-people-have-access-to-electricity-than-ever-before-but-world-is-falling-short-of-sustainable-energy-goals

Youngs, R. (2008). *Energy: A reinforced obstacle to democracy*. CEPS Working Document No. 299.

Zeitoun, M. (2006). *Power and water in the Middle East: The hidden politics of the Palestinian-Israeli water conflict*. London: IB Tauris.

Zeitoun, M., & Mirumachi, N. (2008). Transboundary water interaction I: Reconsidering conflict and cooperation. *International Environmental Agreements, 8*(4), 297–316

Zeitoun, M., & Warner, J. F. (2006). Hydro-hegemony: A framework for analysis of trans-boundary water conflicts. *Water Policy, 8*(5), 435–460.

22

THE ENVIRONMENTAL SECURITY DEBATE IN NEPAL

A perspective from the South

Bishnu Raj Upreti and Evgenia Nizkorodov

> *Now you are diluting the core security concerns by introducing the environment in security debate. It is meaningless. It will confuse military and security officials and policy- and decision-makers; divert national security priority; and ultimately weaken national security. It is just an intellectual exercise for people like you. We have to focus on hardcore security as our national priority, as it is threatened by decade long civil war and external interests.*
>
> — *response from a General of the Nepal Army after a presentation on environmental security at the National Security Council*

Historically, discussions of security have focused on military threats to nations (war, crime, terror) and did not account for the role of environment in national and human well-being. The Brundtland Convention (1987) marked the first entry of "environmental security" into international debates by linking environmental degradation directly with political and military threats (Trombetta, 2009; see also Dalby, Chapter 20). Since then, discourse surrounding the role of the environment in human security has steadily increased and has helped to catalyze a number of international movements such as the formation of the Intergovernmental Panel on Climate Change, the Kyoto Protocol (1997), and the Paris COP21 Agreement (2015).

The goal of environmental security is to decrease the vulnerability of human and ecological systems by mitigating anthropogenic and natural threats (Upreti, 2013a). For instance, natural disasters such as droughts, earthquakes, or landslides can have devastating impacts on the livelihoods of communities and can disrupt public management of resources (i.e., water treatment and solid waste management). Failure to consider the linkages between the environment, conflict, and human security can increase instability within and across political borders.[1] Empirical research suggests that ineffective natural resource management can lead to or prolong conflict (Homer-Dixon, 2010; Matthew, Halle, & Switzer, 2002; Mathew & Upreti, 2005; Upreti, 2001, 2002; 2010a; see also Le Billon, Chapter 4; Unruh, Chapter 5; Asthana, Chapter 6; Lujala et al., Chapter 10), which, in turn, may decrease socioeconomic well-being of individuals, degrade the environment, and increase overall vulnerability of human systems (see Berdal & Malone, 2000; Carius, 2006; Dalby, 2002; Khanal, 2006; Matthew & Upreti, 2009; Upreti, 2004c, 2013a). Ineffective governance of environmental resources can also create a cyclical process of environmental and community stress: degradation of natural resources can exacerbate

DOI: 10.4324/9781315107592-26

scarcity in the lives of people, particularly low-income individuals, and can lead to coping behaviors that further degrade and pollute the environment (Dalby, 2002). The securitization of a state ultimately entails ensuring the safety of communities from environmental, ecological, and climatic stresses (Gleditsch, 2000; Homer-Dixon, 1991; Upreti, 2013a; 2010a, 2004a, 2004c); the effective management of resources and ecosystems (Buckles, 1999; Collier & Hoeffler, 2004; Hurni & Wiesmann, 2011); and the careful consideration of the linkages between food, health, water, climate, energy, and military security (Upreti, 2013a).

Other countries such as the United States have already incorporated environmental security into the nation's security debate and the national security agenda[2] (Floyd, 2008; see also Floyd, Chapter 19). Yet, discussions of security in the South – and in Nepal – often focus solely on issues related to the military and national defense (Upreti, 2013a; Upreti, Bhattarai, & Wagle, 2013). While research on environmental security concerns in Nepal has been increasing since the beginning of the twenty-first century[3] and has sensitized some policy-makers and the general public to the role of environmental security, the large majority of political decision-makers believe that the link between the environment and the security is forced (Upreti et al., 2013). In other words, government agencies and key policy-makers believe agencies should remain siloed and operate under their own jurisdictions. Thus, the discussion of security is still limited to a small circle of people, primarily military personnel and government officials.

A breakthrough in the environmental security debate occurred in 2016. After a number of efforts to generate national debate on environmental security, defense policymakers updated the National Security Policy in 2016 to include safeguarding "Nepali peoples, Nepal's borders, land, water, economy, natural and cultural heritage, and environment" as a Fundamental Objective (Ministry of Defence, 2016, p. 16). The National Security Policy also includes conservation of natural resources and minimizing disaster-induced risks as a strategic objective and outlines a number of measures related to human security, land rights issues, pollution, and environmental governance. Unfortunately, the efforts are still siloed: development policy-makers have not yet integrated environmental security concerns into their national policies and strategies.

This chapter, therefore, highlights the importance of incorporating environmental security discourse into Nepal's National Security Policy and into decision-making. The chapter begins with the current environmental and security challenges of the country and highlights the key drivers of insecurity. Next, we present four case studies to illustrate the complex linkages between human and environmental systems: the Nepal Civil War, natural disasters, pollution and waste management, and the Indian blockade. The chapter concludes with policy recommendations and avenues for future research.

The broader environmental security context in Nepal

Understanding the security context in Nepal requires unpacking the interrelated broader forces that are stressing both human and ecological systems in the country. Currently, the country is experiencing (1) rapid demographic changes and the expansion of unsustainable economic activities; (2) climate change impacts such as droughts, flooding, earthquakes, and glacier melts; (3) governance challenges; and (4) high levels of socioeconomic inequality.

Demographic pressure: population growth and shifts in consumer preferences

One of the major threats toward resources and the environment is demographic pressure. Over the last 30 years, the demographic composition of Nepal has shifted (NPC, 2017a). The population of the country has nearly tripled in 50 years, rising from 10 million in 1960 to 28.6 million in 2019 (World Bank, 2020). While the population has rapidly expanded, the resource base has not changed. The population growth has exerted pressure on and competition for the available resources, leading to exploitation and rapid environmental degradation. The supply of nonrenewable resources in the country is depleting at an unsustainable rate. The Terai region is particularly stressed: while the region occupies only 23% of the total land area, it holds roughly 50.3% of the county's population (Subedi, Simkhada, & Teijlingen, 2016).

Demographic pressure is acute in urban spaces due to internal displacement and migration. While only has 20.1% of the population resides in urban areas (World Bank, 2020), Nepal is one of the fastest urbanizing countries in the world. The rapid rate of urbanization creates an additional strain on and health, education, water, and waste disposal systems. Ineffective and inconsistent policy as well as a lack of housing infrastructure has resulted in large-scale unplanned urban development, with many migrants settling into informal settlements. These settlements pose a high risk to well-being, as many lack proper sanitation systems, safe drinking water, adequate housing, and are located on lands vulnerable to extreme weather events such as flash floods (Deshar, 2013; see also Nizkorodov & Wagle, Chapter 11). For example, due to the rapid unplanned growth, the slums of Kathmandu are one of the most earthquake-vulnerable regions of the world (Muzzini & Aparicio, 2013). Poor waste management and poor regulation within the slums have led to the contamination of the Bagmati and Bishmnumati River. The disposal of waste along the riverbanks, along with rapid groundwater depletion, is causing "irreparable damage" to the fragile ecosystem surrounding the river (Muzzini & Aparicio, 2013, p. 76)

Another demographic stressor to the environment is changing consumer preferences. Consumerism has rapidly increased in Nepal – and all over the world – over the last two decades, leading to further degradation of resources and systems. The rising consumption of processed foods and the accumulation and use of nonessential goods have increased solid waste production and pollution, exacerbating the already stressed solid waste management system in the country. The changes in consumer preferences have also led to an increased rate of resource extraction and land-use changes, thus increasing unequal access to resources within the country (Upreti et al., 2015). Ultimately, the exploitation of available natural and environmental resources such as water, forests, lands, ecosystems services to meet the rising consumer demands of the population has created insecurity in the region (Upreti et al., 2013).

Climate change impacts

Despite emitting only 0.025% of global greenhouse emissions (MoPE, 2004, cited in Upreti et al., 2013), Nepal is ranked as the fourth most vulnerable country to climate change (Eckstein, Hutfil, & Winges, 2019). The country lacks the resources, infrastructure, and governance mechanism to adapt to changing climate conditions (Lamsal, Kumar, Atreya, & Pant, 2017). Nepal also lacks comprehensive climatological and hydrological data, making it difficult to predict and mitigate climate-related risks.

Climate change is a pressing concern for biodiversity and broader ecosystem functions within the country (Lamsal et al., 2017; Upreti et al., 2015). Nepal has a highly varied topography and contains 118 ecosystems, 75 vegetation types, and 35 forest types. While occupying only 0.1% of the global map, Nepal contains 3.2% of the world's flora and 1.1% of its fauna. (MoFSC 2010, cited in MoPE, 2017). Modeling of future climate change scenarios suggests that the lower and mid-hill forest areas will be vulnerable to climate change impacts and can threaten conservation efforts of species. While the degree of impact on biodiversity in Nepal is currently unknown, it is predicted that globally at least 7.9% of species will become extinct from climate change (Urban, 2015).

Climate change will also directly affect human well-being by impacting water quality and quantity, food production, the frequency and magnitude of natural disasters, and energy security (MoPE, 2017; Upreti et al., 2013). Already, climate-related effects are underway: annually, more than one million people in Mid- and Far West Nepal are directly impacted by climate-induced disasters such as drought, landslides, and floods (Upreti et al., 2013). Between 1971 and 2010, climate-related disasters accounted for 25% of deaths and have resulted in an economic loss of $5.34 billion (roughly 76% of economic losses in the country) (MoPE, 2017).

A striking example of climate-related risks is the shifting precipitation patterns in the Himalayas. The Southern Himalayas is considered to be one of the most vulnerable regions in the globe to climate-related hazards such as drought, flooding, and heat stress (Lamsal et al., 2017). The climate variability in the Himalayas may be higher than that in any other place around the globe (Chaulagain, 2006), with temperatures increasing roughly 0.03 to 0.05°C per year (Practical Action, 2009, cited in Lamsal et al., 2017). This variability can pose a great risk to downstream communities: earlier glacial melt can result in Glacial Lake Outburst Floods (GLOFs) or tsunami-like floods of water that are caused by large portions of glaciers breaking off and crashing into nearby lakes. Over the last three decades, Nepal has already experienced 26 GLOFs, 11 of which have had transboundary impacts (ICIMOD & UNDP, 2020). One of the most devastating GLOFs occurred in 1985 when Langmoche valley was flooded within a 30–90 minutes of the initial glacial lake burst (Vuichard & Zimmerman, 1987). The GLOF destroyed forest space, cultivable land, infrastructure, and homes. As a result, the community lost its subsistence base and remains under threat from landslides and further erosion to this day (Bajracharya & Mool, 2009).

Governance challenges

The third challenge to environmental security is weak governance. Robust environmental governance – or the transparent and effective monitoring and regulation of resources and conservation initiatives, political stability, and investment in environmental quality – has been linked to positive environmental outcomes (Amano et al., 2018; Wingqvist, Drakenberg, Slunge, Sjöstedt, & Ekbom, 2012) and adaptation capacity to climate change effects (Dodman & Satterthwaite, 2008). Conversely, ineffective governance has been linked to biodiversity loss (Smith, Muir, Walpole, Balmford, & Leader-Williams, 2003), deforestation (Umemiya, Rametsteiner, & Kraxner, 2010), and a decreased willingness to invest in environmental protection (Harring, 2012).

Corruption is a key contributor to the rapid degradation of the environment in Nepal (Upreti et al., 2015). Transparency International (2019), an organization which ranks countries from least to most corrupt, ranks Nepal 113th out of 180 countries. While Nepal has a comprehensive legal anticorruption framework in place, regulation and enforcement of it are weak (Business Anti-Corruption Portal, 2019). Government agencies and officials have been accused of political interference, red-tapism, favoritism, extremely poor performance in service delivery, and abuse of state resources and power. This corruption has high economic, social, and environmental costs. The illicit capital flows from Nepal, as well as the corruption within the public and judicial sector, have slowed down poverty reduction efforts and have created unequal access to resources such as electricity and water (UNDP, 2014). Corruption provides opportunities for overexploitation of resources, pollution of air and water ways, reductions of biodiversity, and underprovision of vital services that are essential to human well-being (UNODC, 2015; Upreti et al., 2015).

Political instability also poses a critical challenge for biodiversity and ecosystem well-being in Nepal. Between 1991 and 2003, the country underwent a dozen different government structures (Do & Iyer, 2010). Political instability disrupts the provision of critical supplies and services and leads to inefficient management of environmental resources. For example, the political instability during the Civil War (1996–2006) and the recovery period provided an opportunity for poachers and smugglers to violate environmental rules and regulations, laws, and international conventions (Khanal, 2006). Illegal trading of expensive medical herbs and poaching of rhinoceros, elephants, tigers, black bears, and musk deer and other species were rampant during the violent conflict and led to a broader reduction of biodiversity and the degradation of natural habitats (Khanal, 2006; Upreti, 2009).

Resource scarcity, inequality, and environmental stress

It is important to note that the broader conditions that exacerbate environmental insecurity – demographic pressure, climate change effects, and governance challenges – are interrelated and feedback on each other. Governance challenges lie at the root of human and environmental insecurity: inadequate resources, low political will, and siloed decision-making increase Nepal's vulnerability to demographic, climate-related, and environmental stressors. These factors are also disproportionally impacting low-income and marginalized populations. Women, for example, are particularly vulnerable to climate variability and natural disasters (MoPE, 2017). Women have limited opportunities to participate in decision-making and have low access to education, economic markets, and capital. Economically, women are constrained to informal work, childcare, or the agricultural sector. As climate change will decrease agricultural productivity crops such as rice in many parts of Nepal, the livelihoods of women may be severely impacted.

Nepal's political system has historically excluded low-income populations and ethnic minorities from decision-making and development initiatives (Upreti, 2010c). Yet, Nepal faces conditions of acute scarcity. The UNDP (2018) ranks Nepal 147th of 189 countries in terms of human development. Roughly, 25.2% of the population lives below the national poverty line (UNDP, 2014, cited in MoPE, 2017). Poor governance of environmental resources creates a cyclic process of rising vulnerability and inequality (ADB, 2004; see also Beevers, Chapter 14). For instance, when resource degradation and deforestation in Nepal are not sustainably managed, it is more challenging for low-income populations to meet basic resource needs (Upreti, 2013a). As inequality and social stratification increase, poor, marginalized, and discriminated groups may pursue illegal activities as coping strategies. This heightened competition for resources can increase the risk of conflict in the region. Food, water, and land in Nepal, thus, are a perennial source of tension. Ultimately, until governance mechanisms are able to address rampant poverty, unequal distribution of land and other natural resources, and poor environmental management, human and environmental systems in the country will face high insecurity.

Environmental insecurity in Nepal: four case studies

This section builds on the discussion of environmental insecurity conditions by presenting four case studies that illustrate the complex and intertwined linkages between human and ecosystem vulnerabilities. These case studies draw from practitioner and academic literature as well as Dr. Upreti's extensive fieldwork in Nepal.

The environmental security debate in Nepal

Civil war (1996–2006)

The Maoist People's War began in 1996 when members of the Community Party of Nepal-Maoist (CPN-Maoist or CPN-M) attacked a policy post in Rolpa district (Do & Iyer, 2010). The source of conflict is multifaceted (Upreti, 2010c). Widespread poverty; caste, ethnic, and gender discrimination; high corruption; and roughly 238 years of a top-down centralist political and social system led the CPN-Maoist to take up arms to seize political power back from the monarchy (Baral & Heinen, 2005; Upreti, 2010c). While the Maoists primarily targeted government buildings and public agencies, the rebels also seized land in rural areas to gain access to food, shelter, labor for community projects, military training grounds, and revenue for warfare materials (Murphy, Oli, & Gorzula, 2005). Initial efforts to combat insurgency were led by the Nepalese police. However, the assassination of King Birendra and eight members of the Royal family by Crown Prince Dependra led to a more aggressive stance toward the Maoists: the successor, King Gyanendra, dramatically escalated the conflict between the two groups by mobilizing the Royal Nepal Army (Do & Iyer, 2010). In 2006, a Comprehensive Peace Agreement – which stipulated the formal participation of the CPN-Maoist party in the government the abolishment of the monarchy – was signed between the Maoist and the main political parties (Do & Iyer, 2010).

The civil war had drastic economic and social impacts (Baral & Heinen, 2005). It is estimated that 17,886 people were killed, 1,530 people disappeared, 3,142 were abducted, 8,035 were disabled, and 79,571 individuals were forcibly displaced (MoPR, 2013, cited in NIPS, 2013). The war also resulted in the destruction of 17,484 homes, 2,149 schools, 2,072 local and district-level government buildings, 130 municipalities and district development committees, and 101 suspension bridges (MoPR, 2013, cited in NIPS, 2013). The Ministry of Forest and Soil Conservation estimates that the total value of the damaged property from warfare was roughly 354.5 million Nepalese Rupees[4]. Low-income communities were particularly stressed during the conflict, as funds were diverted from development and social support toward security expenditure (Baral & Heinen, 2005). The country also experienced food shortages after farming communities fled Maoist-controlled conflict zones.

The civil war also resulted in high environmental damage (Gleditsch, 2000). Conflict can impact the environment in three primary ways. The first is through "environmental warfare," or the deliberate destruction of the natural environment to weaken or destroy the enemy by using herbicides, chemical bombs or chemical agents, forest fires, purposive salinization of arable land of freshwater reservoirs, or damaging dams and other structures (Floyd, 2008; see also Closmann, Chapter 8). This strategy is not new; the military has historically played a detrimental role in natural environment during the time of war. Conflict can also accelerate environmental degradation through the extraction of resources by the government or insurgent groups (Westing, 1989; UNEP, 2009; see also Lujala et al., Chapter 10). Finally, the large-scale displacement of individuals within the country or across international borders can place an additional strain on resources and vulnerable ecosystems (Nizkorodov & Wagle, Chapter 11). Ultimately, these ecosystem disruptions can reduce biodiversity, pollute water sources, lead to deforestation, and leave a toxic legacy of landmines and weapons in the soil (Rutherford & Ober, Chapter 9). All three mechanisms of environmental degradation were present in Nepal's civil war.

For several decades prior to the conflict, Nepal was at the forefront of conservation. In 1973, His Majesty's Government of Nepal established the Department of National Parks and Wildlife Conservation (NDPWC) and Protected Area Legislation to oversee 16 protected areas and six National Parks (Murphy et al., 2005). These protected spaces amount to almost 24,000 square kilometers or roughly 18.33% of the country's total area (Baral & Heinen, 2005). Protected forest spaces were managed through community-based conservation (CBC) programs such as Forest User Groups (FUGs)[5] and were patrolled by armed forces (Murphy et al., 2005).

During the conflict, both parties incorporated the destruction of protected spaces and natural resource extraction as military tactics. Government security forces captured or waged war in more than 50 community forests across 16 districts (Khanal, 2006). To target insurgents hiding in the forest, the government security forces launched a series of aerial attacks and ignited forests, disrupting FUGs and decreasing the overall biodiversity of the forest spaces.[6] Similarly, Maoists rebels killed forest conservation leaders, bombed NDPWC offices, and targeted NDPWC staff to gain control of protected areas (Baral & Heinen, 2005). The rebels destroyed 47 physical structures and pushed out the Royal Nepalese Army, creating pockets for shelter and training. In 2001, a turning point in the conflict, protected areas saw a 70% reduction in government guard posts. Thus, the royal government was not able to implement its conservation rules in Maoist-controlled areas. It is estimated that the CPN-M attacks resulted in 20.195 million rupees worth of damage (NDPWC, 2007, cited in Upreti 2014).

Forest spaces were further degraded by the contradicting environmental policies and practices from the two competing political regimes. During the conflict, the government diverted 35,608 hectares of community forest across 38 districts to the army and declared many of them as "military training areas" (Khanal, 2006). Moreover, because the government suspected that timber traders might have been willingly or forcefully paying donations to CPN-M, local and regional administrators also imposed a ban on CBC timber trading in more than 22 districts and seized the resources from the local communities.

The CPN-M pursued similar strategies. Through guerrilla tactics and strikes to urban areas, the rebels were able to gain control of roughly 40%–75% of Nepal (Murphy et al., 2005). In 2002, the CPN-M declared its Common Minimum Policy and Program as the ruling regime of the country (Upreti, 2010c). The Maoists also issued a "Forestry Directive" and an "autonomous forest policy" that gave the rebels ownership of forest spaces and allowed them to sell forest products and wild animals to financially sustain the civil war. The rebels imposed a prohibition order in many forests to minimize the risk of information about Maoist activities reaching the Royal forces. To sustain and expand their insurgency efforts, CPN-M collected and sold expensive medical herbs[7] and extorted 70% of revenue generated by FUGs through a "war tax" (*Yuddha kar*)[8] (Upreti et al., 2005).

The actions of both the Maoist and the Royal government ultimately resulted in the delegimitization and reduced efficiency of FUGs in monitoring and protecting vulnerable ecosystems (Upreti, 2010a; Baral & Heinen, 2005). Poaching in protected areas increased, significantly reducing biodiversity and ecosystem function of forest spaces.

The decade-long warfare also led to the displacement of populations within Nepal and across international borders. Government aid to the 500,000 to 1.2 million displaced individuals was limited (Pradhan, 2005), resulting in high environmental and socioeconomic impacts of displacement. Between 1996 and 2002, the government provided a daily compensation and resettlement fund equivalent to $1.30 for victims of the conflict, a sum that was insufficient in providing shelter, food, and clean water to families. Moreover, despite the fact that the Royal Nepalese Army was responsible for a higher rate of destruction and casualties (Do & Iyer, 2010), aid was only offered to individuals who were displaced by the Maoists rather than national security forces (Refugees International, 2004). As a result, most displaced individuals were forced to fend for themselves by settling informally in rural and urban spaces and extracting natural resources illegally. As seen in the next case study, the rapid rise in population, especially in urban areas, strained waste systems and increased pollution of water sources.

The effects of the civil war on the environment have been documented by examining the decline of vulnerable species (see Upreti, 2009) and conservation efforts within the country (see Baral & Heinen, 2005; Murphy et al., 2005). One of the most significant effects of the conflict was the disruption of community forestry users groups. Many FUGs became inactive or were dissolved after government or insurgent troops took ownership of protected land; CBC bank accounts were suspended or frozen (Khanal, 2006); and community groups were forced to pay a dual tax to the government and CPN-M forces on both timber and nontimber forest products (Upreti, 2010a). It is estimated that 40 billion rupees were lost annually due to the mismanagement of nontimber products (Nepal National Weekly, 2005, cited in Upreti, 2006). The reduction in the monitoring of protected spaces by CBCs and the NDPWC and conflicting environmental regulation issues by CPN-M and government officials provided an opportunity for increased poaching and smuggling of herbs, animals, and environmental resources. Both military groups also impacted biodiversity by directly extracting resources from vulnerable spaces and burning or cutting down large swaths of forest spaces.

This case illustrates how conflict can disrupt environmental governance structures and can have a lasting impact on the institutional capacity of the state. The "one-state-two-regimes" political structure provided an easy excuse for inaction, ignorance, or even justification of former wrong-doing (e.g., failing to control corruption in the forestry sector) (Khanal, 2006; Upreti, 2010b; Upreti et al., 2005). Following the warfare, the country experienced a decade of political transition and instability. As a result, current institutions and governance structures are insufficient in addressing emerging environmental threats (Upreti, 2013b). Inter-party conflicts, political instability, corruption, and undue influence be ruling elites, the rule of autocratic royal regime have exacerbated environmental threats to human systems, as well as the rate of environmental degradation within the country.

Natural disasters – earthquakes and flooding

Nepal's abrupt topography and climate make it prone to natural disasters such as earthquakes, landslides, floods, glacial lake outbursts, and forest fires. The country is still recovering from the decade-long Civil War. The lasting challenges of the conflict – high poverty rates, political instability, corruption, violence, and poor provision of resources – increase the threats to well-being from natural disasters.

Nepal is situated in a high seismic zone area. As a result, earthquakes are a major environmental security concern for the country. For example, on April 25, 2015, the country was decimated by a 7.8 magnitude earthquake (the epicenter was the Barpak area of Gorkha district, 80 km west of Kathmandu). The earthquake was followed by 300 aftershocks, all of a magnitude greater than 4.0. Another earthquake of 7.3 magnitude quickly followed on May 12, 2015. The total economic damage and losses from the earthquakes equated to 706.5 billion NPR (approximately US $7.06 billion) or roughly one-third of Nepal's GDP in 2013–2014 (NPC, 2015). The earthquakes resulted in landslides,[9] mudslides, contamination of water sources, energy insecurity due to damaged hydropower projects, damage to agricultural lands, and destruction of road infrastructure. According to the Post Disaster Need Assessment Report, 8,790 people lost their lives, 22,300 were injured, and more than half a million houses collapsed or were damaged (NPC, 2015). It is estimated that roughly 8 million people, or almost one-third of the population from 31 of 75 districts, were affected by the destruction. Fourteen out of 31 districts were declared as "crisis-hit," and another 17 districts were partially affected. Rural areas with poor and vulnerable people were the most severely affected due to a weak emergency communication system, structurally unsound shelters, and the disruption of critical services such as health, education, and water and sanitation. It is estimated that the 2015 disasters pushed at least 700,000 Nepalis (2.5%–3.5% of the population) below the poverty line. Further, it has created space for corruption and malpractices, or what is called "disaster capitalism" in Nepal (see Matthew & Upreti, 2018).

Another key concern to well-being is large-scale flooding. Nepal annually experiences a monsoon season between June and September, receiving 70%–80% of all rain in this four-month time span (Dewan, 2015). Climate change has increased the severity of these monsoons and accelerated the retreat of glaciers. As a result, since the 1970s, the scale, intensity, and duration of floods have increased in Nepal, damaging infrastructure, increasing the risk of disease, and severely disrupting the economy (Dewan, 2015). In the past 10 years, Nepal has experienced three devastating floods:

- 2008: Large-scale flooding occurred in the Koshi River in Southeastern Nepal of Sunsari and Saptari districts, resulting in the displacement of 26,733 people from Sunsari district and 22,751 people in Saptari districts (OCHA, 2008).
- 2017: Incessant rainfall from August 11th to the 14th caused widespread flooding across 35 of 77 districts of Nepal (NPC, 2017b). Heavy landslides and flash floods inundated about 80% of the land in the southern flat plain of the Terai region, resulting in the death of 134 people, the destruction of 190,000 houses, and the displacement of 461,000 people (UN, 2017). It is estimated that and around 1.7 million people were severely affected, with communities facing shortages of food, water, and shelter. The economic damage of the flood is equivalent to $584.7 million (NPC, 2017b). The most flood-affected sectors were the social sector (housing, health, and education), the productive sector (agriculture, livestock, and irrigation), and infrastructure (transportation, water and sanitation, and energy). The monsoon flooding and landslides were among the most severe natural disasters that many of the affected districts have ever experienced.
- 2018: Flooding of Hanamute River from heavy rains washed away infrastructure and the livelihood base of hundreds of thousands of people of Bhaktapur district. The Bhaktapur District Administration Office estimated that the flooding, landslides, and inundation have led to property damage of RS 119.35 million (equivalent to $1.73 million) in the district (Samiti, 2018a).

Over the last decade, the government has developed a number of strategies to mitigate flood risk, including public outreach campaigns to disseminate knowledge on disaster preparedness, the installation of early warning communication systems, and the development of post-flood rehabilitation programs (Dewan, 2015). While these measures have decreased the number of casualties, economic losses are increasing due to the severity of the natural disasters and poorly managed urban development. For example, the high casualties of the 2017 flood have been attributed to i) Indian officials failing to open the flood gates in Koshi Barrage, Gandaki Barrage, and Laxmipur Barrage at the time of the flood crisis and ii) the construction of 1,355-km-long road parallel to the Nepal–India border (Gill & Paswan, 2017). Similarly, the high property damage of the 2018 flood is the result of construction of houses on the riverbank that obstructed the natural flow of water. Hydrologists have also expressed concern that the rise in sand and gravel extraction for commercial purposes has altered sediment deposits and increased riverbank erosion, further exacerbating future flooding risks.

Poor waste management and rising pollution

Nepal faces a number of pollution challenges. Contamination of land, water, and air is high due to poor management of solid, medical, and industrial waste. Additionally, the migration from rural to urban areas has strained service provisions (i.e., health, water, and waste management) and has increased air, noise, water, and land pollution in urban spaces. These negative impacts are disproportionately impacting poor and marginalized people, especially those residing in slum areas.

Poor Waste Management: Waste management in Nepal has been a challenge for decades. In the early 1990s, the responsibility of waste management transitioned from local oversight to the central government. Political instability during the Civil War led to the underdevelopment of infrastructure for the collection, safe disposal, and monitoring of solid waste (NESS, 1996, cited in Pokhrel & Viraraghavan, 2005). The present-day government still lacks the institutional experience and the political will to safely manage waste disposal (Khatoon, 2020). As a result, solid waste is predominantly disposed by illegally dumping hazardous materials in open sites or through poorly monitored incineration at waste disposal sites (Khatoon, 2020; Pokhrel & Viraraghavan, 2005). Out of 58 municipalities, 48 (82.75%) have used rivers as their dumping sites and 7 have dumped waste on public and forest land (Sah, 2008). Waste is not sorted; organic materials are mixed with medical or industrial waste, resulting in a high risk of air pollution from the toxic ash or the leaching of pollutants into the soil and water systems. Members of informal labor markets (women and children) or residents of informal settlements are particularly at risk of exposure to contamination.

Water Contamination: Nepal's overall level of water security is ranked 43rd out of the 48 Asian and Pacific countries (ADB, 2016). In 2015, only 27% of the population had access to safely managed water systems, with 61% having access to only basic water systems (WHO/UNICEF JMP, 2019). Similarly, only 46% of the population had access to basic sanitation systems. As a result of low access to potable water, the prevalence of water-borne diseases in Nepal is high. Poor sanitation is responsible for 70% of childhood illnesses (NEWAH, 2007, cited in Sedhain, 2014).

Water infrastructure in Nepal is underdeveloped and unevenly distributed (Budhathoki, 2019). In urban spaces, water access is unreliable, with people often waiting days for water access. In rural areas, the major sources of water in Nepal are tube wells, dug wells, municipality-provided water, natural springs, rivers, and *dhunge dhara* (tap made of stone placed where the natural spring flows). However, most of these sources of water are not safe for drinking. Bathing, religious activities, and dumping waste along riverbanks and in rivers have contaminated the natural sources of water in the country. Earthquakes and floods also decrease water quality by damaging water systems. Climate change is expected to further increase the prevalence of water-borne diseases (Bhandari, Gurung, Dhimal, & Bhusal, 2013).

Along with climate change effects and population pressure, institutional challenges hinder the provision of potable water (MoUD, 2014). While the country implemented a Sanitation and Hygiene Master Plan in 2011, the national water regulations are weak and broad and thus lack the ability to effectively safeguard consumers' right to water and health. Moreover, despite roughly three-quarters of the population residing in rural areas, provision of water to rural systems has been largely ignored in favor of large-scale water provision projects. Unfortunately, coordination between local agencies and sectors is low, and local government bodies lack the financial and technical resources to address water provision and treatment at a community level. Finally, technicians – especially those in rural areas – lack the training to address water contamination threats.

The technical and institutional shortcomings in addressing water quality can be seen in the rising rates of arsenic contamination among the population. Arsenic is a significant source of soil and groundwater contamination in many developing countries, including Nepal. Studies suggest that concentrations of arsenic in water sources have increased substantially over the last few decades (Shrestha, 2012; Adamsen & Pokharel, 2002). The Terai region, which supports almost 48% of the population of the country, is facing high levels of arsenic contamination. Groundwater is the primary source of drinking water for almost 66% of households (CBS, 2004, cited in Pokhrel, Bhandari, & Viraraghavan, 2009). Due to detrimental health impacts,[10] the World Health Organization recommends limiting arsenic to less than 10 ppb in drinking water (WHO, 2001, cited in Pokhrel et al., 2009). More than 31% of wells in Terai were contaminated with a concentration between 10 and 50 ppb, and 8% of wells had concentrations above 50 ppb (Shrestha, 2012). It is estimated that roughly 3.5 million people in the region have been exposed to arsenic levels between 10 and 50 ppb (Pokhrel et al., 2009), with low-income individuals facing the highest risk of contamination. While the government has recognized the severity of the issue, only 20,000 out of 200,000 wells have been tested (Shrestha, 2012).

Air pollution: According to the Environmental Performance Index (2020), Nepal's air quality is the worst in the world. Rapid urbanization is the primary driving factor of rising outdoor air pollution (Saud & Paudel, 2018). As public transportation is largely underdeveloped, the number of private vehicles increased by 32 times between 2000 and 2015. The inexorable smokes from vehicles, factories, and waste products paint a bleak picture in major cities like Biratnagar, Birjunj, and Kathmandu. Particulate matter (PM2.5 and PM10) in cities is two times higher than the World Health Organization's recommended value (Saud & Paudel, 2018). The exposure to particulate matter has resulted in respiratory illnesses, allergies, and chronic diseases (i.e., lung cancer, stroke, and pulmonary disease) in the country. The Nepal Academy of Science and Technology estimates that 35,000 people lose their lives every year due to air pollution (Samiti, 2018b) and that air pollution in the future will be the cause of 24,000 deaths annually (WHO, 2017).

Another prominent concern is the reliance on dirty energy sources such as biomass fuel usage for indoor use. Roughly 2.7% (8,700 deaths/year) of Nepal's national burden of disease can be attributed to indoor air pollution (WHO, 2009). It is estimated that 77%–84% of households in Nepal rely on biomass fuel (Devakumar et al., 2014; Sharma, 2018), which impairs lung function and exacerbates respiratory diseases. Children and women are at the greatest risk of exposure and illness. Over a 24-hour time span, children are exposed to a particulate mass level of 168 micrograms/m^3, a value that is more than seven times higher than the World Health Organization's recommended maximum (Devakumar et al., 2014).

The government has attempted to address outdoor and indoor pollution by establishing a National Indoor Air Quality Standard (2009) and by promoting improved cookstove stops. However, monitoring of air quality is limited (Saud & Paudel, 2018; Singh, Tuladhar, Bajracharya, & Pillarisetti, 2012). The UN Population Division (2018) predicts that, at a rate of 2.0% of urbanization per year, Nepal will be the second fastest urbanizing country in the world. Thus, failure to regulate and monitor air quality can create a significant environmental burden of disease (Saud & Paudel, 2018).

Noise pollution: Along with air pollution, rapid urbanization has also increased noise pollution in urban areas. In Banepa, for example, a municipal city lying in the east of Kathmandu valley which covers 5.56 square kilometers, there were 3,295 vehicles registered in 2006 (Murthy et al., 2007). The average traffic and environmental noise from vehicles and industrial projects exceeded the maximum acceptable noise pollution values set by other countries. Noise pollution is a critical environmental insecurity concern in the urban areas of Nepal (Murthy et al.,

2007), as noise pollution is a hazard to health and quality of life. Chronic exposure to noise pollution can result in severe headaches, sleep deprivation, and a loss of concentration. Despite these adverse effects, the country currently lacks noise pollution regulations.

Indian Blockade (September 2015 to March 2016)

The Indian Blockade – a manmade humanitarian crisis – occurred only 6 months after two devastating earthquakes struck Nepal in April and May 2015. On September 20, 2015, Nepal promulgated a new constitution that was endorsed by more than 90% out of the 597 Constituent Assembly Members (Pathak, 2015). The constitution promoted a federal republic political system with a three-tier government structure: 7 center government provinces, 4 metropolises, and 481 rural municipalities. Those that opposed the new constitution were from the Madhes region, arguing that the rules on citizenship and marriage[11] reduce political autonomy and prevent them from participation in upper levels of government (Human Rights Watch, 2015). They demanded that the constitution revise the state boundaries so that the Tharu and Madhesi communities in Nepal become separate states. However, due to concerns of loyalty of the Madhes region to India, government officials did not incorporate these demands into the new constitution.

The day after the new constitution was enacted, Madhesi protesters obstructed four out of the 17 transit points between India and Nepal (Pokharel, 2015). In response to the rising agitation, the Indian government abruptly stopped the supply of all food, medicine, and petroleum at all 17 transit points. Nepalese officials termed the trade disruption as an "unofficial trade blockade" by India, arguing that the country has a vested interest in keeping Nepal dependent on its neighboring country. While Indian officials publicly provided support for the constitution and denied India's role in disrupting trade, the blockade lasted over six months.

The blockade created an unprecedented economic and humanitarian crisis in Nepal. As a landlocked country, Nepal is entirely dependent on India for supplies. In fact, trade between the two countries accounts for more than 60% of Nepal's foreign trade (Budhathoki & Gelband, 2016). In the months following the blockade, more than three million children under the age of five were at risk of death or disease due to the acute shortage of fuel, food, medicines, and vaccines (BBC News, 2015). Hospitals across the country were running short of life-saving drugs, with supplies in intensive care units running out within one week of the blockade. The crippling shortage of cooking gas (LPG) put extreme pressure on forest resources, as individuals across the country began illegally logging forests to procure firewood. These shortages exacerbated environmental and human insecurity. The exploitation of natural resources of the Chure area[12] resulted in severe deforestation, large-scale soil erosion, and salinization, ultimately disrupting agricultural production in Terai and increasing food insecurity in the region during the blockade and its aftermath. The lack of supplies also led to a rise of illegal smuggling and black market activity (Pokharel, 2015), promoting the further degradation of forest spaces and the exploitation of low-income individuals who could barely afford the inflated prices of black market goods.

The case highlights how environmental vulnerabilities can be compounded by transboundary conflicts and governance mechanisms. Nepal was still in the process of recovering from the 2015 earthquakes. Landslides, flooding, and road damage have blocked off transit points between China and Nepal, limiting opportunities to receive emergency supplies from other sources. Moreover, at the time of the blockade, many communities still lacked the proper infrastructure for education, health, and water provision. Government funding was diverted away from post-earthquake reconstruction to providing firewood to citizens. As a result, during the blockade, over 200,000 families were residing in temporary shelters and lacked the supplies to survive the harsher weather conditions in the winter (UNICEF, 2015).

Discussion and conclusion

This chapter examined four cases in Nepal to illustrate the interdependencies and feedbacks between human security, national security, and the environment. Climate change, demographic pressure, and governance mechanisms play a critical role in enabling or hindering environmental security. Security challenges are further compounded by the rising socioeconomic inequality, which stems from these broader mechanisms and hastens environmental degradation. In Nepal, large-scale socioeconomic inequality and high rates of corruption in the government over the span of decades were the primary leading causes of the civil war. The threat of conflict, combined with the poaching, deforestation, and smuggling during the war created conditions of economic and food insecurity and forced members of rural communities to flee across borders and to urban spaces. During and after the war, the rapid rise in urban density, the frequent turnover of political systems, and the one-country-two-regimes political model disrupted critical government services such as waste management, welfare, land use planning, and environmental governance, resulting in increased rates of pollution and high vulnerability to natural disasters (earthquakes, floods, etc.) as well as man-made crises such as the Indian blockade. Climate change is expected to further exacerbate food insecurity and increase the frequency and magnitude of natural disasters, resulting in further devastation of Nepali communities and in the displacement of climate refugees. Ultimately, failure to actively link traditional security concerns with environmental and human security considerations has created conditions that have left the people of Nepal vulnerable to crisis. Anthropogenic and natural stressors are deepening inequality and may stoke the flames of another civil war.

Due to the complex linkages between enabling and triggering conditions of security, achieving environmental security in Nepal will be difficult. Currently, there is a low political and economic incentive for policy-makers to respond to growing environmental challenges. Nepal also lacks the financial and institutional capacity to rapidly address all of the broader health, socioeconomic, and environmental challenges affecting the well-being of Nepalese communities. A regional solution also presents unique challenges: while climate change and the environment have been on agenda for the South Asian Association of Regional Cooperation since the 1980s, the forum has failed to achieve its environmental and economic objectives due to a lack of trust among member countries (Bhattacharjee, 2018).

The conditions within Nepal mirror issues faced by fragile states in South Asia and all over the world (see Kakakhel, 2012). Climate change will disproportionally impact countries that have low institutional capacity and resources and will create additional stresses that can increase tensions and conflict between communities. Governments and humanitarian organizations must strive to target vulnerable "hotspots" where populations will be disproportionally impacted by climate change and other anthropogenic stressors. Building resilience will require investing in education and skills – particularly for women – to diversify jobs and to improve standards of living (World Bank, 2019). More research is needed on not only the causes of environmental security in these vulnerable regions but also adaptable, scalable, and cost-effective strategies to mitigate and adapt to changing environmental conditions. Future work must increase monitoring of environmental conditions (levels of pollution, deforestation, biodiversity loss) as well as evaluate the effectiveness of current resource management and development programs. Finally, strengthening environmental security will also require a greater emphasis on collaboration and partnership at various scales. Garnering political at a regional scale will require greater dialogue between member countries on mutual benefits of international cooperation. At a national and a local scale, policy-makers, military personnel, community leaders, and scholars need to pro-actively engage to build a comprehensive dialogue surrounding security and to develop a clear implementation strategy to link environmental and human elements of security. This process requires reflecting on current and past strategies, adapting and amending legislation and policies, and sharing best practices for adaptation and resource management with vulnerable communities (Upreti, 2013a).

Notes

1 See Floyd and Matthew (2013), Floyd (2008), Dalby (2002), Levy (1995), Homer-Dixon (1994, 2010), Myers (1989, 1986), and Westing (1989).
2 For instance, to "enhance readiness" of the country to security risks, the US Department of Defense integrates "restoration, compliance, conservation, pollution prevention, safety, occupational health, explosives safety, fire and emergency services, pest management, environmental security technology, and international activities" into an "integral part" of the agency's daily activities (Landholm, 1998, p 13).
3 For example, Dr. Upreti's past research focused on the resource conflict-political conflict nexus and established the relationship between resource conflict with armed insurgency, by examining the land, water and forest conflict and their link with the UCPN-M insurgency and their effect on environmental insecurity (Upreti, 2001, 2002, 2004a, 2004b, 2004c, 2010a). He also examined the land based agrarian tension and its contribution to armed conflict and source of human insecurity (Shrestha & Upreti, 2011).
4 Equivalent to US $2.96 million.
5 FUGs are CBC groups that managed and restored forest spaces. Harvesting timber product is the primary source of revenue for these communities.
6 For example, the government security forces conducted massive aerial bombings in the community forest areas between Nawalparasi, Arghakhanchi, Palpa, and Tanahun. Consequently, the forest in these forests burned for weeks.
7 Approximately 166 types of medical herbs from the Nepalese mountains are used for medicinal purposes; these sales have an estimated value of 2.5 billion rupees per year (Upreti, 2006). The illegal harvesting and smuggling of herbs such as *Yarsagumba (Cordyceps sinensis), Chiraito (Swertia Chiraita), Jatamasi (Nardostachys grandiflora), Kutki (Picrorhiza scrophulariiflora), Bikhama (Aconitum palmatum), padamchal (Rheum emodi), Panchaunle (Galearis stracheyi), Sunpati (Rhododendron anthopogon), Sughandhawal (Valerina wallichii)* severely disrupted the industry during the Civil War.
8 The CPN-M imposed a 15%–65% tax on forest products in all districts of Rapti Zone, 35% in Sankhuwasasa district, 5% in Dolakha district, 15%–50% in Ramechhap district, 10% tax in timber trading in Far Western districts, 40% in Kailali district, 30% in Terathum, 20% in Banke, 40% in Bardiya district, and 10% in Ilam and Jhapa districts (Khanal, 2006).
9 The most serious example was the repetitive and frequent landslides on the Mugling-Narayanghat Road corridor (considered the lifeline of Nepal), which blocked transportation for several months and created food supply shortage.
10 Arsenic exposure can cause gastrointestinal, cardiovascular, neurological, dermal, respiratory, reproductive illnesses and can severely impact the development of children, even at low arsenic levels (Pokhrel et al. 2009). At concentrations of 60 ppb, arsenic is a lethal concentration for an adult (Adamsen & Pokharel, 2002).
11 While located in southern Nepal, the Madhes region ethnically, linguistically, and culturally aligns closer the Indian states of Uttar Pradesh and Bihar. Due to the fluidity of the border between the two regions, it is common for individuals residing in the Madhes region to marry Indians. Unfortunately, the process of acquiring citizenship takes 15 years; any children born prior the spouse gaining citizenship will hold a "second-class citizenships" (Human Rights Watch, 2015).
12 The Chure area runs between the hills and the Teria region from east to west of Nepal. It is considered to be a highly ecologically fragile area.

Works cited

Adamsen, K. R., & Pokharel, A. (2002). The Arsenic contamination of drinking water in Nepal. *Nepal Water for Health*. Retrieved September 23, 2019, from www.bvsde.ops-oms.org/bvsacd/arsenico/nepal.pdf

Asian Development Bank (ADB). (2016). *Asian water development outlook 2016. Strengthening water security in Asia and the Pacific*. Metro Manila, Philippines: Asian Development Bank.

Asian Development Bank (ADB). (2004). *Country environment analysis for Nepal*. Retrieved from www.adb.org/sites/default/files/institutional-document/32192/nep-sept-2004.pdf

Amano, T., Székely, T., Sandel, B., Nagy, S., Mundkur, T., Langendoen, T., . . . Sutherland, W. J. (2018). Successful conservation of global waterbird populations depends on effective governance. *Nature, 553*(7687), 199.

Asian Development Bank (ADB). (2013). *Solid waste management in Nepal: Current status and policy recommendations*. Manila: Asian Development Bank.

Baral, N., & Heinen, J. T. (2005). The Maoist People's War and conservation in Nepal. *Politics and the Life Science, 24*(1/2), 2–11.

Bajracharya, S. R., & Mool, P. (2009). Glaciers, glacial lakes and glacial lake outburst floods in the Mount Everest region, Nepal. *Annals of Glaciology, 50*(53), 81–86.

BBC News. (2015, December 12). Nepal blockade: Six ways it affects the country. *BBC News*. Retrieved November 19, 2018, from www.bbc.com/news/world-asia-35041366

Berdal, M., & Malone, D. (2000). *Greed and grievances: Economic agendas in civil wars*. Boulder: Lynne Rienner.

Bhandari, G. P., Gurung, S., Dhimal, M., & Bhusal, C. L. (2013). Climate change and occurrence of diarrheal diseases: Evolving facts from Nepal. *Journal of Nepal Health Research Council, 22*, 181–186.

Bhattacharjee, J. (2018). SAARC vs. BIMSTEC: The search for the ideal platform for regional cooperation. *ORF Issue Brief, 226*.

Buckles, D. (Ed.). (1999). *Cultivating peace: Conflict and collaboration in natural resource management*. Ottawa, ON, Canada: International Development Research Center.

Budhathoki, C. B. (2019). Water Supply, Sanitation and Hygiene Situation in Nepal: A Review. *Journal of Health Promotion, 7*, 65–76.

Budhathoki, S. S., & Gelband, H. (2016). Manmade earthquake: The hidden health effects of a blockade-induced fuel crisis in Nepal. *BMJ Global Health, 1*(2), e000116.

Business Anti-Corruption Portal. (2019). Nepal Corruption Report. Retrieved January 20, 2019, from www.business-anti-corruption.com/country-profiles/nepal/

Carius, A. (2006). Environmental cooperation as an instrument for crisis prevention and peacebuilding. Conditions for success. *Adelphi Report, 3*(07).

Chaulagain, N. P. (2006). *Impacts of climate change on water resources of Nepal: The Physical and socioeconomic dimensions* [MSc. Dissertation]. Germany: University of Flensburg.

Collier, P., & Hoeffler, A. (2004). Greed and grievance in civil war. *Oxford Economic Papers, 56*(4), 563–595.

Dalby, S. (2002). *Environmental security*. Minneapolis: Minnesota Press.

Deshar, B. D. (2013). Squatters problems along Bagmati Riverside in Nepal and its impact on environment and economy. *International Journal of Environmental Engineering and Management, 4*(1), 127–142.

Devakumar, D., Semple, S., Osrin, D., Yadav, S. K., Kurmi, O. P., Saville, N. M., . . Ayres, J. G. (2014). Biomass fuel use and the exposure of children to particulate air pollution in southern Nepal. *Environment International, 66*, 79–87.

Dewan, T. H. (2015). Societal impacts and vulnerability to floods in Bangladesh and Nepal. *Weather and Climate Extremes, 7*, 36–42. https://doi.org/10.1016/j.wace.2014.11.001

Do, Q., & Iyer, L. (2010). Geography, poverty, and conflict in Nepal. *Journal of Peace Research, 47*(6), 735–748. https://doi.org/10.1177/0022343310386175

Dodman, D., & Satterthwaite, D. (2008). Institutional capacity, climate change adaptation and the urban poor. *IDS Bulletin, 39*(4).

Eckstein, D., Hutfils, M., & Winges, M. (2019). *Global climate risk index 2019. Who suffers most from extreme weather events? Wather-related loss events in 2017 and 1998 to 2017*. Berlin, Germany: Germanwatch.

Environmental Performance Index. (2020). Nepal. Retrieved November 14, 2020, from https://epi.yale.edu/epi-country-report/NPL

Floyd, R., & Matthew, R. (Eds.). (2013). *Environmental security: Approaches and issues*. London and New York: Routledge.

Floyd, R. (2008). The environmental security debate and its significance for climate change. *The International Spectator, 43*(3), 51–65.

Gill, P., & Paswan, B. (2017, August 18). Floods devastate Nepal's southern plains. *The Diplomat.* Retrieved March 20, 2018, from https://thediplomat.com/2017/08/floods-devastate-nepals-southern-plains/

Gleditsch, N. P. (2000). Armed conflict and the environment. In P. F. Diehl & N. P. Gleditsch (Eds.), *Environmental conflict* (pp. 521–572). Oxford: Westview Press

Harring, N. (2012). Understanding the effects of corruption and political trust on willingness to make economic sacrifices for environmental protection in a cross-National Perspective. *Social Science Quarterly, 94*(3), 660–671.

Homer-Dixon, T. F. (2010). *Environment, scarcity, and violence.* Princeton, NJ: Princeton University Press.

Homer-Dixon, T. (1994). *Environment, scarcity, and violence.* Princeton, NJ, USA: Princeton University Press.

Homer-Dixon, T. (1991). On the threshold: Environmental changes as causes of acute conflict. *International Security, 16*(4), 76–116.

Human Rights Watch (2015). "Like we are not Nepali": Protest and policy crackdown in the Terai Region of Nepal. USA: Human Rights Watch.

Hurni, H., & Wiesmann, U. M. (2011). Global change research for sustainable development. In U. M. Weismann & H. Hurni (Eds.), *Research for sustainable development: Foundations, experiences, and perspectives.* Bern, Switzerland: National Centre of Competence in Research (NCCR) North-South, University of Bern.

International Centre for Integrated Mountain Development (ICIMOD) & United National Development Programme (UNDP). (2020). Inventory of glacial lakes and identification of potentially dangerous glacial lakes in the Koshi, Gandaki, and Karnali river basins of Nepal, the Tibet Autonomous Region of China, and India. Kathmandu, Nepal: ICIMOD and UNPD.

Kakakhel, S. (2012). Environmental Challenges in South Asia. *Institute of South Asian Studies Insights,* 189.

Khanal, D. R. (2006). *Sasastra dundama samudayik ban (Community forestry in armed conflict).* Kathmandu: Federation of Community Forestry Users of Nepal.

Khatoon, A. (2020). Waste management – A case study in Nepal. In S. K. Ghosh (Ed.), *Solid water policies and strategies: Issues, challenges, and case studies* (pp. 185–196). Springer.

Lamsal, P., Kumar, L., Atreya, K., Pant, K. P. (2017). Vulnerability and impacts of climate change on forest and freshwater wetland ecosystems in Nepal: A review. *Ambio, 46,* 915–930.

Landholm, M. (1998). *Defining environmental security: Implications for the U.S. Army.* Atlanta: Army Environmental Policy Institute.

Levy, M. (1995). Is the environment a national security issue?. *International Security, 20*(2), 35–62.

Matthew, R. A., Halle, M., & Switzer, J. (Eds.). (2002). *Conserving the peace: Resources, livelihoods and security* (pp. 1–27). Winnipeg, Canada: International Institute for Sustainable Development.

Matthew, R., & Upreti, B. R. (2018). Disaster capitalism in Nepal. *Peace Review, 30*(2), 176–183. https://doi.org/10.1080/10402659.2018.1458946

Matthew, R., & Upreti, B. R. (2009). Environmental change and human security in Nepal. In R. A. Matthew, J. Barnett, B. McDonald, & K. L. O'Brien (Eds.), *Global environmental change and human security* (pp. 137–154). Irvine: MIT Press.

Mathew, R., & Upreti, B. (2005). Nepal: Environmental stress, demographic changes and the Maoists. *Environmental Change and Security Programme Report, Issue 11.* Washington, DC: Woodrow Wilson International Centre for Scholars, Pp. 29–39.

Matthew, R., Halle, M,., & Switzer, J. (2001). *Conserving the peace: How Protecting the environment today can prevent conflict and disaster tomorrow.* IUCN/IISD Task Force on Environment & Security. Winnipeg, Canada: International Institute for Sustainable Development.

Ministry of Defence. (2016). *National Security Policy.* Kathmandu, Nepal: Government of Nepal

Ministry of Population and Environment (MoPE). (2017). *Vulnerability and risk assessment framework and indicators for National Adaptation Plan (NAP) formulation process in Nepal.* Katmandu, Nepal: Government of Nepal Ministry of Population and Environment.

Ministry of Urban Development (MoUD). (2014). *National water supply and sanitation sector policy 2014.* Government of Nepal. Retrieved from www.humanitarianresponse.info/sites/www.humanitarianresponse.info/files/documents/files/eng_wss_policy_2014_draft-1.pdf

Muzzini, E., & Aparicio, G. (2013). *Urban growth and spatial transition in Nepal. An initial assessment.* Washington, DC: The World Bank.

Murphy, M. L., Oli, K. P., & Gorzula, S. (2005). Conservation in conflict: The impact of the Maoist-Government conflict on conservation and biodiversity in Nepal. Winnipeg, Manitoba, Canada: International Institute for Sustainable Development.

Murthy, V. K., Majumder, A. K., Khanal, S. N., & Subedi, D. P. (2007). Assessment of traffic noise pollution in Banepa, a semi urban town of Nepal. *Kathmandu University Journal of Science, Engineering and Technology, 3*(2), 12–20.

Myers, N. (1989). Environment and security. *Foreign Policy, 74,* 23–41.

Myers, N. (1986). The environmental dimension to security issues. *The Environmentalist,* 251.

National Planning Commission (NPC). (2017a). *Demographic changes of Nepal: Trends and policy implications.* Kathmandu, Nepal: Government of Nepal National Planning Commission.

National Planning Commission (NPC). (2017b). *Post Flood Recovery Needs Assessment. Nepal Flood 2017.* Kathmandu, Nepal: Government

National Policy Commission (NPC). (2015). Post Disaster Need Assessment (PDNA) Report. Volume A: Key Findings. Kathmandu, Nepal: National Planning Commission

Nepal's Institute for Policy Studies (NIPS). (2013). Nepal's peace process: A brief overview. *Policy Paper, 8*(*1*), 1–24.

OCHA. (2008). *Koshi River floods in Sunsari and Saptari.* OCHA Situation Report, No. 7. Retrieved August 31, 2021, from https://reliefweb.int/sites/reliefweb.int/files/resources/6B22E1D1E48A5E59 852574B8005E89FC-Full_Report.pdf

Pathak, B. (2015). Impacts of India's transit warfare against Nepal. *World Journal of Social Science Research, 2*(2), 266–288.

Pokhrel, D., Bhandari, B. S., & Viraraghavan, T. (2009). Arsenic contamination of groundwater in the Terai region of Nepal: An overview of health concerns and treatment options. *Environment International, 35*(1), 157–161.

Pokhrel, D., & Viraraghavan, T. (2005). Municipal solid waste management in Nepal: Practices and challenges. *Waste Management, 25*(5), 555–562.

Pokharel, K. (2015, November 26). The two-month blockade of Nepal explained. *The Wall Street Journal.* Retrieved March 20, 2019, from https://blogs.wsj.com/indiarealtime/2015/11/26/the-two-month-blockade-of-nepal-explained/

Pradhan, S. (2005, July 12). Nepal: Refugee crisis builds up as civil war rages on. *Inter Press Service News Agency.* Retrieved February 15, 2019, from www.ipsnews.net/2005/07/nepal-refugee-crisis-builds-up-as-civil-war-rages-on/#more-16123

Refugees International. (2004, March 23). Forgotten people: The internally displaced people of Nepal. *Relief Web.* Retrieved February 16, 2019, from https://reliefweb.int/report/nepal/forgotten-people-internally-displaced-people-nepal

Sah, R. C. (2008). POPs and Hg in Nepal. Center for Public Health and Environmental Development (CEPHED). Retrieved from www.htap.org/meetings/2008/2008_04/Presentations/09-04-08/Nepal.pdf

Samiti, R. S. (2018a, July 17). Flood damage worth 119.3 million rupees in Bhaktapur. *The Himalayan Times.* Retrieved March 20, 2019, from https://thehimalayantimes.com/nepal/flood-damage-worth-119-3-million-rupees-in-bhaktapur/

Samiti, R. S. (2018b, March 10). Air pollution causes 35,000 deaths annually. *The Himalayan Times.* Retrieved September 26, 2019, from https://thehimalayantimes.com/nepal/air-pollution-causes-annual-death-toll-of-35000/

Saud, B., & Paudel, G. (2018). The threat of ambient air pollution in Kathmandu, Nepal. *Journal of Environmental and Public Health.* https://doi.org/10.1155/2018/1504591

Sedhain, P. (2014). Water sanitation, socioeconomic states, and prevalence of waterborne diseases: A cross-sectional study at Makwanpur District, Nepal. Master's thesis in Public Health.

Sharma, B. P. (2018). Household Fuel Transition and Determinants of Firewood Demand in Nepal. *Economic Journal of Development Issues,* 83–95.

Shrestha, L., & Upreti, B. R. (2011). Reflection on land-based relationship between agrarian tension, armed conflict and human insecurity in Nepal, In K. N. Pyakuryal & B. R. Upreti (Eds.). *Land, agriculture and agrarian transformation.* Kathmandu: COLARP.

Shrestha, R. (2012). Arsenic contamination of groundwater in Nepal: Good public health intention gone bad. *Inquiries Journal/Student Pulse, 4*(09). Retrieved from www.inquiriesjournal.com/a?id=701

Singh, A., Tuladhar, B., Bajracharya, K., & Pillarisetti, A. (2012). Assessment of effectiveness of improved cook stoves in reducing indoor air pollution and improving health in Nepal. *Energy for sustainable development, 16*(4), 406–414.

Smith, R. J., Muir, R. D., Walpole, M. J., Balmford, A., & Leader-Williams, N. (2003). Governance and the loss of biodiversity. *Nature, 426*(6962), 67.

Subedi, Y. P., Simkhada, P. P., & Teijlingen, E. V. (2016). Where Is Nepal in the Demographic Transition within the Wider Context of the Nutrition Transition?. *Open Journal of Social Sciences, 4*(05), 155–166.

Transparency International. (2019). Corruption Perception Index 2010. Retrieved November 14, 2020, from www.transparency.org/en/cpi

Trombetta, M. J. (2009). Environmental security and climate change: Analysing the discourse. *Cambridge Review of International Affairs, 21*(4), 585–602. https://doi.org/10.1080/09557570802452920

Umemiya, C., Rametsteiner, E., & Kraxner, F. (2010). Quantifying the impacts of the quality of governance on deforestation. *Environmental Science & Policy, 13*(8), 695–701.

United Nations. (2017). *Nepal: Flood 2017.* Retrieved January 15, 2019, from https://reliefweb.int/sites/reliefweb.int/files/resources/Nepal%20Flood%20Sitrep%2021%20August%202017.pdf

United Nations Department of Economic and Social Affairs/Population Division. (2018). *World Urbanization Prospects.* https://population.un.org/wup/Publications/Files/WUP2018-Report.pdf

United Nations Development Program (UNDP). (2018). Nepal. *Human development indices and indicators: 2018 statistical update.* Retrieved from http://hdr.undp.org/sites/all/themes/hdr_theme/country-notes/NPL.pdf

United Nations Development Program (UNDP). (2014). *A snapshot of illicit financial flows from eight developing countries: Results and issues for investigation,* United Nations Development Programme, New York, NY. Retrieved February 28, 2019, from www.undp.org/content/undp/en/home/librarypage/democratic-governance/anti-corruption/a-snapshot-of-illicit-financial-flows-from-eight-developing-coun.html

United Nations Environment Programme. (2009). *From conflict to peacebuilding. The role of natural resources and the environment.* Nairobi, Kenya: UNEP.

United Nations International Children's Emergency Fund (UNICEF). (2015). Nepal: Serious shortage of essential supplies threatens millions of children this winter. Retrieved March 25, 2019, from www.unicef.org/media/media_86394.html

United Nations Office on Drugs and Crime (UNODC). (2015). Corruption and the environment. Retrieved from www.anticorruptionday.org/documents/actagainstcorruption/print/materials2012/corr12_fs_ENVIRONMENT_en.pdf

Upreti, B. R., Butler, C., & Maharjan, K. (2015). *Climate insecurity and conflict in South Asia: Climate variability as a catalyst for social tension and insecurity.* New Delhi: Adroit Publishers.

Upreti, B. R. (2014). Armed Conflict in Nepal and its Impacts (in Nepali language). Kathmandu, Nepal: Nepal Centre for Contemporary Research (NCCR).

Upreti, B. R. (2013a). Environmental security: Concepts, issues and problems (Chapter 9). In B. R. Upreti, R. Bhattarai, & S. G. Wagle (Eds.), *Human security: Concepts, issues and challenges.* Kathmandu: Nepal Institute of Policy Studies and NCCR North-South. Pp. 211–250.

Upreti, B. R. (2013b). Environmental security and sustainable development (Chapter 12). In R. Floyd & R. Matthew (Eds.), *Environmental security: Approaches and issues* (pp. 220–233). London and New York: Routledge.

Upreti, B. R. (2012a). Security for peace and stability by 2030. In S. R. Sharma, B. R. Upreti, & K. Pyakuryal (Eds.), *Nepal 2030: A vision for peaceful and prosperous nation* (pp. 93–110). Kathmandu: South Asia Regional Coordination Office of the Swiss National Centre of Competence in Research (NCCR) North-South.

Upreti, B. R. (2012b). Water and food insecurity: Non-traditional security challenges for Nepal. In National Bureau of Asian Research (Ed.), *Non-traditional security challenges in Nepal.* NBR Special Report (36). Seattle and Washington, DC: The National Bureau of Asian Research, pp. 21–34.

Upreti, B. R. (2010a). *Political change and challenges of Nepal: Reflection on armed conflict, peace process and state building.* Volume 1 and Volume 2. Saarbrucken (Germany): Lambert Academic Publishing.

Upreti, B. R. (2010b). Issues to be addressed by the new security policy of Nepal' (Chapter 22) In H. Phuyal & M. Urscheler (Eds.), *The security sector legislation of the Federal Democratic Republic of Nepal: Commentaries.* Geneva Centre for the Democratic Control of Armed Forces, National peace Campaign and Pacific Law Associates. Geneva: Brambauer. Pp. 107–112

Upreti, B. R. (2010c). A decade of armed conflict and livelihood insecurity in Nepal. In B. R. Upreti & U. Muller-Boker (Eds.), *Livelihood insecurity and social conflict in Nepal.* South Asia Coordination Office. Kathmandu, Nepal: Heidel Press Pvt. Ltd.

Upreti, B. R. (2009). *Nepal from war to peace: Legacies of the past and hopes for future.* New Delhi: Adroit Publishers.

Upreti, B. R. (2006). *Nepal's armed conflict: Security implications for development and resource governance.* Kathmandu, Nepal: Swiss National Centre of Competence in Research (NCCR) North-South, South Asia Coordination Office.

Upreti, B. R. (2004a). Land conflict in Nepal: Peasants' struggle to change unequal agrarian social relations. *Journal of Community, Work and Family, 7*(3), 371–394.

Upreti, B. R. (2004b). Resource conflicts and their resolution practices in Nepal. *Mountain Research and Development Journal, 24*(1), 60–66.

Upreti, B. R. (2004c). *The price of neglect: From resource conflict to Maoist insurgency in the Himalayan Kingdom* (p. 446). Kathmandu: Bhrikuti Academic Publications.

Upreti, B. R. (2002). *Management of social and natural resource conflict in Nepal: Reality and alternatives.* Adroit Publishers.

Upreti, B. R. (2001). *Conflict management in natural resources: A study of land, water and forest conflict in Nepal.* [Published PhD Dissertation]. Wagenignen University.

Upreti, B. R., Bhattarai, R., & Wagle, G. S. (Eds.). (2013). *Human security in Nepal: Concepts, issues and challenges.* Kathmandu: Nepal Institute for Policy Studies (NIPS) and South Asia Regional Coordination Office of NCCR (North-South).

Upreti, B. R., Timsina, N. P., Upreti, U., Shivakoti, I. C., Adhikari, K. P., & Upreti, S. (2005). *Searching for new direction: Reorienting NARMSAP to work on the conflict situation in Nepal* (A report on conflict impact assessment of NARMSAP submitted to the Royal Danish Embassy, Kathmandu, Nepal). Kathmandu: Nepal Niti Sarokar (P.) Ltd.

Urban, M. C. (2015). Accelerating extinction risk from climate change. *Science, 348*(6234), 571–573.

Vuichard, D & Zimmermann, M. (1987). The 1985 catastrophic drainage of a moraine-dammed lake, Khumbu Himal, Nepal: Cause and consequences. *Mountain Research and Development, 7*(2), 91–110.

Westing, A. H. (1989). The Environmental Component of Comprehensive Security. *Security Dialogue, 20*(2), 129–134.

Wingqvist, G. Ö., Drakenberg, O., Slunge, D., Sjöstedt, M., & Ekbom, A. (2012). *The role of governance for improved environmental outcomes: Perspectives for developing countries and countries in transition.* Stockholm, Sweden: Swedish Environmental Protection Agency.

World Bank. (2020). *Nepal population data.* World Bank Open Data. Retrieved November 14, 2020, from https://data.worldbank.org/country/nepal

World Bank. (2019). *Building a climate-resilient South Asia.* Retrieved September 23, 2019, from www.worldbank.org/en/news/feature/2018/04/20/building-a-climate-resilient-south-asia

World Health Organization (WHO). (2017). *WHO country estimates of burden of disease from household air pollution for 2016.* Retrieved August 31, 2021, from http://www.who.int/airpollution/data/hap_bod_may2018_v0.xlsx?ua=1

World Health Organization (WHO). (2009). Nepal. *Country profiles on environmental burden of disease.* Retrieved from www.who.int/quantifying_ehimpacts/national/countryprofile/nepal.pdf?ua=1

World Health Organization/UNICEF Joint Monitoring Program (JMP). (2019). Joint Monitoring Program Global Database. Retrieved January 30, 2019, from https://washdata.org/data/household#!/

23
ENVIRONMENTAL PEACEBUILDING AT THE TIJUANA–SAN DIEGO BORDER

Kristen A. Goodrich and Kyle Haines

The Tijuana–San Diego border region illustrates many of the core challenges of binational environmental management, environmental security, and environmental peacebuilding. It does so in the shared social–ecological context of increasing scarcity of key resources, rapid population growth, and expanding economic integration. These trends are manifested in the rhythms of everyday life as well as in ecosystems, in the depletion of surface and groundwater, air and water pollution, exposure to hazardous waste, and widespread degradation of habitat that supports remaining biodiversity (Liverman, Varady, Chavez, & Roberto, 1999).

Straddling the busiest land port of entry in the world, Tijuana, Mexico (MX), and southern San Diego County in the United States (US) are one bioregion, or area characterized by shared watersheds, airsheds, and ocean currents, and populated by common species and biomes of native vegetation (McGinnis, Woolley, & Gamman, 1999; Pezzoli et al., 2014). Tijuana and San Diego constitute the largest pair of cities in the border region and are increasingly sharing vulnerabilities to global-scale ecological change. The cities do not, however, face these changes with equal resources for adaptation, given their widely unequal levels of preexisting social and natural vulnerability.

This vulnerability is important in the face of the widespread change still to come and drives our scholarship, teaching, and practical fieldwork in the US and MX. Approaching it through exclusive social and ecological categories, like trying to solve regional issues in only the US or MX, is both ethically and pragmatically flawed from our perspective. From the context of our work in the binational region, we argue that there are lessons to be learned from the difficult case the Tijuana–San Diego bioregion presents, in particular, (1) the imperative of addressing human security in the most vulnerable areas urgently and given two national governments and (2) the need to adapt approaches for resilient regional governance such as peacebuilding from the ground up through enhanced collaboration and a commitment to social justice.

The Tijuana River Watershed is an approximately 1,750-square mile binational area that includes a diverse and complex drainage system ranging from 6,000-foot pine forest-covered mountains to the tidal saltwater estuary at the mouth of the Tijuana River in the US (TRN-ERR, 2010). Despite intense pressure from urban development at the highly surveilled international border between two major metropolitan areas – San Diego (California, US) and Tijuana (Baja California, MX) – the Tijuana River Valley (TRV) in the US contains one of the largest

279

DOI: 10.4324/9781315107592-27

Figure 23.1 The Canyon-estuary System: Los Laureles Canyon (MX) and the Tijuana River National Estuarine Research Reserve (US).

and last remaining wetland habitats in southern California, the Tijuana River Estuary (Zedler & West, 2008; Goodrich, Boudreau, Crooks, Eguiarte, & Lorda, 2018).

This is in stark contrast to the highly urbanized Mexican side of the border and has major implications for the risks produced and the number of people affected by them. In the adjacent Los Laureles Canyon (LLC) (see Figure 23.1), the focal point of our shared work, residents grapple with flooding and erosion in dense, peri-urban conditions, and the absence of many basic municipal services like sanitation and infrastructure, including sewers and storm drainage. While in the US the TRV is subject to flooding, in contrast to the densely urbanized landscape of Tijuana, it has only some sparse rural housing and equestrian activities and is primarily natural habitat or in agricultural use (TRNERR, 2010). Viewed in separate national lenses, the social and environmental challenges that arise are problematically disconnected and, most importantly, solutions are frustratingly opaque.

The TRV is exposed to various contaminants conveyed by stormwater posing a threat to the US marine environment and its ecosystem services. Upstream, rapid and unplanned growth in LLC – a 4.6 square mile watershed sub-basin adjacent to the TRV – has manifested in urbanization occurring before public infrastructure was planned and built, resulting in an absence of paved roads leading to denuded hillsides and excessive sedimentation. Results from community-based collaborative research and flood modeling point to pluvial flash flooding (i.e., flooding caused directly by rainfall) threats, including debris blockages and barriers to mobility and evacuation (Goodrich et al., 2020).

Imagery from Google earth, boundaries from TRNERR and IMPLAN TJ

Significant investments have been made by federal, state, and local governments in the US to protect and manage the Tijuana River Estuary, and this is primarily carried out by the Tijuana River National Estuarine Research Reserve (TRNERR), a federal–state–NGO partnership. However, the lack of a shared national governance framework with associated regulations and resource bureaucracies to implement them has major implications for planning, practice, and implementation of solutions. While interpreting and assessing the regional effects of global climate change, sea-level rise, and projections of future availability of water and food, there is also a need to focus on the unequal vulnerability among and between these binational communities and impacts on the natural environment and implications for security. Given global trends, many of which will be experienced across this region, prospects for successful adaptation must consider issues of equity and power in the border context. In this chapter, we examine this binational bioregion and the deeply interconnected social and ecological goals of improving community capacities and environmental outcomes (Goodrich et al., 2018).

Centering our analysis on the challenges of shared ecosystems and divided political sovereignty, in what follows, we use the language of resilience and adaptive governance as framings for our pragmatic aim to build alliances of communities, local institutions, and universities. We examine our work as a peacebuilding approach – as Ide et al. (2021) define as *pathways by which the management of environmental issues is integrated in and can support conflict prevention, resolution and recovery* – that reveals the necessity for collaboration and shared social and ecological responsibility as components of any resilient binational adaptation to common ecological change.

In this chapter, we detail some of the issues in the canyon-estuary system and tease out some of the lessons produced by the engagement of these theoretical frameworks in day-to-day practice. Through this experience, we better understand the complex security problems in the border region and evaluate the prospects for environmental peacebuilding strategies in the presence of punctuated conflict (if not war). Pursuing such a project in both field-based and theoretical ways, we argue that strategies developed for environmental peacebuilding can be key tools for the strengthening of local capacity and targeting solutions to urgent needs.

We conclude by emphasizing the potential for community-based and interdisciplinary approaches to enhance social–ecological outcomes based on the ways that our respective organizations have attempted to put these aspirations into practice. Expanding upon these observations through the vocabulary of "adaptive governance" makes a practical case for strengthening local capacity to address key aspects of adaptive policy regimes and guard against instability or even hostility of higher levels of government that may result in advancing degradation and unequal risks. We also reflect upon our roles as practitioners – situated in boundary organizations that interface between the science and policy and transfer knowledge – that seek to implement strategies such as engaging at multiple scales of government, academia, and with community residents and across disciplines on diverse initiatives that focus on the social and ecological health of the binational canyon-estuary system interrupted by the westernmost edge of the US–MX border wall (Gustafsson & Lidskog, 2018).

Dimensions of peacebuilding and strategies for social–ecological resilience

For over a decade, we have worked, researched, and engaged with communities on both the MX and US sides of the shared Tijuana River Watershed. These experiences have resulted in applied research and practice, which, utilizing field-based methods and data collection, have informed our perspective on environmental peacebuilding. While it is uncommon in resource management to identify strategies of the "field" as aimed at building peace, this framework is useful for evaluating such efforts. We structure our assessment of the bottom-up strategies of building collective capacity in terms of dimensions of environmental peacebuilding: security, livelihoods and economy, and politics and social relations (Ide et al., 2021; see also Bruch et al., Chapter 2); this is because peace relies on environmental health and vice versa.

Although there is a rich history of efforts to protect the Tijuana Estuary, US perspectives tend to dominate the narrative. We instead shift our narrative and much of our practical work –in terms of both social capacity-building like education and training workshops and physical interventions to build community resources, reforest key areas and formalize public green space, and work with local government agencies to repair and redesign critical infrastructures like roads and canals – to the MX side of the canyon-estuary system. This approach has the practical advantage of preventing conservation catastrophe rather than reacting, for example, through expansion of infrastructure on the US side of the border, such as the large sediment basins built to intercept sediment and debris at the terminus of the canyon before it enters the estuary and eventually the ocean. These kinds of "end of pipe" solutions are expensive to maintain and do nothing to reduce the social risk borne by upstream communities. We limit our discussion in this chapter to the canyon-estuary system, yet acknowledge the interrelated implications for MX and US communities proximate to this area.

Progress is challenged in the border context, but as identified by adaptive governance scholarship, opportunities for a broader kind of conflict resolution can be realized through an expanded role for boundary-spanning organizations and local communities. The rest of this section builds upon Ide et al.'s (2021) three peacebuilding dimensions of security, livelihoods and economy, and politics and social relations as a framework for elaborating strategies that we deploy and that are unique to the Tijuana-San Diego context, the particular issues of the canyon-estuary social–ecological system, and our positionality:

1   Increase security through natural resource management
2   Amplify improved livelihoods alongside healthier environment
3   Identify failures and imagine governance alternatives

Increase security through natural resource management

Borders can be highly productive, in terms of both material exchange and movement of capital and cultural exchange between residents of each country. Where they open, they enable circulation from distant places to funnel through particular spaces, concentrating flows of people, material, and energy. However, when they close, they can disrupt relationships as played out in policies that separate children from their families and species from their wildlife corridors. Closed borders and hardened security infrastructure place transitory elements into more permanent relationships, like migrants seeking asylum or economic opportunity who become stalled and out of necessity have integrated into the urban fabric of Mexican border cities.

These novelties provide both challenges and opportunities for building resilience and peace in the midst of conflict and inequality. Although not characterized by overt warfare, the border between Tijuana and San Diego is both a symbolic and physical site of conflict. Much of this conflict has to do with explosive population growth in the region over the past 50 years, in part, a product of Mexican border industrialization since the 1960s. Tijuana is a highly desirable location for migration from Latin American and Caribbean countries due to its economic opportunity related to the manufacturing and close proximity to the US. In 2010, the population of the Tijuana–San Diego border region was 4.8 million, making it the largest binational metropolitan area shared between the US and MX (Al-Delaimy, Larsen, & Pezzoli, 2014).

Environmental peacebuilding

In Tijuana, the discrepancy in income ratios relative to nearby markets that attract companies to invest in assembly plants, or *maquiladoras*, is a primary cause of the rapid economic and population growth of the region, especially since the signing of the North American Free Trade Agreement (NAFTA) in 1994 (Kopinak & Soriano Miras, 2013). Nowhere in the region is this more apparent than in LLC, where rapid urban development occurred to meet the housing demands associated with the employment opportunity not matched by increases in actual housing. Despite ongoing economic integration across the border, however, the flow of people and ideas between countries is increasingly inhibited by the security apparatus at the border, a trend intensified in recent years of wall-building during the Trump presidential administration. As a consequence, the region's most essential resources are fragmented and the least-advantaged residents on both sides of the border bear the brunt of exposure and risk that this failure produces.

Although these issues may seem isolated to national governments and residents of cities on each side of the border, a problem-driven interdisciplinary focus underscores the connections between the drivers of social precarity and ecological outcomes and provides a compass for conflict avoidance. It is not apocalyptic to imagine a scenario of scarcity-driven conflict in this region in the not-so-distant future as it suffers from environmental exploitation such as deforestation, development, and pollution. Tensions related to ecological resources can, under unfavorable conditions, turn violent, but inclusive and sustainable management of natural resources, as pursued in this region by boundary-spanning organizations, can help avoid conflicts about or linked to these resources (Ide et al., 2021).

Given the lack of a single entity overseeing the political and governance assemblages at the border, "environmental peacemaking" and its goals of positive-sum cooperation become much more difficult to implement in practice. That these conflicts are highly militarized and nationally contentious only makes local and regional collaboration more essential to improved outcomes, even if treated as "non-defense-related security issues" (Ganster & Lorey, 2004, p. 220). Any idea of environmental security that will be meaningful to resilient outcomes in the binational region will have to also use this expanded idea of security.

Amplify improved livelihoods alongside a healthier environment

Insecurity manifests itself as disruptions to patterns of daily life, to which some are more vulnerable based on relative wealth and power. In turn, well-being (i.e., a sense of fate control and community capacity) and livelihoods (i.e., capabilities, tangible assets, and means of living) are threatened (Kofinas & Chapin, 2009). Furthermore, the entangled nature of social and ecological security has important implications for everyday life and economic stability in the binational bioregion. Despite a shared natural setting and close proximity that entices the massive flows of capital and material from around the world, residents of the two communities largely perceive themselves as culturally separate. At the same time, this feeling of distance is perforated by cross-border travel, family connections, and other social ties that bridge, penetrate, and circulate through the border.

Many times, in our experience on both sides of the border, the "developed" side continues to call for environmental preservation, often not seeing livelihood or social issues as linked to ecological ones. This creates a mismatch in expectations and urgencies and for us poses a critical question: Is it fair, or better yet *effective*, to focus on strategies that emphasize the ecological health and stability of the Estuary, places the vast majority of residents in the riskiest and most precarious conditions will never experience in person or benefit from on the MX side? To focus rhetorically on a narrow strategy of "environmental security" as protecting resources would be (and continues to be) useless without a connection to the real lived conditions of the affected communities themselves, emphasizing the human security gains of integrated conservation and urban renewal planning.

In the case of the canyon-estuary system, this means foregrounding the effects of erosion on housing and roads (rather than on estuarine habitat), solid waste in intensifying flood hazards (rather than becoming marine debris), and contamination on human health (rather than water quality). Emphasis on these social risks does not erase the ecological goals of such a program, rather, it prioritizes gains in human welfare to ethically engage the most precarious and to pragmatically build local capacity to carry out these and more complex, long-term goals. Efforts directed in Tijuana for the protection of an estuary in the US have failed to generate social adoption of much-needed interventions such as soil stabilization, reforestation, and waste management to address the issue at the source. Instead, when hinged to more immediate needs related to livelihoods, interventions with a more direct and immediate impact are more tractable to community and responsible bureaucracies. Addressing concerns related to the protection of the estuary without a cross-border vision and attention to the urgencies created by the social vulnerability is ultimately unproductive.

Identify failures and imagine governance alternatives

The border is both a symbolic line between cultures and also, more prosaically, a physical object that must be planned around by resource managers and politicians alike. The border wall, the physical manifestation of the line drawn between the US and MX in 1848, interrupts social–ecological systems and cements a profound mismatch between political communities. Spatial mismatches between ecosystem boundaries and political borders are mirrored by temporal mismatches in the time horizons of political administrations and rob the region of prospects for resilience.

There has been a policy response to the environmental problems that have plagued this border region, for example, after NAFTA, including the creation of binational entities, the Border Environmental Cooperation Commission (BECC) and the Commission for Environmental Protection (CEC). Ongoing binational coordination through BECC, CEC, the Good Neighbor Environmental Board (GNEB), North American Development Bank (NADB), revisions to the 1944 Colorado Water Compact, and the Border 2012 and Border 2020 initiatives tie institutions from the US and MX to each other and, in a limited but important sense, to local organizations.

That these initiatives remain underfunded and without mandates to build local binational institutions is obvious to those who work at the border; few who live at the border know they exist or experience direct benefit in everyday life. Thus, although there are many government agencies involved in discussions through different treaties and agreements, their practical efficacy to affect ecological outcomes on both sides of the border has been severely limited, evidenced by the many persistent cross-border environmental problems and the radical inequality which exists between relatively affluent and healthy communities in the US and physically proximate communities in MX.

Disconnected at institutional, societal, and linguistic levels, communities' cohabitating shared ecosystems along the border do not have clear and responsive political representation to address their problems *together*. The lack of coordination between the two national communities means that meaningful sites of cross-border collective decision-making, a prerequisite for successful long-term resource management, are largely absent. This governance gap is key to understanding shared issues and potential solutions. Threatened by drought, fires, pollution, and

Environmental peacebuilding

intensifying rainfall (California's Fourth Climate Assessment, 2018), Tijuana and San Diego largely approach their shared risks in isolation despite their common setting.

Adaptive governance from the bottom-up

Ide et al. (2021) and many others claim that persistent challenges like these can be starting points for border-spanning cooperation even where there is a history of conflict and relations are mistrustful. For them, this is because environmental problems are potentially less politically sensitive (relative to immigration or security, for instance) and involve collaboration over longer time horizons. And if, as Barquet (2015) posits, "environmental cooperation can be an efficient instrument for improving relations between states" (p. 14) and "biodiversity is a "low politics" issue that can serve as a starting point for negotiations and peace within regional cooperation" (p. 14) perhaps the Tijuana–San Diego case has the resource (its estuary) at hand to improve collaboration and trust-building that underlies an adaptive governance regime. Our experience supports this: working together on environmental issues can be a gateway to boundary spanning, building trust, and adapting.

This approach is not simply aimed at creating and reinforcing relationships between cross-border organizations and resource bureaucracies but also, we argue here, at building and densifying networks between social groups, universities, and political institutions. These components, working together, are also key to the successful development of novel kinds of science-policy interactions crucial to urgent adaptation to global ecological change, such as "adaptive governance" regimes, a form of policy experimentation and social learning proposed by Folke, Hahn, Olsson, and Norberg (2005) and other scholars.

Adaptive governance is a kind of application of resilience theory that can be useful for expanding the institutional and ecological terms of analysis. At the border, a focus on social capacity and political continuity is troubling for the development of adaptive governance and the comanagement of shared resources for many of the same reasons that we stressed in the section(s) on security and livelihood earlier, with an extra problem in the border region. Adaptive governance regimes have particular prerequisites for success: continuity of political leaders, policy as an experiment, social learning (Armitage et al., 2009). The scarcity of such kinds of institutional, academic, and community collaboration manifests in an extreme form at the border, where the disconnect between institutions, academics, and national cultures produce mixed social and ecological consequences (Kopinak, 2003; Carruthers, 2008; NEJAC, 1999).

This is especially true where, in places like Tijuana and San Diego, borders also represent a division between the "developed" and "developing" worlds. That these worlds exist for San Diego and Tijuana within a few miles only accentuates the threat of increasing separation of communities along the border in times of shared ecological change and uneven vulnerability. This is an important challenge for constructing a more inclusive and regionally meaningful form of environmental security discourse that does not automatically reserve governance to national resource bureaucracies.

One strategy for bridging this divide is to begin in a subsidiary way, building governance capacity from the ground-up and engaging fleeting – and at times, unstable – political institutions with a strengthened core of residents, nongovernmental organizations, and researchers. Doing so is pragmatic as well as in line with guiding principles of fairness and regional community. While ideas like adaptive governance, "common pool resource institutions" (Ostrom, 1990), and "comanagement" (Carlsson & Berkes, 2005) often emphasize local and decentralized solutions, they often do so by assuming a common set of national institutions which can be appealed to and from which power can potentially be devolved. They do not argue that such top-down mechanisms are sufficient to tackle local social–ecological challenges (much of the literature focuses on the benefits of such local governance), but many of these decentralization and autonomy policies are seated in national policy and particularly challenged where key resources for management are transboundary.

From our perspective at the border, we hope national institutions are not *necessary*, but we know from experience that such institutions are not *sufficient* conditions for resilient and healthy outcomes. Even in times of great promise in domestic environmental policy, these gains are not shared across the binational region we work in, and given the unpredictability of times of instability, diminished capacity, and uncertainty, they cannot be a primary strategy for urgent needs for the practical reason that action cannot wait.

This need to act in conditions of uncertainty is one of the drivers in the development of policy experimentation regimes like adaptive governance. Although political challenges associated with security are often assumed to be national in nature, adaptive governance pragmatically localizes this analysis, emphasizing the key roles of researchers and bridging organizations in developing tailored management and effective governance of resources. The border not only complicates this move but also produces new opportunities for boundary-spanning efforts that more centrally involve lower-level actors. Given the seriousness of ecological challenges and fragility of conflicting domestic policies, this is both ethically and pragmatically urgent – the profound scale of social and economic inequality and exposure to environmental risks across the region, in particular, in Tijuana relative to San Diego but with many US localities similarly more vulnerable. The national level cannot, from this perspective, be the sole condition for success.

While the border region, thus, presents extreme challenges to adaptive governance identified by its scholars (e.g., lack of leadership for implementation of the complex problem of adaptive resource management, translating learning into practice, cost and delays associated with gathering information), we think it also represents a fruitful point of critical departure by invalidating by geographic context any purely state-centric idea of environmental security or peacebuilding (Allen & Gunderson, 2011; Armitage, Berkes, & Doubleday, 2010). Failures and mismatches identified, in the pragmatic view we share with adaptive governance theorists, clearly present a list of priorities for further learning and improvement, not dead ends.

Peacebuilding prospects

If linking ecological governance to developing contexts is to be done well, it must be done in a reflexive and hybrid way, at the risk of continued irrelevance or profound gaps in credibility. As environmental challenges grow and prospects for binational collaboration seem distant, social capacity to resolve problems may actually be growing at local and regional levels. Engaging and cultivating this capacity require attention to how residents identify with their surroundings. Laird-Benner and Ingram (2011) found tremendous staying power of human relationships and commitment to place, most powerful to its actors in its context. They also found that face-to-face encounters and positive narratives, albeit increasingly difficult in the face of the growing infrastructure of borders, have favorable effects and can catalyze action.

Such efforts to create a binational political community will necessitate new forms of environmental scarcity–conflict avoidance, peacemaking, and the creation of robust forms of institutional collaboration toward sustained adaptation and resilience. This need for productive forms of peacemaking and empowerment feels particularly urgent at the border at this moment, as we acknowledge and seek a vital shared social and ecological destiny. Central to achieving this are organizations that can span boundaries and, in this setting, also a physical border. TRNERR

Environmental peacebuilding

is a science-based organization with research, education, and training programs that provide a platform for convening partners, leveraging resources, and collaborating. With this mission to protect the Estuary at the forefront, it acknowledges that to do so, issues must be addressed at the source, with a social–ecological lens, and through collaboration.

Likewise, the Center on Global Justice at the University of California San Diego (UCSD) has entered into long-term partnerships with four regional nonprofits to form a comanaged network of Community Stations within which students and researchers from UCSD codesign and implement programming with community leaders. These Community Stations are physical places and, in conjunction with UCSD's Cross-Border Lab, the Center's commitment extends to designing, financing, and building physical infrastructure to house programming and attend to the particular needs of the host communities. Coutilizing each other's infrastructures of engagement, TRNERR, the Center, and other partners work to identify opportunities for bottom-up approaches and community capacity-building toward an adaptive governance paradigm and achievement of improved social and ecological outcomes.

Our perspective and approach do not discard higher levels of organization as prospects for building regional resilience. Where and if opportunities arise, they should be acted on with urgency and commitment. Our experience demonstrates, however, that these changes will not be lasting or meaningful in the lived experience of residents without a primary and durable commitment to building local capacity, both in terms of understanding (e.g., education and scientific baselines) and in terms of collective agency to implement, monitor, and verify. Both of these capacities are identified as the key to the development of adaptive governance and comanagement regimes, which recommend the development of bridging actors and collaboration between sectors which cannot be accomplished in only San Diego or Tijuana.

Resilient futures in the binational region, we have argued, depend on densifying networks of local actors, regional institutions, and resource managers; expanding shared resources for understanding where we are and the changes we confront together; and committing to lasting relationships between researchers, managers, and local residents. These elements build redundancy into the system, making it more resilient to ecological and political shocks. In the terms of adaptive governance, this kind of work can be a key role for universities as bridging actors, cultivating long-term presence and relationships with local actors and curating the building out of new kinds of programmatic and physical infrastructure.

This commitment extends the reach and importance of research while building the capacity to use it to make the everyday life of the most vulnerable places more healthy, verdant, and secure. As for many within the university and national resource bureaucracies, this entails a change in polarity for many focused on environmental security, peacebuilding strategies, and the creation of innovative science-policy regimes like adaptive governance. We have argued, from the vantage point of our divided region, that this change must see across disciplinary boundaries and national borders and begin by creating long-term relationships with local actors to create bulwarks against national and international instability and, crucially, to enable the successful implementation of any such larger scale efforts once agreed upon.

Conclusion

We detailed here how peacebuilding at the US–MX border is distinctly challenged by cultural-linguistic disconnect, susceptibility to changing domestic discourse, lack of continuity of governance and institutional capacity, and the often-divergent emphases and approaches "for" environment and community. The entanglement of binational social, economic, and ecological systems requires working versions of theoretical models of connections between science and policy, themselves oriented around the particular social and ecological priorities of the region. To intervene in highly unequal settings like this requires collaboration and bottom-up approaches. We have taken peacebuilding as one example of these approaches, grounded in strategies that increase security through natural resource management, amplify improved livelihoods alongside healthier environment, and identify governance failures to imagine alternatives.

We cannot ask communities to continue to endure poverty, hazards, and other injustices and expect natural resources to sustain a state of perpetual vulnerability while waiting only for national governments to address manifestations of global change. Even if adequate international and national policies become realities, they would arrive finally at regional and local scale at communities without the basic tools and trusting relationships to manage adaptation and minimize suffering.

Being secure in this environment of ecological change and political disconnection will thus rely even more on the hard, quotidian work of boundary spanning organizations and policy entrepreneurs – the connective tissue between communities, universities, and local government – which can harden into enduring bridges over time. These bridges can then serve as conduits for resources crossing the border, a role almost impossible for state and national institutions limited in their jurisdictional scope, and communicate with residents directly to set the priorities of research and intervention. This is opposed to top-down efforts of treaty organizations or bureaucratic roundtables that rarely dialogue with the residents of particular communities in meaningful ways or involve a wider binational public in debate and decision-making.

There is no simple cure. Tijuana and San Diego, however, share a common natural inheritance and deep history of human residence preceding recent migration despite being separated by human barriers. Adopting a peacemaking perspective demands that this be done with the express intent of creating stewardship and a sense of shared community, beginning at local levels and ascending to higher scales when necessary to meet the scale of the challenges represented. In our view, this particularity is both a cause of many problems and also an opportunity to profit from cross-border visions which see ecological commonalities as central binding forces rather than focusing on cultural, linguistic, and economic disparities. It is only from the base of such a regional community with an understanding of their shared context, awareness of the alternatives to state-centered governance, and focus on building local capacity that peacebuilding and binational adaptive governance will be more than simply an aspiration.

Works cited

Al-Delaimy, W. K., Larsen, C. W., & Pezzoli, K. (2014). Differences in health symptoms among residents living near illegal dump sites in Los Laureles canyon, Tijuana, Mexico: A cross sectional Survey. *International Journal of Environmental Research and Public Health*, *11*, 9532–9552.

Allen, C., & Gunderson, L. (2011). Pathology and failure in the design and implementation of adaptive management. *Journal of Environmental Management*, *92*, 1379–1384.

Armitage, D., Berkes, F., & Doubleday, N. (Eds.). (2010). *Adaptive co-management: Collaboration, learning, and multi-level governance*. Vancouver: UBC Press.

Armitage, D., Plummer, R., Berkes, F., Arthur, R., Charles, A., Davidson-Hunt, I . . . Wollenberg, E. (2009). Adaptive co-management for social-ecological complexity. *Frontiers in Ecology and Environment*, *7*(2), 95–102.

Barquet, K. (2015). Yes to peace? Environmental peacemaking and transboundary conservation in Central America. *Geoforum*, *63*, 14–24.

California's Fourth Climate Change Assessment: San Diego Summary Report (Publication number: SUM-CCCA4–2018–009). (2018). San Diego, CA: University of California, San Diego.

Carlsson, L., & Berkes, F. (2005). Co-management: Concepts and methodological implications. *Journal of Environmental Management*, *75*, 65–76.

Carruthers, D. (2008). The globalization of environmental justice: Lessons from the US-Mexico Border. *Society and Natural Resources*, *21*(7), 556–568.

Folke, C., Hahn, T., Olsson, P., & Norberg, J. (2005). Adaptive governance of social-ecological systems. *Annual Review of Environmental Resources*, *30*, 441–473.

Ganster, P., & Lorey, D. (2004). *Borders and border politics in a globalizing world*. New York: SR Books.

Goodrich, K. A., Boudreau, D., Crooks, J., Eguiarte, A., & Lorda, J. (2018). The role of social capitals in climate change adaptation in a binational community. In P. R. Lachapelle & D. E. Albrecht (Eds.). *Addressing climate change at the community level in the United States*. London: Routledge.

Goodrich, K. A., Basolo, V., Feldman, D. L., Matthew, R. A., Schubert, J. E., Luke, A., Eguiarte, A., . . . Sanders, B. F. (2020). Addressing pluvial flash flooding through community-based collaborative research in Tijuana, Mexico. *Water*, *12*(5), 1257.

Gustafsson, K. M., & Lidskog, R. (2018). Boundary organizations and environmental governance: Performance, institutional design, and conceptual development. *Climate Risk Management*, *19*, 1–11.

Ide, T., Bruch, C., Carius, A., Conca, K., Dabelko, G. D., Matthew, R., & Weinthal, E. (2021). The past and future(s) of environmental peacebuilding. *International Affairs*, *97*(1), 1–16.

Kofinas, G. P., & Chapin, F. S. III. Sustaining livelihoods and human well-being during social – ecological change. (2009). In C. Folke, G. P. Kofinas & F. S. Chapin III (Eds.), *Principles of ecosystem stewardship* (pp. 55–75). New York: Springer.

Kopinak, K. (2003). Maquiladora industrialization of the Baja California peninsula: The coexistence of thick and thin globalization with economic regionalism. *International Journal of Urban and Regional Research*, *27*(2), 319–336.

Kopinak, K., & Soriano Miras, R. M. (2013). Types of migration enabled by maquiladoras in Baja California, Mexico: The importance of commuting. *Journal of Borderlands Studies*, *28*(1), 75–91.

Laird-Benner, W. G., & Ingram, H. (2011, January–February). Sonoran Desert Network Weavers: Surprising Environmental Successes on the U.S.-Mexico Border. *Environment Magazine*, 1–13.

Liverman, D. M., Varady, R. G., Chavez, O., & Roberto, S. (1999). Environmental issues along the United States-Mexico border: Drivers of change and responses of citizens and institutions. *Annual Review of Energy and Environment*, *27*, 607–643.

McGinnis, M. V., Woolley, J., & Gamman, J. (1999). Bioregional conflict resolution: Rebuilding community in watershed planning and organizing. *Environmental Management*, *24*(1), 1–12.

National Environmental Justice Advisory Committee (NEJAC). (1999). *Unheard voices from the border: A report on environmental justice in the US-Mexico border region*. NEJAC International Roundtable on Environmental Justice: National City, CA.

Ostrom, E. (1990). *Governing the Commons*. Cambridge: Cambridge University Press.

Pezzoli, K., Kozo, J., Ferran, K., Wooten, W., Rangel Gomez, G., & Al-Delaimy, W. K. (2014). One bioregion/one health: An integrative narrative for transboundary planning along the US – Mexico border. *Global Society*, *28*(4), 419–440.

TRNERR. (2010). *Comprehensive Management Plan*. Imperial Beach: TRNERR. [WWW document]. Retrieved from http://trnerr.org/about/management-plan/

Zedler, J., & West, J. (2008). Declining diversity in natural and restored salt marshes: A 30-year study of the Tijuana Estuary. *Restoration Ecology*, *16*(2), 249–262.

24

GENDER AND ENVIRONMENTAL SECURITY

Silja Halle

The early twenty-first century has seen a dramatic increase in academic research on the relationship between violent conflict, natural resources, and the environment, together with examples of innovative programming linking these issues on the ground. At the same time, increasingly visible impacts of environmental change have led to a broad political acceptance of the role of environmental factors in destabilizing entire regions, such as the Sahel or the Middle East. Once largely discounted as ancillary to security, issues such as environmental degradation and climate change are now considered defining threats to peace and stability by the UN Security Council and other global security actors, such as the European Union and the African Union.

Similarly, the linkages between gender and security have attracted significant attention since the adoption of UN Security Council Resolution 1325 on Women, Peace, and Security (WPS) in 2000. This resolution and the seven related resolutions that have followed it have generated wide-ranging scholarship and initiatives to strengthen women's roles in all aspects of peace and security and protect women and girls from gender-based violence in situations of armed conflict. As a result, gender issues are now an integral part of the international community's discourse on promoting peace and security.

Until recently, few linkages existed between these two fields of research and practice, but a more comprehensive and nuanced understanding of how gender, natural resources, and the environment are linked in conflict-affected and peacebuilding contexts is now developing. Innovative practices seeking to leverage women's (and men's) agency to support more effective conflict prevention and peacebuilding efforts in countries and regions affected by environmental challenges are also emerging.

Building on the 2013 UN report, *Women and Natural Resources: Unlocking the Peacebuilding Potential* (see UNEP, UN Women, PBSO, & UNDP, 2013) as well as subsequent scholarship and field experiences, this chapter briefly explores the gender dynamics around environment, peace, and security, highlighting both important progress and the gaps that continue to constrain effective responses. Following this overview, we review concrete entry points for addressing this nexus at different stages of the conflict cycle. In the last section of the chapter, we investigate how issues of gender and environment play out in two different conflict-affected settings – Sudan and Colombia – with the aim of providing tangible examples of how these issues can be taken into account in ground-level programming.

DOI: 10.4324/9781315107592-28

Gender dynamics of environment, natural resources, conflict, and peace

Natural resources and the environment underpin livelihoods for the vast majority of populations worldwide and are often the driving force behind economic development, industry, and gross domestic product in conflict-affected settings. Exclusion or restrictions imposed on certain communities and groups of people to own and access natural resources are examples of the structural inequalities and discrimination that can ultimately destabilize a peaceful society. This is most evident with regard to land tenure but also extends to access and usage rights for renewable resources, such as water and forest products, as well as the equitable distribution of benefits from extractive resources.

Gender is an important part of understanding these dynamics, as men and women tend to use and enjoy the benefits of natural resources differently and according to the roles and responsibilities determined by their gender as well as their socioeconomic status. Gendered roles and responsibilities also strongly influence the capacity of individuals to cope with the impacts of shocks and stresses, such as environmental change or violent conflict, including physical and food insecurity, displacement, loss of livelihood assets, or social exclusion.

It is critical to note that gender is only one of many identities carried by any individual. Social shocks and environmental stresses almost invariably exacerbate economic and social hierarchies within a society and often result in marginalization or violence toward particular groups or individuals along economic, political, religious, or cultural lines. Individuals from marginalized ethnic, economic, political, and social groups (such as immigrants or indigenous peoples) as well as very old or young people typically face the harshest discrimination and are likely to be the most vulnerable to violence and ensuing poverty from armed conflict.

In fragile and conflict-affected contexts, different forms of insecurity and violence can emerge when gender roles are disrupted. Men, who often have more difficulty maintaining traditional natural resource-based livelihoods (e.g., livestock herding or day labor), can face intense pressure for recruitment into armed groups. With few employment opportunities overall as well as reduced access to important natural resources such as land, social understandings of masculinity are often challenged or threatened during conflict. This can lead to the adoption of coping strategies that involve violence toward women and other men.

At the same time, these shocks and stresses can also contribute to shifts in gender roles that lead to new responsibilities and opportunities for women, and some men, in economic decisions and activity, political engagement, community arbitration, and mediation. This is often the case when men leave communities to find alternative employment or join armed forces, leaving women in charge of land and households or in situations of displacement, where women often become primary earners for their households by continuing economic activities traditionally associated with their gender roles, such as petty trade and selling in local markets.

Supporting women in their newfound roles can help break down barriers to economic and political empowerment, which are key to sustaining peace. Conversely, failing to understand – or oversimplifying – the gender dimensions of natural resource use and control in conflict-affected settings not only risks rolling back achievements toward greater equality and empowerment but can also lead to important oversights in understanding how different identities – gender and otherwise – intersect and compound marginalization and exclusion, which can undermine the effectiveness of peacebuilding efforts in the long term.

Addressing intersectional gender inequalities and exclusions related to access and benefits from natural resources, or participation in the governance of natural resources – and capitalizing on related opportunities for peace – has been overlooked in both gender-related and natural resource-related peacebuilding programming to date.

Natural resource programming, often a key part of economic recovery efforts in conflict-affected countries, is typically gender-blind. In its regular analyses of development assistance for gender equality, the OECD consistently finds very low levels of dedicated aid for gender equality and women's empowerment programs in the economic and productive sectors, which include agriculture, energy, mining, tourism, and water supply, for example (OECD DAC Network on Gender Equality, 2018). As a result, gains in women's employment and income generation that occur during conflict are often lost after conflict when programs such as economic restructuring, resettlement of displaced populations, and demobilization and reintegration of excombatants do not consider women's needs and opportunities.

Gender programming, similarly, has largely ignored the entry points presented by natural resources for women's political and economic participation and for strengthening women's contributions to peace. Implementation of the UN's WPS agenda has been uneven in focus, greatly emphasizing some topics, such as protecting women from sexual violence and increasing women's participation in (high-level) peace negotiations, over others. Generally speaking, little attention has been paid to addressing the structural inequalities – including those related to natural resources and the environment – that perpetuate exclusion and undermine sustainable peace or to elements of the agenda that could create meaningful opportunities for women's political, social, and economic empowerment.

However, important attempts are now being made within the international community to tackle the nexus of gender, environment, and peace and security. In their 2013 report, UN Environment, UNDP, UN Women, and the UN Peacebuilding Support Office proposed a new framework of analysis for understanding the gender dynamics of natural resource use in conflict-affected settings, reviewing key issues across three main categories of resources: land, renewable resources, and extractives. While many knowledge gaps remain, important research is also ongoing on such issues as the gender dimensions of climate and security, or women's roles in extractive resource exploitation and trading, particularly in artisanal and small-scale mining. New risk assessment tools in different sectors – from mining to business practices – are increasingly combining gender-responsive and conflict prevention approaches. Gender and inclusion dimensions are progressively being reflected in international and multilateral debates and emerging coordination mechanisms around climate and security.

Integrated approaches to gender equality, environment, and security are also being translated into peace and development programming. The most notable example is perhaps the UN's Joint Programme on Women, Natural Resources, Climate, and Peace, which is piloting innovative approaches to gender and environmental security in Sudan and Colombia, with a view to developing guidance and tools to support better integration of these issues across peacebuilding programming (see UNEP, n.d.). Other projects, notably funded through the Gender and Youth Promotion Initiative of the Peacebuilding Fund – which has made addressing "natural resource management and climate change mitigation" one criteria for selection – are addressing various aspects of this nexus in other conflict-affected countries, including Yemen.

In the following section, we seek to identify concrete entry points and lessons learned from these efforts. In this discussion, we focus specifically on women's roles, challenges, and opportunities, as many of the interventions discussed are targeted toward women. As explained earlier, however, a broader intersectional approach to gender in peacebuilding is critically needed. Masculinities and sexual minorities in conflict are also important fields of research and practice, for example, though we do not address those issues here.

Entry points and opportunities along the conflict cycle

Opportunities to strengthen conflict prevention and peacebuilding outcomes by ensuring women's participation in processes that are key to environmental security exist at each stage of the conflict cycle. For the purposes of this discussion, these are organized into three main stages – before conflict, during the conflict, and after the conflict – and further illustrated through the case studies in the following sections.

Conflict prevention, dialogue, and mediation

Since the adoption of Security Council Resolution 1325, there is a growing body of evidence showing that women's participation contributes not only to the conclusion of peace talks but also to the implementation and sustainability of peace agreements. In fact, research has demonstrated that women's participation increases the probability of a peace agreement lasting at least two years by 20%, and by 35% the probability of a peace agreement lasting 15 years (Stone, 2015). While there has been a gradual increase in the number of women formally taking part in mediation and conflict resolution processes since the adoption of the resolution, many barriers remain in ensuring that they have the opportunity to engage substantively and the capacity to influence key outcomes.

Failure to engage women from diverse backgrounds is a significant missed opportunity. As highlighted in the Global Study on the implementation of SCR 1325, "the most important effect of women's engagement in peace processes is not just greater attention to gender-related elements in the deliberations and the text of peace agreements, but a shift in dynamics, a broadening of the issues discussed – increasing the chances of community buy-in and addressing root causes" (UN Women, 2015, p. 2)

Among other issues, women have been shown to consistently prioritize equitable access to natural resources, such as land and water, and more equitable benefit-sharing from extractive resource exploitation, as an important part of peace. This has important implications for sustaining the peace, as structural inequalities and grievances linked to natural resource rights, access, and control have proven to be powerful catalysts for violence.

Although natural resource disputes can vary significantly between different resource sectors, certain characteristics set them apart from other types of conflict. One of these is the dual nature of most resource disputes as both technically complex and politically sensitive. As a result of this dual nature, resource disputes typically fall through the cracks of the international system. Technical agencies shy away from resource disputes because they are too politically sensitive, while the political organizations steer clear due to the technical complexities involved. The result is inadequate attention from the international system to the prevention, mitigation, and resolution of conflict associated with natural resources (UN DPA & UNEP, 2015).

Many women around the world are actively engaged in brokering disputes over natural resources at the community and local levels and, as a result, have critical experience in negotiating usage and benefit-sharing arrangements. However, structural barriers often prevent this experience from being used and capitalized upon in higher-level dialogue processes. Lack of support from the international community for "track 2" and "track 3" negotiations[1] at the local and subnational level also prevents women from building on these roles to increase and/or formalize their engagement.

Failing to engage women, women's groups, and networks in peace negotiations and dialogue processes not only risks weakening how natural resource issues are addressed in the peace process but can also seriously limit the potential for women to participate in natural resource governance and to benefit from resource-related reforms – such as land reform – and resource-based economic development that follow during the peacebuilding process. Strengthening national capacities and support structures with a view to ensuring that women's skills are put to use and their potential realized is an important part of this equation.

At the local level, conflict resolution efforts that build on women's capacity for mediation and influence within their communities have been shown to be particularly successful. For example, in South Kordofan, Sudan, actively involving women pastoralists in local mediation and natural resource governance processes have been essential for preventing conflicts over grazing lands and access to water. In this case, community structures with women representatives were registered as legal bodies, which gave them the legitimacy to carry out work on behalf of their communities, including the demarcation of pastoral corridors, which is a critical component of conflict resolution.

Protection from heightened security risks during conflict

Women in conflict and post-conflict settings often face significant risks when carrying out daily tasks, many of which involve tending to or collecting various natural resources such as fuelwood or water. Population pressures in and around refugee and IDP camps, for instance, can lead to deforestation and water shortages, thereby requiring women to venture further and further away from camps, exacerbating their risk. Experience shows that failure by relief operations, peacekeeping, or peacebuilding interventions to understand and respond to the specific risks and vulnerabilities faced by women and men in the aftermath of conflict can result in continued exposure to insecurity and violence, ultimately undermining recovery.

These risks can be reduced, however, by building awareness of humanitarian aid and peacekeeping actors to the threats faced by women while gathering natural resources as well as by promoting innovative technologies that reduce resource demands within conflict-affected communities. In addition to these measures, peacekeepers and national counterparts can also create secure boundaries and transport to areas most frequented by women. This may include public investment in the removal of land mines where women and young girls collect forest resources or farm. Within camps themselves, this can also involve ensuring women's safety when using water points and sanitation facilities, which has been noted as a rising problem in many refugee settings.

Ensuring infrastructure projects are developed in consultation with women can also help minimize sex-based crimes. Women in areas of protracted conflict often face daily risks when transporting saleable products such as charcoal from forests. Improving this security scenario can multiply the range of economic and social activities in which women are able to participate, from selling in market places to community organizing, providing social services, and other economic activities.

To address the constant risks faced by women with regard to harvesting natural resources in relief settings, a coalition of organizations led by the Women's Refugee Commission (2009) succeeded in placing safe cooking fuel on the same level of priority as water and food on the humanitarian agenda for camp management. These efforts led to the promotion of improved cook stoves, which use less wood and charcoal, minimizing environmental degradation and reducing the amount of smoke and indoor air pollution. Other organizations are now seeking to expand the reach of such initiatives worldwide, including in peacebuilding contexts. For example, the Clean Cooking Alliance (n.d.) has developed a ten-year strategic plan to increase investments, innovation, and operations for a global market for cookstoves.

Physical threats to women can also arise in areas where local conflicts flare up over disputed access to natural resources. Water points and grazing lands, for instance, can become potential flashpoints for violent conflict that put women at particular risk while carrying out their daily tasks. Appropriate responses to these risks can benefit the community as a whole: as the work of Catholic Relief Services in Darfur illustrates, providing separate and more secure water access points for agriculturalists and pastoralist has had the secondary effect of reducing women's risks when accessing water (Warner, 2011).[2] Such measures take into account the vulnerabilities of women in relation to water use, and their role in water management, particularly at the local level.

Finally, engagement and sensitization of men and men's groups are widely recognized as key components of implementing gender-sensitive interventions in conflict-affected and peace-building contexts (Cardona, Justino, Mitchell, & Müller, 2012). Recent efforts in this regard have included the "One Man Can" campaign in Sudan, where men have been engaged in sensitization, education, and communication campaigns to stop violence against women (see Aslund, 2014). These efforts encourage men to speak directly to other community members about the impact of violence against women and to help reduce it by confronting the social norms that allow it to continue.

Sustaining peace through inclusive environmental governance and natural resource programming that supports women's economic empowerment

Interventions around natural resources in post-conflict peacebuilding processes provide significant opportunities to empower women politically and economically and thereby to strengthen their contributions to sustainable peace and development.

Working with natural resource management authorities – from local user councils to national water boards, forestry, and land commissions or national ministries – can help increase women's participation in decision-making and lead to more inclusive and equitable governance of those resources. At the local level, in particular, the knowledge and experience that women may have of a particular natural resource due to their roles and responsibilities can provide a clear entry point for engagement.

However, targeted support is needed for overcoming the structural, social, and cultural barriers to women's formal and informal political participation in conflict-affected settings. This can include measures such as the use of quotas, which have been effective in many different settings, and targeted capacity-building, particularly of local women's organizations and networks. In Chocó, Colombia, for example, the UN's Joint Programme on Women, Natural Resources and Peace has supported grassroots organizations and academic institutions to establish a School of Environmental Leadership that aims to strengthen the capacity of a diverse set of local women's organizations to engage in key environmental governance processes that have a direct link to conflict prevention, such as the implementation of the constitutional court's decision on the protection and rehabilitation of the Atrato River; the river has been a central axis for illegal activities by armed groups (such as drug trafficking and mining), leading to entrenched conflict in the region.

Reestablishing livelihoods and providing opportunities for income generation is a critical step toward sustaining peace, and sustainable natural resource management provides significant opportunities for women's wage and self-employment. In rural areas, where women's productivity is often directly dependent on natural resources, supporting women's economic empowerment includes strengthening their ability to capitalize on their natural resource management roles. This is especially important in post-conflict settings, where women's roles frequently shift or expand to take on income-generating activities traditionally reserved for men. Capitalizing on these shifts not only is essential to supporting women's economic recovery but can also lead to better peacebuilding outcomes.

Building women's capacity for productive and sustainable use of natural resources can include facilitating access to credit and providing technical and capacity-building support but also legal support for enforcement of land rights and other resource rights. The Small Grants Programme of the Global Environment Facility has supported many successful women-led small business ventures related to natural resources, from an artisanal ice-cream company using sustainably harvested forest fruits in Colombia, to a tree nursery that contributed to the restoration of the Kibira forest in Burundi. In Sudan, the UN's Joint Programme has supported women's associations to establish cooperative farms based on adaptive and sustainable farming techniques and helped connect them to the market. These examples also show that collective organizing can be a powerful tool in terms of access to capital and other forms of support.

In the next two sections, we discuss the experience of projects in Sudan and Colombia, which provide an example of the complex and multifaceted environmental and social dynamics of conflict and peace in these regions – but also illustrate some of the emerging opportunities around this nexus of issues.

Gender, climate change, and security in North Kordofan, Sudan

The state of North Kordofan borders North Darfur to its west and South Kordofan to its south – two states that have endured violent armed conflict for several years. This has resulted in an influx of both weapons and internally displaced persons (IDPs) into North Kordofan, which, when combined with limited local economic opportunities, has led to increasing instability.

The locality of Al Rahad in North Kordofan State, comprising approximately 180,000 people, is in many ways emblematic of the prevailing challenges faced by the region. Located some 570 km from the capital Khartoum, on the southern fringe of the Al Baja desert, the area used to be one of the largest gum arabic producers in the country. However, deforestation and drought have damaged and destroyed acacia trees, greatly weakening production. This has had significant negative impacts on the livelihoods of the sedentary population, which have been compounded by the expansion of mechanized agriculture.

Al Rahad has traditionally been an important crossroads for different pastoralist groups, such as the Baggara and the Shanabla, whose migration routes to and from the South have long passed through the locality, leading to robust trade with the sedentary farmer populations, comprised largely the Gawama'a. Recent years, however, have seen a significant increase in the number of pastoralists – and animals – coming through the Al Rahad area as other pastoralist routes have been closed due to conflict in South Kordofan and Darfur.

In addition, due to its proximity to South Kordofan, which has been the scene of violent conflict between the Government of Sudan and the Sudan People's Liberation Army-North (SPLA-N) since 2011, Al Rahad continues to provide a safe haven for tens of thousands of IDPs, which has further stretched the limited basic services and natural resources available in the region, and creates tension between IDPs and host communities.

These significant increases in population have taken place in a context of important variability of rainfall linked to the El-Nino phase, which has contributed to crop failure, water scarcity, and inevitable overcrowding of water and pasture resources. This combination of factors has had two notable types of impacts.

First, violent conflicts between agropastoralists and nomadic groups south of Um-Ruwaba and Al-Rahad localities have increased significantly and had worsening outcomes. According to Al Rahad's Conflict Mediation and Peacebuilding Center, the area witnessed nine violent conflicts between July 2016 and April 2018, which caused 24 deaths. Five of those events and 15 of those deaths took place in a single month, between 11 March and 13 April, indicating an increasing frequency of manifestations of violence. Conflicts occur mainly when cattle nomads trespass on agricultural fields – including gum Arabic tress that is used as fodder for herds – or when farmers cultivate and grow crops on migratory routes, resulting in crop destruction, land degradation, and disputes. For political and historical reasons, traditional conflict resolution mechanisms – such as the "Jodeya mediation" – have become less efficient at resolving conflicts.

Second, the demographic composition of the sedentary community in Al-Rahad is becoming increasingly female, as one response to the economic hardships endured as traditional livelihoods have faltered has been for men, especially younger men, to migrate for increasingly long periods of time to the capital Khartoum, to join agricultural schemes in White Nile State and Gezira State, or to participate in artisanal gold mining operations in other parts of the country.

This feminization of the population is further compounded by the increasing sedentarization of several pastoralist groups, who are not only staying in the area for longer periods of time but often also splitting, leaving women and children behind in the Al Rahad area while men continue on the migration. Sedentarized pastoralist groups – largely women – typically turn to the land to generate income, often renting fields from the local community to graze their sheep and goats or produce small crops.

Women are, therefore, not only heavily impacted by the effects of environmental degradation as heads of household and as farmers, but they are on the frontlines of conflicts opposing different resource user groups. Against this background, engaging with women in addressing the linkages between climate change, environmental degradation, and conflict is paramount. In 2017, UN Environment, UNDP, and UN Women initiated a joint pilot project in Al Rahad to empower women to play a stronger role in the governance and management of natural resources as well as the prevention and resolution of conflicts linked to them.

Building on UNDP's Community Security and Stabilization program activities in the area, the pilot project had three sequential components: (i) ensuring women's economic empowerment through natural resource-based livelihoods; (ii) strengthening women's participation in resource governance through community environmental action planning; and (iii) increasing women's capacity and opportunity to participate in natural resource conflict prevention and resolution.

Using alternative livelihoods and income generation as the entry point was key not only to addressing immediate needs but also to building trust and buy-in for the project. Although women in North Kordofan typically have equal access to land, very few have land ownership rights and thus lack the collateral funding needed for membership in existing cooperatives. Women also lack access to credit as well as extension and production technology. The project, therefore, supported two women's associations in the area to establish cooperative farms and connect to markets, through training, inputs, and formal land allocation, and connected them to credit institutions. At an individual level, women were supported to develop household horticultural schemes that provided additional food for their families while generating extra disposable income. In total, 81% of the women targeted in the livelihood interventions reported a significant increase in their income.

Building on these activities, the project supported committees comprised both sedentary and pastoralist groups representatives in two villages of the Al Rahad area to use joint environmental action planning to identify common challenges, develop mutually agreed solutions, and defuse tensions between different resource user groups. The process, which was conducted through 11 sessions in each village, ensured equal representation of women in all committees and provided a platform for them to engage actively and equally in analysis, action planning, and dialogue.

The project also sought to create more mechanisms and opportunities to strengthen women's roles in natural resource conflict prevention and resolution. Women members of the Community Management Committee and the local Conflict Mediation and Peacebuilding Center received training in conflict mediation skills and environmental peacebuilding, and dialogue forums were created to provide spaces for women to discuss and facilitate exchanges between sedentary and pastoral communities. In parallel, sensitization was conducted in the broader community to shift perceptions of women's roles.

In interviews conducted at the end of the project in September 2018, 100% of respondents – male and female – noted a shift in the communities' perceptions of women's capacities for decision-making and conflict resolution over natural resources. Several notably reported increased representational roles for women, including growing acceptance of women "speaking for the men" in matters related to natural resource governance. Achieving such results does not rely on radically new solutions. Rather, the innovation lies in combining and integrating approaches that have proven effective in one or the other field in ways that lead to more holistic and sustainable results. Success largely depends, therefore, on overcoming entrenched siloed approaches and developing good practices that can be applied more systematically to peace and development programming.

Securing women's roles in environmental peacebuilding in Colombia

With the signature and ratification of the revised peace agreement between the Colombian government and the *Fuerzas Armadas Revolucionarias de Colombia* (FARC) in December 2016, Colombia faces the challenge of building a sustainable and inclusive peace. The process leading up to the agreement – which is seen by many as an exemplary model of a gender-inclusive peace process – has resulted in high expectations for social inequities and injustices to the addressed as a matter of priority in the implementation phase. This is certainly the case for commitments to gender equality and women's rights, which were considered central to the achievement of a sustainable peace by all parties and fully integrated into the text of the peace agreement.

While Colombia is in many ways considered a pioneer in legislation related to women's rights and gender-based violence and is characterized by a vibrant civil society with a long history of women's activism and leadership in peacebuilding, the conflict has had particularly severe impacts on women. Women and youths make up the majority of Colombia's 8 million IDPs[3] (Bouvier, 2016; iDMC, 2020), and more than 3 million women are officially registered as victims of the conflict, including as victims of sexual violence (Unidad, 2015). Women human rights and environmental defenders have also increasingly been threatened and targeted by armed groups (Restrepo, 2016). At the same time, traditional gender roles have shifted during the conflict, as women have taken on roles traditionally ascribed to men in farming or mining, become breadwinners and heads of households, or joined the ranks of the FARC and other armed groups.

In addition to its commitments to promoting and enforcing women's rights, the Colombian peace process has recognized that sound natural resource management and environmental protection are integral to the achievement of peace and sustainable development. Issues related to access to and ownership of land and natural resources were of major importance during the negotiations as unequal land distribution and discrimination against rural people was a key driver of the conflict between the government and the FARC (Bouvier, 2016).[4]

With the cessation of hostilities with the FARC, large areas of valuable and resource-rich land have become accessible for economic activities and infrastructure development. For example, new territories are opening up for industrial mining companies that were previously only

Gender and environmental security

mined through artisanal means, including by women (see ABColombia, 2015; Driver, 2016). Without a concerted effort to develop democratic, transparent, participatory, and inclusive institutions to govern land and natural resources in a sustainable manner, decades-old grievances around unequal benefit-sharing, decision-making, and the impacts of environmental degradation, risk undermining long-term peace.

It is, therefore, critical to ensure that the complex gender dimensions of natural resource use, ownership, governance, and benefit-sharing are fully understood and that women's needs and specific priorities are taken into account in peacebuilding processes, in a manner that helps address systemic social inequity and enables them to fully engage in post-conflict economic revitalization. Against this background, UN Environment, UN Women, and UNDP initiated a pilot project to support the government and civil society of Colombia to realize the vision on gender equality, women's empowerment, and sustainable natural resource management presented in the Havana Accords by (i) strengthening local and national capacities to ensure that the needs and priorities of diverse groups of women related to natural resource use, ownership, governance, and benefit-sharing are clearly articulated and integrated in the policy reforms and programmatic initiatives contributing to the peace process in Colombia and (ii) strengthening women's capacities for conflict prevention and resolution efforts over natural resources.

The project's activities focus on Chocó and Antioquia (Bajo Cauca), two regions in which conflict prevention and peacebuilding challenges relating to natural resources are particularly acute. The two departments alone account for approximately half of all domestic production of metallic minerals, including gold, which is mostly still mined by artisanal and small-scale miners (OECD, 2016). Illegal and informal mining constitute a key source of income for impoverished populations in both departments, with devastating social and environmental impacts linked to the use of heavy machinery, as well as mercury and other toxic chemicals to extract gold (see ABColombia, 2012, 2015; Echavarria, 2014).

Chocó has a poverty rate of 65.9% as compared to 28.5% for Colombia nationally, with 39.1% of the population living in extreme poverty. Gender-based violence is particularly high in the department, where rates of partner violence, legal examinations due to sexual violence, and suicidal behavior in women are double those at the national level. It is also one of the areas in which the dividends of the peace agreement with the FARC as least clear. Territories left by the FARC-EP have been rapidly taken over by other armed actors, which has had the effect of increasing insecurity in many areas. In 2017, an increase in the clashes between public forces, ELN, and other illegal armed groups was witnessed in Chocó (and elsewhere), strongly impacting on communities.

Against this background, the project seeks to develop practical models for the meaningful engagement of diverse groups of women in local environmental governance and peacebuilding processes. This includes supporting local government entities to work in close coordination with civil society organizations, in particular women's organizations and networks not only for post-conflict planning exercises at the local and regional level but also for emblematic processes linking environment and peace, such as the implementation of the Colombian Constitutional Court's landmark 2016 decision on the Atrato River.

The 750-km Atrato River runs through Colombia's northwestern Pacific rainforest, connecting many parts of Chocó. For years, the river has been a central axis for illegal activities by armed groups, such as drug and weapons trafficking and exploitation of gold ore and timber, leading to entrenched conflict as well as humanitarian and environmental crises. In its Decision T-622, Colombia's Constitutional Court recognized the Atrato River basin as having rights to "protection, conservation, maintenance and restoration." The decision aims to offer protection to the Atrato River and guarantee the fundamental rights of the communities that inhabit its banks from a new perspective called "biocultural rights." Under this new paradigm, the court reasoned that the most effective way to protect ethnic communities' rights was through biodiversity conservation and ecosystem restoration on the Atrato River. Awarding rights and achieving them, however, are not the same thing. To achieve protection, conservation, and restoration, action is needed. The peacebuilding potential of the Decision T622 will only be realized through inclusive environmental governance and equitable benefit-sharing.

In parallel, the project is strengthening the capacities of women's organizations themselves to participate in public policy processes related to environmental governance, territorial planning, and conflict prevention over natural resources. Among other activities, the project has established a School of Environmental Peacebuilding and Leadership for Women, which will train women from different backgrounds, including ex-combatants, on key legal and policy frameworks linked to environment and natural resources in Colombia and Chocó; and mediation and dialogue skills for conflict prevention and resolution of conflict over natural resources.

The objective is for these local experiences to inform national-level planning and policy-making. For example, a national forum on the role of women in environmental governance for peacebuilding, with the participation of and based on the experience of women in Chocó. Exchanges between women environmental leaders with women mediator networks from other countries and regions, including the Nordic Women Mediators' network, are also planned.

Conclusion

Failing to examine the gender dimensions of natural resource access, rights, and management in conflict and post-conflict settings misses crucial opportunities for conflict prevention and sustainable peace. While some notable progress in understanding the nuances and complexity of the linkages between these issues has been made, and examples of relevant programming are emerging, more work is needed to ensure that these approaches are further integrated and systematized in peacebuilding practice.

To achieve this, more gender-differentiated research, baselines, and analysis at local and national levels are needed to ensure that peacebuilding interventions are better informed by local realities. This should include a better grasp of power dynamics in respective resource sectors and an understanding of who is involved in the sector, how are they involved, and what the potential impact of any regulations or other natural resource governance efforts in that sector may be. Equally important is to consider differential experiences of various groups of women to determine which groups of women are working in natural resource sectors; who is benefitting; and the specific challenges, threats, and vulnerabilities they face.

At a programmatic level, the inclusion of gender experts with a focus on public policy, natural resource economics, and technical skills related to renewable and extractive natural resource sectors will help programs adapt to changing realities on the ground. Greater emphasis on capacity building and awareness raising with implementing partners, including national and local government agencies, civil society, and private sector, is also key to changing gender biases, in combination with practical, concrete support, such as legal aid services and education around new legislation processes that can impact natural resource rights and access, especially for women.

Notes

1 Peace processes take place through different channels and societal levels (tracks). Track 1 mediation refers to high-level, formal negotiations between military and political leaders (heads of state, leaders of

Gender and environmental security

opposing movements). Track 1.5 brings together government officials in informal, nonofficial dialogue. Track 2 refers to unofficial dialogue and problem-solving activities among nongovernment experts such as academics, religious dignitaries, NGO leaders, and other civil society actors. Finally, track 3 negotiations refer to local-level, grassroots diplomacy; it is focused on transforming attitudes and interactions within communities through intermediaries and can include activities such as community mediation programs, local peace committees (IMSD, 2017)

2 Woodrow Wilson Center for Scholars. (2011). Digging Deeper: Water, Women and Conflict. Environmental Change and Security Program, August 29, 2011. Presentation by Dennis Warner. Woodrow Wilson Center for Scholars: Washington, DC.

3 Estimates on the numbers of IDPs in Colombia vary. For the most recent data on internal displacement in Colombia, see OCHA's (2019) *Humanitarian Needs Overview*

4 The link between armed groups and extractives in Colombia has been the subject of a number of reports and studies, see, for example, the report by The Global Initiative against Transnational Organized Crime (2016).

Works cited

ABColombia. (2015). Fuelling conflict in Colombia: The impact of gold mining in Chocó. London: ABColombia

ABColombia (2012). *Giving it away: The consequences of an unsustainable mining policy in Colombia.* London: ABColombia.

Aslund, S. (2014). *Sonke's one man can campaign supports peacebuilding and gender equality in Sudan.* Cape Town, South Africa: Sonke Gender Justice

Bouvier, V. M. (2016). *Gender and the role of women in Colombia's peace process.* UN Women Background Paper, USIP and UN Women. Retrieved November 18, 2020, from www.usip.org/publications/2016/11/03/gender-and-the-role-of-women-in-colombias-peace-process

Cardona, I., Justino, P., Mitchell, B., & Müller, C. (2012). *From the ground up: Women's roles in local peacebuilding in Afghanistan, Liberia, Nepal, Pakistan and Sierra Leone.* South Africa and London: ActionAid, Institute of Development Studies and WomanKind:

Clean Cooking Alliance. (n.d.). Our Portfolio. Retrieved November 18, 2020, from www.cleancookingalliance.org/market-development/supply-strengthening/our-portfolio.html

Driver, A. (2016, June 27). The courageous Colombian activist going head-to-head with mining interests. Women in the world. Retrieved from https://womenintheworld.com/2016/06/27/the-courageous-colombian-activist-going-head-to-head-with-mining-interests/

Echavarria, C. (2014). What is legal? Formalising Artisanal and Small-scale Mining in Colombia. IIED Research Report. London: International Institute for Environment and Development.

The Global Initiative against Transnational Organized Crime (2016*). Organized Crime and Illegally Mined Gold in Latin America.* Geneva, Switzerland: The Global Initiative against Transnational Organized Crime

Initiative Mediation Support Deutschland (IMSD). (2017). Basics of Mediation: Concepts and Definition. *Peace Mediation and Mediation Support.* https://peacemaker.un.org/sites/peacemaker.un.org/files/Basics%20of%20Mediation.pdf

Internal Displacement Monitoring Center (iDMC). (2020). Women and girls in internal displacement. Retrieved from www.internal-displacement.org/sites/default/files/publications/documents/202003-twice-invisible-internally-displaced-women.pdf

Office of Coordinating Humanitarian Affairs (OCHA). (2019). Colombia – Humanitarin Needs Overview. Retrieved November 18, 2020, from https://reliefweb.int/sites/reliefweb.int/files/resources/290119_hno_2019_enB_0.pdf

OECD (2016). Due Diligence in Colombia's Gold Supply Chain: Gold Mining in Antioquia. Retrieved from www.oecd.org/daf/inv/mne/colombias-gold-supply-chain.htm

OECD DAC Network on Gender Equality. (2018). *Aid to Gender Equality and Women's Empowerment: An Overview.* Paris: OECD.

Restrepo, E. M. (2016). Leaders against all odds: Women victims of conflict in Colombia. *Palgrave Communications, 2.* https://doi.org/10.1057/palcomms.2016.14

Stone, L. (2015). Quantitative analysis of women's participation in peace processes. *Reimagining Peacemaking: Women's Roles in Peace Processes.*

Colombian Unidad para la atención y reparación integral a las victimas (Unidad). (2015). Women build peace, and their reparation contributes to the reconstruction of the social fabric. Retrieved November 18, 2020, from www.unidadvictimas.gov.co/sites/default/files/documentosbiblioteca/fichamujer-esingles2015.pdf

United Nations Department of Political Affairs (UN DPA) & United Nations Environment Programme (UNEP). (2015). *Natural Resources and Conflict: A Guide for Mediation Practitioners*. New York/Geneva.

United Nations Environment Programme (UNEP). (n.d.). Women, natural resource, and peace. Retrieved November 18, 2020, from www.unenvironment.org/explore-topics/disasters-conflicts/what-we-do/recovery/women-natural-resources-and-peace

United Nations Environment Programme (UNEP), United Nations Women, Peacebuilding Support Office (PBSO), United Nations Development Programme (UNDP). (2013). *Women and Natural Resources: Unlocking the Peacebuilding Potential*. New York/Geneva: UNEP, UN Women, PBSO, & UNDP.

United Nations Security Council (UNSC). (2000). Resolution 1325 on Women, Peace and Security.

UN Women. (2015). The Global Study on 1325: Key Messages, Findings, and Recommendations (Fact Sheet). https://wps.unwomen.org/resources/fact-sheets/Fact-Sheet-and-Key-messages-Global-Study-EN.pdf

Warner, D. (2011, August 29). Digging Deeper: Water, Women and Conflict. Environmental Change and Security Program. Presentation at the Woodrow Wilson Center for Scholars. Washington, DC.

Women's Refugee Commission. (2009). Fuel and Firewood Initiative: Leading international efforts to provide safe cooking fuel for refugees. Retrieved November 18, 2020, from www.womensrefugee-commission.org/research-resources/fuel-and-firewood-initiative-leading-international-efforts-to-provide-safe-cooking-fuel-for-refugee/

25

UN ENVIRONMENT'S CONTRIBUTION TO THE EMERGING FIELD OF ENVIRONMENTAL PEACEBUILDING

Key policy milestones and lessons learned

David Jensen and Amanda Kron[1]

Environmental peacebuilding responding to contemporary peace and security challenges

Preventing and resolving conflicts over scarce natural resources is a defining peace and security challenge of the twenty-first century. As the global population continues to rise, the economic demand for resources continues to grow, and the impacts of climate change begin to materialize, competition over natural resources is set to intensify.

At the same time, for countries recovering from violent conflict, natural resources often offer the first opportunity to help stabilize and revive livelihoods and other economic activity. When governments manage their environment and natural resources well and integrate them across a range of peacebuilding activities, they can provide an important pathway to lasting peace and poverty reduction.

At the turn of the millennium, the United Nations' evolving peacebuilding architecture did not reflect the broad and complex role of natural resources across the peace and security continuum (UN Environment, 2015a). As a result, the United Nations was insufficiently prepared to support lasting resolutions to resource conflicts or capitalize on the peacebuilding potential of natural resources and the environment. However, over the past 18 years, significant progress has been made by the United Nations in terms of adopting new policies, programs, and practices to help Member States and local stakeholders address these challenges in a more coherent and coordinated manner.

While there is still much work to accomplish, this chapter reviews some of the major international policy milestones in the evolution of the field of environmental peacebuilding and summarizes some of the key lessons learned. The chapter is based on the policy and fieldwork

303 DOI: 10.4324/9781315107592-29

conducted by the UN Environment Programme (UN Environment) since 1999 when it established a dedicated capacity to conduct post-conflict environmental assessments and support governments in environmental clean-up, restoration, governance, and peacebuilding. From 2008 to 2016, UN Environment also ran a dedicated program called Environmental Cooperation for Peacebuilding (ECP) to catalyze new policies, pilot field approaches, conduct training, establish joint operational programs, and document lessons learned (UN Environment, 2016a).

After a brief introduction to the emerging field of environmental peacebuilding, the chapter introduces four main periods of international policy development from 1999 to 2018 involving UN Environment. Within each period, the major policy milestones are introduced together with a series of lessons learned from field-level work conducted by UN Environment and partners. The final section concludes with suggestions for future work and research in this area.

Environmental peacebuilding

Environmental peacebuilding provides a framework for understanding the positive and negative roles that natural resources and the environment can play throughout the different parts of the conflict lifecycle. In general, environmental peacebuilding is divided into three main areas. The first area of focus is to prevent natural resources and the environment from contributing to or fueling violent conflict. The second involves protecting natural resources and the environment from damage and illegal exploitation during conflict. Finally, the third area pertains to the use of natural resources and the environment to support post-conflict economic recovery, sustainable livelihoods, and confidence building in a manner that contributes to local peace.

Ultimately, it is about using and governing shared natural resources as the basis for cooperation and joint action to prevent conflict or contribute to peace (see Chapter 2 of this volume for a complete overview of the framework). Environmental peacebuilding has emerged from the scholarly literature on environmental security – but it emphasizes the positive contributions that natural resources and the environment can make to conflict prevention and local peacebuilding.

The importance of protecting the environment in times of armed conflict is not a new concept.[2] However, the role that environment and natural resources play as drivers of violent conflict or as opportunities for peacebuilding is still an emerging field of research and policy development. Furthermore, understanding how natural resources present both conflict risks and peacebuilding opportunities across time and at different geographic scales is a major empirical challenge due to the number of variables combined with the political and social dynamics involved.

International policy milestones 1999–2018

The initial wave of international policy action aiming to address the environmental dimensions of conflict occurred in the aftermath of the Vietnam War. Due to the wide-scale use of Agent Orange and plans to weaponize weather as an instrument of warfare, two international legal instruments were adopted. First, in 1976, the Convention on the Prohibition of Military or Any Other Hostile Use of Environmental Modification Techniques (ENMOD Convention). The Convention focuses on the modification of natural processes as a weapon of war, with a focus on weather modification. UN Environment helped convene the negotiations that led to ENMOD – but does not manage it or monitor enforcement (UN Environment, 2009a).

Second, in 1977, the Additional Protocol I to the 1949 Geneva Conventions was adopted. It included two articles (35 and 55) prohibiting warfare that may cause "widespread, long-term and severe damage to the natural environment." This legal instrument was brokered by the International Committee of the Red Cross (UN Environment, 2009b).

While these Conventions were an important starting point, progress then waned for over a decade. The 1991 Gulf War helped spark renewed international policy interest including a debate in the UN General Assembly on armed conflict and the environment (UNGA, 1992). UN Environment also conducted a number of ad hoc regional assessments of the environmental damage resulting from conflict. This spirit of this work was eventually reflected in the Rio Declaration on Environment and Development adopted by governments in 1992. Principle 24 recognized that States shall respect international laws providing protection for the environment in times of armed conflict while Principle 25 noted that peace, development, and environmental protection are interdependent and indivisible. However, few global-level policies or practices emerged following this pulse of activity, including within UN Environment.

The Kosovo conflict of 1999 placed the issue back into the international spotlight prompting a range of more concrete policy and operational responses by the United Nations upon the request of Member States. The subsequent policy landscape involving UN Environment can be divided into four district tracks that roughly correspond to different parts of the conflict lifecycle.

1) **Environmental Impacts:** The first track began in 1999 and involved enhancing UN capacity to conduct independent and scientific assessments of the environmental consequences of conflict.
2) **Conflict drivers:** The second track began in 2005, focusing on strengthening UN capacity in assessing natural resources as drivers of conflict.
3) **Peacebuilding opportunities:** The third track began in 2009, focusing on recognizing and integrating environment, conflict, and peacebuilding linkages within key peace and security reports, policies, and field programs.
4) **Integrated programming and conflict prevention**: The final track is ongoing as of 2015 and consists of stock-tacking, the creation of new integrated programming approaches and emphasizing conflict prevention. This includes understanding the role of the environment and climate change in national and local fragility.

Within each of these tracks, key policy milestones are introduced and important lessons learned by UN Environment and partners are presented.

Track 1: environmental impacts of conflict

In 1999, the international policy landscape on environmental peacebuilding began to heat up. Following the conflict in former Yugoslavia, then UN Secretary-General Kofi Annan requested UN Environment and UN-HABITAT to undertake an independent and scientific assessment of the impacts of the conflict on the environment and human settlements. To carry out this assessment, the UN Balkans Task Force was created in 1999 and was hosted by UN Environment.

This task force was subsequently transformed into a dedicated unit that would focus on conducting post-conflict environmental assessments and helping countries address environmental clean-up, recovery, governance, and peacebuilding. The unit conducted assessments in seven additional countries or regions before it was eventually upgraded into a formal branch by decision 22/1/IV of the UN Environment Governing Council. This included work in the Balkans (e.g., UN Environment, 2004a), FYR Macedonia (UN Environment, 2000a), Albania (UN Environment, 2000b), Afghanistan (UN Environment, 2003a), Iraq (UN Environment, 2003b), the Occupied Palestinian Territories (UN Environment, 2003c), and Liberia (UN Environment, 2004b).

The main lessons learned by UN Environment and partners on the environmental impacts of conflict are highlighted below.

(1) Assessing both direct and indirect environmental damage from conflict

When assessing the environmental damage from conflict, it is useful to consider both direct and indirect impacts from armed conflict. Direct impacts arise from military action during or immediately after conflict, such as direct targeting of the environment and scorched earth tactics, incidental damage, impacts from weapons and military operations (see Closmann, Chapter 8), toxic hazards from damage to infrastructure and industry, as well as financing of conflict through looting of the environment and conflict resources (see Lujala et al., Chapter 10).

Direct damage is often more acute and site-specific than indirect damage. One example is the targeting of hundreds of industrial sites and municipal infrastructure by NATO forces during the Kosovo conflict, resulting in major chemical spills into the environment and at least 100 bomb craters inside national parks and protected areas in Serbia (UN Environment, 1999).

Indirect impacts are secondary impacts that can be credibly linked to the conflict, such as coping and survival strategies of local populations, profiteering and legacies of the conflict economy, breakdown of institutions and local governance, the impact of peacekeeping and humanitarian operations, as well as temporary settlements and infrastructure. These impacts may, in turn, affect human health, livelihoods and contribute to displacement. Indirect impacts are often more chronic, widespread, and long term.

One example of indirect impacts took place in Darfur, where demands for bricks increased five times due to international operations. Since the bricks were kiln-fired, this demand, in turn, contributed to significant deforestation (over 50,000 trees per year) (UN Environment, 2012). In addition, in Iraq, poor resource governance combined with limited regional cooperation and international sanctions paved the way for long-term environmental vulnerabilities and risks relating to water quality, waste management, and the oil industry (UN Environment, 2003b).

(2) Natural resources are a livelihood lifeline during violent conflicts when basic services of society break down

Natural resources frequently become an important economic lifeline for local populations and displaced people during violent conflicts. In many cases, conflict economies emerge, consisting of several distinct but intertwined segments: (i) the remains of the formal economy; (ii) an expanding informal economy; (iii) the international aid economy; and (iv) often an illicit criminal economy (Conca & Wallace, 2012). The main challenge for post-conflict assessments is to understand how these strands provide support to different livelihoods and what kind of environmental impacts different livelihood strategies can cause. Furthermore, as countries move into post-conflict reconstruction, it is essential to understand how incentives can be used to promote a gradual return to regulated and sustainable resource use. In most cases, it is the formal and aid economies that get the most attention from donors and ministries, whereas many people are actually earning a post-conflict living from natural resources in the illicit and informal economies.

The most common activities include artisanal and small-scale mining, charcoal production and wood supply, fisheries, and hunting of wildlife. Such coping strategies and survival livelihoods for local populations and displaced persons during, and after, violent conflicts can have extensive impacts on the environment and such practices often last long into peacebuilding processes. In Afghanistan, for example, UN Environment's post-conflict environmental assessment in 2003 found that at least 90% of the pistachio forests in Badghis and Takhar provinces were heavily degraded due to a combination of direct targeting during the conflict and the survival strategies of local populations. Trees were used for charcoal and building materials and the woodlands were converted into other forms of land use such as pastures or agriculture (UN Environment, 2003a).

One of the most significant United Nations-backed studies on coping and survival strategies used by different livelihood groups was conducted on the camel herding nomads in Darfur known as the Northern Rizaygat. Their notoriety as part of the Janjaweed militia obscured how their lives and livelihoods were affected by conflict and how they adopted maladaptation strategies such as "the use of intimidation and violence as a means of controlling or restricting access to natural resources (e.g., forestry resources, access to cultivable land)" for coping with livelihood collapse (Young, Osman, Abusin, Asher, & Egemi, 2009). The study helped transform the way in which livelihood support programs were being designed and implemented.

(3) Armed conflicts destroy resource governance arrangements, undermine social relationships, and weaken resilience

One of the most significant long-term indirect impacts of violent conflict is the undermining of resource governance arrangements, social relationships, and trust between resource stakeholders. This combination of impacts often weakens resilience to different shocks and stresses, whether natural, social or economic. For instance, in Afghanistan, a wide-scale collapse of local-level water management systems led to reduced and unreliable water supply through uncontrolled well drilling and abstraction. In addition, water quality suffered from contamination from unregulated waste dumping and open sewers (UN Environment, 2003a). Similarly, in Iraq, land registration documents, environmental information, materials, and laboratories were destroyed during the conflicts, leaving governance structures in disarray (Conca & Wallace, 2012; UN Environment, 2007a).

In this context, it is critical to ensure that vulnerable and marginalized groups are protected in the aftermath of conflicts. For instance, women often lack formal access to land, which, in turn, provides access to other resources and rights, such as water and food security (UN Environment-PBSO-UN Women-UNDP, 2013; see also Halle, Chapter 24). For example, in Uganda, a joint UN study found in 2013 that while women were responsible for growing 80% of the food crops in the country, only 7% of landowners were women UN Environment-PBSO-UN Women-UNDP, 2013).

(4) The resource governance vacuum that occurs during armed conflict can make natural resources particularly vulnerable to pillaging and looting

Natural resources are particularly vulnerable to pillage and looting during the governance vacuum that often follows in the wake of armed conflict. During violent conflict, the resulting resource governance and institutional vacuum are often systematically exploited, including through land grabbing, illegal wildlife trade, and the looting of high-value resources (see discussion of Liberia and Angola in UN Environment, 2009a).

The international system has developed tools for addressing such "conflict resources" ranging from voluntary transparency regimes to certification mechanisms and to targeted commodity sanctions (UN Environment, 2015a; see also Beevers, Chapter 14). However, these instruments require context-specific application and improved strategic coordination to be able to respond to the complexity of global supply chains and the dynamic nature of transboundary resource flows. The geographic and technical intricacy of these global supply chains, and their ability to adapt to and thwart regulation, often confound international and domestic legal frameworks, resulting in an unregulated space between the two levels (Conca, 2015). While the existing range of tools is useful, they need to be linked to a broader antitrafficking approach, information exchange, and institutional strengthening to be more effective.

These tendencies are particularly troubling given the rise of environmental crime over the last few decades. In 2015, UN Environment undertook a joint study on illegal exploitation and trade in natural resources in Eastern Democratic Republic of the Congo (DR Congo) together with the peacekeeping mission (MONUSCO) and the Special Envoy of the Secretary-General for the Great Lakes Region. The study found that up to 98% of net revenues from illegal resource theft goes to transnational organized criminal networks, with the remainder to armed groups (UN Environment-MONUSCO-OSESG, 2015). Recent estimates by UN Environment and INTERPOL place the total value of environmental crime, such as wildlife poaching, illegal logging, and illegal extraction of minerals, at up to US $259 billion, which corresponds to twice the amount of global official development assistance in 2015 (OECD, 2016a).

Track 2: assessing drivers of conflict

From 2005 to 2008, the policy focus of UN Environment shifted from assessing the environmental impacts of conflict to understanding how natural resources can drive, fuel, and sustain conflicts. This shift occurred for two main reasons. First, the UN Security Council (UNSC) became increasingly concerned with conflicts resources in places like Sierra Leone, Liberia, and Cote d'Ivoire. Second, many post-conflict recovery and peacebuilding programs were being impacted by local conflicts over access to natural resources, in particular, land and water as well as minerals and oil and gas.

The policy shift began in 2005 when the Governing Council of UN Environment requested a further increase in capacity to conduct post-conflict operations through the establishment of a dedicated branch with core funding. The scope of post-conflict environmental assessments subsequently began to expand to include drivers of conflict from natural resources. For example, the Sudan assessment concluded that natural resources acted as an important conflict driver at several levels: at the *local* level between farming and herding communities, at the *national* level over the control of oil resources, and at the *transboundary* level involving migratory routes and the shared waters of the Nile river (UN Environment, 2007b).

In 2008, UN Member States decided to further upgrade the mandate of UN Environment during the tenth Special Session of the UN Environment Governing Council. Assessing and addressing the environmental causes and consequences of conflicts and disasters were included as one of the six new strategic priorities for the organization's medium-term strategy.

With an increased focus on addressing the environmental dimensions of conflict, UN Environment, together with the International Institute for Sustainable Development, established an Expert Group on Peace and Security consisting of ten leading international experts to provide policy and strategic advice as well as technical expertise. This area of work was managed by a new UN Environment program known as ECP (UN Environment, 2015a, 2016a). One of the goals of the ECP program was to help in systematically sharing the outcomes of field-level assessments with UN peace and security policy development processes to ensure they integrated environment and natural resource risks and opportunities. This was important as a range of policy innovations were advancing across the UN system – particularly on conflict resources including resolutions by the UNSC.[3]

From 2005 to 2008, UN Environment was requested to initiate a number of important field assessments in Somalia (UN Environment, 2005), Lebanon (UN Environment, 2007c), Iraq (UN Environment, 2007a), and Sudan (UN Environment, 2007b). The main lessons learned by UN Environment and partners on the role of natural resources as conflict drivers are highlighted later.

(1) Natural resources contribute to conflict through many unique pathways: the importance of distinguishing between means and motivation

At an overarching level, it is important to distinguish between violent conflicts where natural resources act as an economic *means* for financing conflict versus situations where natural resources contribute to the social and political *motivation* for conflict. For example, in Sierra Leone, it is estimated that between US $25 million and US $125 million worth of raw diamonds were smuggled out per year as a means for financing different rebel groups (UN Environment, 2010). Similarly, in the Angola conflict, so-called blood diamonds are estimated to have been worth US $3–4 billion (UN Environment, 2009a). On the other hand, violent conflicts in places like Nigeria and Bougainville, Papua New Guinea have been motivated, in part, by grievances over environmental damage and unfair revenue sharing. In some cases, such as in Cote d'Ivoire for example, natural resources can play both roles. For example, land played an important role as a conflict driver and source of social grievance, while natural resources such as coffee and cocoa provided conflict financing and also undermined peace incentives (UN Environment, 2015b).

Where natural resources only act as a means for funding the activities of armed groups, they must be secured and restricted from entering the market and generating revenue. Tools include commodity sanctions and trade restrictions, certification schemes, and due diligence requirements around specific resources known to finance conflict such as diamonds or other metals and minerals. Examples include UN timber and diamond sanctions on Liberia, the Kimberly process certification scheme, and the Dodd Frank Act in the United States.

In contrast, conflicts that are motivated by grievances around natural resources must be tackled in different ways. These conflicts typically revolve around one or more drivers that need to be addressed: disputes over ownership; restrictions on resource access; exclusion from consultation and decision making; and/or inequitable distribution of the benefits and risks associated with extraction and use.

A complicating factor is that these drivers often occur at different scales and interact in ways that are nested and interconnected at local, subregional, national, and sometimes transboundary levels. For example, the civil war in Darfur had a series of interconnected conflict drivers, ranging from changes in land administration to competition over resource access and to lack of voice for pastoral groups in decision-making processes. Chronic conflict over natural resources, occurring primarily at the local level, was also interlinked with issues of tribal and state governance (UN Environment, 2014). This situation was compounded by the multiple concurrent drivers of change that livelihoods were adapting to, including climate, population, urbanization, conflict, and economic development.

(2) Social grievances and disputes over natural resources are almost never the sole cause of violent conflict

The drivers of violence are most often multidimensional and can include a range of social, political, and economic grievances as well as opportunism. Resource conflicts can be an important driver, but are rarely, if ever, the sole source of violent conflict. Technical responses are part of the solution, but they need to be connected to a broader political response which aims to help States build and communicate a social contract (UN Environment-UN DPA, 2015).

For example, in Bougainville, the Panguna mine was the flashpoint for starting the decade-long civil war (1990–2001). Most analysts agree that the conflict drivers included environmental damage from the mine combined with the inequitable distribution of benefits, including both revenues and jobs. However, the disputes around the mine were also politicized to amplify a long-standing desire for cultural self-determination and autonomy of Bougainville from Papa New Guinea (UN Environment, 2016a).

(3) Each natural resource has a distinct set of characteristics that can drive conflicts in different ways

Different types of natural resources such as minerals, oil and gas, timber, land, and water can generate unique kinds of conflict between stakeholders, often at different spatial and political scales (see, e.g., European Union and United Nations Interagency Framework Team for Preventive Action, 2010–2012). Typically, the potential for a natural resource to generate risks and vulnerabilities that drive conflict depends on the magnitude and distribution of revenues and benefits they generate, the number of livelihoods they directly support, or the scale of negative impacts they cause when extracted. Many natural resources are influenced by a range of environmental, economic, and social factors, leading to a high level of complexity and uncertainty in their availability, quality, and value that is always context specific.

In addressing this challenge, the United Nations has helped local stakeholders identify conflict risks and suitable mitigation measures. For example, in Sierra Leone (UN Environment, 2010) and along the border region between Haiti and the Dominican Republic (UN Environment-UNDP-WPF, 2013), UN Environment worked with local actors to identify key conflict drivers linked to natural resources and helped develop conflict resolution strategies by the resource sector, including on integrated water resource management and disaster risk reduction measures.

Track 3: addressing environmental peacebuilding opportunities

From 2009 to 2015, the policy scope of UN Environment's work expanded again, from assessing the drivers of conflict to better understanding environment and natural resources as entry points for post-conflict peacebuilding. In particular, UN Environment began assessing how natural resources can contribute to job creation, sustainable livelihoods, and confidence building between divided groups. This happened as the newly established UN Peacebuilding commission began to carry out its work and requested technical assistance from UN Environment on these topics. The commission had a mandate to help conflict-affected countries lay the foundation for sustainable peace (UNSC, 2005). In many countries where the commission

UN environment's contribution

initially worked, such as Sierra Leone, Burundi, and Central African Republic, natural resources such as land underpinned this objective (Lehtonen, 2016). In 2009 alone, three important processes were initiated that had a significant impact on the policy framework for environmental peacebuilding.

First, the newly established Peacebuilding Commission and its Support Office requested assistance from UN Environment to explore the natural resources, conflict, and peace nexus. UN Environment and members of its Expert Group on Peace and Security presented a combination of academic and field evidence to the members of the Peacebuilding Commission in a working group on lessons learned. A joint policy report on the core issues raised during the debate was published in 2009 by UN Environment and the United Nations Peacebuilding Support Office (PBSO) titled *From Conflict to Peacebuilding: The Role of Natural Resources and the Environment* (UN Environment, 2009a).

From Conflict to Peacebuilding has been widely cited across UN publications and in the academic literature. Most importantly, it helped ensure that the successive reports by the UN Secretary-General on Peacebuilding in the Immediate Aftermath of Conflict in 2009, 2010, 2012, and 2014 addressed natural resources. Within this series of reports, the UN Secretary-General formally called on Member States and the United Nations system "to make questions of natural resource allocation, ownership and access an integral part of peacebuilding strategies" (UNGA & UNSC, 2010). On the basis of this call, the UN Development Group (UNDG) and the Executive Committee on Humanitarian Affairs (ECHA) adopted a joint guidance note in 2013 on addressing natural resources in post-conflict transitional settings (UNDG & ECHA, 2013). The process was chaired by UN Environment and eventually endorsed by 38 different UN entities. The intent of the UN guidance note was to improve joint analysis and joint programming for UN country teams on different natural resources ranging from land and water, to extractive resources such as timber, minerals, and oil and gas.

The second major policy milestone that can be traced back to 2009 is the discussion in the General Assembly on climate change and security. Importantly, UNGA Resolution A/63/281 called on the UN Secretary-General to prepare a report on the topic summarizing the views of Member States and international organizations. The UN Department of Economic and Social Affairs (UN DESA) acted as the secretariat for the report while UN Environment provided substantive technical expertise. The Secretary General's report to the General Assembly, titled *Climate Change and its Possible Security Implications*, was released in September 2009 (UNGA, 2009). The report recognizes that increasing competition over climate-sensitive natural resources could increase the risk of domestic conflict as well as have international repercussions. Five channels were identified through which climate change could affect security: increasing vulnerability, undermining development, coping and security, statelessness, and international conflict. The report found that climate change often acts as a threat multiplier by exacerbating threats caused by other drivers.

The SG's report helped catalyze a UNSC debate on the topic in 2011, where UN Environment's Executive Director was invited to directly address the Council about the links between environment, climate, peace, and security. The debate resulted in a UNSC Presidential Statement on climate change and the maintenance of international peace and security that requested the Secretary-General to report on the possible security implications of climate change when such issues are drivers of conflict, represent a challenge to the implementation of Council mandates or endanger the process of consolidation of peace (UNSC, 2011). This statement was particularly important as it requires peacekeeping missions to more actively monitor and report to the Secretary-General on climate change and security dynamics.

The third important policy development process that started in 2009 began with the publication of a joint report by UN Environment, the International Committee of the Red Cross (ICRC), and the Environmental Law Institute titled *Protecting the Environment During Armed Conflict: An Inventory and Analysis of International Law*. Among the findings and recommendations, the report called on the International Law Commission (ILC) to further study the international legal protection of the environment during armed conflicts (UN Environment, 2009b). This recommendation prompted the ILC to place the topic *Protection of the environment in relation to armed conflicts* on its program of work in 2013 and to appoint Dr. Marie G. Jacobsson of Sweden as Special Rapporteur (UNGA, 2013). Dr. Jacobsson adopted a three-year work program for 2014–2016, focusing on identifying and analyzing legal provisions and potential gaps for protecting the environment before, during, and after armed conflicts.

The three reports issued by the ILC Special Rapporteur in 2014, 2015, and 2016, respectively, provide an overarching analysis of the state of environmental protection and suggestions for further development (ILC, 2014, 2015, 2016). The work helped document the practices of States and international organizations in this area. As such, the reports serve as an important source of information submitted by numerous States on their national legislation and means of implementation of their obligations under international law. UN Environment provided technical expertise and input to each of these reports as well as to the 2018 report.

In 2016, the ILC Special Rapporteur proposed a set of draft principles to improve the protection of the environment before, during, and after armed conflict. They include provisions on access to and sharing of information, post-conflict environmental assessments, and protection of zones of major environmental and cultural interest (see, e.g., ILC, 2016). These draft principles continue to be elaborated within the Commission under the leadership of Dr. Marja Lehto, who was appointed as Special Rapporteur in 2017 (ILC, 2018).

In parallel with these higher-level policy processes, UN Environment conducted field assessments in Sierra Leone, Central African Republic, Haiti, Nigeria, and Cote d'Ivoire (UN Environment, 2015b) and managed country programs in DR Congo, Sudan, and Afghanistan. The main lessons learned by UN Environment and partners on post-conflict peacebuilding are highlighted later.

(1) Post-conflict economic recovery strategies should include a blended approach involving both renewable and nonrenewable natural resources

A number of post-conflict countries are rich in high-value natural resources that could support a range of different extractive investments. For example, the potential mineral wealth of DR Congo is estimated to be US $ 24 trillion (UN Environment, 2011c) while Afghanistan has been estimated to range from US $ 1 trillion to US $3 trillion (UN Environment, 2016a). However, extractive resources also carry a number of inherent risks that need to be managed by policy-makers. While extractive industries are often seen as an important opportunity for post-conflict countries to kick-start economic growth, create jobs, and generate revenues, they seldom live up to these expectations and should never be used as the only pathway out of fragility (Beevers, Chapter 14). In most cases, the immediate employment generated by commercial extractives is minimal, with the majority of the population continuing to depend on small-scale subsistence livelihoods. Overreliance on a single extractive industry also heightens vulnerability to price shocks and market downturns.[4] For instance, the government of Afghanistan signed a $3 billion mining concession with the Chinese companies China Metallurgical Construction

Company and Jiangxi Copper Company Limited in 2008, which the World Bank estimated could generate an annual US $541 million for the country (World Bank, 2012). However, the mine has not lived up to these expectations, with reports accusing MCC of corruption, damaging or destroying priceless cultural artifacts, and forcibly displacing locals during the initial construction phase. Falling copper prices and security concerns have also impacted the feasibility of the mine with all operations currently on hold (Global Witness, 2012; UN Environment, 2016a).

Given these challenges, any economic development plan in a peacebuilding context should be geared toward supporting the recovery and improved production of rural livelihoods based on other renewable natural resources, notably agriculture fishing, livestock, and community forestry. This can maximize employment, including for excombatants and women, and contribute to food security. Furthermore, an initial focus on rural livelihoods buys the time needed for countries to build the internal capacity, legal framework, and infrastructure to develop their extractive sector in a more strategic and effective manner.

Where extractive resources form an important part of the economic recovery strategy, countries should consider adopting a resource transformation and economic growth model based on building the institutions and good governance of the resource sector, supporting local employment and value chains, and transforming resource wealth into broader economic development and diversification (McKinsey Global Institute, 2013). The Natural Resource Charter (NRGI, 2014) can provide a sound framework for the good governance of the extractive sector.

(2) Collaboration around natural resources can be used as an entry point for dialogue and for confidence building

Depending on the country context, environmental issues such as pollution, habitat degradation, deforestation, protected areas, or shared natural resources such as water can be an initial entry point for dialogue and confidence building between divided groups and communities. Local peacebuilding may be promoted using natural resources as the basis for rebuilding key relationships if mutual benefits can be identified and a common vision agreed. Over time, cooperation over natural resources can have important "spillover" effects, leading to cooperation in other domains and establishing a basis of trust for continued joint action. Some natural resources or environmental issues seem to have more cooperation and peacebuilding potential than others – much depends on how "politicized" the resource is within the prevailing political context combined with the historical levels of conflict and cooperation around the specific resource.

For example, UN Environment's program in Wadi El Ku, North Darfur, is founded on the idea that shared natural resources can be used to both rebuild relationships between communities and establish new systems of local water governance. By assisting the government in developing mediation and governance strategies for different actors and different resources, the program has contributed to enhance local governance of water resources in the wadi using an integrated water resource management approach (IWRM) (UN Environment, 2014).

(3) Access to neutral and authoritative information is essential for good decision-making

Information around natural resources in conflict-affected countries is often highly contested, with extremely low levels of trust between different stakeholders. In many cases, information asymmetries are exploited to favor the contracting conditions of one party over another – leading to grievances in the longer term. Equalizing the basic information available to all stakeholders is a critically valuable tool in moving from problem analysis to inclusive and equitable action (UN Environment, 2015c). There is value in having an impartial third party, such as the UN, establishing a neutral and scientific set of facts that all parties can trust and use as the basis for decision-making.

The possibility for confidence-building and conflict resolution based on impartial information was tested in Ogoniland, Nigeria. In 2006, the government of Nigeria requested that UN Environment undertake a comprehensive environmental assessment of the oil contamination of Ogoniland, a region with a long history of resource-based conflict. At the time, the government was trying to mediate between the community and the oil producer. UN Environment provided the first independent baseline assessment of the contamination using a scientific methodology to measure the environmental impacts and corresponding risks. To ensure objectivity, this effort was led by international experts; but to ensure transparency and buy-in, local institutions also participated. Indeed, over 23,000 people were directly engaged in the outreach process to build confidence in the assessment process. The assessment determined that the environmental implications of the oil spills were immense, with some regions experiencing levels of benzene 900 times higher than the recommendations of the World Health Organization (UN Environment, 2011a). The assessment ultimately provided a common information base to the parties and a solid technical basis on which they could negotiate a cleanup program.

To strengthen transparency and access to information on the sustainable development of natural resources, and upon request from the g7+ group of fragile States, UN Environment, GRID-Geneva, and the World Bank have developed an online geospatial platform called MapX. The MapX mission is to support the sustainable use of natural resources by increasing access to the best available geospatial information, technology, and monitoring tools. The MapX process focuses on generating actionable insights from geospatial data to inform dialogue and take evidence-based decisions. MapX is designed to build trust among stakeholders, improve transparency, reduce conflict, and improve the contribution of natural resources toward the achievement of the Sustainable Development Goals (SDGs).

Track 4: adopting new frameworks for integrated programming and conflict prevention

At the global policy level, 2015 marked an important year for policy developments that impact the uptake and operationalization of environmental peacebuilding. In particular, a number of important policy reports and processes were generated that were united in a common theme: the need for integrated programming, with an emphasis on conflict prevention.

The first policy development process was anchored in three high-level reviews – on peacekeeping, peacebuilding, and a global study on UNSC Resolution 1325 on women and peace. UN Environment offered expertise and field evidence to all three processes. Importantly, each final report recognized how natural resources can be a structural driver of conflict but can nonetheless play an important role in stabilization and peacebuilding. The 1325 review also acknowledged that natural resources can offer an entry point for women's economic, social, and political empowerment if managed in a sustainable manner (Advisory Group of Experts, 2015; Independent High-level Panel on Peace Operations, 2015; UN Women, 2015; see also Halle, Chapter 24). All three reports stressed the need for more integrated programming that focused on building resilience to multiple shocks and stresses as well as investing more in conflict prevention.

These reports were complemented by a fourth report commissioned by the G7 Foreign Ministers titled *A New Climate for Peace* (see Rüttinger et al., 2015). UN Environment also shared expertise and lessons learned with this process, drawing many important lessons from assessment work conducted in the Sahel (UN Environment, 2011b) and Sudan (UN Environment, 2007b). The final report observed that climate change exacerbates and amplifies existing risks, particularly in fragile states (Rüttinger et al., 2015; see also Crawford and Church, Chapter 7). One of the seven compound climate-fragility risks highlighted by the report focuses on increasing resource competition from climate change and resource scarcity.

As a direct follow-up to these global reports, UN Environment launched two major partnerships. The first is a Joint Programme on Women, Natural Resources, and Peace developed together with UN Women, UNDP, and PBSO. The Joint Programme was established in 2016 to promote natural resource-based interventions as a tool for strengthening women's participation in three areas: (1) dialogue, mediation, and conflict resolution efforts; (2) governance and decision-making at all levels; and (3) contributions to economic recovery and sustainable development. The program is field testing new approaches to women's empowerment through natural resources in Sudan and Colombia (see Chapter 24 for a full overview of these pilot programs).

The second is a joint project on climate change and security in collaboration with the European Union. This partnership was launched in 2017 and aims to assist crisis-affected countries in strengthening resilience to climate-fragility risks. The project works on three levels: (1) at the global level, developing integrated tools to analyze and address climate-fragility risks; (2) at the national level, supporting the integration of a climate-sensitive perspective in peacebuilding strategies and vice versa; and (3) developing a suite of activities that build resilience to climate-fragility risks at the local level. Pilot work is being conducted in Sudan and Nepal (see EU-UN Environment, n.d.).

Perhaps the most important policy milestone for environmental peacebuilding in 2015 was the adoption of the 2030 Agenda for Sustainable Development and the SDGs by the General Assembly (UNGA, 2015). UN Environment is the formal custodian agency for 26 of the SDG indicators (UN Environment-MAP, 2017). Agenda 2030 also provides numerous entry points for environmental peacebuilding (see Figure 25.1), for example, on transparency, participation and access to information (SDG 16), equitable access to resources for men and women (SDG 5), and combating illegal wildlife crime (SDG 15). The key challenge will be measuring the contribution of natural resources and the environment to the various goals in a manner that demonstrates whether conflict was prevented or peace enhanced.

Building on the momentum from 2015, 2016 also brought some important policy advances on environmental peacebuilding. First and foremost, the "Sustaining Peace" resolutions were adopted by the General Assembly and UNSC (UNGA, 2016a; UNSC, 2016). These resolutions were developed in response to the three high-level reviews on peacekeeping, peacebuilding, and UNSC Resolution 1325 on women and peace. The resolution highlights the importance of "a comprehensive approach to sustaining peace, particularly through the prevention of conflict and addressing its root causes."

Second, the UN Environment Assembly (UNEA) passed a ground-breaking resolution on *Protection of the Environment in Areas Affected by Armed Conflict*. The resolution, which was adopted unanimously by the universal membership of the Assembly, stressed "the critical importance of protecting the environment at all times, especially during armed conflict, and of its restoration in the post-conflict period" (UNEA, 2016). It also called again on all Member States to implement applicable international law related to the protection of the environment in situations of armed conflict and to consider the application of other relevant international agreements. The

David Jensen and Amanda Kron

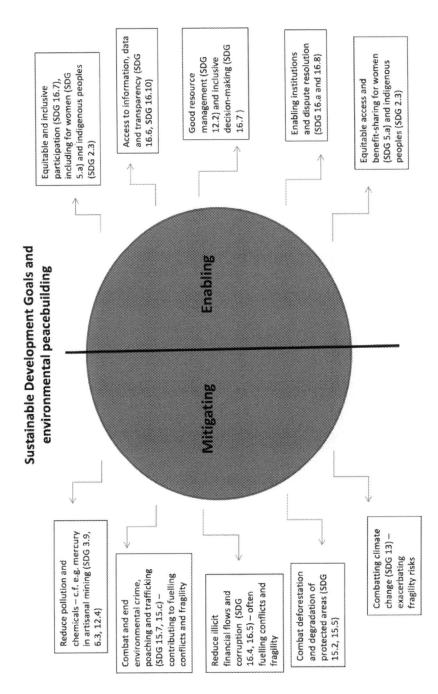

Figure 25.1 Environmental peacebuilding entry points in the SDGs. Unsustainable management of the environment and natural resources can contribute to the outbreak of conflict, fuel and finance existing conflicts, and increase the risk for conflict relapse. Conversely, natural resources can serve as vehicles for durable peace, confidence building, and poverty reduction when governments manage their resources well and integrate them into peacebuilding activities and strategies. Similarly, the SDGs serve to both mitigate fragility, corruption, and environmental hazards on the one hand and enable good governance on the other hand.

ILC Special Rapporteur remarked that this was the most significant UN resolution of its kind since the 1992 Rio Declaration and that the resolution will serve as a critical instrument for international cooperation on this issue going forward (ILC, 2016). In 2017, UNEA adopted a second resolution urging states to minimize and mitigate the health and environmental consequences of pollution caused by armed conflicts and terrorism. It was the first time that a UN decision recognized the diverse means through which conflicts can generate or facilitate pollution (Toxic Remnants of War Network, 2017; UNEA, 2017).

It would also appear that 2017 was a breakthrough year for the UNSC in terms of its own recognition of environmental drives of conflict and the need for integrated approaches to prevention and peacebuilding. In particular, the UNSC issued important resolutions on Lake Chad recognizing "the adverse effects of climate change and ecological changes among other factors on the stability of the region, including through water scarcity, drought, desertification, land degradation, and food insecurity" and emphasizing "the need for adequate risk assessments and risk management strategies by governments and the United Nations relating to these factors" (UNSC, 2017). Similar resolutions and statements on Somalia, West Africa, and the Sahel were issued in 2018 (UNSC, 2018a, 2018b) marking a major shift in the UNSC's treatment of these issues.

Against this policy background, some important lessons learned by UN Environment and partners on conflict prevention and integrated programming are highlighted later.

(1) Preventing and resolving resource conflicts depends on effective institutions, good governance, and a shared vision

The prevention and peaceful resolution of social conflicts over natural resources require effective institutions and good governance based on the principles of inclusion, transparency, accountability, equitable benefit sharing, and sustainability. Communities and other stakeholders should be included within key decisions around natural resources, and there must be some level of equity in the distribution of benefits, costs, and risks. This process should be supported by access to authoritative information and transparent monitoring frameworks on compliance and performance. Grievance redress mechanisms and dispute resolution processes are equally essential to address rising discontent before it can turn violent.

While few countries have all measures and tools in place, some have used these overarching principles as the basis for major institutional and governance reforms in the resource sector. At a local level, both UNDP and UN Environment have worked with stakeholders in Sudan to help establish joint visions for sustainable resource management. These visions have become the foundation for resource management planning and sustainable use in a range of different localities, such as Dar Es Salaam and Kilamendo (UN Environment, 2014). In North Darfur, the Wadi El Ku project developed a Forum where different stakeholders from pastoralist, farmers, and other groups together made joint decisions about water use and access (UN Environment, 2017).

(2) Resilient natural resource programs depend on considering multiple shocks and stresses, including climate change

Repetitive stresses and shocks from disasters and conflicts gradually undermine positive development gains and fundamentally reduce community resilience over time. Climate change has the potential to increase the frequency and magnitude of disasters as well as contribute to increased competition and conflict over scarce natural resources. The interplay between disasters, conflicts, and climate change, as well as the cumulative effects, requires integrated responses to successfully increase community resilience and protect the viability of resource-dependent livelihoods. The revised OECD (2016c) multidimensional fragility framework is a step in the right direction in terms of understanding the multiple political, social, economic, and environmental risks that interact to amplify fragility.

The initial work of UN Environment on climate change and security in Nepal and Sudan, building on the lessons learned from the environmental cooperation for peacebuilding program (UN Environment, 2014, 2016a), further demonstrates the need for integrated approaches to climate-fragility risks using a sustainable livelihoods lens. Ultimately, sustainable livelihoods are the foundation for human security, poverty reduction, and sustainable development. They are also the basis to cope with, recover from, and transform societies in response to climate stresses and shocks. Building trust through shared management of climate-sensitive natural resources can yield double dividends: climate change adaptation and sustainable peace. For integrated and participatory programming to be effective, social inclusion and a gender-responsive perspective are critical.[5] Inclusive participation from the onset of programming strengthens the assessment of intersectional vulnerabilities and opportunities (relating to socioeconomic status, gender, age, faith, occupation).

(3) Strengthen conflict prevention responses through social resilience and trust-building around natural resources management

Natural resource governance decisions are under the sovereign domain of each Member State and any UN program in this area is politically sensitive. The engagement of UN offices in specific resource disputes could signal the limited capacity of domestic actors to resolve disputes and lead to uncertainty and capital flight. For these and other reasons, some Member States have seen the conflict prevention mandate of the United Nations as controversial and narrow.[6]

This perception is starting to change with the recommendations of the UN peacebuilding architecture review, the focus on peace and conflict prevention in the 2030 Agenda for Sustainable Development, and the "Sustaining Peace" resolutions adopted in 2016. In addition, conflict prevention is one of the key focus areas of the new Secretary-General Antonio Guterres. At a UNSC debate on January 10, 2017, Secretary-General Guterres underlined that conflict prevention "is not merely a priority, but *the* priority."

In 2018, the UN Secretary-General's report on Sustaining Peace was released. The report emphasizes the importance of addressing root causes, references the 2030 Agenda for Sustainable Development as "the blueprint of the common vision of society toward which the world is trying to move", and underlines inclusive and sustainable development as "the best defense against the risks of violent conflict" (UNGA-UNSC, 2018, para. 5). The report nonetheless received criticism for not explicitly referencing the role of environment, natural resources, and climate change in sustaining peace (see e.g. Vivekananda, 2018). This is largely due to its adoption of a conservative approach, considering only issues where there was Member State consensus and a track record of existing anchoring resolutions.

Indeed, shortly after the Sustaining Peace report was launched, the UN and World Bank released a more wide-ranging report titled *Pathways for Peace: Inclusive Approaches to Preventing Violent Conflict*. The report references the importance of inclusive and effective management of natural resources to sustain peace as well as the need to address the impacts of climate change within conflict prevention approaches (UN – World Bank, 2018). The report also highlighted the need to address grievances and socioeconomic inequalities, for example, in connection to land as important drivers of conflict (UN – World Bank, 2018).

While these policy shifts are important and promising, the changes have yet to trickle down to building effective local and national capacity for conflict prevention programs on natural resources. One of the key challenges in conflict prevention is that successful interventions are not only about building good governance and dispute resolution processes but also about building trustful and resilient relationships between resource stakeholders in a manner which ensures that disputes are resolved in constructive and nonviolent ways. Understanding how to address some of the structural drivers of conflict and how to influence the prevailing political economy remains huge challenges.

Conclusions, future directions, and recommendations

As has been outlined earlier, UN Environment has engaged on multiple fronts to help establish the international policy and normative framework on environmental peacebuilding on the basis of field evidence from over 20 post-conflict assessments and operations.

Perhaps the most progress has been made in terms of establishing UN capacity to assess and address the environmental consequences of conflict through systematic environmental assessments and recovery programs in partnership with national stakeholders. There has also been an important recognition of the need to use natural resources in a strategic and conflict-sensitive manner to support stabilization and peacebuilding goals. Indeed, UN Environment has observed that many decision-makers now acknowledge that early decisions about resource governance can be critical in affecting whether social relations follow a peaceful or a violent path over the long term. Indeed, in the absence of policy on natural resources during periods of transition, decisions will nevertheless be made by the most powerful actors which often become institutionalized and difficult to undo (UN Environment – DPA, 2015, UNDG-ECHA, 2013).

A number of opportunities and challenges can be identified for further work and research.

First, it remains to be seen how environmental peacebuilding efforts will contribute to informing the realization of SDG 16 (Promote Peace and End Violence) as well as the implementation of the 2030 Agenda for Sustainable Development more broadly. Clearly, natural resources underpin both sustainable development and peace and security objectives. An integrated approach is necessary to deliver on the 2030 Agenda, and opportunities for collaboration and joint programming between UN agencies and other actors will be crucial. The key challenge is how to pilot effective approaches that can be shared and scaled organically without relying on external actors and resources. Another major challenge relates to the measurement of conflict and peacebuilding dynamics together with the impact that natural resource interventions have on these dynamics. Establishing indicators that can be measured and adapted over time at multiple geographic scales is a key need for the field to advance.

Second, while the importance of addressing climate change and fragility risks has been identified and emphasized at the global policy level, additional research and analysis are needed. In particular, research and analysis are needed to identify local, national, and regional programs and actions that contribute to resilience through adopting a climate risk management lens to peacebuilding programs. At the same time, a conflict-sensitivity lens needs to be applied to climate change adaption programs. Developing and furthering such projects and actions could also contribute to operationalizing the 2011 Presidential Statement of the UNSC, as well as the recommendations of a series of policy reports, including *A New Climate for Peace – Taking Action on Climate and Fragility Risks* commissioned by the G7 foreign ministries.

Third, environmental peacebuilding is inherently a bottom-up process that must be driven by local actors. Further analysis to enhance understanding of how to design effective participatory processes that can access trusted and transparent information about natural resources is warranted, particularly in post-conflict contexts where natural resource allocation and management are often characterized as being undertaken in an ad hoc, decentralized, or informal manner (UN Environment, 2009c). Information asymmetries among companies, governments, and local communities are often extreme – leading to an unfair distribution of benefits and risks linked to resource exploitation contacts. Tools such as the UN Environment-World Bank geospatial platform MapX can contribute to strengthening transparency and access to information on the financial, social, and environmental performance of natural resource development. The key challenge is leveraging frontier technologies to support data-sharing and access, citizen science, and the use of big data in a manner that underpins integrated programming, analysis, and impact monitoring.

Finally, protected areas and zones of particular significance to sensitive ecosystems should receive attention in terms of new protection regimes during conflict. In this context, it is promising that the 2016 UNEA resolution speaks to the importance of protecting World Heritage Sites affected by armed conflicts and recommends further collaboration between UN Environment, UNESCO, and other relevant stakeholders to this end (UNEA, 2016). Similarly, the proposed and provisionally adopted set of draft principles of the International Law Commission on the protection of the environment in relation to armed conflicts contains two draft principles on the protection of zones of major environmental and cultural importance before, during, and after armed conflicts (UNGA, 2016).

These efforts will require extensive collaboration between the United Nations, civil society, States, the private sector, and other stakeholders to collect and share good practices and lessons learned. The long-term partnership between the Environmental Law Institute, UN Environment, and a range of other universities and partners serves as one such multistakeholder example. It has led to the development and publication of 150 case studies on environmental peacebuilding covering more than 60 post-conflict countries (see, e.g., Bruch, Muffett, & Nichols, 2016; Jensen & Lonergan, 2012; Lujala & Rustad, 2012; Williams & Unruh, 2013; Weinthal, Troell, & Nakayama, 2014; Young & Goldman, 2015). This work has involved over 225 experts from all over the world, and all of the material is freely available online on the environmental peacebuilding knowledge platform.[7]

The lessons outlined in this chapter demonstrate that natural resources provide numerous entry points for addressing risks and opportunities in conflict-affected environments and highlight some of the ways in which UN Environment can contribute to these efforts by providing information, technical support, and convening platforms for stakeholders to develop solutions informed by the local context. Despite significant progress, research is still needed to show how these endeavors can be measured, further integrated into the global agenda for sustainable development, and connected to climate change adaptation efforts.

Notes

1 The views expressed in the chapter are those of the authors and do not necessarily reflect the views of the United Nations.
2 Even in ancient times, rules existed to ensure access to natural resources essential for survival, such as clean water, lands, and forests, in times of warfare (Deutoronomy 20:19 in Carson, 2013). "When thou shalt besiege a city a long time, in making war against it to take it, thou shalt not destroy the trees thereof by forcing an axe against them: for thou mayest eat of them, and thou shalt not cut them down (for the tree of the field is man's life) to employ them in the siege."
3 For example, the Security Council has condemned the targeting of oil installations, pipelines, and other facilities as well as the use of natural resources such as diamonds, minerals, charcoal, opium poppy, and gold for financing armed conflict. The UNSC has also addressed the natural heritage and natural resources in the context of the conflict in the Central African Republic and the Democratic Republic

UN environment's contribution

of the Congo, for example, Resolution 2121 (2013) condemning the devastation of natural heritage, poaching, and trafficking of wildlife as factors fueling the crisis in the Central African Republic. In resolution 2127 (2013), it condemned the illegal exploitation of natural resources in the Central African Republic which contributed to the perpetuation of the conflict.

See also resolution 2134 (2014) contains provisions on sanctions for individuals, as well as resolution 2149 (2014), regarding the mandate of the United Nations Multidimensional Integrated Stabilization Mission in the Central African Republic.

For a further analysis, see Aldinger, Bruch, and Yazykova (2018).
4 For example, the recent slump in oil prices has contributed to Nigeria's lowest growth rate in almost 20 years (e.g. BBC, 2015; IMF, 2016a; Wallace & Malingha, 2016), while Sierra Leone suffered serious economic setbacks from falling prices in iron ore (IMF, 2016b).
5 For example, the UN Environment – UN Women – UNDP – PBSO Joint Programme on Women, Natural Resources, and Peace, which seeks to strengthen women's roles in local peacebuilding processes over natural resource-based conflicts by building women's capacity to participate more effectively in local planning and decision-making bodies that govern access to and use of natural resources in Al Rahad, North Kordofan. Moreover, the programme aims to support the government of Colombia to realize the vision on gender, rural development, and environment presented in the Havana Accords. See chapter 24 for a complete overview of the Joint Programme.
6 See, for example, General Assembly A/RES/53/242, *Report of the Secretary-General on environment and human settlements*, 10 August 1999.
7 To disseminate this learning, the work has been transformed into a Massive Open Online Course (MOOC) on Environmental Security and Sustaining Peace that is offered by the SDG Academy as of 2018. The first offering of the course attracted over 10,000 participants with a roughly equal distribution between men and women as well as among government, civil society, private sector, and academic sectors. The tremendous level of interest in the course helped catalyze the creation of the Environmental Peacebuilding Association (ENPAx) on Earth Day of 2018. The mission of ENPAx is to improve learning and action on environment, conflict, and peace among academics, practitioners, and policy-makers. More information at www.environmentalpeacebuilding.org.

Works cited

Advisory Group of Experts. (2015). *The challenge of sustaining peace*. The 2015 Review of the United Nations Peacebuilding Architecture. Retrieved from www.un.org/pga/wp-content/uploads/sites/3/2015/07/300615_The-Challenge-of-Sustaining-Peace.pdf

Aldinger, P., Bruch, C., & Yazykova, S. (2018). Revisiting securitization: An empirical analysis of environment and natural resource provisions in United Nations Security Council Resolutions, 1946–2016. In A. Swain & J. Öjendal (Eds.), *Routledge handbook of environmental conflict and peacebuilding*. London: Routledge.

BBC (2015, December 22) Nigeria raises borrowing in budget as oil prices fall. *BBC News*. Retrieved from www.bbc.com/news/business-35162111

Bruch, C., Muffett, C., & Nichols, S. S. (Eds.). (2016). *Governance, natural resources and post-conflict peacebuilding*. Routledge.

Carson, T. (2013). Advancing the Legal Protection of the Environment in Relation to Armed Conflict: Protocol I's Threshold of Impermissible Environmental Damage and Alternatives. *Nordic Journal of International Law*, *82*(1), 83–101.

Conca, K., & Wallace, J. (2012). Environment and peacebuilding in war-torn societies: lessons From the UN Environment Programme's experience with post-conflict assessment. In D. Jensen & S. Lonergan (Eds.), *Assessing and restoring natural resources in post-conflict peacebuilding*. London: Earthscan.

Conca, K. (2015). *An unfinished foundation: The United Nations and global environmental governance*. Oxford, UK: Oxford University Press.

European Union-United Nations Environment Programme (EU-UN Environment). (n.d.). *Climate change and security: Strengthening resilience to climate-fragility risks*. Retrieved November 20, 2020, from www.unenvironment.org/explore-topics/disasters-conflicts/what-we-do/risk-reduction/climate-change-and-security-risks

European Union & United Nations Interagency Framework Team for Preventive Action. (2010–2012). *Toolkits and Guidance Notes for Preventing and Managing Land and Natural Resource Conflicts*. Retrieved from www.un.org/en/land-natural-resources-conflict/

Global Witness. (2012). *Copper Bottomed? Bolstering the Aynak contract: Afghanistan's first major mining deal.* Retrieved from www.globalwitness.org/en/campaigns/afghanistan/copper-bottomed/

Illicit Financial Flows (IFF). (2015). *Report of the High-Level Panel on Illicit Financial Flows from Africa,* Commissioned by the AU/ECA Conference of Ministers of Finance, Planning and Economic Development. Retrieved from www.uneca.org/sites/default/files/PublicationFiles/iff_main_report_26feb_en.pdf

International Law Commission (ILC). (2014). *Preliminary report of the Special Rapporteur,* Submitted by Marie G. Jacobsson, Special Rapporteur, UN Doc. A/CN.4/674 and Corr. 1

International Law Commission (ILC). (2015). *Second report of the Special Rapporteur,* Submitted by Marie G. Jacobsson, Special Rapporteur, UN Doc. A/CN.4/685

International Law Commission (ILC). (2016). *Third report on the protection of the environment in relation to armed conflicts,* Submitted by Marie G. Jacobsson, Special Rapporteur, UN Doc. A/CN.4/700

International Law Commission (ILC) (2018). *First report on the protection of the environment in relation to armed conflicts,* Submitted by Marja Lehto, Special Rapporteur, UN Doc. A/CN.4/720

International Monetary Fund (IMF) (2016a) *NIGERIA: SELECTED ISSUES,* IMF Country Report No. 16/102, April 2016. Retrieved from www.imf.org/external/pubs/ft/scr/2016/cr16102.pdf

International Monetary Fund (IMF) (2016b) *SIERRA LEONE: SELECTED ISSUES,* IMF Country Report No. 16/237, July 2016. Retrieved from www.imf.org/external/pubs/ft/scr/2016/cr16237.pdf

International Peace Information Service (IPIS). (2015). Infographic – Mapping Mining Areas in Eastern DRC. Retrieved November 19, 2020, from https://ipisresearch.be/infographic-mapping-security-human-rights-mining-areas-eastern-drc/

Jensen, D., & Lonergan, S. (Eds.). (2012). *Assessing and restoring natural resources in post-conflict peacebuilding.* London: Earthscan.

Lehtonen, M. (2016). Peacebuilding through Natural Resource Management: The UN Peacebuilding Commission's First Five Years. In C. Bruch, C. Muffett, & S. S. Nichols (Eds.), *Governance, Natural Resources, and Post-Conflict Peacebuilding* (pp. 147–164). Routledge.

Lujala, P., & Aas Rustad, S. (Eds.). (2012). *High-Value Natural Resources and Post-Conflict Peacebuilding.* Routledge. Retrieved from http://environmentalpeacebuilding.org/publications/books/.

McKinsey Global Institute (2013, December). *Reverse the curse: Maximizing the potential of resource-driven economies.* Retrieved from www.mckinsey.com/industries/metals-and-mining/our-insights/reverse-the-curse-maximizing-the-potential-of-resource-driven-economies

Natural Resource Governance Institute (NRGI) (2014). *Natural Resource Charter (Second Edition).* Retrieved from http://resourcegovernance.org/sites/default/files/documents/nrcj1193_natural_resource_charter_19.6.14.pdf

Organization for Economic Cooperation and Development (OECD) (2016a) *Development aid rises again in 2015, spending on refugees doubles,* 13 April 2016. Retrieved from www.oecd.org/dac/development-aid-rises-again-in-2015-spending-on-refugees-doubles.htm

Organization for Economic Cooperation and Development (OECD) (2016b) *States of Fragility 2016: Highlights,* September 2016. Retrieved from www.oecd.org/dac/conflict-fragility-resilience/docs/Fragile-States-highlights-2016.pdf

Organization for Economic Cooperation and Development (OECD) (2016c) *Towards a multidimensional fragility framework for the OECD: Working Paper outlining the methodology for the OECD's monitoring of fragility* Retrieved from www.oecd.org/dac/governance-peace/conflictfragilityandresilience/Multidimensional%20Fragility%20Framework%20OECD.pdf

Office of the High Commissioner for Human Rights (OHCHR) (2016). *Early warning and economic, social and cultural rights.* Retrieved from www.ohchr.org/Documents/Issues/ESCR/EarlyWarning_ESCR_2016_en.pdf

Office of the Prosecutor of the International Criminal Court (2016). *Policy paper on case selection and prioritization* Retrieved from www.icc-cpi.int/itemsDocuments/20160915_OTP-Policy_Case-Selection_Eng.pdf.

Intendent High-level Independent Panel on Peace Operations. (2015). *Report of the High-level Independent Panel on Peace Operations on uniting our strengths for peace: Politics, partnership and people.* UN Doc. A/70/95 – S/2015/446. Retrieved from www.un.org/sg/pdf/HIPPO_Report_1_June_2015.pdf

Rome Statute (1998). Article 8(b) (iv) Retrieved from http://legal.un.org/icc/statute/romefra.htm

Rüttinger, L., Smith, D., Stang, G., Tänzler, D., & Vivekananda, J. with Brown, O., Carius, A., Dabelko, G., De Souza, R-M., Mitra, S., Nett, M. . . . Pohl, B. (2015). *A New Climate for Peace: Taking Action on Climate and Fragility Risks* An Independent Report Commissioned by the G7 Members. Retrieved from www.newclimateforpeace.org

Toxic Remnants of War Network (2017, December 7). *UN passes first ever resolution on conflict pollution.* Retrieved from www.trwn.org/un-passes-first-ever-resolution-on-conflict-pollution/).

United Nations and World Bank (2018). *Pathways for Peace: Inclusive Approaches to Preventing Violent Conflict.* https://doi.org/10.1596/978-1-4648-1162-3.

United Nations Development Group (UNDG) and Executive Committee on Humanitarian Affairs (ECHA) (2013). *Natural Resource Management in Transition Settings*, Guidance Note. Retrieved from https://undg.org/wp-content/uploads/2014/06/UNDG-ECHA_NRM_guidance_Jan20131.pdf

UN Environment -INTERPOL (2016). The rise of environmental crime – a growing threat to natural resources peace, development and security. *UNEP-INTERPOL Rapid Response Assessment* United Nations Environment Programme and RHIPTO Rapid Response – Norwegian Center for Global Analyses.

UN Environment-UNDP (2013). *The Role of Natural Resources in Disarmament, Demobilization and Reintegration: Addressing Risks and Seizing Opportunities*, December 2013. Retrieved from http://postconflict.unep.ch/publications/UNEP_UNDP_NRM_DDR.pdf

UN Environment-UN DPA (2015). *Natural resources and conflict: A guide for mediation practitioners.* Retrieved from http://postconflict.unep.ch/publications/UNDPA_UNEP_NRC_Mediation_full.pdf

UN Environment -UNDP-WPF (2013). *Haiti – Dominican Republic: Environmental challenges in the border zone.* Retrieved from http://postconflict.unep.ch/publications/UNEP_Haiti-DomRep_border_zone_EN.pdf

UN Environment-PBSO-UN Women-UNDP (2011). *Women and natural resources. Unlocking the peacebuilding potential*, 2013, referring to OECD, *Aid in Support of Women's Economic Empowerment.* Retrieved from www.oecd.org/dac/gender-development/aid-women-economic-empowerment.htm

UN Environment-PBSO-UN Women-UNDP (2013). *Women and natural resources. Unlocking the peacebuilding potential.* Retrieved from http://postconflict.unep.ch/publications/UNEP_UN-Women_PBSO_UNDP_gender_NRM_peacebuilding_report.pdf

UN Environment-MONUSCO-OSESG (2015, April). *Experts' background report on illegal exploitation and trade in natural resources benefitting organized criminal groups and recommendations on MONUSCO's role in fostering stability and peace in eastern DR Congo.* Retrieved from http://postconflict.unep.ch/publications/UNEP_DRCongo_MONUSCO_OSESG_final_report.pdf

United Nations Environment Assembly (UNEA) (2016, May 27). *Protection of the environment in areas affected by armed conflict*, UNEP/EA.2/Res.15

United Nations Environment Assembly (UNEA) (2017). *Pollution mitigation and control in areas affected by armed conflict or terrorism*, 30 January 2018, UNEP/EA.3/Res 1

United Nations Environment Programme (1999). *The Kosovo Conflict: Consequences for the Environment and Human Settlements.* Retrieved from https://postconflict.unep.ch/publications/finalreport.pdf

United Nations Environment Programme (2000a). *Post-Conflict Environmental Assessment – FYR of Macedonia.* Retrieved from https://postconflict.unep.ch/publications/fyromfinalasses.pdf

United Nations Environment Programme (2000b). *Post-Conflict Environmental Assessment-Albania.* Retrieved from https://wedocs.unep.org/bitstream/handle/20.500.11822/8615/-Post-Conflict%20Environmental%20Assessment%20-%20Albania-2001313.pdf?sequence=3&isAllowed=

United Nations Environment Programme (2003a). *Afghanistan Post-Conflict Environmental Assessment.* Retrieved from www.unep.org/pdf/afghanistanpcajanuary2003.pdf

United Nations Environment Programme (2003b). *Desk study on the Environment in Iraq.* Retrieved from www.unep.org/pdf/iraq_ds.pdf

United Nations Environment Programme (2003c). *Desk Study on the Environment in the Occupied Palestinian Territories.* Retrieved from http://postconflict.unep.ch/publications/INF-31-WebOPT.pdf

United Nations Environment Programme (2004a). *From Conflict to Sustainable Development: Assessment and Clean-up in Serbia and Montenegro.* Retrieved from http://postconflict.unep.ch/publications/sam.pdf

United Nations Environment Programme (2004b). *Desk Study on the Environment in Liberia.* Retrieved from http://postconflict.unep.ch/publications/Liberia_DS.pdf

United Nations Environment Programme (2005). *The state of the environment in Somalia: A desk study.* Retrieved from http://postconflict.unep.ch/publications/dmb_somalia.pdf.

United Nations Environment Programme (2007a) *UNEP in Iraq: Post-conflict assessment, clean-up and reconstruction.* Retrieved from http://postconflict.unep.ch/publications/Iraq.pdf

United Nations Environment Programme (2007b) *Sudan: post-conflict environmental assessment.* Retrieved from https://postconflict.unep.ch/publications/UNEP_Sudan.pdf

United Nations Environment Programme (2007c) *Lebanon: Post-conflict environmental assessment.* Retrieved from http:// postconflict.unep.ch/publications/UNEP_Lebanon.pdf

United Nations Environment Programme (2009a) *From Conflict to Peacebuilding: The Role of Natural Resources and the Environment.* Retrieved from www.unep.org/pdf/pcdmb_policy_01.pdf

United Nations Environment Programme (2009b) *Protecting the Environment During Armed Conflict: An Inventory and Analysis of International Law.* Retrieved from http://postconflict.unep.ch/publications/int_law.pdf

United Nations Environment Programme (2009c) *Integrating Environment in Post-Conflict Needs Assessments,* Guidance note. Retrieved from http://postconflict.unep.ch/publications/environment_toolkit.pdf

United Nations Environment Programme (2010). *Sierra Leone: Environment, conflict and peacebuilding assessment.* Retrieved from http://postconflict.unep.ch/publications/Sierra_Leone.pdf

United Nations Environment Programme (2011a). *Environmental assessment of Ogoniland* Retrieved from http://postconflict.unep.ch/publications/OEA/UNEP_OEA.pdf

United Nations Environment Programme (2011b). *Livelihood security: Climate change, migration and conflict in the Sahel.* Retrieved from https://postconflict.unep.ch/publications/UNEP_Sahel_EN.pdf

United Nations Environment Programme (2011c) *The Democratic Republic of the Congo Post-Conflict Environmental Assessment. Synthesis for Policy Makers.* Retrieved from https://postconflict.unep.ch/publications/UNEP_DRC_PCEA_EN.pdf

United Nations Environment Programme (2012, May). *Greening the Blue helmets: Environment, natural resources and un peacekeeping operations.* Retrieved from www.un.org/en/peacekeeping/publications/UNEP_greening_blue_helmets.pdf

United Nations Environment Programme (2014). *Relationships and Resources: Environmental governance for peacebuilding and resilient livelihoods in Sudan,* June 2014. Retrieved from http://postconflict.unep.ch/publications/UNEP_Sudan_RnR.pdf

United Nations Environment Programme (2015a) *Addressing the role of natural resources in conflict and peacebuilding: A summary of progress from UNEP's environmental cooperation for peacebuilding programme 2008–2015.* Retrieved from www.unep.org/disastersandconflicts/Introduction/EnvironmentalCooperationforPeacebuilding_/ECPProgressReport/tabid/1060787/Default.aspx

United Nations Environment Programme (2015b) *Côte d'Ivoire post-conflict environmental assessment.* Retrieved from http://postconflict.unep.ch/publications/Cote%20d'Ivoire/UNEP_CDI_PCEA_EN.pdf

United Nations Environment Programme (2015c) *Natural Resources and Conflicts: A Guide for Mediation Practitioners,* February 2015. Retrieved from http://postconflict.unep.ch/publications/UNDPA_UNEP_NRC_Mediation_full.pdf

United Nations Environment Programme (2016a). *Environmental Cooperation for Peacebuilding: Final Report.* November 2016. Retrieved from http://postconflict.unep.ch/publications/ECP/ECP_final_report_Nov2016.pdf

United Nations Environment Programme (2017). *Wadi El Ku Final Report: July 2013 – April 2017.* April 2017.

United Nations Environment Programme – Mediterranean Action Plan (2017). *Follow-up and review of SDG 14 through the Regional Seas programmes,* 6 December 2017, UN Doc. UNEP(DEPI)/MED IG.23/Inf.20. Retrieved from https://wedocs.unep.org/bitstream/handle/20.500.11822/22289/17ig23_inf20_engonly.pdf?sequence=1&isAllowed=y

United Nations General Assembly (UNGA) (2016). Seventy-first session, Supplement No. 10, *Report of the International Law Commission: Sixty-eighth session (2 May-10 June and 4 July-12 August 2016),* UN Doc. A/71/10

United Nations General Assembly (UNGA). (2015). *Transforming our world: The 2030 Agenda for Sustainable Development,* 25 September 2015, UN Doc. A/RES/70/1.

United Nations General Assembly (UNGA) (2013). Official Records, Sixty-Eighth Session, Supplement No. 1, UN Doc. A/68/10

United Nations General Assembly (UNGA) (2009). *Climate change and its possible security implications: Report of the Secretary-General,* UN Doc. A/64/350, 11 September 2009. Retrieved from www.un.org/ga/search/view_doc.asp?symbol=A/64/350

United Nations General Assembly (UNGA) (2001). *Observance of the international day for preventing the exploitation of the environment in war and armed conflict,* Resolution, 5 November 2001, UN Doc. A/RES/56/4

UN environment's contribution

United Nations General Assembly (UNGA) (1999). *Report of the Secretary-General on environment and human settlements*, 10 August 1999, UN Doc. A/RES/53/242

United Nations General Assembly (UNGA) (1992). *Protection of the environment in times of armed conflict*, Resolution, 25 November 1992, UN Doc. A/RES/47/37.

United Nations General Assembly (UNGA) and United Nations Security Council (UNSC) (2010). *Progress Report of the Secretary-General on peacebuilding in the immediate aftermath of conflict*, Report, 16 July 2010, UN Doc. A/64/866; UN Doc. S/2010/386

United Nations General Assembly (UNGA) & United Nations Security Council (UNSC). (2018). *Peacebuilding and sustaining peace: Report of the Secretary-General*, 18 January 2018, UN Doc. A/72/707; UN Doc. S/2018/43

United Nations General Assembly. (2016a). *70/262. Review of the United Nations peacebuilding architecture*, 12 May 2016, UN Doc. A/RES/70/262. Retrieved from http://undocs.org/A/RES/70/262

United Nations Security Council (UNSC) (2005). *Resolution 1645 (2005)*, 20 December 2005, UN Doc. S/RES/1645 (2005). Retrieved from http://undocs.org/S/RES/1645%20(2005)

United Nations Security Council (UNSC) (2011). *Statement by the President of the Security Council*, 20 July 2011, UN Doc. S/PRST/2011/15. Retrieved from https://undocs.org/S/PRST/2011/15

United Nations Security Council (UNSC). (2016). *Resolution 2282 (2016)*, 27 April 2016, UN Doc. S/RES/2282 (2016). Retrieved from http://undocs.org/S/RES/2282(2016)

United Nations Security Council (UNSC). (2017). *Resolution 2349 (2017)*, 31 March 2017, UN Doc. S/RES/2349 (2017). Retrieved from http://undocs.org/S/RES/2349(2017)

United Nations Security Council (UNSC). (2018a). *Resolution 2408 (2018)*, 27 March 2018, UN Doc. S/RES/2498 (2018). Retrieved from http://undocs.org/S/RES/2408(2018)

United Nations Security Council (UNSC). (2018b). Statement by the *President of the Security Council*, 30 January 2018, UN Doc. S/PRST/2018/3. Retrieved from http://undocs.org/S/PRST/2018/3

UN Women. (2015). *Preventing conflict, transforming justice, securing the peace: A Global Study on the Implementation of United Nations Security Council Resolution 1325*. Retrieved from http://wps.unwomen.org/pdf/en/GlobalStudy_EN_Web.pdf

Vivekananda, J. (2018, February 23). Sustaining peace in a climate of change. *Thomson Reuters Foundation News*. Retrieved from http://news.trust.org/item/20180223163215-ptl0r/

Wallace, P., & Malingha, D. (2016, April 22) Nigeria Revenue Drops to 5-Year Low as Tax, Oil Income Fall. *Bloomberg*. Retrieved November 19, 2020, from www.bloomberg.com/news/articles/2016-04-22/nigeria-s-revenue-drops-to-five-year-low-as-tax-oil-income-fall

Weinthal, E., Troell, J., & Nakayama, M. (Eds.). (2014). *Water and Post-Conflict Peacebuilding*. Routledge.

World Bank (2012). *Afghanistan in Transition: Looking Beyond 2014, Volume 2*. Retrieved from http://siteresources.worldbank.org/AfghAn-   istAnexn/images/305983–1334954629964/Aftransition2014vol2.pdf

Williams, R., & Unruh, J. (Eds.). (2013). *Land and Post-Conflict Peacebuilding* (Routledge, 2013). Retrieved from http://environmentalpeacebuilding.org/publications/books/.

Young, H., & Goldman, L. (Eds.). (2015). *Livelihoods, natural resources, and post-conflict peacebuilding*. Routledge. Retrieved from http://environmentalpeacebuilding.org/publications/books/

Young, H., Osman, A. M., Abusin, A. M., Asher, M., & Egemi, O. (2009). *Livelihoods, power and choice: The vulnerability of the Northern Rizaygat, Darfur, Sudan*. Boston, MA: Feinstein International Center, Tufts University.

26

CONCLUSION

Evgenia Nizkorodov and Richard Matthew

The Routledge Handbook of Environmental Security brings together the diverse perspectives of researchers from around the world to critically trace the complex linkages among the environment, security, conflict, and peace across the conflict life cycle. Contributors have examined (1) the various roles that natural resources and different forms of environmental and climate stress and shock can play in causing or otherwise contributing to the *onset of violent conflict*, (2) the ways in which environmental factors can help prolong and sustain conflict as well as the ways in which the environment can suffer *during violent conflict*, and (3) the role of the environment in *conflict resolution, post-conflict recovery and peacebuilding*, ideally helping build the capacity to manage conflict and prevent violence in the future. This book is the first to assemble the findings of some three decades of environmental security research around the concept of the conflict life cycle. In doing so, it also advances the growing field of environmental peacebuilding by reflecting on past programmatic efforts and grounding novel approaches to conflict prevention, peacemaking, and post-conflict recovery in empirical analysis. And, it ushers in an emerging third wave of scholarship that builds on the first wave of theoretical and conceptual work characteristic of the 1990s and on the second wave of ethnographic case study and quantitative research that advanced the field in the 2000s and 2010s.

Several key insights emerge from the book, and in this conclusion, we focus on six of them. First, the authors argue that violent conflict is the outcome of the interplay of complex and contextual factors such as ethnic rivalry, chronic poverty, foreign meddling, and weak government, all of which can be affected by environmental stress and shock. In the 1990s, as concerns about the extent of planetary environmental change moved onto the top of the global agenda, scholars theorized the implications of this for peace and conflict. Building on ideas with roots in thinkers such as Thomas Malthus and David Ricardo, they focused on linking resource scarcity and environmental degradation to conflict in quite direct and causal ways (see, e.g., Homer-Dixon, 1994, 1999). This generated considerable, constructive, and persistent criticism from both practitioners and scholars who stress the importance of moving away from deterministic and oversimplified explanations (see Le Billon, Chapter 4; Asthana, Chapter 6; Krampe et al., Chapter 21; see also Ide, Bruch, et al., 2021). Biogeography is not destiny. The presence or absence of resources does not create a self-fulfilling prophecy of conflict. Instead, understanding the causes of conflict requires examining broader historical processes, geopolitical relationships, and sociopolitical conditions at different scales. Unequal access to resources and the uneven

DOI: 10.4324/9781315107592-30

Conclusion

distribution of benefits derived from resource extraction can create tensions and social discontent. Threats to traditional livelihoods or governance of land and resource rights that is opaque, corrupt, or poorly enforced can transform these tensions into direct confrontation or conflict. Indeed, the pathways from natural resources, climate change, and the environment to violent conflict are fluid and contextual. As the former became more widespread and severe, trends clearly documented in Intergovernmental Panel on Climate Change Assessment Reports (2014, 2018, 2021), Global Environmental Outlook reports (UNEP, 2019), and the recent Ecological Threat Registry (IEP, 2020), these pathways may become more pronounced and alarming.

Second, large-scale perturbations, such as climate change, disproportionately impact low-income and marginalized individuals (UN DESA, 2020; World Bank, 2020). Addressing the root causes of conflict thus requires solutions that secure sustainable livelihoods, particularly among the poorest and disadvantaged – and especially communities that have long been marginalized politically and economically such as indigenous peoples, traditional communities, small-scale farmers and those living in abject conditions of urban and peri-urban poverty (Beevers, Chapter 14; Goodrich & Haines, Chapter 23). Doing so requires providing critical infrastructure services, such as water and sanitation systems, and strengthening the adaptive capacity of communities to both persistent stress and large-scale shocks (Ide, Bruch, et al., 2021; UN DESA, 2020; World Bank, 2020).

Third, while conflict can be a way to correct inequalities and environmental injustices (see Le Billion, Chapter 4; Unruh, Chapter 5), the impacts of warfare can lead to further social–ecological harms. Closmann's (Chapter 8) historical analysis suggests that modern warfare has inflicted unprecedented damage to the environment. The environment can be deliberately targeted to weaken or destroy opposing groups. Valuable resources located inside conflict zones can also be extracted by rebel groups or governments to fund war, thus prolonging conflict (Lujala et al., Chapter 10, Upreti & Nizkorodov, Chapter 22). The environment can also be impacted indirectly during conflict. For instance, large-scale displacement can threaten vulnerable ecosystems, as IDPs or refugees extract resources to fulfill basic survival needs; in urban areas, a sudden influx of formal and informal settlements can strain waste and water systems and increase land, water, and air pollution (Nizkorodov & Wagle, Chapter 11; Maharramli, Chapter 15).

Violent conflict also transforms institutions and governance mechanisms. Not only does violence directly destroy critical infrastructure, but it often forces governments to redirect public resources from social welfare programs to military spending (UNDP, 2020). The state may also have limited capacity to enforce sustainable practices, particularly at the local level. In Nepal, for example, low political stability and corruption during and after the Civil War (1996–2006) rapidly increased the rates of deforestation, delegitimized community-based Forest User Groups, and disrupted critical services such as waste management (Upreti & Nizkorodov, Chapter 22). The impacts to institutions and governance mechanism during warfare ultimately have profound impacts on human health, human capital, and poverty, which can persist for decades or even generations (Corral, Irwin, Krishnan, & Mahler, 2020).

Fourth, the direct and indirect impacts to social–ecological systems can be very long lasting which underscores the importance of conflict-sensitive programs in post-conflict regions. Historically, development and environmental organizations have implemented programs without distinction between regions affected by conflict and those not affected (Ide, Bruch, et al., 2021). Policy interventions in conflict areas are never neutral and can have unintended consequences that are often unevenly distributed along ethnic, social, and gender lines (Ide, 2020; Tänzler & Scherer, 2019; Victor, 2010). Women, for example, may lose gains in employment and income generation as new development or economic restructuring programs are introduced in post-conflict contexts (Halle, Chapter 24; Ide, 2020b). Thus, failing to account for political, economic, and sociocultural context runs the risk of recreating or generating new conflict (Tänzler & Scherer, 2019). At a minimum, programs in conflict-sensitive regions must strive to "do no harm" by ensuring interventions do not reinforce structural inequalities or worsen divisions between conflicting groups. Ideally, interventions pursue an integrated approach that provide opportunities to promote peace and security in the conflict-affected state. Program designs must identify communities vulnerable to social tensions, anticipate and mitigate negative impacts, and monitor for unintended consequences (Bruch et al., Chapter 2; Tänzler & Scherer, 2019; UNDP, 2016).

A fifth theme that resonates through the book, and historically has not received sufficient scholarly attention, is the importance of bottom-up, inclusive governance mechanisms in development and peacebuilding (see also Ide, Bruch, et al., 2021; UNDP, 2020). Effective governance of environment and natural resources across scales (from local to national to international) is critical in the prevention and resolution of conflicts (Bruch et al., Chapter 2; Jensen & Kron, Chapter 25). In the past, peacebuilding initiatives by NGOs, state institutions, and state elites have prioritized national-level security and development, often assuming that reform will trickle down to improve human security at local scales (Beevers, Chapter 14). Swatuk's examination of transboundary peace parks (Chapter 16) reveals that top-down solutions may not achieve expected outcomes in economic development and livelihood at the local level. Instead, for example, peace parks often have resulted in the uncompensated loss of land and resource access. Similarly, Maharramli (Chapter 15) demonstrates that post-conflict reconstruction and economic development programs in Kigali, Rwanda, has exacerbated the housing crisis in the city. The development of business districts has displaced low-income individuals to unplanned settlements, which are located in areas highly prone to flooding and erosion and lack access to basic amenities (see also Baffoe, Ahmad, & Bhandari, 2020). By limiting opportunities for participatory governance and pursuing a top-down approach to planning, the government of Rwanda has set itself on a potentially unsustainable path to post-conflict recovery.

Local-level governance that provides opportunities for inclusive engagement can empower vulnerable and marginalized communities, reconfigure power dynamics, and reduce sources of tension among communities (Halle, Chapter 24; Ide, Palmer, et al., 2021; Johnson, 2021). To maximize opportunities for local economic development, these bottom-up initiatives must be directly scaled up and linked to national and regional development strategies. The authors in this book caution that a strictly top-down approach can create cyclical process of rising vulnerability and inequality (Beevers, Chapter 14) and can undermine the effectiveness of local institutions (see also Ide, Palmer, et al., 2021).

Sixth and finally, to promote sustainable development, peacebuilding must be an integrated approach that accounts for the environment, livelihoods, and human rights. A number of powerful economic, social, and environmental forces – or megatrends – are heightening global disparities (UN DESA, 2020). In the late twentieth century, the global economy was drastically restructured under neoliberal ideology. The financialization of markets and infrastructures has hastened the rate of resource extraction and has created conditions of slow violence for marginalized and low-income communities (Nixon, 2011). At the same time, human activities have radically reshaped the earth at an unprecedented rate and scale, posing new threats to human and environmental systems (IPCC, 2018; UN DESA, 2020). Climate change serves as a threat multiplier, particularly in fragile and low-income countries, by stressing already overburdened institutions and governance mechanisms (Crawford & Church, Chapter 7). Natural disasters and the threats to water and food security can disrupt livelihoods and result in large-scale

Conclusion

displacement. It is estimated that climate change will push an additional 68–132 million individuals into poverty (World Bank, 2020).

The COVID-19 pandemic has further compounded these trends and has forced us to reflect on the effectiveness of our social institutions and governance systems (UNDP, 2020). The World Bank (2021) estimates that COVID-19 has pushed an additional 88–115 million people into extreme poverty in 2020; as many as 150 million people (1.9% of the world's population) may fall into extreme poverty by 2021. The pandemic may accelerate drivers of conflict by heightening economic disparity, reducing social mobility, decreasing access to education, increasing food insecurity, and reducing overall resilience to future shocks and stressors (UNDP, 2020; UN Security Council, 2020; World Bank, 2020). Fragile and conflict-affected countries will be those worst affected in the long term (UN Security Council, 2020; World Bank, 2020). Limited resources and governance structures to combat the pandemic can increase social tensions between ethnic groups, undermine local governance, and ultimately erode gains made to peace (Polo, 2020; UN Security Council, 2020). Recent research reveals alarming trends of increasing violent conflict (Ide, 2020; UNDP, 2020). COVID-19 has created additional opportunities for political and military groups to seize power (Ide, 2020; Polo, 2020). There has been a rise in authoritarian regimes and human rights violations – attacking and arresting critics, spreading misinformation, stifling free speech, withholding information, or using excessive force (Kolvani et al., 2020; Nygard, Methi, & Rustad, 2020).

In the face of these global challenges, contributing authors have emphasized the importance of pursuing joint strategies that link multiple development and peacebuilding objectives to promote sound governance and build the resilience and adaptive capacity of the most vulnerable populations. Peacebuilding features a diverse set of actors, each with their own mandates, resources, and cultures, which can promote siloed approaches. Yet, environmental challenges and threats to livelihood often cross political and organizational jurisdictions. Greater emphasis must be paid to linkages between social and ecological systems in designing and implementing programs: to secure livelihoods, programs must directly target the water–food–energy nexus (Krampe et al., Chapter 21) and should utilize a climate risk management lens (Matthew, Chapter 17; Jensen & Kron, Chapter 25).

Future climate change impacts – and our response to other megatrends – are highly dependent on which security narratives will prevail (Dalby, Chapter 20). Therefore, it is important to critically examine how security discourse narratives are shaped, under what conditions they are accepted, and who the beneficiaries of the subsequent policies are (Floyd, Chapter 19). Jensen and Kron (Chapter 25) provide a detailed account of how over the past 20 years the UN Environment Programme has spearheaded discourse, research, and interventions that link environment and natural resource governance with security and development. While this discourse among and within international organizations has been substantial, changes have yet to trickle down to many local and national governments, particularly in the Global South (Upreti & Nizkorodov, Chapter 22). Promoting holistic approaches, thus, will require shifting discourse and policies from traditional notions of security, a "freedom from fear" perspective, to one that is centered on "freedom from want" (Krampe et al., Chapter 21).

Future directions: a third wave of environmental peacebuilding research and practice

Environmental peacebuilding research has evolved substantially over the last three decades (Ide et al., 2021). Early peacebuilding primarily focused on the international level and examined transboundary water and conservation solutions to conflict prevention and cooperation between states. The second generation (2009 and onward) was heavily influenced by the rising recognition of the role of climate change in the increasing vulnerabilities of states. Research turned toward intrastate-level analysis with scholars and practitioners reflecting critically on past efforts and exploring a variety of factors – education, energy use, legal instruments – that promote resilience of communities. We conclude this book by identifying an emerging, multidisciplinary agenda for a third wave of environmental peacebuilding and security research.

Monitoring and evaluation

To ensure that peacebuilding efforts are making necessary impacts at all scales, there is a need for developing robust monitoring and evaluation (M&E) systems. Environmental peacebuilding is an emerging field of practice and research. Policies are based on intuition, anecdotal evidence, or low-N case studies (Bruch, 2020; Ide, Bruch, et al., 2021; Nanthikesan & Juha, 2012). Yet, a lack of casual evidence can create competing research narratives and can limit the effectiveness of interventions (Walch, Chapter 12).

Evaluations of post-conflict interventions are challenging (Nanthikesan & Juha, 2012). Conflict may weaken institutional and financial capacity to collect data, particularly in rural regions. Moreover, it may take years for the effects of an intervention to become evident. The long-time horizons and a lack of treatment and control cases make it almost impossible to isolate the effects of one particular intervention, especially in post-conflict contexts, where conditions may shift rapidly and are influenced by a number of diverse actors.

There have been a number of developments that can aid scholars and practitioners in developing effective M&E systems in fragile and post-conflict settings. For instance, there has been a shifting focus from attribution to contribution in M&E methods (see, e.g., Forss, Marra, & Schwartz, 2011). Rather than attributing all outcomes to an intervention, analysts quantify the extent to which resources, events, or actions contributed to achieving a set of outcomes. This M&E strategy is particularly useful in a nonexperimental setting (a lack of treatment and control options) and when coupled with a theory of change approach (Mayne, 2008). By developing a theory that explains how a planned intervention will lead to the desired social and environmental changes, practitioners can increase transparency of interventions, review underlying assumptions of the project, and identify appropriate partners on the ground (CARE, 2012; Nanthikesan & Juha, 2012).

Big data, GIS, AI, and other digital technologies

Big data and powerful collection, storage and processing technologies such as the Internet-of-Things planetary web of sensors and other data collection instruments, GIS, Artificial Intelligence, and blockchain present a unique opportunity to not only aid in M&E but also support many other activities relevant to environmental peacebuilding. These include promoting shared understanding of issues, such as the extent of environmental damage; increasing inclusion, especially of historically marginalized voices and perspectives; codeveloping knowledge; building trust in the utility and reliability of science; integrating big historical and real-time data with local knowledge and values to support and coordinate decision-making at multiple scales; clarifying trade-offs for different courses of action; exploring alternative scenarios for the future and assisting with decision making under conditions of deep uncertainty; and experimenting with solutions in high-resolution digital space. These powerful technologies hold considerable promise for helping identify fair and effective ways to increase the resilience of vulnerable communities, articulate a shared and viable vision of the future, quickly accommodate new information, and make progress on achieving the Sustainable Development Goals (Wählisch, 2019; Jensen & Campbell, 2019; ITU | UN, 2020). For several decades, since the late 1980s with the advent of the Worldwide Web or even earlier, the world has been in the midst of an incredibly rapid, wide-reaching, and impactful technological revolution. Advances in machine learning and other forms of artificial intelligence able to extract useful information from big data, identify patterns and trends, and adaptively manage practices such as water treatment, irrigation, and transportation have the potential to transform economies and societies (UN DESA, 2018). This book has presented a number of innovative technical solutions to peacebuilding and environmental security – utilizing remote sensing to plan and manage refugee settlements (Nizkorodov & Wagle, Chapter 11) or sophisticated modeling technologies to codevelop with vulnerable communities strategies for reducing hazard risk and other forms of vulnerability (Sanders, Chapter 19).

Big data and powerful information technologies are generating promising tools for promoting development and aiding peacebuilding initiatives (Orbinksi et al., Chapter 13). The skills required to use these tools can often be acquired through short trainings that can be carried out in any context, and platforms such as the ubiquitous smartphone are more than adequate for many purposes, even when not connected to the Internet and dependent solely on their own processing capacity. However, these novel technologies pose difficult policy challenges that require urgent attention. Unequal access to the benefits of these technologies can reinforce various forms of inequality and can create a new "digital divide." (UN DESA, 2018, 2020). Moreover, big data raises ethical questions about privacy and concerns about misuse or exploitation of data. Imperfect inputs, logics, or interpretations of data may lead to misaligned policy responses or run the risk of reinforcing existing biases and forms of exclusion (Blumenstock, 2018; UN DESA, 2018). And the compelling outputs of these technologies can create a higher level of confidence in them than might be warranted. Currently, no governance frameworks for big data or data sharing exist. Mitigating these data-related risks and minimizing unforeseen consequences will require establishing robust institutions and protocols for data ownership, use, and sharing (UN DESA, 2018).

Inclusive, bottom-up approaches and novel governance mechanisms

The authors in this book have highlighted the importance of differentiating between process and outcome in peacebuilding strategies. It is important to recognize that development is not only about the end result but also the means by which it is achieved (Nanthikesan & Juha, 2012). To promote inclusive development and economic growth, there must be a stronger emphasis on designing effective participatory processes and bottom-up approaches (Maharramli, Chapter 15; Swatuk, Chapter 16). Informal and hybrid institutions are slowly being recognized as critical pathways to climate change adaptation and peacebuilding (Walch, Chapter 12; Johnson, 2021). Further research on bottom-up approaches and novel methods in community-engaged research are critical in identified tailored, robust solutions to complex challenges and identifying best practices.

The third wave of environmental peacebuilding will also require stronger consideration of gender. Historically, while academic and grey literature on gender and the environment has been growing, little attention has been paid to structural inequalities related to gender in natural resource programming. Yet, the impacts of large-scale stressors – such as COVID-19, climate change, or conflict – are not gender neural (Halle, Chapter 24; Grown & Bousquet, 2020; Polo, 2020; Stoler, Jepson, & Wutich, 2020). Oversimplifying or disregarding the gender dimensions of natural resource use and control increases the risk of marginalization and exclusion, thus limiting peacebuilding efforts in the long term (Halle, Chapter 24). Conversely, including women in peace processes broadens the types of issues discussed and promotes equitable access to natural resources, therefore, strengthening community buy-in and trust (see also Dunn & Matthew, 2015). There is a crucial need for a comprehensive research framework that acknowledges women's contribution to environmental resource governance and peace processes (Yoshida & Céspedes-Báez, 2021) and promotes opportunities for long-lasting structural change, rather than short-term effects or symbolic nods to gender (Fröhlich & Gioli, 2015; Myrttinen, Naujoks, & Schilling, 2015).

Innovative partnerships to promote integrated solutions

We have argued that effective peacebuilding requires the use of joint strategies that increases the overall resilience of communities. To achieve holistic peacebuilding and development, there is a critical need for additional research on novel cross-sector partnerships which promote innovative finance mechanisms for critical infrastructures, close information gaps and advance novel data solutions, and increase our understanding of the complex linkages between social and ecological systems. Already, there is work on the role of utilizing "citizen science" to aid in monitoring and evaluation of post-conflict settings (Jensen & Campbell, 2019; Weir, McQuillan, & Francis, 2019). There is also emerging research on the role and the best practices of public–private data collaboratives in aiding decision-making and improving the resilience of natural and human systems (Klievink, Van Der Voort, & Veeneman, 2018; Susha, 2020; Verhulst, 2020). These are emerging and experimental forms of partnership; little is known about their processes and impacts (Blumenstock, 2018; Susha et al., 2019). Research and pilot studies on developing partnerships that bridge the diverse goals and values of cross-sector actors, effectively mobilize and pool resources, and mitigate risks to directly aid communities – rather than third parties – will grow increasingly important in the face of large-scale stressors.

The chapters in this book summarize important research findings of the past three decades while also advancing the field by addressing critical theoretical and empirical gaps on the linkages between security, conflict, peace, and the environment, and thus this volume provides a strong foundation for the emerging third generation of environmental peacebuilding research.

As we finalize this volume, much global attention has been focused on understanding the widespread impacts around the world of COVID-19 and trying to peer into the future of this and other pandemics to clarify vulnerability and develop effective forms of risk management and resilience measures. Sadly, for many people around the planet, COVID-19 has added another layer of hardship and challenge to a world of frequent and increasing stresses and shocks. As we write the conclusion, swarms of locusts have decimated crops in the Horn of Africa, pushing millions toward famine (Godin, 2020). Record-setting numbers of severe storms have battered coastlines (Samenow, Freeman, & Cappucci, 2020). Deadly fires have destroyed homes and livelihoods and released carbon and dangerous microbes into the atmosphere. The four million acres of forest that burned in California in 2020, for example, doubled the previous record set in 2018 (Freedman, 2020). From Sub-Saharan Africa to South America, communities around the world experienced devastating heat waves (Hersher & Sommer, 2020; University of Oxford, 2020). As natural disasters increase in frequency and intensity, the world has also witnessed a steady growth in violent state-related conflict, which in 2019 reached its highest level since the end of World War II (PRIO, 2020). As the authors in this volume make clear, the interactions between environmental factors and violent conflict are complex, and today one can hardly imagine discussing the causes and impacts of war in places like Syria and Yemen, without some mention of the concomitant impacts of drought and years of environmental mismanagement.

Conclusion

As we peer cautiously into the future, we discern many ways in which environmental change and violent conflict could reinforce each other and impact many parts of the world. The *Ecological Threat Register,* for example, released in 2020 argues that as many as 1.2 billion people are highly vulnerable to and could during this century be displaced by the effects of climate change (IEP, 2020). While uncertainty is characteristic of all projections, the science upon which they are based is increasingly clear. For example, *Global Environmental Outlook 2019* concludes that we have reached or almost reached irreversible levels of damage in the socioecological systems upon which all species depend – atmosphere, land, water, oceans, and biodiversity (UNEP, 2019).

Under current conditions, and thinking about the implications of current planetary environmental boundaries, we are comfortable concluding that an inclusive, interdisciplinary, and problem-solving third wave of environmental peacebuilding research and practice is of critical importance.

Works cited

Baffoe, G., Ahmad, S., & Bhandari, R. (2020). The road to sustainable Kigali: A contextualized analysis of the challenges. *Cities*, *105*, 102838.

Blumenstock, J. (2018). Don't forget people in the use of Big Data for development. *Nature*, *561* 170–2

Bruch, C. (2020, March 31). Show me! Laying the foundation for the next generation of environmental peacebuilding. *New Security Beat*. Retrieved December 29, 2020, from www.newsecuritybeat.org/2020/03/show-me-laying-foundation-generation-environmental-peacebuilding/

CARE International UK. (2012). *Peacebuilding with impact: Defining theories of change*. London, UK: CARE International UK.

Corral, P., Irwin, A., Krishnan, N., & Mahler, D. G. (2020). *Fragility and conflict: On the front lines of the fight against poverty*. Washington, DC: World Bank. https://openknowledge.worldbank.org/handle/10986/33324.

Dunn, H., & Matthew, R. (2015). Natural resources and gender in conflict settings. *Peace Review*, *27*(2), 156–164. https://doi.org/10.1080/10402659.2015.1037619

Forss, K., Marra, M., & Schwartz, R. (Eds.). (2011). *Evaluating the complex: Attribution, contribution, and beyond*. New Brunswick, NJ: Transaction Publishers.

Freedman, A. (2020, 5 October). Record-setting California fires surpass 4 million acres burned in a single year. *The Washington Post*. Retrieved March 22, 2021, from www.washingtonpost.com/weather/2020/10/05/california-fires-4-million-acres/

Fröhlich, C., & Gioli, G. (2015). Gender, conflict, and global environmental change. *Peace Review*, *27*(2), 137–146. https://doi.org/10.1080/10402659.2015.1037609

Godin, M. (2020, February 14). Swarms of up to 80 million locusts decimating crops in east Africa, threatening food security for 13 million people. *Time*. Retrieved March 22, 2021, from https://time.com/5784323/un-locust-east-africa/

Grown, C., & Bousquet, F. (2020, July 9). *Gender inequality exacerbates the COVID-19 crisis in fragile and conflict-affected settings*. Development for Peace. Retrieved January 11, 2021, from https://blogs.worldbank.org/dev4peace/gender-inequality-exacerbates-covid-19-crisis-fragile-and-conflict-affected-settings

Hersher, R., & Sommer, L. (2020, December 18). 2020 may be the hottest year on record. Here's The damage it did. *NPR*. Retrieved March 22, 2021, from www.npr.org/2020/12/18/943219856/2020-may-be-the-hottest-year-on-record-heres-the-damage-it-did

Homer-Dixon, T. F. (1994). Environmental scarcities and violent conflict: Evidence from cases. *International Security*, *19*(1), 5–40. https://doi.org/10.2307/2539147

Homer-Dixon, T. F. (1999). *Environment, scarcity, and violence*. Princeton, NJ: Princeton University Press.

Ide, T. (2020a). COVID-19 and armed conflict. *World Development*, *140*, 105355. https://doi.org/10.1016/j.worlddev.2020.105355

Ide, T. (2020b). The dark side of environmental peacebuilding. *World Development*, *127*, 104777.

Ide, T., Bruch, C., Carius, A., Conca, K., Dabelko, G. B., Matthew, R., & Weinthal, E. (2021). The past and future(s) of environmental peacebuilding. *International Affairs*, *97*(1), 1–16. https://doi.org/10.1093/ia/iiaa177

Institute for Economics & Peace (IEP). (2020). *Ecological threat register 2020: Understanding ecological threats, resilience and peace.* Retrieved March 12, 2021, from http://visionofhumanity.org/reports

Intergovernmental Panel on Climate Change (IPCC). (2014). *Climate change 2014: Impacts, adaptation, and vulnerability. Part A: Global and sectoral aspects. Contribution of working group II to the fifth assessment report of the intergovernmental panel on climate change* (C. B. Field, V. R. Barros, D. J. Dokken, K. J. Mach, M. D. Mastrandrea, T. E. Bilir . . . L. L. White, Eds.). Cambridge, UK and New York: Cambridge University Press.

Intergovernmental Panel on Climate Change (IPCC). (2018). *Global Warming of 1.5°C. An IPCC special report on the impacts of global warming of 1.5°C above pre-industrial levels and related global greenhouse gas emission pathways, in the context of strengthening the global response to the threat of climate change, sustainable development, and efforts to eradicate poverty* (V. Masson-Delmotte, P. Zhai, H.-O. Pörtner, D. Roberts, J. Skea, P. R. Shukla . . . T. Waterfield, Eds.). Retrieved from www.ipcc.ch/sr15/

Intergovernmental Panel on Climate Change (IPCC). (2021). Climate Change 2021: The Physical Science Basis. Contribution of Working Group I to the Sixth Assessment Report of the Intergovernmental Panel on Climate Change.

In Masson-Delmotte, V., P. Zhai, A. Pirani, S. L. Connors, C. Péan, S. Berger, N. Caud, Y. Chen, L. Goldfarb, M. I. Gomis, M. Huang, K. Leitzell, E. Lonnoy, J.B.R. Matthews, T. K. Maycock, T. Waterfield, O. Yelekçi, R. Yu and B. Zhou (Eds.). Camrbidge, UK: Cambridge University Press.

International Telecommunication Union (ITU), United Nations Educational, Scientific and Cultural Organization (UNESCO); UN Environment; United Nations Framework Convention on Climate Change (UNFCCC); United Nations Global Compact; United Nations Industrial Development Organization (UNIDO); United Nations Human Settlements Programme (UN-Habitat); United Nations Entity for Gender Equality and the Empowerment of Women (UN-Women); and with the support of United Nations Economic Commission for Europe (UNECE). (2020). *Frontier technologies to protect the environment and to tackle climate change.* International Telecommunication Union.

Jensen, D., & Campbell, J. (2019). *The case for a digital ecosystem for the environment: Bringing together data, algorithms, and insights for sustainable development.* Discussion paper, Science Policy Business Forum. UN Environment.

Johnson, M. F. (2021). Fighting for black stone: Extractive conflict, institutional change and peacebuilding in Sierra Leone. *International Affairs, 97*(1), 81–101.

Klievink, B., Van Der Voort, H., & Veeneman, W. (2018). Creating value through data collaboratives. *Information Polity, 23*(4), 379–397.

Kolvani, P., Pillai, S., Edgell, A. B., Grahn, S., Kaiser, S., Lachapelle, J., & Luhrmann, A. (2020). Pandemic backsliding: Democracy nine months into the COVID-19 pandemic. V-Dem Institute. *Policy Brief No#26*

Mayne, J. (2008). Contribution analysis: An approach to exploring cause and effect. *Institutional Learning and Change Initiative, Policy Brief No. 6.* https://web.archive.org/web/20150226022328/www.cgiar-ilac.org/files/ILAC_Brief16_Contribution_Analysis_0.pdf

Myrttinen, H., Naujoks, J., & Schilling, J. (2015). Gender, natural resources, and peacebuilding in Kenya and Nepal. *Peace Review, 27*(2), 181–187.

Nanthikesan, S., & Juha, I. U. (2012). Evaluating post-conflict assistance. In D. Jensen & S. Lonergan (Eds.), *Assessing and restoring natural resources in post-conflict peacebuilding* (pp. 389–408). London: Routledge.

Nixon, R. (2011). *Slow violence and the environmentalism of the poor.* Harvard University Press.

Nygard, H. M., Methi, F., & Rustad, S. C. A. (2020, June 5). *Coronavirus and the (Wannabe) dictators.* PRIO Blogs. https://blogs.prio.org/2020/06/coronavirus-and-the-wannabe-dictators/

Peace Research Institute Oslo (PRIO). (2020). *Conflict trends: A global overview, 1946–2019.* Oslo, Norway: PRIO.

Polo, S. M. (2020). A pandemic of violence? The impact of COVID-19 on conflict. *Peace Economics, Peace Science and Public Policy, 26*(3). https://doi.org/10.1515/peps-2020-0050

Samenow, J., Freeman, A., & Cappucci, M. (2020, November 10). 2020 Atlantic hurricane season breaks all-time record while leaving Gulf Coast battered. *The Washington Post.* Retrieved March 22, 2021, from www.washingtonpost.com/weather/2020/11/10/record-hurricane-season-atlantic/?fbclid=IwAR2zWOabsiphGYN734JqH_H5lDK64VjPCBW9V-3JChYKeefG3LSg-AduxAI

Stoler, J., Jepson, W. E., & Wutich, A. (2020). Beyond handwashing: Water insecurity undermines COVID-19 response in developing areas. *Journal of Global Health, 10*(1).

Susha, I. (2020). Establishing and implementing data collaborations for public good: A critical factor analysis to scale up the practice. *Information Polity*, (Preprint), 1–22. https://content.iospress.com/articles/information-polity/ip180117

Susha, I., Grönlund, Å., & Van Tulder, R. (2019). Data driven social partnerships: Exploring an emergent trend in search of research challenges and questions. *Government Information Quarterly*, *36*(1), 112–128.

Tänzler, D., & Scherer, N. (2019). *Guidelines for conflict-sensitive adaption to climate change*. Umweltbundesamt

UN Department of Economic and Social Affairs [UN DESA]. (2018). *World economic and social survey 2018: Frontier technologies for sustainable development*. United Nations.

UN Department of Economic and Social Affairs [UN DESA]. (2020). *World social report 2020: Inequality in a rapidly changing world*. United Nations.

UN Development Programme [UNDP]. (2016). *A principled approach to conflict sensitive do no harm programming in the context of Federal Iraq and the Kurdistan Region*. Emergency Livelihoods and Social Cohesion & Cluster.

UN Development Programme [UNDP]. (2020). *Governance for peace: Strengthening inclusive, just, and peaceful societies resilient to future crises*. Thematic paper for the UN Secretary General's 2020 Report on Sustaining Peace and Peacebuilding.

United Nations Environment Programme (UNEP). (2019). *Global environmental outlook 6*. Retrieved from www.unep.org/resources/global-environment-outlook-6?_ga=2.227852510.2120879290.1614713659-1674902825.1613760489

University of Oxford. (2020, July 13). *Climate concern: Extreme heat going unrecorded in Africa*. Retrieved March 22, 2021, from www.ox.ac.uk/news/2020-07-13-climate-concern-extreme-heat-going-unrecorded-africa

UN Security Council. (2020, September 9). *Weakest, most fragile states will be those worst affected by COVID-19 in medium, long term, humanitarian chief tells security council*. United Nations. Retrieved December 24, 2020, from www.un.org/press/en/2020/sc14296.doc.htm

Verhulst, S. G. (2020, April 2). The potential of Data Collaboratives for COVID19. *Medium*. Retrieved from https://medium.com/data-stewards-network/the-potential-of-data-collaboratives-for-covid19–68294 6da7bdc

Victor, D. A. (2010). Peace and conflict sensitive programming. *Journal of Alternative Perspectives in the Social Sciences*, *2*(2).

Wählisch, M. (2019). Big data, new technologies, and sustainable peace: Challenges and opportunities for the UN. *Journal of Peacebuilding & Development*, *15*(1), 122–126. https://doi.org/10.1177%2F1542316619868984

Weir, D., McQuillan, D., & Francis, R. A. (2019). Civilian science: The potential of participatory environmental monitoring in areas affected by armed conflicts. *Environmental Monitoring and Assessment*, *191*(10), 1–17.

World Bank. (2020). *Poverty and shared prosperity 2020: Reversals of fortune*. Washington, DC: World Bank.

Yoshida, K., & Céspedes-Báez, L. M. (2021). The nature of Women, Peace and Security: A Colombian perspective. *International Affairs*, *97*(1), 17–34. https://doi.org/10.1093/ia/iiaa173

INDEX

Note: Page numbers in *italics* indicate a figure and page numbers in **bold** indicate a table on the corresponding page.

9/11 event 48, 230

Abdul Aziz ibn Saud (King) 33
Aberystwyth School, Critical Theory of 236
acacia trees 296
Aceh (Indonesia) 18
adaptive governance 281, 282, 286–287
Adapt Now: A Global Call for Leadership on Climate Resilience (Global Commission on Adaptation) 160
Afghanistan **83**; floods 216; landmines 109; Taliban 58; UN Environment work in 305, 307, 312; mining rights 312–313; wars 107
Africa: civil war 77; coastal communities 62; water rights 76; *see also* Horn of Africa; Sahel; South Africa; sub-Saharan Africa
Agenda for Peace (United Nations) 215
Agenda for Sustainable Development 2030 315
Agent Orange 10, 25, 95, 103, 304
Alexander, J. 57
Algeria 36
Ali, Saleem 191, 194, 198
Alinon, K. 150
Al-Qaeda 86
Al Rahad 296–297
American Civil War *see* Civil War (United States)
Anglo-Persian Oil Company (APOC) 33
Angola 30–31, 46; national parks 195
Anthropocene 240, 242; concepts of 243–244; "good" or "bad" 245–246; security and 247
anthropogenic climate change 207; trends in 70
anthropogenic stressors 272
anthropogenic threats 254, 260
Anti-Personnel Landmine Ban Treaty 108

Arab-Israeli Wars 74
Arab Spring 45, 46, 49; aftermath 59; Yemen 61
arsenic 100, 112, 270; *see also* groundwater
Atlantic Hurricane Basin 161
atomic weapons 101, 102
Atrato River 295, 299–300

Badme 31
Bangladesh 39; floods 77, 84; refugees in 140; water-sharing agreement with India 74
Bannon, I. 172
Barents Protected Area Network 194
Barnett, M. 209
Battle of Wounded Knee (1890) 31
Bay of Bengal 39
Beardsley, K. 150
Beevers, Michael D. 179
Bela Ponte dam, Brazil 76
Benjaminsen, T. 150
Berlin, Germany 101
Berlin Wall, collapse of 197
Besley, T. and Persson, T. 150
Betsill, Michelle 230
Bhopal chemical leak 241
Bhutan 194
Biba, Sebastian 235
big data 163, 210, 320, 330–331
biocultural rights 300
biosphere project *see* International Geosphere Biosphere Project
Birenda (King of Nepal), assassination of 265
Boer War (1900–1902) 99
Boko Haram 86
Bolivia 77, 194

Index

borderlands 193, 194
Bosnia and Herzegovina 107
Boutros-Ghali, Boutros 215
Brady, Lisa 99
Brahmaputra river 39, 73
Brazil 70; Bela Ponte dam, protests over 76; criminal violence in 146; "pre-salt" fields 36; water protests 77
Brown, Lester 205
Brown, Oli 2, 159
Brundtland Convention (1987) 260
"Brundtland Report" 241
Brunei 37
Brzezinski, Zbigniew 32
Buhaug, H. 150, 151
Burke, M. 148
Burma 102
Burundi **83**, 181, 311; Civil War 131; Kibira forest 296
Buseth, J.T. 150
bushfires 132
Bush, George H.W. 30, 34, 35
Bush, George W. 34, 230, 231, 234
bushmeat 131, 137

Caldrón, Felipe 232
California 208, 216–218; forest fires (2020) 332; San Diego 279; wetland habitats 280; *see also* Tijuana River Valley (TRV), California; Tijuana–San Diego border
Cambodia: conflict timber 11, 16; Hun Sen's control of 209
Cameroon **83**, 194, 253
Canada 160, 191, 192, 193; as climate "winner" 204; peacebuilding example of 209; wheat prices affected by weather in 254
Carter Doctrine 30, 34
Carter, Jimmy 30
cattle 70, 95, 99
cattle nomads 297
Centcom *see* United States (US) Central Command (Centcom)
Center for International Stabilization and Recovery (CISR) 109
Central African Republic (CAR) 87
Central Intelligence Agency (CIA) (US) 38
CFM *see* collaborative flood modeling (CFM)
Chad 82, **83**, 87, 253
Chapin, Mac 199
Chernobyl 241
China: Afghanistan mining concession 312–313; drought in 254; emissions, pledge to reduce 160; and Nepal, transit points between 271; rise of 246; Turkmenistan sending gas to 36; and Vietnam, clashes with 29; water conflicts in 76; warfare in 98; *see also* South China Sea
China Metallurgical Construction Company 312

cholera 185
Churchill, Winston 33
CISR *see* Center for International Stabilization and Recovery (CISR)
Civil War (Burundi) 131
Civil War (Nepal) 265–266
Civil War (United States) 99
Clausewitz, C. von *see* von Clausewitz, C.
Clean Cooking Alliance 294
Climate Ambition Summit (2020) 160
climate: landmine removal and 109; Nepal 267; recovery from war and 103; refugee camps and 138; security and 261
climate anomalies and armed conflict 150
climate change 1–3; Anthropocene and 240, 242–247; broad trends linked to 221, 326–333; conflict and 82–89, 327; conflict cycle and 205–208; COVID-19 and 162–163 displacement due to 87–88, 129, 140, 160, 187, 329; environmental peacebuilding and 9–11, 281, 303; extractive sectors and 43, 45, 49; food security and 253–254; gender and 296–298; health risks and 160; information technologies and 161–162; interest in renewable sources of energy and 35, 255–256; Nepal, impacts on 262–263, 268–269, 272, 318; peacebuilding and 203–211, 215; and public health and conflict cycle 155–163; resource wars and 39–40; risks exacerbated by 315, 319; Sahel as hotspot for 84; securitization of 229; Sierra Leone's vulnerability to 184; Sudan 318; as threat multiplier 311, 328; violent conflict and 159; water security and 252; water stress and 39; "water wars" and 66–70, 73, 77–78
climate refugees 126
climate security 227–236, 290; gender dimension of 292
climate shock 148, 326
climate vulnerability and state fragility **83**, 330; *see also* fragile states
"climate wars" 11
Clinton administration 230
Clinton-Gore era (US) 1
Coca-Cola company, water exploitation by 77
Cold War: end of 1, 11, 12, 192, 195; conflicts in the wake of 169; environmental waste, legacy of 102–103; environment viewed as security risk, post- 195; national security models derived from 247; nuclear weapons, concerns regarding 10, 241; peacebuilding agenda, post- 2, 208, 215; United Nations and 12; United States and China, post- 38; violence in the Global South, post- 242
collaborative flood modeling (CFM) 216–218
Collier, P. 148, 172, 205
Colombia: Antioquia 299; Chocó 295, 299, 300; floods in 216, 221; gender and environmental

337

Index

security in 290, 292, 295–300; landmines in 109; land rights 61; sustainably harvested forest fruits in 296; women's roles in environmental peacebuilding 298–300, 315

community-based conservation (CBC) programs 266, 267

Community Party of Nepal-Maoist (CPN-Maoist or CPN-M) 265, 266, 267

Conca, Ken 251

conflict: climate change 82–89, 327; drivers of 308–310; environmental impact of 305–308; root causes of 326–327; water resources and 66–70; *see also* extractives; mining conflicts; water conflicts

conflict bananas 11

conflict cacao 11

conflict cycle and climate change 205–208

conflict diamonds 9, 11

conflict timber 11, 310

Congo *see* Democratic Republic of Congo

Convention on the Prohibition of Military or Any Other Hostile Use of Environmental Modification Techniques (ENMOD Convention) 304

cooking facilities 255

cooking fuel 271, 294

Copenhagen School securitization theory 228–230, 233–236

copper mining 14, 155, 313

corruption 5, 13, 48; abundant resources and 116; community distrust and 52; endemic 171; hydro-bureaucratic 69; land conflicts and 58, 59, 62; mining companies 313; natural resource dependency and 170; natural resource governance and 174; Nepal 263–264, 265, 267, 268, 272; peacebuilding efforts faced with 173; state-level 175; transparency as response to 172; violent conflict linked to 207

Corry, Olaf 234

Cote d'Ivoire 62; ; conflict cacao 11, 205; natural resource conflicts 308, 309, 312

Covid-19 3, 159, 332; effects of 162–163; gender discrimination in resource use 331; poverty acceleration 329; resource diversion 205

CPN-M *see* Community Party of Nepal- Maoist (CPN-Maoist or CPN-M)

Cross River Region, West Africa 194

Crutzen, Paul 240

Dadaab refugee camp 136

Daesh 252

Dar Es Salaam 317

Darfur 16, 60, 307; Catholic Relief Service 295; civil war 309; deforestation in 306; nomads 307; North and South Kordofan and 296; Wadi El Ku 313, 317

DDT *see* Dichlorodiphenyltrichloroethane (DDT)

deforestation: Darfur 306; refugee camps and 132, **134**, 139, 294; ineffective governance linked to 263; Mexico 283; negative transformation of the earth and 240, 242; Nepal 264, 265, 271, 272, 327; Sierra Leone 210; species extinction and 245; urban growth and 184; wartime 98, 100

Demilitarized Zone (DMZ) (Koreas) 110, 192

Democratic Republic of Congo (DRC) 16, 82, **83**, 156; illegal trade of natural resources 308; mineral wealth 312; peace park initiative, suitability for 194; urban refugee settlements 183

Dependra (Crown Prince of Nepal) 265

Derg War (Ethiopia) 55

desecuritization 228, 230–231, 234–236

desertification 130, 139, 317

de Soysa, I. *see* Soysa, I. de

Detraz, Nicole 230

DIADATA dataset 117

diamond data 117

diamond mining (Sierra Leone) 116–117, 184, 205

diamonds 29, 30, 47, 174; alluvial (Liberia) 62; "blood diamonds" 184, 309; rough 171; secondary and primary 120–126; *see also* conflict diamonds

diamond sanctions 309

"diamond wars" 48

Dichlorodiphenyltrichloroethane (DDT) 100

disasters *see* natural disasters

disaster diplomacy 215

disaster capitalism 268

displacement of population: climate change as factor in 87–88, 129, 140, 160, 187, 329; drought as factor in 159, 187, 203; environmental factors in 129–140; natural disasters as factor in 69, 130–131; Tanzania 131, 132, 134, 139; *see also* internally displaced persons (IDPs); refugees

distributional conflicts 50

DMZ *see* Demilitarized Zone (DMZ)

Dodd Frank Act (United States) 309

Donges, J.F. 88

Donner, R.V. 88

drought: American West 76; California 208; China 39, 254; climate change impacts of 260, 261, 263; displacement due to 159, 187, 203; escalating resource conflict and 147; food security and 253; human health and 156, 158; North Kordofan 296; refugee camps and 89; Sahel 84; slow onset disaster 146; Syria 77, 87, 252; threat multiplier of 243; violent interpersonal behavior and 148, 151

Duffield, M. 197

Duffy, Rosaleen 192, 194, 198

dysentery 132

Index

"Earth Summit" (1992) 242
Ebola 186
"ecological crises" 96
Ecological Threat Register 216, 333
ecotourism 191, 192, 194; destinations 197
Ecuador 76, 193
Egypt 39, 72, 73, 254
Ehrlich, Paul 205
EIA *see* environmental impact assessment (EIA)
energy and energy security 32, 44, 255–256; *see also* fossil fuels; Middle East; securitization
ENMOD Convention *see* Convention on the Prohibition of Military or Any Other Hostile Use of Environmental Modification Techniques (ENMOD Convention)
environmental impact assessment (EIA) 135, 137, 138
environmental peacebuilding 12–13; components and objectives of 13; phases of 13–18; sustainable development goals (SDGs), entry points into *316*; Tijuana-San Diego border 279–288; UN Environment and 303–320
environmental peacemaking 12, 16–17, 20n4, 176, 283
environmental security: gender and 290–300
environmental security discourse 236, 240–248; sustainable development and 241–242
Environmental Warfare (Westing) 96
Eritrea 31, **83**
erosion: coastal 84; genetic 102; management of 218; riverbank 268; soil 3, 100, 130–132, 142, 271; war as cause of 95, 97, 98
ERWs *see* explosive remnants of war (ERW)
Ethics and Justice Working Group (EJWG) 109
Ethiopia 31, 72
explosive remnants of war (ERW) 107–113
extinction *see* species extinction
Extractive Industries Transparency Initiative (EITI) 15, 172
extractive, definition of term 45
extractives 17–18; conflict related to 43–52

Falkenmark, M. 251, 252
FAO *see* Food and Agriculture Organization (FAO)
Farakka Water Treaty (1996) 74
FARC *see* Fuerzas Armadas Revolucionarias de Colombia (FARC)
Fearon, J. 117, 120
feminist theory 46
feminization 297
fisheries 10, 18, 44, 77, 307
fish stocks 204
Fishhendler, I. 252
flood 69; Bangladesh 77; Glacial Lake Outburst Flood 263; Hanamute River 268; Pakistan 84

flood hazard information 215–221
Floyd, Rita 179
food 252–254; *see also* water-food-energy nexus
food aid 139
Food and Agriculture Organization 252, 253
food and water: conflict caused by reductions of 147; cooking fuel and 294; disease vectored through 156; distribution of 29–30; future availability of 281; potential contamination of 134; rationing of 131; scarcity of 140, 147
food insecurity 49, 56, 253; drought and 84; Freetown and 185; gender and 291, 294, 297, 307, 313; global expansion and acceleration of 203–204; migration and 129, 203
food production 87, 158; AI solutions for 162; climate change impacting 263
food riots 146
food scarcity 130
food sector 46
food security 18, 58, 69, 72, 158; climate change impacting 211; natural disasters as threats to 328
food shortages 67; Africa and Asia 241; Nepal 266, 268, 271, 272
food supplies, war and 97, 98, 101
forest communities 155
forest cover 118, 120, **122**, 132
forest fires, California 332
Forest Law Enforcement Governance and Trade initiative 171
forestry 203, 295
Forestry Act of 1919 (Great Britain) 100
Forestry Commission (UK) 100
forest regeneration 200
forests: Afghanistan 307; agricultural burning of 95; Burundi 296; denuding of 98; depletion of 130, **134**; firewood and 110; Nepal 262–267, 269, 271–272; old-growth 99; pistachio 307; Tanzania 131; tropical 97; Vietnam 103; World War II, damage to 101; *see also* deforestation; reforestation
forest sector (economic) 205, 267
Forest User Groups (FUGs) 266, 267
fossil aquifers 44
fossil fuels 35–36, 38; climate change related to 227, 240–241; conflicts related to 43–45; energy dependency on 255–256; lobal economic dependency on 243–244, 246–248; greenhouse gas and 203; *see also* Anthropocene
fragile areas 131
fragile regions 135
fragile states 58, 59, 82–88; climate change's impact on 150, 158, 250, 315; COVID-19's impact on 162; G7+ 314; Nepal 272; OECD's principles for engagement with 210
fragile security situation 253
fragility and conflict 250, 252, 291
fragility risks 319

Index

Frankfurt, Germany 102
freedom from. . .: discrimination 175; fear 250, 329; threats 227; want 227, 250, 252, 329
freedom of. . .: movement 138; navigation 37
Freetown, Sierra Leone 181, 184–186; mudslides in 210
Fuerzas Armadas Revolucionarias de Colombia (FARC) 61, 298–299
FUGs *see* Forest User Groups (FUGs)

G7 314, 315, 319
Gaia hypothesis 243
Galtung, Johan 10, 44
Ganga-Brahmaputra river basins 73
Ganga River 74
gas 256, 310; cooking gas 271; *see also* greenhouse gas emissions; natural gas
gas export 255
Gawama'a 296
GEMDATA 117
gender: environmental peacebuilding and 19; environmental security and 290–300; natural resource use and 331
gender-based violence 298
gender discrimination: Nepal 265
gender dynamics: environment and natural resources and 291–292; water scarcity and 68
gender empowerment 200
gender equality 292, 299
gender inequality 85
gender programming 292
Geneva Conventions 11, 304
Germany 97, 100; 1941 invasion of Soviet Union by 101; climate security discourse 231–232; postwar rebuilding of 102
Gezira State 297
glacial lake outbursts 267
Glacial Lake Outburst Floods (GLOFs) 263
Global Commission on Adaptation 160
Google Earth 280–281
Gordon, Stewart 98
Gore, Al 1, 237n8
Gorongosa (Mozambique) 195
gorillas, critically endangered status of 194
gorilla tourism, Rwanda 183, 186
Grant, Ulysses S. (General) 99
"great acceleration" 241
Great Britain 34, 100
Greater Limpopo TFCA (includes the Great Limpopo Transfrontier Park) (GLTFCA) **196**, 198, 199
Greater Virunga Transboundary Collaboration 194
Great Lakes Region 308
Great Limpopo Transfrontier Park (GLTP) 194, **196**
greenhouse gas (GHG) emissions 44, 83, 88, 160
green infrastructure, definition of 179

GRID-Geneva 314
groundwater: contaminated 159, 183, 185, 270; depletion of 262, 279; disputes over 77; polluted 132; replenishment of, failure to consider 135; saltwater intrusion into 156, 203; transboundary 87, 251–252
Gulf War (1990–1991) 10–11, 96, 305; *see also* Persian Gulf oil supply
Guterres (Secretary General, United Nations) 318

Habyarimana (President) 181
hakura system 60–61
Haiti 89, 310, 312
Hallegatte, S. 148, 204
Hamburg, Germany 101–102
Hanson, T. 206
Hardin, Garrett 205
Hayes, Jarrod 230
Himalayas, Nepal 263
Hiroshima and Nagasaki, Japan 102
HMA *see* humanitarian mine action (HMA)
Hoeffler, A. 148, 205
Holocene 240
Homer-Dixon, T. F. 1, 205
Horn of Africa 84, 86
Horton, Richard 157
Hsiang, S. 206
Huachen, Zhang (Rear Admiral) 37
humanitarian mine action (HMA) 109, 111, 113
humility, lack of 199
Hupy, Joseph 99
Hurricane Basin *see* Atlantic Hurricane Basin
hurricanes 187, 204
Hussein, K. and Gnisci, D. 62
Hutu 131, 181
Hutu Power Movement 181

Iban people 99
Ide, T. 280
IDPs *see* integrated development plans (IDPs)
IDPs *see* internally displaced persons (IDPs)
IEDs *see* improvised explosive devices (IEDs)
ILC *see* International Law Commission (ILC)
IMAS *see* International Mine Action Standards (IMAS)
IMPLAN TJ 280–281
improvised explosive devices (IEDs) 107–110, 113
India: Bangladesh, water sharing with 74; Bhopal chemical leak 241; Brahmaputra River, political dangers linked to 39, 73; Cauvery River study 76; drought 84; emissions, failure to curtail 160; geopolitics of 38; intrastate conflicts 75; Kerala 77; Kishanganga hydroelectric project (KHEP) 73–74; oil consumption by 36, 37; raw materials, demand for 49; warfare, history of 98; water-sharing agreement with Bangladesh 74

Index

Indian Blockade of Nepal (2015–2016) 261, 271–272
Indian Ocean 37, 38
Indian Ocean Tsunami 150
India-Pakistan border 192
Indonesia: Aceh 18; Bali 76; and Bhutan, border between 194; Indian Ocean Tsunami, impact on 150
Indus River 39, 73
Indus Water Treaty 73, 87
integrated development plans (IDPs) **196**
Intergovernmental Panel on Climate Change (IPCC) 2, 150, 260; conflict and climate change 158, 160, 206; Nobel Peace Prize awarded to 85; Fifth Assessment Report (AR5) 203; First Assessment Report (AR1) 160; population displacement and climate change 204; Sixth Assessment Report (AR6) 155; species extinction and climate change 203
internally displaced persons (IDPs) 58, 132, 140, 180, 296; conflict and 3, 327; women and youth 298
International Energy Agency (IEA) 35–36
International Campaign to Ban Landmines 109
International Committee of the Red Cross (ICRC) 305, 312
International Geosphere Biosphere Project 243
International Law Commission (ILC) 312; Special Rapporteur 312
International Mine Action Standards (IMAS) 109, 110, 113
International Union for Conservation of Nature (IUCN) 189–195, 197–198; "protected area," definition of 189; Red List 194; transboundary conservation area, two definitions of 190
IPCC *see* Intergovernmental Panel on Climate Change (IPCC)
Iran 33; Iraq, invasion by 31; natural gas reserves 36; nuclear program 45; Persian Gulf, power struggle in 38, 45; war 34
Iraq 33: Army, destruction of oil fields by 96; Iran, invasion of 31; Kurdistan 18; Kuwait, expulsion from 34; Kuwait, occupation of 29; landmines 107, 109; US defense of Saudi Arabia against 30; UN Environment Programme assessment of 305, 306, 307, 309; US invasion of 45, 48, 49; US power struggle with 38
ISIS 45, 86
Israel 39, 72; Palestinian conflict 55, 59; settlements 55
Israel-Jordan Peace Treaty of 1994 74
IUCN *see* International Union for Conservation of Nature (IUCN)

Jacobsson, Marie G. 312
Jägerskog, Anders 252, 253
jaguars 194

Janjaweed militia 60, 61, 307
Jiangxi Copper Company Limited 312
Joint Programme on Women, Natural Resources, and Peace 315
Jordan 252
Jordan River 39, 72; "picnic talks" 74
Jordan Peace Treaty of 1994 74
Jodeya mediation 297
Just Securitization Theory 236

Kagame, Paul (General) 181
Kahl, C. 205
Kailash Sacred Landscape Conservation and Development Initiative 194
Kaplan-Meier estimates 119, 120, 121
Kaplan, Robert 2, 235
Kashmir 192
Katerere, Y. 192
Kathmandu, Nepal 262, 267, 270
Kenya 87; Dadaab refugee camp 136; drought and political violence in 151; Maasai 200n5
Kerala, India 77
Kibira forest, Burundi 296
Kibondo District 131
Kigali, Rwanda 179, 180, 181–186
Kilamendo 317
Kimberly Process Certification Scheme 11, 171, 173, 309
King Philip's War of 1675–1678 31
Kiribati 87
Kishanganga hydroelectric project (KHEP) 73–74
Klare, Michael T. 205
Knox-Hayes, Janelle 230
Koreas, North and South 110, 192
Kosovo conflict 96, 112, 305, 306
Kurdistan (Iraq) 18
Kuwait 71; Iraq's expulsion from 34; Iraq's invasion of 45; Iraq's occupation of 29; Iraq's oil field dispute with 49; oil reserves of 33
Kyoto Protocol 242, 260

Lagos 77
Lake Chad 253, 317
Lake Chad Basin 253
Lake Titicaca 194
"Lancet Countdown, The" 155, 158
Lancet, The 157
Landmine and Cluster Munition Monitor 109
landmines 17, 107–113; biodiversity and 110–111; ecological pressure created by 110; environmental impact of 110; mine action and 111–112; mitigating the impact of 112–113; toxic chemicals and 112, 265; *see also* humanitarian mine action (HMA)
Latour, Bruno 246
Lebanon 134; forests of 97; Jordan River 72; refugees in 132, **133–134**; UN Environment

Index

Programme assessment 309; urban population density in 132
Lehto, Marja 312
Lesotho, South Africa 194
liquefied natural gas (LNG) 36–38
Limits to Growth report 241, 245
Linke, A. 151
littoral states 37
LLC *see* Los Laureles Canyon (LLC)
LNG *see* liquefied natural gas
logging 30, 86; illegal 271, 308; wartime 102
"logic of exception" 234
"logic of the routine" 234
Los Laureles Canyon (LLC) 217–218, 220, 280, 283
Lovelock, James 243
Luengue-Luiana National Park (Angola) 195
Lysenko, I. 192

Mackinder, Halford 1, 32
Mahan, Alfred Thayer 32
malaria 97, 100, 132, 156, 185
Malaysia 37
Maloti-Drakensberg Transfrontier Park (MDTP) 194, **196**
Malthus, Thomas 1, 205, 326; neo-Malthusianism 43, 47, 147
Mandela, Nelson 189
MapX 314
Marshall, F. 159
maquiladoras 283
Mavinga National Park (Angola) 195
Mayan civilization 148
MBT *see* Mine Ban Treaty (MBT)
McQuinn, B. 150
Meadows, Donella 205
measles 132
Mekong 39
Mekong Agreement of 1995 74
Mekong crisis 235
Methman, C. 234
Mexico: criminal violence in 146; flooding 216; negative climate change impacts 204; Tijuana 216, 217, 279, 282 US–Mexico border 194, 280, 282; US–Mexico War 31; securitization of climate change in 232
Middle East foreign policy, US 49
Middle East and North Africa (MENA) region 70, 251–252
Milgrom, J. and Spierenburg, M. 193
Mine Ban Treaty (MBT) 108, 109, 110, 112, 113

mineral industries, conflict related to 45, 46, 49
minerals 18, 29, 44; specialty (cobalt and platinum) 33
mines *see* landmines
mining 18; Afghanistan 312–313; Colombia 295; gold 14, 297; mountaintop removal 44; open-pit 44, 47; resistance to 46, 47, 50, 172, 185; Sierra Leone 185, 186, 210; "sustainable" 45; women in 19, 298; *see also* copper mining; diamond mining
mining conflicts 50–52
Moftakhari, H. 204
monitoring and evaluation (M&E) systems 330
Mozambique: elephants 199; Gorongosa 195; Limpopo National Park 189; RENAMO war 55; *see also* Great Limpopo Transfrontier Park (GLTP)
Myers, Norman 205

NAFTA *see* North American Free Trade Agreement (NAFTA)
National Intelligence Council (NIC) (US) 38
National Union for the Total Independence of Angola (UNITA) 30, 195
natural gas 30–33, 35–39, 115, 255–256
natural disasters: armed conflict and 146–152, 215–216; climate change's impact on 140, 263; displacement caused by 69, 130–131; flow of water during 138; Freetown's and Kigali's vulnerability to 186; Nepal 267–268, 271
Natural Enemy, Natural Ally (Russell) 97
natural habitat 195, 264, 280
Natural Resource Management in Transition Settings (UN) 12
natural resource base, measuring 117
natural resource competition, increasing 86–87
natural resource governance reform 169–176; "blind spots" 174–175; environmental peacebuilding, opportunities for 175–176; security and developmental agenda 170–173
natural resource programs 317–318
natural resources 1–3; Arctic 204; chronic conflict over 309; collaboration around 313; conflict and 9–12, 15–20, 40, 115–117, 179, 205, 290; contested information around 313–314; disputes over 293; economic recovery strategies involving 312–313; environmental peacebuilding and 304; environment and 291–292; exploitation of 262, 271; food security and 253; gender dynamics of 291–295; high value 312; illegal exploitation of 308; as livelihood lifeline during violent conflict 306–307; as means and motivation for violent conflict 309; Model 8 test 121; Nepal 271; nexus with peace and conflict 311; rebel groups impacted by 126; renewable 10, 312, 312; resource wars over 29; risks and opportunities

342

connected to 309; scarce 11, 14, 179, 303, 318; Sierra Leon 184; social conflict related to 14; social grievances and disputes over 310; unique kinds of conflict generate by 310; urban dimensions of 180, 187; war and 96–99, 206; women and 315

natural resources management 179, 193; community-based 199; conflict prevention responses built around 318–319; increased security via 282–283, 288; ineffective 260; women and 19, 295–300

natural resource sector 44, 155

natural water scarcity 70

NB *see* Newport Beach

Nepal 264; civil war 265–267, 272; climate-induced disasters in 263; environmental security debate 260–273; floods 216; Himalayas 263; Indian Blockade 271–272; natural disasters 267–268; natural resource conflicts 16; pollution and poor waste management 269–271; resource scarcity 264; Tharu and Madhesi communities 271; urbanization in 262; see also food shortages; forests

Nepal Civil War 261, 265–267, 272

New Climate for Peace (G7) 315

Newport Beach (NB) 217, *219*

Ngara district 131

Ngaruiya, G. and Scheffran, J. 151

NIC *see* National Intelligence Council (NIC) (US)

Nigeria 194; intrastate conflicts 75; natural resource conflicts 309; offshore oil revenues 116; Ogoniland 314; refugees from 87; UN Environment field assessments 312, 314

Nile Basin Initiative 72, 75, 87

Nile Day 73

Nile River 39, 72, 73, 308

nomads 60, 296, 297, 307

North American Free Trade Agreement (NAFTA) 283, 284

Northern Rizaygat 307

nuclear energy 39

nuclear war 234, 241, 242, 245

nuclear waste 102

nuclear weapons 10, 101

nuclear winter 243

Obama, Barack 38, 231

Occupied Palestinian Territories 306

Oels, A. 232, 237n8

oil *see* Middle East; OPEC oil crisis

O'Loughlin, J. 150

Oman 33

Omelicheva, M. 150

"One Belt One Road" initiative (China) 37

OPEC oil crisis 241

opportunity conflicts 50

Organization for Economic Cooperation and Development (OECD) 33; energy consumption by 36; gender equality analysis by 292; multidimension fragility framework 210, 318; peacebuilding framework adopted by 209

Osborn, Fairfield 205

Ottoman Empire 33

Our Common Future 241–242

ozone layer 240, 241, 243

Pahlavi, Mohammed Reza (Shah) 34

Palestine 72; Occupied Palestinian Territories 306; refugees from 141n1

Palestinian–Israeli conflict 55, 59

Papua New Guinea: Bougainville 14, 115, 309

ParBreZo hydrodynamic mode 217–218

Paris Climate Agreement (2015) 210, 245–246, 260

park for peace *see* peace park

pastoralism 82, 84, 86

pastoralists: Al Rahad 296, 297; Darfur 60, 295, 317; Nigeria 253; Sudan 294

pastoralist systems 59

Peace and Biodiversity Dialogue Initiative 190, 191

peacebuilding 10, 328–329; climate change adaptation and 203–211; urban dimensions of 179–187; *see also* environmental peacebuilding

peacekeeping 10, *14*; failures of 294; impacts of 306; mandates and objectives 17

peacekeeping missions (United Nations) 12, 16, 171, 311, 315; DR Congo 308; Rwanda 209

peacemaking 10, 13, 286, 288; costs and benefits 189; environmental 12, 16–17, 20n4, 176, 283; intercommunal 195; mediation/ peacemaking *14*

peace park 189, 190, 195

Peace Parks Development and Management 191

Peace Parks Foundation (PPF) 189, 195, 198

"peak oil" 45, 49

Pentagon, the (US) 37

peri-urban areas 159, 185, 203, 207, 216, 280; poverty 327

Persian Gulf countries 45

Persian Gulf oil supply 31, 33–35, 38, 40; geopolitics of 49

Peru 193; dam building in 76; water riots in 77; *see also* Lake Titicaca

Peru–Ecuador land use 193

PETRODATA 117

Philippines, the 37; New People's Army 150; rebel groups in 47; resilience of 151; World War II logging in 102

"pivot to Asia" 38

Plato 1, 205

poaching 132, 138, 264, 266, 267, 272, 308; *see also* wildlife

Index

Qatar 36
Quakers 192
Quinn, M. 194, 200n2

Radford Army Ammunition Plant 111–112
rainfall 68–70, 73, 84, 86, 244; floods caused by 268; shortages of 151
rainforest 299
Ramsar sites 190, **196**, 198
Ramutsindela, Maano 198–199
Rapid Deployment Joint Task Force (RDJTF) (US) 34
Reagan, Ronald 34
Red Cross *see* International Committee of the Red Cross (ICRC)
Red List *see* IUCN Red List
reforestation 282, 284
refugee camps 89, 110, 131–132, 137; Dollo Ado 139; population pressures around 294
refugee crisis 130; Syrian 139–140
refugee-host relations 130
refugees 58, 63; antiimmigration backlash to 180; from Central African Republic 87; climate refugees 126, 272; countries most likely to host 129; return of 107; self-settling 131, 132–135; in Tunisia 84; warfare and 182–183
refugee settlements 134, 139, 183, 327, 331
refugee support, per capita cost 136
Renaissance Dam, Ethiopia 72
RENAMO 55, 195
resistance conflicts 49–50
resource curse 12
resource degradation 58
resource depletion 245
resource wars 29–40, 43–44; extractives and 48–49; future geographies of 35–37; geography and geopolitics of 31–32; inherited geographies of 32–35
Revolutionary United Front (RUF) (Sierra Leone) 184, 205, 206
Ricardo, David 205, 326
Richards, P. 62–63
Rio+ 20 conference 255
Rio Declaration on Environment and Development 305, 317
Rio Earth Summit 1992 1, 197
Robbins, Paul 46
Roosevelt, Franklin D. 33, 35
Rothe, Delf 232–234
Rupert, Anton 195
Russell, Edmund 96, 97, 100
Russia 32–33, 36; as climate change beneficiary 204; drought and wildfire in 254; "green belt" border with Finland 101; insurgent groups, support of 48; Yemen and Syria, military involvement in 46

Rwanda 1, 194; civil war 131, 181; Doctors Without Borders in 156; gorilla tourism in 183, 186; *see also* Kigali, Rwanda
Rwandan Genocide 131, 181
Rwanda Patriot Front (RPF) 181, 182

SADC *see* Southern African Development Community (SADC)
Sahara Desert 253
Sahel 150, 256; climate change impacts on 82, 84, 86, 87; environmental factors destabilizing 290; Mopti region 150; UN Environment assessment 315; UNSC resolution 317
Sandwith, T. 199
Saudi Arabia 29–30
Savimbi, Jonas 30
Schleussner, C.-F. 88
Schmitt, Carl 43, 234, 235
Schellnhuber, H. 88
Sea of Galilee 72
securitization and securitization theory 227–236; applied to climate change, studies 229–232; definition of 228–229; see also Copenhagen School
Shanghai Cooperation Organization (SCO) 37
Sheridan, Philip H. 99
Sherman, William Tecumseh (General) 99
Siachen Glacier 192
Sierra Leone 3, 205; civil war in 208; civil war 206, 208; climate change and conflict in 156; conflict diamonds 11, 205; customary tenure in 58; land issues in 62–63; natural resource conflicts 16; rebels in 116; *see also* Freetown, Sierra Leone
Sirleaf, Ellen Johnson 205
sixth planetary extinction event 245
Slettebak, R. 149, 207
small island developing states (SIDS) 84, 85
soil erosion *see* erosion
solar energy 256
Somalia 82, **83**, 86, 87; civil war in 208; conflict bananas 11; Doctors Without Borders in 156; grazing and water disputes 55; refugees from 137; Shari'a courts, emergence of 58; UN field assessments in 309; UNSC statements on 317
South Africa 194; Apartheid, ending of 192; Mandela 189; peace parks 194–200; water resources 77
South Asia 76, 84, 159, 161, 194
South China Sea 29, 37–39
Southeast Asia 140
Southern Africa 195–200
Southern African Development Community (SADC) 192, 195, 197, 198
Southern Cause, the (United States) 99
South Sudan 18, 82, **83**; forest cover, regaining of in 132; population demographics of 86

344

Index

Soviet Union: Chernobyl 241; fall of 192, 197; gas and chemical disposal 102; Germany's invasion of 101

Soysa, I. de 148, 205

species extinction 100, 203, 244, 245

Sri Lanka 150, 186

Strait of Malacca 37

sub-Saharan Africa 159, 161; climate stress impacts on 206; drought 204

Sudan 16, 46, 72, **83**, 87; gender and environment, impact on conflict in 290, 292, 294–298; flood 216; natural resources as conflict driver in 308; "One Man Can" campaign 295; North Kordofan 296–298; South Kordofan 294; UN Environment Programme field assessment in 309, 311, 315, 317–318

Sudan People's Liberation Army–North (SPLA-N) 296

Sunderbans, South Asia 194

Sustainable Development Goals (SDG) 82, 88–89, 314, *316*; SDG7 255; SDG13 88; SDG15 315; SDG16 88, 315, 319

Swain, Ashok 253

Sykes-Picot agreement of 1916 33

Syrian Civil War 253

Taliban 58

Tanzania 5, 76; Game Reserve population, plummeting of 132; refugee and displaced populations in 131, 132, 134, 139

Taylor, Charles 209

Thorsell, J. 191

Thucydides 1, 205

tigers: poaching of 264; Sunderbans, South Asia 194

Tigris-Euphrates 39

Tijuana, Mexico 216, 217, 283–287

Tijuana River Estuary 280, 282, 287

Tijuana River National Estuarine Research Reserve (TRNERR) 279–281, 286–287

Tijuana River Watershed 279, 281

Tijuana River Valley (TRV), California 217–218, 279–280

Tijuana–San Diego border 279–288

Tillerson, Rex W. 35

timber 16, 36, 62, 102; Colombia 299; Extractive Industries Transparency Initiative (EITI) and 172; French 99–100; Liberia 174, 309; Nepal 266–267; pit 100; tracking of 171; *see also* conflict timber

timber traders 266

Tokyo, Japan 102

Transboundary Condor Peace Park 193

Transboundary Protected Area (TBPA) 190, 195

Transboundary Conservation Landscape and/or Seascape (TBCL/S) 190, 195

Transboundary Migration Conservation Area (TBMCA) 190, 195

transfrontier conservation area (TFCA) 189, 193, 195–200

Trombetta, Julia 234

Trump, Donald J. 35, 38, 283

Tsangpo River 39

Tucker, Richard 96, 97, 101, 102

Turkey 39, 232

Turkmenistan 36, 71

Tutsi and Hutu, conflict between 131, 181

Tuvalu 87

typhoid 185

typhoons 150

UCDP/PRIO Armed Conflict Dataset 118–119

Uganda 87, 181, 194, 307

Ukraine 32, 194, 254

Ullman, Richard 205

UNITA rebel group *see* National Union for the Total Independence of Angola (UNITA)

United Nations Convention to Combat Desertification (UNCCD) 159

United Nations Department of Economic and Social Affairs (UN DESA) 311

United Nations (UN) Department of Peacekeeping Operations and Department of Field Support 12

United Nations (UN) Environment Assembly (UNEA) 315, 317, 320

United Nations (UN) Field Missions 12

United Nations Framework Convention on Climate Change (UNFCCC) 242

United Nations (UN) Human Development concept 253

United Nations (UN) Peacebuilding Commission 10

United Nations Refugee Agency (UNHCR) 129, 131, 135–140

United Nations Security Council (UNSC): debate on climate change 230, 235; debate on conflict prevention 318; interest in and resolutions on conflict resources 308, 209; Lake Chad, resolution on 317; Presidential Statement on climate change 311, 319; Resolution 1325 on women and peace 314, 315

United States (US) Central Command (Centcom) 34

United States–Mexico border 279–284, 287

University of California San Diego (UCSD) 287

Urban Environmental Peacebuilding (UEPB) 180, 181, 187

uranium 33, 39, 96

urban green infrastructure 180–181

US–MX *see* United States–Mexico border

Uzbekistan 71

Index

"valuable" resources 30–31
Vasilijevic, M. 190, 194, 197, 198
Viet Cong 10, 95, 103; Operation Popeye 10; Operation Ranch Hand 10; Operation Rome Plow 11
Vietnam 29, 37; forests of 95; South 95, 96
Vietnam War 9–11, 103; aftermath 304; landmines 108
"virtual water trade" 70–71
vital materials 30, 31, 32, 37
"vital interests" 30
"vital" resources 30–31, 33, 38
von Clausewitz, C. 43
von Lucke, F. 231, 232, 234, 235

Wadi El Ku project 313, 317
Walch, Colin 150
War on Terror (US-led) 45, 48–49; American environmental security discourse and 243; climate change and 231, 234, *desecuritization* enabled by 230
war: environmental destruction during 95–103; environmental factors in 129–140; environmental spoils of 115; toxic legacy of 107–113; *see also* Civil War; Cold War; displacement; explosive remnants of war (ERW); landmines; resource wars; water, war, and conflict; World War I; World War II
wastewater 163, 184–185
water: cities/urbanization and 66, 183–185, 262; climate change and 208; displaced people and 130–135, 137–140; disputes over 55; environmental peacebuilding and 19; extractive sectors and 44; farmers and herders competing over 86; fragile states and 84; human societies and 31; national security and 30; resource wars over 29, 88; scarcity 203; security and 251–252; violence over 147, 150; "virtual water trade" 70–71; as vital resource 33; war/conflict and 66–78; women and 19; Yemen 61; *see also* drought; floods; groundwater
water conflicts: dynamics of 71; subnational 75–77; transboundary 71–75
water-food-energy nexus 250–256
water pollution 14, **51**, 132, 265; war as major source of 156
water, sanitation, and hygiene (WASH) system 162, 184, 185

watersheds 180, 185, 186
water stress 39, 204, 207
Waterton-Glacier International Peace Park 190–191, 193
water, war, and conflict *see* water
"water wars" 11
Watts, M. 155, 158
WCED *see* World Commission on Environment and Development (WCED)
Weibull regression models 4
Wellmann, Z. 231, 232
Welzer, Harald 208
Westing, Arthur 101
White Nile State 297
wildlife 12, 18; hunting of 307; illegal wildlife trade 308, 315; landmines and 107, 110; Tanzania 132; see also Transboundary Migration Conservation Area (TBMCA)
wildlife watching 197
Wolmer, W. 191
women *see* gender; Joint Programme on Women, Natural Resources, and Peace; natural resources management
World Bank 162, 204
World Commission on Environment and Development (WCED) 241, 242
World Commission on Protected Areas 191
World Energy Outlook (IEA) 35–36
World Heritage Sites (WHS) 198
Worldometers 162
World War I (WWI) 33; war and the environment during 100
World War II (WWII) 112; DDT, use of 100; Malthusian explanation for 205

Xayaburi dam 76

Yangtze River (China) 98
Yellow River (China) 98
Yellowstone National Park (United States) 190
Yemen 46, 82, **83**, 292, 332
Yemen civil war 61
Yugoslav Wars 112; *see also* Kosovo conflict

Zeitoun, M. and Warner, J.F. 252
Zimbabwe 55, 194, **196**

Printed in the United States
by Baker & Taylor Publisher Services